Foundations of Decentralized Organizations

Foundations of Decentralized Organizations

Blockchain and the Future of Corporate Law

Edited by

KEVIN WERBACH, EVA MICHELER,
AND BIANCA KREMER

OXFORD
UNIVERSITY PRESS

OXFORD
UNIVERSITY PRESS

Great Clarendon Street, Oxford, OX2 6DP,
United Kingdom

Oxford University Press is a department of the University of Oxford.
It furthers the University's objective of excellence in research, scholarship,
and education by publishing worldwide. Oxford is a registered trade mark of
Oxford University Press in the UK and in certain other countries.

Published in the United States of America by Oxford University Press
198 Madison Avenue, New York, NY 10016, United States of America.

British Library Cataloguing in Publication Data
Data available

Library of Congress Control Number: 2025950211

ISBN 978–0–19–894611–3

DOI: 10.1093/law/9780198946113.001.0001

Printed and bound by
CPI Group (UK) Ltd., Croydon, CR0 4YY

The manufacturer's authorised representative in the EU for product safety is
Oxford University Press España S.A. of Parque Empresarial San Fernando de Henares,
Avenida de Castilla, 2 – 28830 Madrid (www.oup.es/en or product.safety@oup.com).
OUP España S.A. also acts as importer into Spain of products made by the manufacturer.

MIX
Paper | Supporting
responsible forestry
FSC® C013604

Contents

Detailed Contents vii
List of Abbreviations xv
List of Contributors xvii

Introduction 1

PART I. DAOs AS AN INNOVATION IN CORPORATE FORM

1. DAO Legal Forms Around the World 13
Nina Reiser

2. Are Bespoke DAO Forms Needed in Organizational Law? 27
Shawn Bayern

3. DAOs and the History of Corporate Law 41
Michael Schillig

PART II. DAO GOVERNANCE

4. DAOs and Corporate Governance 61
Jill E Fisch

5. The Fiduciary Duties of Network Participants of Blockchain Systems 77
Morshed Mannan and Primavera de Filippi

6. DAOs: The Theory of the Firm and Ostromian Perspectives 100
Daniela Gandorfer and Eva Micheler

7. DAOs Are Adaptive Governance Engines 123
Darcy WE Allen, Chris Berg, Aaron M Lane, and Jason Potts

PART III. LEGAL CONSIDERATIONS

8. DAOs in Financial Distress 143
Kara Bruce, Christopher K Odinet, and Andrea Tosato

9. Choice of Court Agreements in Disputes Involving DAOs 163
Florence Guillaume

10. Code, Community, and Conflict: DAO Disputes 184
Bianca Kremer

11. DAOs for Collective Investment: An Emerging Paradigm 215
Nizan Geslevich Packin and Anat Alon-Beck

12. Regulating Decentralized Finance: How Financial Regulation Sheds Light on Governing DAOs 235
Iris H-Y Chiu

PART IV. THE FUTURE OF DAOs

13. The Law of Digital Organizations: A Prospective 259
Jason Grant Allen and Peter Hunn

14. What Do DAOs Really Contribute? 285
Edmund Schuster and Kelvin FK Low

15. Out of Control: DAOs, AI, and the Question of Autonomy 305
Kevin Werbach

Index 325

Detailed Contents

List of Abbreviations xv
List of Contributors xvii

Introduction 1
1. Foundational Concepts 1
2. Background to this Volume 3
3. Highlights of the Volume 5
4. Conclusion 9

PART I. DAOs AS AN INNOVATION IN CORPORATE FORM

1. DAO Legal Forms Around the World 13
Nina Reiser
1. Introduction 13
2. Concept of DAOs 14
3. DAO Model Law 15
4. The US 17
4.1. Classification of DAOs under Company Law 17
4.2. First Laws for DAOs in Individual States 18
4.2.1. Vermont blockchain-based LLC 18
4.2.2. Wyoming's special regimes for DAOs 18
4.2.2.1. DAO LLC 18
4.2.2.2. Decentralized unincorporated nonprofit association (DUNA) 20
4.2.3. Tennessee decentralized organization (DO) LLC 20
4.2.4. First application examples of DAO Model Law 20
5. Cayman Islands 21
6. Guernsey 22
7. Switzerland 23
8. Conclusion and Outlook 25

2. Are Bespoke DAO Forms Needed in Organizational Law? 27
Shawn Bayern
1. Introduction 27
2. Organizational Law and Technological Neutrality 28
2.1. Technological Neutrality and Blockchains 29
2.2. Technological Isomorphism in Decentralized Organizations 30

3. The Generality and Generativity of Conventional Business Organizations 33
3.1. General-Purpose LLCs and DAOs 33
3.2. Benefits of Nonproliferation of Organizational Forms 37
4. The Corporate Transparency Act 39
5. Conclusion 40

3. DAOs and the History of Corporate Law 41
Michael Schillig
1. Introduction 41
2. DAOs and Corporations: A Functional Approach 44
3. Corporate Law History: Lessons for DAOs? 46
3.1. Partnerships: Old and New 47
3.2. The Need for (Further) Accommodation 49
3.3. The Need for (Further) Regulation 53
4. Conclusion 58

PART II. DAO GOVERNANCE

4. DAOs and Corporate Governance 61
Jill E Fisch
1. Introduction 61
2. DAOs and Investment, Ownership, and Membership 62
3. DAOs and Corporate Governance 65
3.1. DAOs and Ministerial Components of Corporate Governance 65
3.2. DAOs and Governance Decisions 66
4. Implications 69
4.1. Authority and Accountability 69
4.2. Fiduciary Duties 71
4.3. Standardization 74
5. Conclusion 76

5. The Fiduciary Duties of Network Participants of Blockchain Systems 77
Morshed Mannan and Primavera de Filippi
1. The Problem of Imposing Implicit Fiduciary Duties 77
2. Fiduciary Duties in Blockchain Systems 79
2.1. Brief Overview of Fiduciary Duties 79
2.2. Academic Debate about Applying Fiduciary Duties to Blockchain Systems 81
3. Are Blockchain Developers and Other Network Participants Fiduciaries? 84
3.1. Tulip Trading Ltd 84
3.2. Law Commission's DAO Scoping Paper 88
3.3. Ooki/bZx 90
3.4. Lido DAO 92
3.5. Takeaways 94

4. Arguments Against Implicit Fiduciary Duties for Blockchain Developers and Participants 96
4.1. COALA DAO Model Law 96
4.2. Regulatory Equivalence 98
5. Conclusion 99

6. DAOs: The Theory of the Firm and Ostromian Perspectives 100
Daniela Gandorfer and Eva Micheler
1. Introduction 100
2. The Theory of the Firm 101
3. Ostrom 102
4. DAOs 105
4.1. Introduction to DAOs 105
4.2. Ideological Origins of DAOs 106
4.3. Autonomy 108
4.3.1. Introduction to autonomy 108
4.3.2. Autonomy as an ideological idea 109
4.3.3. (Autonomous) smart contracts 110
4.3.4. Summary 113
4.4. Decentralization 114
4.5. Summary 117
5. Theory of the Firm and DAOs 117
6. Ostromian Perspectives 119
7. Conclusions 121

7. DAOs Are Adaptive Governance Engines 123
Darcy WE Allen, Chris Berg, Aaron M Lane, and Jason Potts
1. Why Do DAOs Exist? 123
2. How Do DAOs Evolve in Practice? 127
2.1. Shapeshift 128
2.2. Uniswap 132
2.3. Optimism 134
3. What DAOs Really Do 137

PART III. LEGAL CONSIDERATIONS

8. DAOs in Financial Distress 143
Kara Bruce, Christopher K Odinet, and Andrea Tosato
1. Introduction 143
2. Intellectual Foundations, Corporate Form, Owners, Managers, and Creditors 145
2.1. Intellectual Foundations of DAOs 145
2.2. Current Landscape and Definition 146
2.3. Key Organizational Factors 147
2.3.1. Corporate form 147

2.3.2. Managers 148
2.3.3. Assets 150
2.3.4. Creditors 151
3. Liquidation and Bankruptcy of DAOs in Distress 153
3.1. Introduction to Bankruptcy Law 153
3.2. Governance and Decision-making 155
3.3. Disclosure, Notice, and Service 156
3.4. Blockchain Immutability and Avoidance 157
4. Bankruptcy for DAOs?: Policy Implications and Concerns 158
4.1. Choosing Between Purism and Pragmatism 159
4.2. Increased Commercial Complexity and Bankruptcy's Appeal 160
4.3. The Threat of Involuntary Bankruptcy 160
4.4. Bankruptcy Courts as DAO's Court of First Impression 161
5. Conclusion 162

9. Choice of Court Agreements in Disputes Involving DAOs 163
Florence Guillaume
1. Addressing Disputes Involving a DAO 163
2. Establishing Jurisdiction for Disputes Involving a DAO 164
2.1. Characterization of DAOs as Social Organizations 165
2.2. The Challenges of Locating the Jurisdiction for the Dispute 168
3. Assessing the Validity and Effect of Choice of Court Agreements under International and European Legal Instruments 170
3.1. Validity Requirements of a Choice of Court Agreement under the Hague Convention, Lugano Convention, and Brussels I Regulation 171
3.2. Effect on the Courts of a Valid Choice of Court Agreement under the Hague Convention, Lugano Convention, and Brussels I Regulation 173
4. Evaluating the Validity of Choice of Court Agreements in Disputes Involving a DAO 174
4.1. Disputes Between DAO Members 174
4.2. Disputes Between a DAO and a Third Party 176
4.3. DAO-related Disputes 178
5. Conclusion 182

10. Code, Community, and Conflict: DAO Disputes 184
Bianca Kremer
1. Navigating Disputes in the World of DAOs: An Introduction 184
2. From Corporate Disputes to DAO Disputes—A Targeted Definition 187
3. Types of DAO Disputes 190
3.1. Internal DAO Disputes 191
3.1.1. Governance and voting disputes 191
3.1.2. Smart contract bugs, exploits, and their resulting disputes 193
3.1.3. Fund allocation and treasury management disputes 194
3.1.4. Role and authority conflicts 196
3.1.5. Token-holder v DAO disputes 197
3.2. External DAO Disputes 199

4. Major Hurdles to Effective Resolution of DAO Disputes 200
5. The Transparency Paradox 202
6. The DAO Dispute Resolution Spectrum 204
7. The Lived Reality: Synthesizing Insights from DAO Practitioners on Disputes and Their Resolution 208
8. Conclusion 209

11. DAOs for Collective Investment: An Emerging Paradigm 215
Nizan Geslevich Packin and Anat Alon-Beck
1. DAOs as Collective Investment Vehicles 215
1.1. Traditional VC Funding Models 216
1.2. Democratizing Investments: Crowdfunding as an Alternative Funding Model 217
1.3. Democratizing Investments 2.0: DAOs as an Alternative Funding Model 218
1.4. A Deeper Dive: Traditional VC Funding Models and Crowdfunding Platforms v DAOs 220
1.4.1. Advantages of DAOs 220
1.4.2. Challenges and limitations of DAOs 220
1.4.2.1. Potential drawbacks of inclusivity 220
1.4.2.2. Investor protection mechanisms in DAOs 221
1.4.2.3. Lack of support commonly offered by traditional VC 222
1.4.2.4. The legal landscape surrounding collective investments 225
2. Comparative Analysis of DAOs, Traditional VC, and Crowdfunding Platforms 227
3. Future Developments and Challenges 230
3.1. Technological Risks 232
3.2. Governance Issues 233
4. Conclusion 234

12. Regulating Decentralized Finance: How Financial Regulation Sheds Light on Governing DAOs 235
Iris H-Y Chiu
1. Introduction 235
2. DeFi's Internal Governance and the Need for Regulatory Governance 238
2.1. A Brief Primer on DeFi 238
2.2. The Limits of Internal Governance Developed by DeFi DAOs 239
3. Regulatory Intervention to Address Internal Governance Failures 245
3.1. MiCAR's Key Regulatory Tenets for Crypto-Asset Service Providers 246
3.1.1. Authorization to operate 246
3.1.2. Identification and qualities of responsible persons and capital providers 247
3.1.3. Ex ante regulation of constitutional structure, operational program, and business policies 248

3.1.4. Ex ante regulation of internal control, technological, and other risk management policies 248
3.1.5. Ex ante regulation of conflicts of interest management policy and disclosure 252
3.1.6. Duty to act fairly, honestly, and professionally 253
3.1.7. Prudential regulation 254
3.1.8. Users' custodial rights over assets 254
3.1.9. Governance regulation as the basis for achieving broad financial regulatory objectives such as consumer protection? 255
4. Concluding Remarks and Regulatory Insights for DAOs Generally 255

PART IV. THE FUTURE OF DAOs

13. The Law of Digital Organizations: A Prospective 259
Jason Grant Allen and Peter Hunn
1. Introduction 259
2. Organization 260
2.1. Platform and Network Organizations 262
2.2. Affordances (Technical and Legal) 264
2.2.1. Toward a concept of "techno-legal" affordances 266
2.2.2. Isomorphism at the legal-technical interface 269
2.2.3. DLT affordances as techno-legal substrates for organizational coordination 271
3. Techno-Legal Affordances of Digital Organization 273
4. The Digital Company: A Prospective 279
5. Conclusion 283

14. What Do DAOs Really Contribute? 285
Edmund Schuster and Kelvin FK Low
1. The Way of the DAO 285
2. "Secure," "Decentralized" Ledgers? 286
3. DAOist Misadventures: This Way Lies Madness? 287
4. Integrating Law and Blockchains: Theory v Reality 292
5. Real DAOs: Going Beyond BLINOs 296
6. The Self-Driving Corporation: Legal Obstacles 298
7. The Conflict Between DAOs and the Rule of Law 298
8. The Need for a Realignment Mechanism 299
9. Other Legal Challenges 301
10. DAOs and the Boundary of the Firm 302
11. Conclusion 303

15. Out of Control: DAOs, AI, and the Question of Autonomy 305
Kevin Werbach
1. The AI Tidal Wave 305

2. DAOs and AI 307
2.1. DAOs as AI Governance Mechanisms 307
2.2. AI Controlling DAOs 311
2.3. DAOs and AI Agents Converge 313
3. The Question of Autonomy 316
3.1. Autonomy for AI and Corporations 316
3.2. Autonomy and DAOs 318
4. Governing Autonomous DAOs 319
4.1. DAO Legal Responsibility 319
4.2. Regulation for Autonomous Harms 321
4.3. Humans in the Loop 323
5. Conclusion 324

Index 325

Abbreviations

ADR	alternative dispute resolution
AGI	artificial general intelligence
AI	artificial intelligence
AMM	automated market maker
API	application programming interface
AVC	alternative venture capital
BBLLC	blockchain-based limited liability companies
BDAP	Wharton Blockchain and Digital Asset Project
BDC	business development company
BLINO	blockchain in name only
BORG	base organization run by governance
CAO	centralized autonomous organization
CDP	collateralized debt position
CeDeFi	centralized decentralized finance
CFTC	Commodity Futures Trading Commission
COALA	Coalition of Automated Legal Applications
DAC	distributed autonomous corporations
DAO	decentralized autonomous organizations
DeFi	decentralized finance
DIP	debtor in possession
DLT	distributed ledger technology
DORA	Digital Operational Resilience Act
DTCC	Depository Trust and Clearing Corporation
DUNA	decentralized unincorporated non-profit association
EBA	European Banking Authority
ENS	Ethereum Name Service
ESMA	European Securities and Markets Authority
ETH	Ether
EU	European Union
FDV	fully diluted value
FINMA	Swiss Financial Market Supervisory Authority
FTC	Federal Trade Commission
GDPR	General Data Protection Regulation
GPU	graphical processing unit
GUI	graphical user interface
ICC	International Chamber of Commerce
ICO	initial coin offering
IPO	initial public offering
LCAM	London Chamber of Arbitration and Mediation

LLC	limited liability company
LLM	large language model
LLP	limited liability partnership
LLLP	limited liability limited partnership
M&A	mergers and acquisitions
MiCAR	Markets in Crypto-Assets Regulation
NDA	non-disclosure agreement
NFT	non-fungible token
OECD	Organisation for Economic Cooperation and Development
RAG	retrieval-augmented generation
RULLCA	Revised Uniform Limited Liability Company Act
RUPA	Revised Uniform Partnership Act
SEC	Securities and Exchange Commission
SPT	special purpose trust
TVL	total value locked
UCC	Uniform Commercial Code
VC	venture capital

Contributors

Anat Alon-Beck, Professor of Law at Case Western Reserve University School of Law. Her research focuses on corporate law and governance.

Jason Grant Allen, Associate Professor of Law and Director of the Centre for Digital Law at Singapore Management University. His work explores the interface of law, economics, and emerging technology.

Darcy WE Allen, Associate Professor of Economics at RMIT University and Director of the Digital Economy Council of Australia. He regularly publishes on the topics of cryptodemocracy, innovation policy, token airdrops, and Web3 governance.

Shawn Bayern, Larry and Joyce Beltz Professor of Torts and Associate Dean for Technology at the Florida State University College of Law. He is the author of various books, including *Autonomous Organizations* (CUP 2021).

Chris Berg, Professor of Economics at RMIT University. His books include *The New Technologies of Freedom* (American Institute for Economic Research 2020) and *Understanding the Blockchain Economy: An Introduction to Institutional Cryptoeconomics* (Edward Elgar 2019).

Kara Bruce, Graham Kenan Distinguished Professor of Law at the University of North Carolina at Chapel Hill. Her research focuses on bankruptcy law and procedure. She is co-author of *The Law of Bankruptcy* (West Academic Press 2024) and *Problems and Materials on Secured Transactions* (6th edn, West Academic Press 2022).

Iris H-Y Chiu, Professor of Corporate Law and Financial Regulation at the Faculty of Laws, University College London. She has published extensively in the areas of corporate governance and financial regulation, including *Regulating the Crypto Economy: Business Transformations and Financialisation* (Hart Publishing 2023).

Primavera de Filippi, Director of Research at the National Center of Scientific Research (CNRS) in Paris and Faculty Associate at the Berkman Klein Center for Internet & Society at Harvard University. Her books include *Blockchain and the Law: The Rule of Code* (Harvard UP 2018) and *Blockchain Governance* (MIT Press 2024).

Jill E Fisch, Saul A Fox Distinguished Professor of Business Law at the University of Pennsylvania Carey School of Law. She focuses on the intersection of business and law, including the role of regulation and litigation in addressing limitations in the disciplinary power of the capital markets.

Daniela Gandorfer, Lecturer at University of Westminster Law School and Emerging Tech & Innovation Systems Lead at the Institute for Healthy Urban Living at Westminster University. She is also the founder and director of the Logische Phantasie Lab and has a forthcoming book entitled *Matterphorics: On the Laws of Theory* (Duke UP 2026).

Florence Guillaume, Professor of Civil, Private International and Digital Law at the Faculty of Law of the University of Neuchâtel and founder of the LexTech Institute. Her books include *Decentralized Autonomous Organizations in the Legal Landscape: From Decentralized Governance to Legal Frontiers* (Edward Elgar 2025).

Peter Hunn, Founded a leading legal contracts startup acquired by Docusign and previously worked on DAOs as a lawyer at the Law Commission of England & Wales. He writes on the law around digital assets, DAOs, and smart contracts. His books include *Smart Legal Contracts* (OUP 2022).

Bianca Kremer, Senior Fellow at the Wharton School's Blockchain and Digital Asset Project, Postdoc at the Zug Institute for Blockchain Research at the University of Lucerne and Legal Counsel at law firm MME in Zurich. She is co-author of *The DAO Policy Toolkit* (WEF and Wharton BDAP 2023) and wrote an award-winning doctoral dissertation on arbitration law and blockchains (2022).

Aaron M Lane, Senior Lecturer in Law at RMIT University, Senior Fellow at the Competition and Innovation Lab at The George Washington University, and Barrister at the Victorian Bar. His research sits at the intersection of innovation, law, and regulation.

Kelvin FK Low, Professor of Law and Director, Centre for Private Law at the University of Hong Kong. His research interest spans the field of private law but with a particular interest in property, broadly defined. He is co-author of *The Law of Personal Property* (2nd and 3rd edns, Sweet & Maxwell Ltd 2019 and 2021).

Morshed Mannan, Lecturer in Global Law and Digital Technology at the University of Edinburgh. His research focuses on blockchain governance and the wemergence of democratic firms in the digital economy. His books include *Blockchain Governance* (MIT Press 2024).

Eva Micheler, Professor of Law at the London School of Economics. She writes and teaches on company law, corporate finance, the law of securities and digital assets. She is the author of *Company Law: A Real Entity Theory* (OUP 2021).

Christopher K Odinet, Professor of Law and Mosbacher Research Fellow at Texas A&M University School of Law. He focuses on commercial law, consumer finance and banking, and property law. His books include *Foreclosed: Mortgage Servicing and the Hidden Architecture of Homeownership in America* (CUP 2019).

Nizan Geslevich Packin, Professor of Law at the Zicklin School of Business at Baruch College, CUNY. Her primary research interests lie at the intersection of tech policy, consumer protection, and financial regulation. Her works include *The Cambridge Handbook on the Law and Policy of NFTs* (CUP 2024).

Jason Potts, Distinguished Professor of Economics at RMIT University and Director of the Blockchain Innovation Hub at RMIT. He is also a chief investigator on the ARC Centre of Excellence for Automated Decision-Making and Society. His books include *Understanding the Blockchain Economy: An Introduction to Institutional Cryptoeconomics* (Edward Elgar 2019).

Nina Reiser, Professor for Financial Market Law at the University of St Gallen (HSG), Director at the Institute for Law and Economics HSG, co-founder of the Centre for Financial Services Innovation HSG and titular Professor at the University of Zurich. Her fields of research include financial market law, company law, and capital market law. She combines basic research with her many years of practical experience at the Swiss Financial Market Supervisory Authority (FINMA).

Michael Schillig, Professor of Law at King's College London and Professor of International Business Law at the University of Leipzig, Germany. His research and teaching generally focus on financial law from both a regulatory and transactional perspective, as well as on corporate law, corporate insolvency law, and law and technology.

Edmund Schuster, Associate Professor of Corporate Law at the London School of Economics. His research focuses on corporate law, law and finance, takeover regulation, as well as the economic analysis of law. His books include *The Private International Law of Companies in Europe* (CH Beck, Hart Publishing, Nomos 2019).

Andrea Tosato, Professor of Law at SMU Dedman School of Law. He is a leading private law scholar with internationally recognized expertise in the intersection between commercial law and new technologies.

Kevin Werbach, Liem Sioe Liong/First Pacific Company Professor and Chairperson of Legal Studies and Business Ethics at the Wharton School of the University of Pennsylvania. He is the founder and director of the Wharton Blockchain and Digital Asset Project and the Wharton Accountable AI Lab. His books include *The Blockchain and the New Architecture of Trust* (MIT Press 2018).

Introduction

Not all readers will be familiar with decentralized forms of organizations, or with the instantiation that is the focus of this volume, the decentralized autonomous organization (DAO). To those uninitiated to the field, it will be helpful to start with its foundational concepts. Even a conventional business firm, organized as a corporation or similar legal entity, may embody elements of decentralization. Shareholders may be dispersed and separated from management; management teams themselves may distribute authority among themselves and other stakeholders; and units or offices of a firm may operate with degrees of autonomy. Certain well-established organizational structures, such as the cooperative, disperse ownership or governance more explicitly. All of these, however, operate within traditional paradigms of legal authority, governance structures, contractual relationships, and management practices.

A DAO is different. At its core, it is enabled by computer software and takes advantage of three technological ideas: *distributed ledgers* or *blockchains*; *smart contracts*; and *digital assets*.

1. Foundational Concepts

A distributed ledger is a computer-based record-keeping system that stores information securely and reliably, without reliance on a central authority. The distributed ledger is maintained and updated by many record keepers and can only be updated by their consensus. The name blockchain derives from the way in which information is commonly recorded and maintained on a distributed ledger. When someone enters a transaction the information about this transaction is bundled with transactions entered by other participants into a "block" and verified by the record keepers. Before the transactions forming part of the block are added to the ledger the record keepers must agree that these are consistent with it. Once all the transactions in the block have been verified, these are connected to all previous blocks and added to the distributed ledger. Cryptography and game-theoretic software incentives are used to ensure that once blocks are validated, they may not be changed or removed, a concept known as immutability. The technology of distributed ledgers can provide strong guarantees of security and integrity, even with no central administrator or direct legal oversight. This can be true even if the ledger is "permissionless," allowing anyone, without prior identification, to serve as a record keeper or validator.

A smart contract is a computer program that is associated with a programmable blockchain and operates on a distributed ledger. Smart contracts can be thought of as the digital equivalent of a vending machine: you put money into a slot, press a button, and the machine releases a snack. There is no need for a salesperson, and the transaction cannot be reversed. Like the vending machine, a smart contract is programmed to automatically execute a transaction when certain pre-programmed conditions are met. A smart contract can, for example, automatically initiate payment to a supplier when their delivery arrives and is scanned at a warehouse. A smart contract can also automatically release funds when the participants of the smart contract who have signing rights have agreed by a pre-set majority requirement to authorize this transfer. On most major blockchain networks (Bitcoin, as the first blockchain, being one of the exceptions), smart contracts can, in theory, execute programs of arbitrary complexity, although in practice speed and security impose limitations. Software programs built out of smart contracts are known as decentralized applications or dApps.

Digital assets are units created and recorded on a distributed ledger. They are sometimes also referred to as "tokens" and can represent value. With smart contracts, tokens can be created with virtually any desired functionality. These tokens can be used to compensate participants for desired activities, or to grant them powers in connection with a dApp, analogous to the way a vending machine accepts coins to purchase products.

DAOs make use of powerful software applications, combining distributed ledgers, smart contracts, and digital assets to fashion an organization. A DAO is a set of smart contracts, comprising one or more dApps, that govern a group's activities and resources. The smart contracts define the set of activities that the DAO may engage in. Digital assets or tokens associated with the DAO are typically used to provide voting rights for governance, or to compensate participants for their contributions. When someone proposes an action, such as funding a project or changing a rule, tokenholders vote using their tokens. If the proposal passes, the smart contracts may automatically execute the decision. More generally, the technology enables participants to agree on actions. They can be more directly and continuously involved with the management of the DAO's operations, without the need for physical meetings or formal management roles, boards, and officers.

DAOs and similar decentralized organizations (then called distributed autonomous corporations or DACs) were first described by Vitalik Buterin and Daniel Larimer in 2013. This was shortly before the launch of the Ethereum blockchain that first fully implemented smart contracts. DAOs came to the fore in 2016, when the first significant implementation, known simply as *The DAO*, was launched on the Ethereum blockchain. This DAO was intended to operate as a collective investment scheme governed by smart contracts. The smart contracts were designed to enable participants to vote on which project should receive funding from a common pool of contributions. In a now-infamous incident, the DAO's smart contract was used in an unintended way shortly after launch, putting at risk a substantial number of all Ethereum Ether (ETH) tokens in circulation at that time. This led to much controversy and resulted in what is known as a "hard fork" of the Ethereum blockchain, creating Ethereum (where the transfer of the funds to the attacker was ultimately reversed) and Ethereum Classic (where the reversal was not implemented).

This troubled start initially limited adoption of the DAO concept. However, within a few years, new DAOs with more sophisticated mechanisms for security and governance began to appear. Some have aggregated significant stores of digital assets in their treasuries, while others host prominent communities engaging in a variety of activities.

DAOs continue to be used for collective investment,[1] as well as to facilitate financial services such as trading and lending with tokens.[2] However, they have also been set up for other and very diverse purposes. A DAO can, for example, be used to allow musicians to earn return directly from their fans.[3] DAOs arrange collective ownership of art or other assets.[4] They organize collaboration between computer gamers or inhabitants of the metaverse.[5] Some DAOs have social aims coordinating activity to combat climate change or poverty or to enhance education.[6]

2. Background to this Volume

In 2022 and 2023, the Wharton Blockchain and Digital Asset Project (BDAP), in collaboration with the World Economic Forum, issued two working papers drawing on an international group of experts—Decentralized Autonomous Organizations: Beyond the Hype and the Decentralized Autonomous Organization Toolkit.[7] Two of the editors of this volume, Kevin Werbach and Bianca Kremer, were among the leaders of that project. The two papers survey and map an emerging but vibrant DAO landscape. They are directed at policymakers and practitioners intending to set up DAOs or advising their proponents. They also provide researchers with a comprehensive window into the subject.

An important conclusion from this exercise was that, while there were some outstanding academic contributions to the field, there was a need for further research on DAOs, especially from scholars of corporate law and related fields. Many DAOs, or affiliated foundations, engage lawyers to create formal legal arrangements rooted in one or more jurisdictions. DAOs control tens of billions of dollars of assets and manage major blockchain-based applications,[8] all without traditional hierarchical

1 Examples include MetaCartel Ventures <https://metacartel.xyz> accessed July 11, 2025 and LAO <https://docs.thelao.io> accessed July 11, 2025.

2 eg Uniswap DAO <https://gov.uniswap.org> accessed July 11, 2025.

3 Audius DAO <https://audius.org> accessed July 11, 2025.

4 Head DAO <https://opensea.io/collection/headdao> accessed July 11, 2025 and PleasrDAO <https://pleasr.org> accessed July 11, 2025.

5 Yield Guild Games <https://www.yieldguild.io/guilds> accessed July 11, 2025 or Decentraland DAO <https://decentraland.org/dao/> accessed July 11, 2025.

6 Klima DAO <https://www.klimadao.finance> accessed July 11, 2025 or Gitcoin <https://www.gitcoin.co> accessed July 11, 2025.

7 David Gogel and others, *Decentralized Autonomous Organization Toolkit* (January 2023) <https://www3.weforum.org/docs/WEF_Decentralized_Autonomous_Organization_Toolkit_2023.pdf> accessed July 11, 2025; David Gogel and others, *Decentralized Autonomous Organization: Beyond the Hype* (June 2022) <https://www3.weforum.org/docs/WEF_Decentralized_Autonomous_Organizations_Beyond_the_Hype_2022.pdf> accessed July 11, 2025.

8 CoinMarketCap lists 276 DAOs with a market cap over $28 billion: CoinMarketCap, "Top DAO Tokens by Market Capitalization" <https://coinmarketcap.com/view/dao/> accessed July 14, 2025. Deep DAO lists even more DAOs, they monitor at least 2,461 DAOs as of July 14, 2025, Deep DAO, "Organizations" <https://deepdao.io/organizations> accessed July 14, 2025.

management, boards, or equity shareholders. Yet their creators often have little understanding of how traditional firms operate, and they exist in an uncertain legal environment. Correspondingly, experts on major aspects of organizational law and governance have rarely taken DAOs as a subject of inquiry.

This edited volume represents a collaboration of Kevin Werbach, a US-based legal scholar of emerging technologies; Eva Micheler, a UK-based corporate law scholar; and Bianca Kremer, senior fellow of the Wharton Blockchain and Digital Asset Project, and a legal practitioner based in Switzerland. It is unique in that it brings together scholars from the two backgrounds that DAOs relate to. It contains chapters from leading scholars specializing in the law of digital technology and blockchain, along with contributions from eminent corporate law academics. And it does so with a global perspective, focusing primarily on the US, UK, and Europe, with several contributors also based in Asia.

Astute readers will note that the term "DAO" does not appear in the title. There are several reasons for this. We are not interested in fighting definitional battles. Some experts count permissionless blockchains such as Bitcoin as "algorithmic DAOs," while others limit the term to dApps operating on top of blockchains.[9] And whether an organization is sufficiently decentralized, or sufficiently autonomous, to count as a DAO, or is merely "DAO-like," it still raises the questions of corporate law and governance that this volume engages with. Moreover, the attribute of autonomy, which was significant in the original conception of DAOs, has largely been abandoned in most operating DAOs (although as Kevin Werbach explores in his chapter, it may reappear with the integration of DAOs and artificial intelligence (AI)). We believe that viewing DAOs within a continuum of organizational structures, and bringing to bear both traditional and novel perspectives, will shed the most light on the subject.

We hope this book contributes to the academic debate, as well as the development of DAOs in practice, in two ways. First, by providing a robust and rigorous academic analysis of salient DAO topics, and integrating the developments that have occurred since DAOs were initially created. Second, by catering to diverse audiences, including academics, researchers, and students from various fields such as internet law and policy, commercial law, company law, contract law, law and economics, private international law, corporate governance, private ordering, and dispute resolution. In addition to its legal focus, the interdisciplinary nature of blockchain-based organizations also makes this book appealing to scholars in information studies, computer science, economics, political science, and philosophy. Beyond academic readers, the book targets policymakers, business executives, investors, and entrepreneurs interested in blockchain technology and DAOs. By providing a comprehensive legal perspective on a rapidly evolving topic, this book bridges the gap between highly technical engineering literature and superficial popular accounts.

[9] For a source treating blockchains as algorithmic DAOs, Aaron Wright, "The Rise of Decentralized Autonomous Organizations: Opportunities and Challenges" (2021) 4 Stanford Journal of Blockchain Law & Policy 152.

3. Highlights of the Volume

DAOs were originally conceived of as computer code-based structures that operate outside of any legal system and might make corporate law as we know it redundant. In deployment, they have largely moved on from their idealistic origins, although many DAO participants retain those views. The area continues to develop but we can observe that decentralization, which remains an aspiration, has been combined with centralized elements for effectiveness and efficiency of DAO processes. The most prominent example for this development is the integration by DAO proponents of legal entities such as Cayman foundations, Swiss associations, or bespoke legal forms. This development was inspired by a number of jurisdictions characterizing DAOs as partnerships leading to the personal and unlimited liability of their participants toward third parties. The legal entities that are combined with DAOs enable them to interact with the non-crypto native environment and shield participants from personal liability.

There are two contributions in the book that examine the phenomenon of bespoke legal forms for DAOs. Nina Raiser's "DAO Legal Forms Around the World" (Chapter 1) provides a comprehensive overview of the different bespoke legal forms that have been recently created by the US states of Tennessee, Utah, Vermont, New Hampshire, and Wyoming. She also discusses existing legal forms that are frequently used by DAOs such as the Cayman Island foundation, the Guernsey trust, and the Swiss association, and examines a recent proposal for a DAO model law that is tailored to the characteristics and needs of DAOs and their participants. The chapter concludes with the argument that bespoke legal forms are useful as they help prevent the characterization of DAOs as partnerships with unlimited liability of their members. These forms can also be designed more flexibly than general purpose corporate vehicles.

In contrast, Shawn Bayern argues (in Chapter 2, "Are Bespoke DAO Forms Needed in Organizational Law?") that organizational forms should be neutral to private parties' choices of technology. He argues that bespoke legal forms are problematic because it can be difficult to draw clear lines between different technologies as these can easily be strategically designed to emulate one another. A proliferation of legal forms also leads to inconsistencies and loopholes. This can complicate the parties' legal decisions and consequently increase their legal costs. He further concludes that existing general organizational forms such as the limited liability company (LLC) available in US states are sufficiently flexible to serve the needs of DAO proponents.

Michael Schillig (Chapter 3, "DAOs and the History of Corporate Law") examines DAOs through the lens of the history of corporate law. He notes that DAOs replicate certain features of the modern business corporation. They lock in capital in the form of crypto-assets and adopt a participatory governance model based on token holder democracy. He reminds readers that the rampant abuse and speculation, as well as widespread fraud and corruption, that prevailed when the corporate form became freely available did not prevent limited liability corporations from being hailed as "the greatest single discovery of modern times" only a generation later. The author recommends that DAOs should be approached in an incremental way that gradually seeks to accommodate the concept of DAOs within the existing legal framework. This fosters innovation while curbing abuse.

DAOs constitute an attempt to design organizational arrangements outside of established corporate practices. To a corporate lawyer engaged in highly specialized and advanced debates, this is a unique opportunity to examine fundamental questions and principles from a fresh angle while at the same time providing useful advice to DAO proponents and their advisors, who may be unfamiliar with traditional corporate law.

In her chapter entitled "DAOs and Corporate Governance" (Chapter 4), Jill Fisch writes that DAOs challenge traditional conventions about corporate governance in several ways. They enable enterprises to craft customized governance structures and thus challenge the ability of participants to understand and price the businesses that employ novel governance structures. They broaden the scope of who can participate in the governance systems and so respond to the debate on stakeholder governance. Finally, decentralized governance can raise issues for the accountability of decision-makers who may or may not be constrained by fiduciary principles.

Morshed Mannan and Primavera de Filippi examine the extent to which fiduciary duties apply to network participants of blockchain systems (Chapter 5, "The Fiduciary Duties of Network Participants of Blockchain Systems"). They critique the recent UK Court of Appeal decision in *Tulip Trading Ltd v van der Laan*.[10] The case raised the question of whether Bitcoin developers owe a fiduciary duty to Bitcoin users. The court did not decide the substance of this question but rather held that the case should proceed to trial as there was a real prospect of establishing that such a duty exists. The two authors argue it is improper to impute fiduciary duties on network participants as this stifles innovation and threatens the financial stability of blockchains. They favor a more nuanced approach focusing on transparency, stress the non-coercive nature of software updates, and point out that DAO administrators or representatives normally do not hold sufficient discretionary power to be conferred with fiduciary responsibility.

DAOs not only challenge traditional corporate law they also invite analysis from the perspective of the theory of the firm and other institutional perspectives. Here too the book contains two approaches. In their contribution entitled "DAOs: The Theory of the Firm and Ostromian Perspectives" (Chapter 6), Daniela Gandorfer and Eva Micheler examine DAOs through the lens of the theory of the firm. They conclude that DAOs are so diverse that no general statements can be made as to where they lie on the spectrum between markets and firms. In particular, and in contrast to some earlier contributions, the use of smart contracts does not suffice to characterize them as either contractual, firm-like, or hybrid arrangements. DAOs that adopt hierarchical arrangements, however, should be characterized as firms. The two authors further use the framework for institutional analysis developed by Elinor Ostrom to suggest that DAOs should be analyzed, and can be designed, distinguishing different levels of action. They distinguish the operational from the policy, constitutional, and meta-constitutional levels of action. This form of analysis helps academics to identify

[10] [2023] EWCA Civ 83.

the salient features of particular DAOs and guides practitioners in designing their respective bespoke arrangements.

Darcy Allen, Chris Berg, Aaron Lane, and Jason Potts use the framework of new institutional economics to examine whether DAOs should be viewed as merely a new mechanism to economize on transaction costs (Chapter 7, "DAOs Are Adaptive Governance Engines"). Based on case studies of three operating DAOs, they argue that it is the adaptiveness of their governance that actually generates DAOs' economic advantages as an organizational form. The flexibility of DAO governance allows for rapid adaptation to dynamic regulatory, competitive, and financial environments. DAOs, they predict, are likely to be employed where the benefits of such governance mechanisms exceed the costs.

In addition to corporate law, DAOs intersect with other areas of the law. Kara Bruce, Christopher Odinet, and Andrea Tosato examine what happens when DAOs become financially distressed. Their chapter (Chapter 8, "DAOs in Financial Distress") focuses on US bankruptcy law but also contains general remarks for other jurisdictions. Like other contributors to the book, they observe that there is enormous diversity in DAO arrangements and so refrain from drawing general conclusions. They note, for example, that DAOs are sometimes characterized as partnerships and in that capacity can be subject to US bankruptcy law. DAOs eligible for bankruptcy proceedings need to be represented by a human person in court. This individual can be identified by the court but DAOs who seek bankruptcy protection will have to designate their representative for these purposes. Time is of the essence in bankruptcy proceedings. This may pose a challenge for DAOs with a highly decentralized governance structure.

Because blockchains and smart contracts are not tied to nations or their legal regimes, by their very nature DAOs operate across borders. This raises questions of private international law. Florence Guillaume's contribution to the book is entitled "Choice of Court Agreements in Disputes Involving DAOs" (Chapter 9). She sets out the issues that arise when determining the jurisdiction of state courts for disputes that involve DAOs, their participants, or third parties interacting with them, and shows that traditional connecting factors can lead to unpredictable results. For the purposes of private international (rather than domestic private) law, she characterizes DAOs as social organizations, which may or may not have legal personality, and argues that choice of court agreements can be used to identify a state court to hear disputes between DAO participants. The same applies for contracts entered into between a DAO and third parties.

Bianca Kremer explores the complexities of disputes arising within and related to DAOs (Chapter 10, "Code, Community, and Conflict: DAO Disputes"). She notes that DAOs face unique challenges in dispute resolution, such as ambiguity over what constitutes a dispute, pseudonymity of parties, the absence of traditional hierarchical structures, opaque power dynamics, and uncertainties regarding DAOs' real-world structures and legal status. She provides a working definition of "DAO disputes" and then examines both internal conflicts and external challenges to DAOs, drawing from real-world examples, including interviews with DAO practitioners. Her findings show that there are interesting parallels between corporate and DAO disputes and that there is a need for DAOs to plan for conflicts from the outset by establishing clear rules, processes, and guidelines (both on- and off-chain).

As decentralized entities, DAOs pose a significant challenge to regulation. However, it is possible to trace how DAOs relate to different regulatory regimes, and how difficulties might be resolved. Nizan Geslevich Packin and Anat Alon-Beck (Chapter 11, "DAOs for Collective Investment: An Emerging Paradigm") analyze how DAOs are, and can be, used for the purposes of collective investment. They compare this form of DAOs with traditional venture capital models and crowdfunding platforms and note that DAOs provide easy access to early-stage investment opportunities for a broader set of investors. This may give rise to problems of investor protections, which some DAOs attempt to address by engaging third-party firms to audit smart contracts or through insurance protocols covering smart contract failure or hacks. Traditional early-stage financial models normally supply entrepreneurs with valuable expertise and access to professional networks. Collective investment DAOs currently do not supply access to such services. There are also unresolved questions of regulation. The pseudonymous nature of DAOs, for example, provides challenges for regulatory requirements such as those addressing money laundering. There is further uncertainty if and under which circumstances tokens are characterized as securities and, consequently, subject to securities regulation.

Iris Chiu's chapter is entitled "Regulating Decentralized Finance: How Financial Regulation Sheds Light on Governing DAOs" (Chapter 12) and addresses more broadly the implications of financial regulation for DAOs. One of the major areas of DAO activity is in decentralized finance (DeFi). Many of the most prominent DeFi platforms, for on-chain execution of functions such as trading and lending, are overseen by DAOs. Financial services are subject to extensive and specialized regulation in major jurisdictions such as the European Union (EU). This gives rise to the questions of how emerging regulatory policy initiatives may seek financial regulation on DeFi, and how that may shape DAO governance. Financial regulation tenets require ex ante programming and governance provision to meet regulatory objectives in user protection, public interest, and collective good. DAOs have experienced difficulties similar to those which manifest in traditional financial markets, such as conflicts of interests among users, governance controversies, unequal power structures, and disadvantages for non-technically savvy users, as well as the need for dispute resolution in view of incomplete contracting. More ex ante development of governance standards could therefore gain traction in DAOs.

The final three contributions offer broad and forward-looking perspectives on the implications of DAOs.

Jason Allen and Peter Hunn examine how DAOs might integrate into the wider corporate landscape (Chapter 13, "The Law of Digital Organizations: A Prospective"). They follow Lawrence Lessig's modalities of regulation to suggest that computer code is a form of regulation. Coders make design choices that restrict those who use this code and consequently their design choices regulate behavior. They conclude that the challenge will be to design organizations that are both compliant with the law and responsive to the logic of code. They suggest that we should treat legal and technical properties as building blocks of organizations and open our minds to rethink the infrastructure of organizational law in the age of programmable institutions.

Kelvin Low and Edmund Schuster sound a skeptical note (Chapter 14, "What Do DAOs Really Contribute?"). They point out that proponents have argued since The

DAO launched in 2016 that DAOs would solve the principal–agent problem inherent in the corporate form, yet today, they argue, DAOs remain a niche organizational structure that has little to no traction outside of crypto projects. They identify two major reasons for this failure. First, centralization and opacity serve useful functions in business organizations. The decentralization and transparency of DAOs are therefore not necessarily a benefit. Second, the security, transparency, and predictability of blockchains come at a cost, which DAO developers fail to acknowledge. This means that DAOs are ill-equipped to cope with the dangers that investors and business organizations face in the real world.

Kevin Werbach analyzes how DAOs could intersect with artificial intelligence and suggests that there are three ways in which the two technologies can be combined (Chapter 15, "Out of Control: DAOs, AI and the Question of Autonomy"). DAOs can be deployed as a governance mechanism to store, grant access to, and maintain the integrity of data and AI models. Artificial intelligence could be used to take decisions that are automatically enforced through a smart contract. DAOs themselves may function as a form of AI. Both DAOs and AI push on our traditional concept of a corporation by potentially replacing humans with machines. The pace and extent to which DAOs enhance AI, AI enhance DAOs, and autonomous AI DAOs take off remain to be seen. Even if DAOs never grow beyond the DeFi applications and collective investment vehicles which are substantial today, or fizzle out entirely as a concept, they will provide an environment for experimentation with both the governance mechanisms and legal considerations that will have growing stakes as AI development continues.

4. Conclusion

Many of the contributors to the book observe that it is not possible to make general statements about the characteristics of DAOs. There are substantial differences in the purposes and governance arrangements adopted by individual DAOs and their participants. With traditional business corporations we find differences between corporate statutes in different jurisdictions and bespoke constitutional arrangements in corporations, but these differences exist on a relatively smaller scale. Legal questions relating to DAOs cannot be quickly or preliminarily answered by reference to a standardized mental model. Judges and practitioners need to examine individual arrangements to determine the extent to which a particular arrangement is subject to specific legal rules. The contributors to this book suggest ways in which this can be done.

The blockchain field is characterized by boom-and-bust cycles and has its share of both excessive hype and illicit or fraudulent activity. The collapse of several major blockchain-related firms in 2022 fueled skepticism about the sector. Despite this, both business activity and academic interest in blockchain across multiple disciplines has continued. We believe that the contributions by a distinguished international group of corporate law scholars contained in this book raise the intellectual caliber of the field and provide value even for those who remain unconvinced of the significance of blockchains and DAOs.

By highlighting how traditional concepts from corporate law, governance, and dispute resolution may be applied to DAOs, we believe that both practitioners and policymakers will more clearly see gaps calling for new approaches, avoid the tendency to re-invent what already exists, and identify where DAOs truly have a comparative advantage. We also believe that exposure to DAOs will benefit the development of law and governance for traditional corporate entities. DAOs challenge many of the assumptions underpinning the legal, regulatory, and economic attributes of the firm. They are a novel technological experiment that presses us to ask whether governance can in fact be conducted more efficiently, and the familiar accoutrements of the firm done away with. The answers will unfold over time. Blockchain-based phenomena such as DAOs are subject to very rapid evolution, and law is not static either. We hope this volume raises the level of understanding of DAOs and offers foundations for further work across many fields and jurisdictions.

PART I
DAOs AS AN INNOVATION IN CORPORATE FORM

1
DAO Legal Forms Around the World

*Nina Reiser**

1. Introduction

The assignment of decentralized autonomous organizations (DAOs) to a specific legal company form causes enormous difficulties around the world.[1] This phenomenon is partly due to their decentralized and cross-border organization, and partly due to the fact that many of those involved consciously or unconsciously ignore legal issues.[2] Because of the fundamental differences in the organizational structure of DAOs and traditional organizations, various legal problem areas have arisen.[3] For example, the Ooki DAO, a decentralized finance (DeFi) infrastructure, was found by a Californian district court to be responsible for operating an illegal trading platform. The judgment found the Ooki DAO to be an unincorporated association, following which we may deduce joint and several liability of its members for violations of the US Commodity Exchange Act (1936).[4] Similar liability issues could also arise in other countries.[5] After clarifying the concept of DAOs (Section 2) and making some comments on the DAO Model Law (Section 3), this chapter provides an overview of chosen legal forms in different jurisdictions around the world that DAOs commonly use.[6] Without any claim to completeness, it covers the classification of DAOs under company law and the first laws for DAOs in selected states in the US (Section 4), Cayman Islands (Section 5), and Guernsey (Section 6), as well as Switzerland's options *de lege lata* and thought-provoking impulses *de lege ferenda* (Section 7). It concludes with a summary of the results and an outlook (Section 8). Aspects of international private law,[7] as well as

* The author would like to thank Prof Dr Rolf H Weber, for his valuable comments on the text, as well as Michael Kallenberg, MA HSG, Ann Sevray, BA HSG, and Sandro Terzi, BLaw, for their valued support with the research and the management of the footnote apparatus.

[1] Holger Fleischer, *Rechtsformneuschöpfungen im in- und ausländischen Gesellschaftsrecht* (Mohr Siebeck 2024) 681; Biyan Mienert, *Dezentrale autonome Organisationen (DAOs) und Gesellschaftsrecht* (Mohr Siebeck 2022) 81.

[2] Fleischer, *Rechtsformneuschöpfungen im in- und ausländischen Gesellschaftsrecht* (n 1) 681, 685 with further references.

[3] Nina Reiser and Basil Wächli, "Rechtliche Erfassung von Dezentralen Autonomen Organisationen (Teil 1)" (2024) 120 Schweizerische Juristenzeitung SJZ 755, 756.

[4] *Commodity Futures Trading Commission v Ooki DAO* [2023] US District Court, Northern District of California, 3:22-cv-05416-WHO.

[5] eg Stefanie Boss, "DAOs: Legal and Empirical Review" (2023) Amsterdam Law School Research Paper No 27/20235.

[6] For the jurisdictions commonly used by DAOs, eg, Fleischer, *Rechtsformneuschöpfungen im in- und ausländischen Gesellschaftsrecht* (n 1) 681, 688.

[7] Florence Guillaume, "Choice of Court Agreements in Disputes Involving Decentralized Autonomous Organizations (DAOs)" in Kevin Werbach, Eva Micheler, and Bianca Kremer (eds), *Foundations of*

difficulties in connecting with a decentralized form of organization,[8] are deliberately excluded.

2. Concept of DAOs

DAOs differ from simple smart contracts in that they have a form of internal organization that defines the governance of the DAO and the procedure for managing its assets.[9] In this context, the governance of DAOs describes the rules codified in the smart contracts that are used to coordinate and manage the DAO's activities and strategy.[10] A general definition of DAOs has not yet been established.[11] According to Article 3(7) DAO Model Law[12] DAOs are "smart contracts (i.e., blockchain-based software) deployed on a public permissionless Blockchain, which implements specific decision-making or governance rules enabling a multiplicity of actors to coordinate themselves in a decentralized fashion. These governance rules must be technically, although not necessarily operationally, decentralized." In contrast, the actual or operational decentralization of DAOs was a prominent defining feature in a previous draft of the European Union (EU)'s Markets in Crypto-Assets Regulation (MiCAR).[13,14] In the final version of MiCAR, however, the provisions on DAOs were omitted entirely.[15]

Decentralized Organizations: Blockchain and the Future of Corporate Law (OUP 2026); for Switzerland cf eg Reiser and Wächli, "Rechtliche Erfassung von Dezentralen Autonomen Organisationen (Teil 1)" (n 3) 755, 767–69 with further references.

[8] cf for the anchor points of the Swiss Financial Market Supervisory Authority (FINMA), Nina Reiser and Basil Wächli, "Whitepaper Decentralised Finance" (2024) Zeitschrift für Gesellschafts- und Kapitalmarktrecht GesKR 301, 305.

[9] Florence Guillaume and Sven Riva, "Blockchain Dispute Resolution for Decentralized Autonomous Organizations: The Rise of Decentralized Autonomous Justice" in Andrea Bonomi, Matthias Lehmann, and Shaheeza Lalani (eds), *Blockchain and Private International Law* (Leiden 2023) 549, 552–53.

[10] Ding Qinxu and others, "A Survey on Decentralized Autonomous Organizations (DAOs) and Their Governance" (2023) 1 World Scientific Annual Review of Fintech 5.

[11] Sven Riva, "Decentralized Autonomous Organisations (DAOs) in the Swiss Legal Order" in Andrea Bonomi and Gian Paolo Romano (eds), *Yearbook of Private International Law* (Dr. Otto Schmidt 2019/2020) 601, 612; Fleischer, *Rechtsformneuschöpfungen im in- und ausländischen Gesellschaftsrecht* (n 1) 681, 683; for compilations of various definitions Johannes Baur, *Die gesellschaftsrechtliche Außenhaftung für die Verbindlichkeiten von Decentralized Autonomous Organizations* (Peter Lang 2021) 37; Rolf H Weber, "Is There a Need for Regulation of DAOs in Switzerland?" in Florence Guillaume and Sven Riva (eds), *Decentralized Autonomous Organizations in the Legal Landscape: From Decentralized Governance to Legal Frontiers* (Edward Elgar 2025) 143, 145.

[12] COALA, DAO Model Law for Decentralized Autonomous Organisations (DAOs) (2021) 13 <https://coala.global/wp-content/uploads/2022/03/DAO-Model-Law.pdf> accessed May 5, 2025; Section 3.

[13] Regulation (EU) 2023/1114 of the European Parliament and of the Council of 31 May 2023 on markets in crypto-assets and amending Regulations (EU) No 1093/2019 and (EU) No 1095/2010 and Directives 2013/36/EU and (EU) 2019/1937 (Text with EEA relevance), ABl L 150 of 9 September 2023 40 et seq (cited MiCAR [EU]).

[14] Art 3(1)(1a) of European Parliament (2022), "Report on the proposal for a regulation of the European Parliament and of the Council on markets in crypto-assets and amending Directive (EU) 2019/1937", COM[2020]0593 – C9-0306/2020 – 2020/0265 (COD).

[15] Reiser and Wächli, "Rechtliche Erfassung von Dezentralen Autonomen Organisationen (Teil 1)" (n 3) 755, 758.

3. DAO Model Law

In 2021, the Coalition of Automated Legal Applications (COALA) published the DAO Model Law to define a flexible legal framework that is tailored to the features and needs of DAOs and their future development, while providing the necessary legal certainty for DAOs and their participants.[16] Using a principle-based approach, an in-depth survey of corporate law provisions was conducted to identify the policy objectives and the principles underlying current legislation.[17] In accordance with the principles of functional and regulatory equivalence, the DAO Model Law stipulates the technological features that must be fulfilled by a DAO to be considered equivalent to a company.[18] Designed as a best practice guide for DAOs, the DAO Model Law is intended to help states to modernize their corporate law.[19]

A DAO that was established according to the conditions of the transposed or adopted legal rules of the corresponding state qualifies as a legal entity.[20] The DAO Model Law also contains provisions on continuation of the legal personality and limitation of liability in the event of a hard fork,[21,22] a restructuring,[23] or a so-called failure event.[24,25] If the requirements of the DAO Model Law are met, the liability of DAO members is limited.[26] Nevertheless, a minimum capitalization is not mandatory.[27] Additionally, states can authorize an accreditation authority[28] to monitor whether a DAO continues to fulfill the conditions for legal personality[29] when adopting the DAO Model Law.[30] Among other prerequisites, a DAO must be set up on a public blockchain.[31] Beyond that, bylaws that are comprehensible to a layperson[32] have to be

[16] COALA, DAO Model Law (n 12); DAO Model Law for Decentralized Autonomous Organizations (DAOs), LexTech Institute; for an overview of the DAO Model Law, Florence Guillaume and Sven Riva, "DAO, code et loi: Je regime technologique et juridique de la decentralized autonomous organization" (2021) 4 Revue de Droit International d'Assas 206, 217–22; Rolf H Weber, "Neues 'Kleid' für Dezentrale Autonome Organisationen?" (2024) Jusletter from 3 June 2024 N 1 18–23; Nina Reiser and Basil Wächli, "Rechtliche Erfassung von Dezentralen Autonomen Organisationen (Teil 2)" 120 Schweizerische Juristenzeitung SJZ 863, 865.

[17] COALA, DAO Model Law (n 12) 6.

[18] ibid 2–3, 7–9.

[19] ibid 2, 5–7.

[20] ibid 2.

[21] A hard fork means a blockchain software upgrade that is not compatible with previous versions of the blockchain software, and therefore requires all users to upgrade (COALA, DAO Model Law (n 12) Art 3(13), 14; also Kyung TaeckMinn, "Towards Enhanced Oversight of 'Self-Governing' Decentralized Autonomous Organisations: Case Study of The DAO and Its Shortcomings" (2019) New York University Journal of Intellectual Property & Entertainment Law 139 et seq.

[22] COALA, DAO Model Law (n 12) Arts 16, 44–46.

[23] ibid Arts 17, 46–47.

[24] ibid Arts 3(11), 13.

[25] On the whole in detail Weber, "Neues 'Kleid' für Dezentrale Autonome Organisationen?" (n 16) 47–52.

[26] COALA, DAO Model Law (n 12) Arts 5, 24–27.

[27] Reiser and Wächli, "Rechtliche Erfassung von Dezentralen Autonomen Organisationen (Teil 2)" (n 16) 863, 866.

[28] Definition in COALA, DAO Model Law (n 12) Arts 3(1), 12.

[29] ibid Arts 4(1), 18.

[30] ibid Arts 4(4), 19.

[31] ibid Arts 4(1)(a), 18.

[32] Definition in ibid Arts 3(5), 12.

published via a GUI[33] or a public forum.[34,35] Other conditions are the use of a unique public address[36] (instead of a firm)[37] and the at least technical decentralization of governance mechanisms.[38] Instead of a minimum capitalization, the complete software code of the DAO must be in open source format in a public forum, for example on GitHub,[39] to allow anyone to review it.[40] To protect shareholders and creditors, the software on which the DAO is based must be subject to a quality assurance.[41,42] Furthermore, anyone may read the funding situation, the governance, and any token issuance from the permissionless blockchain[43] or the publicly available GUI – which must also be comprehensible to the layperson.[44] Eventually, because of the decentralized nature of DAOs, a physical, registered address becomes redundant. Instead, a publicly specified mechanism that allows a layperson to contact the DAO must exist.[45] In addition, there must be a dispute resolution mechanism.[46] As far as the internal organization is concerned, the founders, administrators, and members of a DAO have considerable leeway.[47] For example, the DAO Model Law contains neither an obligation to hold general meetings nor provisions on their frequency or other modalities.[48] The delegation of tasks to administrative bodies is also optional.[49] To undertake tasks, which cannot be achieved on-chain,[50] DAOs may also have one or more legal representatives.[51] The liability for discretionary decisions of developers, members, participants, and legal representatives of DAOs is limited by the fact that they generally do not have to fulfill any fiduciary duties unless they explicitly hold themselves out as a fiduciary or the DAO bylaws stipulate corresponding duties.[52]

[33] Definition in ibid Arts 3(12), 13.
[34] Definition in ibid Arts 3(30), 15.
[35] ibid Art 4(1)(f), 18.
[36] Definition in ibid Art 3(29), 15.
[37] Reiser and Wächli, "Rechtliche Erfassung von Dezentralen Autonomen Organisationen (Teil 2)" (n 16) 863, 866.
[38] COALA, DAO Model Law (n 12) Arts 4(1)(g), 19; cf Section 2.
[39] GitHub is the most established web server for software projects. In public forums, programmers can publish their code in open source format so that it can be reviewed and further developed by the community (Mienert (n 1) 143 fn 357).
[40] COALA, DAO Model Law (n 12) Arts 4(1)(c), 18.
[41] ibid Arts 3(32), 15–16.
[42] ibid Arts 4(1)(d), 18.
[43] ibid Arts 4(1)(a), 18.
[44] ibid Arts 4(1)(e), 18, 23.
[45] ibid Arts 4(1)(i), 19.
[46] ibid Arts 4(1)(j), 19, 22; Reiser and Wächli, "Rechtliche Erfassung von Dezentralen Autonomen Organisationen (Teil 2)" (n 16) 863, 867–68; Bianca Kremer, "Code, Community, and Conflict: DAO Disputes" in Kevin Werbach, Eva Micheler, and Bianca Kremer (eds), *Foundations of Decentralized Organizations: Blockchain and the Future of Corporate Law* (OUP 2026).
[47] COALA, DAO Model Law (n 12) 35.
[48] ibid Arts 12, 35–36.
[49] ibid Arts 13(1), 37.
[50] ibid Arts 3(22), 14.
[51] ibid Arts 14(1), 38–39.
[52] ibid Arts 15, 39–41; Reiser and Wächli, "Rechtliche Erfassung von Dezentralen Autonomen Organisationen (Teil 2)" (n 16) 863, 869.

4. The US

4.1. Classification of DAOs under Company Law

In the US, DAOs sometimes choose a limited liability company (LLC) as their legal form, preferably from Delaware,[53] even though this state has not recognized DAOs as legal entities. In fact, the Delaware LLC format is to some extent not suitable for the autonomous and decentralized nature of DAOs. Among other issues, for example, under certain circumstances, it may not be possible to maintain the anonymity of the DAO members. However, the Delaware LLC format permits the adaption to DAO principles and procedures to a significant extent. Typically, the LLC is the owner and the beneficiary of the funds that are raised in a DAO's token sale. The functions that will be operated through smart contracts are specified in the LLC's operating agreement. These functions include acting as custodian for assets, issuing interests, registering membership interests, counting the votes of members, and providing notice. Beyond that, the operating agreement ensures restriction of fiduciary duties, limitation on liability, and other DAO characteristics.[54]

Unless a DAO is registered as an LLC or (less likely) a corporation,[55] it should fall under the law of partnerships according to the model legislation, the Revised Uniform Partnership Act (RUPA).[56] The partnership has a default function.[57] Accordingly, the literature to date has almost unanimously come to the conclusion that profit-oriented DAOs "neatly fit the classic default business-entity form of a partnership."[58] This is consistent with the judgment mentioned at the beginning,[59] according to which the Ooki DAO was found to be responsible for operating an illegal trading platform and to qualify as an unincorporated association, following which we may deduce joint and several liability of its members. Partners of a partnership in the US have unlimited, joint and several liability for all contractual and non-contractual partnership liabilities.[60] Against this background and the widespread legal uncertainty regarding the legal status of DAOs, the first states of the US have recently taken corresponding legislative initiatives.[61] The most important of these are briefly explained below.

[53] Fleischer, *Rechtsformneuschöpfungen im in- und ausländischen Gesellschaftsrecht* (n 1) 681, 688.

[54] Gail Weinstein, Steven Lofchie, and Jason Schwartz, "A Primer on DAOs" (2022) Harvard Law School Forum on Corporate Governance <https://corpgov.law.harvard.edu/2022/09/17/a-primer-on-daos/> accessed May 5, 2025.

[55] "A DAO can form as a corporation and state in its articles of incorporation and bylaws that certain decisions are delegated to the DAO members and that the corporation will abide by those decisions. However, in light of the many inconsistencies between a DAO and the corporate form, this route tends to be avoided and best practices for implementing a DAO in corporate form have not been established." ibid.

[56] cf eg *Christian Sarcuni v bZx DAO* [2023] 3:22-cv-00618-LAB-DEB (SD Cal 2023) 17; Laila Metjahic, "Deconstructing the DAO: The Need for Legal Recognition and the Application of Securities Laws to Decentralized Organizations" (2018) Cardozo Law Review 1533, 1553–58.

[57] Sebastian Bong and Felix Jaeger "§ 12 Vereinigte Staaten" in Holger Fleischer (ed), *Personengesellschaften im Rechtsvergleich* (Leinen 2021) 436 et seq, § 12 fn 3.

[58] Carla L Reyes, "If Rockefeller Were a Coder" (2019) The George Washington Law Review 373, 398.

[59] Section 1.

[60] §§ 305 and 306(a) RUPA.

[61] cf for an overview Jordan Teague, "Starting a DAO in the USA? Steer Clear of DAO Legislation. A Primer on DAO Legislation in Multiple States" (*The Defiant*, 2022) <https://thedefiant.io/news/resea

4.2. First Laws for DAOs in Individual States

4.2.1. Vermont blockchain-based LLC

An important initial impetus came from the legislature in Vermont, which created "blockchain-based limited liability companies" (BBLLCs).[62] This statute, passed in 2018, enables an entity to incorporate or reincorporate its business in this form if it is organized "for the purpose of operating a business that utilizes blockchain technology for a material portion of its business activities."[63] Moreover, incorporators are required to "state whether the decentralized consensus ledger or database utilized or enabled by the BBLLC will be fully decentralized or partially decentralized and whether such ledger or database will be fully or partially public or private."[64] Hence, as under the DAO Model Law,[65] the governance rules appear to be technically, but not necessarily operationally, decentralized. Additionally, the utilized blockchain is not mandatorily public.

In practical terms, this company form adopts blockchain not only as an alternative allowed under certain conditions, but as a primary tool from governance to corporate record-keeping.[66] The operating agreement must include a summary of the company's mission or purpose, information on the blockchain technology to be used, protocols for responding to security breaches, voting procedures for certain types of matters, the procedure for becoming a member, as well as the rights and obligations of each group of participants.[67] In addition, it is possible for a participant to perform various functions, such as being both a manager and a developer, on the condition that the person concerned complies with any applicable fiduciary duties, such as refraining from competition with the organization.[68] However, under Vermont's standard LLC law, this duty may be reasonably restricted in the operating agreement. Additionally, the provisions of Vermont's standard LLC law also apply to BBLLCs.[69]

4.2.2. Wyoming's special regimes for DAOs

4.2.2.1. DAO LLC

It was Wyoming that enacted the first law in the US on DAOs, effective from July 1, 2021.[70] To the extent that it is not inconsistent with these special provisions, DAO LLCs are also governed by Wyoming's standard LLC Law.[71] Besides some definitions,

rch-and-opinion/starting-a-dao-in-the-usa-steer-clear-of-dao-legislation> accessed May 5, 2025; <https://www.stinson.com/newsroom-publications-decentralized-autonomous-organization-laws-across-the-us> accessed May 5, 2025.

[62] No 205 An act to blockchain business development (2018) 269; cf Pierluigi Matera, "Delaware's Dominance, Wyoming's Dare: New Challenge, Same Outcome?" (2022) 27 Fordham Journal of Corporate & Financial Law 73, 123.

[63] No 205 An act to blockchain business development (2018) 269.

[64] ibid.

[65] Section 3.

[66] Matera (n 62) 124.

[67] No 205 An act to blockchain business development (2018) 269.

[68] ibid; Teague (n 61).

[69] No 205 An act to blockchain business development (2018) 269; Teague (n 61).

[70] Wyo Stat Ann § 17-31-101–§ 17-31-115 (2024); Matera (n 62) 130; Teague (n 61).

[71] Wyo Stat Ann § 17-31-101(a) (2024); Teague (n 61).

the focus is on the formation requirements, which differ from the ordinary LLC and governance structures.[72] First, the articles of organization must express state its status as a DAO LLC.[73] In addition, its registered name shall "include wording or abbreviation to denote its status as a DAO, specifically 'DAO,' 'LAO,' or 'DAO LLC.'"[74] Finally, a clear and visible warning is required that the rights and obligations of members, such as reduced fiduciary duties, transfer restrictions, and withdrawal or dissolution rights, may differ significantly from those of an ordinary LLC.[75]

The DAO LLC is founded by delivering the articles of organization to the secretary of state for filing by a person who need not be a member of the DAO.[76] Any lawful purpose is possible, whether for profit or not.[77] The articles of organization must include a publicly available identifier of any smart contract that directly manages, facilitates, or operates the DAO.[78] Additionally, the articles of organization and the smart contracts regulate, among other things, the relations among the members and between the members and the DAO, the members' rights and duties, as well as the DAO's activities and the conduct of those activities.[79] The operation of a DAO may be supplemented by an operating agreement.[80] Thereby, the articles of organization take precedence over the operating agreement and the smart contracts over the articles of organization.[81] In contrast, in the case of an ordinary LLC, the operating agreement is the central governance document.[82]

In addition, the articles of organization must include a statement on "how the decentralized autonomous organization shall be managed by its members, including the extent to which the management will be conducted algorithmically."[83] As far as membership rights and obligations are concerned, membership interests in a DAO are generally determined by their contribution of digital assets.[84] Members have no individual right to information.[85] The fiduciary duties imposed on members are greatly reduced.[86] However, all "members shall be subject to the implied contractual covenant of good faith and fair dealing."[87] Finally, it should be noted that the state has the power to intervene in the event of unlawful activity. In this case, the secretary of state can order the dissolution of the DAO.[88]

72 Fleischer, *Rechtsformneuschöpfungen im in- und ausländischen Gesellschaftsrecht* (n 1) 681, 692.
73 Wyo Stat Ann § 17-31-104(a) (2024).
74 Wyo Stat Ann § 17-31-104(d) (2024).
75 Wyo Stat Ann § 17-31-104(c) (2024).
76 Wyo Stat Ann § 17-31-105(a) (2024).
77 Wyo Stat Ann § 17-31-105(c) (2024).
78 Wyo Stat Ann § 17-31-106(b) (2024).
79 Wyo Stat Ann § 17-31-106(c) (2024).
80 Wyo Stat Ann § 17-31-108 (2024).
81 Wyo Stat Ann § 17-31-115 (2024).
82 cf *Elf Atochem N America, Inc v Jaffari* [1999] Supreme Court of Delaware 727 A.2d 286, 291; Fleischer, *Rechtsformneuschöpfungen im in- und ausländischen Gesellschaftsrecht* (n 1) 681, 693; Holger Fleischer, "Die Erfolgsgeschichte der Limited Liability Company in den Vereinigten Staaten Gegenstück zu GmbH oder GmbH & Co. KG?" (2022) Zeitschrift für Gesellschaftsrecht, Unternehmensrecht und Steuerrecht GmbHR 1179, 1184–85.
83 Wyo Stat Ann § 17-31-104(e) (2024).
84 Wyo Stat Ann § 17-31-111(a)(i) (2024).
85 Wyo Stat Ann § 17-31-112 (2024).
86 Fleischer, *Rechtsformneuschöpfungen im in- und ausländischen Gesellschaftsrecht* (n 1) 681, 694.
87 Wyo Stat Ann § 17-31-110 (2024).
88 Wyo Stat Ann § 17-31-114(a)(v) (2024).

4.2.2.2. Decentralized unincorporated nonprofit association (DUNA)

An alternative regime for DAOs is gaining momentum in the US. Wyoming's Decentralized Unincorporated Nonprofit Association Act (Senate File 50), signed on March 7, 2024 and in force since July 1, 2024, allows DAOs to organize as so-called DUNAs—effectively a "digital UNA" in the same way that the 2021 statute created a "digital LLC."[89] In general, UNA laws are suitable for DAOs due to their flexibility in accommodating ad hoc structures and significant informalities.[90] Potential benefits of the technology-agnostic DUNA[91] include liability protections for DAO members, the flexibility to incorporate the DAO's decentralized governance into the legal entity, the support of on-chain voting as a governance principle, and the absence of a mandatory hierarchy of individuals responsible for managing the enterprise (eg directors, officers, or managers).[92] The DUNA only makes available limited administrator roles with authority that can be flexibly defined to execute, where necessary, the directives of the DAO's decentralized governance.[93]

4.2.3. Tennessee decentralized organization (DO) LLC

Less than a year after Wyoming introduced the Wyoming DAO LLC, Tennessee became the second state to introduce a special DAO regulation.[94] In many respects, it is based on the Wyoming model but refers to the new legal form variant of its LLC, abbreviated to decentralized organization (DO).[95]

4.2.4. First application examples of DAO Model Law

The similarity of the text of the following bills to the text of the DAO Model Law indicates that they are based thereon:[96] On January 1, 2024, with the implementation of the Decentralized Autonomous Organization Act (Utah DAO Act),[97] Utah introduced the limited liability decentralized autonomous organization (Utah LLD)[98] as a different legal form that is based on the DAO Model Law, instead of trying to fit DAOs

[89] Miles Jennings and David Kerr, "The DUNA: An Oasis for DAOs" (*a16z crypto*, 2024) <https://a16zcrypto.com/posts/article/duna-for-daos/> accessed June 4, 2025.

[90] David Kerr and Miles Jennings, 'A Legal Framework for Decentralized Autonomous Organizations—Part III: Model Decentralized Unincorporated Nonprofit Association Act' (*SSRN*, March 5, 2024) 2 <https://ssrn.com/abstract=4749245> or http://dx.doi.org/10.2139/ssrn.4749245> accessed June 4, 2025.

[91] ibid 3.

[92] The Nouns Foundation Blog, "Exploring a New Legal Framework for Nouns DAO | The Wyoming DUNA" (2024) <https://foundation.nouns.wtf/> accessed June 4, 2025.

[93] ibid; Kerr and Jennings (n 90) 3, and for further detailed explanation of DUNA's characteristics, 10–14.

[94] Ryan McDowell, "Tennessee Permits Decentralized Autonomous Organization to Organize as LLCs" (*Tennessee Bar Association*, 2022) <https://www.tba.org/?pg=Articles&blAction=showEntry&blogEntry=73474> accessed May 5, 2025; Kathryn Rickmeyer, "Tennessee Becomes Second State to Pass DAO Legislation" (*Nashville Scene*, 2022) <https://www.nashvillescene.com/news/pithinthewind/tennessee-becomes-second-state-to-pass-dao-legislation/article_ecbd4cbe-b5e2-11ec-abe0-77a2385be512.html> accessed May 5, 2025.

[95] For more information Matt Miller, "Beyond a Reasonable DAOubt: Tennessee's Limited Liability Statute for Decentralized Autonomous Organizations (DAOS)" (*K&L Gates Hub*, 2022) <https://www.klgates.com/Beyond-a-Reasonable-DAOubt-Tennessees-Limited-Liability-Statute-for-Decentralized-Autonomous-Organizations-DAOs-8-4-2022> accessed May 5, 2025.

[96] Boss (n 5) 7.

[97] Utah Code § 48-5-101–§ 48-5-406 (2024).

[98] Utah Code § 48-5-105(1)(a) (2024).

into an LLC form.[99] Additionally, on May 15, 2024, the New Hampshire Senate passed the New Hampshire Decentralized Autonomous Organization Act (NH DAO Act),[100] which provides for the introduction of the New Hampshire DAO (NH DAO)[101] as a new corporate form on July 1, 2025, also based on the DAO Model Law.[102]

5. Cayman Islands

In the Cayman Islands, the foundation company, which was introduced under the Foundation Companies Law 2007 and acts similarly to an incorporated trust, is popular in conjunction with DAOs.[103] A foundation company that is unique to the Cayman Islands, is a hybrid corporate vehicle with separate legal personality and limited liability.[104] It has a flexible corporate structure[105] and can function like a trust or a foundation with the possibility of identifying beneficiaries to receive benefits from the foundation over time. In addition, it is possible to confer certain powers on persons or entities other than the directors of the foundation.[106] Beyond that, a foundation can cease to have members (ie shareholders), making it an ownerless vehicle.[107]

For DAOs, the foundation company has several advantages. As noted, the fact that a foundation does not need members fits well with the decentralization of ownership and control.[108] The separate legal personality allows the foundation to execute contracts and token agreements and open exchange or bank accounts.[109] Beyond that, the option to build in control mechanisms to be held by persons other than the directors allows the founding or core team members to have a say in the direction of the foundation. Other advantages include its quick establishment, the fact that the foundation company is a recognized structure in connection with DAOs, its apparently clear regulatory regime, the seemingly high quality of service providers in the Cayman Islands, and the tax advantages. Furthermore, separate bylaws, rather than the constitutional documents, may contain more specific details on how the foundation functions in practice.[110]

99 Boss (n 5) 5; Reiser and Wächli, "Rechtliche Erfassung von Dezentralen Autonomen Organisationen (Teil 1)" (n 3) 863, 869–70.

100 New Hampshire Revised Statutes § 301-B:1-B:20, Annotated (NH RSA) (Hause Bill 645-FN [NH DAO Act] (2023) <https:// gencourt.state.nh.us[bill_status/billinfo.aspx?id=566&inflect=2> accessed May 5, 2025.

101 § 301-B:5(XXIII) NH RSA; also Boss (n 5) 6–7; Reiser and Wächli, "Rechtliche Erfassung von Dezentralen Autonomen Organisationen (Teil 2)" (n 16) 863, 870 et seq.

102 Boss (n 5) 5 et seq; Reiser and Wächli, "Rechtliche Erfassung von Dezentralen Autonomen Organisationen (Teil 2)" (n 16) 863, 870–71.

103 Carey Olsen, "Cayman Islands Foundation Companies for DAOs, Defi and NFTs" (*Carey Olsen*, 2022) <https://www.careyolsen.com/insights/briefings/cayman-islands-foundation-companies-daos-defi-and-nfts> accessed May 5, 2025; "Where to Incorporate a DAO" (*Flag Theory*, 2024) <https://flagtheory.com/where-to-incorporate-a-dao/#cayman-islands6>.

104 Olsen (n 103).

105 Alex Campbell and Harold Koster, "Decentralised Autonomous Organisations: Legal Personality under English Law?" (2023) 34(12) ICCLR 677, 692–93.

106 Olsen (n 103); Foundation Companies Law 2017, ss 2(1) and 8(2).

107 Olsen (n 103).

108 Campbell and Koster (n105) 677, 693; ibid.

109 ibid.

110 Olsen (n 103).

However, the mandatory appointment of supervisors and/or directors creates an agency problem. Since an ideal DAO should be fully decentralized, proposals that the token-holders pass should be automatically enacted by the organization. The fact that actions must be taken by supervisors and/or directors, undermines transparency and certainty by recording decisions and actions on a blockchain. The token-holders must trust in these individuals to enact decisions in accordance with the token-holders' intentions.[111]

6. Guernsey

Guernsey's trust law of 2007 allows for the creation of a non-charitable special purpose trust (SPT). An SPT is established by a written instrument which clearly defines its lawful, non-charitable purposes.[112] Its flexibility in terms of governance structure and on the issue of who can serve as trustees and enforcers make SPTs well-suited for DAOs.[113] Tax advantages should also be mentioned here.[114] The right to direct, add, or remove trustees (and the enforcer) or to terminate the trust and transfer funds is retained by DAO token-holders.[115] The settlor, the legal entity representing the DAO, can be appointed as the "enforcer."[116] Other offshore trusts, however, stipulate that trustees must include a licensed local trust company.[117] This prevents typical DAO committee members from serving as the only trustees.[118]

The Guernsey SPT is particularly commonly used by DAOs.[119] A prominent example is the dYdX trust, a prominent decentralized crypto-token exchange, in which assets are transferred from a smart contract controlled by the DAO to an SPT to issue token-based grants to third parties.[120] The reason for selecting an SPT correlates to the notion of a so-called "entity fit": "[t]he Purpose Trust under Guernsey law allows a DAO to retain all the characteristics of a DAO and continue to minimize trust in any group or person."[121] However, the fact that a DAO vote is able to direct the trustees to

[111] Campbell and Koster (n 105) 677, 694.

[112] Axis Advisory, "Legal Framework" (*subDAO Handbook*) <https://handbook.dydxopsdao.com/post/legal-framework> accessed May 5, 2025.

[113] UK Law Commission, "Decentralised Autonomous Organisations (DAOs): A Scoping Paper" (July 2024) 129 <https://webarchive.nationalarchives.gov.uk/ukgwa/20250109094345mp_/https://cloud-platform-e218f50a4812967ba1215eaecede923f.s3.amazonaws.com/uploads/sites/30/2024/07/DAOs-scoping-paper-110724.pdf> accessed May 5, 2025; Axis Advisory (n 112).

[114] UK Law Commission (n 113) 42.

[115] ibid 129.

[116] Trusts (Guernsey) Law (2007), Art 12(10).

[117] Cayman Islands Trusts Act 2021 (Supplement No 3 published with Legislation Gazette No 19 of 26 February, 2021) 105(1); Virgin Islands Trustee Act (Revised Edition showing the law as at 1 January 2020), ss 84A(1) and 84A(3)(c).

[118] UK Law Commission (n 113) 129.

[119] ibid.

[120] "Purpose Trust Instrument of dYdX Grants Trust" <https://drive.google.com/file/d/1HV97VtmeHSt2Fof920TzR7utuSStBFhZ/view> accessed May 5, 2025; dYdX Foundation, "Legal Framework for Non-U.S. Trusts in DAOs" (*dYdX Foundation*, 2022) <https://www.dydx.foundation/blog/legal-framework-non-us-trusts-in-daos> accessed May 5, 2025.

[121] dYdX Foundation (n 120).

act in a particular way is partially considered to be a "roundabout way" of maintaining the decentralized nature of DAOs being inconsistent with the autonomy of the SPT and the traditional concept of the role of the trustee.[122]

7. Switzerland

Switzerland does not (yet) have a specific legal form for DAOs.[123] As far as the existing company forms are concerned, the principle of a single and uniform registered seat pursuant to Article 56 of the Swiss Civil Code (CC)[124] shows that the Swiss company law system is conceptually designed for centralized forms of organization. Hence, there is a tension with the decentralized structure of DAOs.[125] It is therefore not surprising that the existing Swiss company forms are not, or only to a limited extent, suitable for the legal structuring of DAOs.[126]

Because the liability for the obligations of the association is limited to its assets (unless the articles of association provide otherwise),[127] the nature of association law is flexible and largely dispositive[128] and the formal requirements for the establishment are low, the association, under Article 60 ff CC is generally considered to be the most suitable Swiss company form for the legal organization of DAOs.[129] However, for the following reasons, a complete decentralization of the association is not feasible within the current legal framework.[130] First, some proponents of the doctrine consider the complete renunciation of the executive body to be inadmissible.[131] Secondly, if the

[122] UK Law Commission (n 113) 129.

[123] The comments on Switzerland are largely based on Reiser and Wächli, "Rechtliche Erfassung von Dezentralen Autonomen Organisationen (Teil 1)" (n 3) 755; Reiser and Wächli, "Rechtliche Erfassung von Dezentralen Autonomen Organisationen (Teil 2)" (n 16), 863.

[124] Swiss Civil Code of 10 December 1907 (CC) SR 210.

[125] Arthur Meier-Hayoz and Peter Forstmoser, *Schweizerisches Gesellschaftsrecht* (13th edn, Stämpfli 2023) § 11 fn10; Reiser and Wächli, "Rechtliche Erfassung von Dezentralen Autonomen Organisationen (Teil 1)" (n 3) 755, 769.

[126] Reiser and Wächli, "Rechtliche Erfassung von Dezentralen Autonomen Organisationen (Teil 1)" (n 3) 755, 761–67 and 769.

[127] Art 75a CC.

[128] In detail, Meier-Hayoz and Forstmoser (n 125) § 20 N 34–36.

[129] Weber, "Neues 'Kleid' für Dezentrale Autonome Organisationen?" (n 16) 4, 12; Stephan D Meyer, "Dezentrale autonome Organisationen (DAOs) und das Gesellschaftsrecht der Zukunft. Selbstdurchsetzende Programme als Exekutivorgane globaler Peer-to-Peer-Gesellschaften" (2023) Aktuelle Juristische Praxis AJP 319, 338; Reiser and Wächli, "Rechtliche Erfassung von Dezentralen Autonomen Organisationen (Teil 1)" (n 3) 755, 764–65 with further references; Rolf H Weber, "Is There a Need for Regulation of DAOs in Switzerland?" (n 11) 143, 155, 157–58.

[130] Meyer (n 129) 319, 332; Reiser and Wächli, "Rechtliche Erfassung von Dezentralen Autonomen Organisationen (Teil 1)" (n 3) 755, 764.

[131] Urs Scherrer and Rafael Brägger, "Art. 69 ZGB" in Thomas Geiser and Christiana Fountoulakis (eds), *Basler Kommentar, Zivilgesetzbuch I: Art. 1-456 ZGB* (7th edn, Helbing Lichtenhahn 2022) N 1; Wolfgang Portmann, *Schweizerisches Privatrecht Bd. 11/5: Das Schweizerische Vereinsrecht* (3rd edn, Helbing & Lichtenhahn 2005) N 356; for a different opinion: Hans Michael Riemer, "Vorbemerkung zu Art. 64-69c ZGB" in Regina E Aebi-Müller and Christoph Müller (eds), *Berner Kommentar zum schweizerischen Privatrecht, Zivilgesetzbuch, Die juristischen Personen, Die Vereine: Art 60-79 ZGB, Art. 712m Abs. 2 ZGB (Stockwerkeigentümergemeinschaft)* (2nd edn, Stämpfli 2023) N 26–27; Weber, "Neues 'Kleid' für Dezentrale Autonome Organisationen?" (n 16) 35; left the question open Meyer (n 129) 319, 333–34; Bruno Pasquier and Harald Bärtschi, "Dezentrale Autonome Organisationen für Immobilien" (2024) Zeitschrift für Gesellschafts- und Kapitalmarktrecht GesKR 200, 210.

association is subject to an audit in accordance with Article 69b CC, the external auditors are also mandatory as an additional body.[132] Atypical and *de lege lata* probably associated with legal uncertainty would also be the securitization of membership rights.[133] Last but not least, the association is generally not available for commercial purposes.[134]

Whether Maverick-DAOs[135] qualify as simple partnerships is controversially discussed in the doctrine. It is clear that the simple partnership is generally not suitable as a legal form for DAOs due to its person-related structure, the personal liability of its members, and the existing legal uncertainty in connection with the transfer of tokenized company shares. Nevertheless, there is likely to be at least a practical risk that a court will classify a DAO in Switzerland as a simple partnership with personal liability of its members due to the default function of this company form.[136]

As far as foundations pursuant to Article 80 ff CC are concerned, the foundations' assets must be dedicated to a specific purpose, which is usually, but not necessarily, of an ideal nature.[137] Both foundations and DAOs tie up special-purpose assets, which are protected against misappropriation by the solidification principle under foundation law and by the corresponding programming of the blockchain application.[138] At first glance, DAOs thus have some parallels with foundations.[139] However, the fact that foundations only come into existence upon entry in the commercial register is an argument against structuring DAOs as foundations.[140] Furthermore, the dedicated assets must be separated from the founder and in principle, the founder's will can no longer be changed after establishment.[141] Due to the separation principle mentioned earlier and the associated inadmissibility of "foundations for the founder" this legal form is not suitable for DAOs.[142]

[132] Meyer (n 129) 319, 332 and 335.

[133] ibid 319, 337; Reiser and Wächli, "Rechtliche Erfassung von Dezentralen Autonomen Organisationen (Teil 1)" (n 3) 755, 762 and 765.

[134] In more detail, Reiser and Wächli, "Rechtliche Erfassung von Dezentralen Autonomen Organisationen (Teil 1)" (n 3) 755, 764–65 and 769; Art 60(1) CC.

[135] "Some within the industry think that if you don't subject yourself to the regulatory regime of a given jurisdiction that you're somehow not subject to it. By doing that, you're actually subjecting yourself to all jurisdictions" (Interview with Miles Jennings in *Leo Schwartz*, Wyoming wants to become the Delaware of DAOs with new crypto law for decentralized autonomous organizations, *Fortune Crypto* from May 8, 2024 <https:/ /fortune.com/crypto/2024/03/08/wyomingdao-a16z-crypto-crypto-blockchain-ooki/> accessed May 5, 2025); Reiser and Wächli, "Rechtliche Erfassung von Dezentralen Autonomen Organisationen (Teil 1)" (n 3) 755, fn 234.

[136] Art 520(2) of the Federal Act on the Amendment of the Swiss Civil Code (Part Five: The Code of Obligations) of 30 March 1911 (CO), SR 220; in more detail, Reiser and Wächli, "Rechtliche Erfassung von Dezentralen Autonomen Organisationen (Teil 1)" (n 3) 755, 761–62 and 769 with further references.

[137] Meier-Hayoz and Forstmoser (n 125) § 23 fn 18.

[138] Meyer (n 129) 319, 330.

[139] Weber, "Neues 'Kleid' für Dezentrale Autonome Organisationen?" (n 16) 11; Weber, "Is There a Need for Regulation of DAOs in Switzerland?" (n 11) 143, 154.

[140] Meier-Hayoz and Forstmoser (n 125) § 23 fn 18; Reiser and Wächli, "Rechtliche Erfassung von Dezentralen Autonomen Organisationen (Teil 1)" (n 3) 755, 766.

[141] Meier-Hayoz and Forstmoser (n 125) § 23 fn 18.

[142] Meyer (n 129) 319, 330; Reiser and Wächli, "Rechtliche Erfassung von Dezentralen Autonomen Organisationen (Teil 1)" (n 3) 755, 766; Weber, "Is There a Need for Regulation of DAOs in Switzerland?" (n 11)143, 154–55.

Because of the current uncertainty regarding the legal classification of DAOs, there is a practical need to recognize them under company law as legal entities with their own legal personality and limited liability.[143] Some proponents of the doctrine argue that current association law already largely meets this need. To take account of the technology-related particularities of DAOs and to eliminate existing legal uncertainties in the structuring of DAOs as associations, selective amendments to the law on associations are proposed.[144]

However, since the association is generally not available for commercial purposes, in the author's opinion, the implementation of a Swiss DAO company form *sui generis* should be examined at least for DAOs with commercial purposes,[145] possibly alongside, or as a supplement to, the postulated amendments to association law for DAOs without commercial purposes.[146] The DAO Model Law has created a well-founded basis for the legal structure of a corresponding DAO company *sui generis* on the basis of functional and legal equivalence. Utah and New Hampshire have already implemented the DAO Model Law.[147] In principle, this should also be suitable as a basis for the introduction of a DAO company or legal form in Switzerland. To ensure that the legal enforcement function can also be fulfilled without an entry in the commercial register, the introduction of an accreditation authority to verify the formation requirements or a decentralized DAO register should be examined when implementing the DAO Model Law in Switzerland—similar to the legislation in Utah and New Hampshire. The implementation of an obligation to designate an alternative dispute resolution mechanism for disputes between DAO members and between the DAO and third parties is to be welcomed in principle. However, in deviation from the DAO Model Law, it should not be possible to dispense with compliance with minimum procedural standards. Unlike the DAO Model Law, the principle of a single and uniform registered seat should be maintained. In contrast, the designation of a legal domicile proves to be dispensable when introducing the electronic delivery of official documents, if DAOs are obliged to designate a public communication mechanism. The electronic delivery of official documents would therefore need to be examined in more detail.[148]

8. Conclusion and Outlook

As mentioned at the beginning,[149] this overview on DAO legal forms around the world shows that the assignment of DAOs to concrete legal company forms causes enormous

[143] In detail, Reiser and Wächli, "Rechtliche Erfassung von Dezentralen Autonomen Organisationen (Teil 2)" (n 16) 863.

[144] In detail, Weber, "Neues 'Kleid' für Dezentrale Autonome Organisationen?" (n 16) 39–51; Reiser and Wächli, "Rechtliche Erfassung von Dezentralen Autonomen Organisationen (Teil 2)" (n 16) 863, 871–72; Weber, "Is There a Need for Regulation of DAOs in Switzerland?" (n 11) 143, 158–61.

[145] In detail, Reiser and Wächli, "Rechtliche Erfassung von Dezentralen Autonomen Organisationen (Teil 2)" (n 16) 863, 872–76.

[146] ibid 876.

[147] Section 4.2.4.

[148] Reiser and Wächli, "Rechtliche Erfassung von Dezentralen Autonomen Organisationen (Teil 2)" (n 16) 863, 872–77.

[149] Section 1.

difficulties internationally. That is why some states have recently taken corresponding legislative initiatives. Since DAOs must be covered by company law,[150] states should examine their company law accordingly and adapt it where necessary. Although existing, nonspecific legal forms of certain jurisdictions, such as the Cayman Islands' foundation company,[151] Guernsey's Special Purpose Trust,[152] or Switzerland's association[153] are commonly used by DAOs, they are not completely tailored to the features and needs of DAOs and their future development in order to provide the necessary legal certainty for DAOs and their participants. The DAO Model Law created a well-founded basis for the legal structure of DAO companies based on functional and legal equivalence. Depending on the peculiarities of the respective jurisdiction, selective amendments and/or the implementation of specific company forms for DAOs are conceivable and necessary. Consequently, there is a need for further research in this area.[154]

150 Reiser and Wächli, "Rechtliche Erfassung von Dezentralen Autonomen Organisationen (Teil 2)" (n 16) 863.

151 Section 5.

152 Section 6.

153 Section 7.

154 For Switzerland, Reiser and Wächli, "Rechtliche Erfassung von Dezentralen Autonomen Organisationen (Teil 2)" (n 16) 863, 876–77.

2
Are Bespoke DAO Forms Needed in Organizational Law?

Shawn Bayern

1. Introduction

This chapter questions the need for decentralized autonomous organization (DAO)-specific organizational statutes and entity types in view of several propositions about the theory, structure, and practice of organizational law.

First, it introduces and defends the proposition that organizational forms should be neutral to private parties' choices about technology. That said, while technological neutrality is a useful principle in evaluating organizational statutes, the current wave of bespoke organizational forms probably does little practical harm on this front because of the possibilities for one technology to emulate another: software other than a blockchain, for example, can superficially be cast in the form of a blockchain to meet any statutory requirements. This sort of technological polymorphism, however, may highlight the limits or at least the excess specificity of organizational forms tied to particular software technologies.

Second, the chapter observes that existing general organizational forms, such as the limited liability companies (LLCs) authorized by statutes in US states, are already capable of accommodating DAOs and other new technological structures for organizations. Because the existing forms are adequately adaptable, they are sufficient: using existing forms promotes harmony and simplicity in organizational law, a field that is already too fragmented and in which too many distinct types of entities already exist. The proliferation of organizational forms has led to inconsistencies and loopholes, and it has probably unnecessarily complicated parties' legal decisions and thereby increased their legal costs.

The chapter also discusses the relationship between registered and unregistered organizational forms and how bespoke organizational forms interact (and might interact differently) with the Corporate Transparency Act.

The scope of my analysis here is limited. It takes no position on the desirability of enabling DAOs or encouraging them to interface with the legal system; to say it differently, it assumes for the sake of argument that it is useful to have *some* organizational form through which DAOs operate. My contention is that even given that proposition, bespoke forms are not needed and can cause problems; they have costs but few benefits.

2. Organizational Law and Technological Neutrality

Ordinarily, organizational law should probably aim to remain neutral with respect to the technology that an organization uses to implement internal governance processes and indeed most other processes. This principle of technological neutrality is, if nothing else, justified by liberal theory, under which the state should avoid picking winners and losers.[1] Treating one type of distributed database differently from other types of distributed databases threatens, at least conceptually, to create an artificial incentive to use one technology over another. It also threatens to restrict technological innovation by privileging existing, known forms of technology over future ones that may be developed; if it is easy to set up a blockchain-based LLC, it might be harder for a hypothetical future competitor to blockchain technology to gain a foothold even if it presents advantages over blockchains.

I don't mean to be doctrinaire about the point. State preference for particular technologies can be justified in theory by any number of considerations.[2] If settling on a particular technology as a focal point aids regulators and private parties, or if a technology provides guarantees that regulators believe will lead to less confusion or fraud among private parties, it may be justified for regulations to encourage it. For example, if a single technological mechanism for electronic signatures happened to be superior to others, there would be no reason for a regulator to avoid privileging it in deference to an abstract principle about neutrality.[3] Real-world experience has shown, however, that a requirement to put digital signatures in particular forms is counterproductive;[4] ordinary online commerce doesn't require sophisticated technologies or a public-key infrastructure for parties' signatures any more than in-person commerce required wax seals.[5] Of course, when particular technologies have externalities, common law and regulations can treat them differently from other technologies based on several

[1] cf World Summit on the Information Society, "Declaration of Principles" (December 12, 2003) Doc WSIS-03/GENEVA/DOC/4-E <https://gssd.mit.edu/search-gssd/site/world-summit-information-society-wsis-53802-mon-07-23-2012-0911> accessed January 8, 2025 ("The rule of law, accompanied by a supportive, transparent, pro-competitive, technologically neutral and predictable policy and regulatory framework reflecting national realities, is essential for building a people-centred Information Society. Governments should intervene, as appropriate, to correct market failures, to maintain fair competition, to attract investment, to enhance the development of the ICT infrastructure and applications, to maximize economic and social benefits, and to serve national priorities." See also Marcelo Thompson, "The Neutralization of Harmony: The Problem of Technological Neutrality, East and West" (2012) 18 Boston University Journal of Science & Technology Law 303, 303 ("Technological neutrality in law is, roughly, the idea that law should not pick technological winners and losers, that law should neither help nor hinder particular types of technological artifacts."); Arthur J Cockfield, "What Is Legal Knowledge?: Towards a Law and Technology Theory" (2004) 30 Manitoba Law Journal 383, 410 ("Because the law strives to ensure that substantively similar activities are treated the same way, it generally operates on the basis of what could be called the principle of technological neutrality.").

[2] Brad A Greenberg, "Rethinking Technology Neutrality" (2016) 100 Minnesota Law Review 1495.

[3] Stephen E Blythe, "A Critique of Argentine E-Commerce Law and Recommendations for Improvement" (2011) 17 Annual Survey of International & Comparative Law 75, 85–86 (discussing jurisdictions in the 1990s that required a particular technology for electronic signatures—a requirement that could plausibly have been justified at the time, although in fact it was likely misguided).

[4] Jane K Winn, "The Emperor's New Clothes: The Shocking Truth About Digital Signatures and Internet Commerce" (2001) 37 Idaho Law Review 353 (offering an early critique of digital-signature technologies for recording assent to contractual obligations).

[5] HC McDougal, "The Seal: Its Origin, Evolution and Abolition" (1894) 28 American Law Review 25.

factors, including whether they are commonly used in the locale where they have caused harm.[6]

2.1. Technological Neutrality and Blockchains

No special technological, social, or administrative factors support a privileging of blockchains over any other candidate for the management of decentralized organizations. To be clear, blockchains are not required for decentralized organizations or group processes similar to them; they are merely one technology that enables them. Blockchains have benefited from a cachet that probably results from a variety of factors: their claim to be a focal point of technological interest; their close association with their initial application, cryptocurrencies, which appreciated rapidly in value after their introduction to the public; and their history as a technology that introduced many people to the capabilities of cryptography. But purely as a matter of technological design, blockchains are simply not needed for many of the applications for which they're proposed; they are often in fact a poor fit as a technological matter for particular proposed applications.

For example, blockchains facilitate distributed decision-making in the absence of a trusted third party, so they are not a useful fit for many specific applications that depend anyway on a trusted third party, like the management of rights to land (by, eg, a municipality). A common refrain (in the nature of technological marketing or advocacy) is that blockchains have a technological role to play even in situations that retain a trusted third party because they prevent tampering with records, but as a technological matter they are an extremely heavyweight technology to achieve that goal; much simpler and less expensive public-key cryptosystems that existed decades before blockchains can prevent participants in a system from editing, recalling, or denying the validity of messages that they have transmitted to others. From the perspective of technological design, "blockchain" seems often to mean little more than "database plus public-key cryptosystem." Perhaps it is a way to marshal enthusiasm for technological reform (eg to replace the antiquated information-technology systems of a municipality), a way to benefit from standardization and a now-relatively-known solution to a common set of problems, and so forth, but it is often not necessary as a technological matter.

A decentralized "organization" of at least some kind, moreover, is certainly possible without blockchain technology. As a simple example, any cryptographic mechanism using *Shamir key sharing*, attributable originally to Adi Shamir[7] and Bob Blakely[8] in 1979, permits distributed decision-making enforced by cryptography. In particular,

[6] Restatement (Second) of Torts § 520 (1977) (imposing strict liability on activities, including uses of technology like explosives, that are "not a matter of common usage" in particular geographical areas).

[7] Adi Shamir, "How to Share a Secret" (1979) 22 Communications of the ACM 612; also Ed Dawson and Diane Donovan, "The Breadth of Shamir's Secret-Sharing Scheme" (1994) 13 Computers & Security 69 (offering "new constructions for multipart, multilevel, democratic and prepositioned schemes" that support "detecting cheaters and disenrolling participants").

[8] GR Blakeley, "Safeguarding Cryptographic Keys" (1979) International Workshop on Managing Requirements Knowledge 313.

Shamir key sharing permits the distribution of what we might think of as a technical *power* (a practical technological analogue of a legal-theoretical Hohfeldian power)[9] to transmit information or achieve some other purely technological goal among multiple participants, a particular subset of whom must expressly and objectively concur (within the parameters of the system) in order to do what they've set out to do. In other words, decades before blockchains, distributed cryptographic voting mechanisms were possible without any need for any of the overhead of a blockchain. To be sure, blockchains solve particular technological problems—mainly, what has come to be known as the *double-spending* problem in cryptocurrencies.[10] My point is only that they are not logically or technologically necessary for decentralized organizations and that there is no evident argument that blockchains ought to be privileged by law to crowd out alternative technologies that might implement distributed decision-making procedures.

In short, if a commentator or policymaker generally has no opposition to the notion of decentralized, technology-based organizations and recognizes (1) that blockchains present no special reason to override a general principle of neutrality toward technology and (2) that blockchains are not the only possible basis for distributed organizations, the commentator or policymaker should probably want to avoid statutes or regulations that stifle the development of forms of decentralized organizations that do not depend on blockchains.

2.2. Technological Isomorphism in Decentralized Organizations

Given the discussion in the previous section, statutes that enable decentralized organizations only if they are cast into the form of a blockchain[11] warrant at least skepticism; even if they do not directly prohibit or otherwise stifle potentially desirable, novel private arrangements that don't depend on blockchains, they take a position overtly favoring one form of decentralized organization over another.

That favoritism, however, may be more symbolic than practical. Perhaps that is as it should be; cynically, a natural perception from outside the statehouse is that states pass statutes specifically recognizing blockchain-based LLCs as a result of lobbying or in a desire to drive businesses to organize in their state instead of another.[12] As it turns

[9] Wesley N Hohfeld, "Fundamental Legal Conceptions as Applied in Judicial Reasoning" (1917) 26 Yale Law Journal 710 (defining and classifying "jural relations" including "rights" and "powers"). In drawing this analogy, I mean to refer specifically to the simple ability to change ownership rights or similar incidents as a technological matter, as distinct from the rightfulness of doing so. Particularly, before the commonplace use of cryptocurrency by the public—ie in older discussions of public cryptosystems and in the early days of Bitcoin—it was commonplace for participants to claim that the only arbiter of "rightfulness" in a cryptographically managed system was the technological system itself. In referring to such a state of affairs, which we might think of as *technological positivism*, I don't mean to endorse it.

[10] "Double-spending" (*Wikipedia*) <https://en.wikipedia.org/wiki/Double-spending> accessed January 8, 2025.

[11] eg Vt Stat Ann tit 11, § 4173 (2023) (enabling "Blockchain-Based Limited Liability Companies").

[12] eg Victor Reklaitis, "Crypto Industry's Lobbying Hit a Record in 2023—and Is Off to a Strong Start in 2024" (*Morningstar*, May 10, 2024) <https://www.morningstar.com/news/marketwatch/20240510198/crypto-industrys-lobbying-hit-a-record-in-2023-and-is-off-to-a-strong-start-in-2024> [perma.cc/69GF-QC5F] accessed January 8, 2025; also Mark J Roe, "Delaware's Competition" (2003) 117 Harvard Law

out, even a statute that explicitly permits decentralized organizations only if they are put into the form of a blockchain probably does not prevent organizations that use other technological mechanisms from benefiting from the statute, though it may make their implementation or regulatory compliance more expensive.

The reason that a statute that permits or recognizes only blockchains as the basis for a decentralized organization likely does little harm to other forms of decentralized organization is that it is normally both possible and not difficult to cast any software system into the form of a blockchain. Often even that is not required. For instance, Vermont's statute entitled "Blockchain-Based Limited Liability Companies" does not in fact depend on blockchains even as a formal matter; the statutory definition of "blockchain" in Vermont is "a cryptographically secured, chronological, and decentralized consensus ledger or consensus database maintained via Internet, peer-to-peer network, or other interaction."[13] That is considerably broader than the typical technological definition of a blockchain;[14] the term has essentially been stylized to fit its general usage in a fairly broad statute. Though it is more neutral to technology than requiring a blockchain would be, the statute still depends on a "consensus ledger or consensus database" that is "chronological." From a technological perspective, the definition is rather imprecise, particularly for a statute; for example, the meaning of words like "secured" and "decentralized" are not clear on their own.[15] In particular, it is hard to see how "decentralized" would limit the operation of the statute; if a private party feared that keeping a single copy of a ledger was insufficient, by making a separate copy elsewhere (or giving one to another data controller) perhaps they have made the database "decentralized."[16]

Review 588 (discussing the familiar "race to the bottom" in corporate law in the context of a national market for organizational registrations potentially supervised by federal power).

[13] Vt Stat Ann tit 12, § 1913(a)(1) (2023).

[14] cf Lorenzo Ghiro and others, "A Blockchain Definition to Clarify its Role for the Internet of Things" (19th Mediterranean Communication and Computer Networking Conference, 2021) <https://dx.doi.org/10.1109/MedComNet52149.2021.9501280> accessed January 8, 2025.

[15] The blockchain-based LLC statute in Vermont is quite short overall, comprising only six short sections and contributing to the perception that it is perhaps more a symbolic endorsement than a meaningful statutory enablement or regulation. Vt Stat Ann tit 11, §§ 4171–4176 (2023). Statutes in other states have been observed to follow similar patterns, either tunneling through the state's normal adoption procedures for business-organization statutes or having relatively limited extents; Joan McLeod Heminway, "Tennessee's DAO Act: Positive Innovation or Fringe Legislation?" (2014) 22 Florida State Business Review 171, 173–75 (discussing the circumstances under which Tennessee passed a DAO statute and observing that it "spans only eighteen sections of the Tennessee Code Annotated").

[16] cf Utah Code Ann § 48-5-101 (2023) (defining "[d]ecentralized," in Utah's DAO statute, as "decision-making [that] is distributed among multiple persons"; under that definition a married couple's schooling decisions for their children are "decentralized," as is the functioning of conventional corporations). Some DAO-related statutes implicate specific technologies but only in ways that appear unimportant or unnecessary. For example, Tennessee's "decentralized organization" statute, in a chapter that is titled "Blockchains" but otherwise doesn't contain the word except in a non-operative definition, Tenn Code Ann §§ 48-250-101–48-250-115 (2023), defines the term "Distributed ledger technology" in fairly technology-specific language that requires "distributed, decentralized, shared, and replicated ledger," although to its credit it does not formally require a blockchain. ibid § 48-250-101; The statue's one apparent use of the term in an operative provision is to say that an organization "does not have an obligation to furnish information concerning the organization's activities, financial condition, or other circumstances to the extent the information is available on publicly available distributed ledger technology." ibid § 48-250–111; Presumably the word "publicly" does all the important work in that operative provision—distributed, shared, decentralized "ledgers" can be private—so that the statute's rule about a member's right to inspect the books and records

That sort of minimal workaround is capable of significant generalization. Any software system can be put into the form of a "cryptographically secured, chronological, and decentralized consensus ledger" even if such a ledger has little role in the software. For example, the software might simply write its output into such a ledger. Indeed, any software can be put into the form of a conventional blockchain. This capability can be expressed using a colloquial version of a technical notion known as *Turing completeness.*[17] Essentially, as computer scientist Alan Turing showed, simple computers with a few basic operations are capable of computing anything that can be computed. (Not everything can be computed.)[18] At least one system that implements blockchains, Ethereum, supports a Turing-complete set of operations.[19] Therefore, any computation can be run on a blockchain. In order to meet the terms of a statute that requires a blockchain, then, someone can operate a decentralized organization in some other form; the blockchain may have no functional role other than to comply with or trigger the terms of the statute. Vermont's statute might, for example, be used in theory to enable an artificially intelligent system that has nothing intrinsically to do with blockchains.[20]

As a result of the technical facts I've just outlined, a pro-blockchain statute may not in fact repress or fail to enable any other technology. Still, the need to cast software in the form of a blockchain or in any other specific format may increase the costs to organizers or participants in a decentralized organization; obviously those who didn't intend to use a blockchain face unnecessary implementation costs if they feel the need to comply with or trigger the terms of a statute by adopting a blockchain. So the effect may be distortive even if not prohibitive.

of a covered organization simply depends on the sensible principle that no such right is necessary if the information is already available to the public. It would have been clearer for the statute just to say that—and perhaps to apply it to all organizations, not just decentralized ones. In other words, routing the principle through a technological definition adds little; publicity comes in many forms, not just through decentralized ledgers, and focusing the legal questions that the statutes create on technology seems not to aid courts at all in the resolution of those questions. As an example in the form of a hypothetical dispute before a court applying the statute: suppose the disputed "information is available on publicly available distributed ledger technology," ibid, but only in a form that is encrypted, difficult, or unusually expensive to access, or otherwise unusable for practical purposes.

[17] "Turing Completeness" (*Wikipedia*, June 18, 2024) <https://en.wikipedia.org/wiki/Turing_completeness> accessed January 8, 2025 ("In colloquial usage, the terms 'Turing-complete' and 'Turing-equivalent' are used to mean that any real-world general-purpose computer or computer language can approximately simulate the computational aspects of any other real-world general-purpose computer or computer language."); Marc Jansen and others, "Do Smart Contract Languages Need to Be Turing Complete?" in Javier Prieto and others (eds) *Blockchain and Applications* (Springer 2019) 19; AM Turing, "On Computable Numbers, with an Application to the *Entscheidungsproblem* ("Decision Problem")" (1937) 42 Proc Lond Math Soc 230.

[18] Turing (n 17); see also "Halting Problem" (*Wikipedia*) <https://en.wikipedia.org/wiki/Halting_problem> accessed January 8, 2025.

[19] Jansen and others (n 17).

[20] cf Kevin Werbach, "Out of Control: DAOs, AI, and the Question of Autonomy" in Kevin Werbach, Eva Micheler, and Bianca Kremer (eds), *Foundations of Decentralized Organizations: Blockchain and the Future of Corporate Law* (OUP 2026).

3. The Generality and Generativity of Conventional Business Organizations

Even putting aside concerns about technological neutrality, DAO-specific wrappers are not needed in US organizational law for a simpler and more powerful reason: LLCs and probably other existing organizational forms are already general enough to accommodate DAOs. Using these existing forms, organizational statutes can avoid several matters that they should best avoid: they can avoid favoring particular technologies; needing to specify features of technologies in ways that will likely be either confusing, overly broad, or insufficiently broad;[21] and indeed what amounts to an entirely unnecessary drafting and regulatory exercise. Of course, states may still have reasons to try to encourage businesses to organize in their states versus others (or just to send political signals), but that competitive posturing is likely, in this context, to be a zero-sum game, and policymakers should at the very least recognize it as such before engaging in it. Organizers and participants in DAOs should also not be fooled by it; there is no reason in the general case that a DAO-specific statute will favor DAOs more than a modern, general-purpose LLC statute based on (eg) the Revised Uniform Limited Liability Company Act (RULLCA) will.[22] Indeed, as we'll see, paradoxically it is possible for DAO-specific statutes to impose more limitations on DAOs than general-purposes LLC statutes do.

3.1. General-Purpose LLCs and DAOs

The animating principle of many LLC acts is flexibility and what the acts sometimes call "freedom of contract."[23] The "freedom" that the statutes have in mind is twofold. First, LLCs have no preconceived formalities or structures, in contrast to the way that a classical corporation was, in the legal imagination, specifically a group of shareholders who elect a board on a particular schedule—where each group (the shareholders and the board) held predefined powers constituted by the corporation statute. Corporate statutes provide considerably more flexibility than that today,[24] although they retain some traditional requirements, like the need for at least one shareholder.[25]

[21] See n 13 and accompanying text.

[22] RULLCA is formally the Uniform Limited Liability Company Act (2006, rev 2013), promulgated by the Uniform Law Commission and adopted so far in about half the states in the US; Uniform Law Commission, "Limited Liability Company Act, Revised" <https://www.uniformlaws.org/committees/community-home?CommunityKey=bbea059c-6853-4f45-b69b-7ca2e49cf740> [perma.cc/U6Z9-RCV6] accessed June 19, 2024. I refer to and cite it throughout simply as RULLCA and similarly cite other Uniform Law Commission and ABA acts by their commonplace abbreviations.

[23] eg Fla Stat § 605.0111 (2023) ("It is the intent of this chapter to give the maximum effect to the principle of freedom of contract and to the enforceability of operating agreements ...."); Del Code Ann tit 6, § 18-1101 (2013) ("It is the policy of this chapter to give the maximum effect to the principle of freedom of contract and to the enforceability of limited liability company agreements.").

[24] eg MBCA § 7.32(a) (2020) ("An agreement among the shareholders of a corporation that complies with this section is effective among the shareholders and the corporation even though it is inconsistent with one or more other provisions of this Act in that it ... eliminates the board of directors or restricts the discretion or powers of the board of directors ....").

[25] ibid § 6.01(b); Shawn Bayern, *Autonomous Organizations* (CUP 2021) 54–55 (discussing the implications of the requirement in a comparison of modern corporations and LLCs).

LLCs, by contrast, never had such preconceived structures. LLC statutes typically lay out two standard default paths for LLCs—*member-managed* and *manager-managed* companies[26]—but those are mainly bundles of default rules, not structures to which organizers and participants are tied. Second, and not altogether differently, statutes that emphasize "freedom of contract" tend to oppose the notion of mandatory rules in organizational governance. For example, in Delaware, organizers of an LLC have a freer hand to alter or remove the fiduciary duties of those in control over the organization than do organizers of a corporation.[27]

For our purposes, the first of these freedoms—flexibility in structure and operation—is more important. Modern LLCs provide legal personhood—which, in organizational law's usage of the term, amounts just to an organization's ability to interact with the rest of the legal system[28]—to entirely open-ended organizations that can be structured internally in whatever way suits the organizers' and participants' private wishes. I have explored the general consequences of this combination of features of modern LLC law in earlier work that began, now more than a decade ago, in an early article laying out the application of LLC statutes to DAOs.[29]

The main feature of flexibility in LLC law that matters for our purposes is the ability of that law to give *legal* effect, through a variety of mechanisms or transactional techniques, to a *factual* decentralized organization. As long as the software that expresses the control and governance of the factual organization is *verifiable* to a court (ie as long as it can be proven in hypothetical litigation seeking to define the obligations of the participants), an operating agreement that refers to the software's state, output, or other characteristics effectively recognizes the software, importing or connecting its operation to law.[30] This permits a DAO to operate in the legal system, making contracts, owning and disposing of property, filing lawsuits, and so forth.

As a simple example, suppose some question of legal authority—the powers of a legal agent—are to be determined by a vote within a DAO. Imagine, for instance, that the DAO has amassed funds and needs to make a decision about which human being or corporation is permitted to commit those funds in a contract with a conventional, offline third party (eg to buy the intended target of crowdsourced funding or otherwise to make any deal relevant to the DAO). The LLC that enables the DAO can easily

[26] eg RULLCA § 407 (2006, rev 2013).

[27] Compare Del Code Ann tit 6, § 18-1101(c) (2013) (providing that in LLCs "the member's or manager's or other person's duties may be expanded or restricted or eliminated by provisions in the limited liability company agreement; provided, that the limited liability company agreement may not eliminate the implied contractual covenant of good faith and fair dealing.") with Del Code Ann tit 8, § 102(b)(7) (2022) (listing fiduciary duties that the certificate of incorporation of a corporation "shall not eliminate or limit the liability").

[28] Shawn Bayern, *A Research Agenda for Organizational Law* (Elgar 2024) 10–17.

[29] Shawn Bayern, "Of Bitcoins, Independently Wealthy Software, and the Zero-Member LLC" (2014) 108 Northwestern University Law Review 1485, 1486; also Bayern, *Autonomous Organizations* (n 25).

[30] I borrow the term *verifiable* from contract theory, eg Hans Lind and Johan Nystrom, "The Explanation of Incomplete Contracts in Mainstream Contract Theory: A Critique of the Distinction between 'Observable' and 'Verifiable'" (2011) 7 Evolutionary and Institutional Economics Review 279. The distinction of verifiable information is that it can be proven to courts; without that feature the operating agreement of an LLC does not achieve the legal effects it intends, because the states or outputs of the relevant software system will not have reliable legal consequences. In the terminology of the theory of incomplete contracts, verifiable information is not merely *observable* to the parties but susceptible of legal proof.

have an operating agreement that recognizes legal authority to act for the DAO based on the state or output of a blockchain. It can do this in so straightforward a manner that an example does little more than express what I've already said in the traditional language of a written operating agreement; for example, dependent on some vote or recorded transaction to which the operating agreement specifically refers, "the natural or legal person identified in that record shall have legal authority to act for the LLC, subject to any restrictions also contained in that record." LLC law provides no meaningful limits here; the limits all come from the capabilities of the governing DAO software, the imaginations of the participants, and the political or economic reality of the DAO. LLC law imposes no particular forms or technical hoops to jump through; whatever capabilities the DAO organizers want for their legal agent—or, for example, for legally significant voting mechanisms or the disposition of offline assets—they can specify them in plain language in an LLC operating agreement.

The capabilities of modern LLCs do not stop there. For a DAO's control of an LLC to be meaningful, participants may desire that the operating agreement that recognizes the DAO be unshakeable or immutable, not subject to ready displacement that would hijack the LLC's operation and separate it from that of the governing software. To be clear, this forceful tie between the factual (technological) organization and the legal (offline) one is not a necessary feature of any organization's governance and may not be desirable in every situation. But suppose it is. Modern LLC law provides a ready way to achieve it, because many modern LLC statutes permit the operating agreement of a DAO to be immutable. I have defended this proposition in legalistic detail in previous work,[31] occasionally showing that it can be done through the creation of zero-member LLCs that are permitted under modern LLC law[32]—although that is not the only way LLC operating agreements may become immutable.[33] The simplest way to understand the legal proposition is merely to say that RULLCA, adopted in about half the US states, commits to an LLC operating agreement "the means and conditions" for its own amendment;[34] in a statute that is very careful to mark out rules that are mandatory or subject to modification only when not "manifestly unreasonable,"[35] there are no restrictions in the statute on how amendments to an operating agreement may be restricted.

The result is that LLCs can do everything DAOs need them to do. They can act according to software in whatever way the participants want them to do. They have as flexible a tax treatment under federal US tax law as is currently available.[36] In some states, they can limit fiduciary duties as far as current law permits organizations to do. Perhaps organizers of a DAO will feel more comfortable in a bespoke form that they

[31] eg ibid 68–73.

[32] Bayern, *Autonomous Organizations* (n 25) 58–75.

[33] Shawn Bayern, "Are Autonomous Entities Possible?" (2019) 114 Northwestern University Law Review Online 23, 26–34.

[34] RULLCA § 105(a)(4) (2006, rev 2013).

[35] ibid § 105.

[36] US Treas Reg § 301.7701-3(a) (as amended in 2020) ("A business entity that is not classified as a corporation [under particular regulations] can elect its classification for federal tax purposes as provided in this section.") (known as the *check-the-box regulations*).

know a state legislature has recently created for them,[37] but that is mostly a cultural or perhaps a psychological advantage, not a legal or practical one.

Indeed, general-purpose LLCs can be even *more* flexible—and thus more specifically suited—to DAOs than bespoke statutes can be. For example, the Tennessee DAO statute includes a provision that reads: "A smart contract-managed decentralized organization may only form under this chapter if the underlying smart contracts are able to be amended."[38] This provision, which may have seemed like a sensible way to ensure the law can retain some control over the technical operation of what might have appeared to be an otherwise ungovernable technological entity, restricts the specifically enabled "decentralized organizations"[39] in Tennessee more than the general LLC statute in Tennessee does. That is because Tennessee's general LLC statute is conceptually similar to RULLCA in its support of immutable operating agreements.[40] Accordingly, an organization based on an unamendable smart contract probably finds an easier home in a regular Tennessee LLC than in a more specialized legal "decentralized organization" in the same state.

As a general matter, if the organizers of an LLC can envision a particular control structure or any other feature of the internal governance of an LLC—arbitrarily fractional shares, full separation of economic and voting rights,[41] multiple overlapping control structures with checks and balances, reference to on-chain or off-chain governance, opportunities for judicial or third-party oversight, automatic operation, limited or indefinite ("perpetual") duration,[42] tradeable or non-tradeable membership interests (or "units," or indeed whatever organizers want to call them), use or abandonment of the conventional "membership" structure—the operating agreement under modern statutes can accommodate it. Whether all those capabilities are present in the same way under a new and perhaps hastily written DAO-specific statute is anyone's guess, because the statutes often are not aimed at addressing those basic building blocks of organizational law.

[37] cf Heminway (n 15) 180 ("If we desire to encourage the creation of DAOs as vehicles for conducting business and industry representatives and legal practitioners are not prepared to avail themselves of existing choices of entity for valid reason, then the creation of a new form of entity may be an appropriate option for legislatures to consider.").

[38] Tenn Code Ann § 48-250-104(d) (2023).

[39] ibid § 48-250-101(1).

[40] ibid § 48-206-102(b) ("*Unless otherwise provided in the articles or the operating agreement*, the amendment of the operating agreement shall require the vote of members necessary to amend the articles.") (emphasis added). Section 48-206-102(b) permits voting thresholds and other restrictions in "the articles *or* the operating agreement" (emphasis added), but depending on how courts interpret and apply that section and others in chapters 205–206 of the Tennessee statutes, Tennessee law could perhaps reserve power to the members to amend an LLC's articles of organization in a way that influences their authority to amend the operating agreement. The articles, however, may require a supermajority or unanimous vote for their own amendment; Tenn Code Ann § 48-209-103(f) (2023) ("Unless chapters 201–248 of this title, the articles, or the board of governors (acting pursuant to subsection (c)) requires a greater vote, the amendment to be adopted must be approved by a majority vote of the members entitled to vote thereon."). That opens the door to various transactional techniques to achieve practical immutability, even of the articles; Bayern, "Are Autonomous Entities Possible?" (n 33) 26–34.

[41] RULLCA § 401(d) (2006, rev 2013).

[42] ibid § 108(c).

3.2. Benefits of Nonproliferation of Organizational Forms

General organizational forms, in the general case, are more adaptable than specific forms. They avoid raising unnecessarily legal issues adverted to in the discussion so far, like what precisely counts as "decentralized" or a "ledger." They embrace technological neutrality by default simply by being unconcerned with the underlying implementation of an organization. If an LLC operating agreement can give effect to the verifiable state of *any* software, it doesn't matter whether a novel mechanism for managing wealth or coordinating action is for-profit, not-for-profit, or some hybrid between the two;[43] it also doesn't matter if it's decentralized, where it is located, or how it is implemented. From the law's perspective, these are irrelevant implementation details. LLC law, in recognizing "freedom of contract," permitted private parties to adapt to novel circumstances in their operating agreements long before state legislatures could approve of new technological arrangements. Just as general incorporation statutes are far more flexible than individually chartered corporations, a general-purpose LLC statute is more adaptive than a statute tied to a particular software-based arrangement that may seem stale or out of date in a decade.

In general, when one form of legal organization subsumes the capabilities of another form, there is probably little reason for the continued existence of the other form. (Admittedly, this is not yet a principle on which American organizational law has acted.) Reasons for the preservation of a subsumed form are conceptually possible, of course. They include tradition, inertia, various parties' comfort with existing case law concerning a particular organizational form, a convenient way to specify default rules for different types of legal organizations in statutes, and the difficulty of updating commonly reused forms and pleading boilerplate. None of these reasons is persuasive. For example, to the extent different default rules are useful, they can be accommodated as different paths within the same statute—and they might even come to be more thoughtfully designed to depend on the substance of the parties' decisions or circumstances rather than on the organizational form that they've chosen.[44] Existing case law and forms are made no less certain or predictable by newer forms if organizational statutes are clear and the bench and bar understand their intent. As I have suggested in earlier work, instead of trying to harmonize different organizational statutes—as the Uniform Law Commission is doing, in many cases quite gracefully—there should probably be more of an effort to consolidate them and eliminate redundancies.[45]

There is simply little reason, for example, to have a variety of overlapping forms, some of which—for entirely formal reasons—have different mandatory rules than others.[46] That is just a recipe for confusion and abuse, and it provides an opportunity

43 eg ibid § 108(b).

44 Bayern, *A Research Agenda for Organizational Law* (n 28) 54–59.

45 ibid 31–65.

46 See n 27 and accompanying text. In Bayern, *A Research Agenda for Organizational Law* (n 28) 58–59 I suggest that it could be justified to vary mandatory rules based on substantive rather than formal characteristics of organizations. To be clear, US states are not the only jurisdictions with multiple overlapping organizational forms, but my assertion in the text is that, as a general normative matter, the affirmative case for overlap and choice of mandatory rules on formal grounds alone has yet to be made.

for organizers to detect and take advantage of the potential legal misunderstandings of later participants. Small investors in organizations, including DAOs, often don't have any legal advice and will not read form agreements carefully; to imagine that "freedom of contract" should extend to outright theft via the wholesale elimination of fiduciary duties of managers—and then to condition that opportunity for theft on whether the organizers have chosen an LLC instead of a corporation[47]—is not a demonstration of sound statutory craft. The same is true of the typical modern jurisdiction that maintains forms for limited liability partnerships (LLPs), limited liability limited partnerships (LLLPs), and limited liability companies (LLCs). As the computer scientist Alan Perlis said of computational subroutines, "If you have a procedure with 10 parameters, you probably missed some";[48] the same is true, as I've pointed out previously, of organizational forms.[49] At least in the US, there has not been any thoughtful justification of the state of the sprawling subject as a whole.

Adding to that already overcomplicated state of affairs with bespoke new statutes that reflect enthusiasm for new technology and a desire to attract it to a jurisdiction is likely to lead to more inconsistencies, more loopholes, less sound organizational governance, more difficulty amending statutes, and more confusion among organizers and participants. We've seen some examples of that even in the discussion so far. And local, state-by-state drafting also is likely to be less cautious, coordinated, and thoughtful if it proceeds without any connection to the drafting of the Uniform Law Commission and the benefit of that organization's national experience; drafting novel organizational-law statutes is not as easy as it may appear, in particular because of the complex consequences that relatively minor decisions in organizational law may have on other fields of law.[50] If a modern LLC is flexible enough to accommodate a DAO, legislators should impose a high bar on those who wish to add what will be, at bottom, a redundant organizational form.

Indeed, as it happens, the modern corporation is likely sufficiently flexible to incorporate DAOs, even putting aside all the extreme flexibility of the LLC. Corporate shares are freely tradeable, don't need to be "certificated,"[51] may be arbitrarily fractional,[52] and may be expressed through multiple *classes* or *series*,[53] so that (eg) voting rights and economic rights can be aggregated or disaggregated as suit the organizers' intent. Voting agreements[54] and voting trusts[55] are enforceable under modern corporate law, and shareholder agreements[56] make the corporate form extremely adaptable today. There is little reason to use the corporate form when the LLC is more flexible; my point is just that we already have enough organizational forms.

47 ibid.
48 Alan Perlis, "Epigrams in Programming" (September 1982) ACM Sigplan Notices 7.
49 Bayern, *Autonomous Organizations* (n 25) 60.
50 Bayern, *A Research Agenda for Organizational Law* (n 28) 67–68, 125–54.
51 eg MBCA § 6.25(a) (2020).
52 eg ibid § 6.04(a).
53 eg ibid § 6.01(b).
54 ibid § 7.31.
55 ibid § 7.30.
56 eg ibid § 7.32.

4. The Corporate Transparency Act

DAO organizers and participants may be troubled by the requirements of the Corporate Transparency Act even if they have no intent to launder money or otherwise have a substantive reason to shield their legal identities from FinCEN, the bureau of the US Treasury charged with preventing certain financial crimes. For example, the decentralized and pseudonymous or anonymous nature of some DAOs may make compliance with identity-based reporting requirements difficult even for those with nothing to hide.

Based on early drafts of what became the Corporate Transparency Act,[57] it may have seemed as if DAO-specific statutes might have enabled loopholes against the initial reporting requirements of the Act. That is unlikely to be the case, at least for LLC-based DAO statutes that exist so far. Because of the Supremacy Clause of the US Constitution,[58] state statutes cannot override the force of the Corporate Transparency Act, and the version of the Corporate Transparency Act that Congress passed applies to any "corporation, limited liability company, or other similar entity that is ... created by the filing of a document with a secretary of state or a similar office under the law of a State or Indian Tribe."[59] The "other similar entity" language likely prevents new statutes from sidestepping the force of the statute.

There is a potential loophole, however. The Corporate Transparency Act, as just shown, applies to *registered* entities—those created by filing documents with the state. Organizational law has long supported unregistered organizations: legal entities with all the powers and many of the other characteristics of registered entities like corporations or LLCs, except that they come into being even without any formal registration. For example, modern law recognizes that the general partnership[60] and the unincorporated nonprofit association[61] may come about without registration and even in many cases accidentally. Most such organizational forms arose at common law, but today they are statutory; the statutes explicitly permit the creation of legal entities without any formal registration. This creates the opportunity for litigation and potentially other minor confusion, but on the whole it has proved to be a workable model, free from most of the conceptual confusions that may seem, to some, inherent in the creation of new legal entities through informal processes.

Using existing unregistered entities as a template, states—if they wanted to do so—could aim to permit organizers to avoid the force of the Corporate Transparency Act for DAOs while otherwise permitting DAOs to have legal-entity status. That is, they could adopt statutes that give DAOs legal-entity status without any registration with the state. Doing that would complicate, although not necessarily eliminate entirely, states' abilities to collect registration fees from new businesses; it would not

57 William M (Mac) Thornberry National Defense Authorization Act for Fiscal Year 2021 (to be codified at 31 U S C § 5336) (hereinafter "Corporate Transparency Act").

58 US Const, Art VI, cl 2.

59 Corporate Transparency Act (to be codified at 31 U S C § 5336(a)(11)).

60 RUPA § 202 (2006, rev 2013).

61 UUNAA § 1(11) (2008, rev 2011).

undermine their goal of symbolically or substantively supporting DAOs or attracting them to their jurisdictions.

I almost hesitate to mention this loophole; it arises effectively only from a hole in the Corporate Transparency Act that Congress probably ought to plug. But I have observed this and other incompleteness in the Corporate Transparency Act in earlier work.[62] And presumably states' abuse of the loophole would accelerate Congress's closure of it.[63]

5. Conclusion

LLCs are flexible enough to accommodate DAOs. Perhaps the only legal reason for a separate DAO form might be to provide default rules that better suit the operation of a typical DAO. But a menu of options within the LLC form—much like organizers' ability to select member-managed or manager-managed LLCs under the same statute—would be a better way to accommodate DAO organizers and participants in view of existing features of organizational law, the benefits of harmonizing the subject, and the general advantages of technological neutrality.

[62] Bayern, *A Research Agenda for Organizational Law* (n 28) 152–54.
[63] cf Roe (n 12).

3
DAOs and the History of Corporate Law

Michael Schillig

1. Introduction

Thousands of decentralized autonomous organizations (DAOs) operate in the decentralized finance (DeFi) space today.[1] The purposes for which DAOs are deployed, as well as their respective modes of operation and organizational parameters, are very diverse. Accordingly, there is, as yet, no commonly agreed definition, neither in law nor across the other relevant disciplines, including computer science and economics. The Law Commission's description of a DAO as a "new kind of internet-based collaborative organization that coordinate people and resources using rules expressed in computer code"[2] seems a good starting point for unpacking the features common to most DAOs currently operating in DeFi.

DAOs leverage the "smart contract" capability of blockchain networks allowing for the programmability of assets and their representations. "Smart contracts" are machine-readable instructions (code) that can be run by the participating nodes, and track and store the resulting state changes on the blockchain,[3] allowing parties to automate the performance of contractual relationships that follow a deterministic "if X then Y" logic.[4] These smart contracts—as a DAO's underlying infrastructure—mediate the social interactions among the individuals who participate in a DAO and make up *the DAO community*.

Chronologically, a DAO is likely to originate from one or more developers—forming a more or less stable or fluid community—with an idea for a product or service that can be built and implemented on a blockchain network. The technical aspects, use cases and the envisaged governance structure are usually explained in a White Paper, distributed online and through social media. Immediately following its launch, a DAO may be "decentralized"[5] only in the sense that the smart contract code runs on a decentralized blockchain network: the code is stored at, and executed

[1] CoinMarketCap, "DAO Cryptocurrencies by Market Cap" <https://coinmarketcap.com/view/dao/> accessed December 11, 2024.

[2] Law Commission, *Decentralised autonomous organisations (DAOs)—A scoping paper* (July 2024) para 2.2, <https://lawcom.gov.uk/project/decentralised-autonomous-organisations-daos/> accessed November 4, 2025.

[3] Andreas Antonopoulos and Gavin Wood, *Mastering Ethereum* (O'Reilly 2019) 6–8.

[4] Dan Awrey, "Split Derivatives: Inside the World's Most Misunderstood Contract" (2019) 36 Yale Journal of Regulation 495, 499.

[5] Law Commission (n 2) paras 2.33–2.36.

by, every participating node, making it difficult for third parties[6] to interfere with or halt its execution. This approach stands in stark contrast to building a similar product on a centralized platform, where the provider retains the ability to halt implementation at any point, although developers remain influential at an early stage and possibly throughout. How they structure the DAO varies: they might form a foundation or another legal entity to hold governance tokens or perform certain functions, they might wrap only parts of the DAO in a formal structure, or they might forgo formal incorporation altogether. White Papers are often silent on these decisions, and in some cases even indicate that no traditional business entity is intended.

A DAO will flourish only if its products and services are being used. Accordingly, the interaction of users with the smart contract architecture is vital. By "depositing" crypto-assets with a system of interacting smart contracts, users may obtain tokens that represent a loan, or the participation in a liquidity pool or money market, or grant the privilege to submit project proposals to be funded out of the asset pool. Smart contracts allow for the automation of certain transaction decisions: an algorithmically calculated interest rate payable on a collateralized loan; automated liquidation in case of under-collateralization; an automatically adjusting exchange rate for various assets; or the automated funding of projects approved by majority vote. It is this element of automated transaction decision-making that accounts for the "autonomy" attribute.[7] For a crypto-loan through a DeFi lender, you send in your collateral; based on its quality, the loan will be granted with a collateral-specific interest rate. At your bank the process may also be automated, but the bank can still refuse the loan even though its formal criteria have been met. In a DAO, the underlying decentralized infrastructure can shield the automated decision-making from outside interference and thereby strengthen the idea of "autonomy" as automated execution.

To amount to an "organization,"[8] a DAO must be more than just users relying on a product or receiving a service: a lawyer and their client do not become an "organization" by merely giving and receiving legal advice. Rather, an organization connotes the pursuit of a common interest or purpose by two or more people. This may be the case for the developers who launch the smart contract code. Moreover, as a bootstrapping technique, (initial) users and/or investors who store crypto-assets at the DAO's smart contract address may be rewarded with governance tokens that allow them to vote on certain proposals or parameters of the underlying code: say, what type of collateral is supported; how interest rates should be calculated; and so on. In addition, governance tokens may provide financial incentives, either through rewards or the appreciation of token value. Over time, there may be a trajectory from initially centralized—developer-controlled—governance to ever more decentralized governance with governance token-holders becoming increasingly more influential. Often,

[6] Although once deployed, smart contracts cannot be modified, workarounds do exist. A popular method for ensuring upgradability—to fix bugs, add new features, and comply with regulation—consists in the use of so-called "proxy contracts." A proxy acts as an intermediary, forwarding function calls to the implementation contract that contains the business logic. An upgrade entails the launch of a new—improved—implementation contract and proxy admin allowing for calling the new upgraded logic while retaining the same contract address for users.

[7] Law Commission (n 2) paras 2.37–2.43.

[8] ibid paras 2.62–2.79.

there will be a significant overlap between these constituencies: developers are likely to be the first users and governance token-holders; although, if successful, the user base and governance token-holder base will grow, perhaps resembling intersecting circles with a commonality that decreases over time.

Thus, a DAO will have promoters—the developers—and foundational documents in form of the White Paper and its smart contract code. In exchange for contributions that may be locked-in at a smart contract address for a specific purpose, the DAO may issue tokens that confer on the holder certain control and/or cash flow rights not dissimilar to traditional equity and debt instruments. In the DeFi space, tokens will normally be freely transferable and will be actively traded on liquid secondary markets. Control rights will often be based on the one-token-one-vote principle, like the one-share-one-vote principle in corporate law, rather than the one-member-one-vote idea of cooperative and mutual societies. New projects will often be funded through token emissions, similar to equity financing. Consequently, DeFi DAOs replicate to some extent features traditionally reserved for corporate-type entities, and raise regulatory and governance concerns—minority protection, conflicts of interest, self-dealing, misappropriation of assets, voter apathy—familiar from the corporate law debates.[9] Accordingly, this chapter seeks to ascertain whether and to what extent the history of corporate law can provide valuable lessons for the design and implementation of adequate legal frameworks for capturing the DAO phenomenon in a business context. It advocates for an incremental approach that gradually seeks to accommodate and regulate DAOs within existing legal frameworks. This seems more conducive to fostering innovation whilst also curbing the propensity for abuse, than a new one-size-fits-all bespoke regulatory suit that is likely to be quickly overtaken by technological advancement.

Given that DAOs (without more) are not companies or corporations, drawing on the history of corporate law to gain insights for the regulation of DAOs amounts to a comparative exercise. Thus, in accordance with the received wisdom of comparative law methodology, it is necessary to define in purely functional terms the underlying socio-economic problem that both corporations and DAOs seek to address.[10] Accordingly, the next section seeks to define this *tertium comparationis*. This is then

[9] Romain Rossello, "Blockholders and strategic voting in DAOs' governance" (May 29, 2024) 1 <https://ssrn.com/abstract=4706759> accessed December 11, 2024; Katrin Schuler, Ann Sofie Cloots, and Fabian Schaer, "On DeFi and On-Chain CeFi: How (Not) to Regulate Decentralized Finance" (2024) 10 Journal of Financial Regulation 1, 23. As mentioned earlier, the DAO universe is vary varied (Andrea Pena-Calvin and others, "Concentration of Power and Participation in Online Governance: the Ecosystem of Decentralized Autonomous Organizations" <https://dl.acm.org/doi/pdf/10.1145/3589335.3651481> accessed December 11, 2024. In addition to the many DeFi DAOs that offer on-chain financial applications seeking to replicate traditional financial products or services, there is also a significant number of DAOs with the (nonprofit) purpose of furthering the interests of their members through cooperation and co-creation in a multitude of ways. These DAOs are more akin to traditional cooperative and mutual societies. Still, the company limited by shares or corporation is the predominant vehicle for doing business (at least in Western economies) and is geared toward addressing the issues mentioned in the text above; whereas the law of cooperative and mutual societies is less tightly regulated, because many of the speculative risks associated with freely tradable securities do not occur to the same extent; Zoe Adams and Simon Deakin, "Enterprise Form, Participation, And Performance in Mutuals and Co-Operatives" in Jonathan Mitchie, Joseph Blasi, and Carlo Borzaga (eds), *The Oxford Handbook of Mutual, Co-Operative and Co-Owned Business* (OUP 2017) 227–45.

[10] Konrad Zweigert and Hein Kötz, *An Introduction to Comparative Law* (3rd edn, OUP 1998) 34.

followed by a high-level historical account of corporate law history and the lessons that can be learned for the regulation of DAOs. The final section concludes.

2. DAOs and Corporations: A Functional Approach

The functional starting point is the "horizontal pooling of resources problem," consisting of the following elements: (1) several types of resources are pooled for the attainment of a specific economic purpose; (2) the resources belong to more than one person; (3) all resources are important to the venture; (4) the proceeds of the venture are not the sum of separable outputs attributable to each contributing resource.[11] In short, the essence of "horizontal pooling" is coordination, cooperation, and merging of resources to achieve something more, bigger, or different than the participants would be able to achieve on their own.[12]

Institutional[13] structures are necessary to induce participants to make the requisite investments and discourage wasteful rent-seeking.[14] Internally—among participants—individual contributions must be defined, in addition to access rights to benefits and profits, powers of control over inputs and pool assets, and the process of decision-making as a group ("internal governance structure"). Further, there must be an "external liability structure" defining the asset pool's interaction with others via the market, including the delineation of, and third parties' access to, pool assets. "Internal governance structure" and "external liability structure" do not operate in isolation: a certain external liability structure is a quasi-necessity for a particular internal governance structure.

Corporate law provides this infrastructure: (1) as a separate legal entity, the corporation is distinct from its members and capable of enjoying rights and of being subject to liabilities of its own. Moreover, (2) the shareholders (or directors or employees) are not liable for the corporation's obligations. This external liability structure consisting of (1) and (2) provides the necessary bedrock for an internal governance structure based on (3) investors' interests being represented by shares of common stock as freely transferable items of property, and (4) centralized management of the business,

[11] This is a modification of the "team production problem" as defined by Armen Alchian and Harold Demsetz, "Production, Information Costs, and Economic Organization" (1972) 62 American Economic Review 777, 779. In the original team production problem, the focus is on understanding how individuals can effectively cooperate to produce something as a group when the product of their joint effort cannot be easily traced back to the individual contributions. This makes it difficult to measure and reward individual efforts accurately, which can lead to issues like free-riding or insufficient incentives for optimal teamwork.

[12] Margaret M Blair and Lynn A Stout, "A Team Production Theory of Corporate Law" (1999) 85 Virginia Law Review 248, 260–71. Since Ronald Coase's seminal piece on "The Nature of the Firm," published in 1937, a rich economic literature seeks to explain the integration of resources and the organization of production within firms. Ronald Coase, "The Nature of the Firm" in Oliver Williamson and Sidney Winter (eds), *The Nature of the Firm: Origins, Evolution, and Development* (OUP 1993) 18, 19, first published in (1937) *Economica, New Series IV* (1937) 386.

[13] As "humanly devised constraints that shape human interaction," Douglass North, *Institutions, Institutional Change and Economic Performance* (CUP 1990) 3.

[14] Margaret M Blair, "Locking in Capital: What Corporate Law Achieved for Business Organizers in the Nineteenth Century" (2003) 51 UCLA Law Review 387, 402.

subject to fiduciary duties.[15] Only under an external liability structure consisting of (1) and (2) is it rational for equity investors to take a passive role and leave the day-to-day business of the company to the management,[16] and only under a regime of limited liability will the share price be independent from the identity and personal wealth of the shareholders.[17]

Importantly, separate legal personality requires a special rule of "organizational law" as a "form of property law" committing assets to the firm and granting priority to firm creditors.[18] Contract (in the economic sense of "relationships characterized by reciprocal expectations and behavior"[19]) would be inadequate because transaction costs would be prohibitively high.[20] By contrast, as long as transaction costs are low, no matter what the liability regime, parties will contract so as to allocate the risk to the cheapest cost avoider.[21] Limited liability reflects the normal (default) desires of transacting parties.[22] If in a particular case the shareholders are, by way of exception, cheapest cost avoiders, the parties may contract for unlimited liability, by furnishing personal guarantees. Importantly, contracting for (or around) limited liability is required and will only be effective where the law ensures that agreements are enforceable.

DAOs can perform a similar institutional function within a blockchain network's self-contained techno-sociological normativity without reliance on traditional "organizational" or property law. By transferring Ether (ETH) to a smart contract address, investors can effectively pool these assets for specific purposes in accordance with the objectives of the smart contract (or network of smart contracts). Depending on the embedded logic, neither the investors nor their personal creditors would have access to the amounts of ETH once transferred. The pooled assets can then be utilized to fund the projects that the smart contract was deployed for, perhaps based on a decision-making process that relies on token-holder votes. Thus, just like a corporate treasury, through a smart contract account, crypto-assets can be "owned," exchanged, or traded in interactions with other accounts controlled by humans or other smart contract code.[23] As for (un-)limited liability, the question, if it arises at all, could be

[15] William Klein, John Coffee Jr, and Frank Partnoy, *Business Organization and Finance* (11th edn, Foundation Press 2010) 108–10; Paul Davies, Sarah Worthington, and Chris Hare, *Gower Principles of Modern Company Law* (11th edn, Sweet and Maxwell 2021) paras 2-001–2-033.

[16] Frank H Easterbrook and Daniel R Fischel, *The Economic Structure of Corporate Law* (Harvard UP 1991) 41.

[17] ibid 42–44; Paul J Halpern, Michael J Trebilcock, and Sarah Turnbull, "An Economic Analysis of Limited Liability in Corporation Law" (1980) 30 University of Toronto Law Journal 117, 126.

[18] Henry Hansmann and Reinier Kraakman, "The Essential Role of Organizational Law" (2000) 110 Yale Law Journal 387, 422.

[19] Oliver Hart, "An Economist's Perspective on the Theory of the Firm" (1989) 89 Columbia Law Review 1757, 1764 fn 30; Melvin A Eisenberg, "The Conception that the Corporation is a Nexus of Contracts and the Dual Nature of the Firm" (1998) 24 Journal of Corporation Law 819, 822–23.

[20] Hansmann and Kraakman (n 18) 406–22; Henry Hansmann, Reinier Kraakman, and Richard Squire, "Law and the Rise of the Firm" (2006) Harvard Law Review 1335,1340–43.

[21] Richard A Posner, *Economic Analysis of Law* (9th edn, Wolters Kluwer 2014) 541.

[22] Richard A Posner, "The Rights of Creditors of Affiliated Corporations" (1975) 43 University of Chicago Law Review 499, 506; Posner, *Economic Analysis of Law* (n 21) 541.

[23] Aaron Wright and Primavera De Filippi, "Decentralized Blockchain Technology and the Rise of Lex Cryptographia" (2015) 3 (unpublished manuscript available at <http://ssrn.com/abstract=2580664> accessed December 11, 2024).

addressed based on the social norms prevalent within the network. For example, when TheDAO—an early smart contract-based investment fund—was hacked and more than $50 million worth of investor contributions siphoned off, the Ethereum community seemed unconcerned with holding Slock.it—the software company that launched TheDAO—liable for any losses caused by their buggy code. Rather, the conversation revolved around whether "code is law," that is, the hacker being justified in exploiting loopholes within the code. And in the end, to contain the reputational damage, the Ethereum community effectuated a so-called "hard fork" to restore the "stolen" funds to investors.[24] In other words, the social conventions that may apply within a blockchain network may be so strong as to preclude from arising in the first place the issue of holding developers and token-holders personally liable for a DAO's obligations. Where personal liability is desired—perhaps to enhance the credibility and reputation of a certain project—liability could be assumed by the protagonists under the social norms of the network.

Of course, push comes to shove where a DAO transcends the boundaries of the blockchain's techno-sociological normativity by interacting with users who do not share the ideological purity of blockchain evangelists. When things go wrong, even the latter may seek recourse under the applicable law with a view to breaking the smart contract capital lock-in or holding developers or token-holders personally liable for any losses sustained.[25] It is here that the question arises whether and to what extent a DAO's institutional structure needs, and deserves, support from the legal order. In this respect, perhaps lessons can be learned from the history of corporate law.

3. Corporate Law History: Lessons for DAOs?

What, if anything, can the history of corporate law teach us that is relevant for DAOs today? Early companies were, and DAOs may be, general partnerships, with all the inadequacies this entails. Accordingly, early companies did, and DAOs may, require some further accommodation and recognition by the legal system. For companies, this was driven by a strong business case: the industrial revolution and the rise of the railways. For DAOs today, it remains to be seen whether there is a business case at all. In addition, early companies had, and DAOs have, a propensity to be used by fraudsters and scammers to exploit investors. Following scandals and crises, the necessary regulatory interventions tend to go too far, stifling innovation and hitting fraudulent and legitimate ventures alike. An incremental approach has served companies well, and seems preferable also for DAOs.

[24] Kevin Werbach, *The Blockchain and the New Architecture of Trust* (MIT Press 2018) 67–69.

[25] eg Hector DAO's leadership was sued by token-holders asserting breach of contract, breach of fiduciary duties, and conversion before Hector Enterprises Inc went into a British Virgin Islands (BVI) receivership; Kara Bruse, Christopher Odinet, and Andrea Tosato, "Bankrupt Crypto Organizations" (2025) 43–44 <https://papers.ssrn.com/sol3/papers.cfm?abstract_id=5115277> accessed July 25, 2025.

3.1. Partnerships: Old and New

> The directors of [joint stock] companies being the managers rather of other people's money than of their own, it cannot well be expected, that they should watch over it with the same anxious vigilance with which the partners in a private copartnery frequently watch over their own.... Negligence and profusion, therefore, must always prevail, ...[26]

The general partnership—Adam Smith's "copartnery"—as organizational form connects early companies and modern DAOs. However, as we will see, the reasons for the applicability of partnership law in either case may be quite different, albeit with similar legal consequences for participants and contractual counterparties.

In the fifteenth and sixteenth centuries, merchant companies began to seek incorporation[27] with a view to obtaining a monopoly of trade for their members and exercising governmental power over colonial territory.[28] For these purposes, a license from the sovereign was needed: a Royal charter, concession, or *octroi*.[29] The (English) East India Company was first chartered in 1600, the Dutch East India Company was formed in 1602, followed by companies chartered by other European sovereigns.[30] For most businesses, obtaining a Royal charter was not worth the considerable[31] hassle. In England, firms increasingly operated as unincorporated joint stock companies. Formed by a "deed of settlement," the company's property would be vested in trustees holding the legal title for the benefit of the members as *cestuis que* trust who in turn held transferrable shares as equitable interests in the company's property.[32]

The first two decades of the eighteenth century saw a significant increase in the formation and flotation of these "joint stock companies," both incorporated and unincorporated. Fraud and corruption were widespread with major financial scandals in France and England, including the South Sea Bubble followed by the demise of the South Sea Company.[33] The latter, according to Adam Smith,

> had an immense capital divided among an immense number of proprietors. It was naturally to be expected, therefore, that folly, negligence and profusion should prevail in the whole management of its affairs. The knavery and extravagance of their

[26] Adam Smith, *An Inquiry into the Nature and Causes of the Wealth of Nations*, vol II (RH Campbell and AS Skinner eds, Liberty Press 1976; first published in 1776) 264–65.

[27] Paul Davies, *Gower's Principles of Modern Company Law* (6th edn, Sweet & Maxwell 1997) 19; Alfred F Conard, *Corporations in Perspective* (Foundation Press 1976) 181.

[28] Davies (n 27) 20; David L Perrott, "Changes in Attitude to Limited Liability—the European Experience" in Tony Orhnial (ed), *Limited Liability and the Corporation* (Croom Helm 1982) 81, 89.

[29] Davies (n 27) 18; Klaus Macharzina, "Corporate Forms and Limited Liability in German Company Law" in T Orhnial (ed), *Limited Liability and the Corporation* (Croom Helm 1982) 44, 47; Conard (n 27) 180.

[30] Clive M Schmitthoff, "The Origin of the Joint-Stock Company" (1939) 3 Toronto Law Journal 74, 93.

[31] Phillip I Blumberg, *The Law of Corporate Groups: Tort, Contract, and Other Common Law Problems in the Substantive Law of Parent and Subsidiary Corporations* (Little Brown 1987) 13.

[32] Davies (n 27) 28.

[33] ibid 24–28.

> stock-jobbing projects are sufficiently known, ... Their mercantile projects were not much better conducted.[34]

To prop up South Sea stock by preventing an outflow of cash,[35] the Bubble Act of 1720 made it illegal for an unincorporated company to act as corporate body and to raise transferable stock without legal authority granted by Act of Parliament or Crown charter.[36] The Act made both fraudulent and legitimate ventures more difficult,[37] and most entrepreneurs had to turn to unincorporated companies which started to re-appear after the initial shock had subsided. The Bubble Act was repealed in 1825.

At a time when incorporation was by and large unavailable, the "deed of settlement" company became the vehicle of choice for entrepreneurs. Technically a partnership, promoters tried to replicate some of the advantages of incorporation: Deeds would provide that the trustees could sue or be sued on behalf of the company. Although mostly effective in the courts of equity, actions at common law had to be brought by or against all the partners, thus essentially barring unincorporated joint stock companies from the common law courts.[38] Clauses in the deed tried to limit direct and indirect liability of members to the amount of their stock interest, and contracts with third parties contained clauses stipulating that liability would be limited to the assets of the company.[39] By the middle of the nineteenth century, the latter were confirmed to be valid and effective by the courts in respect of express clauses in insurance policies.[40] By contrast, a clause in the deed of settlement was still deemed to be insufficient even if the creditor had notice thereof.[41] Having said that, in the words of Davies, unlimited personal liability was "a delusion rather than a protection to the public and no handicap at all for the dishonest promoter."[42] In practice, it was almost impossible to obtain judgment against the fluctuating body of shareholders, and even more difficult to enforce it against the members whose identities would often be concealed.[43]

Today, given the right circumstances, DAO developers and governance token-holders may also constitute a general partnership:[44] under English law, provided there is a contractual relationship between the participants, concerning a business carried on in common with a view of profit.[45] The "business" nature of the activities carried out by most DAOs in the DeFi ecosystem—stablecoins, lending and borrowing, automated market makers, derivatives, asset management, insurance—will rarely be in doubt; neither will be the motivation to generate a profit,[46] for the common benefit

[34] Smith (n 26) 264–65.

[35] Charles Kindleberger and Robert Aliber, *Manias, Panics, and Crashes—A History of Financial Crisis* (6th edn, Palgrave Macmillan 2011) 88.

[36] Davies (n 27) 25.

[37] Kindleberger and Aliber (n 35).

[38] ibid 29–31; Perrott (n 28) 96.

[39] Blumberg (n 31) 15.

[40] *Halket v Merchant Traders' Ship, Loan & Insurance Association* (1849) 13 QB 960.

[41] *Re Sea, Fire & Life Insurance Co* (1854) 3 De GM & G 459.

[42] Davies (n 27) 32.

[43] Ronald R Formoy, *The Historical Foundations of Modern Company Law* (Sweet and Maxwell 1923) 35.

[44] *Sarcuni v bZx DAO*, No 22-618 (S D Cal, March 27, 2023); Michael Schillig, "Decentralized Autonomous Organizations (DAOs) under English Law" (2022) 16 Law and Financial Markets Review 68.

[45] Partnership Act 1890, s 1(1); Roderick Banks, *Lindley and Banks on Partnership* (21st edn, Sweet & Maxwell 2022) para 2-02.

[46] Banks (n 45) para 2-08.

of the participants. Consequently, developers acting together to get a DAO off the ground and to maintain it would seem to meet these conditions, depending on the underlying project. For governance token-holders, the situation is less clear. However, a finding that they may (also) be general partners in a DAO partnership is not inconceivable. Still, the risk of personal and unlimited liability for the DAO's debts of developers seems low, and remote for governance token-holders. The evidentiary hurdles for a claimant are high, both in terms of the conditions for partnership and the applicability of any national partnership law, but perhaps even more so for proving that the defendant was a partner at the time the relevant DAO debt was incurred. Given the potentially high fluctuation and mobility of governance token-holders, and perhaps even developers, this will not be an easy task and may often be practically impossible,[47] just as it was with regard to the shareholders in "deed of settlement" companies.

Whereas the promoters of the latter had no other option, DAO developers can not only pick the jurisdiction they deem most suitable but also have a whole menu of organizational forms to choose from: foundations, corporations, limited liability companies (LLCs), possibly even with a DAO-specific bent. These may be used as legal wrappers for all or part of a DAO's business operations. Where developers do not avail themselves of any of these options this could be for a variety of reasons: ideological—the cypherpunk decentralization ethos in its purest form is incompatible with state-sponsored legal wrappers; practical—what is available may still not be suitable for accommodating the novel cooperation and governance arrangements envisaged by the developers; or as a matter of convenience—the developers just hadn't thought of it or thought they didn't need it.

3.2. The Need for (Further) Accommodation

For the "deed of settlement" companies, the legal system eventually offered the necessary accommodation, albeit only following major socio-economic changes during the industrial revolution. It turns out that being a "copartnery" with *de facto* limited liability may be the worst of all worlds: it does not prevent "negligence and profusion" as envisaged by Smith; and may still be too risky for serious investors to support newly emerging industries. Both issues had to be addressed. The history of corporate law shows how hard it is to get the balance right and seems to support a cautious approach going forward, also for DAOs.

Increasing industrialization at the turn of the eighteenth to the nineteenth century resulted in heightened demand for the privileges of incorporation. In England, the charter system was replaced by general incorporation under the Joint Stock Companies Registration and Regulation Act of 1844. This Act had a dual nature of being both enabling and regulatory: It conferred on the unincorporated joint stock company some of the advantages of corporate personality: to sue and be sued, to enter into contracts, and to hold land in its corporate name.[48] At the same time, the

[47] Schillig (n 44).

[48] Michael Lobban, "Corporate Identity and Limited Liability in France and England 1825–67" (1996) 25 Anglo-American Law Review 397, 416.

requirement to publicly register not just the name and business of the company but also the name and place of residence of its promoters was designed to curb the problem of "bubble companies," set up with a view to defrauding investors.[49] Importantly, the 1844 Act was not perceived as creating a new form of business organization; joint stock companies remained partnerships and the shareholders their collective owners. Accordingly, only a genuine partnership, consisting of at least 25, later 7, members could incorporate.[50] In line with partnership principles, the Act initially retained the unlimited liability of members for unsatisfied corporate debts;[51] although creditors had to proceed against the assets of the company first.[52]

This was about to change with the rapid development of the railways after 1844.[53] The railway industry required huge amounts of capital that could only be raised by issuing large quantities of shares with small denominations held by a multitude of investors who could freely trade them on liquid capital markets.[54] At the same time, railways were exposed to potentially exorbitant tort liability which could not be eliminated by contract. Still, limited liability remained a highly contentious political issue.[55] Only after a long and heated debate, was limited liability finally welcomed as a general feature of company law. This was achieved with the Limited Liability Act 1855 and the subsequent Joint Stock Companies Act 1856.[56] After consolidation of various amendments, the Companies Act 1862 emerged as the first modern company law statute in England. These developments culminated in the famous decision in *Salomon & A Salomon & Co Ltd*,[57] decided by the House of Lords in 1897, which consolidated the entity concept and opened the corporate form for all entrepreneurs including small partnerships and sole traders. In the words of Lord Macnaghten:

> When the memorandum is duly signed and registered, . . . , the subscribers are a body corporate "capable forthwith," . . . , "of exercising all the functions of an incorporated company." Those are strong words. The company attains maturity on its birth. There is no period of minority—no interval of incapacity. I cannot understand how a body corporate thus made "capable" by statute can lose its individuality by issuing the bulk of its capital to one person, whether he be a subscriber to the memorandum or not. The company is at law a different person altogether from the subscribers to the memorandum; and, though it may be that after incorporation the business is precisely the same as it was before, and the same persons are managers, and the same hands receive the profits, the company is not in law the agent of the subscribers or trustee for them. Nor are the subscribers as members liable, in any shape or form, except to the extent and in the manner provided by the Act.

[49] Eva Micheler, *Company Law: A Real Entity Theory* (OUP 2021) 39.

[50] Ross Grantham, "The Doctrinal Basis of the Rights of Company Shareholders" (1998) 57 Cambridge Law Journal 554, 561.

[51] Davies (n 27) 38.

[52] ibid 38–39.

[53] Blumberg (n 31) 18–20.

[54] Paddy Ireland, "Capitalism without the Capitalist: The Joint Stock Company Share and the Emergence of the Modern Doctrine of Separate Corporate Personality" (1996) 17 Legal History 41, 67–69.

[55] Davies (n 27) 40–46.

[56] Blumberg (n 31) 19; Davies (n 27) 44–46.

[57] [1897] AC 22.

It has been argued that historically the "industrial revolution" in England did not require general incorporation under limited liability. Ordinary partnerships were largely adequate and dominated the cotton and iron industries. Where the required amount of capital was very high—as with railways—chartered companies were available to accommodate these needs. Entrepreneurs were generally content with ordinary partnerships.[58] According to others, the comparatively late development of limited liability in highly industrialized England had other reasons: Whereas limited liability is most useful for new firms which require the pooling of savings from many individuals, England had well-established industries and wealth was concentrated in fewer hands. These established industrialists did not need the additional funds generated by limited liability to expand. Indeed, limited liability as a general principle meant enhanced competition and potential loss of market share. Hence the resistance to the introduction of limited liability by British industrialists.[59]

Either way, the rise of the railway companies and the rapid growth of a new class of passive investors in search for new investment opportunities made it necessary to make the share "safe" as an object of financial investment.[60] Limited liability as a general principle was, accordingly, not the "natural" result of market forces; rather, it was a conscientious political decision resulting in a top-down regulatory intervention.[61] Despite a *de facto* freedom from liability in large unincorporated joint stock corporations and exclusion of liability by contract, without legislative intervention, according to Davies:

> [L]imited liability could never have been attained in a satisfactory and clear cut fashion, and it was this intervention which finally established companies as the major instrument in economic development.[62]

Thus, for joint stock companies, further accommodation was driven by technological innovation and new business models that required a legal wrapper with specific features. And still, this accommodation was politically highly controversial. The parallels with DAOs today only go so far: *DAOs* constitute a new way of holding new types of assets and of making governance decisions concerning them. DAOs can achieve capital lock-in based on smart contract and blockchain technology, however outside the network's techno-sociological normativity they cannot hold property and enter into contracts in their own name; they cannot have acts attributed to them as separate from the individuals that make up a *DAO's community*. The liability of developers and token-holders may practically be limited (or non-existent), however a residual risk remains which may be too much for some. DAOs and their underlying technology do

[58] Paddy Ireland, "Limited Liability, Rights of Control and the Problem of Corporate Irresponsibility" (2010) 34 Cambridge Journal of Economics 837, 840–41.

[59] Kevin F Forbes, "Limited Liability and the Development of the Business Corporation" (1986) 2 Journal of Law, Economics, and Organization 163, 171.

[60] Ireland (n 58) 842–47.

[61] David Campbell and Stephen Griffin, "Enron and the End of Corporate Governance" in Sorcha Macleod (ed), *Global Governance and the Quest for Justice, Volume II: Corporate Governance* (Hart Publishing 2006) 47, 59–63.

[62] Davies (n 27) 46.

have the potential of creating new capital markets accessible to new constituencies of investors and entrepreneurs outside the traditional venture capital channels—a democratization of finance. Pushback from established players—traditional finance and big tech—is therefore to be expected. A successful rollout of the technology may only be possible by getting these incumbents on board, so that they can leverage the technology for themselves, a tendency we can observe with the growth in centralized decentralized finance (CeDeFi). Whether beyond that, the DAO's value proposition—the "business case" for further compatibility adjustment within the legal environment—is sufficiently strong remains to be seen. Again, incorporation is already widely available for DAO communities. In addition, or alternatively, contract law can be used to mimic some of its features. In any case, re-centralization seems inevitable—contracts need endpoints and corporations a registered office and board of directors. This is true also for the new DAO-specific organizational forms, like the Wyoming DAO LLC.[63] We can go even further: smart contracts as software programs have no legal significance other than that deriving from explicit or implicit agreements—a contractual framework in the traditional sense—between the DAO's participants: developers, users, governance token-holders. This contractual framework—with endpoints—exists by necessity. A case can be made to enhance it with a statutory underpinning, perhaps along the lines of Armour and Whincop's analysis of corporate law as consisting of a "contractual superstructure" and "proprietary foundations," giving certain governance arrangements third-party effect,[64] specifically tailored to DAOs.

Whether DAO entrepreneurs and communities are asking for this is an interesting empirical question. Regardless, further accommodation by way of enabling legislation that DAOs can opt into seems harmless enough: the worst that can happen is the promulgation of a new legal framework that remains (largely) unused, a waste of time and money on the part of policymakers and legislators. Given that very flexible options are already available, there is a risk that any new corporate suits also won't be a perfect fit and may be quickly overtaken by technological developments: DAO technology is constantly evolving and at this stage is by no means settled. Therefore, and given that the business case, for now, seems comparatively weaker than for early companies, an incremental adjustment that seeks to gradually accommodate DAO technology within existing legal frameworks, seems preferable.

One could think, for example, of a legal recognition that a smart contract (address) can be the holder of crypto-assets, similar to the idea of a purposeful pool of assets (*Zweckvermögen*) that is not owned by anyone but can be the allocative endpoint of property rights itself;[65] so that there would be no need for using a foundation for these purposes. It is also not inconceivable that, given the right circumstance, courts could gradually accept the validity and effectiveness of limited liability clauses in White Papers duly published in accordance with MiCAR.[66] Which brings us back to the second aspect of the 1844 Act: the need for further regulation.

[63] Wyoming Decentralized Autonomous Organization Supplement, File No SF0038, Enrolled Act No 73, Senate, 66th Legislature of the State of Wyoming, 2021 General Session.

[64] John Armour and Michael Whincop, "The Proprietary Foundations of Corporate Law" (2007) 27 OJLS 429.

[65] Alois Brinz, *Lehrbuch der Pandekten, Dritter Band (Das Zweckvermögen)* (Andreas Reichert 1888).

[66] MiCAR, Arts 4–9.

3.3. The Need for (Further) Regulation

> I weigh my words, when I say that in my judgment the limited liability corporation is the greatest single discovery in modern times ... Even steam and electricity are far less important than the limited liability corporation, and they would be reduced to comparative impotence without it.[67]

The introduction of general incorporation was followed by rampant abuse and speculation, colorfully summarized by the eminent German jurist Rudolf von Ihering:[68]

> Under the eyes of our legislators, joint stock corporations have become organised fraud and robbery institutions whose secrete history bears witness to greater meanness, dishonour and villainy than any penitentiary, except that the robbers and fraudsters do not lie in chains but sit in gold.

Whereas the Bubble Act with its near blanket ban on incorporation went too far, the regulatory aspects under the 1844 Act—registration and compliance with a few formalities—also proved to be inadequate. Still, the lesson to be drawn for DAOs today is not to come down with a regulatory sledgehammer as soon as possible. Here, much more than when it comes to accommodation within the legal framework, a tentative and incremental approach seems to be in order.

Unfortunately, the European Union (EU)'s MiCAR[69] seems to be doing the opposite: The Regulation contains stringent requirements for crypto-asset services providers and the issuers of stablecoins. Its effect on many DeFi DAOs will largely depend on how Recital (22) —exempting "crypto-asset services ... provided in a fully decentralised manner without any intermediary" from the scope of the Regulation—will be interpreted. On a strict reading, there currently seems to be not a single DeFi DAO that can be said to be "fully decentralized" in that sense. Consequently, depending on its business model, a DAO may need a banking or e-money license (for the issuance of e-money tokens), may have to incorporate in a Member State and obtain authorization (for the issuance of asset-referenced tokens, or as a crypto services provider), and will be subject to various conduct of business, governance, and prudential requirements. The risk of stifling innovation is real, as is the risk of forcing budding enterprises offshore.

The history of corporate law shows that it doesn't have to be this way. Ever since incorporation became widely available, the law tried to tighten the leash of promoters/directors to commit them to the investors' cause. The same direction of travel seems feasible and preferable for DAOs. Adam Smith neatly explained what much

[67] "Politics and Business," Address of Nicholas Murray Butler President of Columbia University, CXLIII. Annual Banquet of the Chamber of Commerce of the State of New York (New York: Press of the Chamber of Commerce 1911) 47.

[68] Rudolf von Jhering, *Der Zweck im Recht 1. Band* (Breitkopf & Härtel 1877) 222.

[69] Regulation (EU) 2023/1114 of the European Parliament and of the Council of 31 May 2023 on markets in crypto-assets, and amending Regulations (EU) No 1093/2010 and (EU) No 1095/2010 and Directives 2013/36/EU and (EU) 2019/1937 OJ EU 2023 L150/40.

later became known as the principal–agent problem:[70] promoters and directors know much more about their own skills and intentions and the envisaged business venture than any outside investors, resulting in an asymmetry of information combined with formal powers on the part of the promoters/directors that exceed their substantive entitlements. Being entrusted with the investors' contributions there is always the temptation to syphon off value for their own benefit—perhaps outright, or disguised as an arm's length transaction, investment in a risky venture, or by issuing new shares at a discount to themselves. For DAOs we may add the exploitation of admin privileges or re-entrancy vulnerabilities, and other smart contract-specific risks.

The development of fiduciary principles is a pertinent example of how abusive behavior was gradually weeded out. This also has great potential for DAOs. The first cases in which directors were held liable for "breach of trust" concerned corporations proper, not unincorporated joint stock companies.[71] As early as 1854 it was held in *Aberdeen Railway Co v Blaikei Bros*[72] that:

> [t]he directors are a body to whom is delegated the duty of managing the general affairs of the company. A corporate body can only act by agents, and it is, of course the duty of those agents so to act as best to promote the interests of the corporation whose affairs they are conducting. Such an agent has duties to discharge of a fiduciary character towards his principal, and it is a rule of universal application that no one having such duties to discharge shall be allowed to enter into engagement in which he has or can have a personal interest conflicting or which possibly may conflict with the interests of those whom he is bound to protect.

And by 1894 it was well established that:

> Although directors are not properly speaking trustees, yet they have always been considered and treated as trustees of money which comes to their hands or which is actually under their control; and ever since joint stock companies were invented directors have been held liable to make good moneys which they have misapplied upon the same footing as if they were trustees ...[73]

The fiduciary obligations of trustees properly so called became a template for formulating the duties of company directors, who unlike trustees proper, do not hold legal title to the property under their control which instead vests in the company as a separate legal entity.[74] In adopting the established case law by way of analogy to directors, it had to be adjusted to address important differences and deviations.[75] In doing so,

[70] Michael C Jensen and William H Meckling, "Theory of the Firm: Managerial Behavior, Agency Costs, and Ownership Structure" in Michael C Jensen (ed), *A Theory of the Firm: Governance, Residual Claims, and Organizational Forms* (Harvard UP 2003) 83, 86.

[71] Lon S Sealy, "The Director as Trustee" (1967) 25 Cambridge Law Journal 83, 84–86.

[72] [1843–60] All ER Rep 249, per Lord Cranworth LC.

[73] *Re Land Allotment Co* [1894] 1 Ch 616 per Lindley LJ.

[74] Alan Dignam and John Lowry, *Company Law* (12th edn, OUP 2022) 300.

[75] Lon S Sealy, "The Director as Trustee" (n 71) 86–90.

the law occasionally reacted directly to the misbehavior of promoters and directors. The evolution of the no-profit rule is an instructive example.[76]

In the 1862 case of *Tyrrell v Bank of London*,[77] a solicitor (Tyrrell) acting for their client (Bank of London) had received a piece of land as a "bribe" from the seller (Read) in exchange for inducing their client to purchase other property. It was held that the client could not lay claim to the property received by the solicitor as a "bribe." Lord Chelmsford explains:

> [L]et it be supposed that Tyrrell had acquired no interest in the property, but that Read had offered him £5000 to induce the Respondents to purchase, and that they had been persuaded by Tyrrell to buy at an excessive price.... could they, in any manner, have obtained the £5000 on the ground that it belonged to them? ... the £5000 itself ... they could in no manner have recovered. The unsold part of the property, in the same manner, cannot be directly reached by any proceedings of the Respondents.

However, throughout the 1870s, company promoters and directors developed various schemes to exploit the investing public. In its simplest form, company promoters would pay a commission to their initial directors to induce them to accept appointment and adopt a purchase by the company from the promoters. Out of the purchase price, the company directors would then receive their commission. The company could recover such payment as in equity the money still belonged to the company.[78] However, faced with ever more elaborate schemes, the courts gradually moved away from the traditional fiduciary principle that a profit made by the fiduciary in breach of their duties could only be recovered on the basis that, unlike the "bribe" in *Tyrrell v Bank of London*, in equity it was still the property of the beneficiary.[79] By 1880, it was well established that a fiduciary must hand over to the beneficiary any payment received from the opposite party with whom the fiduciary had negotiated, although such a claim could now be statute-barred.[80] *Metropolitan Bank v Heiron*[81] concerned a former director who had received a bribe from a company debtor with a view to facilitating a favorable compromise of their debt. According to Cotton LJ,

> [h]ere the money sought to be recovered was in no sense the money of the company, ... It is a suit founded on breach of duty or fraud by a person who was in the position of trustee, his position making the receipt of the money a breach of duty or fraud. It is very different from the case of a *cestui que* trust seeking to recover money which was his own before any act wrongfully done by the trustee.

Subsequently, the new principle was extended so that a beneficiary could recover sums they never could have obtained for themselves; and that *mala fides* on the part of

[76] LS Sealy, "Some Principles of Fiduciary Obligations" (1968) 26 Cambridge Law Journal 119, 132–35.
[77] (1862) 10 HLCas 26.
[78] Sealy, "Some Principles of Fiduciary Obligations" (n 76) 133.
[79] ibid 134.
[80] ibid 133.
[81] (1880) 5 Ex D 325.

the fiduciary or loss on the part of the beneficiary didn't matter at all.[82] This culminated in a strict no-profit rule as summarized by Lord Russell of Killowen in the seminal case of *Regal (Hastings) Ltd v Gulliver*:[83]

> The rule of equity which insists on those, who by use of a fiduciary position make a profit, being liable to account for that profit, in no way depends on fraud, or absence of bona fides; or upon such questions or considerations as whether the profit would or should otherwise have gone to the plaintiff, or whether the profiteer was under a duty to obtain the source of the profit for the plaintiff, or whether he took a risk or acted as he did for the benefit of the plaintiff, or whether the plaintiff has in fact been damaged or benefited by his action. The liability arises from the mere fact of a profit having, in the stated circumstances, been made. The profiteer, however honest and well-intentioned, cannot escape the risk of being called upon to account.

The adoption and strengthening of fiduciary principles had an important signaling effect: fiduciaries are more likely to take the performance of their duties seriously and to perform them with due care and diligence. Fiduciary principles provide an accountability standard that is in line with the significance of their tasks at hand. The strict enforcement of fiduciary principles ensures a reduction of bonding and monitoring costs (and the residual loss), making companies as an organizational form more efficient.[84]

This is of great relevance for DAOs. The issue of whether core developers of Bitcoin and Ethereum should be characterized as fiduciaries and be subject to the corresponding duties has already come up.[85] In *Tulip Trading Limited v van der Laan and others*,[86] a decision concerning an interim application to serve proceedings out of the jurisdiction, the Court of Appeal was of the view that whether the core developers of Bitcoin can be fiduciaries vis-à-vis the holders of the cryptocurrency was "a serious issue to be tried." According to Birss LJ:

> ... I recognise that for Tulip's case to succeed would involve a significant development of the common law on fiduciary duties.... However there is, it seems to me, a realistic argument along the following lines. The developers of a given network are a sufficiently well defined group to be capable of being subject to fiduciary duties. Viewed objectively the developers have undertaken a role which involves making discretionary decisions and exercising power for and on behalf of other people, in relation to property owned by those other people. That property has been entrusted into the care of the developers. The developers therefore are fiduciaries. The essence of that duty is single minded loyalty to the users of bitcoin software. The content of the duties includes a duty not to act in their own self interest and also involves a duty to

[82] Sealy, "Some Principles of Fiduciary Obligations" (n 76) 134.

[83] [1942] 1 All ER 378.

[84] Angela Walch, "In Code(ers) We Trust—Software Developers as Fiduciaries in Public Blockchains" in P Hacker and others (eds), *Regulating Blockchain* (OUP 2019) 58, 70.

[85] ibid.

[86] [2023] EWCA Civ 83.

> act in positive ways in certain circumstances. It may also, realistically, include a duty to act to introduce code so that an owner's bitcoin can be transferred to safety ... [87]

It is important to emphasize that the case does not settle the matter, as it was strictly on the procedural issue of serving proceedings abroad. However, the line of reasoning espoused in *Tulip Trading Limited v van der Laan* applies with even greater force to most DAOs where authority and power tend to be (even) more concentrated[88] than in public blockchain networks.[89] An incremental development of the law in this respect could reduce the potential cost of stifling innovation. Fiduciary principles could be developed in a way that is commensurate to the value at stake. In other words, the core developers of a DeFi application with total value locked (TVL) of $millions or billions could be held to a much higher standard than the developers of a DAO that has not gone beyond an experimental stage. Again, this seems preferable to a new one-size-fits-all regulatory crackdown. Of course, imposing fiduciary duties on DAO developers and promoters and perhaps other constituencies does not sit well with blockchain's and DeFi's decentralization ethos.[90] Obviously, this would not prevent courts from imposing fiduciary duties where doing so seems justified, which then raises the further issue of the appropriate limitation and tailoring of the ensuing duties in the underlying contractual framework.

How is it then that within a generation, Ihering's "organized fraud and robbery organizations" became the "greatest single discovery in modern times." This is a complex empirical question, but it seems plausible that legal development played a major role. An enabling legal framework with separate legal personality and limited liability was ready to accommodate changing socio-economic needs. By tightening the leash on promoters and directors, a signal was sent to investors and the market more generally that their investment was (relatively) safe, whilst simultaneously reducing bonding and monitoring costs.

DAOs today also face the problem of costly signaling: how can high-quality DAOs distinguish themselves from low-quality DAOs and send credible signals to the market?[91] The obvious answer is incorporation using one or a combination of the available organizational forms, and perhaps actively seeking compliance with applicable regulatory frameworks (MiCAR), where suitable. The risk is that this might be incompatible with an innovative business model. For these cases, which for now

[87] ibid [86].

[88] Matthias Nadler and Fabian Schär, "Decentralized Finance, Centralized Ownership? An Iterative Mapping Process to Measure Protocol Token Distribution" (2020) <https://arxiv.org/abs/2012.09306> accessed December 11, 2024; Mitchell Goldberg and Fabian Schär, "Metaverse Governance: An Empirical Analysis of Voting within Decentralized Autonomous Organizations" (2023) 160 Journal of Business Research 1.

[89] Cesare Fracassi, Moazzam Khoja, and Fabian Schär, "Decentralized Crypto Governance? Transparency and Concentration in Ethereum Decision-Making" (*SSRN*, 10 January 2024) <https://ssrn.com/abstract=4691000> accessed December 11, 2024.

[90] Walch (n 34) 71; *Tulip Trading Limited v van der Laan* [2023] EWCA Civ 83 [33]; Law Commission [n 2] para 3.142.

[91] Darcy Allan and others, "On costly signalling in DAOs: A research agenda" (*SSRN*, 22 May 2024) <https://ssrn.com/abstract=4837504> accessed December 11, 2024.

seem to be rare, the law can, and should be, developed incrementally to accommodate DAOs and their underlying technology.

4. Conclusion

DAOs and corporations are both a type of infrastructure that allows for a capital lock-in and the allocation of cash flow and control rights over a pool of assets. Both can easily be used by unscrupulous promoters and developers to exploit investors. The history of corporate law has seen many asset bubbles, scams, and crashes. Still, the modern corporation has emerged as the preferred organizational form for doing business, at least in Western capitalist societies. An ever more sophisticated legal framework accompanied the rise of the corporation from "organised fraud and robbery institutions" to the "greatest single discovery in modern times." Whether DAO technology will experience a similar meteoric rise remains to be seen. It is clear however that to reach its full potential, some form of legal recognition and accommodation will be necessary. However, at the current stage of development, DAO communities do not seem to need a new and bespoke legal framework. The technology that they rely on can be accommodated more effectively by incrementally adjusting existing legal frameworks. This may entail the recognition of asset ownership of smart contract addresses, the validity of limited liability clauses in White Papers, and the development of fiduciary principles to hold developers and other powerful DAO constituencies to account. There are signs that the law could follow this trajectory. However, this will depend on whether and to what extent DAO technology's value proposition remains strong.

PART II
DAO GOVERNANCE

4
DAOs and Corporate Governance

Jill E Fisch

1. Introduction

A decentralized autonomous organization (DAO) is a business organization that maintains its ownership structure and conducts some or all of its operational decisions through decentralized computer technology, specifically blockchains.[1] Supporters of DAOs tout their potential to democratize businesses by facilitating member input and avoiding the need for complex organizational structures that increase agency costs. As one commentator explains, "Whereas executives and boards govern traditional organizations, DAOs are owned and operated by their community."[2]

The types of businesses that can potentially benefit from the DAO structure and the extent to which DAOs offer advantages over the traditional corporate form remain to be seen. At a minimum, the use of a DAO requires an evaluation of the need for standard governance features such as centralized authority and fiduciary duties. DAOs challenge conventions about which participants in an enterprise should be treated as members and afforded governance rights as well as the range of issues to which those governance rights should attach. In addition, the autonomous nature of DAOs stems from the fact that a variety of decisions are hardwired into the smart contract coding, raising issues if there are gaps between members' perceptions of the decision-making rules and the manner in which the code implements those rules.[3] Finally, DAOs highlight the competing claims as to the extent to which business forms should privilege standardization over customization, a debate that extends beyond DAOs to other contract-based business forms such as limited liability companies.

This chapter considers the corporate governance implications of DAOs and explores the ways in which DAOs differ from traditional corporations. In so doing, the chapter reflects on the governance challenges of the DAO system and the potential implications of the DAO's distinctive features.

[1] David Lucking, "Decentralized Autonomous Organizations" (*Allen & Overy LLP*, 2016) <https://www.allenovery.com/en-gb/global/news-and-insights/publications/decentralized-autonomous-organizations> accessed November 14, 2024.

[2] Rayne Steinberg, "Enhancing Traditional Corporate Governance with DAOs" (*Forbes*, 31 May 2022) <https://www.forbes.com/sites/forbesfinancecouncil/2022/03/31/enhancing-traditional-corporate-governance-with-daos/?sh=737cbaf76256> accessed November 14, 2024.

[3] Shaanan Cohney and others, "Coin-Operated Capitalism" (2019) 119 Columbia Law Review 591, 598.

2. DAOs and Investment, Ownership, and Membership

Fundamentally, a DAO is a structure that is organized for some purpose and that uses smart contracts executed on the blockchain rather than persons to make some or all of its decisions. A smart contract is a standing computer program that, in response to some trigger or event x, executes a response y.[4] Not every use of a smart contract or blockchain involves a DAO, however.[5] A classic DAO sells digital tokens to purchasers, typically in exchange for cryptocurrency, on the promise of delivering a product, providing a financial return, achieving some specified goal, or achieving a combination of objectives.[6] In some cases, DAOs also distribute tokens in exchange for services that are provided to them.[7] The proceeds from the sale of tokens can be used to develop a product, to create an ongoing business, or to accomplish a specific task. The Constitution DAO, for example, was created to raise money and bid at an auction to purchase an edition of the US Constitution.[8]

Token sales enable those forming a business or creating a product to raise capital. In turn, the tokens give their purchasers economic rights, governance rights, or a combination of the two. Economic rights include the right to receive the product or service that is developed by a DAO or the right to a return from a DAO's operations. Governance rights may include the right to make proposals to a DAO or its membership, the right to vote on proposals made by others, a role in selecting future products, and a say on other organizational decisions.

A DAO need not be organized as a formal legal entity. Nonetheless, entity status is valuable for a variety of reasons. One important feature of entity status is legal personhood—it allows a DAO to enter into contracts, take title to assets, and sue and be sued in its own name. Entity status may also provide participants in a DAO with limited personal liability and simplify issues of authority and tax treatment. For these reasons, DAOs are increasingly using formal business structures. Toward that end, a variety of structures are viable. DAOs have been organized as limited liability companies (LLCs), business trusts, nonprofit entities, including ownerless foundations, and public benefit corporations. Because they typically lack a physical presence, DAOs can choose from the entity structures available in a range of jurisdictions.[9]

Some jurisdictions have created special entities expressly designed for DAOs. In the US, three states have created DAO-specific business forms—Vermont's

[4] Carla L Reyes, "Autonomous Business Reality" (2021) 21 Nevada Law Journal 437, 446.

[5] I exclude from this discussion digital assets that are intended to function as currency or a form of payment, such as Bitcoin.

[6] Yuliya Guseva, "A Conceptual Framework for Digital-Asset Securities: Tokens and Coins as Debt and Equity" (2020) 80 Maryland Law Review 166.

[7] Gail Weinstein, Steven Lofchie, and Jason Schwartz, "A Primer on DAOs" (*Harvard Law School Forum on Corporate Governance*, September 17, 2022) <https://corpgov.law.harvard.edu/2022/09/17/a-primer-on-daos/> accessed November 14, 2024.

[8] Bernard Marr, "The Best Examples of DAOs Everyone Should Know About" (*Forbes*, 25 May 2022) <https://www.forbes.com/sites/bernardmarr/2022/05/25/the-best-examples-of-daos-everyone-should-know-about/?sh=1126dc2f40c3> accessed November 14, 2024.

[9] Irina Heaver, "The Ultimate Crypto Legal Guide to Structuring Your DAO" (*Forbes*, August 14, 2023) <https://www.forbes.com/sites/irinaheaver/2023/08/14/the-ultimate-crypto-legal-guide-to-structuring-your-dao/?sh=684973ad7b81> accessed November 14, 2024.

blockchain-based limited liability company, Wyoming's DAO LLC, and Tennessee's DAO LLC.[10] Although these forms are tailored to DAOs, some commentators have argued that they create additional disclosure and regulatory burdens beyond those required for LLCs without providing any distinctive advantages.[11]

An interesting aspect of the DAO structure is the extent to which DAOs can exist independently of human members. On the one hand, as discussed further below, a fully autonomous DAO is designed to enable computer software to make all operational decisions. Whether individual humans or artificial entities possess economic rights in a DAO, those economic rights can, at least in theory, be determined completely through smart contracts, avoiding the need for individuals to exercise governance rights. At the same time, every DAO requires people to create its smart contract programming and draft its White Paper.[12] Moreover, to the extent that there are deficiencies in a DAO's programming[13] or successful efforts to hack its code or misappropriate assets, human intervention is likely to be necessary.[14] Nonetheless, as detailed in the next section, DAOs vary in the degree to which they rely on automation to perform management functions that, in the traditional business enterprise, are performed by officers and directors.[15]

Another interesting issue concerns the extent to which DAO tokens are properly classified as securities for purposes of the federal securities laws. DAO tokens can take a variety of forms and be used for a variety of objectives. Nonetheless, to the extent that DAOs issue what essentially are investment tokens, those interests are no different than interests in traditional corporations, which are subject to regulation under the federal securities laws. In 2017, the Securities and Exchange Commission (SEC) issued an investigative report concluding that the tokens issued by "The DAO" were securities.[16] Subsequently, the SEC has applied the test for an investment contract from *SEC v Howey*[17] to a variety of digital assets and concluded, in many cases, that those assets constitute securities.[18] In contrast, utility tokens and currency tokens,

[10] Jordan Teague, "Starting a DAO in the USA? Steer Clear of DAO Legislation" (*The Defiant*, June 7, 2022) <https://thedefiant.io/starting-a-dao-in-the-usa-steer-clear-of-dao-legislation> accessed November 14, 2024.

[11] ibid.

[12] Cohney and others (n 3) 608.

[13] Wei Jiang and Tao Li, "Corporate Governance Meets Data and Technology" (*SSRN*, March 23, 2024) <https://papers.ssrn.com/sol3/papers.cfm?abstract_id=4746141> accessed November 14, 2024.

[14] Participants may disagree factually on whether a particular action constitutes a "hack" or is consistent with the rules of the DAO. Tatiana Cutts, "Smart Contracts and Consumers" (2019) 122 West Virginia Law Review 389, 428.

[15] Reyes (n 4) 463–64.

[16] Securities and Exchange Commission, "SEC Issues Investigative Report Concluding DAO Tokens, a Digital Asset, Were Securities" (*SEC*, July 25, 2017) <https://www.sec.gov/news/press-release/2017-131> accessed July 24, 2024.

[17] *SEC v W. J. Howey Co.* [1946] 328 US 293.

[18] James J Park and Howard H Park, "Regulation by Selective Enforcement: The SEC and Initial Coin Offerings" (2020) 61 Washington University Journal of Law & Policy 99. In 2019, the SEC published a framework providing guidance on the relevant factors in analyzing when a digital token is a security. Securities and Exchange Commission, "Framework for 'Investment Contract' Analysis of Digital Assets" (2019) <https://www.sec.gov/files/dlt-framework.pdf> accessed November 14, 2024.

which do not meet the *Howey* test, are unlikely to be classified as securities.[19] The legal status of governance tokens is unclear.[20]

Classification as a security affects how DAO tokens are sold, the platforms on which they are traded, and the disclosures required by founders and participants. To the extent that DAO tokens are offered or sold to the public through an internet-based platform, the issuance of those tokens may constitute a public offering.[21] Although it is, in theory, possible for issuers to use one of the exemptions from the registration requirements, as a practical manner, it is unclear whether any of those exemptions will be suitable.[22] Exemptions such as Regulation A require issuers to make disclosures, although those disclosure are more limited than those required for the full registration process; Regulation Crowdfunding limits the amount of capital that an issuer can raise; and Regulation D limits, in most cases, the offering to accredited investors.[23]

Further, if an ICO is conducted in accordance with the registration requirements, a DAO will be subject to the periodic reporting requirements applicable to public companies under the Securities Exchange Act of 1934. The securities laws which enable reporting companies to "go dark" and continue to be publicly traded,[24] would conceivably allow DAOs to raise capital through an ICO and subsequently cease to be a reporting company. As a practical matter, however, unlike the large private companies such as unicorns, DAOs are public companies regardless of their reporting status. A final complication in the application of the federal securities laws is the decentralization of a DAO. When smart contracts result in the issuance of tokens, it is not clear that a DAO itself is doing the offering. The issue is pending in the SEC's investigation of Uniswap Labs in which Uniswap claims the SEC is improperly targeting software

[19] Toshendra Kumar Sharma, "Security Tokens vs. Utility Tokens: A Concise Guide" (*Blockchain Council*, May 10, 2024) <https://www.blockchain-council.org/blockchain/security-tokens-vs-utility-tokens-a-concise-guide/> accessed August 1, 2024.

[20] Kyle Bersani, "Separating Governance Tokens from Securities: How the Utility Token May Fall Short of the Investment Contract" (2022) 43 Cardozo Law Review 1305 (proposing four-factor framework to determine whether a governance token is a security).

[21] A DAO may raise capital through an initial coin offering (ICO) or through an ongoing series of transactions. The federal securities laws apply to all public offerings. 15 United States Code Annotated §§ 77(c)(a)(2), 77(e). Offerings made over the internet or marketed to the general public constitute public offerings. *In the Matter of Paragon Coin Inc.*, Rel No 10674 [November 16, 2018] [45]–[47] <https://www.sec.gov/files/litigation/admin/2018/33-10574.pdf> accessed November 14, 2024 (explaining that Paragon's sales of tokens to the general public constituted a public offering in violation of § 5). Exchanges that allow secondary trading of tokens would be subject to registration as national securities exchanges as well. Existing crypto exchanges have not so registered; eg Cryptocurrency/ICOs, US Securities and Exchange Commission (*SEC*, March 8, 2024) <https://www.sec.gov/securities-topics/ICO> accessed November 14, 2024 ("If a platform offers trading of digital assets that are securities and operates as an 'exchange,' as defined by the federal securities laws, then the platform must register with the SEC as a national securities exchange or be exempt from registration."); also Press Release, "SEC Charges EtherDelta Founder With Operating an Unregistered Exchange," US Securities and Exchange Commission (November 8, 2018) <https://www.sec.gov/news/press-release/2018-258> accessed November 14, 2024 (announcement of settlement of SEC action against digital token trading platform for operating "as an unregistered national securities exchange").

[22] Simona Mola, An Wang, and Michael Liftik, "ICOs As Exempt Securities Offerings: An Economic Analysis" (*Law360*, June 28, 2018) <https://www.law360.com/articles/1057426/icos-as-exempt-securities-offerings-an-economic-analysis> accessed November 14, 2024.

[23] ibid (observing that "the question of whether [existing securities law exemptions] are generally suitable for ICOs remains open").

[24] Jesse M Fried, "The Going-Private Phenomenon: Firms Gone Dark" (2009) 76 University of Chicago Law Review 135.

developers.[25] Although the federal securities laws extend responsibility to those who control a public offering, the analysis of who is exercising control is likely to be complex in a DAO context.[26]

3. DAOs and Corporate Governance

When examining the corporate governance of DAOs, blockchain technology has the potential to address two distinct concerns. The first involves the cost, reliability, and transparency of ministerial tasks such as verifying ownership, effecting transfers, and voting. The second involves how business decisions are made. This chapter will focus primarily on the latter issue and its impact.

3.1. DAOs and Ministerial Components of Corporate Governance

Corporate and securities law reflects a variety of concepts that have their roots in an era of paper communication and record-keeping. Many of these concepts are out of date and stunningly inefficient.[27] For example, shareholder ownership records are fragmented across multiple platforms and providers. Ownership itself is intermediated initially through the Depository Trust and Clearing Corporation (DTCC) and subsequently through banks and brokerage firms, and only the intermediaries have the information necessary to identify the true beneficial owners of the underlying shares.[28] As a result, neither issuers nor other investors have ready access to a full list of shareholders, and communications often require complex systems in which intermediaries must forward materials to beneficial owners and, in the case of a shareholder vote, collect voting instructions.[29]

This fragmentation gives rise to a variety of concerns. Intermediaries may overvote by submitting votes for a greater number of shares than they actually hold.[30] Intermediaries may also fail to determine which shareholder has the legal authority to vote specific shares accurately—an issue further complicated by margin lending.[31] Reliance on a paper process and the use of the mail both to distribute voting materials and to collect voting instructions requires time and, as a result, state law requires issuers to set a record date, typically well in advance of a shareholder meeting, to enable

[25] MacKenzie Sigalos and Kaan Ogu, "Uniswap fights back against SEC as the ethereum crackdown continues" (*CNBC*, May 21, 2024) <https://www.cnbc.com/2024/05/21/uniswap-fights-back-against-sec-as-the-ethereum-crackdown-continues.html> accessed November 14, 2024.

[26] See nn 66–80 and accompanying text.

[27] Securities and Exchange Commission, "Concept Release on the U.S. Proxy System" Exchange Act Release No 34-62495, 75 Fed Reg 42,982, 42,984–85 (22 July 2010).

[28] Spencer Nord, "Blockchain Plumbing: A Potential Solution for Shareholder Voting?" (2019) 21 University of Pennsylvania Journal of Business Law 706, 713.

[29] Jill E Fisch, "Standing Voting Instructions: Empowering the Excluded Retail Investor" (2017) 102 Minnesota Law Review 11, 29.

[30] Ronald Oral, "Trian Talks Proxy Plumbing after Peltz's P&G War" (*The Deal*, March 2018) <https://trianpartners.com/wp-content/uploads/2018/03/The-Deal-Trian-Talks-Proxy-Plumbing-After-Peltzs-PG-War.pdf> accessed November 14, 2024.

[31] ibid.

shareholders to receive the necessary information and to submit voting instructions. The gap between record date and the vote, however, makes it possible for a shareholder to submit multiple proxies during the voting period, creating challenges in determining how the shareholder actually wants to vote.[32] In addition, the gap results in a disaggregation of economic interest and voting power for shares traded between the record date and the actual vote.[33]

Blockchain technology simplifies the verification of ownership rights, the verification of voting rights, and the mechanical process of counting votes. David Yermack, for example, has highlighted the advantages blockchain offers for improving liquidity as well as the transparency of securities ownership.[34] Spencer Nord has explored the advantages and disadvantages of using blockchain technology to address persistent problems with the mechanics of the voting process.[35]

Notably, blockchain technology can be used to address these governance issues in a traditional corporation or LLC. What distinguishes a DAO is the decentralized and autonomous manner in which the technology is used. In contrast, a traditional corporation's use of blockchain technology would be under the control of its officers and directors.

Blockchain can also be used to automate compliance. Smart contracts can automatically identify and report when an owner triggers the disclosure requirements of sections 13(d) and 16(a) of the Securities Exchange Act.[36] DAOs could simplify other compliance and reporting issues as well, including foreign ownership reporting and compliance with money laundering regulations.[37]

3.2. DAOs and Governance Decisions

Centralized management is a key component of the corporate form. Corporate officers and directors make most operational and governance decisions, and the business judgment rule shields those decisions, except in rare cases, from judicial oversight. Shareholders, despite their economic stake, play a limited decisional role, participating primarily through the process of electing directors, and voting on a small number of particularly consequential decisions such as amending the corporate charter or approving a merger.

Centralized management has a variety of advantages. It reduces collective action problems, provides a mechanism for resolving inter-shareholder disagreements, and allows corporations to benefit from expertise. Managerial decision-making is also

[32] ibid (describing the difficulty of accurately verifying voting results in public company election contests).

[33] Henry TC Hu and Bernard Black, "The New Vote Buying: Empty Voting and Hidden (Morphable) Ownership" (2006) 79 Southern California Law Review 811, 832.

[34] David Yermack, "Corporate Governance and Blockchains" (2017) 21 Review of Finance 7, 21–22.

[35] Nord (n 28) 713.

[36] Lucian A Bebchuk and Robert J Jackson, Jr, "The Law and Economics of Blockholder Disclosure" (2012) Harvard Business Law Review 39.

[37] Aniruddh Vadlamani and Sarthak Sharma, "Bridging the Divide Between DeFi and Regulators: Showcasing Decentralized Autonomous Governance as the Future for Self-Custody Wallet Regulation" (2023) University of Illinois Journal of Law, Technology & Policy 373.

viewed as reducing information asymmetries. At the same time, it has potential disadvantages. Corporate law has focused, in particular, on the managerial agency costs that result from the separation of ownership and control.[38]

In addition, the corporate form relies heavily on standardizing both the nature of these decisions and the authority of the applicable decision-maker. Although commentators generally describe corporate law as enabling, and many statutory provisions operate merely as default rules that can be modified in the corporate charter or bylaws, principles such as board primacy, the scope of shareholder power, the minimum requirements of the corporation's governing documents, and the applicability of fiduciary principles are largely considered to be hardwired into corporate law. Although commentators have criticized a one-size-fits-all approach to corporate law, there is evidence that standardization reduces information and transaction costs and may therefore be valuable, particularly for diversified investors.[39]

Blockchain can address issues of decision-making authority by automating the process by which a decision is made. This can have the effect of removing the need for management entirely or reducing the scope of management decision-making. Blockchain can also automate the role of shareholders or other participants in operational or governance decisions, either directly by using smart contracts instead of people to make the decisions, or indirectly by using technology to engage those with participation rights.

Many commentators categorize DAOs based on the extent to which they require outside, typically human, input, as opposed to implementing decisions automatically through their programming. DAOs offer two distinctive governance models. In the fully autonomous or algorithmic DAO, decisions are implemented through software, and human participants play a minimal role.[40] Highly automated DAOs are obviously best suited for relatively simple projects that do not require ongoing external inputs or responses to changed circumstances.[41] For example, it may be difficult to automate investment decisions without knowing the nature of the projects that will be submitted for funding. Even autonomous DAOs may require human interaction. A given contract may not operate as intended. Someone can interfere with the operation of the software through a hack, as was the case with "The DAO."[42] And ongoing real-world developments may require modification in the DAO's operations.[43]

Participatory DAOs respond to these concerns by vesting certain governance rights in the DAO's members, such as the right to set the parameters within which a smart contract will operate or to change the terms of the contract itself. The DAOs

[38] Adolf A Berle, Jr and Gardiner C Means, *The Modern Corporation and Private Property* (Macmillan 1932).

[39] Reilly Steel, "Proxy Access and Optimal Standardization in Corporate Governance: An Empirical Analysis" (2017) 23 Fordham Journal of Corporate & Financial Law 173, 195.

[40] Kelsie Nabben, "Experiments in Algorithmic Governance Continue" (*Kelsie—on the cataclysmia of digital infrastructure Substack*, July 29, 2021) <https://kelsienabben.substack.com/p/experiments-in-algorithmic-governance> accessed November 14, 2024; Lynn M LoPucki, "Algorithmic Entities" (2018) 95 Washington University Law Review 897.

[41] Steinberg (n 2).

[42] Usha R Rodrigues, "Law and the Blockchain" (2019) 104 Iowa Law Review 679.

[43] Aaron Wright, "The Rise of Decentralized Autonomous Organizations: Opportunities and Challenges" (2021) 4 Stanford Journal of Blockchain Law & Policy 152, 166.

programming hardwires the issues for which human interaction is required and provides an automated mechanism affording participation to those who own tokens with governance rights. The software determines the range of issues on which tokenholders engage as well as the process for engagement and the procedure for determining when a decision has been reached. Subsequently, the code automatically implements the result of the decision.

To be sure, the difference between algorithmic and participatory DAOs is somewhat overstated, as both models involve degrees of both participation and automation.[44] At the same time, the distinction is important in that algorithmic DAOs explicitly contemplate embedding a broader range of decisions directly in the code and, as a result, provide a more limited role for human participants.

Unlike the corporation, in which a combination of legal rules and practice norms standardize the decision-making roles of officers, directors, and shareholders, DAOs can allocate participation rights however they see fit. In practice, participatory DAOs have implemented several differences from traditional corporate law. First, DAOs typically adopt a flattened governance structure. DAOs typically operate without a board of directors or an executive team, making decisions through a combination of smart contracts and decentralized governance mechanisms, such as token-holder voting. Thus, a key distinction between DAOs and traditional corporations is that DAOs provide a decentralized decision-making structure.[45]

Second, DAOs can extend governance rights more broadly than corporations. Rather than limiting voting power to shareholders, for example, dOrg provides its employees with governance tokens that accrue when the employees complete projects for the company.[46] DAOs can also use airdrops to distribute free tokens to current or prospective community members.[47]

Third, corporations generally allocate decisional rights in proportion to economic power, applying the principle of one-share-one-vote.[48] DAOs may customize voting power, implementing participation rights on a per capita basis, providing voting power to those who lack an economic interest, or implementing unequal voting rights. An example is the Curve vote escrow token design in which holders of governance tokens "lock up" their tokens for a period of time, during which they may not sell them.[49] In exchange for their loyalty, the holders receive voting power in proportion to the length of the lockup. DAOs can also implement customized procedures for determining who is eligible to submit an issue for a vote, communicating information

[44] Nabben (n 40); LoPucki (n 40).

[45] Vitalik Buterin, "DAOs are not corporations: where decentralization in autonomous organizations matters" (*Vitalik Buterin's Website*, September 20, 2022) <https://vitalik.eth.limo/general/2022/09/20/daos.html> accessed July 24, 2024.

[46] Andrew R Chow, "No Bosses: What It's Like Working at a DAO" (*Time*, March 24, 2022) <https://time.com/6146406/working-at-dao-dorg/> accessed July 24, 2024.

[47] Jiang and Li (n 13) 62–63.

[48] Jill E Fisch and Steven Davidoff Solomon, "Dual Class Stock" in Jeffrey N Gordon and Wolf-Georg Ringe (eds), *Oxford Handbook of Corporate Law and Governance* (2nd edn, OUP 2025) <https://papers.ssrn.com/sol3/papers.cfm?abstract_id=4436331> accessed November 14, 2024; Paul H Edelman, Wei Jiang, and Randall S Thomas, "Will Tenure Voting Give Corporate Managers Lifetime Tenure?" (2019) 97 Texas Law Review 991.

[49] Robert Mullins, "veGood, veBad, and veUgly" (*Outlier Ventures*, November 16, 2022) <https://outlierventures.io/article/vegood-vebad-and-veugly/> accessed November 14, 2024.

about an upcoming vote, and providing which token-holders are eligible to vote on a particular issue.[50]

These features enable DAOs to offer both greater flexibility and greater customization than traditional business entities. This ability to provide customized participation structures, including flexibility in terms of which decisions are made by participants, and who participates, has the potential to make DAO governance more participatory. In this sense, DAOs both eliminate the formal separation of ownership and control and engage a wider group of potential decision-makers. Technology can reduce the collective action problems associated with this approach both by reducing information asymmetries and reducing the costs of collective action.

4. Implications

4.1. Authority and Accountability

The foregoing structure creates several governance challenges for DAOs. One is the lack of centralized authority. Jiang and Li term this a "governance void."[51] Although the blockchain mechanism would appear to provide a trustworthy system in that its programming is hardwired and thereby protected from individual misconduct, "[b]lockchains are vulnerable to selfish behavior, attacks, and manipulation."[52]

In addition, to the extent the DAO needs to take an unanticipated action—whether that involves implementing a hard fork in response to a hack or liquidating a DAO because accomplishing its objective has become impossible—DAOs typically do not provide a default person or entity that can make that decision. Similarly, there is no ready way for an automated decision-making process to address problems that are outside the scope anticipated by its programming. Most businesses need to respond on a continual basis to new inputs and external developments, and an entity's corporate governance provides the structure by which those responses occur. A business that lacks such flexibility is likely to be more limited in its scope and duration. That is not to criticize algorithmic DAOs, but simply to recognize that their use is likely to be limited to contexts in which the need for flexibility in response to external inputs is likely to be most limited.[53]

The response to this governance void are participatory DAOs. Indeed, commentators defend participatory DAOs as replacing centralized authority with a decentralized governance structure that both reduces the agency costs inherent in corporate governance and offers a more inclusive decision-making process. Participatory DAOs

[50] Anne Lafarre and Christoph Van der Elst, "The Viability of Blockchain in Corporate Governance" (2023) ECGI Working Paper Series in Law N 712/2023, 8 <https://www.ecgi.global/sites/default/files/working_papers/documents/theviabilityofblockchainincorporategovernance_0.pdf> accessed November 14, 2024.

[51] Jiang and Li (n 13) 42.

[52] Kevin Werbach, "Trust, but Verify: Why the Blockchain Needs the Law" (2018) 33 Berkeley Technology Law Journal 487, 494.

[53] The same issue potentially applies to participatory DAOs that lack a sufficient override mechanism.

typically resolve governance issues that are not handled through smart contracts through blockchain-based voting. The voting process of DAOs typically allows those who possess governance tokens to participate in these governance decisions, and the blockchain voting structure, as noted above, makes the voting process more transparent and efficient than in the traditional corporation. In particular, a wide range of stakeholders may own such governance tokens in DAOs, providing a formal mechanism through which they can exercise governance rights.[54]

Nonetheless, governance in participatory DAOs presents distinctive concerns about the potential for abuse. One of the critical economic rationales for vesting corporate voting power in shareholders is the fact that shareholders are the residual claimants in the corporation.[55] As a result, shareholders' economic interests discipline their voting decisions, leading them, in most cases, rationally to vote in favor of actions that enhance corporate value.[56] Most DAOs operate in a way that is fundamentally different, in which token-holders merely have contractual claims rather than being residual claimants.

By separating participation rights from economic interests, DAOs jeopardize this discipline.[57] In addition, affording governance rights to other stakeholders complicates the aggregation of preferences. Stakeholders such as employees or members of the public may have economic or noneconomic preferences that are not aligned with the maximization of firm economic value. The participation of stakeholders with a variety of noneconomic preferences in DAO governance increases the risk of unstable voting results because the voting process no longer provides a viable took for aggregating multidimensional preferences.[58]

At the same time, DAOs may provide greater versatility in voting structures. For example, traditional voting does not adequately enable voters to express the intensity of their preferences.[59] There are voting options that respond to these concerns. "Some DAOs are allocating more weight to decisions based on how long a member supports a given proposal to approximate voting 'conviction' and rewarding the votes of long-standing members of a DAO".[60] Another option that allows voting to take intensity of preferences into account is quadratic voting.[61]

Providing governance rights through tokens also facilitates opportunistic practices such as vote-buying and capture.[62] Those same stakeholders that lack an economic stake in the firm may be willing to part with their governance rights at too low a cost or

[54] Wright (n 43) 166.

[55] Jill E Fisch, 'Measuring Efficiency in Corporate Law: The Role of Shareholder Primacy' (2006) 31 Journal of Corporation Law 637, 657.

[56] Frank H Easterbrook and Daniel R Fischel, 'Voting in Corporate Law' (1983) 26 Journal of Law and Economics 395, 403.

[57] Jiang and Li (n 13) 47; Hu and Black (n 34) 832; Lucian A Bebchuk and Kobi Kastiel, 'The Perils of Small-Minority Controllers' (2019) 107 Georgetown Law Journal 1453, 1461.

[58] Robert D Cooter and Michael D Gilbert, 'A Theory of Direct Democracy and the Single Subject Rule' (2010) 110 Columbia Law Review 687, 701.

[59] Yair Listokin, 'The Vickrey-Clarke-Groves "Pivotal Mechanism" as an Alternative to Voting for Organizational Control' (2015) 16 Theoretical Inquiries in Law 267, 268; Saul Levmore, 'Voting with Intensity' (2000) 53 Stanford Law Review 111.

[60] Wright (n 43) 166.

[61] Del Wright Jr, 'Quadratic Voting and Blockchain Governance' (2019) 88 UMKC Law Review 475.

[62] Jiang and Li (n 13) 47.

be willing to transfer those rights to a buyer with a propensity to engage in self-dealing or otherwise harming the corporation.

Most troubling is that tokenizing governance rights, instead of making DAO governance more democratic, can actually lead to a more concentrated governance structure.[63] As Jiang and Li observe, "Perhaps counter-intuitively, rather than democratizing decision-making (which was the main mission of DAOs), a small number of entities exert control in most DAOs."[64] Most token-holders simply do not participate in DAO governance.[65] This stems both from the fact that stakeholders who lack economic interests are less likely to participate in DAO governance and the fact that, as in the traditional corporation, dispersed small investors engage in rational apathy.

A 2022 vote on a proposed restructuring at MakerDAO illustrates these concerns.[66] Founder, Rune Christensen, proposed a radical restructuring plan for the DAO, that, according to at least some commentators was "incomprehensible."[67] MakerDAO's ownership structure was nominally highly decentralized—"MakerDAO puts every important decision to a community vote, open to anyone who buys a special kind of token called MKR."[68] Nonetheless, the low voting turnout led to what appeared to be 80 percent support, even though effectively only two voters mattered, Christensen, who owned roughly 10 percent of the MKR supply, and venture capital firm Andreessen Horowitz, which owned 6 percent.[69]

4.2. Fiduciary Duties

The DAO's governance void also reduces accountability. The officers and directors who make the majority of decisions for the corporation owe duties to the corporation and its shareholders through fiduciary principles and can be held liable for actions that are careless, conflicted, or lacking in good faith. Shareholders who exercise control over a corporation may be subject to similar fiduciary duties.[70]

An ongoing debate concerns the role of fiduciary duties in a DAO—whether, as a default matter, participants in a DAO should owe fiduciary duties to each other and the DAO, whether the law should enable DAO participants to limit or eliminate fiduciary duties, and, if not, the situations in which fiduciary duties might apply. Significantly, fiduciary duties do not play the same role in DAOs as in corporations for several reasons. First, DAOs lack any counterpart to the officers and directors who manage

[63] Igor Makarov and Antoinette Schoar, "Cryptocurrencies and Decentralized Finance (DeFi)" (2022) Brookings Papers on Economic Activity 141, 145.

[64] Jiang and Li (n 13) 59.

[65] Alex Dolphin, "Scaling DAOs Through Fiduciary Duties" (2022) 48 Brigham Young University Law Review 977, 993 ("Across the top three DAO platforms, the average tokenholder participation rate is 16.35%").

[66] Joel Khalili, "This Billion-Dollar Crypto Collective Is Tearing Itself Apart" (*Wired*, November 10, 2022) <https://www.wired.com/story/makerdao-rune-christensen-decentralize/> accessed November 14, 2024.

[67] ibid.

[68] ibid.

[69] ibid.

[70] *Ivanhoe Partners v Newmont Mining Corp* 535 A.2d 1334, 1344 (Del Supr 1987).

traditional corporations. In corporate law (and elsewhere), fiduciary duties are generally understood to be a response to the principal–agent problem.[71] Contractual rather than fiduciary duties are the norm in the absence of a principal–agent relationship. This difference perhaps explains why some DAO-specific legislation, such as the statutes in Tennessee and Wyoming, have eliminated default fiduciary duties.[72] In Chapter 5 of this volume, Morshed Mannan and Primavera de Filippi similarly argue that courts should not impose "implicit" fiduciary duties on DAO participants, arguing that those participants do not possess the same level of decision-making authority as traditional corporate law fiduciaries.[73]

Similarly, it is impractical to view smart contracts as fiduciaries and, even if they were, it would be difficult to establish the causal chain between a smart contract that acted improperly and those who contributed to its programming.[74] Although some have sought to impose fiduciary duties on open source software developers, most commentators view that effort as misguided.[75] The concern is both that much of the potential for self-dealing results not from the coding but from the manner in which subsequent participants use the code and that the imposition of liability on developers will unduly quash innovation.[76]

In participatory DAOs, token-holders, similar to corporate shareholders, are unlikely to be viewed as fiduciaries as a general matter when they exercise their governance rights, most commonly through voting.[77] The lack of structural controls over the exercise of these rights, however, increases the potential for them to be exercised selfishly by those who do not represent the interests of a majority of the DAO's participants.

A further question arises with respect to actions by those who can exercise controlling power over the actions of a DAO. Recent developments in corporate law have evinced growing concern about the potential for controlling shareholders to behave opportunistically. Courts have responded to this concern by implanting a flexible and context-specific definition of control and extending the application of fiduciary principles to transactions in which a controlling shareholder obtains a benefit not shared by the minority shareholders.[78]

As noted above, DAOs present significant opportunities for shareholders to exercise substantial control even without holding a majority of the DAO's economic interest or formal voting rights. In the DAO context, the entity that sets up the DAO and writes

[71] Robert H Sitkoff, "The Economic Structure of Fiduciary Law" (2011) 91 Boston University Law Review 1039, 1040; Wulf A Kaal, "Blockchain-Based Corporate Governance" (2020) 4 Stanford Journal of Blockchain Law & Policy 3, 6.

[72] Joan MacLeod Heminway, "The Fiduciary-ness of Business Associations"' (2023) 24 Transactions: The Tennessee Journal of Business Law 255, 276.

[73] Morshed Mannan and Primavera de Filippi, "The Fiduciary Duties of Network Participants of Blockchain Systems" in Kevin Werbach, Eva Micheler, and Bianca Kremer (eds), *Foundations of Decentralized Organizations: Blockchain and the Future of Corporate Law* (OUP 2026).

[74] *Francis v United Jersey Bank* 87 NJ 15, 39 (NJ Sup 1981).

[75] Reyes (n 4) 1879.

[76] ibid 1898.

[77] Nathan Tse, "Decentralised Autonomous Organisations and the Corporate Form" (2020) 51 Victoria University of Wellington Law Review 313, 335; Douglas R Cole, "E-Proxies for Sale? Corporate Vote-Buying in the Internet Age" (2001) 76 Washington Law Review 793.

[78] *Tornetta v Musk* 310 A.3d 430 (Del Ch 2024).

the code is technically separate from the DAO, but its power and control may not just result from the voting tokens it holds but also from its design of the code, as well as its ability to take action in response to emergencies or new developments.[79] As a result, DAOs present a similar potential for opportunism by controllers, raising the question of whether fiduciary principles are necessary to protect the minority token-holders and the DAO itself from controller self-dealing.

At the same time, DAOs may lack other protections available to dissenting or minority investors that are available through the corporate form. These include appraisal rights, which protect minority shareholders in the context of mergers and sometimes other transactions. As discussed above, minority shareholders in publicly-traded entities, which include many LLCs and limited partnerships, are also protected through the disclosure requirements of the federal securities laws.[80] Although minority investors may be protected through the market mechanism of exit, the extent to which DAO tokens trade in an efficient market is unclear, especially for DAOs that do not make public disclosures. As a result, that exit will not necessarily reflect a fair value for the tokens. While some argue that reputational constraints offer a meaningful level of protection,[81] the anonymity associated with blockchain transactions inherently limits the effectiveness of such constraints.[82]

If DAOs adopt governance structures that provide an active role for stakeholders or the general public, those structures further complicate the application of fiduciary principles.[83] One issue is the extent to which governance decisions should be made in the interests of stakeholders.[84] If so, would a failure to consider those interests constitute an actionable breach of fiduciary duty? Although US law has not adopted the stakeholder approach, the Canadian Supreme Court in the *BCE* case adopted a legal requirement that corporate directors and officers "take into account the interests of all corporate stakeholders, including 'shareholders, employees, suppliers, creditors, consumers, governments and the environment.'"[85] Another is the extent to which stakeholders with conflicting objectives have the right to act selfishly in pursuing their

[79] Daniel Kuhn, "Uniswap Vote Delay Shows DeFi Stakeholders Aren't All in It Together" (*Coindesk*, June 3, 2024) <https://www.coindesk.com/tech/2024/06/03/uniswap-vote-delay-shows-defi-stakeholders-arent-all-in-it-together/> accessed November 14, 2024.

[80] *Dieckman v Regency GP LP* 155 A.3d 358, 367 (Del 2017).

[81] Kaal (n 71) 6.

[82] Dolphin (n 65) 993.

[83] Corporate law has recognized the limitations both of fiduciary duties and investor litigation to enforce those duties as tools for ensuring officer and director accountability eg Paul D Weitzel, "The Case Against Officer Fiduciary Duties" (2023) 102 Nebraska Law Review 344 (arguing for the elimination of officer fiduciary duties). Indeed, concerns about the effect of investor litigation led states to authorize corporations to limit the personal liability of officers and directors for breaches of their fiduciary duties; eg Del Gen Corp L § 102(b)(7).

[84] Mark E Van Der Weide, "Against Fiduciary Duties to Corporate Stakeholders" (1996) 21 Delaware Journal of Corporate Law 27; Brett H McDonnell, "From Duty and Disclosure to Power and Participation in Social Enterprise" (2018) 70 Alabama Law Review 77.

[85] J Anthony Vanduzer, "BCE v. 1976 Debentureholders: The Supreme Court's Hits and Misses in its Most Important Corporate Law Decision Since Peoples" (2010) 43 University of British Columbia Law Review 205, 206, quoting *BCE Inc v 1976 Debentureholders* [2008] 3 SCR 560, 301 DLR (4th) 80 (SCC) [39].

individual interests at the expense of other stakeholders. Both these concerns have been raised in the ongoing debate over stakeholder governance in corporate law.[86]

Even if DAO participants were subject to default fiduciary duties, DAOs that are organized as LLCs, limited partnerships, or similar entities can typically limit or eliminate those fiduciary duties by including appropriate language in their governing documents.[87] Alternative entity law, however, does not permit participants to eliminate the implied covenant of good faith and fair dealing.[88] The extent to which the implied covenant applies to DAOs and, if so, to whom is unclear, but at least some commentators have argued that "the implied covenant might serve a critical function for a DAO."[89] Whether courts will impose such a duty in the DAO context, however, remains uncertain.

4.3. Standardization

Finally, the lack of standardization associated with DAO governance can be both a feature and a bug. DAO governance offers participants unprecedented flexibility, and in their short history, DAOs have adopted new governance features that lack precedent in the antecedent structures of prior business entities.[90] The ability to adopt such features enables DAOs to adopt customized structures that are well suited to each DAO's particular enterprise.[91] The potential for such customization is appealing. Even within corporate law, commentators have argued against standardized corporate governance structures, explaining that a one-size-fits-all approach prevents firms from efficiently tailoring their governance structures to meet their individual needs.[92] This argument supports the evolution of corporate law into a series of default rules that are subject to individual tailoring through private ordering.[93] It further supports the use of alternative entities, such as LLCs, in which participants enjoy even greater contractual freedom.

At the same time, the degree to which such customization is efficient remains unclear. For one thing, it creates transaction costs.[94] Market participants must evaluate and price each non-standard feature in order to understand the risks and benefits that

[86] Lucian A Bebchuk and Roberto Tallarita, "The Illusory Promise of Stakeholder Governance" (2020) 106 Cornell Law Review 91, 120–22.

[87] Dolphin (n 65) 993.

[88] *Boardwalk Pipeline Partners LP v Bandera Master Fund LP* 288 A.3d 1083, 1108 (Del 2022), quoting Delaware Revised Uniform Limited Partnership Act, s 17-1101(f); *Dieckman v Regency GP LP* 155 A.3d 358, 367 (Del 2017).

[89] Matthew J O'Toole and Christopher N Kelly, "Delaware May Be the Right Jurisdiction for 'Smart' Orgs" (*Law360*, February 15, 2018) <https://www.law360.com/articles/1013208/delaware-may-be-the-right-jurisdiction-for-smart-orgs> accessed November 14, 2024.

[90] Rodrigues (n 42) 707.

[91] Reyes (n 4) 1878; Wright (n 43) 166.

[92] Steel (n 39) 175.

[93] Megan Wischmeier Shaner, "Corporate Resiliency and Relevancy in the Private Ordering Era" (2022) Columbia Business Law Review 804.

[94] Michael Klausner, "Robert Clark's Corporate Law: Twenty Years of Change: The Contractarian Theory of Corporate Law: A Generation Later" (2006) 31 Iowa Journal of Corporate Law 779, 794.

it presents.[95] The resulting costs contribute to a lack of efficient pricing that, in turn, reduces the available protection for investors through market-based token sales and purchases. Some commentators have argued that these costs limit, in particular, the ready transferability of investment interests in entities with a high degree of customization, an argument that would explain the high degree of standardization in the governance structures of publicly-traded corporations.[96]

Customization may also lead to inferior terms, particularly when those terms are not individually negotiated but instead drafted unilaterally by a DAO sponsor and then imposed on passive public investors. As a practical matter, efficient customization is most likely to take place when the terms of an entity's structure and governance are the product of informed negotiation by sophisticated participants.[97] There are reasons to question the extent to which this process occurs in the typical DAO.

In addition, the lack of standardization can increase the potential for litigation. Two distinguished Delaware jurists explain that the contractual freedom associated with alternative entities such as LLCs has, counter-intuitively, increased litigation risk both because parties and their lawyers have increased ability to argue for differing interpretations of complex and non-standardized terms and because it is more difficult to predict how a judge will interpret complex and unique contractual provisions.[98] As a result, they argue that "some degree of standardization could well be desirable."[99] Michael Klausner further observes that the relative infrequency with which customized governance provisions are litigated increases uncertainty even with respect to matters that do go to court, because the development of case law interpreting those provisions—a process Klausner terms "judicial updating"—does not occur.[100]

The extent to which the benefits of standardized governance terms outweigh the costs is unclear, even outside the DAO context. At a minimum, however, these costs suggest that DAO sponsors should consider carefully the adoption of bespoke governance provisions. To the extent, however, that DAOs are successful in developing and implementing customized governance mechanisms, that success offers a powerful argument for corporate law to authorize greater contractual freedom.[101]

[95] Leo E Strine, Jr and J Travis Laster, "The Siren Song of Unlimited Contractual Freedom" in Robert W Hillman and Mark J Loewenstein (eds), *Research Handbook on Partnerships, LLCs and Alternative Forms of Business Organizations* (Edward Elgar Publishing 2015) 12; Dorothy Lund, "In Search of Good Corporate Governance" (2022) 131 Yale Law Journal Forum 854, 863.

[96] Steel (n 39) 175.

[97] Strine and Laster (n 95).

[98] ibid.

[99] ibid 17.

[100] Klausner (n 94) 794.

[101] In July 2024, the Delaware legislature took a step in this direction, adopting Del Gen Corp L § 122(18) which broadly authorizes corporations to implement a variety of governance mechanisms through shareholder agreements; Philip C Babler, Nicholas O'Keefe, and Douglass D Lightfoot, "Delaware Enacts Controversial Market Practice Amendments to Its General Corporation Law" (*Foley Insights*, July 18, 2024) <https://www.foley.com/insights/publications/2024/07/delaware-market-practice-amendments-general-corporation-law/> accessed November 14, 2024.

5. Conclusion

DAOs are an exciting new business structure that offers the potential to modernize many outdated and inefficient features of corporate law and structure. DAOs also offer unprecedented corporate governance flexibility by allowing participants to customize voting, the degree to which decisions are executed automatically, and to embrace more inclusive and democratic forms of participation rights. This flexibility, however, comes with challenges. Customized governance structures pose challenges for those who design DAOs' programming both in implementing the desired design features and allowing smart contracts to incorporate outside business developments. They also pose challenges for market participants both in understanding and evaluating non-standardized structures and terms. As such, the success of DAOs is likely to contribute valuable evidence to the longstanding debate over the value of standardization in corporate governance.

Any customized governance structure also raises questions about the constraints on participants' ability to act out of self-interest or opportunism. Whether and when DAO participants will be constrained by fiduciary principles remains an important open issue. Even for DAOs that adopt a business form characterized by a substantial degree of contractual freedom to modify or eliminate such principles, like an LLC, how DAOs exercise that contractual freedom and the extent to which courts defer to those decisions remain uncertain.

5
The Fiduciary Duties of Network Participants of Blockchain Systems

Morshed Mannan and Primavera de Filippi

1. The Problem of Imposing Implicit Fiduciary Duties

Over the past 15 years, there has been growing concern about the social and economic impact of using cryptocurrencies and deploying blockchain technologies in various sectors. From a public policy perspective, concerns have ranged from its use to allegedly facilitate money laundering activities and finance terrorism to the exploitation of vulnerable unsophisticated investors to the destabilization of traditional financial markets to having adverse effects on a wider unsuspecting public if these experimental technologies malfunction in some way (eg in the provision of public services, such as debt collection).[1] Naturally, these concerns have led to questions about the responsibilities, duties, and liabilities of developers and other blockchain network participants that are responsible for deploying and maintaining blockchain protocols and blockchain-based applications.

Some scholars have argued that the responsibilities of, for instance, software developers of blockchain protocols, are fiduciary in nature.[2] The issue of whether or not software developers are fiduciaries has also been explored in the ongoing *Tulip Trading Ltd* litigation, with the High Court[3] and Court of Appeal[4] of England and Wales arriving at contrasting preliminary assessments. Relatedly, recent litigation against decentralized autonomous organizations (DAOs) in courts across the US reveal that in some instances, courts are willing to categorize these blockchain-based systems as general partnerships or unincorporated associations.[5] These cases show

[1] Gert Meyers and Esther Keymolen, "Realizing a Blockchain Solution without Blockchain? Blockchain, Solutionism, and Trust" (n/a Regulation & Governance, 2023) <https://onlinelibrary.wiley.com/doi/abs/10.1111/rego.12553> accessed December 5, 2024; Primavera De Filippi and Morshed Mannan, "Regulatory Equivalence in Blockchain Systems: The Role of Public Values and Legitimacy" in Jurgen Goossens, Esther Keymolen, and Antonia Stanojević (eds), *Public Governance and Emerging Technologies* (Springer 2025).

[2] Angela Walch, "In Code(Rs) We Trust: Software Developers as Fiduciaries in Public Blockchains" in Philipp Hacker and others (eds), *Regulating Blockchain: Techno-Social and Legal Challenges* (OUP 2019).

[3] *Tulip Trading Ltd v Bitcoin Association* [2022] EWHC 667 (Ch).

[4] *Tulip Trading Limited v van der Laan and others* [2023] EWCA Civ 83.

[5] *In the Matter of Bzerox, LLC; Tom Bean; and Kyle Kistner, Respondents*, CFTC No 22-31, 2022 WL 4597664 (September 22, 2022); *CFTC v Ooki DAO*, No 3:22-CV-05416-WHO, 2022 WL 17822445 (N D Cal December 20, 2022); *Sarcuni v bZx DAO*, No. 22-CV-618-LAB-DEB, 2023 WL 2657633 (S D Cal March 27, 2023); *Andrew Samuels v Lido DAO*, et al., No 3:23-cv-06492-VC (N D Cal, November 18, 2024).

that courts may deem founders, developers, investors, and even ordinary governance token-holders of a DAO to be general partners in a partnership, depending on the specific facts of a given case. This is significant as being a partner in a general partnership can expose each partner to joint and several liability for the liabilities of the organization. As partners in a general partnership can have fiduciary duties toward one another, these developments make the attribution of duties and liabilities to network participants a topic of increasing importance. In the years ahead, it is possible that more claims will be brought against DAO participants under US federal financial legislation, such as the US Securities Act of 1933,[6] as Acts such as these enable courts to exercise nationwide personal jurisdiction over any natural or legal person that has minimal contacts with the US,[7] a requirement that has been relatively easy to satisfy for many DAOs given the prominence of the US in the blockchain ecosystem.

In light of these recent developments, we will argue that *imputing implicit fiduciary duties* on network participants is improper and can lead to unjust consequences. While traditional corporate entities have well-established rules governing fiduciary duties, the decentralized nature of blockchain-based systems complicates the application of such duties.[8] We contend that imposing fiduciary duties on these parties could not only stifle innovation and threaten the financial viability of blockchain systems but also deter broad-based participation in these decentralized systems. We advocate instead for a more nuanced approach: rather than imposing implicit fiduciary duties on network participants because of their status, regulators should focus more on fostering system-wide trust, transparency, and accountability, promoting best practices while incentivizing the creation of novel governance and liability frameworks that align with the principles of autonomy and decentralization. We will build our argument against implicit fiduciary status using relevant case law analysis and industry examples, while also drawing on our practical experience designing the Coalition of Automated Legal Applications (COALA) DAO Model Law (2022) as members of COALA.

In the second section, we briefly introduce the concept of fiduciary duties, focusing in particular on why they are an important component of corporate law globally and the criteria that is generally applied to determine the existence of fiduciary duties in the UK and in US states such as Delaware. We then survey the early academic debates concerning the fiduciary duties of blockchain developers. In Section 3, we provide a detailed overview and analysis of the main case law pertaining to fiduciary duties in this space, before building our argument against the imposition of implicit fiduciary duties in Section 4. We outline the COALA Model Law approach toward excluding implicit fiduciary duties before showing how a *co-regulatory* approach grounded in the principle of *regulatory equivalence* can meet the public policy objectives of imposing fiduciary duties while still acknowledging the distinctive distributed nature of blockchain systems.

[6] Securities Act of 1933, 15 USC §§ 77a–77aa (2024).

[7] *SEC v Ross*, 504 F.3d 1130, 1139 (9th Cir, 2007).

[8] Raina Haque and others, "Blockchain Development and Fiduciary Duty" (2019) 2 Stanford Journal of Blockchain Law & Policy 139.

2. Fiduciary Duties in Blockchain Systems

2.1. Brief Overview of Fiduciary Duties

The literature on fiduciary duties is voluminous, and our intention is mainly to highlight some key points that are relevant for understanding the case law discussed in Section 3 and our proposals against the imposition of fiduciary duties in Section 4. Fiduciary relationships arise in a number of contexts, but as we primarily discuss DAOs in this chapter, we will focus on the fiduciary duty of loyalty within business organizations.

The duty of loyalty is primarily a duty of "unselfishness."[9] It is mainly intended to address *self-dealing transactions* between a person and the company they serve as a director, and the *use of corporate opportunities* (ie business opportunities that the director personally avails himself of, even if the company they serve as a director may benefit from it instead.) In the UK, there are statutory duties to deter self-dealing, namely the duty not to accept benefits from third parties,[10] the duty to declare directors' interest in a proposed transaction with the company,[11] and a general duty to avoid conflicts of interest.[12] If an ex ante declaration of interest in a proposed transaction or arrangement is made,[13] this transaction is valid and does not require further approval by the company's members. The members also have the opportunity to ratify this breach of duty, disregarding the votes of a connected person unless the members consent to their inclusion.[14]

In relation to corporate opportunities, the statutory duty to avoid conflicts of interest extends to avoiding the exploitation of any property, information, or opportunity that belongs to the company, regardless of whether the company avails itself of that opportunity.[15] If the business opportunity is wholly outside the scope of the company's activities, then a corporate opportunity did not arise.[16] Subject to certain conditions, disinterested directors can authorize the use of corporate opportunities.[17]

In the US, similarly, state jurisdictions like Delaware have sought to deter conflicts of interest between directors and the principals the fiduciaries serve. Directors owe a duty of loyalty to the corporation and its shareholders, which entails refraining from "doing anything that would work injury to the corporation, or to deprive it of profit or advantage which his skill and ability might properly bring to it, or to enable it to make in the reasonable and lawful exercise of its powers."[18] Self-dealing transactions are not automatically void,[19] but are permitted so long as there is a disclosure of these

[9] Andrew Gold, "On the Elimination of Fiduciary Duties: A Theory of Good Faith for Unincorporated Firms" (2006) 41 Wake Forest Law Review 123, 132.
[10] Companies Act 2006, s 176.
[11] Companies Act 2006, s 177.
[12] Companies Act 2006, s 175.
[13] Companies Act 2006, s 182.
[14] Companies Act 2006, s 239.
[15] *Bhullar v Bhullar* [2003] BCC 711.
[16] *Wilkinson v West Coast Capital* [2007] BCC 717.
[17] Companies Act 2006, s 175(4)–(5).
[18] *Guth v Loft, Inc*, 5 A.2d 503, 510 (Del. 1939).
[19] Blake Rohrbacher, John Mark Zeberkiewicz, and Thomas A Uebler, "Finding Safe Harbor: Clarifying the Limited Application of Section 144" (2008) 33 The Delaware Journal of Corporate Law 719, 724.

transactions to disinterested directors and the transaction is approved by a majority of disinterested directors acting in good faith.[20] Alternatively, a majority of shareholders can ex ante approve the transaction or the transaction can be found to be fair to the corporation when it was authorized.[21]

In terms of corporate opportunities, the Delaware Supreme Court has sought to prevent directors making use of corporate opportunities, but on narrower terms than in the UK. In addition to the opportunity being in the line of business of the corporation, the corporation should also have both the financial ability and interest in making use of the opportunity. It should also be clear that by making use of this corporate opportunity, the fiduciary is less able to fulfill their duties to the corporation.[22] It is possible for specific corporate opportunities to be waived by the board of directors or through the certificate of incorporation.[23]

A series of other directors' duties are derived from the fiduciary duty of loyalty, including the duty of good faith (ie acting to advance the best interest of the corporation), duty to monitor (ie implementing information and reporting systems to monitor compliance with applicable laws), duty of confidentiality (ie keeping corporate information confidential), and the duty of disclosure (ie fully disclosing all relevant facts and circumstances that shaped directors' decisions).[24] Of particular relevance here, pursuant to the duty to monitor, directors would be expected to take measures to counter cybersecurity and other technological risks, and have policies in place to address such risks.[25] However, as the duty to monitor in the UK is part of the duty of skill and care instead of the duty of loyalty, this duty is not fiduciary in nature in the UK.

In contrast to the UK, in the US, the duty of care is seen as being fiduciary in nature. In Delaware, a director that exercises duty of care has to take into account all of the "material information" that is reasonably available to him, which involves soliciting information, critically evaluating information and advice that he received, and taking sufficient time to make decisions.[26] The standard Delaware courts apply to determine violation of this duty is that of "gross negligence," which is defined as "reckless indifference to or a deliberate disregard of the whole body of stockholders or actions which are without the bounds of reason."[27]

In Delaware, it is ordinarily presumed that directors act in accordance with these duties and courts will not try to second-guess and intervene in the rational commercial decisions of business people.[28] Breaches of the duty of loyalty can be used to rebut

[20] Delaware General Corporation Law, s 144(a)(1).

[21] Delaware General Corporation Law, s 144(a)(2)–(3).

[22] *Broz v Cellular Info Sys*, 673 A.2d 148 (Del 1996).

[23] Delaware General Corporation Law, s 122(17).

[24] William M Lafferty, Lisa A Schmidt, and Donald J Wolfe, "A Brief Introduction to the Fiduciary Duties of Directors Under Delaware Law" (2012) 116 Penn State Law Review 837, 847–48; Randy J Holland, "Delaware Directors' Fiduciary Duties: The Focus on Loyalty" (2009) 11 University of Pennsylvania Journal of Business Law 675, 698; Marc Moore and Martin Petrin, *Corporate Governance: Law, Regulation and Theory: 1* (1st edn, Red Globe Press 2017) 171–94, 218.

[25] Florian Möslein, "Contract Governance in the Network Economy: Implications for Company Law and Directors' Duties" (2024) 35 European Business Law Review 383, 398–99.

[26] Lafferty, Schmidt, and Wolfe (n 24) 842–43.

[27] *Benihana of Tokyo, Inc v Benihana, Inc*, 891 A.2d 150, 192 (Del Ch 2005).

[28] *Cede & Co v Technicolor, Inc*, 634 A.2d 345, 361 (Del 1993).

this presumption, with the board having to satisfy the court the decision or transaction in question "was the product of both fair dealing *and* fair price."[29] Case law in the UK has also referred to courts' deference to business or commercial judgment,[30] and gives courts the ability to relieve fiduciaries who have breached duties if they have acted "honestly and reasonably" and ought to be excused.[31] If there is cause to still pursue a breach of duties, there are a number of ways for members/shareholders to seek remedies for this breach including through a derivative suit on behalf of the corporate entity itself.[32]

As discussed in section 3, these fiduciary duties are also relevant in the context of unincorporated firms (eg general partnerships), and even unregistered entities (eg DAOs), as fiduciary relationships can be read into the governance structure of these entities. As Berry explains, with regard to the English context, "[p]artners are subject to a common law duty of good faith which gives rise to fiduciary duties" between the partners.[33] The fiduciary relationship between the general partners means that they each have to act as if they were trustees, with the other general partners being beneficiaries.[34] Under the Partnership Act 1890, general partners are subject to three statutory duties, which apply unless there is an agreement that provides otherwise.[35] These statutory duties are: (1) a duty to fully disclose information that affect the partnership;[36] (2) a duty to account for any benefits derived from general partners' connection to the partnership that were not consented to by the other partners;[37] and (3) a duty to account for profits that a general partner makes from a similar business that competes with the partnership, without obtaining consent from the other partners.[38]

The existence of fiduciary relations is a crucial issue, as it can have several unintended outcomes. A corollary to this is the issue of carving out fiduciary duties, a topic that has been relevant to general partnerships, limited liability companies (LLCs), and other legal entities in the past and now relevant for DAOs.

2.2. Academic Debate about Applying Fiduciary Duties to Blockchain Systems

Angela Walch offers a provocative lens on this issue by asserting that core blockchain developers should be viewed as fiduciaries.[39] According to her, core developers play a crucial role in shaping the technical and policy framework of blockchain networks,

[29] ibid.

[30] Carsten Gerner-Beuerle and Michael Schillig, *Comparative Company Law* (1st edn, OUP 2019).

[31] Companies Act 2006, s 1157(1).

[32] Holland (n 24) 679; Companies Act 2006, s 260(3).

[33] Elspeth Berry, *Partnership and LLP Law* (2nd edn, Wildy, Simmonds and Hill Publishing 2018) 4. That the duty of good faith gives rise to fiduciary relations in a partnership is mentioned by Pennycuick V-C in *Thompson's Trustee in Bankruptcy v Heaton* [1974] 1 W L R 605, 613.

[34] Berry (n 33) 60.

[35] ibid 62–66.

[36] Partnership Act, 1890, s 28.

[37] ibid s 29.

[38] ibid s 30.

[39] Walch (n 2).

exercising power that mirrors the authority traditionally held by corporate directors, lawyers, and other professionals who hold positions of trust. Indeed, despite the widespread perception that public blockchains are decentralized systems, Walch claims that governance within these systems often rests with identifiable individuals or groups who wield significant influence over their operations.

To sum up her argument, core developers, in particular, are responsible for the technical implementation of new features or code changes, and are therefore essential to the system's operations. They oversee software integrity, manage updates, and, in some cases, directly intervene to resolve crises, such as hard forks following system breaches or operational failures. These actions are analogous to corporate governance decisions that shape a company's trajectory and affect shareholder value—except that in the case of blockchain networks, the stakeholders are the users, the token-holders, and the businesses that depend on the network's functionality and security.[40]

As such, Walch contends that, to the extent that core developers—by the nature of their work—are entrusted with significant responsibilities, they act as *de facto* leaders, whose choices have far-reaching implications on the blockchain system they work on. Walch argues, then, that fiduciary duties are equally relevant to blockchain developers, who should therefore be subject to obligations of care (requiring them to operate with competence and diligence) and duties of loyalty (requiring them to act in the best interests of those they serve, while avoiding conflicts of interest).

Walch's analysis is based on the recognition that blockchain systems—even if typically touted as "trustless" or "trust-minimized" systems—do not eliminate trust but rather displace it. In the context of public blockchains, trust is transferred from centralized intermediaries to a small group of core developers who are in charge of designing, implementing, and managing the network. Walch believes that failure to acknowledge the risks in this concentration of power exposes users to vulnerabilities—such as conflicts of interest, assets loss, or unintended consequences due to poorly conceived updates.[41]

Walch argues that recognizing that core developers owe fiduciary duties would not only hold them accountable for their actions, but also compel them to make carefully-considered and ethical decisions, as well as consult relevant experts to mitigate risks of harm to stakeholders. Additionally, imposing fiduciary responsibilities on core developers would reduce risks of conflicts of interest—such as those resulting from financial ties between developers and private companies or the foundations supporting blockchain projects[42]—which can compromise impartiality and prioritize the interests of a few over the collective interests of the network.

[40] The need to apply a corporate governance framework to blockchain-based systems, including imposing fiduciary duties on core developers, was also advanced in Philipp Hacker, "Corporate Governance for Complex Cryptocurrencies? A Framework for Stability and Decision Making in Blockchain-Based Organizations" in Philipp Hacker and others (eds), *Regulating Blockchain: Techno-Social and Legal Challenges* (OUP 2019) 157–58. For a different approach to applying corporate governance models to blockchain protocols, that does not rely on the imposition of fiduciary duties on blockchain developers, Carla Reyes, "(Un)Corporate Crypto-Governance" (2019) 88 Fordham Law Review 1875.

[41] Walch (n 2) 66–67, 70.

[42] Primavera De Filippi and others, "Report on Blockchain Governance Dynamics" (*Project Liberty and BlockchainGov*, 2024) <https://www.research.ed.ac.uk/en/publications/report-on-blockchain-governance-dynamics> accessed June 16, 2025.

Her argument is controversial because it challenges prevailing norms in the technology and legal landscapes, where open source software developers are often shielded from responsibility for any involuntary flaw or vulnerability in their software. Walch recognizes that assigning fiduciary duties to blockchain developers could hinder innovation and reduce participation by fear of liability; yet, she believes that the benefits will outweigh these costs. Treating core blockchain developers as fiduciaries will help navigate the tension between innovation and accountability, ensuring that blockchain systems are developed with the interests of all stakeholders in mind. This fiduciary framework, she claims, will serve as a critical foundation for the long-term sustainability and credibility of public blockchain networks.

Haque and others present a counterpoint to Walch's argument by asserting that fiduciary duties are ill-suited for the Bitcoin and Ethereum blockchain networks due to the lack of centralized control.[43] Unlike corporate governance structures where fiduciaries can bind the organization through their decisions, public blockchain networks operate under distributed consensus, and no single participant or group (including the core developers) has the authority to unilaterally enforce changes on the network. Instead, decisions are made collectively, and network participants must voluntarily adopt protocol modifications by updating their software. This undermines the traditional elements of fiduciary relationships, such as the entrustment of authority and the ability to bind others with a decision.

Haque and colleagues argue that developers are fundamentally different from traditional fiduciaries because their role has not been directly entrusted by users or investors, nor do they pose the same risks as traditional fiduciaries (such as directors of corporations) who hold recognized positions of authority and power. They point out that traditional corporate fiduciaries are typically well-compensated for their role and the risks they take on, while Bitcoin and Ethereum developers are not directly compensated for contributing code.[44] The quantity of contributions by open source developers may vary considerably, from those who contribute one line of code to those who "contribute a high volume of lines over a long period of time."[45] This is distinct from the quality and value of their contributions, with some work being more essential than others.[46] It would thus be untenable and unjust for all of these developers, with their widely varying contributions, to be deemed to be fiduciaries. Even when focusing on a narrower group of "core developers" (eg developers who have "commit access" and can thus make changes to the code repository), they lack the capacity to coerce network participants into downloading code changes[47] or act on behalf of the entire public permissionless network, which is governed by distributed consensus mechanisms rather than hierarchical control.

Hence, Haque and others claim that imposing fiduciary duties on blockchain developers would not only be impractical, but also potentially harmful. It creates the possibility that any network participant (eg a token-holder) could file a lawsuit against a

[43] Haque and others (n 8) 140–41.
[44] ibid 185.
[45] ibid 183.
[46] ibid.
[47] ibid 147.

protocol developer for proposing a code update which they perceive as being harmful to them and breaching their purported duty of loyalty to network participants.[48] Aside from the risk of opening the floodgates of litigation, courts may struggle to apply traditional fiduciary frameworks to decentralized open source environments where participants often operate under pseudonyms and without formalized structures. The threat of legal liability could stifle innovation in the blockchain space by dissuading developers from contributing to open source blockchain projects. According to Haque and others, this makes fiduciary duties ultimately incompatible with the realities of decentralized public blockchain networks.

Accordingly, while Walch advocates for fiduciary accountability to address potential harms and governance gaps in blockchain systems, Haque and others underline the fundamental tension between fiduciary obligations and the decentralized ethos of blockchain systems. This debate exposes a deeper philosophical and practical divide: Walch's perspective challenges the narrative of decentralization in public blockchain networks, highlighting the latent power that core developers allegedly wield, while Haque and others defend the claim of decentralization by emphasizing the distributed, voluntary, and non-binding nature of developer contributions. The crux of this disagreement lies in reconciling the need for accountability within the decentralization principles that underpin blockchain technology. This tension not only raises questions about governance and liability but also reflects broader challenges in adapting traditional legal frameworks to distributed technologies that do not easily fit within established categories. In particular, this debate underscores an urgent need to craft new regulations that can balance the protection of stakeholders with the preservation of open source innovation and the decentralized ideals of blockchain technology.

3. Are Blockchain Developers and Other Network Participants Fiduciaries?

3.1. Tulip Trading Ltd

After years of academic debate, the *Tulip Trading Ltd* litigation was the first to explore the fiduciary duties of public permissionless blockchain network developers. Initially, this case concerned a claim brought by Craig Wright, an Australian entrepreneur who had for several years declared that he was Satoshi Nakamoto, the mysterious and (until then) anonymous founder of the Bitcoin blockchain. In his initial claim he contended that his company, Tulip Trading Ltd (TTL), had been hacked and consequently he lost access to private keys that gave him access to, and control over, Bitcoin that was worth approximately £3 billion in value at the time.

One of the grounds of TTL's claim was that the core developers of the Bitcoin network, as well as its various spin-off networks, had fiduciary duties toward TTL and other users of the network. As a consequence, the developers were legally obliged

[48] ibid 185.

to help users regain control over their crypto-assets after a hack had taken place. In the claimant's view, it would not be difficult for developers to implement a patch that could return any crypto-assets that had been transferred and for a replacement set of private keys to be generated.[49] This was premised on the claimant's belief that developers have a significant influence over these blockchain networks and the ability to propose software updates for the network to adopt.[50] As these developers had failed to return these assets to him, they had breached their fiduciary duties and were liable to pay him compensation.[51]

In several cases concerning blockchain-based systems, defendants don't appear in court in an effort to preserve their anonymity and avoid the coercive power of the court in which proceedings have been initiated. In this instance, the defendants that did appoint legal representatives made four main arguments as to why blockchain developers should not be deemed to be fiduciaries. First, it was argued that the developers were a large and ever-changing group of contributors. Second, developers could not unilaterally bind Bitcoin miners with their decisions, as the miners could refuse to run new software updates. Third, the ability of network participants to fork a blockchain protocol means that it is not possible for these participants to coerce one another. Fourth, relatedly, if network participants such as developers attempted to coerce other participants through off-chain means (eg using their social influence to sway governance decisions), the reputation of these network participants would be harmed.[52]

At this stage of proceedings, the claimant only had to demonstrate that there was an arguable case that Bitcoin blockchain developers had fiduciary duties toward the claimant and other users of the Bitcoin blockchain network. If jurisdiction was accepted over the matter, then the proceedings would go to a full trial that would establish the facts about the relationship between blockchain developers and users of the network. In evaluating whether Bitcoin core developers were fiduciaries, the High Court defined a fiduciary as "someone who has undertaken to act for or on behalf of another in a particular matter in circumstances which give rise to a relationship of trust and confidence. The distinguishing obligation of a fiduciary is the obligation of loyalty."[53] Moreover, this status was not based on the parties' intentions but turned on the objectively determined factual nature of the relationship between the parties.[54] It is possible and common for a fiduciary to act on behalf of multiple principals, and when doing so the fiduciary is expected to act in good faith in the interests of each principal and not privilege one over others.[55]

After explaining how fiduciary status is established, Justice Falk of the High Court applied this legal concept to the facts of the case. The court held that the claimants had not established a "seriously arguable" case that the Bitcoin core developers owed fiduciary duties to TTTL and other network participants.[56] The fact that these developers

[49] *Tulip Trading Ltd v Bitcoin Association* [2022] EWHC 667 (Ch) [21].
[50] ibid [33].
[51] ibid [53].
[52] ibid [34].
[53] *Bristol and West Building Society v Mothew* [1998] Ch 1, 18A.
[54] *Tulip Trading Ltd* [60].
[55] ibid [61].
[56] ibid [72].

are a "fluctuating, and unidentified" group militated against the claim that these participants had entrusted their property to them or that there was a continuing positive obligation for these developers to remain as developers and deploy patches or other updates to the Bitcoin core network software.[57] Nor was Justice Falk persuaded that asymmetrical power relations between the developers and the network participants was sufficient to establish that a fiduciary relationship existed between them. Given the nature of the relationship between core developers and network participants, it would be unjust to hold that the former had assumed the risks and liabilities of being a fiduciary simply by contributing software code.[58]

Even assuming that the developers had a positive duty of loyalty to the network participants, being required to deploy a software patch to benefit one set of users (eg TTL) could be to the detriment of other users who may want to preserve the immutability and tamper-proof properties of the Bitcoin blockchain network.[59] This would compromise the developers' purportedly undivided loyalty to network participants as a class. It was on the basis of this analysis, along with the High Court's findings on other forms of liability, that the claim was dismissed without a further trial.[60]

This decision was later appealed on four grounds.[61] The appellants contended that a full trial on the facts was required due to this topic engaging an undeveloped and complex area of law (first ground). Instead, the first instance court made assumptions about the facts in drawing its conclusions that were impermissible (second ground), and drew upon documents, like the England & Wales Law Commission project on digital assets, that were inadmissible (third ground). The High Court was also wrong in finding that the appellants had no real prospect of establishing that a fiduciary relationship exists in these circumstances (fourth ground).

In summary, counsel for the appellants contended that while the Bitcoin network is indeed permissionless, core developers have commit access and ultimately "decide what amendments, if any, are made to the software."[62] Core developers are also those individuals who decide what constitutes a software bug, how the bug should be fixed, and when such a fix should be introduced.[63] Counsel for the appellants also referred to the research of Angela Walch, to note that there is "independent support" for the claim that the Bitcoin blockchain was not decentralized—or at least that it was arguable that it is not decentralized.[64] Indeed, the fact that there was a factual dispute regarding the decentralization of the Bitcoin blockchain itself necessitated a full trial.[65]

Lord Justice Birss of the England & Wales Court of Appeal returned to the *Mothew* judgment that Justice Falk had used to define the concept of fiduciaries. In his interpretation of that precedent, being a fiduciary involves "acting for or on behalf of another person in a particular matter and also that there is a relationship of trust and

[57] ibid [73]–[75].
[58] ibid [81].
[59] ibid [76], [78]–[79].
[60] ibid [171].
[61] *Tulip Trading Limited v van der Laan and others* [2023] EWCA Civ 83 [67].
[62] ibid [29].
[63] ibid [31].
[64] ibid [36].
[65] ibid [39].

confidence between the putative fiduciary and the other person."[66] Fiduciaries have a duty to act in good faith, to avoid conflicts of interest and taking profits from their role, and should not act for their own personal benefit without gaining the consent of their principal.[67] There is no fixed limit to the range of fiduciary relationships and it is possible for new fiduciary relationships to emerge by way of analogy, as has happened in the past under English common law. In Justice Birss' view, the fact that the role of developers "bears some relationship to the interests of... the owners of bitcoins" satisfies one of the necessary criteria for determining whether an individual is a fiduciary.[68]

As with the first instance decision of the High Court, the Court of Appeal was concerned with determining if there was an arguable case that developers have fiduciary obligations toward users, rather than definitively establishing if such duties exist on the facts. The main objective of this judgment was to assess if there was a serious issue to be tried in this matter.[69] Justice Birss agreed with the appellants that the identity of the developers—if they are indeed a fluctuating and unidentified group—was contested and needed to be established through a trial.[70] While Justice Falk had relied on certain assumptions about the facts to hold that the developers were not fiduciaries, there were other aspects of the relationship between developers and network participants that indicated a sufficiently identifiable group that can feasibly hold fiduciary duties toward others. He considered that developers enjoy a degree of authority within blockchain networks due to their "control of access to the source code" and had discretionary decision-making capacities that can affect all network participants, including Bitcoin owners.[71] The property of these Bitcoin owners had effectively been entrusted into the care of the developers.

The possible existence of a fiduciary relationship meant that the developers can have both negative and positive duties toward network participants such as Bitcoin owners like Tulip Trading Ltd. The court acknowledged that developers have certain powers and decision-making abilities, thus leading them to conclude that developers can have a duty not to benefit themselves by introducing technical features that could potentially weaken the security of Bitcoin owners.[72] Conversely, as it was arguable that core developers had passwords to the "bitcoin software account in Github" they also could have the power to fix software bugs—and could have a positive duty toward Bitcoin owners to address these bugs.[73] The fact that Bitcoin owners may have varying interests, including in maintaining the immutability of the Bitcoin blockchain, did not mean a fiduciary relationship did not exist between the developers and the Bitcoin owners as a class. Fiduciary obligations arose as soon as Bitcoin owners were not able to access their Bitcoins.[74]

66 ibid [70].
67 ibid [42].
68 ibid [70].
69 ibid [91].
70 ibid [77].
71 ibid [74].
72 ibid [75].
73 ibid [78]–[79].
74 ibid [80]–[81].

The presiding Justice summarized the analysis above as follows:

> Pulling all this together, I recognise that for Tulip's case to succeed would involve a significant development of the common law on fiduciary duties. I do not pretend that every step along the way is simple or easy. However there is, it seems to me, a realistic argument along the following lines. The developers of a given network are a sufficiently well defined group to be capable of being subject to fiduciary duties. Viewed objectively the developers have undertaken a role which involves making discretionary decisions and exercising power for and on behalf of other people, in relation to property owned by those other people. That property has been entrusted into the care of the developers. *The developers therefore are fiduciaries. The essence of that duty is single minded loyalty to the users of bitcoin software.*[75] (Emphasis added.)

Both the High Court and the Court of Appeal considered the *Mothew* judgment to ascertain if a fiduciary relationship exists: if someone had "undertaken to act for on behalf of another in circumstances which give rise to a relationship of trust and confidence."[76] However, they came to contrasting conclusions about whether, in the instant circumstances, it was arguable that a fiduciary relationship exists. Yet, even when finding it arguable that developers are fiduciaries, the Court of Appeal acknowledged that this would represent a significant development of the common law on fiduciaries.

While the judgments in the *Tulip Trading* litigation provide insight into how the higher courts in England and Wales view the novel question of software developers being fiduciaries, the Court of Appeal clarified that their judgment was not a definitive conclusion that the Bitcoin developers did have a fiduciary duty toward Bitcoin owners. The main outcome of their decision was to show that there was a "serious issue to be tried" in this matter.[77] However, this trial is not going to take place as the claimants discontinued their claim in April 2024.[78] This ultimately leaves the question of whether developers are fiduciaries unresolved.

3.2. Law Commission's DAO Scoping Paper

The Law Commission of England & Wales has, however, weighed in on the fiduciary duties of open source software developers, reflecting on both developers of blockchain networks and DAO developers.[79] In this subsection and the remainder of Section 3,

[75] ibid [86].

[76] *Mothew* (n 53).

[77] *Tulip Trading Limited v van der Laan and others* [2023] EWCA Civ 83 [91].

[78] Emma Probyn and others, "Self-Proclaimed Creator of Bitcoin Found to Have Lied by English Court: Crypto Open Patent Alliance v Wright" (*Freshfields TechnologyQuotient*, 24 May 2024) <https://technologyquotient.freshfields.com//post/102j8iq/self-proclaimed-creator-of-bitcoin-found-to-have-lied-by-english-court-crypto-op> accessed 14 February 2025.

[79] Law Commission of England & Wales, "Decentralised Autonomous Organisations (DAOs): A Scoping Paper" (Law Commission of England & Wales, July 2024) <https://webarchive.nationalarchives.gov.uk/ukgwa/20250109094345mp_/https://cloud-platform-e218f50a4812967ba1215eaecede923f.s3.amazonaws.com/uploads/sites/30/2024/07/DAOs-scoping-paper-110724.pdf> accessed June 16, 2025.

we turn to the question of whether fiduciary duties are owed by certain participants in DAOs.

In its DAO Scoping Paper, the Commission acknowledged that open source software developers have the ability to update and release new source code, with some developers (ie "maintainers") being able to enact changes to the code directly and others (ie "contributors") being limited to proposing changes.[80] They note, however, that developers maintaining open source software, such as the Bitcoin and Ethereum blockchain networks, cannot coerce network participants to run specific software nor force them to accept an update.[81] In contrast, they contend that the situation with DAOs is slightly different, as the internal rules of the DAO may allow for smart contracts to be unilaterally updated by DAO developers (but see Section 4.1 on how this is not common), and these changes invariably have an impact on all users.[82] Depending on the governance design of a specific DAO (eg the bZx DAO discussed in Section 3.3), its token-holders can demand that major technical updates and modifications only take place after community discussions and formal voting (ie the voice option) or they can sell their tokens (ie the exit option). While this is not addressed by the Law Commission, DAO token-holders can also opt to fork the DAO.

Although blockchain networks and DAOs are different, the Law Commission opined that the *Tulip Trading* litigation held valuable lessons for both blockchain networks and DAOs: "If a developer exercising developer software publishing power could have a fiduciary obligation imposed on them for doing so, then that might theoretically also be true of a DAO or its participants that either exercised similar power or provided oversight or checks on that power."[83] However, the Commission noted that the "current law of England and Wales does not recognise such a developed fiduciary obligation" and observed that the recognition of such an obligation was unlikely to be a positive development from a legal or practical perspective.[84] Echoing the view of Justice Falk, the Commission considered whether it was realistically practicable for open source blockchain developers to demonstrate single-minded loyalty and contended that such loyalty to a particular owner or owner class would be "extremely difficult to describe and delineate,"[85] and ignored the conflicting interests open source software developers may have, and their lack of effort to act loyally. Depending on the internal rules of a DAO, the wide distribution of governance powers may further limit any discretionary power over software updates and modifications developers may have. Instead, alternative forms of liability may be more appropriate for DAO members. Imposing fiduciary duties going forward would constrain developers' personal autonomy and chill open source software development in England and Wales.[86]

80 ibid 77.
81 ibid.
82 ibid 78.
83 ibid 80.
84 ibid 78.
85 ibid.
86 ibid 81.

3.3. Ooki/bZx

On the other side of the Atlantic, the regulatory enforcement action and litigation against bZx DAO, and its successor Ooki DAO, raised issues regarding partnership liability, which also bears on the development of fiduciary liability in the blockchain space.

The bZx Protocol (later the Ooki Protocol) facilitated the lending of crypto-assets and margin trading. This protocol was first launched by bZerox LLC, a limited liability company co-founded and controlled by Tom Bean and Kyle Kistner. This LLC had considerable powers over the protocol as, according to the Commodity Futures Trading Commission (CFTC), it could "access and control the operation of, and the funds held in, the smart contracts" involved in crypto-asset lending and margin trading.[87] The CFTC also found evidence that these administrator keys were used to pause transactions and suspend protocol users' ability to withdraw funds after various hacking attempts. Bean and Kistner also spearheaded the marketing and business development of the protocol.

The two eventually decided to dissolve the LLC and transfer control over the protocol to its community of users through the creation of a new bZx DAO. The decision to do this was not out of altruism or community-mindedness but rather to avoid securities liability by decentralizing ownership of the protocol: "[R]eally what we're going to do is take all the steps possible to make sure that when regulators ask us to comply, that we have nothing we can really do because we've given it all to the community."[88] The transfer of control was completed in August 2021.

In this new governance arrangement, bZx DAO token-holders were given control over the protocol, in a manner identical to how Bean and Kistner previously controlled the protocol through bZerox LLC. As with many DAOs, token-holders were required to submit a new proposal to a community forum for discussion and a non-binding vote. Only those proposals that received a sufficient level of support were subsequently formally voted upon and the decision executed on-chain. These proposals were used to make a wide range of decisions, including the approval of a compensation plan for victims of a cybersecurity incident and the renaming of bZx DAO as Ooki DAO. At the same time, it was these token-holders who funded the further technical development and maintenance of the protocol.

The "exit" of Bean and Kistner to community ownership[89] did not give them the protection from regulatory enforcement they hoped. As bZx's activities involved offering commodities worldwide, including to US persons, they fell within the jurisdiction of the CFTC, who charged them with inadequate Know Your Customer (KYC) diligence and failure to register as a designated contract maker and futures commission merchant. Section 13(b) of the Commodity Exchange Act attributes liability for breaches of commodity laws to the controlling persons behind the entity that was in

[87] *In the Matter of Bzerox, LLC; Tom Bean; and Kyle Kistner, Respondents*, CFTC No 22-31, 2022 WL 4597664 (September 22, 2022) 5.

[88] ibid.

[89] Morshed Mannan and Nathan Schneider, "Exit to Community: Strategies for Multi-Stakeholder Ownership in the Platform Economy" (2021) 5 Georgetown Law Technology Review 1.

breach. This led to the allegation that Beans and Kistner were personally liable before the transfer of control, while Ooki DAO (which still included Bean and Kistner) was liable after the transfer. This, in turn, required the CFTC to classify this DAO as a legal entity.

The CFTC deemed Ooki DAO to be a for-profit unincorporated association because it was "a voluntary group of persons [ie Ooki token-holders], without a charter, formed by mutual consent for the purpose of promoting a common objective."[90] The common objective in this instance was to govern the Ooki protocol, generate revenue through fees for its products and services, and redistribute some of this revenue as proceeds to Ooki token-holders.[91] The CFTC also clarified that in such an entity, individual members (ie Ooki token-holders) are personally liable for the entity's debts and violations of law. Bean and Kistner were thus considered to be personally liable as members of the Ooki DAO unincorporated association and charged a civil monetary penalty.

Later, when the CFTC sought to serve notice on Ooki DAO, a court in California confirmed the CFTC's claim that Ooki DAO was a for-profit unincorporated association under California law and that it could be sued as an entity.[92] The test for determining the existence of an unincorporated association in California is similar to that applied by the CFTC: "an unincorporated group of two or more persons joined by mutual consent for common lawful purpose, whether organized for profit or not."[93] Voter apathy among token-holders or the lack of unanimous decisions was not sufficient to dispel the presumption that such an unincorporated association was created. Failure to appear before court eventually led to a default judgment to be entered against the DAO in 2023.

The regulatory activity of the CFTC was complemented by private litigation brought against Bean and Kistner for their negligence in averting a cybersecurity attack.[94] On November 5, 2021, a hacker took control of a private key of a bZx developer through a phishing attack and then used the private key to transfer all assets held by the DAO on the Polygon and Binance Smart blockchains. For the plaintiffs, this amounted to a loss of US$1.7 million out of a total of US$55 million. To compensate the victims, a compensation plan was recommended by bZx DAO, which would partially be in the form of replacement tokens and "debt tokens" to be later purchased by bZx DAO.[95] In deciding whether to dismiss the suit or not, the court found there to be a plausible case that the defendants had a duty of care to avoid causing harm and this duty had been breached.

This led the court to consider who would be responsible for remedying this breach. In particular, they assessed whether bZx could be deemed to be a general partnership under California law, with the consequent implications of finding the general partners to be jointly and severally liable for the harms caused by the general partnership.

[90] *In the Matter of Bzerox, LLC* (n 87) 9.

[91] ibid 10–11.

[92] *CFTC v Ooki DAO*, No 3:22-CV-05416-WHO, 2022 WL 17822445 (N D Cal December 20, 2022) 7.

[93] Cal Corp Code § 18035(a) (West 2024).

[94] *Sarcuni v bZx DAO* et al, No 3:2022cv00618 (S D Cal March 27, 2023). As discussed above, the duties arising out of negligence are not considered to be fiduciary in nature in the UK.

[95] ibid 9.

bZx DAO would be considered a general partnership if the plaintiffs established that it is "(1) the right of the purported partners to participate in the management of the business; (2) the sharing of profits and losses among the purported partners; and (3) contributions of money, property, or services by the purported partners to the partnership."[96] The active participation limb is particularly important in determining the existence of a general partnership, while profit sharing is not as essential. The court held that the bZx token-holders were able to participate in the management of the business through the use of the governance rights attached to their tokens. They also pointed out that "limited governance rights don't divest a partnership of its essential nature—a partnership can still exist when individual partners only control a part of the enterprise." The token-holders were also able to share in the profits of the DAO, if they wished, through a governance proposal,[97] and they implicitly agreed to share in the losses of the DAO by foregoing the use of a limited liability entity to shield themselves from joint and several liability. bZx DAO was, therefore, a general partnership comprising all the bZx token-holders, including Bean and Kistner themselves, with fiduciary duties of loyalty and care to other partners.[98] Bean and Kistner's use of LLCs when formally interacting with the bZx DAO did not prevent the court from piercing the veil and holding them personally liable, as they were held liable as partners of the general partnership not as members of their respective LLCs.[99]

3.4. Lido DAO

In a more recent lawsuit,[100] the crypto-"staking" platform Lido DAO was sued for allegedly failing to register as securities the Lido DAO tokens (LDO) offered to the plaintiff, thereby rendering Lido DAO liable for the plaintiff's investment losses. In a proof-of-stake system like Ethereum, validators are required to stake their own Ether (ETH) and while they can be rewarded if they are selected to validate transactions, they also risk having their stake slashed if they validate transactions in an incorrect or dishonest manner. Running a validator service individually can be relatively expensive, requiring the staking of at least 32 ETH, as well as dedicated computing resources. As the court explained, staking service providers enable users to pool cryptocurrencies, stake ETH, receive pay-outs, deduct fees for the service provider, and distribute proceeds to users.[101] Lido DAO provided such a service, with the LDO token-holders being able to vote to choose the validators that would stake ETH,[102] with voting power being on a one-token-one-vote basis.

In contrast to the bZx/Ooki cases discussed above, Lido DAO had significant institutional investor involvement from an early stage. Out of the 1 billion LDO tokens

[96] ibid 12–13.

[97] ibid 16.

[98] Cal Corp Code § 16404(a) (West 2024).

[99] However, the court lacked personal jurisdiction over Bean as he didn't have minimum contact with California.

[100] *Andrew Samuels v Lido DAO* et al, No 23-cv-06492-VC (N D Cal November 18, 2024).

[101] ibid 3.

[102] ibid 4.

minted, only 36 percent was reserved for the DAO's treasury, with the remainder being distributed to the founders and early investors. Paradigm Operations, Andreessen Horowitz, and Dragonfly Digital Management are three of the venture capital funds that purchased a significant number of tokens in this early period, making them controlling voters.[103]

The plaintiff bought 132 LDO tokens through a crypto-exchange and eventually sold them at a loss, leading him to initiate the securities litigation. The first question the court had to consider, as with bZx/Ooki, was whether Lido DAO could be sued at all. Lido DAO, who were represented through an LLC acting as a "functional gateway,"[104] argued that the DAO was "just autonomous software that runs without human management."[105] This is similar to the argument that was made with respect to the Tornado Cash software system that helps obfuscate the origin and destination of crypto-asset transfers.[106] While the Fifth Circuit Court of Appeals has recently agreed that the immutable smart contracts providing this privacy-enhancing service are "just software code,"[107] the judge in the *Lido* case was not convinced by the defendant's argument. In his view, Lido DAO was not autonomous software as the protocol software was deployed by people, who can vote, maintain a treasury, and hire employees.

Nor was the court persuaded by the other institutional investors' arguments that they were not in a general partnership. Using the same test for determining the existence of a general partnership in *Sarcuni*, the court found that the formation of a for-profit Ether staking service was adequate to allege that a general partnership existed. However, departing from *Sarcuni*, the plaintiff's allegations of *who* was a general partner was narrower. Instead of every token-holder being a general partner, Samuels contended that only those token-holders who "have the ability to meaningfully participate in DAO governance" are general partners.[108] While this would include the three institutional investors who have substantial voting power, it would not include every LDO token-holder. The judge did not deem it necessary to take a stance on the preferability of a broad or narrow approach to determining who the general partners are, as he was convinced that the Lido founders had formed a general partnership and admitted the institutional investors as new general partners.

This has a broader significance. Under California's partnership law, a general partnership agreement can arise through writing, orally, or through conduct, and this agreement can thereby change default partnership rules under statute (eg entering and exiting a partnership).[109] An explicit agreement on profit-sharing is not required for the existence of a general partnership, and legal entities such as corporations and LLCs can be its members.[110] Instead, participation in governance is key to

[103] ibid 4, 7.

[104] Morshed Mannan and Primavera De Filippi, "The 'Best of Both Worlds': Functional Gateways for DAOs to Comply with Employment, Social Security, and Tax Laws" in Lachlan Robb and John Flood (eds), *The De Gruyter Handbook of Blockchain and Society* (De Gruyter forthcoming).

[105] *Andrew Samuels v Lido DAO* et al (n 100) 8.

[106] Primavera de Filippi, Wessel Reijers, and Morshed Mannan, *Blockchain Governance* (MIT Press 2024).

[107] *Van Loon v Dep't of Treasury*, No 23-50669, F.4th, 2024 WL 4891474 (5th Cir November 26, 2024) 28, 32: the court does not comment on whether Tornado Cash itself is an entity.

[108] *Andrew Samuels v Lido DAO* et al (n 100) 11–12.

[109] ibid 13.

[110] ibid 14.

determining if a particular legal entity is part of the general partnership, with these three institutional investors being partners as they made explicit announcements about participating in governance, acquired governance tokens, exercised voting power, and expressed views on governance generally.[111] In terms of liability, although partners cannot be directly liable for violating section 12 of the Securities Act, a general partnership is a "person" for the purposes of this section and can be a "co-obligor, under state law, for the partnership's liability."[112] As the general partnership implicitly provided for joint and several liability for the general partners, the three institutional investors would be jointly and severally liable for any future judgment.[113] While not explicitly mentioned in the order, as Californian partnership law was applicable in this case, these institutional investors as general partners had fiduciary duties of loyalty and care to other partners.[114]

After finding that a general partnership existed, the court also ruled that Lido DAO had violated section 12(1)(a) of the Securities Act by soliciting the purchase of LDO tokens (a security). The court explained that this solicitation does not have to be through the direct sale of the security, but can be through comprehensive involvement in "the design, operation and monetization of a cryptocurrency enterprise."[115] These enterprises can include both the deployment of blockchain protocols (eg Tezos) and DAOs. An example of involvement in the former would be establishing a foundation to market and monetize the protocol, while examples of the latter would be marketing native tokens, encouraging exchanges to list these tokens, and making governance decisions about them. The general partners comprising Lido were involved in this latter manner in promoting LDO, and there were thus sufficient grounds to hold they were soliciting the purchase of a security.[116]

3.5. Takeaways

Two broad takeaways emerge from this emerging case law concerning the duties and liabilities of various network participants, including blockchain developers. First, courts in both the UK and US have been willing to *apply* longstanding tests regarding fiduciary duties and the existence of general partnerships by applying them to the distinct context of blockchain-based systems. The judgments of the High Court and Court of Appeal in the *Tulip Trading* litigation also demonstrate the difficulties in applying fiduciary duties to blockchain-based systems.

The same dilemma is posed by the application of partnership law. The judge in the *Sarcuni* case contended that the recognition of bZx DAO as a general partnership would not be a "radical expansion and alteration of long-standing principles of

[111] ibid 5, 15.
[112] ibid 17.
[113] ibid 18.
[114] Cal Corp Code § 16404(a) (West 2024).
[115] *Andrew Samuels v Lido DAO* et al (n 100) 19, citing *Houghton v Leshner*, No 22-cv-7781, 2023 WL 6826814 (N D Cal September 20, 2023) 3; *In re Tezos Securities Litigation*, No 17-CV-6679, 2018 WL 4293341 (N D Cal August 7, 2018) 9.
[116] *Andrew Samuels v Lido DAO* et al (n 100) 20.

partnership law [that] should not be countenanced."[117] Courts outside of the US have not had to grapple with the entity status of DAOs to the same extent, but this view on the flexibility of partnership law does not necessarily accord with the view of policymakers in other Anglo-Commonwealth jurisdictions. When considering "pure DAOs,"[118] the Law Commission for England and Wales stated that "general partnerships do not seem to be a good fit … and it might be unfortunate (for DAOs/DAO participants and, potentially, for the law of general partnerships) if they were characterised in this way."[119] Instead, for some pure DAOs, an unincorporated association may be a more accurate characterization, as fewer strict default rules apply.[120]

Second, the *Ooki/bZx* and *Lido* cases reflect the *increasingly expansive* approach of district courts in California toward characterizing DAOs as general partnerships. While these cases focus on the joint and several liability of general partners, this characterization is also significant for the topic of fiduciary duties. This is because, in both the US and England and Wales, partners owe each other fiduciary duties, with the duty of loyalty being common to both jurisdictions.[121] This duty requires the duty holder to not act against the interests of the person to whom the duty is owed, including subordinating their own interests to that of the latter. The Law Commission of England & Wales explains that partners can act in conformity with their duties of loyalty and good faith by not personally profiting from business that should be the firm's, by disclosing conflicts of interest, not competing with the partnership's business without the permission of the other partners, and not personally profiting from information obtained through the partnership.[122] Conversely, if partners fail to abide by these duties, they cannot apply for relief to courts on the grounds of having acted honestly and reasonably—unlike directors of companies.[123]

Similarly, the 2017 amendment to the Revised Uniform Partnership Act (RUPA) of 1997 places similar obligations on a partner to uphold their duty of loyalty.[124] Under RUPA, partners can modify, but not eliminate, the duty of loyalty (or the duty of care).[125] In California, the duty of loyalty can be adjusted, but not eliminated altogether.[126] In Delaware, exceptionally, it is possible to both modify and eliminate fiduciary duties of partners.[127] As RUPA provides model rules for how US states and districts govern partnerships, and continues to be the prevailing approach, its provisions are especially significant in understanding the status quo in the US.

[117] *Sarcuni v bZx DAO* et al (n 94) 17.

[118] The Law Commission of England & Wales defines pure DAOs as "[a]rrangements implemented through smart contracts with very limited off-chain activity, no incorporated legal structure and, often, a rejection (deliberately or otherwise) of dependence on law and legal institutions for their existence (although they may well still attract legal and regulatory consequences)." DAO Scoping Paper (n 79) xi.

[119] ibid 51.

[120] ibid.

[121] Emeka Duruigbo, "Inadvertent Partnerships and Fiduciary Duties" (2020) 14 Virginia Law and Business Review 65, 94–95. DAO Scoping Paper (n 79) 60.

[122] DAO Scoping Paper (n 79) 60 (citations omitted).

[123] ibid.

[124] Duruigbo (n 121) 101.

[125] Revised Unif P'ship Act § 103(b) (Unif Law Comm'n 1994).

[126] Cal Corp Code § 16103(b)(3) (West 2024).

[127] Del Code Ann tit 6, § 15-103(f) (2018).

"Traditionalists" have long argued that fiduciary duties can help build trust and investor confidence as well as reduce opportunistic behavior by partners, while one set of "contractarians" have suggested that the existence of implicit fiduciary duties can reduce the cost of bargaining and provide rules to govern incomplete contracts.[128] We are part of what Duruigbo describes as the second "sub-group" of contractarians who believe that fiduciary duties should not be imposed by default and should only be opted into deliberately and voluntarily—as has become possible with LLCs and LPs in several US states. This is because such duties cannot be readily transposed into the context of most pure DAOs, given their distinct technical properties and distribution of governance power. Moreover, the imposition of default fiduciary duties may not only place unjust burdens on small-scale, individual token-holders, but in some cases also impose fiduciary obligations of loyalty in relationships where network participants are not and cannot be loyal to each other as a matter of fact. Hence, even if it is possible for courts to develop more sophisticated criteria for identifying the existence of a fiduciary relationship in pure DAOs and other technological arrangements, alternative approaches to accountability may be preferable to searching for individuals or organizations to impose fiduciary duties on.[129] As discussed in Section 4, we call for new approaches to achieving the policy aims and objectives behind the imposition of fiduciary duties, which will uphold public interests without requiring wholesale changes to the technology or punitive actions against network participants.

4. Arguments Against Implicit Fiduciary Duties for Blockchain Developers and Participants

4.1. COALA DAO Model Law

The COALA DAO Model Law (2022)—which emerged from extensive collaborative efforts including contributions from the two authors of this chapter—provides a comprehensive framework that addresses, amongst other things, the challenges of applying implicit fiduciary duties to participants in DAOs. In the commentary to Article 15, the DAO Model Law explains why traditional fiduciary principles are ill-suited for the majority of DAOs, due to their inherent operational transparency, the non-coercive nature of their software upgrades, as well as the unique operational features of these decentralized organizations. This stance foreshadows the approach taken by the Law Commission of England & Wales in discouraging the imposition of implicit fiduciary duties on open source developers in all but exceptional circumstances.[130] This stance also reflects the experience of some of the co-authors in drafting DAO member agreements where fiduciary duties had to be explicitly excluded.

[128] Duruigbo (n 121) 97–100.

[129] For another approach that seeks to help DAOs mitigate risks, "without sacrificing common DAO organizational goals of pseudonymity, flexible fiduciary duty regimes, and failure to trigger securities regulations when issuing governance tokens," see Carla Reyes and Christine Hurt's suggestion for creating a "contractarian joint venture"; Carla Reyes and Christine Hurt, "The Contractarian Joint Venture" (2025) 76 Alabama Law Review 741.

[130] DAO Scoping Paper (n 79) 82.

First, there is—at least in theory—a high degree of transparency embedded in the operations of DAOs. The code underpinning most DAOs is made publicly available on platforms like GitHub, and is verifiable through platforms like Etherscan. This, combined with the transparency and auditability of every blockchain transaction, makes it possible for tech-savvy individuals to scrutinize, audit, and understand the mechanics of the DAO. This level of openness reduces information asymmetry, and as a consequence, the power imbalance, which—in traditional contexts—has been addressed through the imposition of fiduciary duties.

Second, even if the decision-making power in a DAO is concentrated among a small group of actors, they do not ordinarily have the capacity to unilaterally modify the underlying operations of the DAO. Once the smart contracts governing the DAO have been deployed on the blockchain, the code can no longer be altered or modified, unless the code specifically provides for an amendment procedure (eg through the use of proxy contracts). While these amendment procedures are becoming common practice in the DAO ecosystem, amendments cannot be implemented unilaterally, they can only be adopted through the explicit consent of the participating members—a majority of whom must agree to upgrade one of the smart contracts governing the DAO. This stands in contrast with centralized platforms where the online operators have the authority to force all users to automatically accept any software update.

Moreover, the Model Law explains why fiduciary relationships cannot arise merely from the roles or titles of participants within a DAO, disclaiming the assumption that administrators or representatives within a DAO hold sufficient discretionary power to be conferred fiduciary responsibilities. Indeed, legal representatives or administrators often function in limited administrative capacities, executing the decision taken collectively by the DAO rather than acting as fiduciaries with decision-making authority.

Third, the Model Law questions the practice of imposing collective liability on DAO members or participants. Individuals may exert influence on a DAO through the submission of or voting on proposals, but—similar to general partnerships or unincorporated associations—no single member possesses absolute control over the DAO's operations. Holding all members in an often large, globally distributed, mostly pseudonymous organization liable for decisions they did not directly partake in would be inherently unjust and potentially harmful to the DAO because it would ultimately dissuade participation.

Finally, the Model Law advocates for an opt-in approach to fiduciary duties, describing a mechanism for DAOs to explicitly designate such responsibilities, either by stipulating them directly in their bylaws, or through an explicit action of the opt-in fiduciaries. This opt-in mechanism makes it possible for DAOs to experiment with novel governance structures that better accommodate their needs, without undermining the legal status of DAO participants that do not want to have fiduciary duties imposed on them.

As such, the DAO Model Law paves the way for a more effective legal framework for decentralized organizations, which recognizes that governance innovation comes hand-in-hand with technological innovation. Instead of requiring DAOs to subject themselves to the same rules and responsibilities of traditional corporate forms, it recognizes the unique features of DAOs and proposes a regulatory framework that better accommodates these features. Notably, jurisdictions like Utah and New

Hampshire have already transposed aspects of this Model Law into their own jurisdiction, as a testament to its desirability and practical viability.[131]

4.2. Regulatory Equivalence

The regulatory approach to blockchain-based organizations should shift from attempting to impose traditional fiduciary duties toward adopting new regulatory compliance models that both respect the decentralized nature of blockchain technology and ensure that fundamental policy objectives are met. We describe this as the *regulatory equivalence*.[132] This approach requires explicit articulation of *public values* (ie what are the underlying policy objectives that justify the establishment of fiduciary duties) while acknowledging the contribution toward these objectives of novel *technological guarantees* that can (but do not necessarily) emerge in blockchain-based systems. Hence, regulatory equivalence entails an acknowledgment by policymakers that the adoption by DAOs of specific technological guarantees (eg quasi-immutable rules, strict auditability of transactions, etc) might provide a degree of protection that is at least equivalent to that provided by the imposition of fiduciary duties. If DAOs implement these technological guarantees in the way that the regulators have recognized as legitimate, then they will not need to be subject to fiduciary constraints because they have opted to achieve regulatory compliance through technological means.

In the context of DAOs, the question of governance in the relationship between technological guarantees and fiduciary obligations cannot be avoided. Core developers, for instance, cannot reasonably be held to fiduciary standards, as their role primarily involves technical implementation rather than discretionary decision-making power over users' assets or interests. However, DAOs operating through multi-signature wallets, where a small group of identified individuals maintain direct control over collective assets, may indeed give rise to implicit fiduciary obligations due to the concentration of power and responsibility.

Conversely, DAOs implementing polycentric governance—characterized by distributed decision-making processes and multiple overlapping centers of authority[133]—inherently resist the application of fiduciary duties. This governance model, rather than creating a vacuum of responsibility, actually contributes to better governance outcomes by fostering alternative, appropriately-tailored accountability mechanisms. The absence of traditional fiduciary relationships in such structures incentivizes the development of robust transparency measures and accountability frameworks (eg the "proof-of-reserve" mechanism introduced by major cryptocurrency exchanges) that

[131] Nina Reiser, "DAO Legal Forms Around the World" in Kevin Werbach, Eva Micheler, and Bianca Kremer (eds), *Foundations of Decentralized Organizations: Blockchain and the Future of Corporate Law* (OUP 2026).

[132] Primavera de Filippi and Morshed Mannan "Regulatory Equivalence in Blockchain Systems: The Role of Public Values and Legitimacy" in Jurgen Goosens, Esther Keymolen, and Antonia Stanojević (eds), *Public Governance and Emerging Technologies* (Springer 2025).

[133] Paul D Aligica and Vlad Tarko, "Polycentricity: From Polanyi to Ostrom, and Beyond" (2012) 25 Governance 237.

are native to blockchain technology, rather than imported from traditional corporate governance models.

This regulatory equivalence approach serves a dual purpose: it not only provides legal clarity but also creates powerful incentives for improved governance. The explicit acknowledgment that certain DAO structures do not give rise to fiduciary duties compels participants to exercise greater due diligence in evaluating the governance frameworks of DAOs they wish to join. Rather than relying on the protective umbrella of fiduciary duties, participants must actively scrutinize governance structures, voting mechanisms, and risk allocation frameworks. This increased scrutiny, in turn, creates market pressure for DAOs to implement more transparent and accountable governance systems, achieving through market mechanisms what traditional fiduciary duties seek to accomplish through legal obligations.

5. Conclusion

In this chapter, we have provided an overview of how the topic of fiduciary duties has come to be of critical importance for blockchain-based systems, including both blockchain protocols and DAOs. After surveying both the general corporate fiduciary literature and the early academic debates on the possible application of fiduciary duties to blockchain developers, we closely analyzed the enforcement actions and case law that either applied these duties to participants of blockchain-based systems or highlighted fact patterns that demonstrate the risks of imposing fiduciary duties on these network participants. In view of the problems posed by applying existing legal approaches and the increasingly expansive view that district courts in California are taking toward construing DAOs as general partnerships, it becomes ever more urgent to shield network participants from fiduciary liability. We proposed the COALA DAO Model Law approach to exclude implicit fiduciary duties by default and the adoption of a co-regulatory approach, grounded in the principle of regulatory equivalence, to meet the public policy objectives inherent in imposing fiduciary obligations.

6

DAOs: The Theory of the Firm and Ostromian Perspectives

*Daniela Gandorfer and Eva Micheler**

1. Introduction

In this chapter we will analyze decentralized autonomous organizations (DAOs) from two perspectives, the theory of the firm and the analytical perspectives developed by Elinor Ostrom. We will conclude that no general statements as to the economic or institutional nature of DAOs can be made. Some but not all DAOs adopt firm-style hierarchical arrangements and insofar as they have done so should be characterized as firms. Either way, and in contrast to the predictions made in early academic contributions, the use of smart contracts does not determine if or to what extent DAOs are either contractual, firm-style, or hybrid arrangements.

We will further demonstrate that an analysis relying on the work developed by Elinor Ostrom reveals that DAOs are organizational arrangements that combine technology with other institutional elements such as values, beliefs, and legal organizational forms.

The chapter is structured as follows. In Section 2 we will discuss the theory of the firm and explain that firms are characterized by a hierarchical structure through which an entrepreneur instructs owners of production factors such as workers to carry out certain actions. Section 3 will introduce Elinor Ostrom's work, which is sometimes referenced by DAOs and their participants. We will examine the principles she developed for the analysis of common pool resources and the framework she suggested for the analysis and development of institutions. In Section 4 we will examine DAOs and their properties. We will look at their ideological roots and define the concepts of autonomy and decentralization. We will conclude that both concepts are primarily aspirations and have not been fully implemented in practice. Section 5 will discuss DAOs from the perspective of the theory of the firm and conclude that there is too much variety in DAO arrangements to support general conclusions about them. Whether a specific DAO qualifies as a firm depends on its structure. DAOs that have incorporated firm-style arrangements should be characterized as firms. Section 6 will demonstrate that the analytical framework developed by Ostrom and adapted by Gindis and Micheler for the analysis of corporate law is useful for the academic

* The authors are very grateful to Vanessa Villanueva Collao, David Gindis, and Kevin Werbach for their generous comments and pointers to further literature. All mistakes are ours.

analysis of DAOs. The framework can also be used by practitioners who develop a particular DAO structure.

2. The Theory of the Firm

The theory of the firm addresses the question of why firms exist, what determines their boundaries, and how they are different from markets. It derives its origin from Ronald Coase's seminal 1937 paper entitled, "The Nature of the Firm."[1] Coase posed the question: If markets are efficient, why do firms exist?

In a market, buyers and sellers search for offers to match their preferences amongst a range of sellers and buyers, negotiate terms, and enter contracts. Markets are decentralized.[2] Participants enter individual spot transactions with each other.

Coase observed that market transactions have certain costs. These are expenses incurred in finding suitable trading partners and relevant information, resources spent on negotiating and drawing up contracts, or expenses related to ensuring that the other party adheres to the agreement.

He argued that firms exist for exchanges that are associated with high transaction costs and so are more efficiently organized through the hierarchy of the firm rather than through the open market. His work laid the foundation for understanding firms as entities that emerge to avoid the transaction costs associated with market exchanges. The theory further suggests that a firm will expand until the costs of organizing an extra transaction within the firm become equal to the costs of carrying out the same transaction in the open market.

In contrast to a market, a firm establishes a hierarchy. Decisions are taken by an entrepreneur, who instructs the owner of a production factor such as a worker supplying labor to carry out certain actions. The relationship between the entrepreneur and the owner of the production factor is hierarchical in nature. The latter has agreed to be bound by the decisions of the former.

Oliver Williamson built on Coase's work. He argued that transactions have three key dimensions: asset specificity, uncertainty, and frequency.[3] An asset is specific to a transaction if its value outside that transaction is lower than within it. A bespoke component part that serves a particular machine, for example, is specific. A standard part that has many use cases is not. Uncertainty is about the frequency and intensity of disturbances in a particular environment. Frequency refers to the number of times parties transact with each other. These three dimensions help to determine whether a transaction is more efficiently conducted in markets or within firms through hierarchies. High asset specificity, high uncertainty, or high frequency can lead to higher transaction costs in markets, making it more efficient to carry out a particular transaction within the boundaries of the firm.[4]

1 Ronald Coase, "The Nature of the Firm" (1937) 4 Economica 386.

2 Harold Demsetz, *The Economics of the Business Firm: Seven Critical Commentaries* (CUP 1995).

3 Oliver Williamson, "The Governance of Contractual Relations" (1979) 22 Journal of Law and Economics 116, 118.

4 Oliver Williamson, "The Modern Corporation: Origins, Evolution, Attributes" (1981) 19 Journal of Economic Literature 1537, 1546.

Further, a distinction can be drawn between ex ante and ex post costs. For markets, ex ante costs include, for example, searching for and negotiating with a contractual partner. For a firm, ex ante costs are high. It needs to be established through a bureaucratic process, it has to hire managers and employees, and set up and run a system of monitoring, reporting, and dispute resolution.[5]

Ex post costs in markets are the costs arising when a contract needs to be adapted to changes in circumstances of either party. This includes the cost of re-negotiating or the cost of enforcing the contract through the courts. In firms, changes in circumstances are resolved by managers imposing orders from above. Consequently, firms have relatively low ex post costs.[6] Indeed, the firm is a form of governance that is designed with a view to adapting to changes in circumstances.[7] The adaptability of the firm nevertheless comes at a price. The incentives of participants of the firm are muted in comparison to the incentives of participants in markets.[8]

Williamson added further depth to this distinction by discussing hybrid forms that operate between the market and the firm and contain limited managerial structures.[9] This happens when the parties anticipate that adaptation to changes in circumstances will be required. Hybrid forms of governance are particularly useful when the parties anticipate high levels of uncertainty.[10]

3. Ostrom

Elinor Ostrom's work is sometimes referenced by those involved in DAOs.[11] Two bodies of her work are of particular interest. She developed principles for the management of common pool resources. This aspect of her work engaged with the claim that common pool resources inevitably find a tragic end because rational actors maximizing their own respective utility are predicted to overuse the resource leading to its depletion. Ostrom carried out empirical work to discover that under certain

[5] Hanna Halaburda, Natalia Levina, and Semi Min, "Digitization of Transaction Terms with TCE: Strong Smart Contracts as a new Mode of Transaction Governance" (2023) 3 <https://ssrn.com/abstract=4501318> accessed November 1, 2025.

[6] ibid 3.

[7] Oliver Williamson, "Comparative Economic Organization: The Analysis of Discrete Structural Alternatives" (1991) 36 Administrative Science Quarterly 269, 274–81.

[8] ibid 275.

[9] Williamson, "The Modern Corporation" (n 4); Halaburda, Levina, and Min (n 5) 6; *contra* Geoffrey M Hodgson, "The Legal Nature of the Firm and the Myth of the Firm-Market Hybrid" (2002) 9 International Journal of the Economics of Business 37.

[10] Halaburda, Levina, and Min (n 5) 3 and 6.

[11] eg Ilia Murtazashvili and others, "Blockchain Networks as Knowledge Commons" (2022) 16(1) International Journal of the Commons 108; Kevin Carson, "Governance, Agency and Autonomy: Anarchist Themes in the Work of Elionor Ostrom" (*Centre of a Stateless Society Paper No 16*, Second Half 2013) <https://c4ss.org/wp-content/uploads/2014/01/Anarchist-Themes-in-the-Work-of-Elinor-Ostrom.pdf> accessed November 1, 2025; David Rozas, Antonio Tenorio-Fornés, and Samaer Hassan, "When Ostrom Meets Blockchain: Exploring the Potentials of Blockchain for Commons Governance" (2021) 11(1) Sage Open <https://doi.org/10.1177/21582440211002526> accessed November 1, 2025; Sinclair Davidson, "Decentralised Autonomous Organisations as Commons" (*SSRN*, 2024) <https://papers.ssrn.com/sol3/papers.cfm?abstract_id=4795629> accessed November 1, 2025.

conditions common pool resources are sustained over time. She expressed these conditions in the form of eight design principles.[12]

These principles are: (1) the boundaries of the resource and the rights of individuals or households are clearly defined; (2) the rules for expropriating from the resources and the rules for contributing labor, materials, and/or money to the resources are related to the local conditions; (3) most individuals affected by the operational rules governing the resources can participate in modifying them; (4) those who monitor appropriation behavior are identical with or accountable to those who appropriate from the resource; (5) appropriators who violate operational rules are likely to receive graduated sanctions; (6) there is rapid access to low-cost conflict resolution mechanisms; (7) the rights of appropriators (users of the resource) to devise their own institutions (rules) are not challenged by external governmental authorities; and (8) large common pool resources are organized in multiple layers of nested enterprises.[13]

Ostrom's principles for the management of common pool resources have inspired a narrative model for the governance of business firms. In 2012, Simon Deakin proposed an approach that conceptualizes the corporation as a commons.[14] In this view the corporation is a shared resource the sustainability of which depends on the participation of multiple constituencies in its governance. These constituencies are shareholders, employees, core suppliers, and customers. He argues that this model of the corporation as a shared resources better describes the legal structure of the firm where managers make decisions in relative autonomy from the shareholders or any other constituency. He further stresses that, at a normative level, the conceptualization of the corporations as a commons will help to sustain the corporate enterprise and deliver benefits for its stakeholders as well as for society as a whole.

Along similar lines, Janine S Hiller and Scott J Shackelford observe for the US that, at a positive level, benefit corporations can be understood as providing a mechanism for the management of common pool resources.[15] Like Deakin, they believe that conceptualizing the business enterprise as a common pool resource normatively changes the conversation. The question for corporate law is transformed from how to manage the relationships between share- and stakeholders to how to develop and sustain the resources attributed to the corporations through collaboration by and for the benefit of its participants.

In addition to researching common pool resources and the factors securing their sustainability, Ostrom developed a framework for the analysis of and development of institutions.[16] This framework is not limited to common pool resources and applies

[12] Elinor Ostrom, *Governing the Commons: The Evolution of Institutions for Collective Action* (CUP 1990); Elinor Ostrom, *Understanding Institutional Diversity* (Princeton UP 2005); Elinor Ostrom, "Beyond Markets and States: Polycentric Governance of Complex Economic Systems" (2010) 100(3) The American Economic Review 641.

[13] Elinor Ostrom and James Walker, "Neither Markets nor States: Linking Transformation Processes in Collective Action Arenas" in Michael D McGinnis (ed), *Polycentric Games and Institutions* (Michigan UP 2000) 427, 437–40.

[14] Simon Deakin, "The Corporation as Commons: Rethinking Property Rights, Governance and Sustainability in the Business Enterprise" (2012) 37 Queen's Law Journal 339.

[15] Janine S Hiller and Scott Shackeford, "The Firm and Common Pool Resource Theory: Understanding the Rise of Benefit Corporations" (2018) 55 American Journal of Business Law 5.

[16] Elinor Ostrom, *Understanding Institutional Diversity* (Princeton UP 2005).

to institutions more generally. It uses action situations as its focus point. An action situation arises when participants with diverse preferences interact. Examples of such interactions are the exchange of goods or services in markets, the collective solving of problems in meetings, dominating one another or arguing.[17] This perspective encourages researchers to examine such interactions between people by identifying and analyzing the effect of factors such as the biophysical and material conditions the action situation is embedded in, the attributes of the community the participants are part of (eg their shared beliefs), and the rules governing the situation.[18]

Relying on broader institutional thought, one of us (Micheler) proposed a theory explaining the company as a legal tool facilitating autonomous organizational actions.[19] In this perspective, organizations or firms bring about behavior that would not exist but for the organizational context. They are real in their consequences. The corporate form acknowledges, supports, and legitimizes these effects of organizational action by providing separate legal personality and procedural rules for organizational decision-making and action. Separate legal personality facilitates not only autonomous contractual actions by firms and organizations, it also makes it possible for the legal system to hold incorporated organizations and firms liable in tort and criminal law.[20]

Connecting this approach with the work of Oliver Williamson and Elinor Ostrom, David Gindis and Eva Micheler have recently set out a narrative model of the company.[21] This model builds on Ostrom's framework for the analysis and development of institutions. It characterizes the firm as an organization that is governed in several nested levels. The meta-constitutional level consists of a Companies or Corporation Act enabling individuals to set up a company by registering certain documents with Companies House and taking decisions about the content of its constitution. At the constitutional level, the shareholders and directors rely on the respective legislation and the corporate constitution to make decisions on how the company is managed. In large companies they set the strategies that inform the activities at the lower levels. At the policy level, senior and lower ranking managers translate these policies into instructions that inform the operational level. At the operational level, participants take and execute everyday decisions. Like Ostrom's work, the model does not advance a normative agenda. It is analytical in nature and aims to provide a granular tool informing the development and implementation of normative interventions. The model can assist those preferring to orient corporate law toward the normative idea of efficiency and shareholder value as well as for those preferring normative concepts such as equality or social welfare. It invites scholars and practitioners interested in corporate law to consider that there is more to organizational action than decisions taken by directors and that corporate law needs to solve more problems than the

[17] ibid 14.

[18] ibid 15.

[19] Eva Micheler, *Company Law—A Real Entity Theory* (OUP 2021).

[20] Eva Micheler, "Separate Legal Personality—an Explanation and a Defence" (2024) 24 Journal of Corporate Law Studies 301.

[21] David Gindis and Eva Micheler, "Institutional Theory For Corporate Law: An Invitation" (2024) 24 Journal of Corporate Law Studies 401.

alignment of incentives. It helps, for example, to integrate insights on the effect of individual beliefs, social context, and corporate culture into the normative analysis of corporate law.

4. DAOs

4.1. Introduction to DAOs

DAOs can be defined as entities that use blockchain, digital assets, and related technologies to direct resources, coordinate activities, make decisions, and distribute value. Vanessa Villanueva Callao reports that some scholars adopt a wide definition that characterizes blockchain organizations such as Ethereum as DAOs rather than as the systems on which DAOs run.[22] We do not follow this approach here. We conceptualize DAOs as *using* rather than operating certain blockchains.[23]

Use cases are diverse but cluster around the unifying themes of enthusiasm for and familiarity with blockchain technology, and the possibility for organizing trustless and transparent systems that operate without centralized control.

Participants have a "shared social or economic mission,"[24] and use DAOs to serve a broad range of purposes. There is much diversity in the way DAOs are used.[25] Some share similarities with business corporations. Members make contributions in the form of money or other resources including labor. In return they receive specific rights such as a portion of the organization's profit or losses or the right to take part in the organization's decision-making process.[26] Others are like cooperatives or charities giving members the right to access, manage, or transfer the resources or services that the DAO controls.[27]

[22] Vanessa Villanueva Callao, "Decentralized Governance (DeGov) An Experimental Study" 15 (draft on file with authors).

[23] ibid; David Gogel and others, "Decentralized Autonomous Organization Toolkit" (January 2023) 6 <https://www3.weforum.org/docs/WEF_Decentralized_Autonomous_Organization_Toolkit_2023.pdf> accessed November 1, 2025; David Gogel and others, "Decentralized Autonomous Organization: Beyond the Hype" (June 2022) 5 <https://www3.weforum.org/docs/WEF_Decentralized_Autonomous_Organizations_Beyond_the_Hype_2022.pdf > accessed November 1, 2025; for a literature overview on the origin and evolution of the term, Samer Hassan and Primavera de Filippi, "Decentralized Autonomous Organization" (2020) 10 Internet Policy Review 2; Law Commission of England & Wales, "Decentralised Autonomous Organisations (DAOs): A Scoping Paper" (July 2024) vi, paras 1.1 and 2.6 < https://lawcom.gov.uk/project/decentralised-autonomous-organisations-daos/> accessed November 1, 2025.

[24] Aaron Wright, "The Rise of Decentralized Autonomous Organizations: Opportunities and Challenges" (2021) 4(2) Stanford Journal of Blockchain Law & Policy 152, 156.

[25] Charles Kerrigan, *Crypto and Digital Assets Law and Regulation* (Sweet & Maxwell 2024) 481; Law Commission (n 23) para 1.5 and chs 3–5.

[26] For a recent analysis, Wulf A Kaal, "DAO Market Meta Analysis 2024" (2024) University of St Thomas (Minnesota) Legal Studies Research Paper No 24-15 <https://ssrn.com/abstract=4900875> accessed November 1, 2025; Wright (n 24) 156; Laila Metjahic, "Deconstructing the DAO: The Need for Legal Recognition and the Application of Securities Law to Decentralized Organizations" (2018) 39(4) Cardozo Law Review 1533.

[27] Morshed Mannan, "The Promise and Perils of Corporate Governance-by-Design in Blockchain-Based Collectives: The Case of dOrg" in Julian Manley, Anthony Webster, and Olga Kuznetsova (eds), *Co-operation and Co-operatives in 21st-century Europe* (Bristol UP 2023) 78–99; Wright (n 24) 156.

DAOs are shaped by the social norms and values prevailing in the environment from which they originate. Vanessa Villanueva Callao and Kevin Werbach and others stress that informal relationships and social norms play an important role in establishing trust and enabling collaboration between DAO participants.[28] Sinclair Davidson draws a parallel between DAO and open source software communities and, relying on Steven Weber,[29] identifies several beliefs prevalent in this environment. These include beliefs such as "Access to computers should be unlimited," "Judge people only on the value of what they create, not who they are or what credentials are present," "People can create art or beauty on computers," and "Computers can change human life for the better."[30]

DAO participants have developed their own usage of the English language creating a bond among them and drawing a boundary between their community and others.[31] The interactions of DAO participants are further informed by the practices of social media and online communication platforms, which play an important role in the development as well as the ongoing management of DAOs. Founders, for example, use social media to attract interest, raise funding, and launch projects.[32]

Today, DAOs serve broad ideological and political preferences. It is nevertheless useful to understand their libertarian origins. These will be examined in the next subsection. After that we will analyze the concepts of "autonomy" and "decentralization." We will see that both autonomy and decentralization are theoretical aims that have not been fully implemented in practice.

4.2. Ideological Origins of DAOs

Before we analyze the concepts of "autonomy" and "decentralization," we will briefly explain some of the ideological foundations of DAOs.

One of us (Gandorfer) shows that DAOs and the blockchain technology through which they are built share ideological roots with the early internet. Both innovations are deeply entangled with three overlapping libertarian movements forming in the late 1980s and early 1990s: extropians,[33] cypherpunks,[34] and anarcho-capitalists.[35]

[28] Vanessa Villanueva Collao, "Understanding the Role of Informal Relationships, Social Norms and Emerging Power Structures in Decentralized Governance" (draft on file with authors); Kevin Werbach and others, "Blockchain Governance in the Wild" (2024) (3) 1 Cryptoeconomic Systems 1.

[29] Steven Weber, *The Success of Open Source* (Harvard UP 2004).

[30] Davidson (n 11) 6.

[31] Sandra Faustino, "How Metaphors Matter: An Ethnography of Blockchain-Based Re-descriptions of the World" 12 (2019) Journal of Cultural Economy 478.

[32] Gogel and others, "Decentralized Autonomous Organization: Beyond the Hype" (n 23) 6; Jungsuk Han, Jongsub Lee, and Tao Li, "A Review of DAO Governance: Recent Literature and Emerging Trends," European Corporate Governance Institute Finance Working Paper No 1044/2025 5-7 <https://ssrn.com/abstract=5074046> accessed November 1, 2025.

[33] The *Oxford English Dictionary* (OED) defines "extropy" as "A theoretical tendency or force which opposes entropy; a tendency for order to increase over time, either within a particular context or universally." The founders of the Extropy Journal, Max More and Thomas Bell, frame "extropy" as a futurist movement, philosophy, and mode of living and thinking that defies entropy and celebrates the limitless outward expansion purportedly inherent in human nature—a sentiment they openly tie to frontierism (Daniela Gandorfer, *Matterphorics* (Duke UP 2025)).

[34] The OED defines a "cypherpunk" as "A person who advocates the use of cryptographic techniques to ensure privacy and anonymity in electronic communications."

[35] Gandorfer, *Matterphorics* (n 33).

Extropians, now known as the US version of transhumanists,[36] and closely align with anarcho-capitalists, adopt a futurist perspective, emphasizing the role of technology in transcending human and societal limitations. Like anarcho-capitalists, they criticize what they see as government overreach but apply this critique to fields such as biotech and longevity research. VitaDAO, a contemporary transhumanist DAO, exemplifies this by challenging conventional regulatory constraint on early-stage biomedical research in longevity, a domain extropians critique as constrained by inefficiency and overregulation.[37] We will see below that VitaDAO also experiments with legal concepts such as intellectual property (IP) rights, drawing funding not only from web3 entities and prominent crypto entrepreneurs such as Balaji S Srinivasan but also from established biotechnology companies such as Pfizer.

The cryptography- and privacy-focused cypherpunk movement seeks, as John Perry Barlow proclaimed in his *Declaration of Independence of Cyberspace*, a "new Social Contract" for the internet—a world that is "both everywhere and nowhere," "where identities have no bodies," yet are "distributed across multiple state jurisdictions."[38] The declaration was a response to the Telecommunications Act of 1996 and contains a strong US libertarian rejection of governments and, importantly, legal concepts, including "property, expression, identity, movement, and context."[39]

Anarcho-capitalists expand this vision by focusing on privatizing governance and creating competitive markets for legal and societal systems. Timothy May, a key figure in both the cypherpunk and anarcho-capitalist movements, outlined in his book, *Crypto Anarchist Manifesto*, a world where "individuals and groups [can] communicate and interact with each other in a totally anonymous manner," relying on "public-key encryption" and "zero-knowledge interactive proof systems."[40] His ideas anticipated blockchain's capacity to facilitate trust, reputation, and unregulated transactions without centralized authorities.[41]

Anarcho-capitalists, with a strong libertarian stance and a decades-long tradition of advocating for competitive governance, spontaneous order, and private legal systems grounded in Austrian School Economics, have invested substantial hope and significant resources into blockchain technology as a means to realize these ideals.[42] Notable examples include DAOs designed to support startup cities or pop-up villages (eg Zuzalu),[43] and "network states."[44] The term "network state" refers to the idea

[36] The OED defines "transhumanism" as "a belief that the human race can evolve beyond its current limitations, especially by the use of science and technology."

[37] VitaDAO, "VITA-FAST—Revolutionizing Governance in Longevity Research" (*Medium*, June 30, 2023) <https://vitadao.medium.com/vita-fast-revolutionizing-governance-in-longevity-research-9cf1d2fc0cd1> accessed November 1, 2025.

[38] Daniela Gandorfer, "Down and Dirty in the Field of Play: Startup Societies, Cryptostatecraft, and Critical Complicity" (2022) 33(3) Law and Critique 355; John Perry Barlow, "A Declaration of the Independence of Cyberspace" (February 8, 1996) Electronic Frontier Foundation <https://www.eff.org/cyberspace-independence> accessed November 1, 2025.

[39] Barlow (n 38).

[40] Timothy May, "Crypto Anarchist Manifesto" <https://groups.csail.mit.edu/mac/classes/6.805/articles/crypto/cypherpunks/may-crypto-manifesto.html> accessed November 1, 2025.

[41] ibid.

[42] Gandorfer, *Matterphorics* (n 33) ch 1.

[43] <https://www.zuzalu.city/> accessed November 1, 2025.

[44] <https://thenetworkstate.com/> accessed November 1, 2025.

of building a state-like structure in a digital environment through blockchain technology.[45] The concept was popularized in the former Coinbase Chief Technology Officer Balaji Srinivasan's book entitled *The Network State*.[46] It envisions corporations evolving into state-like entities that privatize governance services—such as legal systems, courts, police, and healthcare—and offer them in competitive markets driven by supply and demand. These projects are often associated with high profile individuals, who have recently gained political traction in the United States, among them Peter Thiel and Elon Musk.

Tracing the roots of blockchain and DAOs is useful for understanding the origins and implications of terms such as "autonomy" and "decentralization." However, it is equally important to avoid reducing blockchain-based governance and DAOs to purely libertarian tools. DAOs have diverse use cases outside of their original libertarian environment. They are used to organize unions, cooperatives, commons-based communities, and initiatives supporting vulnerable groups such as refugees or smallholder farmers. They are also set up to address governance challenges in corrupt or conflict-affected regions.[47]

Either way we can note that all DAO projects are experiments in (self-)governance that aim to challenge traditional legal frameworks and institutional arrangements, such as international organizations, states, corporations, and (regulated) markets. They are informed by the belief that blockchain technology can offer alternative forms of governance, addressing the challenges typically encountered in cooperative human endeavors.

Having set out the ideological origins of DAOs in this section we will discuss the concept of "autonomy" in the next section.

4.3. Autonomy

4.3.1. Introduction to autonomy

The adjective "autonomous" in "decentralized autonomous organization" refers to two related ideas: (1) the aspiration of DAO participants to achieve independence from the law and traditional (and centralized) economic and societal structures, and

[45] Balaji Srinivasan, eg, offers the following definition: "A network state is a social network with a moral innovation, a sense of national consciousness, a recognized founder, a capacity for collective action, an in-person level of civility, an integrated cryptocurrency, a consensual government limited by a social smart contract, an archipelago of crowdfunded physical territories, a virtual capital, and an on-chain census that proves a large enough population, income, and real-estate footprint to attain a measure of diplomatic recognition." <https://thenetworkstate.com/the-network-state-in-one-sentence> accessed November 1, 2025. However, the term is now defined in different ways by different groups in the blockchain space (eg <https://www.afropolitan.io/≥ accessed November 1, 2025; <https://vitalik.eth.limo/general/2022/07/13/networkstates.html≥ accessed November 1, 2025; <https://theblockchainsocialist.com/category/podcast/overthrowing-the-network-state/≥ accessed November 1, 2025).

[46] Balaji Srinivasan, *The Network State* <https://thenetworkstate.com> accessed November 1, 2025.

[47] eg Ukraine DAO, Eric Mank, "How the Influence of Crypto in Ukraine's Resistance Goes Beyond Money" (*Forbes*, April 7, 2022) <https://www.forbes.com/sites/ericmack/2022/04/07/how-the-influence-of-crypto-in-ukraines-resistance-goes-beyond-money/≥ accessed November 1, 2025 or Joe Noss, "DAO-nions: The Future of Labour Unions" (*LinkedIn*, February 21, 2023) <https://www.linkedin.com/pulse/dao-nions-future-labour-unions-joe-noss/≥ accessed November 1, 2025.

(2) the characteristics of smart contracts, which are computer programs that automatically enforce rules and decisions.[48] We will see in this section that both forms of autonomy are theoretical ideas, which have not been fully implemented in practice.

4.3.2. Autonomy as an ideological idea

The first idea denotes autonomy in a broad ideological sense: autonomy from national and international legal systems, from dominant market players, or from incumbent corporate structures. This idea of autonomy is articulated by various participants in the field. Nathan Schneider, for instance, emphasizes the importance of DAOs for experimenting with self-governance and advocates for a "renaissance of creative governance possibilities,"[49] while Melanie Swan anticipates a multiplicity of personalized and privatized legal frameworks.[50] Vitalik Buterin similarly envisions DAOs as social coordination tools, emphasizing governance systems that allow value-aligned communities to deliberate collectively and independently from centralized state control. Drawing from participatory and democratic traditions, these models could, he emphasizes, help DAOs navigate complex social, economic, and environmental challenges beyond market logic.[51] Ukraine DAO, for example, was set up by individuals disillusioned by traditional institutions organizing humanitarian aid.[52]

Some DAOs are specifically set up to circumvent government regulations and laws. Darcy WE Allen and others mention the case of Shapeshift, a cryptocurrency exchange that initially operated as a centralized platform. Its libertarian founder later decentralized its governance structure, a move explicitly aimed at circumventing regulatory constraints while preserving operational autonomy.[53]

We have already mentioned VitaDAO's experimentation with legal concepts such as non-fungible token (NFT)-based IP rights. They propose mechanisms for commodifying data and sharing revenue from scientific inventions that operate outside of traditional corporate structures.[54]

The proponents of VitaDAO are also concerned with the bureaucracy involved in having experiments and drugs approved by national regulators and propose an

[48] Law Commission (n 23) para 2.37.

[49] Nathan Schneider, "Beyond Cryptoeconomics: Platform Cooperativism and the Future of Blockchain Governance" (*The Reboot*, October 14, 2021) <https://resources.platform.coop/resources/beyond-cryptoeconomics-platform-cooperativism-and-the-future-of-blockchain-governance/≥ accessed November 1, 2025; Daniel Kuhn, "'We've Seen Breakdowns of Trust': Nathan Schneider on How to Democratize the Web" (*Coindesk*, March 26, 2024) <https://www.coindesk.com/consensus-magazine/2024/03/26/weve-seen-breakdowns-of-trust-nathan-schneider-on-how-to-democratize-the-web≥ accessed November 1, 2025.

[50] Melanie Swan, *Blockchain: Blueprint for a New Economy* (O'Reilly Media 2015) 17.

[51] Vitalik Buterin, ""DAOs are not corporations: Where decentralization in autonomous organizations matters"" (*Vitalik Buterin Blog*, 2022) <https://vitalik.eth.limo/general/2022/09/20/daos.html> accessed November 1, 2025.

[52] <https://ukraine-dao.notion.site/Ukraine-DAO-3a0e63c6190b4796890dec5c72a94872> accessed November 1, 2025.

[53] Darcy WE Allen and others, "DAOs Are Adaptive Governance Engines" in Kevin Werbach, Eva Micheler, and Bianca Kremer (eds), *Foundations of Decentralized Organizations: Blockchain and the Future of Corporate Law* (OUP 2026).

[54] Tyler Golato and Paul Kohlhaas, "VitaDAO White paper V1.0" 3 <https://github.com/VitaDAO/whitepaper/blob/master/VitaDAO_Whitepaper.pdf> accessed November 1, 2025.

alternative form for granting approval for conducting research and licensing outcomes.[55] This echoes May's prediction that "emerging information markets and crypto anarchy" could reshape IP rights. His aforementioned manifesto highlighted already in 1988 cryptography's potential to create alternative legal concepts and polycentric legal structures: "Just as barbed wire enabled the fencing-off of vast ranches, redefining land and property rights in the frontier West," a minor mathematical discovery—in his view, cryptography—could become the "wire clippers" dismantling the barbed wire around intellectual property.[56]

At the same time, blockchain technology is used to create funding and governance structures for public goods (eg Funding the Commons)[57] and environmental regeneration (eg Celo and Regen),[58] providing a tool for local self-governance and enabling governance models built around values difficult to quantify in conventional market terms.

It remains to be seen to what extent DAOs will succeed in either operating outside of the law or the traditional market economy.[59]

4.3.3. (Autonomous) smart contracts

The second idea of autonomy is narrower. It refers to the fact that DAOs began as an attempt to replace traditional legal arrangements with "smart contracts."[60] Smart contracts are computer programs which run on certain blockchains and define and/or automatically enforce some or all of the terms of an arrangement entered into by the participants.[61] They are referred to as "smart" because of this automation.

Because smart contracts govern "the standards and procedures of anyone interacting with, or taking part in, a DAO," they are considered to be "the primary glue to manage member-to-member transactions."[62] Unlike simpler blockchains such as Bitcoin, this functionality is limited to programmable blockchains and, despite inherent risks, enables a broader range of design possibilities and facilitates DAOs. Examples of such protocols are Ethereum,[63] Polkadot,[64] Solana,[65] or Cardano.[66]

[55] Morgan J Weaver, "A Beginner's Guide to Vitalia" (February 22, 2024) <https://www.vitadao.com/blog-article/a-beginners-guide-to-vitalia> accessed November 1, 2025.

[56] Timothy C May, "The Crypto Anarchist Manifesto" (1988) <https://nakamotoinstitute.org/library/crypto-anarchist-manifesto/> accessed November 1, 2025.

[57] <https://www.fundingthecommons.io/> accessed November 1, 2025.

[58] <https://celo.org/> accessed November 1, 2025; <https://regen.foundation> accessed November 1, 2025.

[59] Law Commission (n 23) paras 2.76–2.78, ch 6 and app 4; for an early contribution on the question of how to regulate financial technology, Christopher J Brummer and Yesha Yadav, "Fintech and the Innovation Trilemma" (2019) 107 Georgetown Law Journal 235.

[60] Wright (n 24) 152–53; Law Commission (n 23) paras 2.12–2.17.

[61] This definition is adapted from Law Commission, "Smart Legal Contracts Advice to Government" (CP 563 Law Com 401, 2021) vii < https://lawcom.gov.uk/project/smart-contracts/> accessed November 1, 2025.

[62] Wright (n 24) 155; Oscar Borgogno and Edoardo Martino, "Decentralised Autonomous Organisations: Targeting the Potential Beyond the Hype" (2024) 16 Law, Innovation and Technology 392, 395–98.

[63] "Introduction to Smart Contracts" (*Ethereum*, 12 February 2025) <https://ethereum.org/en/developers/docs/smart-contracts/> accessed November 1, 2025.

[64] <https://wiki.polkadot.network/docs/build-smart-contracts> accessed November 1, 2025.

[65] <https://solana.com/docs/core/programs> accessed November 1, 2025.

[66] <https://developers.cardano.org/docs/smart-contracts/> accessed November 1, 2025.

Automatic enforcement is particularly beneficial in the context of DAOs because participants often have diverse interests, voices, and preferences and may be in different geographical regions.[67] DAOs commonly enable members to act under pseudonyms, using blockchain wallet addresses instead of real-world identities.[68] In this case participants are unable to evaluate their respective individual qualifications or trustworthiness. The automatic execution of agreements through smart contracts is a tool for ensuring reliability.

Because the DAO's self-executing smart contracts operate on blockchain networks, they are considered immutable, meaning their code cannot be altered unless such alterations are enabled in the design.[69] Smart contracts produce a highly predictable structure. They can, for example, be programmed such that funds can only be released following a formal vote of certain participants.[70] They are therefore more deterministic in nature than contracts or hierarchies.[71] This has the advantage of requiring lower levels of trust between participants as the program ensures that pre-agreed terms are enforced automatically when a trigger event occurs. Primavera de Filippi and Aaron Wright stress that the rigidity of code acts like a layer of control facilitating cooperation between participants.[72]

Smart contracts, while creating high levels of certainty, also have disadvantages. Unlike legal contracts, which can be adapted by the courts to changes in circumstances, smart contracts are not necessarily modifiable in this way. They are therefore less suitable for environments that are uncertain.[73] Their rigidity can cause problems, for example, when there is a "bug, issuer or regulatory concern."[74] This disadvantage is addressed in practice by programming smart contracts such that they can be modified.[75] Some DAOs also provide exit options, which will be discussed below.

Smart contracts are used in several situations, such as proposal management and members onboarding.[76] We will analyze two particular situations below: (1) rewarding participants for their contributions and (2) voting.

Smart contracts facilitate the determination and payment of rewards for contributions, which are made, for example, by providing funding, operational support, participating in governance, giving advice, or supporting "community building," for example by organizing events, discussions, or collaboration.[77]

67 Gogel and others, "Decentralized Autonomous Organization Toolkit" (n 23) 3.

68 Gogel and others, "Decentralized Autonomous Organization: Beyond the Hype" (n 23) 17; Gogel and others, "Decentralized Autonomous Organization Toolkit" (n 23) 11; Law Commission (n 23) paras 2.16 and 2.18.

69 Wright (n 24) 158.

70 ibid 162; Law Commission (n 23) para 2.62.

71 Wright (n 24) 161.

72 Primavera de Filippi and Aaron Wright, *Blockchain and the Law* (Harvard UP 2018) 135; Wright (n 24) 163; Davidson (n 11) 10; Borgogno and Martino (n 62) 426.

73 Halaburda, Levina, and Min (n 5) 16.

74 Wright (n 24) 158.

75 Werbach and others (n 28) 1, 6.

76 Law Commission (n 23) paras 2.53–2.61; Shaanan Cohney and others, "Coin-operated Capitalism" (2019) 119(3) Columbia Law Review 591 analyzed 50 Initical Coin Offerings (ICOs) and compared the promises made in their respective White Papers with the code implemented. They found that there were significant discrepancies. This question will not be further discussed here.

77 Zack High, "DAO Community Building: Strategies and Best Practices" (*Elkpenn Blog*, February 16, 2024) <https://elkpenn.com/blog/dao-community-building/> accessed November 1, 2025; <https://www.fundingthecommons.io/> accessed November 1, 2025.

The use of smart contracts for facilitating rewards comes with challenges. If DAOs are used to reward contributors for work, for example, there can be a problem with uncertainty of compensation.[78] To address this problem, DAOs have integrated reputation-based frameworks such as Colony.[79] Members of DAOs which use the Colony framework earn "reputation" by completing tasks, successfully managing projects, or otherwise contributing to the DAO's goals within specific domains. The level of reputation achieved informs the voting power, which in turn affects the remuneration paid. A smart contract then automates reward distribution. DAOstack facilitates proposal evaluation and resource allocation through reputation-weighted voting.[80]

The rigidity of smart contracts is further modified by functions that enable participants to exit. Moloch DAO, for example, incorporates a "rage quit" function,[81] allowing members to exit the organization and withdraw a proportionate share of the treasury if they disagree with governance decisions. In addition, DAOs can be reset through a "fork," where the underlying blockchain protocol is modified allowing part of the community to choose a different path.[82] A well-known example is the 2016 Ethereum fork following The DAO hack, which resulted in the creation of Ethereum Classic.[83] Other exit mechanisms include token redemption systems, enabling members to exchange tokens for treasury assets; buyback and burn programs (MakerDAO), where DAOs repurchase tokens from members;[84] and exit auctions, where tokens can be sold transparently to other members or external buyers. In some DAOs, time-locked vesting schedules or delegation reassignment (a form of transferability) offer partial exit possibilities (Gitcoin DAO),[85] while full liquidation events occur when DAOs wind down, distributing remaining assets proportionally to tokenholders. There are also arbitration mechanisms and systems that DAOs can adopt to resolve conflicts. An example for this is Kleros.[86]

[78] For an analysis of DAOs from the perspective of labour economics, Nataliya Ilyushina and Trent Macdonald, "Decentralised Autonomous Organisations: A New Research Agenda for Labour Economics" (2022) 5(1) The Journal of The British Blockchain Association 50.

[79] "What is reputation-based governance in DAOs?" (*Colony Blog*, 2025) <https://blog.colony.io/what-is-reputation-based-voting-governance-in-daos/#:~:text=Earning%20Reputation%3A%20Members%20earn%20reputation,the%20meritocratic%20ethos%20of%20Colony> accessed November 1, 2025.

[80] Alex Rea and others, "Colony Technical White Paper" (February 16, 2018 version cb41534) <https://uploads-ssl.webflow.com/61840fafb9a4c433c1470856/639b50406de5d97564644805_whitepaper.pdf≥ accessed November 1, 2025.

[81] Davidson (n 11) 14.

[82] ibid; Kevin Werbach, *The Blockchain and the New Architecture of Trust* (MIT Press 2018) 68–69; Borgogno and Martino (n 62) 418.

[83] David Z Morris, "CoinDesk Turns 10: 2016—How The DAO Hack Changed Ethereum and Crypto" (*Coindesk*, May 15, 2023) <https://www.coindesk.com/consensus-magazine/2023/05/09/coindesk-turns-10-how-the-dao-hack-changed-ethereum-and-crypto≥ accessed November 1, 2025.

[84] Vikash Malik, "Inside Maker DAO's Token Buyback Strategy" <https://tradedog.io/inside-makerdaos-token-buyback-strategy/> accessed November 1, 2025.

[85] <https://gov.gitcoin.co/t/how-should-i-change-my-delegations-h2-2023/16831> accessed November 1, 2025; "The Token Holder's Guide to Delegation" (*Aragon Blog*, December 11, 2023) <https://blog.aragon.org/the-token-holders-guide-to-delegation/> accessed November 1, 2025.

[86] <https://kleros.io>; also digital, non-territorial governance software such as ULEX Open Source Legal System <https://www.decentralizedgovernance.institute/ulex> accessed November 1, 2025; Bianca Kremer, "Code, Community, and Conflict: DAO Disputes" in Kevin Werbach, Eva Micheler, and Bianca Kremer (eds), *Foundations of Decentralized Organizations: Blockchain and the Future of Corporate Law* (OUP 2026).

Another application for smart contracts is voting. For many DAOs, voting decisions organized through a smart contract are automatically enforced, provided they reach the required threshold.[87] The technology facilitates participation of stakeholders located in different places and is credited with a high level of tamper-resistance.[88] This compares well to the system currently in places for voting shares.[89] Digital voting also makes it possible for different weighing mechanisms to be implemented.[90] Voting rules can be programmed to encourage voters to participate actively in the governance of a DAO.[91] The availability of a voting mechanism that is not only easily accessible but also designed to incentivize participation does, nevertheless, not entirely overcome voter apathy.[92]

Moreover, DAO voting occurs both on-chain and off-chain.[93] While on-chain voting ensures security and transparency through blockchain-based records, it can be costly due to "gas" and transaction fees.[94] Off-chain voting on services such as Twitter (X), Discord, Telegram, or Snapshot, potentially limits the transparency and accountability of DAO governance.[95]

We have seen in this subsection that both in relation to designing and paying rewards and organizing voting, smart contracts have been supplemented with functions modifying their rigidity. In addition, some DAOs have adopted founding documents, such as constitutions, to articulate principles and goals more explicitly.[96] All of this has to some extent undermined but not eliminated the ethos of "code is law."

4.3.4. Summary

We have seen in this section that DAOs aspire for autonomy in both a wider ideological and a narrower technological sense. Both goals are theoretical aims that have been implemented with some concessions. We will analyze the concept of decentralization in the next section.

[87] Law Commission (n 23) para 2.65.

[88] Wright (n 24) 160 and 16–65.

[89] Eva Micheler and Elena Zaccaria, "Digitising the UK Securities Market: The Case Against and a Proposal to Enfranchise Indirect Investors" [2024] Cambridge Law Journal 519; Eva Micheler, "Custody Chains and Asset Values: Why Crypto-securities are Worth Contemplating" [2015] Cambridge Law Journal 533; also de Filippi and Wright (n 72) 133–36; Michael A Schillig, "'Lex Cryptographi(c)a', 'Cloud Crypto Land' or What?—Blockchain Technology on the Legal Hype Cycle" (2022) 86 Modern Law Review 31, 45–49.

[90] For an overview of these, Han, Lee, and Li (n 32) 13–14.

[91] Wright (n 24) 160 and 165.

[92] De Filippi and Wright (n 72) 139–40; Wright (n 24) 165.

[93] On off-chain voting and other off-chain governance practices, Werbach and others (n 28) 1.

[94] Gas fees are transaction costs on the Ethereum blockchain, paid in Ether (ETH) or gwei, compensating validators for securing the network. They fluctuate with supply, demand, and network congestion: Coinbase, "What are gas fees" <https://www.coinbase.com/learn/crypto-basics/what-are-gas-fees#:~:text=Gas%20fees%20are%20transaction%20costs,during%20periods%20of%20network%20congestion> accessed November 1, 2025.

[95] Gogel and others, "Decentralized Autonomous Organization Toolkit" (n 23) 12 and 15; Davidson (n 11) 5.

[96] Gogel and others, "Decentralized Autonomous Organization Toolkit" (n 23) 14; Gogel and others, "Decentralized Autonomous Organization: Beyond the Hype" (n 23) 13.

4.4. Decentralization

Decentralization in the context of DAOs refers to distributing decision-making power among participants rather than concentrating it within a central authority. Decentralized means that decisions are made by all participants without power being allocated in the form of a hierarchy.[97]

Decentralization is connected to but also independent of autonomy. It is possible to imagine a system that is "autonomous" while being centralized. We can imagine a libertarian elite setting up a regime that is intended to be outside of the state but nevertheless dominated by its founders. The Soviet Union was an example of an economy that did not operate through a traditional market but was centralized.

In the context of DAOs, however, an aspiration for decentralization is a characteristic ingredient. The connection between autonomy and decentralization can be traced to the ideological roots of DAOs.[98] Cypherpunks, for example, critique centralized state power and believe that decentralization is the way to achieve a better society. Anarcho-capitalists favor an unregulated free market economy and believe that decentralization is a mechanism to create it. Both groups would like to "exit" or withdraw from specific legal jurisdictions through decentralization. Some speak of *crypto-secession*.[99]

Along similar lines, the proponents of Ukraine DAO have, as noted above, used decentralized blockchain-based crowdfunding to coordinate global humanitarian aid because they have no trust in existing institutional arrangements.[100]

Decentralization can also be a way of avoiding regulation, which connects to particular lead actors. If an activity is organized in a decentralized manner these cannot be identified and, *prima facie*, the activity consequently falls outside of the letter of the law. We have already mentioned that Shapeshift adopted a decentralized model of decision-making to circumvent Securities and Exchange Commission (SEC) regulations.[101]

Technologically decentralization is implemented through smart contracts which organize functions that would normally be performed by a central decision-maker such as the allocation and payment of rewards or the organization of voting.

Because, at least at the most general level, DAOs consist of people "loosely working together with a shared purpose" regardless of their physical location,[102] they are sometimes used by digital nomads seeking fluid, borderless economic and social structures.[103] An example for this is Decentraland, a virtual world governed by its

[97] For a comprehensive analysis of the concept, Thibault Schrepel, *Blockchain + Antitrust* (EE Elgar 2021) 51–66.

[98] Law Commission (n 23) paras 2.34 and 2.37–2.40.

[99] Trent J MacDonald, *The Political Economy of Non-Territorial Exit: Cryptosecession* (Edward Elgar Publishing 2019).

[100] <https://ukraine-dao.notion.site/Ukraine-DAO-3a0e63c6190b4796890dec5c72a94872≥ accessed November 1, 2025.

[101] Allen and others (n 53).

[102] De Filippi and Wright (n 72) 138; Wright (n 24) 152–53.

[103] On digital nomads, "52 Digital Nomad Statistics 2024—The Nomad Almanac" <https://thenomadalmanac.com/digital-nomad-statistics/> accessed November 1, 2025; some countries offer tax advantages and special visas to attract digital nomads (Emma Agyemang, "Countries wooing corporate digital nomads hope to make them stay" (*Financial Times*, May 18, 2024) <https://on.ft.com/3KrQjqZ> accessed November 1, 2025).

community through a DAO, demonstrating how decentralization enables users to create and manage assets without being bound by physical or legal territories.[104]

Like autonomy, decentralization is primarily a theoretical idea and unlikely to be implemented in pure form.[105] Several elements of centralization and hierarchy have emerged in practice.

Different DAO participants can have different responsibilities where some exercise more influence than others. This introduces hierarchical elements into DAOs. For example, DAOs are normally set up by a relatively small founding team,[106] who at least initially determines and controls their design and processes.[107] From the perspective of these founders, decentralization is an aim or an aspiration rather than part of the original setup with DAOs adopting "progressive approaches" to decentralization.[108]

David Gogel and others note that disproportionate power for early contributors can be a problem.[109] This is confirmed by an empirical analysis conducted by Robin Fritsch and others.[110] They find that the governance systems of three prominent DAOs reveal "extreme centralisation," resembling shareholder meetings where a few large investors dominate decision-making.[111] These are sometimes referred to as "whales."[112] However, the authors also observe that these large delegates rarely exercised their full voting power, often aligning their decisions with those of smaller token-holders, thus mitigating potential governance imbalances in practice.[113] Wulf A Kaal recently analyzed 50 DAOs and also found that many of these have centralized features.[114]

DAOs are not formally run by boards or managers,[115] but, in some, delegates are appointed to representative councils, which, according to David Gogel and others, act

[104] Esteban Ordano and others, "Decentraland White Paper" <https://decentraland.org/whitepaper.pdf> accessed November 1, 2025.

[105] Angela Walch, "Deconstructing 'Decentralization': Exploring the Core Claim of Crypto Systems" in Chris Brummer and others (eds), *Cryptoassets: Legal, Regulatory, and Monetary Perspectives* (OUP 2019) 39; also Rozas, Tenorio-Fornés, and Hassan (n 11) 2; Davidson (n 11) 10–12.

[106] Davidson (n 11) 6, citing Carlos Santana and L Albareda Vivo, "Blockchain and the Emergence of Decentralized Autonomous Organizations (DAOs): An Integrative Model and Research Agenda" (2022) 182 Technological Forecasting and Social Change 121806, 5.

[107] Michael A Schillig, "Decentralized Autonomous Organizations (DAOs) under English Law" (2022) 16 Law and Financial Markets Review 68, 70–71.

[108] Werbach and others (n 28) 26–28; Gogel and others, "Decentralized Autonomous Organization Toolkit" (n 23) 11, 13, and 23.

[109] Gogel and others, "Decentralized Autonomous Organization Toolkit" (n 23) 11; Ellie Rennie, Jason Potts, and Joshua Tan, "The 'Natural State' of Blockchains: An Etnography of Validator Governance" (2024) <https://ssrn.com/abstract=4741076> accessed November 1, 2025; Romain Rossello, "Blockholders and strategic voting in DeFi DAOs' governance" (2024) <https://papers.ssrn.com/sol3/papers.cfm?abstract_id=4706759> accessed November 1, 2025.

[110] Robin Fritsch, Marino Müller, and Roger Wattenhofer, "Analysing Voting Power in Decentralized Governance: Who Controls DAOs?" (2024) 5(3) Blockchain: Research and Applications 100208.

[111] ibid 3 and 6.

[112] Han, Lee, and Li (n 32).

[113] Fritsch, Müller, and Wattenhofer (n 110) 5; Chainalysis Team, "Exploring DAOs: Uncovering Web3 Ownership Realities" (*Chainalysis Blog*, June 27, 2022) <https://www.chainalysis.com/blog/web3-daos-2022/> accessed November 1, 2025; Sangita Gazi, "In Code We Trust: Blockchain's Decentralization Paradox" (2025) 27 Vanderbilt Journal of Entertainment & Technology Law 59; Vanessa Villanueva Collao, "Understanding the Role of Informal Relationships, Social Norms and Emerging Power Structures in Decentralized Governance" (draft on file with authors), who shows that hierarchy can also arise off-chain.

[114] Kaal (n 26).

[115] Wright (n 24) 152.

as quasi-boards.[116] These councils introduce a hierarchical element into those DAOs which adopt this structure.

We have already mentioned that DAOs rely on infrastructure built on blockchain technology. This leads to the separation of specific roles with different levels of influence.[117] Developers code and deploy the smart contract on a blockchain protocol.[118] Miners or validators authorize transactions that occur between token-holders.[119] Smart contracts can be programmed to reward different contributors in different ways.[120] Some DAOs have core contributors entitled to receive tokens for ongoing contributions, and token-holders or investors, which are the broadest category of DAO participants and do not receive tokens on an ongoing basis.[121]

Multi-signature authorization programs also create points of hierarchy. They may enable some but not other participants to initiate and approve certain actions.[122] They are used, for example, to authorize changes to smart contracts or to control assets held by some DAOs.[123] Such assets are referred to as "treasury," which has been said to resemble corporate capital, and normally managed through multi signature wallets.[124] Founders sometimes retain the ability to control the funds held in these wallets.[125] But even if they do not, those whose authorizations are required to release the treasury of a DAO have the power to take decisions affecting other participants.

Hyejin Park and others use literature examining constitutional arrangements in nation-states to suggest three dimensions for measuring the extent to which DAOs are decentralized.[126] They evaluate DAOs in terms of political decentralization (number of accounts actively participating in voting and number of accounts actively proposing changes), administrative decentralization (dispersion of tokens, majority requirements), and economic or financial decentralization (quorum requirements and pass rate of proposals with quorum decisions).[127] In this model, a high number of actively participating accounts, which not only vote but also propose changes, widely dispersed token-holders and high majority requirements, high quorum requirements and a large number of proposals that are adopted with these quorum requirements in place suggest very high levels of decentralization.[128] The absence of such characteristics indicates levels of centralization.

[116] Gogel and others, "Decentralized Autonomous Organization Toolkit" (n 23) 16.

[117] Law Commission (n 23) paras 2.22 and 2.79–2.80.

[118] Uniswap DAO, eg, operates based on a code developed by Uniswap Labs, which is legally incorporated in Delaware as Universal Navigation Inc; Han, Lee, and Li (n 32) 4.

[119] Davidson (n 11) 5.

[120] De Filippi and Wright (n 72) 137.

[121] Gogel and others, "Decentralized Autonomous Organization Toolkit" (n 23) 12; Davidson (n 11) 5.

[122] Law Commission (n 23) ix.

[123] Gogel and others, "Decentralized Autonomous Organization Toolkit" (n 23) 16.

[124] Gogel and others, "Decentralized Autonomous Organization Toolkit" (n 23) 11, 12, and 13; also Law Commission (n 23) xii.

[125] Gogel and others, "Decentralized Autonomous Organization: Beyond the Hype" (n 23) 6, 7 (Constitution DAO) and 16 (BadgerDAO); Gogel and others, "Decentralized Autonomous Organization Toolkit" (n 23) 12.

[126] Hyejin Park, Ivan Ureta, and Boyoung Kim, "Developing Dimensions and Indicators to Measure Decentralization in Decentralized Autonomous Organizations, (2023) 13 Administrative Science 1.

[127] ibid 4–5.

[128] ibid 3–5.

Another aspect of centralization derives from the desire to create a link between DAOs and non-crypto native organizations, such as banks and other service providers. To connect decentralized governance with real-world legal frameworks, some DAOs use "wrappers." These are legal entities incorporated, for example, as foundations and operate bank accounts, hold other assets, or employ staff on behalf of the DAO community.[129] Those who control these entities have powers that affect the other participants, introducing elements of hierarchy.

We have seen in this subsection that, like autonomy, decentralization is an aspirational idea. DAOs have not completely avoided hierarchies. These have emerged because there are participants that have more influence than others. They also occur when DAOs use legal entities to connect with the real world. We will come back to this point when we examine DAOs through the lens of the theory of the firm.

4.5. Summary

We have seen in this section that DAOs serve a diverse range of purposes. While some DAO structures explicitly aim to replace the state with a blockchain-based libertarian model of governance, others pursue a profit motive and can be compared with corporations, and still others pursue entirely different goals. Some are built to experiment with democratized decision-making and incentive models outside of traditional corporate structures. Some of these share similarities with cooperatives or charities.

We have further argued in this section that DAOs have their roots in particular ideological ideas but are used for a much broader spectrum of projects. They are designed to achieve the theoretical idea of autonomy, which is implemented through the theoretical idea of decentralization. In practice, both concepts are aspirations of DAO proponents and participants that have been implemented to a varied degree.[130] In the following section we will examine DAOs through the lens of the theory of the firm.

5. Theory of the Firm and DAOs

As we have seen in Section 2, the theory of the firm distinguishes markets, firms, and hybrid forms, and predicts that transaction costs explain which form of economic organization prevails. In Section 4 we concluded that DAOs aspire to organize activity in a less hierarchical manner and that smart contracts and reputation systems are a technology through which decisions can be taken and executed without appointing a central decision-maker.[131] Academic scholars have begun to analyze the effect of DAOs on economic structure.

[129] Werbach and others (n 28) 17–19; Gogel and others, "Decentralized Autonomous Organization Toolkit" (n 23) 11 (NounsDAO), 16 (Optimism Foundation), and 18; Borgogno and Martino (n 62) 420; Law Commission (n 23) para 2.21; Christopher J Brummer and Rodrigo Seira, "Legal Wrappers and DAOs" (*SSRN*, May 30, 2022) <https://ssrn.com/abstract=4123737> or <http://dx.doi.org/10.2139/ssrn.4123737> accessed July 9, 2025.

[130] Law Commission (n 23) paras 2.20–2.23 and 2.36.

[131] Sinclair Davidson, Primavera de Filippi, and Jason Potts, "Blockchains and the Economic Institutions of Capitalism" (2018) 14 Journal of Institutional Economics 639; Jason Potts, "Douglass North and the

Hanna Halaburda and others write that digital technology has led to firms increasingly making decisions to outsource activity to the market causing the balance between firms and markets to shift toward the latter.[132] They believe that smart contracts will add to this effect and shift economic structure further toward the market in the future.[133] Along similar lines, Primavera de Filippi and Aaron Wright suggest that DAOs will increase the prevalence of markets. They argue that smart contracts reduce the cost of coordination. Smart contracts could, for example, be used to develop a ride-sharing system that operates without a centralized operator allowing drivers to keep a larger share of their revenue.[134] Ultimately, in their view, DAOs might reduce or even eliminate the reliance on traditional business organizations.[135]

There is more than one perspective on the effect of smart contracts. Hanna Halaburda and others, for example, caution that smart contracts have ex ante costs as they need to be programmed to account for all future states, including rare events and so require a stable environment with low levels of uncertainty.[136] In contrast Darcy WE Allen and others observe that DAOs are highly adaptable because they can be set up and adapted at low cost.[137] They provide a case study of three DAOs and show how these have experimented with governance models in response to changes in regulation and market conditions. In their view, DAOs are adaptive governance engines.[138] It is possible that the first view reflects the properties of the early and immutable versions of smart contracts. We have mentioned that more recent smart contracts have integrated mechanisms that enable their modification, responding to the problems associated with the rigidity of their earlier predecessors.

We could draw a comparison between DAOs and digital platforms. These have been characterized as hybrid forms sitting somewhere between the market and the firm.[139] This would be a mistake, however. Arrangements are so varied that general statements of this type are best avoided. The same is true also for digital platforms. We have seen this in the *Uber* case. The digital nature of the platform notwithstanding, drivers have been characterized as employees by the UK Supreme Court.[140] This was because the platform designed the digital relationships of drivers in a hierarchical manner.

Crypto-Economy" (*SSRN*, September 24, 2023) <https://ssrn.com/abstract=4581716≥ or <http://dx.doi.org/10.2139/ssrn.4581716≥ accessed November 1, 2025; Schillig (n 89) 40–43; Borgogno and Martino (n 62) 410–11.

[132] Halaburda, Levina, and Min (n 5) 7; Wright (n 24) 163.

[133] Halaburda, Levina, and Min (n 5) 10.

[134] De Filippi and Wright (n 72) 138–39; Darcy WE Allen and others, "Blockchain and the Evolution of Institutional Technologies: Implications for Innovation Policy" (2020) 49 Research Policy 103865; and Halaburda, Levina, and Min (n 5) 10–11; also the hypothetical example of a "pure" DAO developed in Law Commission (n 23) ch 3.

[135] Wright (n 24) 169–70; also Borgogno and Martino (n 62) 426–27.

[136] Halaburda, Levina, and Min (n 5) 16.

[137] Darcy WE Allen and others, "DAOs Are Adaptive Governance Engines" in Kevin Werbach, Eva Micheler, and Bianca Kremer (eds), *Foundations of Decentralized Organizations: Blockchain and the Future of Corporate Law* (OUP 2026).

[138] Allen and others (n 53) 4 and 6–10.

[139] eg Laurent Baronian, "Digital Platforms and the Nature of the Firm" (2020) 54 Journal of Economic Issues 214.

[140] *Uber BV v Aslam* [2021] UKSC 5. Regarding digital platforms and hierarchies also Nofar Sheffi, "We Accept: The Constitution of Airbnb" (2020) 11 Transnational Legal Theory 484.

We have seen above that a gap has opened between the theoretical aims of autonomy and decentralization and their practical implementation. Hierarchical elements have been integrated into DAOs in several ways. Different participants have different roles and powers to make decisions that bind other participants. Founders appear to retain significant influence. DAOs use legal entities to open bank accounts or otherwise contract with other businesses or individuals. These are controlled by some but not other participants. While there is agreement that DAOs have potential to create less hierarchical structures than in other organizational environments, it is nevertheless clear that some DAOs have adopted firm-style hierarchical elements. The use of smart contracts, which was originally said to place DAOs into the market structure, has not turned out to have this effect.

We believe that no general statements should be made about whether DAOs are markets, firms, or hybrids. Different DAOs adopt different structures.[141] They also change over time. Characteristics that we observe now may be outdated in a few months' time. Whether a DAO is a firm is a matter of degree rather than principle. Corporations, cooperatives, and charities also operate some of their relationships in the form of spot contracts or contracts with limited managerial adaptability. Moreover, there is a broad range of designs within traditional organizational forms. Different jurisdictions make available different legal forms and give more or less influence to their respective participants. The hypothetical example of a peer-to-peer ride-sharing system aside DAOs which adopts firm-style hierarchical elements is to this extent a firm.

6. Ostromian Perspectives

We have mentioned that Simon Deakin has characterized the corporation as a form of a common pool resource. This argument can also be found in relation to DAOs. Ilia Murtazashvili and others, for example, argue that blockchain networks represent knowledge commons governance because they rely on "collectively-managed technologies to pool and manage distributed information."[142] In their perspective, blockchain technology is a form of "community governance to produce resources that both support and reflect collective action and self-governing communities with respect to business objectives and other purposes."[143] Along similar lines David Rozas and others describe the technology as potentially enabling the creation of an artifact that facilitates decentralized (non-hierarchical) cooperation.[144] Ilia Murtazashvili and others further point to research that has shown that there is "tremendous diversity" in the ways in which blockchains are organized.[145]

141 Werbach and others (n 28) 1.

142 Murtazashvili and others (n 11) 108; Michael J Madison and Ilia Murtazashvili, "The Decentralized Autonomous Organisation as Knowledge Commons" in David Gindis and Pavel Kuchar (eds), *Governing Corporate Knowledge Commons* (CUP 2025) (forthcoming).

143 Murtazashvili and others (n 11) 109.

144 Rozas, Tenorio-Fornés, and Hassan (n 11) 2.

145 Murtazashvili and others (n 11) 111; Charles Kerrigan, *Crypto and Digital Assets Law and Regulation* (Sweet & Maxwell 2024) 481 and Werbach and others (n 28) 1.

Sinclair Davidson also characterizes DAOs as knowledge commons and uses Elinor Ostrom's framework for the analysis and development of institutions to examine DAOs through the three analytical criteria referred to earlier in the chapter: resource characteristics, attributes of the community, and rules in use. He further concludes that DAOs have adopted all of the eight design principles identified in Elinor Ostrom's research and predicts that DAOs have the potential to operate as an organizational form in the longer term.[146]

From the perspective of the narrative model proposed by David Gindis and Eva Micheler, we can develop insight into DAOs by distinguishing different levels of governance. The meta-constitutional level is the basis on which the constitutional framework of an organization is set up. For corporations the meta-constitutional level consists of a Corporation Act, based on which individual actors register a particular company or corporation. We noted earlier that some DAOs use legal entities to enable them to interact with the legal system. For these DAOs the legislative documents governing how they are registered and operated form the meta-constitutional level. At this level we also find the regulatory environment that motivates the organizers of some projects to attempt to avoid regulation by adopting a decentralized model.[147] In addition, the meta-constitutional level of a DAO is shaped by the blockchain protocol within which it is programmed. These protocols each have their strengths and limitations and, as such, enable different ways of designing smart contracts. If a DAO adopts a conflict resolution system, the properties of this technology shape the meta-constitutional level. This level is also characterized by the formal rules and informal practices prevalent on the social media platforms, such as Discord or Snapshot, used by the respective DAO participants to launch and promote a DAO project.

The constitutional level concerns the governance of a specific DAO. At this level the analysis focuses on the rules that determine how a DAO takes and implements policy and operational decisions. We determine the purpose for which a DAO has been established and the values and beliefs which participants consider themselves bound by. Libertarian DAO projects, for example, value individual autonomy, freedom of speech, or free market entrepreneurialism. Participants in DAOs that are set up to reject the traditional capitalist economy identify with values such as equality, social justice, inclusion, or community (bottom-up) governance.[148] The properties of the specific smart contract rewarding contributors to the DAO for their work or other contributions are also part of the constitutional level. We further examine the methods available for modifying this contract or other ways in which the DAO can be adapted to changes in circumstances. We have mentioned that some DAOs have adopted a constitutional document or a particular conflict resolution system, which would also be relevant to determine the functioning of a DAO.

[146] Davidson (n 11) 5.
[147] Allen and others (n 53) 4 and 6–10.
[148] For an example setting out a vision for "community (bottom-up) governance," Puja Ohlhaver, Eric Glen Weyl, and Vitalik Buterin, "Decentralized Society: Finding Web3's Soul" (*SSRN*, 2022) <https://ssrn.com/abstract=4105763> accessed November 1, 2025.

The operational level concerns ways in which DAOs affect their material and social environment. At this level we determine the extent to which constitutionally adopted rules are implemented in practice and the outcomes that they produce. We establish if and how the values adopted by a specific DAO inform operational outcomes. From a technological perspective we observe how well automated functions operate and how DAO decisions that are not automated are executed. Voting that is carried out off chain, for example, will need to be implemented formally in a DAO. A decision to reprogramme a smart contract or the release of treasury tokens will also require specific implementation.

An analysis that distinguishes different levels of governance not only assists academic scholars. It also helps practitioners to identify and frame the questions that need to be addressed when DAOs are set up and developed. Advisors and participants need to identify the meta-constitutional blockchain protocol that hosts the DAO and the legal and regulatory environment that they will be affected by. At the constitutional level they need to determine the purpose of a particular DAO and decide the properties of the smart contract and its interactions with the external environment. DAO practitioners are further well advised to consider the likely consequences of their design on the operational level.

We have seen in this section that the research tools developed by Elinor Ostrom are useful to guide research on how DAOs function and can assist practitioners in designing and developing DAOs.

7. Conclusions

In this chapter we analyzed DAOs from the perspective of the theory of the firm and from the perspective of the work of Elinor Ostrom. The theory of the firm characterizes economic arrangements as either markets or firms. Markets consist of peer-to-peer spot transactions. Firms adopt hierarchical structures. Elinor Ostrom has developed analytical tools for the analysis of institutions and is sometimes referenced by participants in DAOs.

We traced the libertarian ideological origins of DAOs and argued that they have evolved from these roots to support a broad range of purposes and ideological preferences. We also analyzed the concepts of "autonomy" and "decentralization." We concluded that DAOs are set up to achieve autonomy from either the state or traditional corporate arrangements through decentralization. However, neither concept is not fully implemented in practice.

DAOs have many structures. It is not possible to develop a general statement as to their economic nature as either a market, a firm, or hybrid. Each DAO needs to be assessed individually to determine the extent to which hierarchies are present. Smart contracts automate the enforcement of certain elements of arrangements. As in the case of platforms, the use of this technology does not per se predicate whether an arrangement is a contract, a firm-style hierarchy, or something in between.

We concluded finally that the research tools developed by Elinor Ostrom for the analysis of institutions can usefully be applied to DAOs. Some DAOs can be characterized as knowledge commons where the design principles set out by Ostrom can be identified. We also argued that the narrative model recently advanced by David Gindis and Eva Micheler in relation to the corporation can be usefully adapted to the analysis and development of DAOs.

7
DAOs Are Adaptive Governance Engines

Darcy WE Allen, Chris Berg, Aaron M Lane, and Jason Potts

1. Why Do DAOs Exist?

A long time ago, a young Ronald Coase asked and answered a question: why do organizations exist?[1] That became the analytic foundation of the modern field of New Institutional Economics. Prior to Coase, it was obvious why organizations exist—firms organize production.[2] Coase's genius was to observe that markets also organize and coordinate production through the price mechanism, and that the relevant question is what is the factor that determines the margin of the economizing on production technologies. His surprising answer was to invoke his new conception of transaction costs, as the costs of using a market. Transaction costs are those of setting up and using market institutions. To understand why organizations exist, we should observe these *at the margin* of the costs of operating a firm. Firms exist because transaction costs of markets are positive, and at some margin the costs of using a firm, which are also positive but load on different factors, are the more economically efficient solution.[3] Coase, in other words, developed the core insight of the "marginal revolution" to the study of phenomena that were previously under the ambit of study by economic history (as soon recognized by Douglass North, and others), industrial organization and managerial decision-making (as soon recognized by Oliver Williamson and others), and law (as recognized by an older Coase and others).[4]

Coase answered that firms exist, and are the size and shape they are, because they are a transaction cost-minimizing solution to the problem of economic organization and governance.[5] The insight that firms internalize the costs of writing, bargaining, enforcement, and monitoring contracts and exchange was developed by Oliver

[1] Ronald Coase, "The Nature of the Firm" (1937) 4 Economica 386.

[2] Donald Boudreaux and Randall Holcombe, "The Coasian and Knightian Theories of the Firm" (1989) Managerial and Decision Economics 147.

[3] Neil Kay, "Coase and the Contribution of 'The Nature of the Firm'" (2015) 36 Managerial and Decision Economics 44; "Institutions are the humanly devised constraints that structure human interaction and they exist to reduce the ubiquitous uncertainty arising from that interaction.... Transaction costs are the costs associated with the measurement and enforcement of agreements" in Douglass C North, "Institutions and Credible Commitment" (1993) 149 Journal of Institutional and Theoretical Economics 11; "The organisations that come into existence will reflect the opportunities provided by the institutional matrix." Douglass C North, "Economic Performance Through Time" (1994) 84(3) The American Economic Review 359–68, 361.

[4] Oliver Williamson, *Markets and Hierarchies: Analysis and Antitrust Implications* (Free Press 1975); Oliver Williamson, *The Economic Institutions of Capitalism* (Free Press 1985); Ronald Coase, "The Problem of Social Cost" (1960) 56 Journal of Law and Economics 837.

[5] Ronald Coase, "The Institutional Structure of Production" (1992) 82 American Economic Review 713.

Williamson.[6] His analysis focused on hazards of opportunism in organizations due to asymmetric information and asset specificity, and studied various organizational and institutional solutions to these problems (further developed by David Teece, Oliver Hart, and others).[7] Those studying decentralized autonomous organizations (DAOs) have long recognized that the Coasean framework also applies to the question of why DAOs exist.[8] DAOs are novel governance mechanisms that challenge traditional firm–market structures by reducing transaction costs in new ways. In this chapter, we further develop the transaction cost approach to DAOs by observing the evolution of DAOs in practice.

The idea of decentralized organizations has long been discussed in mechanism design literature. But the modern blockchain-based concept of a DAO was first theorized in 2013 by Vitalik Buterin and Dan Larimer.[9] The opportunity to construct a DAO was realized in 2014 with the smart contract-based Ethereum blockchain, and was first fully operationalized in the Slock.It White Paper, which in turn gave rise to the first DAO, eponymously called The DAO.[10] It has long been obvious to blockchain scholars working in business and law school contexts that Coase's fundamental insight of institutional economics also carries over to DAOs.[11] Hassan and de Filippi

[6] Oliver Williamson, "Transaction-cost Economics: The Governance of Contractual Relations" (1979) 22 Journal of Law and Economics 233; Oliver Williamson, "The New Institutional Economics: Taking Stock, Looking Ahead" (2000) 38 Journal of Economic Literature 595.

[7] For instance, David J Teece, "Profiting from Innovation in the Digital Economy: Enabling Technologies, Standards, and Licensing Models in the Wireless World" (2018) 47 Research Policy 1367; Oliver Hart, "Incomplete Contracts and Control" (2017) 107 American Economic Review 1731.

[8] "As described by Ronald Coase ... people exhibit a natural tendency to organise into more or less formalised institutions-associations, partnerships, companies, corporations, or other types of organisations referred to by economists as 'firms'—when the costs of engaging in market transactions are too high" in Primavera de Filippi and Aaron Wright, *Blockchain and the Law* (Harvard UP 2018); Trent MacDonald, *The Political Economy of Non-Territorial Exit* (Edward Elgar Publishing 2019).

[9] Werner Dilger, "Decentralized autonomous organization of the intelligent home according to the principle of the immune system" (IEEE International Conference on Systems, Man, and Cybernetics. Computational Cybernetics and Simulation, 1997) 351; Daniel Larimer, "Bitcoin and the Three Laws of Robotics" (*Let's Talk Bitcoin*, 2013) <https://letstalkbitcoin.com/blog/post/bitcoin-and-the-three-laws-of-robotics> accessed October 2, 2024; Vitalik Buterin, "Response to Jeffrey Evans" (*Medium*, 2016) <https://medium.com/@VitalikButerin/i-invented-the-term-in-2013-and-daniel-larimer-came-up-with-dacs-s-organization-corporation-a-ef86db1524d5> accessed October 2, 2024; Vitalik Buterin, "Bootstrapping a Decentralized Autonomous Corporation: Part I" (*Bitcoin Magazine*, September 19, 2013) <https://bitcoinmagazine.com/technical/bootstrapping-a-decentralized-autonomous-corporation-part-i-1379644274> accessed October 2, 2024.

[10] Christoph Jentzsch, "Decentralized Autonomous Organization to Automate Governance" (*Slock.It White Paper*, November 2016); Quinn Du Pont, "Experiments in Algorithmic Governance: A History and Ethnography of The DAO, a Failed Decentralised Autonomous Organization" in M Campbell-Verduyn (ed), *Bitcoin and Beyond* (Routledge 2018); Ellie Rennie, Jason Potts, and Joshua Tan, "The 'natural state' of blockchains: An ethnography of validator governance" (*SSRN*, 2024) <https://papers.ssrn.com/sol3/papers.cfm?abstract_id=4741076> accessed October 2, 2024.

[11] Darcy WE Allen and others, "Blockchain and the Evolution of Institutional Technologies: Implications for Innovation Policy" (2020) *49 Research Policy* 103865; Chris Berg, Sinclair Davidson, and Jason Potts, *Understanding the Blockchain Economy: An Introduction to Institutional Cryptoeconomics* (Edward Elgar Publishing 2019); Sinclair Davidson, Primavera de Filippi, and Jason Potts, 'Blockchains and the Economic Institutions of Capitalism' (2018) 14 Journal of Institutional Economics 639; Nataliya Ilyushina and Trent Macdonald, "Decentralised Autonomous Organisations: A New Research Agenda for Labour Economics" (2022) The Journal of the British Blockchain Association; Jason Potts, "Douglass North and the Crypto-Economy" (*SSRN*, 2023) <https://ssrn.com/abstract=4581716≥ accessed October 2, 2024; Kevin Werbach, *The Blockchain and the New Architecture of Trust* (MIT Press 2018).

provide a comprehensive overview of the origin and definition of DAOs and provide a guide to the academic literature on them.[12] Singh and Kim define a DAO as:

> an organization whose essential operations are automated, agreeing to rules and principles assigned in code without human involvement. A DAO is a novel, scalable, self-organizing coordination on the blockchain, controlled by smart contracts.[13]

De Filippi and Hassan define a DAO as a "self-governed organization controlled only and exclusively by an incorruptible set of rules, implemented under the form of a smart contract."[14] The significance of transaction costs and agency problems to the economic logic of blockchains and DAOs economizing on trust is well-recognized in the literature.[15] For instance, Kaal observes that "inexpensive open-source smart contracts eliminate a major motivation for creating a firm under Ronald Coase's transaction cost theory."[16] Kaal continues, noting that "Barzel's [1997] motivation for the existence of a firm, the added efficiency of a centralised production monitoring agency, is also largely irrelevant with efficient smart contracting, as the smart contract performs the production monitoring function and largely removes the agents."[17] And Davidson explains, "the crucial assumption underpinning the viability of DAOs as being that smart contracts must suppress agency costs."[18] So, the now standard approach to the theory of DAOs in institutional economics and corporate law is the Coasean insight about the structure of economic organization as a function of the relative cost of governance combined with the arrival of a new technology of economic

[12] Samer Hassan and Primavera de Filippi, "Decentralized Autonomous Organization" (2021) 10 Internet Policy Review 2.

[13] As distinct from a centralized autonomous organization (CAO), which conducts decision-making from top management down. Madhusudan Singh and Shiho Kim, "Blockchain Technology for Decentralized Autonomous Organizations" (2019) 115 Advances in Computers 115, 117.

[14] Samer Hassan and Primavera de Filippi, "Decentralized Autonomous Organization" (2021) 10 Internet Policy Review 12; and Delphi Labs definition of a DAO, one of the most comprehensive, at <*https://delphilabs.medium.com/assimilating-the-borg-a-new-cryptolegal-framework-for-dao-adjacent-entities-569e54a43f83*> accessed October 2, 2024.

[15] David Yermack, "Corporate Governance and Blockchains" (2017) 21 Review of Finance 7; Primavera de Filippi, Morshed Mannan, and Wessel Reijers, "Blockchain as a Confidence Machine: The Problem of Trust & Challenges of Governance' (2020) 62 Technology in Society 101284; Trent MacDonald, *The Political Economy of Non-Territorial Exit* (Edward Elgar Publishing 2019) Robbie Morrison, Natasha Mazey, and Stephen Wingreen, "The DAO Controversy: The Case for a New Species of Corporate Governance?" (2020) 3 Frontiers in Blockchain 25; Fabrice Lumineau, Wenqian Wang, and Oliver Schilke, "Blockchain Governance—a New Way of Organizing Collaborations?" (2021) 32 Organization Science 500; Aaron Wright, "The Rise of Decentralized Autonomous Organizations: Opportunities and Challenges" (2021) 4 Stanford Journal of Blockchain Law & Policy 151; Joshua Tan, "Exploring DAOs as a new kind of institution" (*Medium*, March 2021) <https://medium.com/commonsstack/exploring-daos-as-a-new-kind-of-institution-8103e6b156d4> accessed October 2, 2024; Marvin Hanisch and others, "Digital Governance: A Conceptual Framework and Research Agenda" (2023) *162 Journal of Business Research* 113777; Asma Alawadi and others, "Decentralized Autonomous Organizations (DAOs): Stewardship Talks but Agency Walks" (2024) 178 Journal of Business Research 114672; Sinclair Davidson, "The nature of the DAO" (*SSRN*, 2024) <https://ssrn.com/abstract=4808295> accessed October 2, 2024.

[16] Wulf Kaal, "Blockchain-based Corporate Governance" (2020) 4 Stanford Journal of Blockchain Law & Policy 3.

[17] Yoram Barzel, *Economic Analysis of Property Rights* (CUP 1997).

[18] Sinclair Davidson, "The nature of the DAO" (*SSRN*, 2024) <https://ssrn.com/abstract=4808295> accessed October 2, 2024.

governance based on smart contracts with a lower cost function for transaction and governance costs of corporations.

Yet, at the time of writing (circa late 2024), the reality, however, is that the "lower cost function," as the manifest Coasean starting point for governance analysis of DAOs, has repeatedly proven to be mostly an implicit assumption that has often been empirically rejected on a number of interesting and even surprising margins. Rather, the more interesting hypothesis that has emerged is that economically viable DAOs exist as islands of prospective effective governance in a high-dimensional sea of community norms, organizational forms, and regulatory environmental contexts. DAOs are interesting because they increase the frontiers of possible organizational forms and types of governance that can exist in the world. They provide possible exit options for organizations that are currently constrained in the space of particular forms by increasingly ossified regulations.[19] We conjecture that in that increased potential space of possible forms lie some good opportunities to create value. The problem is that these specific targets and the exit paths are not *prima facie* obvious, but must be discovered through specific trial and error discovery of costs and benefits.

The simple Coasean equation is not a generalized cost function, that is, in which substituting DAO governance for centralized corporate governance lowers transaction costs, but one of entrepreneurial discovery of particular organizational structures and contexts in which the opportunity for DAO substitution exists. Haussman and Rodrik once characterized economic development as a process of self-discovery, emphasizing that entrepreneurial innovation in discovering local comparative advantage due to particular configurations of resources and relative prices, which are always changing due to innovation, represented a kind of information good spillover for other entrepreneurs operating in the context of uncertainty about opportunities.[20] The same argument can be made about DAO opportunities as self-discovery of comparative governance costs. Yet, pointing to "technological opportunities" in the application for DAOs is almost meaningless advice to an entrepreneur or manager, for the specific opportunity will depend very much on the particular matrix of governance and transaction costs and the organizational, cultural, and regulatory context in which they are incurred.[21] The actual messy and specific details of exactly how DAO substitution or application is implemented, operationalized, culturally legitimated, and legally enforced in order to create value—has been, and will likely continue for some time, to be a largely experimental entrepreneurial endeavor fraught with costly discoveries and billable legal hours.

[19] Darcy WE Allen, "Entrepreneurial Exit: Developing the Cryptoeconomy" in Melanie Swan and others (eds), *Blockchain Economics: Implications Of Distributed Ledgers-Markets, Communications Networks, And Algorithmic Reality* (World Scientific 2019) 197.

[20] Ricardo Hausmann and Dani Rodrik, "Economic Development as Self-Discovery" (2003) 72 Journal of Development Economics 603.

[21] "Entrepreneurs and members of organisations invest in skills and knowledge which lead to revised evaluation of opportunities, which induce alteration of the rules or gradual revision of informal constraints. The kinds of skills and knowledge perceived to have a high value payoff will reflect the incentives embodied in the institutional framework" in Douglass North, "Institutions and Credible Commitment" (1993) 149 Journal of Institutional and Theoretical Economics 11.

So, details matter. Nevertheless, in this chapter we seek to try and draw inductively from several case studies some of the possible lessons that can be extracted and offer an at least partially generalized analysis of these early experiments. There are many DAO applications, and a growing number of these have been studied in detail using digital ethnography techniques.[22] Other case studies have explored how DAOs solve information problems.[23] These case studies are useful not only for analysis of behaviors and context, but also to examine how governance has evolved over time, that is, toward decentralization, and the problems that these changes were trying to solve. Our analysis emphasizes the entrepreneurial discovery process involved in DAO development and suggests that DAOs increase institutional diversity by offering innovative governance solutions within evolving legal frameworks. The implications of our analysis suggest that DAOs not only lower governance costs but also expand the potential design space for organizational forms, fostering experimentation in governance that could reshape institutional boundaries and offer new solutions in response to regulatory and market pressures. All of these properties enable an organization that has transitioned to a DAO to use adaptive governance as an instrument to exist in dynamic regulatory, competitive, or financial environments.

2. How Do DAOs Evolve in Practice?

The transaction cost-based theory of corporate governance provides a framework for analysis of how corporate forms have evolved under different institutional regulatory environments.[24] This tradition includes comparative analysis of different regulatory costs that induce different entry into markets.[25] Others have studied the effect of different relative costs of factors and technological dynamics.[26] We can extend this framework to analyze how particular, competitive, financial, and regulatory environments shape the particular structure of DAOs by considering several case studies below. Before analyzing these examples of DAO evolution in practice, we have summarized the key takeaways in Table 7.1.

[22] Tara Merk, "Why to DAO: a narrative analysis of the drivers of tokenized Exit to Community" (*arXiv*, 2024) <https://arxiv.org/abs/2407.14327> accessed October 2, 2024; Ellie Rennie, "What is a good DAO and how do we know?" (*Medium*, 2024) <https://ellierennie.medium.com/what-is-a-good-dao-and-how-do-we-know-2efa2943997b> accessed October 2, 2024; Ellie Rennie and Jason Potts, 'The DAO: A radical experiment in decentralised governance' (*The Conversation*, May 16, 2016) <https://theconversation.com/the-dao-a-radical-experiment-that-could-be-the-future-of-decentralised-governance-59082> accessed October 2, 2024; Du Pont (n 10).

[23] Darcy WE Allen and others, "The Exchange Theory of web3 Governance" (2023) 76 Kyklos 659.

[24] Andrei Shleifer and Robert Vishny, "A Survey of Corporate Governance" (1997) 52 Journal of Finance 737.

[25] Simeon Djankov and others, "The Regulation of Entry" (2002) 117 The Quarterly Journal of Economics 1.

[26] Oliver Williamson, "Transaction-Cost Economics: The Governance of Contractual Relations" (1979) 22 Journal of Law and Economics 233.

Table 7.1 Summary of case studies

Example	DAO evolutionary path
Shapeshift	Shapeshift began as a traditional centralized firm and later decentralized in response to regulatory pressures (both actual and perceived). It transitioned to a DAO structure by shutting down its corporate entity and handing over assets and operations to token-holders.
Uniswap	Uniswap started as a centralized protocol and gradually moved toward decentralization by introducing governance tokens and community voting. It implemented a phased approach to decentralization, balancing developer influence with increasing token-holder control over time.
Optimism	Optimism evolved from a centralized non-profit to a public benefit corporation, then to a unique bicameral governance structure. It implemented an iterative approach to governance, experimenting with various mechanisms through community input and revealing costs in practice.

2.1. Shapeshift

Shapeshift offers a unique example of a cryptocurrency application that made choices around centralization and decentralization according to the business, regulatory, and technical environment they faced. Founded in 2014 by an early Bitcoin pioneer, Erik Voorhees, Shapeshift was one of the oldest "on-chain" cryptocurrency exchanges as a company incorporated in Switzerland with employees largely operating out of Denver, Colorado.[27] As a result, it was the first to face some of the challenges and opportunities that this category of blockchain application experienced more prominently when decentralized finance led the blockchain ecosystem's development after 2020. The company's disassociation and handover of operations to a decentralized autonomous organization provides a clear case study of decentralization as a response to regulatory action (and the possibility of action).

Shapeshift had a number of novel features which distinguished it from the more traditionally structured cryptocurrency exchanges which were then emerging such as Coinbase (founded in 2012) and Mt Gox (which entered liquidation in April 2014). Users could interact with the Shapeshift website to send one cryptocurrency from their blockchain wallet and would be sent another form of cryptocurrency in return according to the exchange rate. First, it was a "non-custodial" exchange, in that the Shapeshift firm did not control user assets. This minimized the trust that users had to have in Shapeshift, as Shapeshift as a firm could not lose or abscond with user funds (as had occurred in the Mt Gox case). Second, it did not require users to create an account in order to exchange, meaning that Shapeshift could not collect any information about its users other than that available on the public blockchain record. In order to facilitate user exchanges, Shapeshift controlled pools of company-owned

[27] Erik Voorhees, "Way of the DAO" (*Money and State*) <https://moneyandstate.com/blog/way-of-the-dao> accessed October 2, 2024.

cryptocurrency assets that it would deposit and withdraw from on demand, functioning as what Voorhees described as a cryptocurrency "vending machine."

From its earliest establishment, Shapeshift as a firm was highly sensitive to the regulatory environment. In response to the "BitLicense" regulatory framework introduced by New York State in 2015 (which would have required Shapeshift to collect identifying information about users) it blocked users in New York State from accessing its service.[28] It responded similarly when the state of Washington introduced its own blockchain licensing scheme in 2017, including moving a recent corporate acquisition, the hardware wallet KeepKey, out of Washington where it had established its headquarters.[29] Voorhees, self-described as a "libertarian" who believed that much regulation displaced market solutions to economic and social problems, was attracted initially to Bitcoin as an alternative to fiat currencies.[30] The firm operated entirely on Bitcoin, "so it ha[d] no bank accounts and no fiat passing through its books."[31]

The practical limitations of moving operations outside the regulated jurisdictions became clear around 2017, however, when Shapeshift began to make operational decisions to comply—or at least be consistent with—policy statements and intimations from the US government. In mid-2017, the Securities and Exchange Commission (SEC) released what has colloquially become known as "The DAO Report," which argued that capital raising using cryptocurrency tokens would be classified as the creation of investment contracts under US securities law. Shapeshift announced that it would begin a legal audit of the tokens offered on the platform to identify whether any of those met the tests determined by the SEC, and to avoid being classified as a securities exchange as a result.[32]

A more serious blow to the vision of Shapeshift occurred in September 2018, when it introduced—apparently under real or perceived duress—a Shapeshift membership model.[33] Shapeshift membership allowed users to have their own accounts on the platform to which they would sign in, and the account-based user model would provide them with features such as the histories of their transactions and email notifications. User accounts also allowed Shapeshift to introduce a loyalty program using a newly launched token, FOX, where rewards would accrue. But the most important

[28] Kevin Dugan, "Lawsky's new bitcoin rules akin to 'spying' on users: critic" (*New York Post*, June 11, 2015) <https://nypost.com/2015/06/11/lawksys-new-bitcoin-rules-akin-to-spying-on-users-critic> accessed October 2, 2024.

[29] "Notes on Leaving the State of Washington" (*ShapeShift Blog*, August 27, 2017) <https://web.archive.org/web/20191214072110/https://info.shapeshift.io/blog/2017/08/27/blog-2017-08-27-notes-leaving-state-washington/> accessed October 2, 2024.

[30] "Erik Voorhees on Understanding Libertarianism" (*What Bitcoin Did Podcast*, September 24, 2019) <https://www.whatbitcoindid.com/podcast/erik-voorhees-on-understanding-libertarianism> accessed October 2, 2024.

[31] Grace Caffyn, "ShapeShift Raises $525k, Reveals Erik Voorhees as Creator" (*Coindesk*, March 11, 2021) <https://www.coindesk.com/markets/2015/03/10/shapeshift-raises-525k-reveals-erik-voorhees-as-creator/> accessed October 2, 2024.

[32] "ShapeShift and Tokens as Securities" (*ShapeShift Blog*, August 27, 2017) <https://web.archive.org/web/20171211093637/https://info.shapeshift.io/blog/2017/08/17/shapeshift-and-tokens-securities> accessed October 2, 2024.

[33] "Introducing ShapeShift Membership" (*ShapeShift Blog*, September 4 2018) <https://web.archive.org/web/20180905000219/https://info.shapeshift.io/blog/2018/09/04/introducing-shapeshift-membership/> accessed October 2, 2024.

driver for the introduction of membership was the perceived necessity to track some information about Shapeshift users, including compliance with Know Your Customer (KYC) rules. Membership was initially voluntary but would become mandatory. Announcing the membership model, Voorhees wrote that "Yes, that last detail sucks," but justified it on the grounds that:

> The practice of requiring customers to hand over personal private information is one we've struggled with since inception. To the extent that digital asset technology remains a legal grey area, we need to be prudent and thoughtful in our approach as we navigate the regulatory environment.

This was a severe crisis of confidence for Shapeshift's mission and libertarian ethos. Voorhees told a conference a few months later that "I felt like I had to do something morally wrong to allow the company to persist... It's a really awful position to be in."[34] Voorhees later clarified that the policy was proactive, rather than in response to any direct regulatory intervention. But one hint at the pressure Shapeshift felt at the time was published in the *Wall Street Journal* a few weeks after the membership program was announced: a report claiming that nearly US$10 million of "potentially criminal" funds had been sent through Shapeshift into privacy-preserving cryptocurrencies.[35] That "tainted" transaction volume was disputed by Voorhees and later independent blockchain analytics firms.[36] However, in 2020, Shapeshift subsequently removed support for the privacy coins which were subject of the accusations.

The consequences of these increasingly hemmed-in offerings provided by Shapeshift led the firm to implement two major reforms to Shapeshift's business and governance in 2021. The first major change was a radical restructuring of its offering and business model. Throughout 2020 the blockchain ecosystem saw the growth of a new class of decentralized finance ("DeFi") protocols that allowed for more decentralized and autonomous trading than was possible through Shapeshift—for example, by allowing users to make exchanges through open pools of funds rather than through Shapeshift's own-controlled liquidity. In January, it announced that it was phasing out the business model it had pioneered at its launch six years earlier, and was instead going to integrate two major DeFi platforms (0x and Thorchain) to serve Shapeshift users directly. One of the consequences of this was that it would also shut down the requirements for users to KYC with Shapeshift.[37]

[34] Christine Kim, "Rethink, Renew: ShapeShift CEO Erik Voorhees to Rebrand Crypto Exchange" (*Coindesk*, February 17, 2019) <https://www.coindesk.com/markets/2019/02/17/rethink-renew-shapeshift-ceo-erik-voorhees-to-rebrand-crypto-exchange> accessed October 2, 2024.

[35] Justin Scheck and Shane Shifflett, "How Dirty Money Disappears into the Black Hole of Cryptocurrency" (*The Wall Street Journal*, September 28, 2018) <https://www.wsj.com/articles/how-dirty-money-disappears-into-the-black-hole-of-cryptocurrency-1538149743> accessed October 2, 2024.

[36] "Shining Light on WSJ's Attack on ShapeShift and Crypto" (*Shapeshift Blog*, October 1, 2018) <https://web.archive.org/web/20191029162107/https://info.shapeshift.io/blog/2018/10/01/shining-light-on-wsjs-attack-on-shapeshift-and-crypto/> accessed October 2, 2024; Leigh Cuen, "WSJ's ShapeShift Exposé Overstated Money Laundering by $6 Million, Analysis Says" (*Coindesk*, March 20, 2019) <https://www.coindesk.com/markets/2019/03/20/wsjs-shapeshift-expose-overstated-money-laundering-by-6-million-analysis-says/> accessed October 2, 2024.

[37] William Foxley, "ShapeShift Is Going Full DeFi to Lose KYC Rules" (*Coindesk*, January 7, 2021) <https://www.coindesk.com/business/2021/01/06/shapeshift-is-going-full-defi-to-lose-kyc-rules/> accessed October 2, 2024.

A more radical move was made in July, when Shapeshift announced that it was shutting down the corporate entity and handing all Shapeshift assets, brand, and identity over to a DAO. While a staged decentralization is a common path for blockchain projects to take, this was a unique strategic and organizational move; Shapeshift had not been intended to be anything but a centralized firm at its establishment. In an essay published in 2022, Voorhees emphasized the significant administrative and legal overhead required to operate as a corporation: physical office space, human resources and the associated policy development, and executive management across all of "Marketing, Engineering, Product, Customer Support, Legal, HR, Operations." In addition, at one stage Shapeshift was paying for a monthly legal bill in excess of US$1 million.[38] Converting to a DAO would involve completely shutting down most of these functions, or, where this wasn't possible, replacing them with DAO-run infrastructure.

Here too the evolution of blockchain technology provided a space for Shapeshift to move into: DAOs had been discussed extensively by some blockchain pioneers (particularly future founder of Ethereum, Vitalik Buterin and future founder of EOS, Dan Larimer) but were not a serious and implementable policy when Shapeshift was founded in 2014.[39] By 2021, however, DAOs had gone through a significant early stage of experimentation and the infrastructure for on-chain organizations had evolved significantly.[40] In order to effect the conversion to a DAO, governance was transferred over to holders of the FOX token, now a "governance token" (again, neither the Ethereum blockchain nor the Ethereum token standard that FOX used was available to Voorhees when Shapeshift was established). FOX tokens were simultaneously distributed to blockchain addresses that had interacted with the Shapeshift protocol in the past, at the time one of the largest cryptocurrency airdrops by capitalization.[41] Token-holders were then given the power to vote on all future decisions and development of the protocol, including how the large treasury of FOX tokens should be used for further investment or distribution.[42]

Shapeshift began as a traditional firm with no public intention to decentralize, faced regulatory risk, and decentralized. Has the move to a DAO and the transition to DeFi been a success? Given the regulatory drive toward decentralization, it has (at the time of writing) allowed Shapeshift to continue to operate. In 2024 the SEC issued an order to the remaining Shapeshift legal entity (which it accepted "does not currently have any revenue or full-time employees") to cease offering crypto-assets classed as

[38] Erik Voorhees, "Way of the DAO" (*Money and State*) <https //moneyandstate.com/blog/way-of-the-dao> accessed October 2, 2024.

[39] Vitalik Buterin, "Bootstrapping a Decentralized Autonomous Corporation: Part I" (*Bitcoin Magazine*, September 19, 2013) <https://bitcoinmagazine.com/technical/bootstrapping-a-decentralized-autonomous-corporation-part-i-1379644274> accessed October 2, 2024.
Daniel Larimer, "Overpaying for Security" (*Let's Talk Bitcoin*, 2013) <https://web.archive.org/web/20140209061238/http://letstalkbitcoin.com/is-bitcoin-overpaying-for-false-security/> accessed October 2, 2024.

[40] Darcy WE Allen and others, "The Exchange Theory of web3 Governance" (2023) *76* Kyklos 659.

[41] Darcy WE Allen, Chris Berg, and Aaron M Lane, "Why Airdrop Cryptocurrency Tokens?" (2023) 163 Journal of Business Research 113945.

[42] Erik Voorhees, "Way of the DAO" (*Money and State*) <https://moneyandstate.com/blog/way-of-the-dao> accessed October 2, 2024.

securities. Shapeshift settled for a $275,000 fine. It is significant in light of Shapeshift's actions after the release of The DAO Report that the SEC did not identify which of the assets formerly traded on the Shapeshift platform were regulated investment contracts.[43] As a pure business move it has been less successful. By shifting its product offering to using alternative exchange providers, Shapeshift has been competing in a crowded DeFi market, and not necessarily successfully. While token prices do not necessarily reflect underlying product value or consumer surplus, the fully-diluted market capitalization of the FOX token has declined from above $70 million between November 2021 and May 2022 to around $16 million in August 2024.

2.2. Uniswap

Uniswap provides an example of a more gradual move to DAO governance following a period of centralization, allowing it to maintain developer influence while providing more control to token-holders over time. As the name suggests, Uniswap is a protocol that enables a single user to swap tokens in real time without needing a counterparty. Created in 2018 by developer Hayden Adams, Uniswap's automated market maker (AMM) model transformed blockchain trading by replacing traditional order books (matching buyers and sellers) with liquidity pools (where the protocol's smart contracts holds a reserve supply of tokens).

The original version of the Uniswap protocol (V1) was deployed by Adams to the Ethereum blockchain.[44] Adams' autobiographical account of Uniswap's history is that the V1 protocol was controlled by him, albeit in the context of making the code open source on GitHub, advice and support from high-profile individuals in the Ethereum community (including founder Vitalik Buterin), and engagement with blockchain professionals (including company Kyokan).[45] Uniswap protocol V2 was deployed by Uniswap Labs, a development company founded by Adams. While V1 enabled Ethereum to ERC20 token swaps, V2 enabled ERC20 to ERC20 token swaps, among other changes. V3, released in 2021, provided more complex liquidity features.[46]

The incorporation of Uniswap Labs in 2019 marked an important milestone in the protocol's journey toward decentralized governance. It is likely that the motivation for incorporation was a combination of factors including legal liability, regulatory risk, and a mechanism for obtaining external financial investment. For instance, venture capital firm Andreessen Horowitz led a Series A funding round along with several investors.[47] But the effect of incorporation and external investors was to formally bring

[43] Hester M Peirce and Mark T Uyeda, "On Today's Episode of As the Crypto World Turns: Statement on ShapeShift AG" (*US Securities and Exchange Commission*, March 5, 2024) <https://www.sec.gov/newsroom/speeches-statements/peirce-uyeda-statement-crypto-world-turns-03-06-24> accessed October 2, 2024.

[44] Hayden Adams, "A Short History of Uniswap" (*Uniswap Labs Blog*, February 11, 2019) <https://blog.uniswap.org/uniswap-history> accessed October 2, 2024.

[45] ibid.

[46] Uniswap Team, "Introducing Uniswap V3" (*Unswap Labs Blog*, March 23, 2021) <https://blog.uniswap.org/uniswap-v3> accessed October 2, 2024.

[47] Uniswap Team, "Series A" (*Uniswap Labs Blog*, August 6, 2020) <https://blog.uniswap.org/uniswap-raise> accessed October 2, 2024.

additional decision-makers into the governance of the company (even if those parties were not involved in the day-to-day management of the protocol as such).

The next step of Uniswap's transition toward decentralization occurred with the launch of governance token, UNI, in September 2020.[48] One billion UNI tokens were distributed to a variety of stakeholders over a vesting schedule, with 40 percent allocated to the development team, early investors, and advisors. The remaining 60 percent of UNI tokens were allocated to "community" interests including tokens earmarked for a treasury (ie benefiting future users) and an airdrop of 15 percent (ie benefiting past users). The airdrop was strategically significant. Uniswap's decision to airdrop UNI tokens to existing users, rather than using it as a marketing tool to attract new users, was a deliberate move to decentralize governance to those who already had a vested interest in the protocol's future.[49] Although the effect was to reward early users—those who had contributed liquidity or made trades—Uniswap ensured that the recipients of governance tokens were individuals who understood and valued the protocol. By waiting two years into Uniswap's operations, the protocol was able to decentralize with over 250,000 active user addresses and almost 50,000 active liquidity providers.[50]

Uniswap governance token-holders obtained real decision-making power. First, token-holders control all UNI vested to the Uniswap treasury (worth almost $3 billion at the time of writing)—voting to allocate treasury funds to grants, development, research, and other economic incentives aimed at improving the protocol. For example, the community has voted on proposals to fund liquidity mining programs, educational initiatives like the DeFi Education Fund, and other protocol-related projects. Although there was an initial "grace period" for community control over the treasury, with a 180-day period in order to "provide the Uniswap community enough time to familiarize itself with the governance system, bring in a diverse and high-quality set of protocol delegates, and begin discussions and communications around potential governance proposals."[51] It was hoped that a community-managed treasury would "see a variety of experimentation" and "set the benchmark for responsible but radical, long-term aligned on-chain governance systems."[52]

Additionally, UNI token-holders are responsible for voting on protocol upgrades. These include modifications to the core functionality of the AMM, such as changes to trading fees, liquidity provisioning mechanisms, or the development of new features. While Uniswap Labs continues to lead development, these protocol changes are now subject to broader community approval.

Uniswap's governance process has evolved since the launch of the UNI token in 2020. Initially, the governance system allowed anyone holding or delegating at least

48 Uniswap Team, "Introducing UNI" (*Uniswap Labs Blog*, September 16, 2020) <https://blog.uniswap.org/uni> accessed October 2, 2024.

49 Darcy WE Allen, Chris Berg, and Aaron M Lane "Why Airdrop Cryptocurrency Tokens?" (2023) 163 Journal of Business Research 113945.

50 Uniswap Team, "Introducing UNI" (*Uniswap Labs Blog*, September 16, 2020) <https://blog.uniswap.org/uni> accessed October 2, 2024.

51 ibid.

52 ibid.

1 percent of UNI's total supply to propose changes to the protocol.[53] There is a trade-off that occurs with this threshold. On one hand, it limits proposals so that there is stability in the operation of the protocol, and limits the making of those proposals to those that have the most stake in the outcome. On the other hand, it concentrates constitutional power in a small token-holder base and excludes smaller holders from proposing governance changes. Over time, it became clear that this bar was set too high. In 2021, the proposal threshold was lowered to 2.5 million UNI.[54] In 2023, the proposal threshold was lowered again to 1 million UNI.[55] It should be noted that users can delegate votes, which means that coalitions can form to meet this minimum threshold.

The current governance process incorporates off-chain governance tools, which lower the costs of decision-making by providing users with further information in an informal forum and not requiring users to incur transaction fees associated with on-chain governance activity. The first stage is a "request for comment" which is a post on the Uniswap governance web forum that is "meant to allow the community to digest a proposal, comment, and ask questions about a particular proposal."[56] The second stage is a "temperature check" using Snapshot—an open-source off-chain polling tool—with a quorum of 10 million UNI as compared to the on-chain vote.[57] The final stage is the on-chain governance proposal with a higher quorum of 40 million UNI.[58]

2.3. Optimism

Optimism, a Layer 2 blockchain network, has shifted from a centralized and developer-led structure to a decentralized governance structure emphasizing governance iteration and experimentation. Its evolution can be understood through a transaction cost lens both statically (how the multiple houses and voting mechanisms of the DAO compare to alternatives) and dynamically (as a process of continuous governance experimentation drawing on community member suggestions).

Optimism emerged in 2019 as a developer-led project focused on scaling Ethereum through optimistic rollups.[59] The centralized non-profit Plasma Group relied on donations from bodies including Consensys and Gitcoin. The Plasma Group's aim was to scale Ethereum through plasma chains, including research and development on scaling technology. But this traditional centralized governance structure had limitations, including its ability to sustain long-term growth through grants. Indeed, they

53 ibid.

54 0xA13a5a31b891F3DA7074b740B694769BD0f1bb23, "Reduce the UNI proposal submission threshold to 2.5M" (*Boardroom.io*, 2021) <https://boardroom.io/uniswap/proposal/cHJvcG9zYWw6dW5pc3dhcDphcmNoaXZlOjQ=> accessed October 2, 2024.

55 Devin Walsh, "Community Governance Update' (*Uniswap Labs Blog*, January 2023) <https://gov.uniswap.org/t/community-governance-process-update-jan-2023/19976> accessed October 2, 2024.

56 ibid.

57 ibid.

58 ibid.

59 Messari, "Optimism Profile" (*Messari*) <https://messari.io/project/optimism/profile> accessed September 26, 2024.

directly noted that creating "secure, production code requires far more resources than PoCs—beyond what we could raise in donations."[60] The core problem with the centralized structure was seen as one of sustainably funding public goods.

In 2021 the Plasma Group donated their remaining funds to Gitcoin and wound down.[61] They evolved to a new governance structure by launching the Optimism Public Benefit Corporation (PBC).[62] This transition was a strategic shift from research to implementation, acknowledging the need for a new funding model. The Optimism PBC was the "main agent narrating the Optimism transition" toward a more decentralized model, driving the early development from testnet to mainnet.[63] The focus turned to how Optimism could create a Layer 2 to "re-architect the network's economics and close the loop: value produced by the network can be recycled to grow and sustain it."[64] The move to the new structure enabled the Optimism PBC to attract $3.5 million in venture funding.[65]

In June 2022, Optimism established the Optimism Foundation and the Optimism Collective, representing a significant push toward the goal of decentralization. The Optimism Foundation, a Cayman Islands non-profit company, is intended as a transitional body to "steward the early evolution of Collective self-governance."[66] The core benefit of the Foundation is described through the legal lens of it being able to enter into limited liability legal agreements, such as service providers, and to "sometimes act more quickly, predictably, or safely" to support the Collective.[67] The long-term goal of the Foundation is to progressively decentralize its power and transition responsibilities to the broader Optimism community. The board members of the Foundation are elected through token-holder votes, connecting the decentralized governance of the token-holders with some of the benefits of a centralized formal entity.

The Optimism Collective has a bicameral governance system consisting of two "houses." Its design is intended to ensure the fair and efficient allocation of resources and to prevent the concentration of power within the ecosystem. The Collective's unique structure has been described as "a large-scale experiment in digital democratic governance."[68] The two houses, each with different institutional structures, were designed to mitigate some of the shortcomings of existing token-based governance DAO structures (including capture by large token-holders) with the benefits of community input and control.

[60] Optimism, "Optimism" (*Optimism PBC Blog*, January 16, 2020) <https://medium.com/ethereum-optimism/optimism-cd9bea61a3ee> accessed October 2, 2024.

[61] Optimism, "On to New Beginnings" (*Plasma Group Blog Medium*, January 10, 2020) <https://medium.com/plasma-group/on-to-new-beginnings-e9d76b170752> accessed September 26, 2024.

[62] ibid.

[63] Tara Merk, "Why to DAO: a narrative analysis of the drivers of tokenized Exit to Community" (*arXiv*, 2024) <https://arxiv.org/abs/2407.14327> accessed October 2, 2024.

[64] ibid.

[65] Optimism, "Optimism" (*Optimism PBC Blog*, January 16, 2020) <https://medium.com/ethereum-optimism/optimism-cd9bea61a3ee> accessed September 26, 2024.

[66] "What is the Optimism Foundation?" (*Optimism Docs*, August 15, 2024) <https://community.optimism.io/welcome/faq/what-is-the-optimism-foundation> accessed September 26, 2024.

[67] ibid.

[68] The Optimism Collective, "Introducing the Optimism Collective" (*Optimism Collective Mirror*, April 27, 2022) <https://optimism.mirror.xyz/gQWKlrDqHzdKPsB1iUnI-cVN3v0NvsWnazK7ajlt1fI> accessed September 26, 2024.

The Token House follows a fungible token-based governance model of one-token-one-vote. The Token House is designed for discussing and voting on proposals related to protocol upgrades, project incentives, inflation adjustments, director removal, and treasury funding. This institutional structure is familiar to many DAOs, where OP token-holdings provide proportional voting power, and the process of governance draws on the local knowledge and preference of token-holders to influence the direction of the protocol, including the allocation of its resources. This structure might reduce some information costs, by tapping into the distributed knowledge of the community, and token-holders may be incentivized to influence protocol development to increase token price. The Citizen House, with its non-fungible token-based "soulbound" membership, attempts to complement the Token House with a more egalitarian "one-person one-vote system which roots power not in financial capability, but in identity."[69] The governance powers of the Citizen House are primarily to vote on retroactive public goods funding (a novel mechanism for funding public goods under constraints and allocating capital to projects through time and under uncertainty) and to hold veto powers over some key Token House proposals.

The structure of the two houses of the Optimism Collective are guided through several stated principles, including governance minimization and iteration, which can be understood as mechanisms to discover the transaction costs of governance and adapt to them over time.[70] The iterative approach to governance emphasizes that governance structures are experimental and that we can learn from the application of new institutions in practice.[71] For instance, Optimism has implemented seasons of airdrops, has a working constitution, and there are often discussions and experiments with new governance means in their community forums. Compared to more rigid organizations, the governance of Optimism has seen multiple rounds of redesign, responding to knowledge discovered through previous experiments.[72]

Optimism's iterative governance draws both on experimental knowledge of implementing governance in practice, as well as the knowledge of community members experiencing governance costs in different ways. The iterative approach to governance is a type of institutional learning. For instance, Optimism introduced committees that segment governance into smaller focused groups. This change emerged directly from problems with token-based governance including the need to "reduce delegate overload" of understanding and voting on proposals, as well as the

[69] The Optimism Collective, "Introducing the Citizens" House: 10m OP to Public Goods" (*Optimism Collective Mirror*, December 7, 2022) <https://optimism.mirror.xyz/wqk1Yeyn2OhV9paDzbRXvQ0m0JYDu2npbSkMClwk1rY> accessed September 26, 2024.

[70] The Optimism Collective, "The Future of Optimism Governance" (*Optimism Collective Mirror*, July 19, 2023) <https://optimism.mirror.xyz/PLrAQgE1EGRo7GRrFoztplFChnUZda4DFGW3dkQayxY> accessed September 26, 2024.

[71] Optimism Collective, "This Governance Will Self-Destruct" (*Optimism Collective Mirror*, May 18, 2022) <https://optimism.mirror.xyz/r888e4B5iiNQi-3_mO26ixgv-plQ099XWgqEOv9iWKA> accessed September 26, 2024.

[72] The Optimism Collective, "Introducing the Citizens' House: 10m OP to Public Goods" (*Optimism Collective Mirror*, December 7, 2022) <https://optimism.mirror.xyz/wqk1Yeyn2OhV9paDzbRXvQ0m0JYDu2npbSkMClwk1rY> accessed September 26, 2024.

need for expert information to respond to different governance challenges.[73] Not only can community members shape decisions within existing rules, but the community is drawn upon to make proposals to the governance structure itself. At the time of writing, Optimism is experimenting with new "deliberative governance" processes. In the announcement of those processes the forum post directly mentions the change was "inspired by a community member's post."[74]

The shift of Optimism over time from a centralized model in the Plasma Group to the comparatively decentralized Optimism Collective was driven by a desire to reduce transaction costs associated with public goods funding in blockchains. For instance, the decentralized governance of the multiple houses is intended to draw on the local knowledge and information costs of members of the ecosystem, rather than a centralized team of researchers.

While we have focused on the ways that Optimism governance has evolved in an attempt to reduce transaction costs in unique ways, it is important to note that their approach also introduces new transaction costs. For instance, the design and implementation of their governance systems, including the development of new governance mechanisms (some of which are complex) require significant resources not only to develop, but for the community to understand and navigate them. More broadly, coordinating a comparatively large and diverse community inevitably involves communication and coordination overheads.

3. What DAOs Really Do

It is readily apparent that the shifting frontier of DAOs is an emergent form of governance innovation. In this chapter, through the framing of transaction cost economics theory and institutional cryptoeconomics, we have asked why DAOs exist. Reviewing the emerging empirical and theoretical literature on DAOs, we pinpointed some theoretical reasons why DAOs might exist and persist as part of the institutional mix of an economy. But while DAOs can indeed reduce certain transaction costs, such as agency costs, the implications of their emergence are far broader than a simple shift in cost efficiencies. As we have argued in this chapter, DAOs are adaptive governance engines that enable communities to dynamically adapt their governance in response to pressures and organizational needs. The proximate reasons for DAO adoption is often portrayed as related to lowered costs of organization due to smart contract automation, which is entirely in line with Coasean predictions. But the ultimate reason, as the function that is seemingly under competitive selection, as we discovered in our case studies, is that DAOs enable an organization to have what we have called here an "adaptive governance engine."

[73] Ben-chain, "Introducing governance committees" (*Optimism Governance Forum*, August 6, 2022) <https://gov.optimism.io/t/introducing-governance-committees/3238> accessed September 26, 2024.

[74] Optimism, "Experimenting with Deliberative Processes in the Collective" (*Optimism Governance Forum*, April 29, 2024) <https://gov.optimism.io/t/experimenting-with-deliberative-processes-in-the-collective/8041> accessed September 26, 2024.

DAOs represent more than a simple reduction in costs along some existing institutional trajectories, as per the standard Coasean analysis. Rather, from a more evolutionary dynamic perspective, revealed by close study of how DAOs actually behave in the world, our claim is that they represent a new expanded scope of institutional evolution. DAOs create new frameworks for collective action, and those frameworks help propel an open evolutionary process of experimentation. This theory predicts that, irrespective of the reasons and motivations for DAO adoption and use (eg cultural, technological, regulatory, lowered cost, community participation, etc), the economic selection mechanism operating over DAOs will be selecting for fast, cheap governance adaptation. In other words, DAOs are valuable not because they lower the cost of governance, but because they lower the cost of changing governance (while also simultaneously opening up a much larger institutional space of governance).

We argue, therefore, that the blockchain-based tools underpinning DAOs represent not just an expansion of possible organizational forms, which was mostly apparent in the early years of DAOs, but also an ability to move quickly through that new space, which is a functional adaptive property that only became apparent through entrepreneurial experience. The case studies presented above illustrate how the existence of this larger institutional space and the adaptive properties of being able to move quickly (whether defensively or in pursuit of valuable opportunities) must be discovered through a process of entrepreneurial experimentation. Through this lens, not only does blockchain infrastructure expand the design space of organizational forms, but it also provides an alternative governance structure for groups of people to exit from existing institutional frameworks. Our perspective aligns with the Hayekian view of institutions as emergent orders, suggesting that DAOs may serve as laboratories for institutional innovation at an accelerated speed and scale.

Any particular DAO is a point in high-dimensional institutional space, and how it gets there is, at this stage in the history of this new technology, still mostly by an entrepreneurial discovery procedure. The DAOs that we have analyzed have emerged and evolved in a particular historical and local context. Rather than being static and deterministic coded structures, DAOs evolve as their goals change and the institutional environment around them changes. As we observed with Optimism, some DAOs are explicitly embedding efforts to evolve to new ideas and pressures raised by their community, treating their governance as experimental. Their focus is on the discovery of different institutions as they progressively decentralize. As we finalize this chapter, there are current and rigorous community discussions about disbanding the foundation, toward a more decentralized model.[75] Other DAOs, such as Shapeshift, have been shaped by regulatory pressures to decentralize. They have evolved over time in response to these institutional forces. This suggests that there are no panaceas in DAO governance, nor is there a blueprint for DAO members to follow.

[75] GFX Labs, "Accelerated Decentralization Proposal for Optimism" (*Optimism Forum*, September 18, 2024) <https://gov.optimism.io/t/accelerated-decentralization-proposal-for-optimism/8875> accessed October 2, 2024.

Related to this, the discovery of DAO governance rules is an entrepreneurial discovery process within a particular local context. This lens has parallels to what Haussman and Rodrick describe as the development process for developing economies—that is, that the process of economic development is a competitive entrepreneurial process of discovering comparative advantage in times of uncertainty.[76] There are also complex externalities and learning that occurs between DAOs. Governance failures—such as exploits and hacks—should not be dismissed as setbacks, but rather, viewed as externalities that contribute to the broader learning and evolution of governance across DAOs. Future research could focus on developing frameworks for evaluating the success of these governance experiments and identifying best practices for iterative governance design.

Our case studies also illustrate how the boundaries between firms, markets, and networks are becoming increasingly blurred. While hybrid governance forms are often seen as residuals from alternative institutional forms, the blurriness of the boundaries in DAO evolution may necessitate a new theoretical framework that can account for these fluid organizational forms. This challenges us to reconsider fundamental assumptions in organizational theory and economics about the nature of the firm and the delineation of market boundaries. This also has implications for how we consider the regulatory and policy environment of DAOs.

While it is tempting to seek some general design principles for DAOs, there are few examples of mature ecosystems yet. Nobel Laureate Elinor Ostrom spent decades studying comparatively stable common pool resource systems to reveal design principles.[77] Her efforts identified a set of design principles that various scholars have attempted to apply to a blockchain-based context. But our analysis reveals two challenges for this approach to DAOs. First, if there are design principles that relate to DAO governance, those principles must be dynamic—that is, they must respond to the reality that DAOs evolve over time in response to their community needs. Second, it is simply too early to develop any robust design principles—even some of the most established DAOs have not yet settled into some steady decentralized state. This observation suggests that the study of DAOs may require a fundamental shift in how we approach institutional analysis, moving from a search for stable principles to an understanding of governance as a continuous, adaptive process.

Our theory of the selection value of DAOs as adaptive governance engines also has implications for policy responses to DAOs. Traditional legal frameworks assume stable organizational structures.[78] But our analysis reveals that DAOs adapt their governance mechanisms in different ways—responding to community needs, regulatory pressures, and market conditions. The iterative governance processes seen in DAOs like Optimism suggest legal frameworks might benefit from built-in adaptation mechanisms. Policymakers may need new tools to evaluate and regulate organizations that

[76] Ricardo Hausmann and Dani Rodrik, "Economic Development as Self-Discovery" (2003) 72 Journal of Development Economics 603.

[77] Elinor Ostrom, *Governing the Commons: The Evolution of Institutions for Collective Action* (CUP 1990).

[78] Aaron M Lane, Darcy WE Allen, and Chris Berg, "Towards Legal Recognition of Decentralised Autonomous Organisations" (2024) 52 Australian Business Law Review 96

are ongoing governance experiments. DAOs also blur the boundaries between firms, markets, and networks, challenging traditional legal distinctions that involve more binary classifications. Regulators should consider fostering environments that allow controlled experimentation with new governance models (eg regulatory sandboxes or safe harbor provisions) as well as mechanisms to deal with DAO adaptiveness.

PART III
LEGAL CONSIDERATIONS

8
DAOs in Financial Distress

Kara Bruce, Christopher K Odinet, and Andrea Tosato[*]

1. Introduction

Crypto evangelists herald decentralized autonomous organizations (DAOs) as the future of economic and social coordination.[1] DAOs are designed to function through automated decision-making, ostensibly without the centralized management that typifies traditional entity structures. The vision of DAOs as decentralized, democratic, community-driven, and future-oriented entities has sparked narratives about their potential to upend a host of domains. Enthusiasts state that DAOs "have the potential to fundamentally change the way we coordinate as a species,"[2] and policymaking in the US and beyond has moved in a DAO-friendly direction.

Yet, as DAOs rapidly scale up in their activities and expand their treasuries, we think a legal reckoning looms large on the horizon. What happens if insolvency, litigation threat, or another predicate of bankruptcy affects DAOs? Would DAOs turn to US bankruptcy law, a body of substantive and procedural rules for court-supervised debtor–creditor interactions built on compelled information disclosures and transparency? Could such a system realistically govern organizations characterized by decentralized and automated decision-making, organizations which primarily own digital assets, are controlled by pseudonymous crowds of token-holders, and establish amorphous creditor relationships?

[*] The authors thank the editors of this book for their invitation to contribute this chapter, as well as the participants of the Wharton-Harvard Insolvency & Restructuring Conference at the Harvard Law School, of the Foundations of Decentralized Organizations Author Workshop at the London School of Economics, and of the Corporate Restructuring and Insolvency Seminar, of the Faculty Colloquium at the Indiana University Kelley School of Business, of the ComplianceNET Conference at the Fordham University School of Law, and of Professor Edward Janger's "Debt in the Real World" Symposium at the Brooklyn Law School for their helpful comments and critiques. The authors also thank Zachary Brown, Matthew Norton, and Tripper Warlick (all Texas A&M Law Class of 2026) for their helpful editing and research assistance. All errors belong to the authors alone.

[1] eg David Cain, "DAOs: A New Paradigm for Collaboration and Governance" (*LinkedIn*, August 26, 2023) <http://www.linkedin.com/pulse/deciphering-dao-paradigm-navigating-new-frontier-structures-cain/> accessed August 30, 2024; KAF, "DAOs Will Change Everything: Web3, NFTs, Social Tokens, and the Metaverse" (*Medium*, January 5, 2022) <https://medium.com/bankless-dao/daos-will-change-everything-b955588eeedc> accessed August 30, 2024; Polygon Labs, "Why DAOs Will Change Social Media as We Know It" (*Polygon*, April 18, 2022) <https://polygon.technology/blog/why-daos-will-change-social-media-as-we-know-it> accessed August 30, 2024.

[2] Kain Warwick and others, "How DAOs Will Change Everything" (*Bankless Youtube Channel*, August 18, 2021) <https://www.youtube.com/watch?v=dZ4o6wma4js> accessed September 2, 2024.

Lest one be skeptical, the question of DAO bankruptcy is not merely theoretical. First, the bankruptcy filings of crypto giant FTX, as well as Blockfi, Celsius, Voyager, and several others,[3] show that crypto entities may turn to bankruptcy as a forum to gain control in the wake of sharp market downturns, poor strategic decisions, and fraud.

Second, bankruptcy has been a notorious refuge for companies facing sprawling litigation or mass tort judgments, and we should expect that DAOs facing legal liability might follow suit. Indeed, as of this writing, one DAO has filed for bankruptcy under those circumstances.[4] In mid-June 2024, Hector Enterprise Inc. entered into receivership in the Virgin Islands and its receivers filed an ancillary Chapter 15 proceeding for its affiliated DAO in bankruptcy court in New Jersey.[5]

Third, the *threat* of bankruptcy can be a powerful negotiating tool, even if no bankruptcy case is ever filed. As we discuss in these pages, both creditors and DAO members may find involuntary bankruptcy a lever to usurp control over existing DAO governance structures.

Yet, despite the attractiveness of bankruptcy's restructuring tools, the avant garde tenets of decentralized and autonomous governance that permeate DAOs are in tension with bankruptcy's centralized, court-supervised processes. This chapter confronts that tension. We contribute to the emerging body of scholarship on DAOs by undertaking the first focused analysis of their potential insolvency and interaction with American bankruptcy law.[6]

Section 2 undertakes a structural analysis of DAOs, exploring their intellectual foundations and key organizational features through a bankruptcy-focused lens.[7] Section 3 unpacks the tensions between the blockchain-based, decentralized membership of DAOs on the one hand and the transparency and consolidation principles that undergird bankruptcy law on the other.[8] We ultimately conclude that those DAOs that fully embrace decentralization make poor candidates for the bankruptcy system but note that involuntary bankruptcy could be imposed upon the DAO by disgruntled stakeholders.[9] Finally, Section 4 recognizes bankruptcy's use for those organizations that adopt a more hybrid governance model—one that blends aspects of DAO's unique architecture with more traditional corporate structures.[10]

[3] For a discussion of the FTX and other crypto bankruptcies, Diane Lourdes Dick, Christopher K Odinet, and Andrea Tosato, "Debt Tokens" (2025) 173 University of Pennsylvania Law Review 1103; Kara Bruce, "Crypto Failure in the Shadows" (2024) 69 Villanova Law Review 127; also Diane Lourdes Dick and Christopher K Odinet, "The Questionable Virtues of Chapter 11 in the FTX Bankruptcy" (*CLS Blue Sky Blog*, December 7, 2022) <https://clsbluesky.law.columbia.edu/author/diane-lourdes-dick-and-christopher-k-odinet> accessed August 30, 2024; Diane Lourdes Dick and Christopher K Odinet, "The Public and the Private of the FTX Bankruptcy" (*Harvard Bankruptcy Roundtable*, January 31, 2023) <http://blogs.harvard.edu/bankruptcyroundtable/tag/diane-lourdes-dick> accessed August 30, 2024.

[4] Becky Yerak, "Crypto Collective Hector Files U.S. Bankruptcy to Stave Off Lawsuit" (*WSJ*, June 18, 2024) <http://www.wsj.com/articles/crypto-collective-hector-files-u-s-bankruptcy-to-stave-off-lawsuit-ce0f212f> accessed August 30, 2024.

[5] *Re Hector DAO* [2024] (Bankr DNJ, 17 June 2024) No 24-16067.

[6] This chapter summarizes and restates our analysis in Kara Bruce, Christopher K Odinet, and Andrea Tosato, "Bankrupt Crypto Organizations", North Carolina Law Review *forthcoming* 2025 (hereinafter *BCO*).

[7] Section 2.

[8] Section 3.

[9] Section 3.

[10] Section 4.

Examining bankruptcy law's application to DAOs is critical given the rapid scaling of blockchain-based financial activity. As decentralized models continue gaining traction, the fates of failed DAOs—and the losses absorbed by their members, participants, and creditors—may spur significant legal reckonings. Resolving these issues is imperative for developing appropriate policy responses and legal frameworks capable of governing the ever-evolving digital asset economy.

2. Intellectual Foundations, Corporate Form, Owners, Managers, and Creditors

This section lays the groundwork for our subsequent inquiry into DAOs in US bankruptcy. Here we examine the intellectual roots of these novel organizations and survey the current DAO landscape, studying the different economic activities of these organizations and their governance models. We touch on themes discussed elsewhere in this collection, including corporate form, ownership structure, management, asset holdings, and creditor relationships, with an insolvency-focused lens. This analysis reveals significant distinctions between DAOs and traditional organizations, with profound implications for bankruptcy.

2.1. Intellectual Foundations of DAOs

As noted elsewhere in this volume, the intellectual foundations of DAOs are diverse, extending beyond distributed ledger technology, Bitcoin, and Ethereum. They incorporate theories from various disciplines, including organization and corporate law theory, and draw their distinctive ethos from the cypherpunk movement and the concept of crypto anarchy.

Emerging in the late 1980s, cypherpunks advocated for individual freedom through digital encryption technology.[11] Their emphasis on building anonymous communication networks and markets resistant to government interference became a blueprint for decentralized coordination mechanisms.[12] Crypto anarchy, articulated by Timothy C May, envisioned a future where cryptography and digital communications would fundamentally alter governmental regulation, economic activity, and private interactions.[13] This vision of technological self-determination and resistance to centralized authority continues to resonate in many DAO communities, which use the

[11] Eric Hughes, "A Cypherpunk's Manifesto" (1993) <http://www.activism.net/cypherpunk/manifesto.html> accessed August 3, 2004.

[12] Gabriella E Coleman and Alex Golub, "Hacker Practice: Moral Genres and the Cultural Articulation of Liberalism" (2008) 8(3) Anthropological Theory 255.

[13] Timothy C May, "The Crypto Anarchist Manifesto" (1988) <https://groups.csail.mit.edu/mac/classes/6.805/articles/crypto/cypherpunks/may-crypto-manifesto.html > accessed September 2, 2024; Timothy C May, "The Cyphernomicon" (1994) <https://cdn.nakamotoinstitute.org/docs/cyphernomicon.txt> accessed September 2, 2024.

developments of distributed-ledger technology (DLT) and blockchain protocols to transform these theoretical constructs into algorithmic reality.[14]

2.2. Current Landscape and Definition

It is estimated that there are currently 20,000 DAOs in operation, with 3.2 million participants and total treasury assets over $20 billion.[15] DAOs pursue diverse economic activities, including decentralized finance (eg Uniswap for trading, Compound for lending), investment and asset management (eg Mantle, Olympus DAO), infrastructure development (eg ENS, Polkadot), digital art and entertainment (eg Decentraland, Axie Infinity), community initiatives (eg Friends With Benefits, VitaDAO), and media and education (eg Bankless DAO).[16]

The range of economic activities undertaken by DAOs is paralleled by their varied governance frameworks, spanning from direct democracy and delegated voting to multi-tiered decision-making processes. Organizational approaches also vary significantly, with some DAOs creating autonomous working groups or sub-DAOs, while others employ steward-led teams or elected councils.[17] Voting mechanisms also differ, including token-weighted voting, quadratic voting, conviction voting, and holographic consensus.[18] Some DAOs incorporate unique features like allowing dissenting members to exit with their assets or implementing time-locked escrow periods for tokens.[19]

The remarkable heterogeneity of DAOs stems from their unique nature as organizations shaped by code. The fusion of DLT networks, smart contracts, peer-to-peer communications, and digital assets offers an unprecedented level of organizational and operational flexibility. This technological malleability enables the creation of structures and processes that are either infeasible or impractical in traditional organizations relying on little or no automation. Moreover, it results in significant diversity among DAOs, fostering an ecosystem in which each entity can adopt a distinctive architecture and functionality tailored to its specific goals. Innovation and diversity are particularly pronounced regarding stakeholders' direct participation in management, and the allocation and distribution of resources. The diverse structures, governance models, and functions are the primary cause for the lack of a universally accepted definition for DAOs.

[14] Jaya Klara Brekke, "Hacker-engineers and Their Economies: The Political Economy of Decentralised Networks and 'Cryptoeconomics'" (2021) 26(4) New Political Economy 646.

[15] DeepDAO, "Organizations" <https://deepdao.io/organizations> accessed August 15, 2024; L Suss, "State of the DAOs #24: The DAO Landscape in 2023" (*Bankless*, January 11, 2023) <https://banklessdao.substack.com/p/state-of-the-daos-24-the-dao-landscape> accessed August 15, 2024.

[16] eg Uniswap <https://uniswap.org>; Compound <https://compound.finance>; Mantle <https://www.mantle.xyz>; ENS <https://ens.domains>; Decentraland <https://decentraland.org>; Friends With Benefits <https://www.fwb.help>; Bankless DAO <https://www.bankless.community> all accessed August 31, 2024.

[17] For an example of working groups or sub-DAOs for specific functions, Ethereum Name Service (ENS) <https://ens.domains> accessed August 15, 2024. For a DAO with steward-led teams, Gitcoin DAO <https://www.gitcoin.co> accessed August 15, 2024.

[18] Gitcoin, Crypto Unicorn DAO, Aragon, Hive, and DAOstack respectively.

[19] MolochDAO is an example of the former, and Curve DAO of the latter.

2.3. Key Organizational Factors

Much existing scholarship has examined DAOs by observing their technological, organizational, and economic components. We depart from this scholarship by adopting a novel analytical prism that focuses on attributes most relevant to bankruptcy:

2.3.1. Corporate form

A DAO's corporate form can impact bankruptcy eligibility, the allocation of liability between a DAO and its token-holders, and the distribution of decision-making authority in bankruptcy, affecting the decision to file a bankruptcy petition and permeating through every large and small decision that follows.

Initially viewed as a "new frontier" punctuated by unknowns,[20] the prevailing view is presently that, in theory, DAOs can adopt almost any of the existing corporate forms.[21] In practice, this choice of form tends to be influenced significantly by the views and ethos of the individuals involved in a particular project.

Some founders disregard legal considerations entirely, focusing solely on code deployment for their DAO. Despite vacuous claims of existing outside the law, these entities are inevitably classified under the residual corporate form applicable in the relevant jurisdiction.[22] In the US, this typically results in such DAOs being classified as a general partnership with unlimited liability for its participants.[23]

By contrast, other founders choose to engage with a formal legal framework, such as corporations and limited liability companies (LLCs). This approach offers benefits such as liability shields and clear legal standing, yet their structural and governance requirements may conflict with the ethos and ideals prevalent in this ecosystem.

As DAOs have risen in prominence, various middle-ground approaches have emerged.[24] Some DAOs, as exemplified by Uniswap, have adopted hybrid models combining a traditional LLC with an on-chain governance mechanism. Moreover, several jurisdictions have recently introduced novel corporate forms specifically designed for DAOs, offering limited liability, enabling governance through tokenized voting systems, and providing flexibility in organizational structure to accommodate the unique needs of these entities.[25]

[20] Seth Bannon, "The Tao of 'The DAO' or: How the Autonomous Corporation Is Already Here" (*TechCrunch*, May 16, 2016) <https://techcrunch.com/2016/05/16/the-tao-of-the-dao-or-how-the-autonomous-corporation-is-already-here/> accessed September 4, 2024; Christoph Jentzsch, "Decentralized Autonomous Organization to Automate Governance" (*Slock.it*, 2016) 1–2 <https://download.slock.it/public/DAO/WhitePaper.pdf> accessed September 4, 2024.

[21] Carla L Reyes, "If Rockefeller Were a Coder" (2019) 87 George Washington Law Review 373; Lynn M LoPucki, "Algorithmic Entities" (2018) 95 Washington University Law Reveiw 887.

[22] Robert D Snook, "The Liability of Dissolved Corporations Under CERCLA: The Importance of Being 'Dead and Buried'" (1992) 66 Connecticut Bar Journal 397, 418 (referencing the applicability to default business entity law in the absence of a formal corporate selection).

[23] NY Partnership Law § 26 (McKinney); *Sarcuni v bZx DAO*, 664 F Supp 3d 1100 (SD Cal 2023).

[24] Bruce, Odinet, and Tosato, *BCO* (n 6) 17–19 (discussing these developments).

[25] David M Grant, Eric M Kirby, and Steven Hawkins, "DAO L Survey Results" (2023) (unpublished survey, on file with authors); also Gail Weinstein, Steven Lofchie, and Jason Schwartz, "A Primer on DAOs" (*Harvard Law School Forum on Corporate Governance*, September 17, 2022) <https://corpgov.law.harvard.edu/2022/09/17/a-primer-on-daos/> accessed August 31, 2024.

2.3.2. Managers

Managers play a delicate role in bankruptcy. In Chapter 11 reorganizations, incumbent management typically remains in control as the "debtor-in-possession," tasked with developing and implementing a plan of reorganization.[26] In Chapter 7 liquidations, managers are less influential, as a trustee is appointed to wind down the business and distribute assets, but managers must nevertheless fulfill statutory duties and cooperate with the trustee.[27] As discussed below, the bankruptcy system contemplates that a debtor will have the capacity to make large and small corporate decisions to drive the case forward, the manpower to comply with bankruptcy's extensive disclosure requirements, and a human representative to appear on behalf of the debtor when required.

DAOs present a more varied managerial landscape than traditional organizations, with meaningful diversity stemming from the differing degrees of decentralization and automation implemented in decision-making and strategy execution. To illustrate this heterogeneity, we can use a 2x2 matrix (Figure 8.1), where the horizontal axis

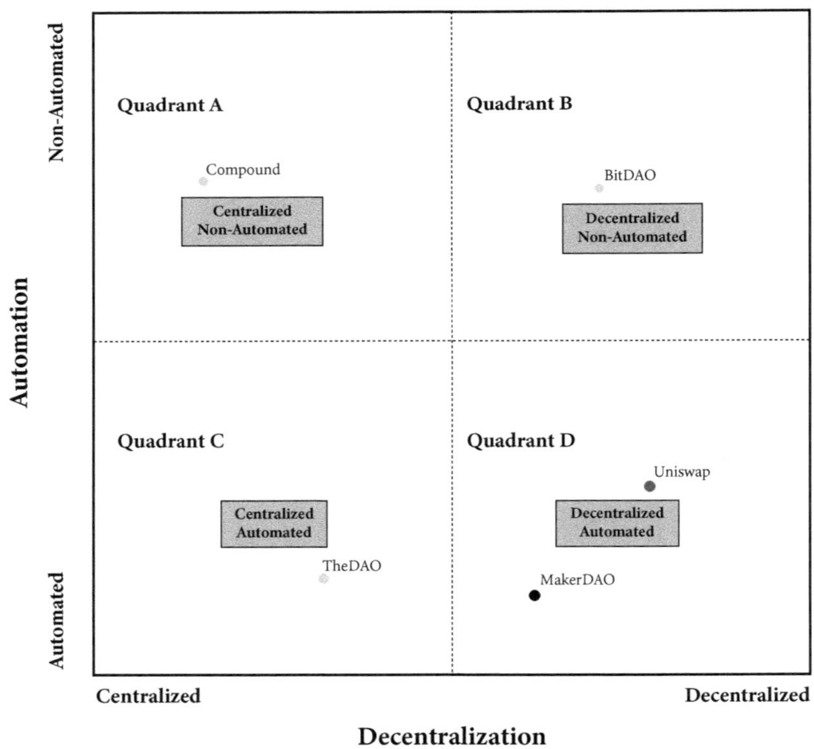

Figure 8.1. DAO Decentralization & Automation Management Matrix

[26] 11 USC s 1107(a) (2018).
[27] 11 USC s 701 (2018).

represents the spectrum from "decentralized" to "centralized," and the vertical axis depicts the range from "automated" to "non-automated."

In quadrant A (top-left) lie DAOs where a concentrated group, typically founders or early developers, make most decisions with limited code reliance. These organizations exhibit limited decentralization and automation, adopting a managerial structure not dissimilar to that of traditional corporate structures. For example, Compound had this type of managerial structure in its early days.[28] Quadrant B (top-right) includes DAOs with widely distributed decision-making power, typically among token-holders, who execute strategies through discretionary actions and limited reliance on code. These entities have decentralized management but limited automation, akin to partnerships, albeit with token-based management powers. BitDAO falls in this category.[29]

DAOs in Quadrant C (bottom-left) are characterized by highly automated, code-driven operations, but with strategic decisions controlled by a small group or foundation. While these entities are highly automated, they lack decentralization, resulting in a unique management structure without direct parallels in traditional organizations. For example, "The DAO" was highly automated, yet decision-making powers rested primarily with Slock.it. Quadrant D (bottom-right) contains DAOs where decision-making powers are distributed among many participants, and strategies are executed primarily via code. These entities are both highly decentralized and automated, differing significantly from conventional organizations. Arguably, Uniswap exemplifies this category, with its governance token-holders voting on protocol changes implemented through smart contracts.[30]

It should be noted that the management structure of a DAO is dynamic, not static. The software-centric nature of these entities allows for evolution over time. Many DAOs begin in Quadrant A (centralized and non-autonomous) and progressively attempt to shift toward Quadrant D (decentralized and autonomous). However, this trajectory is not unidirectional, and changes are neither fluid nor transparent. Some DAOs may adopt more centralized decision-making structures as they grow in complexity or need to delegate operational tasks, moving from Quadrant D toward A or C, leading to internal conflicts amongst participants. Governance purists argue that any form of centralization contradicts core DAO principles, viewing it as fundamentally undemocratic.[31] For example, Sushi DAO experienced periods of decentralization followed by re-centralization due to token accumulation by certain individuals.[32]

Although a DAO's management structure does not directly affect bankruptcy outcomes, we discuss below how the ethos surrounding governance can affect whether DAOs will voluntarily enter bankruptcy. This is because DAOs must adopt some

[28] Compound, "Governance" <https://compound.finance/governance> accessed September 2, 2024.

[29] BitDAO, "Governance" <https://docs.bitdao.io/litepaper-1/governance-overview> accessed September 1, 2024.

[30] Uniswap, "Governance" <https://docs.uniswap.org/protocol/concepts/governance/overview> accessed September 1, 2024; Alfred Lehar and Christine A Parlour, "Decentralized Exchange: The Uniswap Automated Market Maker" (2025) Journal of Finance 321-374 .

[31] Primavera de Filippi and others, "Blockchain as a Confidence Machine: The Problem of Trust & Challenges of Governance" (2020) 62 Technology in Society 101284.

[32] James Hunt, "Controversial sushi DAO treasury proposal passes signal vote' (*The Block*, April 10, 2024) <https://www.theblock.co/post/287588/sushi-dao-treasury-proposal-passes-signal-vote> accessed September 3, 2024.

measure of centralized control in order to interface with the bankruptcy process. Those entities in the lower levels of the matrix may find that such centralization, together with bankruptcy's procedural rigor and focus on transparency, to be too great of a sacrifice.

2.3.3. Assets

DAOs primarily hold digital assets in their treasuries, ranging from cryptocurrencies to stablecoins to non-fungible tokens (NFTs) to governance tokens.[33] This composition, however, creates unique legal and technological challenges during bankruptcy proceedings. Such legal complications begin with determining the governing law, as jurisdictions vary widely in their treatment of digital assets. While the bankruptcy estate is a federal concept, property interests are defined by non-bankruptcy law. Thus, determining the scope of a DAO's estate involves determining first the governing law, a matter that lacks an established conflict-of-laws framework, and second the nature of the DAO's rights in property.[34]

In the US, cryptocurrencies and NFTs are recognized as intangible personal property with clear transfer and ownership frameworks under the revised Uniform Commercial Code (UCC).[35] However, certain digital assets present uncertainties, such as stablecoins when it comes to redemption rights.[36] The same is true for tokenized assets (representing ownership of physical assets, intellectual property (IP), or artwork) due to the fact that these assets are governed by laws specific to the underlying assets.[37]

Regulatory oversight further complicates treasury asset-related issues. Agencies like the Securities and Exchange Commission (SEC) have intervened in crypto bankruptcies (Voyager, FTX) to challenge reorganization plans involving token repayments to creditors, arguing they constituted unauthorized distributions of securities.[38]

Technological vulnerabilities also pose risks.[39] Despite blockchain security, weaknesses in code have triggered bankruptcies (as with Hector DAO) and can ultimately disrupt insolvency processes. Human error and software bugs affecting self-custodied assets present additional risks, especially given DAOs' automated nature. And lastly, while DAOs may also hold conventional assets like IP rights, these assets typically constitute a lesser portion of DAO treasuries and do not present the unique legal and

[33] We explore issues related to the intersection of DAO treasuries and bankruptcy more fully in other work. Bruce, Odinet, and Tosato, *BCO* (n 6) 24–27; also Giuliano G Castellano and Andrea Tosato, "Commercial Law Intersections" (2021) 72 Hastings Law Journal 999.

[34] *Butner v United States*, 440 US 48, 55 (1979). It should be noted that there are unification efforts underway at The Hague Conference on Private International Law and at the International Institute for the Unification of Private Law (UNIDROIT), but they are still in their infancy.

[35] Andrea Tosato and Christopher K Odinet, "Digital Assets and the Property Question" (2026) 78(1) Florida Law Review (forthcoming) available at <https://papers.ssrn.com/sol3/papers.cfm?abstract_id=5151907> accessed July 14, 2025.

[36] Kara J Bruce, Christopher K Odinet, and Andrea Tosato, "The Private Law of Stablecoins" (2022) 54(4) Arizona State Law Journal 1073.

[37] Juliet M Moringiello and Christopher K Odinet, "The Property Law of Tokens" (2022) 74 Florida Law Review 607; R Wilson Freyermuth, Christopher K Odinet, and Andrea Tosato, "Crypto in Real Estate Finance" (2023) 75 Alabama Law Review 93; Christopher K Odinet and Andrea Tosato, "The Intersection of NFTs and Structured Finance" (2023) 103 Boston University Law Review 1005; Christopher K Odinet and Andrea Tosato, "Floating Liens Over Crypto-in-Commerce" (2023) 99 Indiana Law Journal 367.

[38] Bruce, Odinet, and Tosato, *BCO* (n 6) 26–27.

[39] ibid 27.

technological bankruptcy challenges associated with the digital assets that comprise the bulk of DAO holdings.[40]

2.3.4. Creditors

We now turn our attention to creditors, the key stakeholders in a bankruptcy case. In principle, any person, legal or natural, can be owed an obligation by a DAO for monetary debts or in-kind commitments. Under US bankruptcy law's expansive treatments of debt, any such persons will qualify as a "creditor" with a "claim" against a DAO's bankruptcy estate.[41] One of the most pronounced implications of this broad definition is that a DAO's token-holders, who one might assume have the status of "equity" in bankruptcy, might be classified instead as creditors in bankruptcy. This classification would have profound distributional effects in the bankruptcy case.

We can identify several likely types of creditors in a DAO's US bankruptcy case:

(1) *Token-holders:* As discussed elsewhere in this volume, DAOs typically raise capital by minting and offering tokens to the general public in exchange for various digital assets. These tokens are commonly presented as governance tokens, utility tokens, instruments granting pro rata access to profits, or a combination thereof. We have earlier noted evidence of such tokens being deemed functionally equivalent to partnership interests, thus representing an ownership stake in a DAO.[42] However, this is only one possible configuration for such token offerings in the eyes of the law. As we discuss extensively elsewhere, some tokens might qualify as debt instruments or present complex hybrid characteristics requiring more nuanced analysis.[43]

(2) *Lenders:* Currently, there is no evidence of traditional business lenders—such as banks, credit unions, business development companies (BDCs), private equity firms, venture capital funds, or other alternative lenders—extending financing to DAOs. However, nascent lending activities have emerged either between DAOs or from blockchain-focused businesses to DAOs. MolochDAO, for instance, has provided grants and investments to various Ethereum-based projects, occasionally employing loan-like structures.[44]

The default of such loans could present novel challenges in bankruptcy. These transactions often feature unconventional structures, involving tokens and smart contracts, which raise complex questions concerning the underlying obligations. For instance, if the loan is denominated in cryptocurrency, determining the precise value and legal nature of the claim in a bankruptcy proceeding could prove problematic. Moreover, if the loan is extended by another DAO, its behavior as a creditor might diverge significantly from that of traditional financiers due to their decentralized and autonomous decision-making processes. Conventional negotiations and restructuring discussions might be impeded,

[40] ibid.

[41] H R Rep No 95–595, 95th Cong, 1st Sess 309 (1977); S Rep No 95–989, 95th Cong, 2d Sess 22 (1978).

[42] See section 2.3.4.

[43] Bruce, Odinet, and Tosato, *BCO* (n 6) 28–29.

[44] Liam Kelly, "Investment Sorcery: MetaCartel Launches DAO Venture Fund" (*Crypto Briefing*, December 17, 2019) <https://cryptobriefing.com/metacartel-launches-dao-based-venture-fund/> accessed May 14, 2025.

potentially complicating bankruptcy proceedings and creditor coordination in ways unforeseen in traditional financial contexts.

(3) *Trade creditors*: A third source of obligations for DAOs arises from their ordinary course of business activities. The diverse economic pursuits of these novel entities result in a correspondingly varied group of potential creditors. Most notably, DAOs often offer services to users in exchange for cryptocurrency payments.[45] Failure to fulfill these commitments could potentially lead to claims in bankruptcy.[46] Similarly, non-payment for professional services such as software development, accounting, and legal counsel could likewise result in claims.[47] Moreover, as DAOs extend their reach beyond distributed ledger technology networks into "real world," brick-and-mortar businesses, they are likely to incur obligations from trade suppliers.

(4) *Government creditors:* DAOs may also incur obligations to governmental entities. As their activities expand, they might become liable for taxes and other regulatory dues. Additionally, DAOs with IP assets may incur ongoing obligations. For example, MakerDAO, which has registered trademarks, will likely owe periodic renewal fees to various state and federal agencies to maintain its trademark protections.[48] These obligations can also include involuntary obligations owed to governmental entities for violations of regulatory requirements, such as US securities laws.

(5) *Tort claimants:* DAOs may engage in conduct giving rise to tortious, criminal, or other forms of liability, resulting in financial or performance obligations to injured parties or claimants. Evidence of such obligations impacting DAOs has already emerged. The *bZx* case, as discussed elsewhere (n 6), originated from a class action lawsuit filed by users against the DAO, alleging negligence following a series of hacks that led to substantial losses. A more recent illustration of how involuntary obligations can precipitate bankruptcy filings is the Hector DAO insolvency.[49] Hector DAO's receivership and subsequent Chapter 15 filing was triggered by a series of events, most notably a lawsuit brought by investors against the DAO. In this action, plaintiffs alleged, among other claims, that the DAO's managers were liable for breach of fiduciary duty and conversion.[50] Moreover, DAOs have faced enforcement actions from the SEC[51] and the

[45] For instance, RaidGuildDAO operates as a decentralized collective of Web3 product builders, offering development services to clients in exchange for cryptocurrency. "RaidGuild—Hire Web3 Talent" <https://www.raidguild.org/> accessed September 2, 2024.

[46] eg in both *In re bZx* and *Newton AC/DC Fund L P v Hector DAO*, Civil Action 24-722 (RK) (JBD) (DNJ February 13, 2024) the plaintiffs alleged that bZx and HectorDAO had breached their contractual obligations giving rise to damages claims.

[47] eg Jason Gottlieb, Daniel Isaacs, and Alexandra Wang, "How to Do Business as a DAO" (*CoinDesk*, October 20, 2021) <https://www.coindesk.com/policy/2021/10/20/how-to-do-business-as-a-dao> accessed May 14, 2025.

[48] MakerDAO, "The Maker Foundation Transfers Trademarks and Software IP to Independent Dai Foundation" (*MakerDAO Blog*, December 31, 2019) <https://web.archive.org/web/20241004032511/https:/blog.makerdao.com/the-maker-foundation-transfers-trademarks-and-software-ip-to-independent-dai-foundation/> accessed September 2, 2024.

[49] *Newton AC/DC Fund L P v Hector DAO*, Civil Action 24-722 (RK) (JBD) (DNJ, February 13, 2024).

[50] ibid.

[51] US Securities and Exchange Commission, "BarnBridge DAO Agrees to Stop Unregistered Offer and Sale of Structured Finance Crypto Product" (*SEC Press Release*, December 22, 2023) <https://www.sec.

Commodities Futures Trading Corporation.[52] These types of actions may give rise to claims in bankruptcy.

3. Liquidation and Bankruptcy of DAOs in Distress

DAOs that reach the end of their lifespan do not always need bankruptcy to wind up their affairs. If a DAO wishes only to distribute the treasury among token-holders and cease operations, the DAO's existing decision-making structures can likely facilitate that action.[53] As we explain below, however, bankruptcy may be attractive to DAOs that face insolvency, litigation threats, creditor disputes, or fraud.

3.1. Introduction to Bankruptcy Law

The US Bankruptcy Code offers a comprehensive process for addressing a debtor's financial distress either through liquidation[54] or reorganization.[55] A key benefit of bankruptcy is its collective and compulsory nature—it can bind *all* creditors in a single process.[56] From the moment of filing and until relief is granted, those creditors are prevented from acting in their individual self-interest. Most litigation is halted, and all must interface with the bankruptcy process.[57] This serves several goals: it facilitates equality in treatment between creditors, preserves the entity's value against a destructive race to the assets that might occur if all creditors are left to their own desires, and offers debtors the opportunity to attempt a reorganization that allows the company, in some respect, to continue as a going concern.

US bankruptcy law also offers a variety of tools for businesses to shed the financial burdens of their past operations and enhance the value of the bankruptcy estate.[58] An entity can use bankruptcy's debtor-friendly tools to adjust its obligations on outstanding contracts, assuming or assigning profitable contracts and rejecting unprofitable contracts.[59] Debtors can unwind certain pre-bankruptcy transfers and recover

gov/newsroom/press-releases/2023-258> accessed September 2, 2024 (describing settlement of charges brought by the SEC against a DAO called BarnBridge for the sale of securities).

[52] Statement of CFTC Division of Enforcement Director Ian McGinley on the Ooki DAO Litigation Victory, Commodity Futures Trading Commission (June 9, 2023) <https://www.cftc.gov/PressRoom/PressReleases/8715-23> accessed September 2, 2024.

[53] Bruce, Odinet, and Tosato, *BCO* (n 6) 34.

[54] A business's liquidation in bankruptcy can be achieved under both Chapter 11 or Chapter 7 of the Bankruptcy Code, and generally involves the selling of assets to satisfy creditors' claims. At the conclusion of the bankruptcy case, the debtor no longer exists.

[55] A business can use Chapter 11 of the Bankruptcy Code to reorganize, which can involve a standalone restructuring, sale of the company as a going concern, or a variety of other paths through distress.

[56] Charles Tabb, Kara Bruce, and Laura Coordes, *The Law of Bankruptcy* (6th edn, West 2024) sections 1.1, 1.2.

[57] Generally 11 USC s 362 (providing that the filing of a petition in bankruptcy operates as a stay of an expansive variety of collection activities).

[58] The filing of a bankruptcy case creates an estate that includes all of the debtor's property. 11 USC s 541 (describing the scope of property of the estate).

[59] 11 USC s 365 (governing the debtor's rights and obligations respecting executory contracts).

their value for the benefit of all creditors,[60] and can sell property of the estate free and clear of all liens.[61] As noted, bankruptcy has become an attractive venue for companies facing mass tort liabilities, as it allows even a solvent company to comprehensively address the claims of tort victims regardless of when these claims arise. Many of these features might be attractive to a DAO that seeks reorganization. But even where the DAO does not wish to reorganize, the bankruptcy process can achieve a liquidation that is more controlled than that available outside of bankruptcy.

While the novelty and heterogeneity of DAOs makes it difficult to conclusively predict how DAOs will enter bankruptcy, we think several scenarios are plausible:

First, as we have seen, decentralized finance is a volatile form of finance in which one entity's collapse can have a contagion effect on others. DAOs that engage in decentralized finance (DeFi) transactions may find themselves facing "bank-runs" similar to those faced by Celsius, Voyager, and FTX. Each of those entities chose US bankruptcy as the forum to gain control of the crisis, and DAOs in similar positions might follow suit.

Second, the bankruptcy filing of Hector DAO demonstrates that litigation threats can be a driving force of DAO bankruptcy. This case was preceded by market volatility, several hacks resulting in lost assets, and the collapse of the Terra UST stablecoin, followed by a liquidation process derailed by a further hack.[62] But the immediate predicate was that certain stakeholders filed a lawsuit in federal court in New Jersey accusing the DAO's managers of breach of contract, fiduciary duty failures, and conversion. Nine days later, Hector Enterprises entered receivership in the British Virgin Islands and, shortly thereafter, commenced its bankruptcy case.[63]As such, DAOs that receive a significant judgment or commit an act that exposes the DAO to a large number of individual lawsuits might join the ranks of Hector and other non-DAO defendants that have sought bankruptcy protection to address litigation or legal liability. Finally, a DAO's creditors or token-holders might place or threaten to place the DAO into bankruptcy involuntarily.

Given that many DAOs exist without a defined corporate form, a preliminary issue is whether DAOs are "persons" eligible to file for bankruptcy protection in the US.[64] As we discuss elsewhere in more depth, we believe it likely that courts will construe this term expansively and will not allow corporate form to present a barrier to bankruptcy relief.[65] But even if DAOs are eligible for bankruptcy, DAOs must recognize that bankruptcy requires significant procedural rigor, requiring a level of coordination and disclosure that may be in tension with the cypherpunk ideals and crypto-anarchic ethos on which DAOs were founded. In the subsections that follow, we highlight several pronounced tensions between DAOs and bankruptcy.

60 11 USC ss 544, 547, 548 (describing bankruptcy's avoidance powers).
61 11 USC 11 s 363(f).
62 ibid.
63 ibid; *Newton AC/DC Fund, L.P. v Hector DAO* et al [2024] US District Court for the District of New Jersey [2024] No 3:24-cv-00722.
64 11 USC para 109(a).
65 Bruce, Odinet, and Tosato, *BCO* (n 6) 37–39.

3.2. Governance and Decision-making

First, bankruptcy's robust and time-intensive procedures would strain most DAO's governance structures. By way of example, the first step in commencing a bankruptcy case—filing a voluntary bankruptcy petition—is an act that must be properly authorized by the entity seeking bankruptcy protection.[66] From there, each petition, list, schedule, and statement must be verified and signed by an authorized representative of the debtor under penalty of perjury.[67] And, shortly after filing, "the debtor" is required to appear at a meeting of creditors and submit to examination under oath.[68] The court may designate a representative with control of the entity to appear on behalf of the debtor and might require more than one person to appear.[69] All of these requirements mean that, at a minimum, a DAO seeking bankruptcy protection would need to designate a person or set of persons to act as a human representative of the organization in order to enter through the courthouse doors.

After a bankruptcy case is commenced, a variety of financial and operational decisions relating to the path of the bankruptcy case arise.[70] The norm in reorganization cases is for the debtor's current managers to operate the business as a "debtor in possession," or "DIP."[71] The DIP will make critical decisions about the pathway of the case and must also engage in the rigorous and detail-oriented work of assembling the massive amount of operational information required to satisfy bankruptcy's extensive disclosure requirements. To be sure, a third party is appointed as "trustee" to manage Chapter 7 cases and can be appointed in Chapter 11 in rare circumstances.[72] But even then, the debtor is not completely out of the picture. Rather, the debtor has a variety of statutory duties to perform, many of which relate to disclosure requirements, and the debtor likewise has a statutory obligation to cooperate with any trustee

[66] Whether a bankruptcy filing was authorized is a question of applicable non-bankruptcy (eg state corporate) law; eg *Franchise Servs of N Am v United States Trs (Re Franchise Servs of N Am)* 891 F3d 198 203 (5th Cir 2018) ("[T]he issue of corporate authority to file a bankruptcy petition is left to state law."). If a partnership enters bankruptcy without the consent of all general partners, courts will treat the filing as an involuntary bankruptcy petition. Notice must be sent to the partners who did not consent to the filing; eg *Re Beltway Law Group LLP* 514 BR 341, 344 (Bankruptcy Court for the District of DC 2014) ("Section 303(b)(3) allows a general partner (as opposed to a limited partner if the debtor is a limited partnership) to file an involuntary petition against the debtor.").

[67] Fed R Bankr P 1008; 28 USC s 1746.

[68] 11 USC ss 341, 343.

[69] Fed R Bankr P 9001(5) ("When any act is required by these rules to be performed by a debtor or when it is necessary to compel attendance of a debtor for examination and the debtor is not a natural person: (A) if the debtor is a corporation, 'debtor' includes, if designated by the court, any or all of its officers, members of its board of directors or trustees or of a similar controlling body, a controlling stockholder or member, or any other person in control; (B) if the debtor is a partnership, 'debtor' includes any or all of its general partners or, if designated by the court, any other person in control.").

[70] Chapter 11 debtors typically hire professionals, obtain financing, make decisions about treatment of executory contracts, and use or sell property outside of the ordinary course of business, all of which require entity decision-making and court approval. To conclude a successful Chapter 11 case, the debtor files a plan of reorganization and a detailed disclosure statement. Not only that, but other parties with an interest in the bankruptcy case, such as employees, creditors, or the bankruptcy watchdog, can file motions seeking relief that the debtor may wish to oppose.

[71] 11 USC ss 1106(a)(1), 704(a)(22).

[72] This most frequently occurs when a company enters liquidation-style bankruptcy under Chapter 7 but can also occur if the debtor's creditors file a successful motion to appoint a trustee in a Chapter 11 case; 11 USC s 1104.

or auditor appointed in the case.[73] All of this indicates that DAOs that seek bankruptcy relief would need some mechanism to facilitate the decision-making required by bankruptcy's procedural machinery, as well as the manpower to fulfill a debtor's duties.

Bankruptcy's extensive, nuanced, and ongoing procedural requirements would strain many DAOs' governance systems. Not only that, but the act of preparing a company for bankruptcy and navigating the critical early days of a bankruptcy case are often harried, time-intensive events. To the extent that DAOs' voting protocols have mandatory notice periods preceding a vote, these may make it difficult or impossible for DAO democracy to keep up with bankruptcy's timelines. Further, the sheer amount of paperwork required to interface with a bankruptcy process, particularly in reorganization cases, would likely strain even the most dedicated of a DAO's participants.

These tensions can be resolved if DAOs embrace pragmatic centralization. Indeed, it is likely that DAOs seeking bankruptcy protection would have to vest some degree of decision-making authority to determinate persons, creating a centralized management structure. We consider alternatives for imposing this structure elsewhere.[74] For this chapter, it is sufficient to emphasize that bankruptcy's centralized governance layers may be unpalatable, if not outright anathema, for DAOs that strongly embrace decentralized and automated decision-making.

3.3. Disclosure, Notice, and Service

Bankruptcy's disclosure norms present additional theoretical conflicts and practical conundrums. US bankruptcy law is a "fishbowl," premised on strong notions of information-sharing and disclosure.[75] Sharing information about the debtor's operations and descent into bankruptcy "enables the parties to detect misbehavior that otherwise might have gone unnoticed" and "gives every constituency an opportunity to watch the firm during its transition period, and thus to reassess their relationship with the debtor."[76]

To that end, a debtor who files for bankruptcy protection must submit an extensive amount of information about the organization's financial health over the course of the bankruptcy case.[77] Disclosure is mandatory and disclosure requirements arise throughout the bankruptcy process.[78] Bankruptcy's disclosures are presumptively matters of public record, and exceptions that allow sealing require debtors to satisfy extraordinarily stringent standards.[79] Further, creditors or other interest holders can

[73] Generally 11 USC s 521 (outlining the debtor's duties in a bankruptcy case).
[74] Bruce, Odinet, and Tosato, *BCO* (n 6) 43.
[75] Alan S Trust, "Bankruptcy as a Fish Bowl of Disclosure" (2010) 29(5) American Bankruptcy Institute Journal 48.
[76] ibid.
[77] Generally Kara Bruce, "Crypto Failure in the Shadows" (forthcoming 2024) Villanova Law Review (discussing these disclosure requirements in more detail).
[78] ibid.
[79] ibid; also 11 USC s 107.

demand greater levels of transparency by seeking examination of the debtor[80] or appointing a trustee or examiner.[81]

Although DAOs embrace transparency within their protocol, the transparency demanded by the Bankruptcy Code may conflict with the strong principles of pseudonymity that undergird DAOs and other blockchain-based organizations. Consider that mandatory bankruptcy disclosures require the names and addresses of a DAO's members to be publicly listed on the debtor's schedules.[82] The debtor might be able to obtain relief that shields some of this information from public view to avoid identity theft, but this is a controversial practice that relies on a judge agreeing to waive bankruptcy's typical operational rules. A more pressing problem is that DAO membership is traditionally pseudonymous, and the debtor entity may have no way of satisfying this legal requirement.

The pseudonymity of DAO membership also presents significant due process concerns. Bankruptcy is a court-supervised process with significant distributive consequences for third parties. Stakeholders are entitled to receive notice regarding the activities occurring in the bankruptcy case. The Bankruptcy Rules generally contemplate that notice be made by mail, which may be infeasible if stakeholders cannot be identified. Similarly, litigation that occurs within the bankruptcy case requires service of process. Achieving service on DAO participants likewise presents a logistical challenge.[83]

3.4. Blockchain Immutability and Avoidance

Finally, the existence of avoidance actions in bankruptcy stands in theoretical tension with the immutability of blockchain-based transactions. A defining feature of the blockchain is that the system cannot be altered, corrupted, unwound, or revised. Conversely, the Bankruptcy Code bestows the trustee or DIP with significant power to unwind transactions that occurred before bankruptcy and claw back their value to the debtor's estate.[84] These powers include the powers to avoid preferences, transfers

[80] Fed R Bankr P 2004.

[81] ibid.

[82] Whether the DAO's members are classified as creditors or equity, the Bankruptcy Rules contemplate that the names and addresses of token-holders will be disclosed on the debtor's schedules and statements; eg Fed R Bankr P 1007(a)(3) (requiring the names and addresses of equity security holders of the debtor to be disclosed within 14 days of the date of filing the petition unless the court orders otherwise); Fed R Bankr P 1007(a)(1) (requiring the names and addresses of all creditors to be filed along with the bankruptcy petition).

[83] eg Order Concluding that Service has been Achieved, *CFTC v Ooki DAO*, No 22-cv-05416 (ND Cal December 20, 2022).

[84] We do not wish to overstate this clash of values. As other commentators have noted, the immutability of blockchain may be more "philosophical" than realistic. Carla L Reyes and others, "Panel i: Blockchain and the Law" (2019) 34 University of Illinois Chicago John Marshall Journal of Information Technology & Privacy Law 1, 16; also Raina S Haque and others, "Blockchain Development and Fiduciary Duty" (2019) 2 Stanford Journal of Blockchain Law & Policy 139, 164–65 (describing "hard forks" as "the ever-present escape valve" that allows the community to respond to an undesired change). Not only that, but the *Hector DAO* case, which we explore further in Section 4, demonstrates that members of an insolvent DAO might welcome a legal remedy that restores missing value to the estate, regardless of any philosophical tensions it produces.

immediately before bankruptcy that prefer certain creditors over others,[85] and fraudulent transfers, transfers with the intent or effect of hindering, delaying, or defrauding creditors.[86]

To the extent that the DAO's pre-bankruptcy activities involve the transfer of crypto-assets that meet the statutory requisites for avoidance, and no defenses or safe harbors exist, then the Bankruptcy Code will permit the avoidance of the transaction.[87] This process will not directly erase the original transaction from the blockchain, as distributed ledger technology (DLT) systems are fundamentally "add-only" ledgers whereby prior entries remain. Instead, it will require a transferee who does not have a defense or safe harbor to return the assets or value thereof to the estate. The economic equivalent of unwinding the prior transaction could then be achieved on-chain by executing a new transaction that is identical but opposite to the one being avoided. However, compelling such a corrective transaction in a DLT environment presents considerable practical difficulties.[88]

To be sure, application of the avoidance powers is a complicated undertaking, and there are many outstanding questions regarding how these powers and the related safe harbors and exceptions apply to transactions involving crypto-assets. Further, while the prospect of recovering assets might appeal to affected parties, the digital nature of a DAO's holdings can render the enforcement of avoidance actions particularly complex, potentially influencing stakeholders' decisions regarding the pursuit of a bankruptcy case.

4. Bankruptcy for DAOs?: Policy Implications and Concerns

The rise of DAOs has brought forth a unique set of challenges relating to bankruptcy structures. In this section, we seek to reconcile the conflicting principles by narrowing in on the most salient policy dimensions at play.

[85] 11 USC s 547(b). There are numerous defenses to preference liability, including a safe harbor specific to certain securities-related payments, which protects the broader securities markets from the effects of avoidance litigation. 11 USC s 546(e). This safe harbor, which also applies to constructively (but not actually) fraudulent transfers, could conceivably apply to certain DAO-related transfers.

[86] Actual fraudulent transfers are transfers made with the subjective intent to hinder, delay, or defraud creditors. Constructively fraudulent transfers do not require fraudulent intent but instead require a transfer for less than reasonably equivalent value combined with some evidence of insolvency. Tabb, Bruce, and Coordes (n 56) sections 6.32–6.33 (describing the requirements in more detail).

[87] For a thoughtful exploration of how transfer of DAO tokens might give rise to avoidance actions, Ryan Levin, "Bankrupting the Matrix DAOs and the Code" (2024) 40 Emory Bankruptcy Developments Journal 456, 482–85.

[88] 11 USC s 550. Dilip Kumar Patairya, "Can the Ethereum blockchain roll back transactions? Understanding the limits and risks" (*Cointelegraph*, February 28, 2025) <https://cointelegraph.com/explained/can-the-ethereum-blockchain-roll-back-transactions-understanding-the-limits-and-risks> accessed June 4, 2025 ("A rollback is theoretically possible but highly debatable, particularly on a large blockchain like Ethereum.... A rollback in blockchain can be achieved through a soft fork or hard fork, both of which involve modifying the blockchain's history.... In both cases, reversing transactions on such a significant ecosystem would require overwhelming consensus from the network participants, making it an extremely complex and controversial decision with potentially unexpected and equally calamitous fallouts.").

4.1. Choosing Between Purism and Pragmatism

The preceding sections highlighted a clash of values between DAOs and bankruptcy. The decision to embrace or reject bankruptcy protection is a sensitive one and requires commitment to the procedural requirements and transparency goals of bankruptcy. For the staunchest of DAO purists, the centralization and disclosure requirements that we discussed in Section 3 represent a significant compromise of the DAO core values that we discussed in Section 2. DAO mainstream principles center on anonymity and decentralized decision-making, which may be viewed as definitional and sacrosanct.

As discussed in Section 2, DAO values are grounded in a multifaceted intellectual foundation spanning organizational theory on decentralized structures, corporate law scholarship examining algorithmic control and corporate personhood, and cypherpunk ideologies promoting digital freedom and resistance to centralized authority. In turn, blockchain technologies have provided the technical infrastructure to actualize these concepts, resulting in both anonymous, democratic, community-focused organizations and structures resembling traditional corporations. As DAOs increasingly operate within traditional economic frameworks, their stance on bankruptcy emerges as a critical crossroads—requiring careful balance between pragmatic recognition of bankruptcy's benefits on the one hand and fidelity to core DAO principles of decentralization, anonymity, and direct governance on the other. As such, certain DAOs may be unwilling to surrender even a modicum of these principles in exchange for the legal protections and benefits that bankruptcy furnishes.

Hector DAO, in contrast, chose pragmatism in filing for receivership and bankruptcy. Indeed, the receivers submitted statements in support of the Chapter 15 case that emphasized as *benefits* some of the very attributes of bankruptcy that conflict with core DAO principles. First, a significant driver of the Chapter 15 filing was to prevent litigation from duplicating the efforts of the receivers and distracting from the receivership's goals.[89] Put another way, the receivers sought to centralize the legal fallout from Hector's collapse in a single forum. Another driver of the Chapter 15 filing was, surprisingly, bankruptcy's disclosure regime. The receivers sought to harness the power of bankruptcy's disclosures to uncover information relating to assets lost in the hacks preceding the bankruptcy filing.

It is essential, however, to recognize one important feature of Hector DAO that no doubt facilitated this choice: Hector DAO was able to make the decision to file for bankruptcy protection in large part because it had a centralized management structure that had the authority to place Hector's affiliated corporation into receivership, followed by receivers who had the authority to place the DAO into bankruptcy. A DAO with a large and dispersed management structure would likely struggle much more with the balance of pragmatic compromise and ideals.

[89] *In re Hector DAO*, Case No: 24-16067, Bankruptcy Court for the District of New Jersey (June 17, 2024) [Doc No 3].

4.2. Increased Commercial Complexity and Bankruptcy's Appeal

As DAOs evolve in terms of the scope of their activities and particularly if they begin to interact with traditional business structures in the real economy of goods and services, the appeal of bankruptcy protection may become more compelling. As DAOs mature and their operational complexities develop, these organizations may find themselves grappling with a wider array of creditors than they have in the past. This may include not only the DAO's users who may have interacted with the organization for purposes of trading or lending digital assets as part of DeFi transactions, but also as traditional lenders, suppliers, employees, tort victims, and regulatory creditors. In these scenarios, the benefits of bankruptcy—such as debt restructuring, avoidance, and the automatic stay—will more likely outweigh the perceived costs of compromising core DAO principles.

So, too, the specter of litigation can drive bankruptcy filings, as the Hector DAO's bankruptcy filing makes clear. We can expect that other DAOs facing similar litigation pressure will likewise find their way into bankruptcy.

4.3. The Threat of Involuntary Bankruptcy

There is also the chance that a DAO may find itself in bankruptcy, whether it desires to be or not. This is due to the threat of involuntary bankruptcy, which can be initiated by disgruntled creditors.[90] What is more, if a DAO is characterized as a general partnership, then fewer than all of the partners can initiate an involuntary bankruptcy case against the partnership. This means that a subset of disgruntled DAO token-holders could use either the machinery of bankruptcy or the threat of bankruptcy to drive outcomes involving the DAO.

An involuntary bankruptcy case can be commenced under Chapter 7 or 11 of the Bankruptcy Code, and can be filed by either a group of entities holding non-contingent, non-disputed claims exceeding statutory amounts,[91] or if the debtor is a partnership, by fewer than all of the general partners.[92] If the involuntary petition is not controverted in a timely manner, than the court will issue an order of relief that formally commences the bankruptcy case. Representatives of the debtor or other general partners of a partnership debtor can, however, contest the involuntary bankruptcy by filing an answer to the involuntary petition.[93] In that case, the court will enter an order of relief only if the debtor is generally not paying its debts as they become due, unless those debts are subject to a bona fide dispute as to liability or amount; or if, within 120 days before the petition date, a custodian was appointed.[94]

With this framework in mind, we can imagine a situation whereby a DAO's creditors can use bankruptcy to prohibit an insolvent DAO from favoring its token-holders

[90] 11 USC s 303.

[91] 11 USC s 303(b)(1)–(2) contains details on the number of creditors and the aggregate amount of claims necessary to commence an involuntary petition.

[92] 11 USC s 303(b)(3).

[93] 11 USC s 303(d).

[94] 11 USC s 303(h).

over creditors, imposing bankruptcy's distribution framework on the DAO to enhance their recoveries. Not only that, but an involuntary bankruptcy case would require the DAO to comply with invasive disclosure and centralization requirements. In this way, the threat of involuntary bankruptcy could be a powerful lever to drive a DAO's decisions on ordering payments outside of bankruptcy.

It is also possible that a DAO could find itself with a subset of token-holders who are unsatisfied with the DAO's direction and who are concerned with the entity's continued solvency. It is common for DAO members to vote with their feet by "rage quitting"—that is, cashing in their stake in the DAO when the member is dissatisfied with the DAO's operations or the outcome of a vote.[95] These DAO members might find the threat of involuntary bankruptcy to be a powerful governance lever to drive outcomes, including preserving the DAO's assets, enjoining collection activities or litigation against the DAO, or even unwinding transfers that the token-holders believe have negatively affected the entity and are avoidable under applicable bankruptcy law.[96] In this respect, bankruptcy is a "nuclear" option that would immediately interrupt the DAO's activities with the procedural machinery described above.

But while token-holders might be drawn to this powerful lever, they must be aware of the significant repercussions for filing an involuntary petition without sufficient basis. If an involuntary petition is filed and answered, the court will permit the case to move forward only if the court finds that the debtor is generally not paying its debts as they become due or a custodian has been appointed. If the court dismisses the petition, the petitioners may be responsible for the debtor's costs and attorneys' fees. And any petitioner that is found to have filed the involuntary petition in bad faith can be liable for damages proximately caused by the filing, as well as punitive damages. These powerful disincentives mean that it is unlikely for DAO members to commence involuntary bankruptcy cases absent a valid economic basis for the filing.

4.4. Bankruptcy Courts as DAO's Court of First Impression

If a DAO chooses the path of bankruptcy, the Bankruptcy Code will demand judicial resolution of key interpretive questions surrounding the nature of DAOs. The bankruptcy process requires a comprehensive understanding of the scope of the DAO's estate, the number and nature of claims and interests in the estate's assets, and how the DAO's assets should be characterized and valued. The possibility of joint and several liability between a DAO and its members raises additional questions, including whether a DAO's bankruptcy filing can halt litigation against non-debtor members, the extent to which a plan can release non-debtor members from liability, and the extent to which fraudulent transfer and preference liability can attach to membership machinations that occur before bankruptcy. Classification of the DAO's digital assets as currency, commodities, or securities will have a significant effect on the

[95] Osato Avan-Nomayo, "Why 'rage quitting' is a growing DeFi trend that's upending DAOs" (*DL News*, September 13, 2023) <http://www.dlnews.com/articles/defi/what-is-rage-quitting-and-why-has-it-become-so-popular/> accessed September 1, 2024.

[96] 11 U S C §§ 362 (automatic stay), 544 (avoidance), 548 (fraudulent conveyances).

applicability of various Code provisions, most notably the safe harbors from avoidance liability.

As we have seen in the bankruptcy cases of other blockchain-based organizations, bankruptcy courts have been a primary source of decisional law, providing an analytical framework for how the legal system as a whole will conceive of and respond to these organizations. Consequently, if DAO bankruptcies begin to be filed in greater numbers, bankruptcy courts might again become a significant driver of precedent.

5. Conclusion

As DAOs continue to grow in number, size, and complexity, the potential for financial distress becomes an increasingly pressing concern. This chapter has explored the tensions between the decentralized ethos of DAOs and the centralized, court-supervised processes of traditional bankruptcy law. Our analysis reveals that while fully decentralized DAOs may struggle to align with existing bankruptcy frameworks, hybrid models could potentially benefit from bankruptcy protection. Elsewhere, we explore these issues in more detail, and also consider the extent to which blockchain-based restructuring regimes could offer a workable alternative to bankruptcy.[97] As the digital asset economy evolves, so too must those who create and champion DAOs, as the future of insolvency resolution for these organizations may require innovative solutions that bridge the gap between blockchain-based governance and traditional legal structures.

[97] Bruce, Odinet, and Tosato, BCO (n 6) 50–60; Kara Bruce, Christopher K Odinet, and Andrea Tosato, "Decentralizing Bankruptcy: Insolvency in Web 3" (2024) 44 Bankruptcy Law Letter 11.

9
Choice of Court Agreements in Disputes Involving DAOs

Florence Guillaume

1. Addressing Disputes Involving a DAO

While decentralized autonomous organizations (DAOs) could, in theory, exist solely within the Web3 ecosystem, unbound by state laws and governed purely by code and crypto-economic principles, the reality is far more intricate. Every DAO is anchored to real-world individuals—founders, financiers, members, developers, and others with financial or contractual stakes—who operate outside the digital realm and hold legitimate claims and expectations. Thus, while DAOs thrive within the Web3 ecosystem, they inevitably intersect with legal frameworks that shape their relationships with these real-world individuals. Often, these intersections surface when disputes arise—whether over governance issues, hacks, or contractual breaches—compelling DAOs to engage with the legal systems of specific states.

Internal disputes within a DAO—such as conflicts about the governing rules or disagreements about how to reconcile its activities with the DAO's core values—can arise just as they do in any other organization. They cannot be entirely eliminated, even though the architecture of smart contracts can be designed to reduce their likelihood. Conflicts can negatively affect the functioning, reputation, and long-term viability of DAOs, as well as undermining trust and cooperation among their members. This is why DAOs require effective internal dispute resolution mechanisms to function properly, enhance collaboration among members, improve operational efficiency, and promote the stability of the organization. The choice of dispute resolution methods should be tailored to the specific structure and objectives of each DAO: there is no one-size-fits-all solution in this area. Moreover, it is crucial that these mechanisms remain aligned with the evolving aspirations of the DAO members over time. For this reason, dispute resolution mechanisms must be continuously adapted in order to keep pace with the DAO's ongoing development.

A DAO-specific moderation system—that is, a system for resolving disputes among members, according to rules established by the DAO community—can be set up within the DAO. A collaborative approach is typically favored for resolving disputes within DAOs, ensuring that decisions reflect the collective will of the community. Therefore, the most basic moderation system is member voting, which can be structured in various ways to ensure transparency, democracy, fairness, and legitimacy. Generally, any decision-making process within a DAO begins with initial discussions on a community forum. Proposals are then subject to a vote on platforms like Snapshot, following which—in case of approval—the proposal is implemented on-chain. A dispute resolution mechanism may incorporate algorithmic governance based on smart contracts, the use of oracles, and artificial intelligence (AI). The digitally-native architecture of DAOs allows for the relatively seamless integration of AI, opening up new possibilities,[1] particularly for resolving disputes among DAO members. But the implementation of internal dispute resolution mechanisms raises primarily technological questions which fall outside the scope of our research.[2]

In this chapter, we will focus on the resolution of civil or commercial disputes involving a DAO. Such disputes may arise among the members of a DAO, between the DAO and its members, as well as with third parties.[3] The matter may be submitted to a state court or to a private dispute resolution mechanism such as arbitration or mediation. We will address here solely cases where dispute resolution is entrusted to a state court, specifically when jurisdiction arises from a choice of court agreement.

We will begin the analysis by outlining the issues which arise when determining the jurisdiction of state courts in relation to disputes involving DAOs (Section 2). We will then examine in detail how to assess the validity and effect of a choice of court agreement under the main international and European instruments which establish legal frameworks for ensuring the effectiveness of choice of court agreements in civil and commercial matters (Section 3). This will lead us to explore the legal implications of a choice of court agreement in disputes involving a DAO, with an analysis of its impact on the DAO, its members, and third parties (Section 4). We will conclude with a few final remarks (Section 5).

2. Establishing Jurisdiction for Disputes Involving a DAO

When a DAO is involved in a dispute which must be decided by state courts, the unique nature of the DAO raises several legal issues. As a digital entity created without reliance on traditional legal frameworks, a DAO's legal status is uncertain and will vary according to the applicable legal system. Even the classification of DAOs remains unclear, fluctuating between the realms of contract law and corporate law.[4] In our

[1] Ori Shimony, "AI-Driven DAOs" in Florence Guillaume and Sven Riva (eds), *Decentralized Autonomous Organizations in the Legal Landscape: From Decentralized Governance To Legal Frontiers* (Edward Elgar 2025) 348.

[2] eg William George, "Kleros and UMA: A comparison of Schelling-point based blockchain oracles" (June 29, 2022) <https://blog.kleros.io/kleros-and-uma-a-comparison-of-schelling-point-based-blockchain-oracles> accessed October 10, 2024; Amy J Schmitz and Colin Rule, "Online Dispute Resolution for Smart Contracts" (2019) Journal of Dispute Resolution 103.

[3] Florence Guillaume, "Decentralized Autonomous Organizations (DAOs) Before State Courts: How Can Private International Law Keep up with Global Digital Entities?" in Madalena Perestrelo de Oliveira and António Garcia Rolo (eds), *Decentralized Autonomous Organization (DAO) Regulation: Principles and Perspectives for the Future* (Mohr Siebeck 2024) 135; Florence Guillaume and Sven Riva, "Blockchain Dispute Resolution for Decentralized Autonomous Organizations: The Rise of Decentralized Autonomous Justice" in Andrea Bonomi, Matthias Lehmann, and Shaheeza Lalani (eds), *Blockchain and Private International Law* (Brill 2023) 549.

[4] Guillaume, "Decentralized Autonomous Organizations (DAOs) Before State Courts" (n 3) 141–48; also Michael Schillig, "DAOs and the History of Corporate Law" in Kevin Werbach, Eva Micheler, and Bianca Kremer (eds), *Foundations of Decentralized Organizations: Blockchain and the Future of Corporate Law* (OUP 2026).

view, DAOs can be regarded as social organizations and, at least by analogy, the rules governing companies should apply to them. However, this analogy does not resolve all of the legal issues that arise in connection with these blockchain-based entities. In particular, the question of a DAO's capacity to sue or be sued in state courts is complex and must be addressed prior to the filing of an action on behalf of, or against, a DAO. We will briefly revisit this issue by examining the characterization of DAOs as social organizations (Section 2.1.).

We will then outline the difficulties which can arise when determining the jurisdiction of state courts to adjudicate civil or commercial disputes involving DAOs. The jurisdiction of state courts must be based on valid grounds—namely, where there is a connection between the parties or the case and the forum. This raises sensitive issues when a DAO is involved, as the location of both the parties and the subject matter of the dispute is often difficult to determine. These questions will be briefly revisited in order to fully understand the impact of the international context in which DAOs operate when considering dispute resolution before state courts (Section 2.2.).

2.1. Characterization of DAOs as Social Organizations

DAOs are organizations rooted in blockchain technology that were initially designed by engineers to allow blockchain users to pool resources for the purpose of achieving a common goal. They have since become a cornerstone of the crypto economy. DAOs can be described as digital organizations governed by smart contracts on a blockchain, collectively owned and managed by their token-holding members, who form part of a community. Legal scholar Kevin Werbach was one of the first to define DAOs as "a new algorithmic organizational form."[5]

While it can be convenient to refer to DAOs as digital organizations, their nature is more complex, reflecting a blend of various organizational structures—such as corporations, associations, and foundations—operating through smart contracts and blockchain technology.[6] The variety of DAOs makes it impossible to create an exhaustive list of the purposes they can serve. Essentially, DAOs represent all types of organizational structures typically found in national legal systems, transposed into the digital realm without traditional legal constraints.[7]

[5] Kevin Werbach, *The Blockchain and the New Architecture of Trust* (MIT Press 2018) 110; Daniela Gandorfer and Eva Micheler, "DAOs: The Theory of the Firm and Ostromian Perspectives" in Kevin Werbach, Eva Micheler, and Bianca Kremer (eds), *Foundations of Decentralized Organizations: Blockchain and the Future of Corporate Law* (OUP 2026).

[6] For more on the concept of a DAO, with an analysis of its evolution, core components, and various interpretations, Florence Guillaume, "Notion of DAO: Transforming Digital Code into a Legal Entity" in Florence Guillaume and Sven Riva (eds), *Decentralized Autonomous Organizations in the Legal Landscape: From Decentralized Governance to Legal Frontiers* (Edward Elgar 2025) 20, 23–29.

[7] Guillaume, "Notion of DAO" (n 6) 27. Same opinion: Joshua Tan and others, "Open Problems in DAOs" (October 29, 2023, version 1) arXiv:2310.19201, 6 <https://arxiv.org/abs/2310.19201> accessed October 10, 2024; also Adam Miller and Leo Henkels, "The Future of Human Organization and Solving the Legal Entity Problem for Decentralized Autonomous Organizations (DAOs)" in Madalena Perestrelo de Oliveira and António Garcia Rolo (eds), *Decentralized Autonomous Organizations (DAOs) in Various Jurisdictions: from Old Rules to Innovative Approaches* (AAFDL Editora 2025) 135, 137; Schillig (n 4).

This makes them difficult to classify into a specific form or even a category of legal entity.[8]

A DAO is more than just a network of smart contracts[9] as it embodies a collective interest that qualifies it as a social organization. In this context, the term "social organization" broadly refers to a structured group of individuals or entities that come together to pursue common goals—potentially with or without legal personality. The term does not refer to any specific type of legal entity and may encompass structures such as a partnership or a company, depending on the classification applicable under the relevant legal framework.

DAOs exemplify an evolution of the corporate concept toward a more modern organizational model with a typical flat hierarchy in which the community members not only possess ownership but also participate in the decision-making process.[10] This organizational evolution is also reflected in the term "DAO member," which may encompass various categories of persons depending on the DAO's governance design and structural features. It may include the DAO's founders, token-holders with governance or purely financial rights, as well as mere holders of its native tokens (although the latter are more commonly referred to as "DAO participants"). For the purposes of this chapter, the term "DAO members" refers to individuals or entities holding governance tokens—that is, tokens conferring voting rights or other forms of participation in the DAO's decision-making processes.

These social organizations are community-driven structures that coordinate human and financial resources through blockchain-based governance mechanisms to pursue common goals. To achieve these goals effectively, they operate with governance models that incentivize members to optimize both the DAO structure and token value, thereby promoting the overall growth of the community. This has led us to conclude that DAOs embody an "*animus communitatis*," reflecting the collective intent of DAO members to pool resources, goods, or activities in pursuit of a common goal.[11]

Scholars have nevertheless highlighted key differences between DAOs and traditional organizations, particularly in their structure and operation.[12] One of the main distinctions is that DAOs are native to the blockchain, meaning that, unlike traditional organizations, their existence is based on computer code rather than legal rules. As "creations of code," DAOs lack legal personality and therefore, also unlike traditional corporations, do not provide legal protection to their members.

[8] eg Sinclair Davidson, "The nature of the DAO" (March 2024) 12 <https://ssrn.com/abstract=4808295> accessed October 10, 2024; Florence Guillaume, "L'effet disruptif des smart contracts et des DAOs sur le droit international privé" in Alexandre Richa and Damiano Canapa (eds), *Droit et économie numérique* (Stämpfli 2021) 35, 46–47.

[9] The definition proposed by Werbach (n 5) 110: A DAO is "a business conceived as a nexus of contracts, built entirely in software."

[10] Florence Guillaume and Sven Riva, "The DAO: From the First Big Cryptocurrency Craze to a New Era of Legal Frameworks" in Florence Guillaume and Sven Riva (eds), *Decentralized Autonomous Organizations in the Legal Landscape: From Decentralized Governance to Legal Frontiers* (Edward Elgar 2025) 113, 125–27, with further references.

[11] Guillaume, "Notion of DAO" (n 6) 34.

[12] eg Aaron Wright, "The Rise of Decentralized Autonomous Organizations: Opportunities and Challenges" (2021) 4(2) Stanford Journal of Blockchain Law & Policy 152; Wulf A Kaal, "Blockchain-Based Corporate Governance" (2020) 4(1) Stanford Journal of Blockchain Law & Policy 3, 10–11.

Recognizing DAOs as entities with legal status distinct from their members requires granting them a specific legal status. To date, only a few states have taken this step by enacting DAO laws, including the US states of Vermont, Tennessee, Wyoming, Utah, and New Hampshire, as well as the Marshall Islands.[13] DAOs established under the laws of these states are hybrid entities whose structure and operation are defined not only by code but also by the law of the state of incorporation.[14] Thus, so-called "regulated DAOs" are companies established under the law chosen by their founders whose legal status is defined by the law of their state of incorporation.

In other states, the legal status of DAOs remains uncertain, depending not only on the applicable law—which itself hinges on the ability to anchor the DAO to the territory of a particular state—but also on which entity within that legal system is considered to be the most equivalent to the DAO in question, in light of its intrinsic characteristics.[15] The current trend in Western countries is to classify so-called "unregulated DAOs" as general partnerships or civil law partnerships,[16] which generally results in imposing joint and several liability on the DAO's members (or certain categories of members).[17] This indicates that DAOs are not recognized as a legal entity separate from their members.

It is also worth noting the particular case of where a DAO associates itself with a traditional company or legal entity by undergoing a "legal wrapping" process. This is feasible when a state's law is flexible enough to allow a DAO to use another company as a legal wrapper.[18] This arrangement allows DAOs to outsource administrative tasks to the legal entity, enabling it to enter into valid contracts with third parties, and to perform other functions that it would otherwise be unable to carry out in the physical world. A DAO with a legal wrapper gains legal recognition through this wrapper, rather than existing solely in an algorithmic form.[19]

In the context of this chapter, the focus is on the legal treatment of DAOs that resemble traditional types of organizational structures, setting aside "Big DAOs" such as Bitcoin and Ethereum.[20] The concept of DAOs is thus understood not as a blockchain network, but rather as an "organization deployed as smart contracts on top of an existing blockchain network."[21]

[13] Guillaume, "Notion of DAO" (n 6) 44.

[14] ibid 48–49.

[15] ibid 49–50.

[16] For a global overview, eg Florence Guillaume, "Adapting the Legal Landscape for DAOs" in Florence Guillaume and Sven Riva (eds), *Decentralized Autonomous Organizations (DAOs) in the Legal Landscape: From Decentralized Governance to Legal Frontiers* (Edward Elgar 2025) 2. For further references, Guillaume, "Notion of DAO" (n 6) fn 108; also Schillig (n 4).

[17] *Sarcuni v bZx DAO* (SD Cal, 27 March 2023, Case No 22-cv-618-LAB-DEB) <https://casetext.com/case/sarcuni-v-bzx-dao> accessed October 10, 2024; also Schillig (n 4).

[18] eg in Switzerland, DAOs are often associated with legal entities such as associations and foundations, Michael Kunz and Kiril Haslebacher, "Incorporating DAOs in Switzerland" in Florence Guillaume and Sven Riva (eds), *Decentralized Autonomous Organizations (DAOs) in the Legal Landscape: From Decentralized Governance to Legal Frontiers* (Edward Elgar 2025) 162.

[19] For an analysis of the different ways of adapting legal frameworks to the challenges of DAOs, Guillaume and Riva, "The DAO" (n 10) 132–40.

[20] For more on the concept of "Big DAOs," Guillaume, "Notion of DAO" (n 6) 29.

[21] In the words of Samer Hassan and Primavera de Filippi, "Decentralized Autonomous Organization" (2021) 10(2) Internet Policy Review 2, 3 <https://doi.org/10.14763/2021.2.1556> accessed October 10, 2024.

The question of the legal regime applicable to a DAO typically arises when the authorities of a state take an interest in the activities of the DAO or its members. This can happen, for instance, when a dispute involving a DAO is brought before a civil court. In such a situation, one of the key legal issues is whether the DAO has the capacity to sue or be sued.[22] The answer to this question depends on the legal framework within which it is considered. For example, in the *bZx* case,[23] which involved a damages claim following the hack of the code of the bZx DAO, a Californian court classified the DAO as a general partnership under California law. Based on this classification, the court determined that the DAO had the capacity to be sued in a Californian court. If the same question had been examined by a Swiss court, it is likely that they would have ruled that the bZx DAO was to be classified as a simple partnership and therefore would not have had the capacity to be sued before a Swiss court.[24]

This example underscores the notion that the plaintiff indirectly determines the legal framework applicable to a DAO by selecting the state in which to file the lawsuit. Given the absence of universally applicable conflict of jurisdiction rules to determine state court jurisdiction in civil or commercial matters, it is possible for proceedings to be initiated in multiple states. As a result, the plaintiff will choose the forum that promises the most favorable outcome, weighing the advantages and disadvantages of each available option.[25] The court in that state will determine whether a DAO has legal status and has the capacity to be sued by applying the rules of its own legal system. The disparities between different jurisdictions in how they approach this issue leads to significant legal uncertainty. Understanding these dynamics is crucial for DAO members and stakeholders, as the lack of a consistent legal regime across jurisdictions can affect their ability to engage in legal transactions and enforce their rights.

2.2. The Challenges of Locating the Jurisdiction for the Dispute

DAOs have the capacity to bring together a large number of members from all over the world. When they operate on public permissionless blockchains, DAOs are inherently international entities.[26] This is the reason why a dispute involving a DAO is, in most cases, international in nature.[27] Private international law rules must therefore be

[22] Guillaume, "Decentralized Autonomous Organizations (DAOs) Before State Courts" (n 3) 138–48.

[23] *Sarcuni v bZx DAO* (n 17).

[24] Guillaume and Riva, "Blockchain Dispute Resolution for Decentralized Autonomous Organizations" (n 3) 558–59.

[25] Guillaume, "Decentralized Autonomous Organizations (DAOs) Before State Courts" (n 3) 148–58. Apart from the capacity of a DAO to be sued, one must also consider the procedural difficulties associated in effecting service of process on a DAO (ibid 160–62), and the challenge of enforcing the judgment if the DAO does not voluntarily comply with any decision rendered against it (ibid 158–60); also Guillaume and Riva, "Blockchain Dispute Resolution for Decentralized Autonomous Organizations" (n 3) 588–90.

[26] Guillaume, "Decentralized Autonomous Organizations (DAOs) Before State Courts" (n 3) 141; Primavera de Filippi, Morshed Mannan, and Wessel Reijers, "The Alegality of Blockchain Technology" (2022) 41 Policy and Society 358, 365–66; Wright (n 12); Sven Riva, "Decentralized Autonomous Organizations (DAOs) in the Swiss Legal Order" (2019–2020) 21 Yearbook of Private International Law 601, 620.

[27] However, rare exceptions must be made where the situation can be classified as non-international.

applied in order to determine the appropriate jurisdiction in which the dispute can be brought before a civil court.[28]

Conflict of jurisdiction rules include connecting factors that help determine whether the parties or the subject matter of the dispute can be located within the territory of a state. A state will assert jurisdiction and offer the protection of its courts when there are sufficient connections between its territory and one of the parties or the subject matter of the dispute. This mechanism provides legal certainty because it gives parties advance knowledge of which state's courts may have jurisdiction in the event of a dispute, enabling them to anticipate how the case might be resolved. Once the jurisdiction of the courts has been established, the parties will have a clearer understanding of which law will be applied to resolve the case, thereby providing a certain degree of predictability with regard to the substantive outcome.

However, applying conflict of jurisdiction rules to disputes involving DAOs presents challenges due to the difficulty of using traditional connecting factors.[29] For example, if a DAO enters into a contractual relationship—implying that it has the legal capacity to assume rights and obligations in its own name—and then fails to properly perform the contract, how can the other party determine which state's forum corresponds to the domicile of the defendant? It would require the DAO's domicile to be identified or, by analogy with a company, its statutory seat, registered office, or place of administration. Similarly, if a dispute arises between DAO members concerning the governance of the DAO, how can the forum of the DAO's "seat" be determined? For a DAO that is not incorporated within any legal system, the absence of the traditional connecting factors of a statutory seat, registered office, or place of administration means that determining the appropriate jurisdiction on this basis leads to a dead end.

It is also challenging to apply a ground of jurisdiction based on the location of the subject matter of the dispute. For example, how can one determine the place of performance for a contractual obligation that a DAO must fulfill? When a DAO is not anchored in the real world—either through incorporation in a state whose laws allow the creation of DAOs or potentially through a legal wrapper—the place of performance of the DAO's obligation can generally only be located on-chain. One could think, for example, of the payment of a sum in cryptocurrency, but this is also true for any service that the DAO is required to perform. Locating the place of performance in the process of identifying a forum can therefore be very difficult, if not virtually impossible.

It is not only in contract law that applying connecting factors based on the location of the subject matter of the dispute presents challenges. In tort law, for example, the place of the tort is a commonly used connecting factor. How can the tort be precisely located when the dispute relates to the alleged negligence of the DAO in its handling

[28] Guillaume, "Decentralized Autonomous Organizations (DAOs) Before State Courts" (n 3) 148–58.

[29] For a detailed analysis, ibid; Guillaume and Riva, "Blockchain Dispute Resolution for Decentralized Autonomous Organizations" (n 3) 569–91.

of the security of its protocol?[30] The location of the tort can generally not be identified in the physical world but only within the virtual environment, thereby resulting in an infinite multiplication of forums. Indeed, a tort arising from any online activity is characterized by its ubiquitous nature, leading to considerable legal uncertainty.

These examples show that establishing sufficient connections between a DAO or between a case involving a DAO and the physical world is a complex process that often leads to situations in which state courts either lack jurisdiction or, alternatively, they have jurisdiction, but this is based on factors that are too unpredictable to ensure legal certainty.

To avoid the possibility of a denial of justice arising in cases where the application of objective connecting factors results in no state court having jurisdiction, the parties to a dispute in civil or commercial matters may choose a forum by agreement. A choice of court agreement offers the benefit of bypassing connecting factors that may be unsuitable in the context of disputes involving a DAO. This allows the selection of state courts that seem best equipped to handle such cases, such as a jurisdiction that is blockchain-friendly or particularly familiar with DAOs.[31] A choice of court agreement has binding legal effects not only on the parties—who must submit any potential disputes to the agreed court—but also on the courts themselves, which are generally obligated to accept jurisdiction and adjudicate the dispute. However, this binding effect assumes that the choice of court agreement meets the necessary conditions for validity.

3. Assessing the Validity and Effect of Choice of Court Agreements under International and European Legal Instruments

When the jurisdiction of a civil court is based on a choice of court agreement, the validity and effect of such an agreement must generally be assessed under private international law, given the typically international nature of disputes involving a DAO. It is not possible to examine, in this chapter, all state rules for assessing the validity of choice of court agreements in civil and commercial matters, nor the effects that such agreements have on state courts. We will therefore limit our analysis to the main international and European legal instruments—namely, the Hague Convention on choice of court agreements, the Lugano Convention, and the European Brussels I Regulation. We will begin by analyzing the validity requirements for choice of court agreements as defined by these instruments (Section 3.1.), followed by an examination of their effect on the courts (Section 3.2.).

[30] eg in a preliminary ruling in the *bZx DAO* case (n 17), a Californian court held that the plaintiffs failed to demonstrate that one of the defendants had sufficient contact with California for the court to exercise jurisdiction over him. Guillaume, "Decentralized Autonomous Organizations (DAOs) Before State Courts" (n 3) 156–58.

[31] Guillaume, "Decentralized Autonomous Organizations (DAOs) Before State Courts" (n 3) 146.

3.1. Validity Requirements of a Choice of Court Agreement under the Hague Convention, Lugano Convention, and Brussels I Regulation

The validity of a choice of court agreement is examined by the court before which an action is brought, either because it is the court designated in the choice of court agreement (the so-called "chosen court") or because it is another court (the so-called "derogated court"). If the court concludes that the choice of court agreement is valid, they must then assess the scope of the agreement to determine whether they have jurisdiction to decide the dispute to which the agreement applies, or whether they should suspend or dismiss the proceedings. For example, an exclusive choice of court agreement designates the courts of one state to the exclusion of any other courts, meaning that any court other than the chosen one shall decline to decide any dispute to which the choice of court agreement applies.

In an international context, the situation is even more complex because the different courts that may claim jurisdiction are located in different states. Judges assess the validity and scope of a choice of court agreement based on their national rules of private international law. As a result, different courts may reach different conclusions. One court may find the choice of court agreement valid and therefore binding, while another court in another state may determine that the clause is invalid and thus non-binding. This leads to a risk of conflicting decisions on the merits.

To avoid this unsatisfactory situation, some international instruments have unified the rules applicable to choice of court agreements between contracting states, notably the Hague Convention of 30 June 2005 on choice of court agreements, which currently includes 38 states, among which are the 27 European Union (EU) Member States.[32] This instrument is applied by the courts of contracting states when the parties have agreed to an exclusive choice of court agreement in favor of the courts of a contracting state (Arts 1 and 3).

On a smaller scale, but still relevant to the EU Member States, as well as Iceland, Norway, and Switzerland, the Lugano Convention of 30 October 2007 on jurisdiction and the recognition and enforcement of judgments in civil and commercial matters[33] also contains specific provisions on choice of court agreements. This convention has a material scope of application that is nearly identical to that of the Hague Convention.[34]

However, the two instruments differ in the definition of their personal scope of application. While both require that the chosen court be located in a contracting state, the Lugano Convention further requires that one of the parties be domiciled in a contracting state (Art 23 para 1). The courts of a contracting state of both instruments must apply the Lugano Convention when determining their jurisdiction based on a choice of court agreement in cases where at least one of the parties is domiciled in a

[32] Hague Conference on Private International Law, "Choice of Court Section" (*HCCH*) <https://www.hcch.net/en/instruments/conventions/specialised-sections/choice-of-court> accessed October 10, 2024.

[33] Swiss Federal Department of Justice and Police, "Lugano Convention 2007" (*Federal Office of Justice (FOJ)*, November 24, 2021) <https://www.bj.admin.ch/bj/en/home/wirtschaft/privatrecht/lugue-2007.html> accessed October 10, 2024.

[34] Both instruments apply "in civil and commercial matters." The material scope of application of the Hague Convention is defined in Art 2, while that of the Lugano Convention is set out in Art 1 paras 1 and 2.

state bound by this convention (Art 26 para 2 of the Hague Convention).[35] Conversely, when neither party is domiciled in a state bound by the Lugano Convention, the courts of a contracting state of both instruments must apply the Hague Convention when determining their jurisdiction under a choice of court agreement.

At the regional level, it is worth mentioning the Brussels I Regulation (EU) No 1215/2012 of 12 December 2012 on jurisdiction and the recognition and enforcement of judgments in civil and commercial matters (Brussels I Regulation)[36] which sets out rules on choice of court agreements, primarily applicable between EU Member States. This regulation has a material scope of application that is nearly identical to the two aforementioned conventions.[37] The courts of EU Member States apply the regulation to determine their jurisdiction based on a choice of court agreement "regardless of the parties' domicile" (Art 25 para 1). Courts of an EU Member State must apply the Brussels I Regulation when determining their jurisdiction based on a choice of court agreement in cases where at least one of the parties is domiciled in an EU Member State (Art 26 para 6 of the Hague Convention).[38]

It follows from the above that the Hague Convention applies, notably, when the parties are domiciled in two different states that are neither EU Member States nor contracting states of the Lugano Convention. The application of either of these instruments has implications for the validity of a choice of court agreement, as the conditions for validity set out in each are not identical.

The main differences lie in the formal requirements for validity. Under the Hague Convention, a choice of court agreement is valid if it is "concluded or documented (i) in writing, or (ii) by any other means of communication which renders information accessible so as to be usable for subsequent reference" (Art 3(c)). In contrast, according to the Lugano Convention, a choice of court agreement "shall be either: (a) in writing or evidenced in writing; or (b) in a form which accords with practices which the parties have established between themselves; or (c) in international trade or commerce, in a form which accords with a usage of which the parties are or ought to have been aware and which, in such trade or commerce, is widely known to, and regularly observed by, parties to contracts of the type involved in the particular trade or commerce concerned" (Art 23 para 1, third sentence). Additionally, "any communication by electronic means which provides a durable record of the agreement shall be equivalent to 'writing'" (Art 23 para 2). The wording of the Brussels I Regulation is identical to that of the Lugano Convention (Art 25 para 1, third sentence, and Art 25 para 2).

The formal requirements of these texts reflect an evolution in commercial practices that now incorporate the use of electronic means for data transmission or storage. The Hague Convention is more accommodating of this as it does not strictly require

[35] Trevor Hartley, *Choice-of-Court Agreements under the European and International Instruments* (OUP 2013) N 6.16 ff.

[36] European Parliament and Council Regulation (EU) 1215/2012 on jurisdiction and the recognition and enforcement of judgments in civil and commercial matters (recast) [2012] OJ L 351/ 1.

[37] Art 1 of the Brussels I Regulation.

[38] Trevor Hartley and Masato Dogauchi, *Convention of 30 June 2005 on Choice of Court Agreements—Explanatory Report* (Permanent Bureau of The Hague Conference 2005) N 292 ff; also Hartley (n 35) N 6.48 ff.

the text to be in written form or evidenced in writing. That said, despite the difference in wording, all three texts allow for the formal validity of a choice of court agreement in electronic form, regardless of how the agreement is stored, as long as it remains retrievable for subsequent use or reference.[39]

The other requirements for assessing the validity of a choice of court agreement set out by these three instruments are nearly identical: There must be an agreement between the parties, the agreement must designate the courts of a contracting state (an EU Member State, as regards the Brussels I Regulation), and the designation must be for the purpose of deciding disputes which have arisen or may arise in connection with a particular legal relationship. The Hague Convention requires also that the choice of court agreement must designate the courts of one contracting state (or one or more specific courts in one contracting state) as having exclusive jurisdiction (Art 3(a)), noting that in all three instruments, a choice of court agreement is presumed to be exclusive.[40]

3.2. Effect on the Courts of a Valid Choice of Court Agreement under the Hague Convention, Lugano Convention, and Brussels I Regulation

When the choice of court agreement is valid, the chosen court is required to hear the case. This rule applies under the Hague Convention and the Brussels I Regulation; it also applies under the Lugano Convention, provided that at least one of the parties is domiciled in a state bound by the convention.[41] The chosen court cannot decide to decline jurisdiction on the grounds that a court in another state would be a more appropriate forum than the chosen court (*forum non conveniens*).[42]

The choice of court agreement is also binding on courts other than the chosen court, resulting in any non-chosen court being precluded from hearing the case. This rule applies provided that: the choice of court agreement is exclusive; the claim falls within the scope of the choice of court agreement; and both the chosen court and the non-chosen court are in contracting states (Hague Convention and Lugano Convention) or EU Member States (Brussels I Regulation). The derogated court

[39] Under Art 3(c)(ii) of the Hague Convention, the agreement can be concluded or documented "by any other means of communication which renders information accessible so as to be usable for subsequent reference": a form of wording intended to clarify that electronic communications are covered. Hartley and Dogauchi (n 38) N 112; Fausto Pocar, *Convention on jurisdiction and the recognition and enforcement of judgments in civil and commercial matters, signed in Lugano on 30 October 2007—Explanatory report*, OJ C 319 /1 , N 109.

[40] Art 3(b) of the Hague Convention; Art 23 para 1, second sentence of the Lugano Convention; Art 25 para 1, second sentence of the Brussels I Regulation. However, a contracting state of the Hague Convention may declare that its courts will apply the convention not only in case of an exclusive choice of court agreement, but also where there is a non-exclusive choice of court agreement (Art 22 para 1). To date, Switzerland is the only state which has made such a declaration.

[41] Art 5 para 1 of the Hague Convention; Art 23 para 1, first sentence of the Lugano Convention; Art 25 para 1, first sentence of the Brussels I Regulation.

[42] This rule, which is expressly stated in Art 5 para 2 of the Hague Convention, applies in all three instruments.

cannot decide to hear the case on the grounds that it would be a more appropriate forum than the chosen court (*forum conveniens*).[43]

4. Evaluating the Validity of Choice of Court Agreements in Disputes Involving a DAO

The above considerations concerning the validity and effect of choice of court agreements will now be applied to cases where a choice of court agreement is concluded in the context of a contractual relationship. When a dispute involves a DAO, it is important to distinguish between a situation in which the contractual relationship binds only the DAO members (Section 4.1.) and one in which the contractual relationship involves the DAO and a third party (Section 4.2.). In the second scenario, the DAO itself may be a party to the contractual relationship if it has the capacity to acquire rights and obligations. In a third scenario of disputes involving a DAO, it is the legal relationship between the DAO and its members that is at stake (Section 4.3.). It is then worth examining whether the forum can be determined on the basis of a choice of court clause included in the DAO's "statutes."

4.1. Disputes Between DAO Members

According to our analysis, DAOs should, in principle, be classified as social organizations rather than contracts.[44] While this assertion allows us, as a general principle, to consider DAOs as entities distinct from their members, it does not provide a precise legal characterization of DAOs. Such a characterization can only be made by examining the features of the various types of legal entities recognized under national laws. However, if the analysis is limited to the realm of private international law for the purpose of assessing the validity of a choice of court agreement, it is sufficient to consider a DAO as a form of social organization, which may or may not have legal personality depending on the law applicable to it. For example, under Swiss private international law, the category of "companies" includes any social organization, which may encompass both "organized associations of persons" and "organized units of assets." A DAO will therefore be classified as a "company" under Swiss private international law, regardless of the specific type of legal entity it may resemble under substantive law.[45]

However, there may be exceptions where a DAO falls under a contractual classification, depending on the applicable legal framework.[46] This approach is even advocated by some legal scholars who classify DAOs as civil law partnerships of a contractual nature.[47] When a DAO is classified as a contract, it is not a separate entity from its

[43] Hartley (n 35) N 8.34. However, Art 6 of the Hague Convention lays down a number of exceptions to the obligation of the derogated court to decline jurisdiction.

[44] Section 2.1.

[45] Guillaume, "Decentralized Autonomous Organizations (DAOs) Before State Courts" (n 3) 141–45.

[46] ibid 145–48.

[47] The classification of a DAO as either a company or a contract depends on the characterization of the relationship between a company and its shareholders within the legal system of reference. In some legal

members, and the legal relationship among the DAO members is governed solely by contract law. A choice of court agreement can then be included in the partnership agreement.[48]

Such an agreement is binding on all partners, provided it is valid. To verify the validity of the choice of court agreement, it is first necessary to determine which rules should be applied to assess its validity. If the Hague Convention, Lugano Convention, or Brussels I Regulation applies, then the choice of court agreement must meet the validity conditions set out in that instrument.[49]

All three instruments allow for the validity of a choice of court agreement if: there is an agreement between the parties; the agreement designates the courts of a contracting state (or an EU Member State, in the case of the Brussels I Regulation); and the designation is for the purpose of deciding disputes that have arisen or may arise in connection with a specific legal relationship. These validity requirements do not pose any particular difficulties with regard to a choice of court clause included in a partnership agreement.

A formal validity issue could arise from the requirement of a written form when the partnership agreement is formalized through smart contracts rather than in writing. For instance, the choice of court agreement could be embedded in the code of a smart contract. In our view, such a forum selection clause should be considered valid if any of the instruments analyzed above apply. Indeed, all three instruments permit the formal validity of a choice of court agreement in electronic form. The Lugano Convention (Art 23 para 1(b)) and the Brussels I Regulation (Art 25 para 1(b)) even expressly recognize the formal validity of a choice of court agreement concluded "in a form which accords with practices which the parties have established between themselves." However, the clause must be drafted in a format that is understandable to all parties to the partnership agreement to ensure their consent. Furthermore, it must be accessible at all times. This last condition is clearly stated in the Hague Convention, whose Article 3(c) specifies that if the choice of court agreement is not in writing, then it must be "concluded or documented by any other means of communication which renders information accessible so as to be usable for subsequent reference." To meet the requirement of consent, the choice of court clause must be written in plain language where the partners do not have the technical expertise needed to interpret a smart contract.

If all the validity requirements for the choice of court agreement are met, the parties to the partnership agreement are bound, and must, in case of a dispute, bring any legal action arising from the agreement before the agreed court. It is important, however, to keep in mind that the court hearing the case may question the validity of the partnership agreement itself, for instance when it is based solely on smart contracts. Legal scholars are indeed divided on the issue of the legal effect of smart contracts.[50]

systems, this relationship is characterized as contractual, while in others, it is considered institutional. This conceptual divergence probably influences the classification of DAOs as advocated by legal scholars.

[48] Since the legal relationship between DAO founders before the DAO is formed is also contractual in nature, the same reasoning can be applied to this situation.

[49] Section 3.1.

[50] For a recent analysis under French law, Claire Leveneur, *Les smart contracts—Étude de droit des contrats à l'aune de la blockchain* (Dalloz 2024) 360–89.

However, the nullity of the partnership agreement would have no impact on the validity of the choice of court agreement. When a choice of court agreement is part of a contract, it must be treated as independent from the other terms of the contract. This means that the validity of the choice of court agreement cannot be challenged solely because the contract itself is invalid. This rule is explicitly provided for in each of the three instruments mentioned above.[51]

4.2. Disputes Between a DAO and a Third Party

In the scenario where there is a contract between a DAO and a third party, and it has been agreed that any dispute arising from this legal relationship will be submitted to a particular civil court, the question arises as to who is bound by the contract and, consequently, by the choice of court agreement.

This issue again turns on the legal characterization of the DAO and its capacity to enter into binding agreements. When a DAO is a party to a choice of court agreement, the first question that arises is whether it has the legal capacity to do so. As legal capacity falls outside the scope of the international and European instruments analyzed above,[52] it must be assessed independently. It follows that the court will apply the law designated by their own choice of law rules regarding capacity, regardless of whether it is the chosen court or the derogated court. Consequently, the question of a party's capacity to validly enter into a choice of court agreement may be assessed under different laws, depending on whether the issue is examined by the chosen court or the derogated court.

This matter is clearly addressed in the Brussels I Regulation which specifies that the chosen court is bound by the choice of court agreement "unless the agreement is null and void as to its substantive validity under the law of that Member State" (Art 25 para 1, first sentence). It follows that the chosen court will apply the law designated by its own choice of law rules regarding capacity. The same rule applies for the derogated court: it must also resolve the issue of legal capacity by applying the same law as the chosen court.[53]

A similar rule is found in the Hague Convention, which specifies that the chosen court is bound by the choice of court agreement "unless the agreement is null and void under the law of that state" (Art 5 para 1). Consequently, the chosen court must suspend or dismiss proceedings, particularly in cases where one of the parties lacks capacity under the law designated by its own choice of law rules regarding capacity. Similarly, a derogated court is not bound by a choice of court agreement if one of the

[51] Art 3(d) of the Hague Convention; Art 25 para 5 of the Brussels I Regulation. Even though this rule is not expressly stated in the Lugano Convention, it is undisputed that it also applies.

[52] For legal capacity of natural persons, Art 2 para 2(a) of the Hague Convention; Art 1 para 2(a) of the Lugano Convention; Art 1 para 2(a) of the Brussels I Regulation.

[53] This rule is not included in the Lugano Convention. The issue of legal capacity to conclude a choice of court agreement should therefore, in principle, be examined according to the law designated by the forum's conflict of law rules. This could lead to conflicting rulings on the validity of the choice of court agreement between contracting states when this issue is examined under different national laws by the chosen court or the derogated court. However, legal scholars suggest applying the same rule as in the Brussels I Regulation to avoid different outcomes. Hartley (n 35) N 7.113.

parties lacks capacity under the law designated by the choice of law rules of the state of the chosen court (Art 6(a)) or under their own choice of law rules (Art 6(b)).[54] The Hague Convention therefore requires the derogated court to assess the legal capacity to conclude a choice of court agreement not only under the law designated by its own conflict of law rules but also under the law designated by the conflict of law rules of the state of the chosen court.

It follows from the above that a DAO's legal capacity to enter into a binding choice of court agreement must be assessed under the law applicable to the DAO,[55] as determined by the conflict of law rules of the chosen court. However, if the question arises before the derogated court that is examining the validity and effect of the choice of court agreement pursuant to the Hague Convention, the DAO's legal capacity must also be assessed under the law designated by its own conflict of law rules. Once a court has been able to link a DAO to a particular state, it can then identify the form of legal institution within that state's legal system that is applicable to that DAO, in order to determine whether the latter has the legal capacity to enter into binding agreements. This assessment must be carried out on a case-by-case basis, with the following elements serving as guidance in the process.

When a court determines the law applicable to a DAO and then transposes the DAO into that legal system, it may, as we have seen,[56] conclude that the DAO qualifies as either a "regulated" or an "unregulated" DAO. In the latter case, the court must identify the legal institution under the applicable law that the DAO in question most closely resembles. The applicable legal regime will likely be that of general partnerships or civil law partnerships, meaning that the DAO generally does not have legal personality and lacks the capacity to enter into contracts. Consequently, only the DAO members—namely, those considered to be the partners in the general or civil law partnership—will assume the rights and obligations arising from the contract. The assessment of the validity of the choice of court agreement can then be conducted by applying the requirements set out in the applicable European or international instrument. In all cases, particular attention must be paid to whether the parties have indeed consented to the choice of court agreement, especially when it is embedded in computer code.[57]

However, in certain legal systems, the court may determine that the legal institution most closely resembling a DAO possesses legal personality or, at the very least, has the capacity to enter into contractual relations. For instance, under Swiss private international law, a DAO is highly likely to be classified as a company.[58] Accordingly, this classification may also apply when transposing the DAO into the Swiss legal order, potentially leading to the analogous application of the legal regime governing a type of company endowed with legal personality or with the capacity to act independently of its members.[59] But such a scenario is likely to remain exceptional in the case of unregulated DAOs.

[54] Hartley and Dogauchi (n 38) N 150.

[55] Guillaume, "Notion of DAO" (n 6) 42–47; Guillaume, "Decentralized Autonomous Organizations (DAOs) Before State Courts" (n 3) 138–48; Guillaume and Riva, "Blockchain Dispute Resolution for Decentralized Autonomous Organizations" (n 3) 557–69.

[56] Section 2.1.

[57] Section 3.1.

[58] Section 4.1.

[59] Guillaume, "Notion of DAO" (n 6) 47–51.

In the very specific case in which a DAO is associated with a legal entity, such as a Swiss association,[60] the DAO can enter into valid contracts with third parties, using the association as its representative in the physical world. However, in such a case, the DAO is a party to the contractual relationship "through" the legal wrapper, meaning that it is the association that is engaged in the contractual relationship. The exact scope of the choice of court agreement will then depend on the legal construction adopted through the use of a legal entity serving as a legal wrapper for the DAO.

In contrast, for regulated DAOs—those governed not only by computer code but also by the company law of the state in which they are incorporated—the question of whether the DAO has the legal capacity to enter into a binding choice of court agreement depends on whether its law of incorporation confers legal personality. For example, a DAO limited liability company (LLC) from Wyoming has legal personality and can acquire rights and obligations in its own name. In such a case, the choice of court agreement is legally binding on the DAO.

This analysis indicates that a choice of court agreement concluded with a DAO for adjudicating disputes arising from a contractual relationship between the DAO and a third party may, depending on the circumstances, be recognized as valid. The application of the European and international instruments discussed above may, however, face an additional difficulty in circumstances where it is conditional on the parties (or one of the parties) being domiciled within the territory of a state bound by the instrument.[61] To determine whether this condition is met, the domicile of the DAO's members or that of the DAO itself may be decisive, depending on how the DAO is legally characterized. The DAO's domicile would generally be deemed to be the place of its seat. This would again raise questions about the location of the statutory seat, registered office, or place of administration of the DAO, but this time with the aim of determining whether the Hague Convention, Lugano Convention, or Brussels I Regulation applies to the assessment of the validity of the choice of court agreement.

4.3. DAO-related Disputes

When the dispute concerns issues directly related to the DAO itself, such as its internal governance or the rights of its members, it is the legal relationship between the DAO and its members that is at stake. It is interesting to examine, for this particular type of DAO-related dispute, the scenario in which the choice of court agreement is included in the founding documents of the DAO. Assuming DAOs are classified as social organizations, an analogy can be drawn with the situation in which a choice of court clause is found in a company's articles of association or statutes.

In order to determine the validity of a choice of court clause included in the company's articles of association or statutes, the first legal issue to be examined is how to classify the relationship between the shareholders and the company, following its formation. The answer to this question depends on the applicable legal framework. In legal systems where this relationship is deemed to be contractual, a civil court may

[60] Section 2.1.
[61] Section 3.1.

recognize the existence of an agreement between the shareholders and the company with regard to the choice of forum. In contrast, meeting the requirement for a mutual agreement between the parties may be more challenging in jurisdictions where the relationship between the company and its shareholders is not deemed to be one that is contractual.

When a civil court applies an international legal instrument to assess the validity of a choice of court clause, the classification of the relationship between the company and its shareholders is generally determined on an autonomous basis within the legal framework of the convention. For example, when the Lugano Convention applies, the relationship between the company and its shareholders has, following a judgment by the Court of Justice of the European Union (CJEU) in the 1990s,[62] been deemed to be contractual in nature. In light of this characterization of the company–shareholder relationship, the CJEU extrapolated that when applying the Lugano Convention,[63] a choice of court clause included in a company's articles of association or statutes constitutes an agreement between the company and its shareholders. Since a company's articles of association or statutes must generally be formalized in writing—and in some cases even in the form of an official deed—the CJEU ruled that the inclusion of a choice of court clause in such a document will satisfy the requirement for it to be in written form.

However, the question arises as to whether a choice of court clause included in the company's articles of association or statutes binds shareholders who have not expressly consented to it. This is particularly relevant for shareholders who joined the company after its formation. The answer to this question depends on the applicable legal framework and can vary significantly from one legal system to another.

It can be argued that a choice of court clause contained in the statutes of a company binds all shareholders, including future ones. Indeed, any new shareholder has assented to the company's statutes, along with all the rights and obligations they entail, at the time of acquiring shares. This view helps to avoid creating different legal regimes among shareholders—an approach which could be particularly detrimental to a company with numerous shareholders spread across multiple countries. This trend can be illustrated by the decision referred to above, in which the CJEU ruled that a choice of court clause included in a company's statutes binds all shareholders. More precisely, "every shareholder is deemed to be aware of that clause and actually to consent to the assignment of jurisdiction for which it provides"—at least when the statutes are recorded in a public register or are lodged in a place to which the shareholders may have access.[64]

The Hague Convention does not explicitly address the validity of a choice of court clause included in a company's articles of association or statutes. The classification of such a clause as contractual—and therefore the possibility for recognizing an agreement between the company and its shareholders—will depend on the national legal system applied by the court tasked with examining the validity of the clause. For example, if a Swiss court is asked to address this issue under Swiss law, it is difficult

[62] CJEU, Case C-214/89 *Powell Duffryn plc v Wolfgang Petereit* [1992] ECR I-1745, ECLI:EU:C:1992:115.

[63] The analysis related to the Lugano Convention also applies to the Brussels I Regulation.

[64] *Powell Duffryn plc v Wolfgang Petereit* (n 62) [28].

to predict its response, as the matter is not clearly addressed by legislation, has not been definitively settled by case law, and remains highly controversial in Swiss legal doctrine.

In the author's opinion, this issue can be compared with the case of an arbitration clause being inserted into a company's statutes. A recent revision of Swiss law has clarified that an arbitration clause included in the statutes of a Swiss company limited by shares (*société anonyme; Aktiengesellschaft*) is valid by law and binding on all shareholders.[65] The company's entry in the corporate registry must indicate that the statutes contain an arbitration clause, ensuring that new shareholders are informed of its existence, consistent with the principles of disclosure underpinning corporate registration. By way of analogy, the inclusion of a choice of court clause in statutes which are registered in the corporate registry should be considered as binding on all shareholders under Swiss law. This view is especially true in light of the principle of good faith, according to which the shareholders could or should have known about the existence of the choice of court clause.[66]

In the author's view, the principles just discussed in the context of companies can be applied to the domain of DAOs. These principles apply without modification to regulated DAOs that are incorporated as companies in jurisdictions that allow it. They can also apply, with necessary adjustments, to unregulated DAOs. A choice of court clause included in the DAO's founding documents may be considered as binding for all DAO members in legal systems where DAOs qualify as social organizations, provided that such a clause is regarded as contractual in nature when inserted into a company's articles of association or statutes. However, this reasoning will often represent a broad interpretation of the existing legal system and, therefore, remains subject to uncertainty.

In any case, there must be an agreement between the DAO and its members in which a state is designated as the forum for its civil courts to deal with any disputes arising in connection with matters relating to the DAO. This mutual consent presumes that the DAO has the legal capacity to enter into binding agreements. Furthermore, assuming that all DAO members have consented—at least implicitly—to a choice of court clause situated in the DAO's founding documents, it remains to be seen whether such a clause could be considered valid. It is not possible to provide a general answer to this question, as it will depend on the applicable legal framework. Several basic principles can nevertheless be established to guide this analysis.

[65] Art 697*n* of the Swiss Code of Obligations states that "[t]he articles of association [of a company limited by shares] may provide that disputes under company law be adjudicated by an arbitral tribunal that has its seat in Switzerland. Unless the articles of association provide otherwise, the arbitration clause is binding on the company, the corporate bodies of the company, the members of the corporate bodies, and the shareholders." This provision also applies to a limited liability company (*société à responsabilité limitée; Gesellschaft mit beschränkter Haftung*) according to Art 797*a* of the Swiss Code of Obligations. When arbitration is international, "[t]he arbitration agreement must be made in writing or any other means of communication allowing it to be evidenced by text" (Art 178 para 1 of the Swiss Private International Law Act). Art 178 para 4 of the Swiss Private International Law Act specifies that this provision applies by analogy to "an arbitration clause in a unilateral transaction or in articles of association".

[66] In our opinion, any choice of court clause included in the statutes of a company governed by Swiss law, regardless of the form of the company, should be considered valid and binding on all shareholders if, according to the principle of good faith, they could or should have known about the existence of the choice of court clause.

The requirement of consent demands that the choice of court clause be written in plain language, ensuring that all DAO members are aware of its existence. This requirement is important because the rules governing a DAO are encoded in smart contracts deployed on a blockchain. These smart contracts serve as the founding documents, establishing the internal rules for the DAO's operation and governance, such as voting rights, voting procedures, and fund management. Given that data recorded on a public blockchain can be accessed by anyone, the deployment on the blockchain of a smart contract containing this core information on the DAO fulfills the objective of public disclosure underpinning the registration of a company's articles of association or statutes in a corporate registry, and so can be considered as its equivalent.[67] It is therefore crucial that DAO members without the technical expertise to interpret a smart contract are able to identify the presence of a choice of court clause. Furthermore, the requirement for it to be set out in writing may present difficulties when such a clause is embedded in a smart contract. We have seen in the Hague Convention, Lugano Convention, and Brussels I Regulation that the written form is broadly defined to include electronic formats,[68] but this rule does not apply in all national legal systems.

However, a choice of court clause would typically be included in the written documentation associated with the deployment of the DAO on the blockchain, such as a White Paper, bylaws, or governance documents, which outline the objectives, values, and organizational structure of the DAO. These documents are often published in plain text on online platforms (eg Snapshot). It is important that the written documentation containing the choice of court clause is located in an easily accessible place, allowing for it to be retrieved for future use or reference,[69] and so that it can be assumed, in accordance with the principle of good faith, that every DAO member could or should have been aware of its existence. It is indeed crucial to avoid a DAO member being taken by surprise by the assignment of a dispute to the forum of a particular jurisdiction.[70]

The inclusion of choice of court clauses in a DAO's founding documents (eg smart contract, White Paper, bylaws) is particularly useful for determining the jurisdiction

[67] Constance Choi and others, *Model Law for Decentralized Autonomous Organizations (DAOs)* (COALA 2021) 8–9, <https://coala.global/wp-content/uploads/2022/03/DAO-Model-Law.pdf> accessed October 10, 2024. These authors pointed out that the deployment of DAOs on a public (permissionless) blockchain is "regulatory equivalent" to the registration of corporate entities in a corporate registry.

[68] Section 3.1.

[69] It is interesting to note in this regard that Swiss law allows companies limited by shares (as well as limited liability companies) to issue their shares in the form of tokens on a blockchain (Art 622 para 1 of the Swiss Code of Obligations; so-called "ledger-based security"; *droit-valeur inscrit*; *Registerwertrecht*). The issuance can be accompanied by written documentation associated with the register to which the token refers (eg the terms of the token issuance). It is possible to include in the associated documentation, for instance, a choice of court clause (Art 973*d* of the Swiss Code of Obligations).

[70] The COALA Model Law for DAOs recommends in its set of best practices for DAOs that each DAO should "refer to or provide a Dispute Resolution Mechanism that the DAO, Members, and Participants will be bound by" (Art 4 para 1(j)). The Model Law specifies that this mechanism should be included in the DAO's bylaws, which must be "comprehensible to a layperson [and] be publicly accessible via a GUI or a Public Forum" (Art 4 para 1(f)). The commentary to the Model Law explains this requirement by stating that publishing the bylaws through a graphical user interface (GUI) or public forum facilitates understanding and access to the DAO's rules for a wide audience, including DAO members and the general public, thereby enhancing transparency and accessibility. Choi and others (n 67).

of state courts to resolve contractual claims between the DAO and its members. DAOs are social organizations inherently international in nature, composed of a community of individuals or entities holding governance tokens from around the world and subject to frequent changes thanks to the generally easy process for exchanging DAO tokens. Such a clause therefore provides a level of predictability with regard to the forum which would otherwise be unattainable. A choice of court clause, however, must be valid if jurisdiction is to be attributed to the chosen court to the exclusion of all other courts. The assessment of the validity of such clauses is simplified where the Hague Convention, Lugano Convention, or Brussels I Regulation applies. Furthermore, these instruments help achieve greater predictability regarding the binding effect of a choice of court agreement on the courts.[71]

Finally, it is worth mentioning that the Hague Convention, Lugano Convention, and Brussels I Regulation exclude the possibility for a valid choice of court agreement to be made in proceedings concerning the validity, nullity, or dissolution of companies or other legal entities, as well as the validity of decisions made by their governing bodies.[72] A choice of court agreement concerning a dispute in relation to one of these matters would be considered as null and void by the courts of the states bound by these international and European instruments. However, these instruments apply to company-related disputes that arise in connection with legal relationships not covered by this exclusion, such as contractual or tort claims between the company and its shareholders.[73] Subject to these limitations, as well as those mentioned above, the international and European instruments discussed here can be applied to DAO-related disputes.

5. Conclusion

The analysis conducted in this chapter highlights that a choice of court agreement provides a certain degree of predictability with regard to the forum, reducing the risk of a dispute being assigned to a court that may be unsuitable for reasons beyond the parties' control. However, a choice of court agreement does not eliminate all uncertainties. Determining the validity of a choice of court agreement is especially complex in a context where activities are primarily conducted on-chain and involve actors whose capacity to enter into binding agreements is uncertain, given their lack of legal personality or pseudonymity.

Bringing a civil or commercial dispute involving a DAO before a state court still presents legal limitations. Moreover, it is essential to remember that the challenges

[71] Predictability is achieved, notably, by ensuring that the parties' choice of a specific court is respected, thereby guaranteeing the fulfillment of their genuine expectations. Dan Jerker B Svantesson, "The Choice of Courts Convention: How Will it Work in Relation to the Internet and E-Commerce?" (2009) 5(3) Journal of Private International Law 517, 522–24.

[72] In these matters, the courts of the company's seat have exclusive jurisdiction under the Lugano Convention (Art 22 para 2) and Brussels I Regulation (Art 24 para 2). This rule applies to companies having their seat in a contracting state, respectively an EU Member State. To account for this exclusive jurisdiction, the Hague Convention excludes these matters from its subject-matter scope (Art 2 para 2(m)).

[73] CJEU, Case C-47/14 *Holterman Ferho Exploitatie BV and Others v F.L.F. Spies von Büllesheim* [2015] ECLI:EU:C:2015:574.

in seeking justice do not end once a court that has jurisdiction over the dispute is found: ultimately, the ability to enforce the judgment remains the most critical practical consideration.

One of the advantages of submitting a dispute to the jurisdiction of a state court designated by a choice of court agreement is the enforceability of the judgment. When a judgment on the merits has been rendered by a court in a state bound by the Hague Convention or the Lugano Convention, it will be easily recognized and enforceable in all other contracting states to the applicable convention. Recognition and enforcement of judgments are even simpler among EU Member States under the Brussels I Regulation. Certainty with regard to the enforceability of a judgment is particularly useful when it needs to be enforced in the physical world, such as an order to pay a sum of money or to transfer ownership of a tangible asset. In contrast, when the judgment must be enforced entirely online, as is the case with an order to transfer crypto-assets held by a DAO or to modify a DAO's protocol, obtaining assistance from state authorities to carry out on-chain enforcement can present a particular challenge where the losing party fails to comply voluntarily.[74]

[74] Guillaume and Riva, "Blockchain Dispute Resolution for Decentralized Autonomous Organizations" (n 3) 588–90

10

Code, Community, and Conflict

DAO Disputes

Bianca Kremer[*]

1. Navigating Disputes in the World of DAOs: An Introduction

At first glance, dispute resolution and decentralized autonomous organizations (DAOs) seem fundamentally opposed.[1] Dispute resolution introduces a third-party neutral as an intermediary to resolve conflicts, whereas DAOs—just like blockchains—try to eliminate any central points of authority.[2] DAOs—having their origin in libertarian movements[3]—are built on values of self-governance, transparency, and autonomy, offering an alternative to traditional corporate structures that concentrate decision-making power in the hands of a few.[4] DAOs are used for a variety of activities and blend the potential of blockchain technology with innovative models of governance and decision-making for organizations.[5] While certain DAOs emerge without significant pre-planning such as if a particular idea catches fire on the

[*] I am very grateful to Jonatan Baier, Eliane Fischer, David Gogel, Suren Gomtsyan, Amy Jung, Anne-Grace Kleczweski, Nathan Vandy, Dominik Vock, Roger Wattenhofer, Kevin Werbach, and Nadira Zellweger-Ferhat for excellent comments and constructive feedback on the drafts of this chapter. I would like to thank all my interviewees for generously giving their time and answering my questions. Research for and writing of this chapter, as well as my role as co-editor of the book, were supported by the Lido Ecosystem Grants Organization.

[1] Bianca Kremer, *Blockchains, Smart Contracts, and International Arbitration—The Emergence of a Crypto Autonomous Legal Order* (Doctoral Dissertation, University of St. Gallen 2022) 117 et seq.

[2] ibid.

[3] Daniela Gandorfer and Eva Micheler, "DAOs: The Theory of the Firm and Ostromian Perspectives" in Kevin Werbach, Eva Micheler, and Bianca Kremer (eds), *Foundations of Decentralized Organizations: Blockchain and the Future of Corporate Law* (OUP 2026).

[4] Kaal sees agency problems in traditional corporate structures as unsolvable within the existing theoretical and legal infrastructure and explains that "[b]lockchain-based technology has started to offer alternatives to the existing corporate governance solutions." Wulf A Kaal, 'Blockchain-based corporate governance' (*SSRN Electronic Journal*, 2019) 4 <https://papers.ssrn.com/sol3/papers.cfm?abstract_id=3441904> accessed April 26, 2025. Kleczweski describes the way DAOs enable all members to participate, "akin to expanding a roundtable, typically effective for small groups, to accommodate hundreds or even thousands of participants," Anne-Grace Kleczweski, "Connecting Worlds: Reconciling DAOs and traditional Organizations for Better Collective Governance" in Florence Guillaume and Sven Riva (eds), *Decentralized Autonomous Organizations in the Legal Landscape* (Elgar 2025) 53–72.

[5] Ben Schechter, "The Future of Work Is Not Corporate—It's DAOs and Crypto Networks" (*a16z Crypto*, December 12, 2021) <https://a16zcrypto.com/posts/article/the-future-of-work-daos-crypto-networks/> accessed April 26, 2025.

internet,[6] most are the result of blockchain-based open source projects' "path to decentralization," with a vision of handing governance over to the community.

In an ideal implementation of a DAO framework, token-holders exercise governance by voting on key issues, and smart contracts automatically enforce decisions in a decentralized fashion. This creates a system that functions without the oversight of traditional corporate management or the enforcement mechanisms of the legal system. However, as DAOs grow in scale and complexity, they often deviate from this ideal in practice and conflicts become inevitable—whether they arise from disagreements over governance decisions, disputes about fund allocation, contracts that DAOs enter into with other contracting parties, or external pressures like regulatory compliance.[7]

Unlike traditional corporations with stable, hierarchical structures, DAOs are hard to grasp under traditional concepts of corporate law[8] because of their oftentimes opaque, unofficial, and hard-to-identify structures, trying to survive as "bodies without organs."[9] This departure from hierarchical control offers opportunities for transparency, autonomy, and community-driven governance.[10] However, as boundaries and responsibilities are redefined organically rather than by clear, top-down instructions, a host of novel challenges—particularly when disputes arise within or around DAOs—follow.

Dispute resolution is traditionally embedded in formal legal procedures and judicial authority. Traditional corporate entities operate within well-defined frameworks,

[6] Examples include ConstitutionDAO which started as a joke on Twitter and raised $47 million to participate in a Sotheby's auction to buy a copy of the US Constitution, Nilay Patel, "From a meme to $47 million: ConstitutionDAO, crypto, and the future of crowdfunding" (*The Verge*, December 7, 2021) <https://www.theverge.com/22820563/constitution-meme-47-million-crypto-crowdfunding-blockchain-ethereum-constitution> accessed April 25, 2025. Another example is CityDAO, which started with a simple tweet by Scott Fitsimones saying: "Starting a DAO to buy and tokenize land in Wyoming, who wants in?" and today governs 40 acres of land in Wyoming, Scott Fitsimones, "Could a DAO Build the Next Great City" (*TED*, July 28, 2022) <https://www.youtube.com/watch?v=zTStDvUtQWc> accessed April 25, 2025.

[7] Florence Guillaume and Sven Riva, "Blockchain Dispute Resolution for Decentralized Autonomous Organizations: The Rise of Decentralized Autonomous Justice" in Andrea Bonomi and others (eds), *Blockchain and Private International Law* (Brill Nijhoff 2023) 569.

[8] UK Law Commission, "Decentralised Autonomous Organisations (DAOs): A Scoping Paper" (UK Law Commission, 2024) vi <https://webarchive.nationalarchives.gov.uk/ukgwa/20250109094345mp_/https:/cloud-platform-e218f50a4812967ba1215eaecede923f.s3.amazonaws.com/uploads/sites/30/2024/07/DAOs-scoping-paper-110724.pdf> accessed April 26, 2025; Ethereum Foundation, "What is a DAO?" (*Ethereum Foundation*, 2025) <https://ethereum.org/en/dao> accessed April 26, 2025 ("There is no CEO who can spend funds on a whim or CFO who can manipulate the books. Instead, blockchain-based rules baked into the code define how the organization works and how funds are spent."); Primavera de Filippi and Aaron Wright, *Blockchain and the Law: The Rule of Code* (Harvard UP 2018) 146; Vitalik Buterin, "DAOs, DACs, DAs and More: An Incomplete Terminology Guide" (*Ethereum Blog*, 2014) <https://blog.ethereum.org/2014/05/06/daos-dacs-das-and-more-an-incomplete-terminology-guide> accessed April 26, 2025.

[9] Interviewee 2 during ETH Brussels 2024. The two French philosophers Gilles Deleuze and Félix Guattari coined the expression *corps sans organes* ("body without organs" (BwO)) in Capitalisme et schizophrénie 1: L'Anti-Œdipe (1972) and developed it further in Capitalisme et schizophrénie 2: Mille plateaux (1980), both originally published by Les Editions de Minuit, Paris. Interviewee 2 also mentions that DAOs struggle with what he calls the "tyranny of structurelessness." This metaphor is used for an assemblage that resists the "organism," or in the DAO context an "organization," privileging potentiality, flow, and becoming over fixed identity or function. Yet, as Deleuze and Guattari warn, a fully undifferentiated BwO risks collapse if pursued without care. Therefore, some structure is needed.

[10] UK Law Commission (n 8) 12.

overseen by regulatory authorities and governed by rules of fiduciary duty, shareholder rights, and contract law. When disputes arise, they can be addressed through processes such as litigation or arbitration, and the decisions rendered by judges or arbitrators are typically enforceable.[11] DAOs, by contrast, are borderless, with legal seats difficult to pinpoint, often involving pseudonymous members who interact through blockchain protocols. These characteristics make it difficult, if not impossible, to apply conventional legal processes to DAO disputes or find an appropriate forum to enforce decisions once they are rendered. In addition, while DAOs often aspire to resolve issues in code, some conflicts exceed what code can handle and without effective dispute resolution mechanisms, DAOs risk internal dysfunction or vulnerability to external commercial disputes.[12] Moreover, DAOs frequently grapple with defining and managing roles, as roles evolve with organizational needs, all the while struggling to balance decentralization with decision-making powers.[13]

It is important to highlight a specific nuance in this regard. While some DAOs exist with no formal entity whatsoever (often called "pure DAOs"),[14] others use a hub-and-spoke structure, placing a core foundation, association, or trust structure in a jurisdiction with clear regulatory frameworks, such as Switzerland, and spinning up sub-DAOs (or other entities) elsewhere.[15] Still others adopt newer models such as Wyoming's DAO limited liability company (LLC) or the decentralized unincorporated non-profit association (DUNA).[16] This variance in legal designs, including evolving laws in jurisdictions that aim to clarify DAOs' legal rights and obligations, adds yet another layer of complexity when regulators or counterparties try to sue or locate accountability.

Kunz and Haslebacher observe that when a DAO chooses to attach itself to a conventional legal entity, it tends to fall into one of three "relationship archetypes."[17] In a "social-signaling" setup, a project company launches the network or application and maintains custody of both on-chain and off-chain assets.[18] This entity often quietly retains a veto power over any proposal passed by token-holders.[19] While this setup provides a counterparty in courts or arbitration, it significantly diminishes the real power

[11] Rui Pereira Dias, "Corporate Disputes Arbitration" in André Pereira da Fonseca and others (eds), *International Arbitration in Portugal* (Kluwer Law International 2020); also on mediation as a way to resolve corporate disputes, Valentina Allotti, "Mediation and Corporate Disputes: An Opportunity" (2017) 14(2) European Company Law 50 .

[12] Alexandra Sims, "Decentralised Autonomous Organisations: Governance, Dispute Resolution and Regulation" (SSRN Electronic Journal, 2021) 5 <https://www.ssrn.com/abstract=3971228> accessed April 26, 2025.

[13] In this regard, Hats Protocol <https://www.hatsprotocol.xyz> accessed April 26, 2025—which offers a full-stack solution for organizing onchain roles in DAOs, which are called "hats."

[14] eg the UK Law Commission outlining a "spectrum of DAOs" and mentioning "pure DAOs", UK Law Commission (n 8) 37 et seq.

[15] Nina Reiser, "DAO Legal Forms Around the World" in Kevin Werbach, Eva Micheler, and Bianca Kremer (eds), *Foundations of Decentralized Organizations: Blockchain and the Future of Corporate Law* (OUP 2026).

[16] ibid.

[17] Michael Kunz and Kiril R Haslebacher, "Incorporating DAOs in Switzerland" in Florence Guillaume and Sven Riva (eds), *Decentralized Autonomous Organizations in the Legal Landscape* (Elgar 2025) 162 et seq.

[18] ibid.

[19] ibid.

of token-holders. In a "principal–agent DAO," the DAO's treasury remains on-chain, but a company is established to handle off-chain tasks and provide services.[20] Because the DAO itself often lacks legal standing, enforcing promises made by the agent can be difficult.

The "legal wrapper" setup is where a conventional legal entity, such as an association, foundation, trust, or LLC, envelops the DAO.[21] This wrapper provides a clear jurisdiction and a recognizable counterparty for legal purposes. However, it also re-introduces many of the very "frictions" that DAOs were designed to escape, such as the concentration of power in a few directors or multi-signature signers, reviving concerns about fiduciary duties and agency costs. Even with a legal wrapper, enforcement remains complex. Smart contracts are designed to be rigid: they execute code, not court orders. Therefore, a judgment that aims to reallocate tokens or rewrite protocol functions still requires implementation on-chain, typically by multi-signature wallet signers.

As DAOs continue to evolve and expand their influence, dispute resolution will remain a critical issue. Finding effective ways to address conflicts while preserving core principles is essential for the growth of these (r)evolutionary organizations.

This chapter first gives a targeted definition of DAO disputes by drawing on the definition of corporate disputes. It then delves into the most significant categories of DAO disputes, enriched with real-world examples. Drawing on the types of DAO disputes identified, the chapter then highlights some major hurdles to DAO dispute resolution and introduces the Transparency Paradox—the measures that promote DAO accountability and community involvement can also make DAOs vulnerable to external pressures and complicate legal strategies. The chapter then presents a DAO dispute resolution spectrum, examining the toolbox available to resolve DAO disputes, from negotiation, mediation, arbitration, and litigation to novel and experimental approaches. Results from data collected during semi-structured interviews is presented in condensed tables to give a first-hand account of DAO practitioners' lived realities. The closing section presents some final reflections.

2. From Corporate Disputes to DAO Disputes—A Targeted Definition

A key challenge lies in the very definition of a "dispute" within the context of DAOs, as there is no clear or widespread agreement on what this term encompasses. To navigate the uncharted waters of DAO disputes, it is therefore useful to first anchor our understanding in the more familiar concepts of traditional corporate law.

Traditional corporate disputes often involve clearly defined legal entities, national laws, and precedent. Yet even within these clearly defined frameworks, the notion of a "corporate dispute" lacks a universally adopted definition, and its scope can vary significantly across jurisdictions.[22] In Anglo-Saxon legal systems, for example, terms like

[20] ibid.
[21] ibid; Reiser (n 15).
[22] Christian Borris, "Gesellschaftsrechtliche Streitigkeiten in der Schiedspraxis" (2018) 16(4) SchiedsVZ-German Arbitration Journal 243.

"corporate dispute" or "corporate litigation" are interpreted broadly, encompassing any disputes related to corporate law or even commercial entities more generally.[23]

Some scholars have proposed distinguishing corporate disputes by their subjective and objective links to the corporation:[24] Subjectively, the company or its shareholders, directors, or officers must be involved in the dispute. Objectively, the dispute must concern core aspects of the corporate relationship and relate to company law.[25] On this view, disputes between companies arising from ordinary commercial contracts would not qualify as corporate disputes.[26] In contrast, disputes over shareholder agreements, articles of association, internal governance, membership, administration, or corporate dissolution would fall within this definition.[27]

Corporate disputes arise in various forms throughout the lifecycle of a company, from its formation and ongoing operations to dissolution. These disputes may involve conflicts between shareholders, directors, and external parties, typically centered around issues of governance, accountability, and the management of financial or operational affairs.[28] For instance, governance disputes in traditional companies typically involve challenges to resolutions passed by the general meeting of shareholders or the board of directors. Shareholders may contest these decisions if they believe they violate the law, the company's articles of association, or their rights as shareholders.[29] Governance disputes can also extend to broader conflicts about a company's strategic direction, including issues of transparency, decision-making power allocation, and the enforcement of shareholder agreements.[30]

Liability and accountability disputes are another critical area in corporate settings, often centered on the fiduciary duties of directors and officers. These individuals are required by law to act in the best interest of the company and its shareholders, and when they fail to meet these standards—through negligence, fraud, or self-serving decisions—they can be held legally accountable.[31] Shareholders or the

[23] ibid.

[24] Zongyao (Eric) Li, "Revisiting the Arbitrability of Corporate Disputes: Proposing a Unified Approach" (2024) 41(6) Journal of International Arbitration 655–57.

[25] ibid.

[26] ibid.

[27] ibid

[28] eg Jon Rees, "How Barclays CEO Won the Battle vs. Activist Investor" (*S&P Global Market Intelligence*, May 10, 2021) <https://www.spglobal.com/market-intelligence/en/news-insights/articles/2021/5/how-barclays-ceo-won-the-battle-vs-activist-investor-64156800> accessed April 25, 2025; also Reuters, "Tesla Shareholder Sues Musk to Return Billions in Alleged Unlawful Profits" (*Reuters*, June 12, 2024) <https://www.reuters.com/legal/tesla-shareholder-sues-musk-return-billions-alleged-unlawful-profits-2024-06-11/> accessed April 25, 2025.

[29] eg Martin Gelter, "Mapping Types of Shareholder Lawsuits Across Jurisdictions" (2017) N363/2017 European Corporate Governance Institute - Law Working Paper <https://papers.ssrn.com/sol3/papers.cfm?abstract_id=3011444> 2 et seq accessed April 25, 2025.

[30] eg Giulio Piovaccari, "Italian and Chinese shareholders in Pirelli clash over governance" (*Reuters*, March 25, 2025) <https://www.reuters.com/business/autos-transportation/pirellis-italian-chinese-shareholders-clash-over-governance-2025-03-25/> accessed April 25, 2025.

[31] On fiduciary duties in the context of DAOs and blockchain systems, Morshed Mannan and Primavera de Filippi, "The Fiduciary Duties of Network Participants of Blockchain Systems" in Kevin Werbach, Eva Micheler, and Bianca Kremer (eds), *Foundations of Decentralized Organizations: Blockchain and the Future of Corporate Law* (OUP 2026).

company itself may bring lawsuits against directors for damages caused by their actions.[32]

Minority rights disputes are also common in corporate law, particularly in companies where majority shareholders dominate decision-making.[33] Minority shareholders may claim that their interests are being disregarded, leading to disputes over issues like dilution of shares, unfair voting processes, or exclusion from critical decisions.[34] In mergers and acquisitions (M&A), disputes may arise over the terms of the transaction, share valuation, cross-border scrutiny, financial and operational performance, as well as regulatory compliance.[35] Similarly, disputes arise during the insolvency or liquidation of a company.[36] Directors may also face claims for wrongful trading if they continued to operate the company despite knowing it was insolvent.[37]

Although translating these forms of disputes into the DAO context is imperfect, elements of these appear in the DAO space as well and are thus informative when exploring disputes in DAOs. DAOs represent a diversity of activities and setups, ranging from art collectives to investment funds, in various stages of development as either "pure DAOs" with no connecting legal anchors to the real world or through connections via the relationship archetypes discussed in Section 1, such as a social signaling, principal–agent or a legal wrapper setup.[38] This complicates the process of defining disputes, aside from the fact that disputes may arise between members of a DAO (internal DAO disputes) or between the DAO (or at least one of its members) and the external world (external disputes).

Acknowledging that DAOs, despite their deviations from traditional corporate structures,[39] frequently face analogous conflicts, such as governance disagreements, membership conflicts, and post-M&A disputes,[40] this chapter adopts and adapts the

[32] eg Daniel L Stein and others, "Directors' Duties: The US Perspective" (*Global Investigations Review*, January 14, 2022) <https://globalinvestigationsreview.com/guide/the-practitioners-guide-global-investigations/2022/article/directors-duties-the-us-perspective> accessed April 25, 2025.

[33] Joseph Lee, "Intra-Corporate Dispute Arbitration and Minority Shareholder Protection: A Corporate Governance Perspective" (2017) 83(1) The International Journal of Arbitration, Mediation and Dispute Management 85 et seq.

[34] ibid.

[35] Heiko Daniel Ziehms, *M&A Disputes: How They Happen, How to Resolve Them, How to Avoid Them* (Kluwer Law International 2023); Benjamin Yost, "Litigation Risk and Strategic M&A Valuation" (*Harvard Law School Forum on Corporate Governance*, August 1, 2024) <https://corpgov.law.harvard.edu/2024/08/01/litigation-risk-and-strategic-ma-valuation> accessed July 13, 2025; BRG, "M&A Disputes Report 2025" <https://media.thinkbrg.com/wp-content/uploads/2025/03/18063551/MA-Disputes-Report-2025_F.pdf> accessed July 13, 2025.

[36] eg Suzzanne Uhland and others, "Insolvency Litigation" (*Lexology GTDT*, December 21, 2021) <https://www.lw.com/admin/upload/SiteAttachments/Insolvency%20Litigation.pdf> accessed July 13, 2025.

[37] Andrew Keay, "Wrongful Trading and the Liability of Company Directors: A Theoretical Perspective" (2005) 25(3) Legal Studies—The Journal of the Society of Legal Scholars 431.

[38] A possible taxonomy of DAOs into means (activity, value transfer, or social) and objectives (generative, associative, or ad hoc) can be found in David Gogel and others, "Decentralized Autonomous Organization Toolkit" (*WEF Insight Report*, January 2023) 28 <https://www3.weforum.org/docs/WEF_Decentralized_Autonomous_Organization_Toolkit_2023.pdf> accessed April 25, 2025.

[39] On DAO governance and how it is rooted in history and what can be learnt from history, Andrew Hall and Porter Smith, "Lightspeed Democracy: What web3 organizations can learn from the history of governance" (*a16z Crypto*, June 29, 2022) <https://a16zcrypto.com/posts/article/lightspeed-democracy-what-web3-organizations-can-learn-from-the-history-of-governance/> accessed April 25, 2025.

[40] eg Joshua Tan and others, "State of DAO M&A" (*SSRN*, April 23, 2025) <https://papers.ssrn.com/sol3/papers.cfm?abstract_id=5164782> accessed July 13, 2025.

corporate dispute definition. This allows for a focused and structured examination of the most pertinent organizational conflicts arising amidst the multitude of potential conflicts relating to DAOs. It also lays down common ground on which to build.

"DAO Disputes" can thus be understood as conflicts that exhibit both a subjective and an objective link to a DAO. In a subjective sense, at least one party must be the DAO itself (whether wrapped in a legal entity or not) or one of its actors, for example, token-holders, members, delegates, contributors, elected councils, smart contract signers, or developers. In an objective sense, the controversy must center on matters impacting or relating to the DAO, that is, governance and decision-making, treasury, assets and resource allocation, protocol integrity or code maintenance, membership and contributor relations, as well as existential events (eg mergers, splits, forks, legal liability from hacks and external contracts). In contrast to the objective link for corporate disputes, this definition is wider and may include contractual disputes or issues that do not necessarily fall within the corporate relationship, but relate to matters impacting the DAO, such as intellectual property, off-chain assets and others.

We thus come to the following working definition of "DAO Disputes":

> A DAO Dispute may be characterized as any conflict that (1) involves the DAO itself or one of its actors, such as token-holders, members, delegates, contributors, developers, councils, or wrapper entities (subjective link); and (2) concerns a matter intrinsic to the DAO, such as governance decisions, treasury use, asset management, code integrity, membership relations, or existential events such as forks or mergers (objective link).[41] A formal proposal vote or treasury allocation is evidence that the dispute materially affects a DAO. Internal disputes arise solely between the DAO and/or its actors, whereas external disputes involve at least one non-DAO actor.

3. Types of DAO Disputes

This chapter attempts to broadly categorize DAO Disputes based on the definition adopted above, where the subjective and the objective links are present. The following list is not exhaustive but rather open and bound to develop with further research und understanding of DAO Disputes. It outlines some prevalent categories of DAO Disputes, with their unique challenges and governance dynamics. A functional division can be drawn between internal and external DAO Disputes, bearing in mind that the boundary is porous and the list necessarily provisional.

Internal DAO Disputes arise among DAO members or between different factions within the DAO, often concerning the interpretation of rules, the allocation of resources, or the exercise of governance power. While traditional corporations face shareholder versus director and shareholder versus shareholder disputes, DAOs' unique structure introduces specific complexities.

[41] Both examples in (1) and (2) are non-exhaustive.

External DAO Disputes involve the DAO's interactions with entities or individuals outside its on-chain ecosystem, often touching upon traditional legal concepts and requiring engagement with established legal systems. Depending on whether the DAO adopts a legal entity or remains a "pure DAO," challenges may arise due to the absence of a clear place of incorporation and/or entity to represent the DAO in legal proceedings.

3.1. Internal DAO Disputes

This section delves into five frequently intertwined categories of internal disputes: governance and voting disputes; smart contract bugs, exploits, and their resulting disputes; fund allocation and treasury management disputes; role and authority conflicts; and investor disputes. While each type presents unique challenges, disputes within DAOs often do not occur in isolation and thus the categories may overlap and exacerbate one another, demanding nuanced approaches to resolution.

3.1.1. Governance and voting disputes

When a DAO is established, two critical elements for effective operation are its governance framework and voting processes. These components define how the DAO functions, how decisions are made, and how contributors interact within the system.[42] DAO governance typically begins with the choice of a framework—a bundle of smart contracts that acts as the on-chain equivalent of a company's bylaws, codifying a DAO's purpose, the roles and responsibilities of contributors, and incentive structures.[43] A well-designed framework aligns with the DAO's vision.[44]

Governance tokens are typically issued and allocated to participants to enable voting within a decentralized and pseudonymous environment.[45] Distribution methods for these tokens vary; for example, Uniswap[46] allocated its UNI tokens to team members, early investors, and users through an airdrop.[47] Once in circulation, these tokens become tradable, allowing individuals to acquire tokens—and thus voting influence—over time.[48] In this way, governance tokens resemble company shares with voting rights attached.[49] In contrast to shareholder meetings, where participation rate among shareholders of US companies is about 72 percent, voting participation rates are strikingly low in DAOs.[50] According to Fritsch and others, in three studied DAO governance systems, less than 10 percent total tokens participate

[42] Gogel and others (n 38) 15 et seq.
[43] ibid.
[44] ibid.
[45] Robin Fritsch and others, "Analyzing Voting Power in Decentralized Governance: Who Controls DAOs?' (2024) 5(3) Blockchain: Research and Applications 1–2.
[46] Uniswap <https://app.uniswap.org/> accessed April 25, 2025.
[47] ibid.
[48] ibid.
[49] ibid.
[50] Konstantinos Zachariadis and others, "Free-Riders and Underdogs: Participation in Corporate Voting" (2020) N 649/2020 European Corporate Governance Institute-Finance Working Paper 2; Fritsch and others (n 45) 4.

in votes.[51] Not only does this study show that participation rate is low, but that voting power is highly concentrated.[52]

Some thus perceive voting as "governance theater"—where formal voting and consensus mechanisms are presented as democratic but lack genuine debate such as when decisions are portrayed as collective but, in reality, favor a subset of influential participants.[53] This can lead to disillusionment within the community. In addition, signaling polls on Snapshot that may not be binding in contrast to binding on-chain votes can also lead to confusion.[54]

To counter this, DAOs should carefully design voting protocols that encourage genuine debate and include minority voices to build a governance framework reflecting true community sentiment. One possible mechanism to achieve this is delegated voting, also known as "liquid democracy."[55] In this system, token-holders either choose to vote directly on issues or to delegate their voting power to another member or a group of members, who are often more engaged or possess specialized knowledge. This allows smaller or less active voters to have their voices represented without needing to participate in every proposal directly. In addition, there are diverse voting processes that enable contributor participation, ranging from straightforward token-based quorum voting to more nuanced methods like elected councils and conviction voting[56] to non-fungible token (NFT)-based voting and quadratic voting,[57] all designed to mitigate issues like rational apathy and plutocracy.[58]

An interesting event presented itself in 2020, when Justin Sun, the founder of Tron, acquired Steemit, holding about 20 percent of the Steem blockchain's native token supply.[59] Because Justin Sun attained control of the Steem blockchain through delegates and tokens held by exchanges, the community resorted to an *ultima ratio* and decided to hard fork Steem into a new blockchain called Hive,[60] by copying all token

[51] ibid.

[52] Fritsch and others (n 45).

[53] eg Juan Esquivel, "Governance Theater: Lessons from AIP-1" (*StableLab*, April 7, 2023) <https://stablelab.xyz/blog/governance-theater-lessons-from-aip-1> accessed April 25, 2025.

[54] eg Fei's founder Joey Santoro explaining this difference to Blockworks in Jack Kubinec, "Fei Flips Again, Repays Crypto Hack Victims" (*Blockworks*, September 21, 2022) <https://blockworks.co/news/fei-flips-again-repays-crypto-hack-victims> accessed July 10, 2025.

[55] Many DAOs today incorporate some version of liquid democracy. However, this model also has many imperfections. Andrew Hall, "What happens when anyone can be your representative? Testing liquid democracy in web3" (*a16zcrypto*, October 31, 2024) <https://a16zcrypto.com/posts/article/testing-liquid-democracy/> accessed June 7, 2025.

[56] This allows voters to continuously signal their preference by staking tokens on proposals with the weight of their support growing over time, accumulating "conviction" until it reaches a predefined threshold (eg Gardens platform); Gogel and others (n 38) 15 et seq.

[57] Quadratic voting, used by DAOs like Gitcoin, reduces the influence of large token-holders by counting votes based on their square root, but needs to combat Sybil attacks where one actor creates multiple wallets; Gogel and others (n 38) 15 et seq.

[58] Gogel and others (n 38) 15 et seq.

[59] Vitalik Buterin, "The Most Important Scarce Resource is Legitimacy" (*Vitalik Blog*, March 23, 2021) <https://vitalik.eth.limo/general/2021/03/23/legitimacy.html> accessed April 25, 2025; Brady Dale, "Justin Sun Bought Steemit. Steem Moved to Limit His Power" (*CoinDesk*, September 13, 2021) <https://www.coindesk.com/tech/2020/02/24/justin-sun-bought-steemit-steem-moved-to-limit-his-power> accessed April 25, 2025.

[60] Hive <https://hive.io> accessed April 25, 2025.

balances, except Justin Sun's.[61] This shows a community's ability to fork a blockchain to regain voting power.

In another case, the community either had less power or decided not to resort to such extreme measures. In late 2024 when Uniswap Labs rolled out its own Layer-2 network, *UniChain*, it did so without first consulting or informing the Uniswap DAO. Delegates complained that such a strategic pivot should have been put to a token vote.[62] The episode sparked a debate over community governance, transparency, and decentralization,[63] highlighting how unclear legal setups (different entities involved with hybrid or legal wrapper structures) and community participation mandates can ignite disputes even in otherwise well-engineered DAOs.[64]

Together these episodes underscore that token ownership rarely maps neatly onto community legitimacy and decision-making power.

3.1.2. Smart contract bugs, exploits, and their resulting disputes

Smart contracts are at the heart of DAO operations, but disputes can occur when there are errors, bugs, or ambiguities in the execution of these contracts. Since smart contracts are self-executing and immutable once deployed,[65] any unforeseen bugs can lead to disputes over the intent and fairness of the outcomes. This highlights a fundamental tension within the "code is law" philosophy often associated with smart contracts, where the literal execution of the code dictates the outcome, even if it contradicts the original human intent or leads to unintended consequences.

A prominent example of such a dispute—which overlaps with governance disputes[66]—is the infamous "The DAO" incident in 2016.[67] A vulnerability in the smart contract code of The DAO, which was the first DAO project on the Ethereum blockchain, allowed an attacker to drain a significant portion of its Ether (ETH) holdings. This incident led to a contentious debate within the Ethereum community and ultimately resulted in a hard fork of the Ethereum blockchain to reverse the transactions and restore the stolen funds, demonstrating the complexities and real-world implications of "code is law" in practice.[68]

Another important example in this context which also falls under governance disputes[69] and fund allocation disputes[70] are exploits that turn into a governance crisis

[61] Buterin (n 59).

[62] Mehab Qureshi, "Uniswap Faces Criticism after Launching Unichain Without DAO Approval" (*The Defiant*, October 22, 2024) <https://thedefiant.io/news/defi/uniswap-faces-criticism-after-launching-unichain-without-dao-approval> accessed April 25, 2025; Crypto News Flash, "Uniswap Faces Governance Crisis Over Unichain L2 Launch" (*Bitget*, March 7, 2025) <https://www.bitget.com/news/detail/12560604625320> accessed April 25, 2025.

[63] Section 5 on the "Transparency Paradox."

[64] Jose Maldonado, "Strong criticism against Uniswap for the launch of Unichain" (*bit2me Crypto News*, October 23, 2024) <https://news.bit2me.com/en/uniswap-launch-unichain-receives-criticism> accessed April 25, 2025.

[65] Unless they are designed to be "upgradeable."

[66] Section 3.1.1.

[67] For an analysis on this incident in the context of dispute resolution, Kremer (n 1) 133 et seq.

[68] ibid 135 et seq. This dispute was finally resolved by a so-called "hard fork," splitting Ethereum into its original version, now called Ethereum Classic, and the new version, in which the hack was undone.

[69] Section 3.1.1.

[70] Section 3.1.3.

over fund allocation and the complete winding down of a DAO. A 2021 DAO M&A of Fei Protocol's FEI Stablecoin and Rari Capital's permissionless-lending pools led to the merger of two blockchain communities and the creation of one of the largest decentralized finance (DeFi) DAOs at the time: "Tribe DAO."[71] However, in 2022, a major hack caused nearly $80 million in losses across Rari's liquidity pools, leading to governance and voting disputes over user reimbursement and the winding down of both the Fei Protocol and the Tribe DAO.[72]

Another case is MakerDAO's "Black Thursday" market crash of March 2020. During this black swan event of extreme network congestion and price volatility, MakerDAO's price oracle failed to update and allowed opportunistic bidders to purchase collateralized debt positions (CDPs) with zero-bid auctions.[73] This resulted in significant losses for users whose collateral was liquidated for next to nothing, triggering years of litigation and a subsequent $1.16 million settlement.[74]

What is the lesson to be drawn from these cases? According to Fei's founder Joey Santoro, "[t]he biggest lesson here is that DAOs should not have to make decisions like this after the fact. An explicit upfront policy, ideally with on-chain enforcement, would have saved the DAO from needing to venture into uncharted governance territory."[75] While proactive safeguards are clearly desirable, it is impossible to plan for all eventualities, unless one implements advanced artificial intelligence (AI) systems capable of alerting the community to emerging issues and assisting in their resolution before they escalate.[76] Nonetheless, establishing clear policies with escalation ladders of how to effectively handle disputes (both on- and off-chain) from the outset, and adapting them over time, offers meaningful long-term potential.[77]

3.1.3. Fund allocation and treasury management disputes

Some DAOs manage substantial treasuries, funded by token sales or community contributions.[78] Disputes can emerge over how funds are allocated or managed, particularly when some members feel that funds are being misused or allocated unfairly. Internal disagreements on how to distribute resources for projects, grants, or operational expenses can create tension within a DAO, especially if transparency and

[71] Andrew Thurman, "Rari Capital, Fei Protocol Token Holders Approve Multibillion-Dollar DeFi Merger" (*CoinDesk*, May 11, 2023) <https://www.coindesk.com/tech/2021/12/21/rari-capital-fei-protocol-token-holders-approve-multibillion-dollar-defi-merger> accessed July 10, 2025. This is also an interesting case in the context of post-DAO M&A disputes, which one may consider its own category of disputes.

[72] eg Ryan Holloway and Traver Normandi, "Governor Note: The Fei Unwind" (*Messari*, August 24, 2022) <https://messari.io/report/governor-note-fei-unwind> accessed July 10, 2025.

[73] Liesl Eichholz, "What Really Happened to MakerDAO?" (*glassnode insights*, March 17, 2020) <https://insights.glassnode.com/what-really-happened-to-makerdao/> accessed April 25, 2025.

[74] Shalini Nagarajan, "Maker firm settles for $1.16M with users liquidated in Covid crash" (*Blockworks*, June 23, 2023) <https://blockworks.co/news/maker-settle-black-thursday; https://www.theblock.co/post/61797/maker-foundation-class-action-lawsuit-black-thursday> accessed April 25, 2025.

[75] Joey Santoro (*X*, September 19, 2022) <https://x.com/0xJoeysantoro/status/1571898753271103488> accessed July 10, 2025.

[76] On AI and DAOs, Kevin Werbach, "Out of Control—DAOs, AI and the Question of Autonomy" in Kevin Werbach, Eva Micheler, and Bianca Kremer (eds), *Foundations of Decentralized Organizations: Blockchain and the Future of Corporate Law* (OUP 2026).

[77] *Contra* Section 4 on dispute resolution hurdles and that even when such policies are established, they may lack proper enforcement and may thus result in being ineffective.

[78] DeepDao <https://deepdao.io/organizations> accessed April 25, 2025.

consensus are lacking. One way to address such challenges is a mechanism introduced by MolochDAO called "rage quit" in 2019, which allows DAO members who no longer agree with the direction in which the DAO is heading, to exit the DAO and withdraw their proportional share of the treasury.[79]

A leading example of a dispute over fund allocation is Nouns DAO which has spent millions of dollars from their treasury for a variety of projects to increase awareness of the Nouns brand, including the right to name a newly discovered species of glass frog in Ecuador.[80] However, different views on treasury management ultimately led to a fork in Nouns DAO.[81] The ability to fork, prevalent in layer 1 blockchains, such as Ethereum with its fork into Ethereum Classic,[82] is not widespread for DAOs without a layer 1.[83] As opposed to a rage quit which focuses on the individual member, a fork needs several members to agree.[84] In an ambition to innovate, increase decentralization, and protect dissenting opinions, Nouns DAO introduced forking in 2023 as a "last-resort minority protection mechanism."[85] This new mechanism had far-reaching consequences and some say it backfired.[86] Over half of Nouns DAO's holders exercised their fork right in 2023, forking away with roughly \$27 million.[87] Then Nouns DAO forked again and again.[88]

Another prominent example of internal DAO disputes, particularly concerning fund allocation and treasury management, emerged in the Aragon project. In May 2023, the Aragon Association (AA), a Swiss-based legal entity acting as the steward of the Aragon project's treasury, intervened in the—at the time—recently deployed Aragon DAO. This action was a direct response to what the AA described as a "coordinated attack" by "Risk Free Value Raiders" who acquired a majority voting power (a 51% attack) within the Aragon DAO, reportedly aiming to extract value for personal financial gain rather than advancing the project's mission.[89] The AA asserted its

[79] Ragequit <https://moloch.daohaus.fun/features/ragequit> accessed July 10, 2025.

[80] Nouns Proposal 16, "Proposal to name a recently discovered species of glass frog after Nouns" <https://www.nouns.com/vote/16> accessed July 10, 2025. Other examples include a Super Bowl commercial, appearance in an indie film, a comic book series and much more, Andrew Hayward, "Nouns Fork: Disgruntled NFT Holders Exit With \$27 Million from Treasury" (*decrypt*, September 15, 2023) <https://decrypt.co/197400/nouns-fork-disgruntled-nft-holders-exit-27-million-from-treasury> accessed July 10, 2025.

[81] Nouns DAO <https://nouns.wtf/> accessed April 25, 2025.

[82] For a discussion on The DAO incident, which lead to the hard fork of Ethereum, see Section 3.1.1.

[83] verbs, "Introducing Nouns Fork: A Last-Resort Minority Protection Mechanism" (*Mirror*, May 11, 2023) <https://mirror.xyz/verbsteam.eth/iN0FKOn_oYVBzlJkwPwK2mhzaeL8K2-W80u82F7fHj8> accessed July 10, 2025.

[84] ibid.

[85] ibid.

[86] Danny Nelson, "A \$27M Crypto Loss Reveals a Toxic Mix of Money-Hungry Traders and DAO Idealists" (*CoinDesk*, September 21, 2023) <https://www.coindesk.com/business/2023/09/21/nouns-daos-27m-revolt-reveals-toxic-mix-of-money-hungry-traders-and-blockchain-idealists> accessed July 10, 2025.

[87] ibid.

[88] Overview of all Nouns DAO forks <https://nouns.wtf/fork> accessed July 10, 2025; also Jack Kubinec, "Nouns DAO is forking again" (*Blockworks*, October 10, 2023) <https://blockworks.co/news/nouns-fork-two-dao-treasuries-spending> accessed July 10, 2025.

[89] Aragon, "Aragon Association Takes Action to Safeguard the Mission of the Aragon Project and its Community of Builders" (*Aragon Blog*, May 9, 2023) <https://blog.aragon.org/aragon-repurposes-dao-to-ensure-treasury-serves-its-mission/> accessed June 7, 2025; also Joshua Tan, "The Ends of Aragon" (*Coindesk*, December 14, 2023) <https://www.nasdaq.com/articles/the-ends-of-aragon> accessed July 13, 2025.

responsibility to safeguard the treasury and its mandate, temporarily halting further large transfers to the DAO and instead announcing a grants program to ensure funds reached builders aligned with the mission.[90] This contentious move, which ultimately led to the AA's decision in November 2023 to dissolve itself and allow Aragon Network Token (ANT) holders to redeem their tokens for ETH, highlights the inherent tension between the decentralized, on-chain governance of a DAO and the fiduciary duties and legal stewardship obligations of an underlying legal entity tasked with protecting a project's long-term mission and assets, especially when faced with perceived hostile takeovers through token governance mechanisms.[91]

This internal conflict escalated further when, in November 2023, Aragon token-holders voted to initiate legal action against the Aragon Association itself, allocating 300,000 USD Coin (USDC) to fund a lawsuit aimed at challenging the Association's decision to dissolve and manage the ANT redemption without a DAO vote.[92] This illustrates a critical escalation where an internal governance dispute leads the DAO community to seek recourse in traditional courts against its own legal wrapper.

3.1.4. Role and authority conflicts

In a decentralized organization, the roles and responsibilities of contributors, developers, and key decision-makers are not always clearly defined, creating uncertainty regarding leadership, project management, or the control of treasury assets. This can lead to role and authority conflicts, where members dispute who has the authority to make decisions on behalf of the DAO.

Unlike the structured and continuous employment model in companies, DAO contributors may engage intermittently, which can heighten misunderstandings and operational frictions. This sporadic engagement model introduces complexities in both governance and execution, as contributors may have limited context or background when making decisions. In a flat structure where power is theoretically distributed, the need for decision-making frequently creates conflict.

A decentralized structure thus calls for a more flexible approach to dispute resolution, allowing DAOs to address disagreements that arise due to uneven information distribution and sporadic involvement. Hats Protocol tries to tackle this problem by creating accountability relationships and the possibility to revoke "hats" (ie roles), where certain roles are granted temporary centralization of power, but only under the strict oversight of the DAO's governance mechanism through accountability.[93] This setup therefore allows DAOs to allocate roles of high responsibility curtailing the risks of unchecked power.

[90] Aragon (n 89).

[91] Aragon, "A New Chapter for the Aragon Project" (*Aragon Blog*, November 2, 2023) <https://blog.aragon.org/aragon-repurposes-dao-to-ensure-treasury-serves-its-mission/> accessed June 7, 2025.

[92] Samuel Haig, "Aragon Tokenholders Vote to Sue Aragon Association" (*The Defiant*, November 22, 2023) <https://thedefiant.io/news/defi/aragon-tokenholders-vote-to-sue-aragon-association> accessed June 7, 2025.

[93] eg Hats Protocol <https://www.hatsprotocol.xyz/> accessed April 25, 2025. Hats Protocol is a full-stack solution for on-chain organizations, enabling the creation of roles and introduces accountability for contributors; Hats Protocol Documentation <https://docs.hatsprotocol.xyz/> accessed July 10, 2025.

Disputes can also stem from issues related to incentives and recognition regarding roles and unequal weight given to different roles. An example is the Token Engineering Commons, where a system intended to reward contributions unintentionally led to resentment.[94] A "praise" mechanism rewarded DAO members for attending meetings, creating an imbalance because high-value contributors, such as engineers working on critical projects, often missed out due to their work commitments that prevented them from attending as frequently.[95] This issue illustrates how poorly designed incentive systems can unintentionally undermine internal harmony and lead to disputes over perceived value and contributions.

A further layer of complexity and potential conflict arises from the fundamental differences between a DAO's on-chain community and its off-chain legal structures, often compounded by a lack of clear understanding within the community regarding these nuances. Whether a project relies on a purpose-built foundation or an independent corporate developer, real-world control over wallets, intellectual property (IP), and contracts often rests with directors who are only loosely—if at all—bound by token votes.[96] When the foundation's board pre-spends funds before asking the DAO to ratify the move (as Arbitrum's foundation did in 2023),[97] or a core development company launches a major product without consulting token-holders (Uniswap Labs' "UniChain" in 2024),[98] the community suddenly discovers that on-chain roles and off-chain authority do not always align.

3.1.5. Token-holder v DAO disputes

Some disputes are brought against the DAO by token-holders and challenge the legal status of DAOs and the potential personal liability of their participants, while also challenging a DAO's token qualification.

One example of such dispute is *Samuels v Lido DAO*, where a US class action lawsuit filed against Lido DAO (a liquid staking platform) in the United States District Court for the Northern District of California raises critical questions about the legal status of DAOs and their capacity to participate in legal proceedings.[99] The lawsuit

[94] Juan Bell, "Praisemageddon" (*CommonsBuild Github*, July 2, 2021), <https://github.com/CommonsBuild/IH-intervention/issues/11> accessed April 25, 2025; Jeff Emmett "Pre-Hatch Impact Hours Distribution Analysis" (*TEC Forum*, May 11, 2021) <https://forum.tecommons.org/t/pre-hatch-impact-hours-distribution-analysis/376> accessed April 25, 2025.

[95] ibid.

[96] See Section 1 for a discussion on social signaling DAOs; also Kunz and Haslebacher (n 17).

[97] The Arbitrum Foundation's first governance proposal (AIP-1) in April 2023, seeking to allocate 750 million ARB tokens (approximately $1 billion) for operational costs and grants, ignited significant community backlash. The controversy stemmed from the Foundation's announcement that this was a ratification of a pre-existing decision, not a proposal, and that some tokens had already been moved or converted to stablecoins *before* the community vote concluded. This led to accusations of a lack of transparency and questions about the true decentralization and authority of the DAO's token-holders; Ana Paula Pereira, "Arbitrum's first governance proposal sparks controversy with $1B at stake" (*Cointelegraph*, April 2, 2023) <https://cointelegraph.com/news/arbitrum-s-first-governance-proposal-sparks-controversy-with-1b-at-stake?> accessed April 25, 2025.

[98] Section 3.1.1.

[99] Sage D Young, "Lido Governance Authorizes $200,000 To Engage Law Firm in Dismissing Class-Action Lawsuit" (*Unchained Crypto*, July 9, 2024) <https://unchainedcrypto.com/lido-governance-authorizes-200000-to-engage-law-firm-in-dismissing-class-action-lawsuit/> accessed April 25, 2025.

claims that Lido DAO is a general partnership, and its governance token, LDO, an unregistered security.[100]

Lido DAO token-holders voted to authorize Dolphin CL, LLC, a Delaware limited liability company, to represent the DAO in court.[101] Dolphin CL, LLC was tasked with hiring legal counsel and filing a motion to dismiss the lawsuit.[102] The motion contends that Lido DAO, being software, is not a legal entity capable of being sued.[103] This strategy sought to provide the court with a tangible entity to interact with so as to not run the risk of a default judgment against Lido DAO.[104]

The lawsuit also names several venture capital firms invested in Lido DAO as defendants, alleging their involvement makes them partners in a general partnership.[105] These firms have sought to distance themselves from Lido DAO, arguing that they are not part of the organization and should be dismissed from the lawsuit.[106]

One of the core issues highlighted by this case is the absence of a formal legal personality for pure DAOs. Without recognition as a legal entity, the DAO faces significant hurdles in responding to legal actions and protecting its interests within the judicial system. It also exposes DAO participants to legal risks, including personal liability, if the DAO is deemed a general partnership by default. The decision to authorize Dolphin CL, LLC to represent the DAO in court reflects an attempt to navigate these challenges by creating, *ad hoc*, a bridge between the DAO and the traditional legal framework. The court expressed skepticism, suggesting that such an appointment might inadvertently affirm the DAO's capacity to be sued, potentially undermining arguments that the DAO, as software, lacks legal personhood.[107]

The Lido DAO case highlights the tension between decentralized governance and the legal system. While DAOs strive to distribute control and decision-making among participants, they may need to incorporate centralized elements or legal structures to interact effectively with national legal systems and regulatory authorities.

Establishing a legal wrapper can provide DAOs with legal personhood, enabling them to own assets in the "off-chain" world, enter contracts, and represent themselves in legal proceedings. This approach can also limit the liability of participants, shielding them from personal exposure related to the DAO's activities. However, introducing centralized legal structures raises concerns about compromising the decentralization that is fundamental to the DAO model. Balancing these considerations requires innovative legal and organizational solutions that preserve the DAO's core principles while ensuring compliance and protecting participants.

[100] *Andrew Samuels v Lido DAO,* et al, No 23-cv-06492-VC (ND Cal, amended complaint April 3, 2024).

[101] kadmil, "Appoint Entity to Respond to Pending Class Action Litigation Against Lido DAO" (*Lido Forum*, July 2, 2024) <https://research.lido.fi/t/appoint-entity-to-respond-to-pending-class-action-litigation-against-lido-dao/7791> accessed April 25, 2025; Young (n 99).

[102] ibid.

[103] *Andrew Samuels v Lido DAO*, et al, No 23-cv-06492-VC (ND Cal, Dolphin CL LLC's reply in support of motion to dismiss the amended complaint August 22, 2024), section B: "Lido DAO does not exist as a legal entity because it is mere software."

[104] Matthew Bultman, "Community-Run Crypto Project Tests Legal Standing by Forming LLC" (*Bloomberg Law*, September 16, 2024) <https://news.bloomberglaw.com/securities-law/community-run-crypto-project-tests-legal-standing-by-forming-llc> accessed April 25, 2025; kadmil (n 101).

[105] *Andrew Samuels v Lido DAO,* et al, No 23-cv-06492-VC (ND Cal, amended complaint April 3, 2024).

[106] Young (n 99).

[107] Bultman (n 104).

3.2. External DAO Disputes

When a dispute moves beyond the DAO and its internal actors and enters the "off-chain world," disputes may be brought by the DAO or its actors against external parties or by an external party against the DAO and its participants.

A key example of an external dispute is the Ethereum Name Service (ENS) dispute over the eth.link domain. ENS is a decentralized domain name system built on the Ethereum blockchain.[108] It allows users to create human-readable names for their Ethereum addresses, making it easier to send and receive cryptocurrency.[109] For example, instead of sending ETH to a long and complex string of characters, users can send it to a name like "example.eth." For ENS domains to resolve in standard web browsers, "eth.link" was set up.[110] The domain, initially assigned to ENS Labs, expired while its owner, Virgil Griffith, was incarcerated.[111] Domain registrar GoDaddy subsequently sold it to Dynadot, which auctioned it off to Manifold Finance.[112]

ENS Labs sued GoDaddy, Dynadot, and Manifold Finance to reclaim the domain.[113] A federal district court in Phoenix, Arizona, issued a preliminary injunction ordering the return of the domain to ENS Labs while the case was being resolved.[114] Manifold Finance then proposed a settlement, offering to relinquish its claim to the domain name in exchange for a payment of $300,000 from ENS Labs, coupled with "confidentiality and non-disparagement agreements."[115]

ENS Labs put the settlement offer to a vote by the ENS DAO, which overwhelmingly approved it.[116] The DAO also voted to reimburse ENS Labs for its legal expenses, which had totaled $750,000.[117] ENS Labs subsequently dropped the lawsuit against GoDaddy and Dynadot.

[108] Ethereum Name Service (ENS) <https://ens.domains/> accessed April 25, 2025.

[109] ENS, "What Is ENS?" <https://support.ens.domains/en/articles/7900404-what-is-ens> accessed April 25, 2025.

[110] Andrew Allemann, "Eth.link domain sold for $852k in unique situation" (*Domain Name Wire*, September 7, 2022) <https://domainnamewire.com/2022/09/07/eth-link-domain-sold-for-852k-in-unique-situation/> accessed April 25, 2025.

[111] The domain was first registered in 2018 by Griffith, a former employee of ENS. Vishal Chawla, "Company behind Ethereum Name Service files lawsuit over domain sale" (*The Block*, September 8, 2022) <https://www.theblock.co/post/168579/company-behind-ethereum-name-service-files-lawsuit-over-domain-sale> accessed April 25, 2025. US Department of Justice, "U.S. Citizen Who Conspired to Assist North Korea in Evading Sanctions Sentenced to Over Five Years and fined $100,000" (*DOJ Press Release*, April 12, 2022) <https://www.justice.gov/opa/pr/us-citizen-who-conspired-assist-north-korea-evading-sanctions-sentenced-over-five-years-and> accessed April 25, 2025.

[112] Andrew Allemann, "Ethereum Name Service drops lawsuit over eth.link" (*Domain Name Wire*, August 23, 2024) <https://domainnamewire.com/2024/08/23/ethereum-name-service-drops-lawsuit-over-eth-link> accessed April 25, 2025.

[113] ibid; *ENS Labs Ltd v GoDaddy Inc* (D Ariz, No 2:22-cv-01494).

[114] *True Names Ltd* et al *v GoDaddy Inc* (D Ariz, No CV-22-01494-PHX-JJT) <https://storage.courtlistener.com/recap/gov.uscourts.azd.1309358/gov.uscourts.azd.1309358.19.0_4.pdf> accessed April 25, 2025.

[115] Jesse Coghlan, "ENS to end eth.link domain suit after DAO greenlights $300k settlement" (*Cointelegraph*, February 27, 2024) <https://cointelegraph.com/news/ens-dao-approves-300k-domain-manifold-lawsuit-settlement> accessed April 25, 2025.

[116] nick.eth, "[EP5.2] [Social] Determine ENS Labs' next steps in eth link litigation" (*Snapshot ENS Proposal*, February 20, 2024) <https://snapshot.org/#/ens.eth/proposal/0x456ccb438eed5d189cbe51e5e36a88d2bb4dc0c61f12f6d9e310a7ba4798d5fc> accessed April 25, 2025.

[117] Coghlan (n 115).

One of the takeaways from the ENS case is the DAO's reliance on traditional legal mechanisms to resolve disputes involving off-chain assets. The "eth.link" domain, although integral to ENS's functionality, exists outside the blockchain and is subject to conventional domain registration processes. When the domain expired and was subsequently auctioned off, the ENS DAO found itself compelled to engage with the traditional legal system to assert its rights and recover the domain.

This reliance highlights a fundamental challenge for DAOs: while they can effectively manage and govern on-chain assets using smart contracts and decentralized decision-making, they often lack the legal personality required to interact with off-chain entities and assets. In ENS's case, ENS Labs—a legally recognized entity—had to represent the DAO's interests in court.

The dispute also sheds light on the risks associated with key assets being under the control of individual members rather than the DAO collectively. The initial assignment of the "eth.link" domain to Virgil Griffith and its subsequent expiration during his incarceration reveal vulnerabilities in asset management practices. DAOs must ensure that critical resources are held and managed in a manner that guarantees continuity and mitigates risks associated with individual circumstances.

Another theme observed in this case is the manifestation of the "transparency paradox" or how to balance transparency v strategic confidentiality,[118] which may have led to higher costs in the end. The DAO spent approximately $750,000 on legal fees—an amount that significantly exceeded the $300,000 settlement offer from Manifold Finance. This outcome prompts a critical evaluation of the DAO's decision-making processes, particularly regarding cost-benefit analyses in conflict resolution. The preference for legal action over first entering into negotiation may not only have increased financial costs but also prolonged the dispute.

Another example of an external dispute where instead of being on the side of the plaintiffs, a DAO was a defendant, is the Commodity Futures Trading Commission's (CFTC) enforcement action against Ooki DAO, which shows how regulatory bodies can hold DAOs accountable in federal courts under existing laws.[119]

4. Major Hurdles to Effective Resolution of DAO Disputes

Taken together, these internal and external DAO disputes reveal a common pattern: once a dispute meets the subjective/objective test, claimants run into recurrent obstacles, such as identifying parties, choosing a forum, and enforcing outcomes. This section explores some of these hurdles.

DAOs exist in a diverse landscape, spanning various activities. As mentioned in Section 1 above, they may span a continuum from "pure" on-chain DAOs with no legal personality to hybrids wrapped in conventional entities, each at their own stages

[118] On the "transparency paradox," Section 5.

[119] *CFTC v Ooki DAO*, No 3:22-CV-05416-WHO, 2022 WL 17822445 (N D Cal December 20, 2022). For an in-depth discussion of the case, Morshed Mannan and Primavera de Filippi, "The Fiduciary Duties of Network Participants of Blockchain Systems" in Kevin Werbach, Eva Micheler, and Bianca Kremer (eds), *Foundations of Decentralized Organizations: Blockchain and the Future of Corporate Law* (OUP 2026).

of "progressive decentralization." As a result, the selection of hurdles examined in this section may surface differently depending on the precise structure of the DAO in question, whether it is a "pure," hybrid, or "wrapped" DAO structure.

A prominent hurdle is the identification of parties in DAOs.[120] In most DAOs, governance maps to pseudonymous wallet addresses, some of which may contain millions of tokens and dominate key votes. While that pseudonymity preserves user privacy and guards against retaliation, it frustrates the two classic pillars of legal proceedings: knowing *who* did what and deciding *who* must answer for it.[121]

In traditional corporate disputes, parties are easily identifiable as shareholders, directors, or employees. Although some DAOs are increasingly adopting Know Your Customer (KYC) standards and experimenting with zero-knowledge proof in KYC verification,[122] the anonymous or pseudonymous nature of participants still reigns supreme, making it much more complex to identify responsible parties and enforce legal actions.[123]

These intertwined questions—*who is behind the wallets* and *who may legally represent the DAO*—forces DAOs to create real-world legal persons in an *ad hoc* manner or rely on legal entities already created to defend themselves and reconcile representation with decentralization.[124]

When the DAO is not the defendant but the plaintiff, such as when the "eth.link" domain expired, it did not go to court itself but its development company, the ENS Labs had to sue GoDaddy and Dynadot in an Arizona federal court because domain-name law—not smart-contract code—governed the asset.[125] The borderless DAO still had to rely on a legal entity to go before a court in a specific jurisdiction for an off-chain dispute.

Closely interlinked with the pseudonymity of parties is another hurdle: jurisdictional issues. These often arise in pure DAOs, which have no fixed corporate seat, while their contributors, assets, and governance tokens may span dozens of legal systems. This opens up the question—what court, if any, has jurisdiction when things go wrong? Unlike traditional companies, which are typically incorporated in a specific country and subject to its laws, DAOs may not be based in any particular legal jurisdiction, complicating the application of national laws.[126] This makes it hard to identify a particular jurisdiction for disputes, even when DAOs have entered choice of court agreements.[127] Further challenges arise relating to the capacity to sue or be sued and service of process.

[120] Kremer (n 1) 224 et seq.

[121] ibid. It also makes it difficult to establish whether a party has legal capacity; ibid 226 et seq.

[122] eg Michelangelo Frigo, "Zero-Knowledge Proof: The Future of Secure KYC" (*Zyphe Blog*, May 21, 2025) <https://www.zyphe.com/resources/blog/what-is-zero-knowledge-proof-in-kyc-verification> accessed May 25, 2025.

[123] Kremer (n 1) 225 et seq.

[124] Section 1 on the discussion of different DAO legal structures; also Section 3.1.5.

[125] Section 3.2. for a discussion on the eth.link dispute.

[126] At least when it comes to "pure DAOs"; Section 1; UK Law Commission (n 8) 37 et seq.

[127] For a deeper analysis of these challenges, Florence Guillaume, "Choice of Court Agreements in Disputes Involving Decentralized Autonomous Organizations (DAOs)" in Kevin Werbach, Eva Micheler, and Bianca Kremer (eds), *Foundations of Decentralized Organizations: Blockchain and the Future of Corporate Law* (OUP 2026).

In *CFTC v Ooki DAO*, the court found that the CFTC had sufficiently pleaded facts showing that Ooki DAO is an unincorporated association under California law with legal capacity.[128] In this case, the court also allowed service via online forums.[129]

In addition, the lack of enforceability of internal codes of conducts and other policies—adopted by some DAOs—[130] creates its own challenges for resolving disputes. Even when DAOs have specific guidelines and policies in place, enforcement remains difficult without appropriate mechanisms. And once enforcement bodies or committees are created, further questions arise regarding their legitimacy, how to mitigate risks of power concentration or abuse, and how to manage conflicts of interest.[131] For effective dispute resolution, DAOs require procedural infrastructures for decision-making and enforcement, which are often at odds with the crypto ethos. To bridge this gap, projects like Optimism have explored and experimented with mechanisms for decentralizing enforcement, while Q Protocol is developing a system that enables the decentralized enforcement of non-deterministic rules.[132]

Another important aspect concerns the enforcement of off-chain court judgments or arbitral awards, which can be challenging in the context of a DAO.[133] In traditional companies, such decisions are enforced by state authorities against identifiable legal entities or their shareholders, directors, and officers. In DAOs, however, enforcement becomes complicated: decisions involving real-world assets require not only locating the asset but also identifying against whom enforcement may be sought. When the decision concerns digital assets and is not the result of a crypto-native mechanism—such as Kleros, which may enable automatic on-chain enforcement, or Q Protocol, which requires its nodes to comply with off-chain arbitral awards—enforcement ultimately hinges on voluntary cooperation. This usually means cooperation from multi-signature wallet signers (when assets are self-custodied) or from crypto exchanges (when assets are held on exchanges). Finality then needs code, courts, and community.

5. The Transparency Paradox

Navigating DAO disputes requires a consideration of the unique social mechanisms that govern these organizations, coupled with an acknowledgment of the inherent tension between transparency, trade secrets, IP, and strategic advantage. This interplay creates what is termed here the “transparency paradox” in DAO dispute resolution. The desire for transparency, a cornerstone of the DAO ethos, can thus create a paradox when it comes to resolving disputes. While transparency is intended to

[128] *CFTC v Ooki DAO*, No 3:22-CV-05416-WHO, 2022 WL 17822445 (N D Cal December 20, 2022).

[129] ibid.

[130] eg Optimism DAO’s Code of Conduct.

[131] eg Optimism Foundation, “Council Dissolution Proposal” (*Optimism Forum*, November 26, 2024) <https://gov.optimism.io/t/code-of-conduct-council-dissolution-proposal/9321> accessed July 13, 2025. There, the Optimism Foundation notes community feedback expressing the perceived conflicts of interest in the Code of Conduct Council, responsible for enforcement of the Code of Conduct.

[132] ibid. However, the Code of Conduct Council was later dissolved; Q Protocol <https://q.org/> accessed April 25, 2025.

[133] Guillaume and Riva (n 7) 588.

promote accountability and community involvement, it can also make DAOs vulnerable to external pressures and complicate legal strategies.

This transparency paradox is clearly illustrated by Uniswap's announcement of Unichain.[134] In this case, the core team's decision to launch a new product without community consultation sparked controversy, even though the decision might ultimately have benefited the DAO. This tension is similarly evident in the Optimism Foundation's approach to private token sales, where the need for discretion—the Foundation stated that "the terms and purchaser are not able to be disclosed"—has stirred debate within crypto circles, as it requires the community to place trust in the foundation's unilateral decisions.[135]

The transparency paradox also became evident in the "eth.link" domain case, in which the ENS DAO's commitment to transparency, intended to align with DAO principles, may have inadvertently weakened its negotiating position.[136] By openly discussing strategies and decisions regarding a legal dispute, DAOs provide their counterparty with insights into its intentions and limits. This transparency may reduce the DAO's leverage in negotiations, potentially leading to less favorable dispute outcomes or settlement terms.

The transparency feature of DAOs can create significant legal weaknesses, particularly in common law jurisdictions where broad discovery requirements exist. While DAOs inherently strive for public disclosure and transparency in governance and operations, this creates significant challenges in protecting privileged information, such as dispute resolution strategies, confidential information, and non-disclosure agreements (NDAs), as sharing them with the broader DAO community through discussion forums could inadvertently waive privilege.[137] This waiver also risks inviting opponents to pursue more expansive discovery requests, compelling the production of additional documents and records that might otherwise remain shielded.[138]

DAOs must strike a balance between the need for transparency with the strategic considerations for confidentiality when operating in a competitive and often adversarial landscape. While openness fosters trust and community engagement, there are circumstances—particularly involving legal disputes or negotiations—where discretion is important.

DAOs may thus need to develop protocols for handling sensitive matters privately to protect their interests without compromising their foundational values of transparency and community governance. The DAO Coalition of Automated Legal

134 Maldonado (n 64).

135 eg Tim Craig, "Optimism Foundation sells another $90m worth of OP in 'private token sale'" (*DL News*, March 8, 2024) <https://www.dlnews.com/articles/defi/optimism-foundation-sells-more-op-tokens-in-private-sale/> accessed April 25, 2025; Optimism Foundation, "Token Sale—March 2024" (*Optimism Collective Forum*, March 7, 2024) <https://gov.optimism.io/t/token-sale-march-2024/7760> accessed April 25, 2025.

136 Section 3.2.

137 Deborah R Meshulam and others, "Privilege Issues in Cross-Border Investigations Around the World" (*GIR*, December 7, 2023) <https://globalinvestigationsreview.com/guide/the-guide-international-enforcement-of-the-securities-laws/third-edition/article/privilege-issues-in-cross-border-investigations> accessed July 7, 2025.

138 eg "The Consequences of Waiving the Attorney-Client Privilege" (*Mintz*, June 24, 2015) <https://www.mintz.com/insights-center/viewpoints/2451/2015-06-consequences-waiving-attorney-client-privilege> accessed July 7, 2025.

Applications (COALA) Model Law, for example, recognizes this in respect to member privacy and states in its Article 4 on formation requirements that "[s]ensitive information may be redacted from the By-Laws before their publication, if those redactions are necessary to protect the privacy of individual Members or Participants in the DAO."[139]

To mitigate the tension between transparency and strategic advantage, DAOs may adopt "legal wrappers" for privilege preservation, though this compromises decentralization. Some DAOs are therefore experimenting with legal funds that can handle dispute-related matters requiring legal action more privately without necessarily having to compromise on decentralization.

6. The DAO Dispute Resolution Spectrum

Now that prevalent dispute types and the hurdles to dispute resolution have been discussed, this chapter turns to mechanisms that DAOs may employ to resolve disputes. There is a whole spectrum of dispute resolution tools, ranging from traditional off-chain methods like negotiation, mediation, arbitration, and court adjudication to experimental on-chain solutions embedded within blockchain protocols.

As disagreements cannot be coded away preemptively, and are a natural part of organizations of any size and configuration, effective dispute resolution becomes essential. Absent effective and enforceable ways to resolve disputes, they may turn into a power play, ultimately benefiting the "stronger" party.

Several projects have begun to experiment with dispute resolution to overcome limitations inherent in both traditional legal systems and basic on-chain voting. Traditional systems may be too slow, opaque, or misaligned with DAO principles, while on-chain voting can be vulnerable to manipulation by large token-holders and may not effectively resolve complex disputes. Novel mechanisms include on-chain rage kicking or rage quitting, reputation systems, security councils, and hybrid models that blend on-chain and off-chain processes. By adopting these experimental approaches, DAOs seek to create tailor-made systems for dispute resolution that uphold decentralization while ensuring effective governance.

From the outset, there is a significant oversight in many DAOs which is also true for companies: the lack of upfront conflict resolution planning. By establishing transparent conflict resolution guidelines at the outset, DAOs may mitigate potential conflicts and provide contributors with a clear understanding of the governance processes they are joining.

Most controversies in DAOs are relatively simple internal community disputes that start out small and are first discussed informally on Discord, Telegram, or in governance forums and are resolved within the community itself through negotiation, without the need for a neutral third party. These exchanges are entirely voluntary and

[139] Coalition of Automated Legal Applications (COALA), "Model Law for Decentralized Autonomous Organizations (DAOs)" (2021) <https://coala.global/wp-content/uploads/2022/03/DAO-Model-Law.pdf> accessed July 7, 2025.

hinge on reputational pressure rather than enforceable sanctions. DAOs may employ forum moderation for such disputes or *ad hoc* working groups.

"Rage quitting" as mentioned in Section 3.1.3 was popularized by MolochDAO and enables members to protect their interests if they disagree with the DAO's direction, which could be considered a form of dispute prevention.[140] The opposite of rage quitting would be "rage kicking", where DAOs rely on social slashing (delegitimizing bad actors). LidoDAO is experimenting with a similar approach they term "Dual Governance," where dissatisfied token-holders may exit the DAO.[141]

Some DAOs have attempted to create off-chain mediators to deliver non-binding recommendations. In 2024, Optimism Foundation, for example, introduced a mediation mission and is continuously experimenting with governance mechanisms and effective forms of decentralizing enforcement.[142] These methods can be faster than on-chain voting but often lack the transparency inherent in blockchain-based solutions. Moreover, they may not align seamlessly with the decentralized ethos that underpins DAOs.

To obtain a (binding) outcome without state-court formalities,[143] DAOs experiment with crypto arbitration such as Kleros.[144] Kleros offers decentralized, blockchain-based arbitration solutions leveraging game theory and crowdsourced jurors.[145] Despite their potential, such crypto-native arbitrations have yet to achieve widespread adoption due to legal uncertainties and integration complexities with existing frameworks.

While these crowdsourced tribunals promise expert decision-makers and global enforceability under the New York Convention,[146] national law still needs to recognize the dispute as *arbitrable*. Arbitrability concerns the threshold question whether a given category of dispute may be removed from the jurisdiction of state courts and entrusted to a private arbitral tribunal. Under most national laws, a dispute is arbitrable when the subject matter of the dispute is capable of settlement by arbitration.[147] Classic examples of non-arbitrability are criminal liability and some aspects of family law.

Corporate conflicts sit between the poles: many are commercial in substance, yet they frequently implicate third-party interests, such as creditors, employees, and public interests through regulatory bodies, including tax authorities and public registries. That tension may explain the long-running debate over whether corporate

[140] MolochDAO <https://molochdao.com/docs/introduction/wtf-is-moloch/> accessed April 25, 2025.

[141] Lido, "Dual Governance: An Overview" (*Lido Blog*, April 13, 2024) <https://blog.lido.fi/dual-governance-overview/> accessed April 25, 2025.

[142] opjulian, "Foundation Mission Request S6 Mediation Mission [ABANDONED]" <https://github.com/ethereum-optimism/ecosystem-contributions/issues/237> accessed June 10, 2025.

[143] Whether such outcomes can be binding is disputed. For an analysis, Kremer (n 1) 247 et seq.

[144] For an in-depth discussion of Kleros as "crypto arbitration," Kremer (n 1) 209 et seq.

[145] Kleros <https://kleros.io> accessed April 25, 2025. For an in-depth discussion of Kleros as "crypto arbitration," Kremer (n 1) 209 et seq.

[146] Convention on the Recognition and Enforcement of Foreign Arbitral Awards, is a crucial international treaty in the field of international commercial arbitration. It was adopted by a United Nations diplomatic conference on June 10, 1958, in New York City, and entered into force on June 7, 1959.

[147] Nigel Blackaby and others, *Redfern and Hunter on International Arbitration* (OUP 2015) para 2.124; also Arts II(1) and V(2)(a) of the New York Convention and UNCITRAL Model Law, Art 34(2)(b)(i) and 36(1).

disputes can ever be entrusted to arbitrators.[148] EU law reinforces those doubts: Article 24(2) of the Brussels I (Recast) Regulation assigns exclusive jurisdiction over the "validity of the constitution" and "nullity or dissolution" of companies to the courts of the seat, and Article 24(3) does the same for public registers, signaling that those matters lie beyond party autonomy.[149]

Arbitral institutions and legislative reforms have nonetheless pushed the boundary outward by crafting procedural frameworks that accommodate company law issues without surrendering the field to the courts.[150] However, DAO disputes raise several difficulties that do not appear, or appear in different form, in the corporate context, such as giving notice to a DAO,[151] having an "agreement in writing" under the New York Convention for blockchain-based arbitrations,[152] as well as consent and legal capacity of token-holders.[153] Where a wrapper entity exists, capacity follows automatically but where it does not, the increasingly common practice of treating a group of token-holders as a partnership probably comes into play.

To address this, projects like Q Protocol, for example, are experimenting with dispute resolution, including arbitration, directly integrated into their core governance framework.[154] Q Protocol establishes a comprehensive decentralized governance layer that aims to provide a legal backstop for DAOs by combining on-chain rules with off-chain dispute resolution mechanisms, including the use of established institutions like the International Chamber of Commerce (ICC) for arbitration.[155] This approach seeks to offer a legally enforceable dispute resolution pathway from the outset of a DAO's operation.

LexPunk, meanwhile, has circulated a model "LexDAO Arbitration" clause referencing the UNCITRAL arbitration rules,[156] and Immunefi, the bug bounty coordination platform adopted by several DAOs and blockchain protocols, partnered with the London Chamber of Arbitration and Mediation (LCAM) to draft arbitration rules specific to Immunefi's bug bounty program.[157] These rules illustrate what a DAO-specific arbitration mechanism looks like in practice. Immunefi's support

[148] Li (n 24).

[149] Regulation (EU) No 1215/2012, Art 24; Pilar Perales Viscasillas, "Arbitrability of (Intra-)Corporate Disputes" in Loukas A Mistelis and Stravos L Brekoulakis (eds), *Arbitrability: International and Comparative Perspectives* (Kluwer 2009) 14–26.

[150] eg Swiss Arbitration Centre, *Supplemental Swiss Rules for Corporate Law Disputes* (2023); Article 697n of the Swiss Code of Obligations, which permits companies to include an arbitration clause directly into their articles of association.

[151] However, eg, Steve Kaaru, "CFTC justified in issuing summons to Ooki DAO through help chat box, judge rules" (*Coingeek*, October 7, 2022) <https://coingeek.com/cftc-justified-in-issuing-summons-to-ooki-dao-through-help-chat-box-judge-rules/> accessed July 10, 2025.

[152] Kremer (n 1) 213 et seq.

[153] ibid 222 et seq.

[154] Q Protocol <https://q.org/> accessed April 25, 2025.

[155] ibid; specifically para 4.6 of the Q White Paper <https://q.org/files/Q_Whitepaper_v1.0.pdf> accessed July 24, 2025 and Art 13 of the Q Constitution <https://q.org/constitution#_article_13_applicable_law_and_dispute_resolution> accessed July 24, 2025.

[156] Kremer (n 1) 198–99; LexDAO Arbitration <https://github.com/lexDAO/Arbitration> accessed July 10, 2025.

[157] Immunefi, "Immunefi Arbitration: A New Era for Onchain Dispute Resolution" (*Medium*, January 21, 2025) <https://medium.com/immunefi/immunefi-arbitration-a-new-era-for-onchain-dispute-resolution-bc24af9bdafa> accessed May 25, 2025.

documentation describes the system as an e-mail document-based arbitration, which comes into play when the parties involved are unable to reach a consensus through Immunefi's standard mediation process, after which any party has 12 months to submit a request for arbitration.[158]

LCAM then appoints a neutral arbitrator to oversee the case.[159] Once the arbitrator closes the proceedings, a legally binding decision (the arbitral award) is issued within two weeks.[160] Depending on the outcome and if the project's Immunefi vault holds sufficient collateral, the payment can be issued directly from the vault.[161] Should the vault lack adequate funds, the project is expected to add the necessary collateral to fulfill the award.[162] Critically, if a project refuses to honor the award, in whole or in part, the LCAM decision becomes legally enforceable in more than 170 countries, all signatories of the New York Convention.[163] This global enforceability provides a powerful recourse and a strong incentive for projects to comply.

Another way to resolve disputes in DAOs is through simple community voting, where token-holders vote on proposals related to the dispute. However, this method can be slow and cumbersome, especially for time-sensitive issues. Additionally, it is vulnerable to governance attacks, where a group of token-holders collude to sway outcomes in their favor. Moreover, large token-holders can wield disproportionate influence, leading to outcomes that may not reflect the broader community's will and may lead to further disputes over voting fairness, necessitating off-chain mechanisms for complex or contentious disputes.[164]

To mitigate threats that could destabilize the DAO, some organizations have established security councils—small groups empowered to make rapid decisions in emergencies. During security breaches or attacks, DAOs face the challenge of balancing the need for swift action with their decentralized governance principles.[165] An example is Curve's Emergency DAO, which has nine democratically elected members with the authority to suspend project functionalities during crises, except for withdrawals.[166] This mechanism allows for rapid response, bypassing the delays of community voting, but it also raises concerns about centralization within decentralized systems.[167]

The Emergency DAO exemplifies the trade-off between maintaining decentralization and ensuring quick, effective responses to emergencies, highlighting the challenge of having to compromise decentralization for security and stability—a

[158] Immunefi Arbitration Overview <https://immunefisupport.zendesk.com/hc/en-us/articles/26081514838673-Arbitration-Overview> accessed May 25, 2025.

[159] ibid.

[160] ibid.

[161] ibid.

[162] ibid.

[163] The New York Convention is one of the most successful international treaties, with over 170 contracting states. It has played a pivotal role in the growth and reliability of international commercial arbitration, providing a predictable and efficient mechanism for businesses to resolve disputes globally. It is often referred to as the "cornerstone" of international arbitration.

[164] Section 3.1.1.

[165] Bianca Kremer and Kanye Ye Wang, "DeFi Attacks and the Role of DAOs" in Madalena Perestrelo de Oliveira and António Garcia Rolo (eds), *Decentralised Autonomous Organization (DAO) Regulation* (Mohr Siebeck 2024) 233.

[166] Curve Emergency DAO <https://dao.curve.fi/emergencymembers> accessed April 25, 2025.

[167] Kremer and Wang (n 165).

challenge analogous to dispute resolution, which requires a third-party authority.[168] While these councils offer a mechanism for swift action, ambiguity surrounding their authority and intervention criteria can lead to internal disputes and concerns over centralization.[169]

Another approach involves the use of reputation systems designed to prevent disputes from arising in the first place. Members earn reputation scores based on past behavior and contributions, influencing their weight in decision-making processes. Platforms like Colony utilize reputation to align incentives and encourage positive contributions.[170] While reputation systems can enhance trust and accountability, they may not be as scalable for large, distributed DAOs.

For hacks and similar exploits, DAOs have also begun to use negotiation with "attackers" in a way that compensates them so they return the tokens they extracted for a "white-hat bounty."[171] Negotiation has proven quite effective in many such cases.

For complex disputes and in situations where disputes extend beyond the DAO and blockchain ecosystem, recourse to traditional litigation or alternative dispute resolution (ADR) may become unavoidable, especially when they involve external parties, off-chain assets, or regulatory authorities.[172]

7. The Lived Reality: Synthesizing Insights from DAO Practitioners on Disputes and Their Resolution

Drawing on the insights from DAO practitioners, this section synthesizes the lived realities of DAO operations, disputes, and resolution, weaving a practical "red thread" through the theoretical framework established in the preceding sections. The interviews reveal a complex, often paradoxical, landscape where idealized decentralization collides with practical necessities, human behavior, and external legal pressures.

This chapter has been inspired by a qualitative approach, with data gathered through 17 semi-structured interviews from July 2024 to December 2024. Interviews in July 2024 ranged between 10–30 minutes as they were done spontaneously and in person during ETH Brussels at events which gathered many DAO participants. The later interviews were conducted online on Microsoft teams, Zoom, or Google Meet, and lasted between 45–60 minutes, with some extending beyond this duration when participants had more insights to share, focusing on participants' experiences, perspectives on disputes and dispute resolution mechanisms within DAOs, case studies, and their insights into current challenges and developments in DAO governance.

168 ibid.

169 Section 3.1.4.

170 Colony <https://colony.io/> accessed April 25, 2025. Another example is the Grantee Accountability Protocol (GAP) DAO <https://gap.karmahq.xyz/> accessed July 10, 2025.

171 eg the GMX DAO with GMX, a decentralized spot and perpetual exchange governed, offering its attacker $5 million to return the stolen funds, André Beganski, "GMX Hacker Goes White-Hat, Returns $40 Million—Sends Rest to Tornado Cash" (*decrypt*, July 11, 2025) < https://decrypt.co/329821/gmx-hacker-white-hat-returns-40-million-sends-rest-tornado-cash> accessed July 13, 2025.

172 eg *CFTC v Ooki DAO*, No 3:22-CV-05416-WHO, 2022 WL 17822445 (N D Cal December 20, 2022); *ENS Labs Ltd v GoDaddy Inc* (D Ariz, No 2:22-cv-01494).

To guide the interviews and gather targeted insights, the following key questions were asked:

1. DAO Disputes: Based on your experience, what types of disputes have you encountered or observed in DAOs, both internally (eg governance disagreements) and externally (eg with third parties)?
2. Resolution Methods: What dispute resolution methods have been most effective in your experience? What are the limitations or challenges of these methods, particularly when compared to traditional legal systems?
3. Case Study Contributions: Can you share insights from specific disputes involving DAOs that could serve as case studies? What lessons were learned, and how did these outcomes shape your approach to conflict resolution within DAOs?

The conversations with leading practitioners in the DAO space illuminate that disputes are not merely theoretical constructs but an inevitable and inherent aspect of DAO operations. Governance, at its core, involves trade-offs and the allocation of scarce resources, making conflict a natural outcome, akin to any human organization from a corporation to a book club. Far from being a flaw, some even view healthy disagreement as a sign of a robust ecosystem, fostering dialectic and leading to a deeper understanding of problems and solutions.

To respect the chapter's length limit, this section provides overview tables for each of the three questions, keeping the emphasis on patterns rather than full anecdotes. Tables 10.1, 10.2, and 10.3 offer a concise, at-a-glance digest of the most insightful points raised during the interviews. Table 10.4 lists details of the interviewees.

8. Conclusion

While the rise of DAOs represents many opportunities in governance and institutional design, it also presents unique challenges to dispute resolution. These get aggravated by uncertainty regarding DAOs' real-world structures, legal status, and power dynamics. As explored in this chapter, DAOs challenge traditional notions of hierarchy and legal authority, while facing internal as well as external disputes, ranging from day-to-day friction to existential, high-stakes disputes.

Effective internal dispute resolution may hinge on the design of clear rules and processes established from the outset. Transparent accountability mechanisms may reduce the frequency and severity of disputes, while adopting hybrid models that combine decentralized governance with legal recognition may provide DAOs with a promising path to interact with traditional legal systems without compromising their decentralized nature.

The very difficulties DAOs face today can be catalysts for innovation leading to more dispute-proof systems that may even be driven by AI to resolve issues before they escalate. There is much to be learned, and the journey of DAOs is still unfolding. As DAOs continue to mature and expand their influence, the development of effective dispute resolution will be critical to their success.

Table 10.1 Categories of DAO Disputes and Key Insights from Interviews

Question 1 – What kinds of DAO disputes show up in practice?		
Dispute Category	**Insight**	**Interviewees**
Role and ownership ambiguity, conflicts of interest	"Who is supposed to do what?"; unclear mandates and escalation paths; risk of self-interest and self-coup power grabs; intransparent power structures; opaque designs	2, 3, 5, 7, 8, 10, 13, 15, 17
Governance/voting conflicts	Matters if the outcome of the vote is binding or not; on-chain proposal does not execute as expected – what happens then? Revotes, quorum failure, whale capture, behind the scenes actions, token-accumulation "attacks"; online v vast silent offline presence and the dynamics of voting; token weighted voting v reputation	3, 6, 7, 8, 10, 11, 12, 13, 14, 16
Fund-allocation and treasury spending rules/management	Treasury drains, misspent grants, skewed reward systems ("praiseflation"); clear treasury spending rules are important as well as documentation made available to the community	1, 3, 11, 12, 13, 15, 16
Power-grabs/hostile takeovers	Founders or whales seek control or dissolve treasury safeguards	3, 13, 14, 16
External asset and IP battles	Domain names, trademarks, real-world contracts draw DAOs into court	8, 9, 13, 15, 16
Technical conflicts and the complexity of technology	Important to specify elements that are upgradeable and those that aren't; have documented immutability; also disputes can arise when the technology gets too complex and people no longer understand the system; with multiple chains, bridges, cross-chains, and DAOs, dispute resolution becomes more around infrastructure, validators, staking, forking the network in addition to the social layer	6, 8, 12, 16
Interpretations and "code is law"	Did the system act as expected? There is a fine line between what is an attack or playing the game of the system; disputes can happen when interpretations around these differ	14
Community conduct (eg forum harassments)	A simple type of dispute, may be interpersonal, moderation needed	8
Regulatory/liability shocks	Regulatory agency actions ("general partnership" rulings) create personal risk fears	8, 9, 12, 16
"Structurelessness," loss of trust and coordination problems	Early DAOs collapse under vague hierarchy or after merging communities and unclear distribution of governance and rights; crowd momentum blocks nuance	2, 3, 7, 8
Design edge cases and technical disputes	Bridge-tech choices, code of conduct breaches, unforeseen voting outcomes	8, 10, 14, 16
Categorization and definition of disputes into phases, layers, spectrums and scales, from subjective to objective and vice versa	From smaller peer-to-peer disputes, informal disagreements to big forum discussions with two opposing camps and more formal disputes with external lawsuits; difference to be made between objective and subjective; social and tech consensus layer	6, 7, 10, 12, 14

Table 10.2 Interview Insights on DAO Dispute Resolution Methods, Examples, Advantages, and Disadvantages

Question 2 – What dispute resolution methods work, and where do they stumble?			
Method family	**When it works best**	**Key limitations / challenges**	**Interviewees**
Prevention, social escalation and peer mediation (including "simple escalation ladder")	Early stage of conflict, everyday interpersonal friction; low-stakes role questions	Relies on goodwill; no legal finality	2, 8, 10, 14, 17
Role-based tools with retroactive accountability (Hats Protocol, functional sub-groups)	Clarifying authority, preventing mandate overlap	Needs thoughtful setup; can recentralize power	1, 2, 17
On-chain deterrents, slashing, clawback, rage quit, rage kick v fork, veto	Objective, verifiable failures; mostly on-chain; for subjective exit option pressure; forks are ultima ratio; vetoes are a hard stop	Only covers what can be coded; expensive or irreversible	6, 10, 12, 13, 14, 15, 16, 17
"Dispute games," delay function	After a proposal passed or decision made – window of time to deliberate on the outcome and dispute it, after which it becomes complete	Based on negotiation game principles, someone will lose and stakes are economic	14
Off-chain/hybrid/third-party arbitration (Kleros, Q Protocol + ICC); Security Councils; smart escrow; off-chain negotiation before on-chain deployment	Kleros for low-value claims; LexDAO, Q protocol for high stakes cases that necessitate fact-finding, interpretation, etc; cross-jurisdiction assets; security councils for hacks and matters that do not resolve on-chain	Cost, speed, adoption, uncertainty regarding legal and actual enforceability; uncertainty regarding liability	2, 7, 11, 12, 14, 15
Legal wrappers, proxy entities, "mirror DAOs," legal funds	Off-chain assets, litigation, IP protection; liability protection; minimize transparency paradox	Re-imports corporate frictions; creates hierarchical structures; reduces transparency	4, 9, 13, 14 16

Continued

Table 10.2 Continued

Question 2 – What dispute resolution methods work, and where do they stumble?			
Method family	**When it works best**	**Key limitations / challenges**	**Interviewees**
Futarchy-based methods	To help make decisions based on predictions, with people who may have more information than others	Requires an oracle for different matters, difference between objective and subjective matters	14
Preference signaling, veto-guarded, reputation/attestation-driven governance	Fast-moving DAOs; contributor heavy; reduces vote load; "proceed unless objection"	Mapping signals to action; veto abuse; fair reputation; Sybil resistance	4, 7, 11
Up-front design and prevention (governance minimization, manifesto clauses), automated transparent monitoring (including AI) that alerts DAO when it needs to pay attention to a particular dispute	Reduces dispute frequency by baking rules in early; a working governance system leads to fewer disputes because the rules are known and engaging in a conflict becomes costly and time consuming	Needs foresight; hard to retrofit into live DAOs	1, 2, 4, 8, 12

Table 10.3 DAO Dispute Cases Referenced in Interviews

Question 3 – Case studies			
Case	Year	Dispute type	Interviewees
Bitcoin Blocksize Wars	2015–2017	Technical dispute over scaling of blockchain block's size	12
The DAO hard fork	2016	Major exploit, historical case study, "code is law" discussions, fork	12, 13, 14
MakerDAO Black Thursday	2020	Technical basis; Black swan event, could not have been predicted; pressure on system due to global event	6, 14, 16
Constitution DAO Sotheby's bid	2021	Not a dispute per se but shows the difficulty of moving beyond the DAO space; transparency paradox	13, 17
Tribe DAO collapse	2022	Post M&A dispute, exploit consequences	8
Mango Markets Exploit	2022	External; exploit consequences, trader civil lawsuits, criminal charges, regulatory action; broader regulatory scrutiny by SEC and CFTC; leading to Mango Markets shutdown	6
OokiDAO	2022–2023	External; CFTC enforcement action	6, 14
ENS *eth.link* lawsuit	2022-2024	Off-chain asset dispute	9, 13
Aragon DAO; Aragon treasury dispute	2023	Fund allocation and governance dispute	11, 13, 14, 15, 16
Uniswap BNB Chain Deployment	2023	Governance and voting dispute	16
NounsDAO	2023	Forking (as opposed to rage quitting)	4, 16
Compound "governance attack"	2024	Token accumulation push, enough delegation, "attack" or "hostile takeover"	14, 16
Pocket Network founder takeover bid	2024	Governance dispute, hostile takeover, founding team v community v foundation	3
SushiSwap DAO – Treasury Transfer Proposal	2024	Governance dispute; fund allocation and treasury management dispute	11, 16
Unichain Launch	2024	Governance dispute; role and authority conflicts	11

Table 10.4 List of Interviewees

Interviewee #	Name	Function and Affiliation
1	Jeff Emmett	Research and Communications at BlockScience
2	Ven Gist	Systems Designer with Applied Cybernetics Guild. Former dungeonmaster (Governance Lead) with Metacartel
3	Dermot O'Riordan	Former Director of POKT Network Foundation
4	Donny Lewis	Director Web3 Partnerships at Viridis, Contributor at KokonutDAO
5	Marco Germanier Torrado	Contributor at Token Engineering Commons and the Bonding Curve Research Group and researcher at Wonderland
6	David Gogel	COO at dYdX Trading
7	Eugene Leventhal	Research Director at Metagov
8	Justine Humenansky	Head of Governance at Optimism Foundation
9	Alexander Urbelis	General Counsel of the Ethereum Name Service
10	André Geest	VP of Growth at Safe Ecosystem Foundation
11	Etienne Le Roux	Growth Lead at Colony
12	Martin Schmidt	Co-initiator of Q Protocol
13	Fabrizio Romano Genovese	Founder of 20 squares
14	Amy Jung	Governance at Eigen Foundation, formerly at Safe Foundation, former Head of Community at MakerDAO
15	Klaus Bravenboer	Founder at Hack Humanity
16	kadmil	Contributor of DAO Operations Workstream at Lido DAO
17	Spencer Graham	Founder of Hats Protocol

11

DAOs for Collective Investment

An Emerging Paradigm

Nizan Geslevich Packin and Anat Alon-Beck

1. DAOs as Collective Investment Vehicles

The digital age enabled by the latest internet iteration[1] has ushered in revolutionary changes in how we conceptualize and execute collective investments.[2] Central to this revolution is the emergence of decentralized autonomous organizations (DAOs), which represent a novel paradigm that challenges traditional business associations, business entrepreneurship models, and financing models.[3] This chapter explores DAOs not merely as operational entities, but as innovative platforms for pooling capital, and offering a decentralized and democratized approach to investment. Indeed, DAOs could serve as an alternative means for venture-backed startups and private or public companies, a novel way to attract investors. By leveraging blockchain technology, they have recently gained prominence as collective investment vehicles that broaden access to capital. Unlike traditional venture capital (VC) models that are often hindered by geographical limitations, high entry barriers, and opaque governance, some believe that DAOs offer a transparent, inclusive, and efficient alternative. Through smart contracts, DAOs enable investors to pool resources, vote on investment decisions, and share profits in a trustless environment, revolutionizing the concept of collective investment.

[1] Generally Leon Anidjar, Nizan Geslevich Packin, and Argyri Panezi, "The Matrix of Privacy: Data Infrastructure in the AI-Powered Metaverse" (2023) 18 Harvard Law and Policy Review 59 (discussing this digital, decentralized era, which is also known as Web3.0).

[2] Nizan Geslevich Packin and Yafit Lev-Aretz, "Crypto Native Credit Score: Between Financial Inclusion and Predatory Lending" (2024) 45(3) Cardozo Law Review 845 (describing how decentralized finance (DeFi) is different from the traditional finance).

[3] eg Brian J Broughman and Jesse M Fried, "Do Founders Control Start-Up Firms that Go Public?" (2020) 10 Harvard Business Law Review 49, 64 tbl 2 (discussing venture capital (VC) financing and control-related issues); Eva Micheler and Dionysia Katelouzou, "Investor Capitalism, Sustainable Investment and the Role of Tax Relief" (2022) 23 European Business Organization Law Review 217 (referencing the evolution of investor capitalism and highlighting regulatory impacts on sustainable business practices); Will Gornall and Ilya A Strebulaev, "The Contracting and Valuation of Venture Capital-Backed Companies" in B Espen Eckbo, Gordon M Phillips, and Morten Sorensen (eds), *Handbook of the Economics of Corporate Finance: Private Equity and Entrepreneurial Finance*, vol 1 (North Holland 2023) (describing how startups attract late-stage VCs, and how later investment rounds better protect investors from risk); Brian J Broughman and Matthew Wansley, "Risk-Seeking" (2023) 76 Vanderbilt Law Review1209 (discussing VC's traditional role and proposing a new corporate governance theory in which VCs mainly seek to persuade risk-averse founders to pursue high-risk strategies); Yifat Aran and Elizabeth Pollman, "Ousted" (2024) 25(1) Theoretical Inquiries L 231 (highlighting the limits of founders-CEOs' power and shedding light on why investors might accept certain control structures in startup initial public offerings (IPOs)).

1.1. Traditional VC Funding Models

To understand the potential impact of DAOs on investment, it is essential to examine traditional VC funding models. The traditional venture capital ecosystem plays a crucial role in supporting the development of VC-backed startups by offering not just financial investment but also strategic guidance.[4] This system, which has been extensively explored in recent legal and entrepreneurial research, involves a variety of key participants, each contributing in unique ways.[5]

Entrepreneurs form the core of this ecosystem, often funding their initial operations through personal finances or contributions from their network, known as the "three Fs"—friends, family, and fools. As startups grow and require more capital, they turn to formal investment sources, marking their entry into the traditional VC ecosystem.[6]

At the heart of this system are VC firms, which are usually structured as limited partnerships. These firms consist of general partners (GPs), who manage the firm and make investment decisions, and limited partners (LPs), who provide the majority of the capital but are not involved in day-to-day operations.[7] LPs often include institutional investors, such as pension funds, endowments, and sometimes banks, while GPs use their expertise and networks to actively participate in the governance of startups, often by securing board positions to guide the companies' strategic directions.[8]

The compensation model for GPs generally includes a management fee and a share of the profits (carried interest), aligning their financial incentives with the success of the startups. This structure motivates VCs to ensure the growth and performance of their portfolio companies.[9]

VCs typically negotiate for preferred stock, which grants them liquidation preferences, giving them priority in the event of a sale or liquidation. This preferential

[4] Yael V Hochberg, Alexander Ljungqvist, and Yang Lu, "Networking as a Barrier to Entry and the Competitive Supply of Venture Capital" (2010) 65(3) Journal of Finance 829, 829 ("examin[ing] whether strong networks among incumbent venture capitalists (VCs) in local markets help restrict entry by outside VCs, thus improving incumbents' bargaining power over entrepreneurs").

[5] Paul Gompers and others, "How Do Venture Capitalists Make Decisions?" (2016) National Bureau of Economic Research, Working Paper 22587, 2 <https://www.nber.org/system/files/working_papers/w22587/w22587.pdf> accessed October 18, 2024. Anat Alon-Beck, "The Coalition Model, A Private–Public Strategic Innovation Policy Model for Encouraging Entrepreneurship and Economic Growth in the Era of New Economic Challenge" (2018) 17 Washington University Global Studies Law Review267.

[6] Darian M Ibrahim, "Financing the Next Silicon Valley" (2010) 87 Washington University Law Review 717, 720.

[7] Josh Lerner and Paul Gompers, "The Money of Invention: How Venture Capital Creates New Wealth" (*Ubiquity*, January 2002) <http://ubiquity.acm.org/article.cfm?id=763904> accessed October 18, 2024; Joseph A McCahery, Erik PM Vermeulen, and Andrew M Banks "Corporate Venture Capital: From Venturing to Partnering" in Douglas Cumming (ed), *The Oxford Handbook of Venture Capital* (OUP 2012) 211.

[8] Anat Alon-Beck, "Unicorn Stock Options—Golden Goose or Trojan Horse?" (2019) Columbia Business Law Review107.

[9] Victor Fleischer, "Two and Twenty: Taxing Partnership Profits in Private Equity Funds" (2008) 83 New York University Law Review 1, 9. Many have also written on VCs' exit at IPO; eg Christopher Barry and others, "The Role of Venture Capital in the Creation of Public Companies: Evidence from the Going Public Process" (1990) 27 Journal of Financial Economics447; William L Megginson and Kathleen A Weiss, "Venture Capital Certification in Initial Public Offerings" (1991) 46 J Fin Econ 879; Paul A Gompers, "Grandstanding in the Venture Capital Industry" (1996) 42 J Fin Econ 133; Peggy M Lee and Sunil Wahal, "Grandstanding, Certification, and the Underpricing of Venture Capital Backed IPOs" (2004) 73 Journal of Financial Economics 375.

treatment highlights the substantial influence VCs have within the startup ecosystem. Additionally, the funding provided by VCs is often delivered in stages, contingent upon the startup achieving specific milestones. This staged approach allows VCs to manage their risk while maintaining control over the startup's trajectory through board involvement and contractual covenants that require VC approval for major business decisions.[10]

As startups progress, alternative venture capital (AVC) participants, such as hedge funds and corporate venture capital arms, may join at later stages. These non-traditional investors bring different financing approaches and governance mechanisms, further influencing the company's development through innovative equity structures and contractual agreements.[11]

If we compare the traditional VC ecosystem with the structure and operation of a DAO, we will find that VC investors provide funding to startups in exchange for equity.[12] VC investors often gain control over major decisions through seats on the board or voting rights based on this equity ownership. The VC system relies on hierarchical governance, where VCs guide startups by offering strategic direction, expertise, and resources.[13]

1.2. Democratizing Investments: Crowdfunding as an Alternative Funding Model

While traditional VC models have their merits, alternative funding models have emerged to address their limitations. Crowdfunding platforms provide an accessible and decentralized alternative to traditional VC funding models by allowing

[10] JK Sharma and Smita Tripathi, "Staged Financing as a Means to Alleviate Risk in VC/PE Financing" (2016) 19(2) Journal of Private Equity 43; D Gordon Smith, "Team Production in Venture Capital Investing" (1999) 24 Journal of Corporation Law 949.

[11] Anat Alon-Beck, "Alternative Venture Capital: The New Unicorn Investors" (2020) 88 Tennessee Law Review 983; Anat Alon-Beck, Robert N Rapp, and John Livingstone, "Investment Bankers as Underwriters: Barbarians or Gatekeepers? A Response to Brent Horton on Direct Listings" (2020) 73 Southern Methodist University Law Review 251; Gad Weiss, "A Theory of Seed Financing" (2025) 5 University of Illinois Law Review 1831.

[12] Abraham Ravid and Ola Bengtsson, "The Geography of Venture Capital Contracts" (2009) <http://papers.ssrn.com/sol3/papers.cfm?abstract_id=1361827> accessed October 18, 2024; also Ola Bengtsson and David H Hsu, "How Do Venture Capital Partners Match with Startup Founders?" (2010) 1 <https://papers.ssrn.com/sol3/papers.cfm?abstract_id=1568131> accessed October 18, 2024) ("A central feature of the venture capital market is that matching between borrower and investor is two-sided. On the financial capital supply side, venture capitalists (VCs) select which handful of startups to fund among the several hundred business plans it reviews every year (Fried & Hisrich, 1994; Boocock & Woods, 1997). This selection is difficult because startup quality is widely dispersed and hidden quality problems can be severe in that entrepreneurs may have better information about project quality relative to investors (Gompers & Lerner, 2001; Cochrane, 2006). On the demand side, the entrepreneur must make a decision on which VCs will most reliably provide not only financial capital but also professional services which can spur startup corporate development (Macmillan et al., 1989; Gorman & Sahlman, 1990; Hellmann & Puri, 2000, 2002; Brander et al, 2002).").

[13] David H Hsu and Martin Kenney, "Organizing Venture Capital: The Rise and Demise of American Research & Development Corporation, 1946–1973" (2005) 14 Industrial and Corporate Change 579 (2005); Charles R Korsmo, "Venture Capital and Preferred Stock" (2013) 78 Brooklyn Law Review 1163, 1169.

large groups of individuals to pool resources and invest in startups.[14] Platforms such as Kickstarter, Indiegogo, SeedInvest, and Crowdcube democratize investment by enabling participation from diverse investors.[15] This approach not only diversifies investment perspectives but also facilitates innovative and successful ventures.[16] Crowdfunding also introduces transparency, with platforms providing detailed project information to build trust and foster investor confidence.

Platforms like Kickstarter and Indiegogo have revolutionized creative and technological sectors by offering startups a direct route to capital, bypassing traditional financial intermediaries.[17] These platforms enable projects to gain funding through contributions from backers worldwide. On the other hand, SeedInvest and Crowdcube focus on equity crowdfunding, allowing everyday individuals to gain equity in startups, emphasizing regulatory compliance and investor protection, creating a safer investment environment. This combination of accessible investment and regulatory oversight makes crowdfunding platforms a popular alternative to VC.

Moreover, by broadening access to funding, crowdfunding allows individuals with even modest amounts of capital to participate, leveling the playing field and giving more people the opportunity to support promising startups.[18] The diversity of investors can lead to the identification and support of innovative projects that may otherwise be overlooked by traditional VC firms focused on specific industries or markets. Crowdfunding also fosters a sense of community, with investors often providing valuable feedback and support beyond financial investment.[19]

1.3. Democratizing Investments 2.0: DAOs as an Alternative Funding Model

Building on the democratizing momentum sparked by crowdfunding, DAOs still rely on decentralized capital-pooling. At the same time, they push even further away from

[14] Generally Michelle Black, "Equity Crowdfunding: What Is It & How Does It Work?" (*Forbes Advisor*, March 31, 2022) <https://www.forbes.com/advisor/business-loans/equity-crowdfunding/> accessed November 4, 2024; "Learn" (*SeedInvest*) <https://www.seedinvest.com/learn> accessed June 13, 2024; "Investors" (*Crowdcube*) <https://www.crowdcube.com/explore/investors> accessed June 13, 2024.

[15] ibid; also "What are the basics?" (*Kickstarter*, September 9, 2024) <https://help.kickstarter.com/hc/en-us/articles/115005028514-What-are-the-basics> accessed November 4, 2024; "How It Works – Crowdfunding" (*Indiegogo*) <https://learn.indiegogo.com/how-it-works-crowdfunding/> accessed 13 June 2024.

[16] Ethan Mollick and Alicia Robb, "Democratizing Innovation and Capital Access: The Role of Crowdfunding" (2016) 58 California Management Review 72; Ethan Mollick and Venkat Kuppuswamy, "Crowdfunding: Evidence on the Democratization of Start-Up Funding" in Josh Lerner and Scott Stern (eds), *Innovation Policy and the Economy*, vol 16 (University of Chicago Press 2016).

[17] Generally Andrew A Schwartz, *Investment Crowdfunding* (OUP 2023).

[18] eg Thomas Young, "Alternative Investments: Equity Crowdfunding" (*RocketDollar Blog*, July 20, 2022) <https://www.rocketdollar.com/blog/alternative-investments-equity-crowdfunding> accessed October 18, 2024 (describing how "[a]nyone can participate in equity-based crowdfunding, even with modest amounts. In some cases, the minimum investment required is only $1,000.").

[19] Jordana Viotto da Cruz, "Beyond Financing: Crowdfunding as an Informational Mechanism" (2018) 33 Journal of Business Venturing 371 <https://www.sciencedirect.com/science/article/abs/pii/S0883902618301174> accessed October 18, 2024 (examining the informational value of crowdfunding to entrepreneurs and showing "evidence that crowdfunding is also an informational mechanism, providing feedback about the presented ideas").

conventional financial structures. DAOs enable large numbers of investors to collectively pool their resources and vote on investment decisions through blockchain-based governance. As mentioned, they operate without intermediaries, leveraging smart contracts to ensure that governance and investment decisions are executed automatically and transparently.

Like crowdfunding, DAOs democratize access to investment opportunities by allowing participants to contribute small amounts of capital. This approach opens up funding to a more diverse group of individuals. This decentralization offers advantages such as broader participation and greater investor autonomy, as the contributions come from a distributed network of investors or token-holders. Governance is driven by the community through smart contracts and voting mechanisms, giving every token-holder a say in key decisions. There is no central authority; instead, the rules are set in code, and decisions are made collectively.

Additionally, and more importantly, DAO participants are generally token- holders or stakeholders who have voting rights. They are not passive investors. The traditional roles found in DAO ecosystems are decentralized, with no clear hierarchy. Stakeholders collectively propose, vote on, and implement changes. Each participant's power is proportionate to the tokens they hold.

However, DAOs face significant challenges related to legal frameworks and regulatory uncertainty. Unlike crowdfunding platforms that operate within well-established regulatory environments, DAOs lack legal certainty, potentially exposing investors to greater risks, including those that are associated with cross-jurisdications-related issues.[20]

Also, unlike VCs, the decisions in a DAO are typically slower due to the need for consensus through voting. While this ensures transparency and participation, it can also slow down critical decision-making processes, especially in times of crisis. The legal and financial risks can be more significant as DAOs can face regulatory challenges due to their decentralized nature and the lack of formal legal structures.

While DAOs can bring in a wide range of perspectives and expertise, similar to crowdfunding platforms, their reliance on blockchain technology offers unique benefits, such as enhanced transparency and security. Nevertheless, the regulatory uncertainty surrounding DAOs, especially when compared to crowdfunding platforms that adhere to existing financial regulations, presents a key challenge. Despite this, DAOs represent a promising model for decentralized investment, particularly in sectors related to blockchain technology and cryptocurrencies.

[20] Generally Oscar Borgogno and Edoardo D Martino, "Decentralised Autonomous Organizations: Targeting the Potential Beyond the Hype" (2024) European Banking Institute Working Paper Series 161 <https://ssrn.com/abstract=4692754> accessed October 17, 2024; Florence Guillaume, "Decentralized Autonomous Organizations (DAOs) Before State Courts. How Can Private International Law Keep Up With Global Digital Entities?" in Madalena Perestrelo de Oliveira and António Garcia Rolo (eds), *Decentralised Autonomous Organisation (DAO) Regulation—Principles and Perspectives for the Future* (Mohr Siebeck 2024).

1.4. A Deeper Dive: Traditional VC Funding Models and Crowdfunding Platforms v DAOs

1.4.1. Advantages of DAOs

A key distinction between traditional venture capital funds, most accredited investor crowdfunding rounds, and DAOs is the gatekeeping. Platforms such as OurCrowd, SeedInvest, and Crowdcube usually confine offerings to accredited investors, meeting regulatory safeguards but shutting out most retail participants. Scholars echo this trade-off. Cicchiello and others show how investor protection rules in crowdfunding law narrow eligibility,[21] while Professor Darian Ibrahim notes that compliance costs push platforms toward limited "qualified" pools.[22] DAOs invert that logic. By using blockchain governance tokens and smart contracts, they let virtually anyone buy in, vote, and share upside—no accreditation thresholds, geographic barriers, or intermediaries. The result is a funding environment that is markedly more open and inclusive than either venture capital or regulated crowdfunding.

This inclusiveness is one of the defining characteristics of DAOs, which operate outside of traditional financial frameworks and allow for a greater number of participants. The broader participation model DAOs foster offers investors of all backgrounds the chance to engage in early-stage financing, without the stringent regulatory requirements that crowdfunding platforms must adhere to in many jurisdictions. Thus, DAOs remove the barriers to entry that typically limit investor involvement in early-stage startups, democratizing investment opportunities in ways that even the most accessible crowdfunding platforms cannot fully match.[23]

1.4.2. Challenges and limitations of DAOs

While DAOs open investment opportunities to a broader audience, there are certain challenges associated with this openness, which require further analysis and exploration.

1.4.2.1. Potential drawbacks of inclusivity

The DAOs' inclusivity can expose uninformed, inexperienced, or less tech-savvy investors to significant risks. The complexity of blockchain technology and smart contracts may not be fully understood by all participants, leading to uninformed decision-making.[24] Moreover, the absence of intermediaries or regulatory oversight can increase the risk of fraudulent activities, scams, and Ponzi schemes within the DAO ecosystem.[25] For instance, the lack of mandatory disclosures or due diligence

[21] Generally Antonella Francesca Cicchiello and others, "Entrepreneurial Dynamics and Investor-Oriented Approaches for Regulating the Equity-Based Crowdfunding" (2021) 10 Journal of Entrepreneurship and Public Policy 27 <https://www.emerald.com/insight/content/doi/10.1108/JEPP-03-2019-0010/full/html> accessed October 18, 2024.

[22] Darian M Ibrahim, "Equity Crowdfunding: A Market for Lemons" (2015) 100 Minnesota Law Review 561.

[23] Generally Cicchiello and others (n 21).

[24] eg Teuta Franjkovic, "Solana's Mango Markets Seeks SEC Settlement Following Eisenburg Exploit" (*CCN*, August 20, 2024) <https://www.ccn.com/news/crypto/mango-markets-seeks-sec-settlement-eisenburg-fraud/> accessed October 18, 2024 (discussing how the exploit exposed significant vulnerabilities in the decentralized platform, including arguably voting to forgive the attacker).

[25] ibid.

processes can result in investors supporting projects without adequate information about their viability or legitimacy.

Additionally, there are challenges associated with the volatility of cryptocurrencies and tokens used in DAOs that can lead to substantial financial losses. Uninformed investors may not be prepared for such volatility or may not have diversified portfolios to mitigate risks. The democratization of investment through DAOs, while innovative, necessitates a careful approach to educate and protect investors from potential pitfalls associated with complex financial instruments.

1.4.2.2. Investor protection mechanisms in DAOs

Unlike traditional investment vehicles that operate under stringent regulatory frameworks designed to protect investors, DAOs often lack formal mechanisms to safeguard participants' interests. However, some DAOs implement innovative approaches to address this gap that include (1) code audits and security measures, using third-party firms that can audit their smart contracts, reducing the risk of vulnerabilities;[26] (2) insurance protocols, which some DAOs utilize to provide coverage against smart contract failures or hacks;[27] (3) governance structures that implement robust governance models, such as requiring multi-signature approvals for significant transactions;[28] and (4) dispute resolution platforms that offer decentralized arbitration services, allowing DAOs to resolve disputes among members or with third parties in a transparent manner.[29]

In addition, as further described below in Section 3 of this chapter, DAO members may have limited options for legal recourse in cases of fraud or mismanagement, given that their legal status remains largely unsettled and jurisdiction-dependent.[30] Similarly, the pseudonymous nature of blockchain can make it difficult to hold bad actors accountable.[31] Finally, efforts to comply with Know Your Customer (KYC) and anti-money laundering (AML) regulations are inconsistent, potentially exposing stakeholders to risks associated with illicit activities.

[26] eg DAOs like Aave have undergone extensive security audits. "Security" (*Aave*) <https://docs.aave.com/security> accessed October 30, 2024 (stating that "Aave's official audit reports and verifications from independent security companies.").

[27] eg Nexus Mutual. Danny Nelson, "DeFi Insurer Nexus Mutual Requests $153K for 6-Month Budget" (*CoinDesk*, March 8 2024) <https://www.coindesk.com/business/2024/01/29/defi-insurer-nexus-mutual-requests-153k-for-6-month-budget/> accessed October 18, 2024.

[28] "Decentralized Power: Exploring Multisignature Wallets for DAO Governance" (*Medium*, January 29, 2024) <https://tozex.medium.com/decentralized-power-exploring-multisignature-wallets-for-dao-governance-0457d6afec39> accessed October 18, 2024.

[29] eg "About Kleros" (*Kleros*) <https://kleros.io/about/> accessed October 18, 2024 ("Kleros is an open source online dispute resolution protocol which uses blockchain and crowdsourcing to fairly adjudicate disputes.").

[30] Generally Kara Bruce, Christopher K Odinet, and Andrea Tosato, "DAOs in Financial Distress" in Kevin Werbach, Eva Micheler, and Bianca Kremer (eds), *Foundations of Decentralized Organizations: Blockchain and the Future of Corporate Law* (OUP 2025).

[31] eg Nizan Geslevich Packin, "How Hector DAO's Bankruptcy Case Is Shaping the Future of DeFi" (Bloomberg Law, August 20, 2024) <https://news.bloomberglaw.com/us-law-week/how-hector-daos-bankruptcy-case-is-shaping-the-future-of-defi> accessed April 29, 2025) (highlighting Hector DAO's collapse to show that blockchain's pseudonymous wallets often mask real-world identities, making it extraordinarily hard for courts or creditors to trace misappropriated assets and hold insiders accountable).

1.4.2.3. Lack of support commonly offered by traditional VC

Beyond writing a cheque, VC firms and leading crowdfunding portals wrap founders in a dense web of non-financial assistance—strategy coaching, operational hand-holding, marketing muscle, and warm introductions to customers, partners, and later-stage investors. Delivered by veteran entrepreneurs, sector specialists, and professional investors, this "smart-money" package often matters more to a young company's survival than the cash itself. LPs supply most of the capital, but general partners contribute the bootstrapping know-how:[32] they choose deals, sit on boards,[33] and plug portfolio CEOs into networks that an unaided start-up could never reach. The discussion that follows unpacks this value-add in three buckets—strategic, operational, and networking support—and then explains why investment-focused DAOs, despite their fundraising prowess, still struggle to replicate it.

First, strategic support. Traditional VC funds and leading equity crowdfunding portals contribute far more than capital. General partners—often former founders, sector specialists, and professional investors—sit on portfolio company boards,[34] nominate additional directors, and appoint board observers who monitor performance, assist with budgeting and financial planning, and secure later funding rounds.[35] They refine business models, develop go-to-market road maps, position firms for scalability, help founders make important decisions, and navigate high-stakes governance conflicts such as pivoting strategy or replacing a founder-manager.[36] For instance, given the distinct skill sets and expertise required to establish a company versus managing a larger one, disputes between founders-managers and directors are particularly prevalent in the startup context.[37] These disputes can involve decisions like changing the company's direction over the founder-manager's objection, or even firing the founder-manager, and typically mirror the growth and development of the startup, so outside guidance could be very useful. Moreover, sector-focused funds can

[32] Bernard S Black and Ronald J Gilson, "Venture Capital and the Structure of Capital Markets: Banks Versus Stock Markets" (1998) 47 Journal of Financial Economics 243, 245 (noting that VCs are specialized in providing portfolio companies with monitoring and advisory services, as well as financial and reputational capital).

[33] Ronald J Gilson, "Engineering a Venture Capital Market: Lessons from the American Experience" (2003) 55 Stanford Law Review 1067, 1070–71.

[34] Jeffrey A Sonnenfeld, "What Makes Great Boards Great" (*Harvard Business Review*, September 2002) <https://hbr.org/2002/09/what-makes-great-boards-great> accessed October 18, 2024 (discussing the importance of having skilled board members).

[35] Generally Nizan Geslevich Packin and Anat Alon Beck, "Board Observers" (2025) 5 University of Illinois Law Review 1507 (describing how the VC-backed startups have board observers listen in and observe their board activities, with the main drawback being that board observers do not formally have a fiduciary duty to act in the best interest of the company and its shareholders).

[36] Shrishti Bhardwaj, "What is Venture Capital (VC)?" and "How Venture Capital Works?" (*Smallcase*, October 19, 2023) <https://www.smallcase.com/learn/vc-venture-capital/#how-venture-capital-works> accessed October 18, 2024; Joy Samuel, "Understanding Venture Capital: What It Is And How It Works" (*startup geek*) <https://startupgeek.com/blog/venture-capital/> accessed October 18, 2024.

[37] Noam Wasserman, "The Founder's Dilemma" (*Harvard Business Review*, February 2008) <https://hbr.org/2008/02/the-founders-dilemma> accessed October 18, 2024 ("[T]he faster that founder-CEOs lead their companies to the point where they need outside funds and new management skills, the quicker they will lose management control. Success makes founders less qualified to lead the company .... 'Congrats, you're a success! Sorry, you're fired,' is the implicit message that many investors have to send founder-CEOs.").

add tailored insight in technology, healthcare, clean energy, and other verticals, giving startups a competitive edge that raw money cannot provide.[38]

Second, operational support. VC teams and curated portals tackle day-to-day execution. They optimize supply chains, streamline product development cycles, and install scalable processes so young companies can grow efficiently. Their deep talent networks help recruit key engineers, sales leaders, and C-suite executives—crucial hires that fledgling firms struggle to attract alone. By advising on financial planning, cash flow management, and resource allocation, VC observers and operating partners guide startups through growth and scalability possibilities, past common pitfalls, and even prepare them for future investment rounds.[39] They also issue LP-style quarterly reports that track portfolio performance and risk, setting a transparency baseline investors now expect. The impact of these actions, especially on young entrepreneurial companies, is particularly significant during the early stages of the startups' growth.[40]

Third, networking support. Equally valuable is the web of relationships that VCs, leading crowdfunding portals, and these types of intermediaries provide. VCs and platforms connect founders to seasoned mentors, institutional investors, corporate partners, and early customers, using regular, verifiable metrics shared across the investor syndicate that make these relationship building and maintenance far smoother. For example, OurCrowd's network of advisors and mentors helps startups navigate

[38] eg John Paul Hampstead, "Why Venture Capitalists Must Specialize: The Rise of Sector-Based VC Firms" (*FreightWaves*, August 17, 2020) <https://www.freightwaves.com/news/why-venture-capitalists-must-specialize> accessed October 18, 2024; Willow Shah-Neville, "Meet the 'Biotech Mafia': How Specialized Biotech VC Firms Are Dominating Industry Funding Once Again" (*Labiotech.eu*, November 20, 2023) <https://www.labiotech.eu/in-depth/specialized-biotech-vc-firms-funding/> accessed October 18, 2024.

[39] Mia Sullivan, "How to Build Startup Ecosystems" (*Hubspot Blog*, July 22, 2024) <https://blog.hubspot.com/sales/startup-ecosystem> accessed October 18, 2024; Adam Hayes, "What Is Venture Capital? Definition, Pros, Cons, and How It Works" (*Investopedia*, October 18, 2024) <https://www.investopedia.com/terms/v/venturecapital.asp> accessed October 18, 2024.

[40] For more on the role of VCs and investment in startups, Jill E Fisch, "A Lesson from Startups: Contracting Out of Shareholder Appraisal" (2022) 107 Iowa Law Review 941 (focusing on the corporate notion of appraisal, including its importance and relevance for investments in startups). For more on the distinction between cash flow and control rights, William A Sahlman, "The Structure and Governance of Venture Capital Organizations" (1990) 27 Journal of Financial Economics 473; Paul A Gompers and Josh Lerner, *The Venture Capital Cycle* (MIT Press 1999) 127–31; Manuel A Utset, "Reciprocal Fairness, Strategic Behavior & Venture Survival: A Theory of Venture Capital-Financed Firms" (2002) 2002 Wisconsin Law Review 45, 55 (writing that "Venture capitalists in most instances negotiate to get outright control of the board."); Steven N Kaplan and Per Strömberg, "Financial Contracting Theory Meets the Real World: An Empirical Analysis of Venture Capital Contracts" (2003) 70 Review of Economic Studies 28; William W Bratton and Michael L Wachter, "A Theory of Preferred Stock" (2013) 161 University of Pennsylvania Law Review 1815, 1875 (stating that "[VCs] holding preferred sometimes take voting control and can dominate the boards of directors even when holding a minority of the votes."); Zohar Goshen and Richard Squire, "Principal Costs: A New Theory for Corporate Law and Governance" (2017) 117 Columbia Law Review 767, 784–85; Robert P Bartlett and Eric Talley, "Law and Corporate Governance" in Benjamin E Hermalin and Michael S Weisbach (eds), *The Handbook of The Economics of Corporate Governance*, vol 1 (North Holland 2017) 177, 185–86 ("privately held firms tend historically to grapple with 'horizontal' governance dilemmas, involving disputes among competing shareholders (or classes of shareholders) who seek to enhance their influence and control relative to other shareholders To the extent this trend continues, the study of governance in privately held firms is likely to become more critical to important policy debates."); Yifat Aran, "Beyond Covenants Not to Compete: Equilibrium in High-Tech Startup Labor Markets" (2018) 70 Stanford Law Review 1235, 1239 (note) (describing how a combination of economic and legal conditions enables successful startup managements' to delay their companies' going public, weakening some corporate governance mechanisms).

the challenges of scaling a business and provides valuable insights that can enhance the company's growth trajectory.[41] Similarly, SeedInvest provides startups with access to a vast network of institutional investors, corporate partners, and industry experts, in addition to a post-funding support program, which enables startups to leverage the expertise and networks of SeedInvest's community.[42] Crowdcube, another leading equity crowdfunding platform, provides startups with marketing assistance to help them effectively promote their funding campaigns. Crowdcube's team of marketing experts works closely with startups to develop compelling campaign strategies, create engaging content, and reach a broader audience. This marketing support can significantly increase the visibility of a startup's campaign, attracting more investors and increasing the chances of successful fundraising.[43] These examples illustrate how despite having more of a decentralized nature than a typical VC, crowdfunding investing platforms can and do go beyond merely providing financial capital. They offer a holistic support system that includes mentorship, strategic advice, marketing assistance, and access to extensive networks. Regular, verifiable metrics shared across the investor syndicate make these relationship introductions far smoother. This integrated support helps bridge the gap between innovative ideas and successful businesses, ensuring that startups have the resources and guidance needed to achieve long-term success that a stand-alone startup could rarely have.[44]

By contrast, the DAO model, which also delivers capital, still falls short on the surrounding "smart-money" infrastructure. Indeed, investment-focused DAOs excel at pooling funds quickly and democratizing access, yet their decentralized, volunteer-driven structure makes sustained, accountable support uneven. Without designated partners or board seats, DAOs struggle to provide systematic strategic guidance, hands-on operational help, or curated networks. Mentorship "workstreams" and Discord channels do exist, but participation is optional and expertise inconsistent, leaving founders without consistent, accessible, and reliable advice on scaling, talent recruitment, or market entry. Additionally, DAOs still lack a universally accepted reporting standard or audit framework, leaving many token-holders uncertain about true performance and risk. Until DAOs formalize clear roles and incentives for delivering these non-financial services, they will continue to supply capital and crowd

[41] eg "Ultimate FAQ: OurCrowd, What, How, Why, When" (*FasterCapital*, June 23, 2024) <https://fastercapital.com/content/Ultimate-FAQ-OurCrowd--What--How--Why--When.html> accessed October 18, 2024 (describing under the "Access to Expertise" section that "OurCrowd provides investors with access to a network of industry experts and mentors who can offer insights and guidance/ . . . .").

[42] "Does SeedInvest Provide Any Support Or Resources for Startups After They Raise Funds?" (*FasterCapital Blog*) <https://fastercapital.com/topics/does-seedinvest-provide-any-support-or-resources-for-startups-after-they-raise-funds.html> accessed October 18, 2024 (describing how the platform offers "ongoing support and resources to help startups succeed even after their fundraising rounds. From investor relations and reporting to mentorship, . . . SeedInvest provides a comprehensive suite of services to assist startups" and "recognizes the value of mentorship and offers guidance to startups through their network of experienced advisors and industry experts.").

[43] eg "Where Can I Get More Support for My Campaign?" (*Crowdcube*) <https://help.crowdcube.com/hc/en-us/articles/115001549324-Where-can-I-get-more-support-for-my-campaign> accessed October 18, 2024 (detailing on its site its hands-on support including "offering extensive marketing and PR services to help businesses create a buzz around their brand and crowdfunding raise").

[44] Angelina Graumann, "How to Get Into Venture Capital: A Beginner's Guide" (*Visible*, April 5, 2024) <https://visible.vc/blog/how-to-get-into-venture-capital/> accessed October 18, 2024.

sentiment but prove less effective in offering the holistic support ecosystem that distinguishes traditional VC and vetted crowdfunding platforms.

1.4.2.4. The legal landscape surrounding collective investments

Traditional VC firms operate in a well-defined regulatory compliance landscape, providing legal certainty through established frameworks that ensure adherence to securities laws, investor protections, and standardized reporting requirements, thereby fostering a stable and predictable investment environment.[45]

Similarly, leading crowdfunding platforms benefit from a well-defined regulatory compliance landscape so that crowdfunding investments are conducted in a transparent and secure manner, reducing the risks associated with emerging funding mechanisms. Therefore, the user-friendly legal nature of these platforms means that even those without extensive technical knowledge can easily navigate the investment process.

A major advantage traditional VC and financing models (including crowdfunding investing platforms) have over DAOs is that they offer legal certainty. One of the most formidable barriers to the widespread adoption of DAOs is the lack of clarity regarding their legal status. In particular is the issue of regulation by enforcement,[46] which is "a historically widely criticized practice, [that] occurs when a regulator or government agency creates a piecemeal rule by taking enforcement actions or via interpretive letters, therefore bypassing the traditional process of regulation creating."[47] And while historically this criticism was largely directed at the Securities

[45] Anat Alon-Beck, "Delaware Beware" U Ill L Rev (forthcoming 2025) <https://papers.ssrn.com/sol3/papers.cfm?abstract_id=4921048> accessed October 19, 2024; Hilary J Allen, "Interest Rates, Venture Capital, and Financial Stability" (2025) 5 University of Illinois Law Review 1695 <https://papers.ssrn.com/sol3/papers.cfm?abstract_id=4513037> accessed October 19, 2024; Anat Alon-Beck, "Incorporating Unicorns: An Empirical Analysis" (2025) 62 University of Houston Law Review 891 <https://houstonlawreview.org/article/138612 > accessed October 19, 2024.

[46] Chris Brummer, Yesha Yadav, and David Zaring, "Regulation by Enforcement" (2023) 96 Southern California Law Review 1297; Nizan Gelsevich Packin and Hadar Jabotinsky, "Blocking as Regulating? Blacklisting Generative AI", 73 American University Law Review (forthcoming 2024); also Roberta S Karmel, *Regulation by Prosecution: The Securities and Exchange Commission v. Corporate America* (Simon & Schuster 1982) 95 ("The evils of combining prosecutorial and adjudicative functions have been exacerbated by the predilection for formulating regulatory policy through the prosecution of enforcement cases."); Harvey L Pitt and Karen L Shapiro, "Securities Regulation by Enforcement: A Look Ahead at the Next Decade" (1990) 7 Yale Journal on Regulation 149, 155 (describing that many agencies have not maintained a "vigorous, highly-visible, and largely successful enforcement profile"); Donna M Nagy, "Judicial Reliance on Regulatory Interpretations in SEC No-Action Letters: Current Problems and a Proposed Framework" (1998) 83 Cornell Law Review 921, 937 (explaining interpretive letters as the letters which agencies send in response to a request for guidance on the applicability of a particular regulation); Committee on Capital Markets Regulation, *Interim Report of the Committee on Capital Markets Regulation* (2006) 66 <https://capmktsreg.org/wp-content/uploads/2022/11/Interim-Report-of-the-Committee-on-Capital-Markets-Regulation-1.pdf> accessed October 19, 2024 ("bank regulators, concentrating on the 'safety and soundness' of the financial system, take a prudential approach to supervision and generally do not broadly publicize their enforcement actions"); James J Park, "The Competing Paradigms of Securities Regulation" (2007) 57 Duke Law Journal 625, 635–37 (describing how regulation by enforcement happens when agencies or regulators use interpretive letters to create a rule that otherwise does not actually clearly exist); generally Douglas C Dreier, "The Lending-Limit Combination Rules: Regulation by Enforcement at the OCC" (2013) 62 Duke Law Journal 1747 (explaining how regulation-by-enforcement is relevant to other government agencies beyond the SEC, including other banking regulators).

[47] Packin and Jabotinsky (n 46) fn 245.

and Exchange Commission (SEC), other regulators have also relied on this practice as part of their rulemaking, often justifying it by using former Secretary of the Treasury Timothy Geithner's rationale that "it is imperative [in some situations to] ... be able to adapt quickly to innovation and to changes."[48]

Traditional legal frameworks do not easily accommodate entities that operate without centralized leadership or a clear jurisdictional base, making it difficult to classify DAOs within existing corporate structures or regulatory regimes.[49] Many view DAOs as partnerships due to their collaborative nature and the involvement of multiple parties in decision-making processes. This classification has significant legal implications, as partnerships generally imply joint and several liability for all members. Such a perspective can deter participation in DAOs due to the potential legal risks involved.[50] Different states have begun addressing these challenges by creating new rules to avoid classifying DAOs as partnerships.[51] For example, Wyoming has been at the forefront of this regulatory innovation. The state introduced legislation to recognize DAOs as distinct legal entities, thereby providing a clearer legal framework for their operation.[52]

Finally, there are securities law compliance issues that pose challenges. Indeed, many DAOs issue tokens that could be classified as securities under various jurisdictions, which subjects them to stringent regulatory requirements concerning registration, disclosure, and compliance. As mentioned above, the case of "The DAO" prompted the SEC to assert that digital tokens could be considered securities, underscoring the need for DAOs to navigate complex securities laws.

[48] Julie A Hill, "Bank Capital Regulation by Enforcement: An Empirical Study" (2012) 87 Indiana Law Journal 645, 695 (referring to the letter from Timothy F Geithner, US Secretary of the Treasury, to Representative Keith Ellison on 11 January 2010), arguing that the alternative could "produce an ossified safety and soundness framework that is unable to evolve to keep pace with change and to prevent regulatory arbitrage").

[49] Generally Florian Möslein and Daniel Ostrovski, "Legal Personality of Decentralized Autonomous Organizations (DAOs): Privilege or Necessity?" in Madalena Perestrelo de Oliveira and António Garcia Rolo (eds), *Decentralised Autonomous Organisation (DAO) Regulation—Principles and Perspectives for the Future* (Mohr Siebeck 2024) (examining the different DAO classifications including the partnership possibility).

[50] Generally Biyan Mienert, "Limited Liability as Applied to DAOs" in Madalena Perestrelo de Oliveira and António Garcia Rolo (eds), *Decentralised Autonomous Organisation (DAO) Regulation—Principles and Perspectives for the Future* (Mohr Siebeck 2024) (discussing the liability issue).

[51] Chris Brummer and Rodrigo Seira, "Legal Wrappers and DAOs" (30 May 2022) <https://ssrn.com/abstract=4123737> accessed October 19, 2024 (providing a comprehensive overview of the legal structures available to DAOs and examining the unique characteristics of DAOs, such as dispersed memberships and blockchain-based governance, which do not align well with traditional legal entities like corporations, nonprofits, and partnerships. The paper explores various legal wrappers that can be used to mitigate issues related to liability, tax treatment, and regulatory compliance).

[52] Leo Schwartz, "Wyoming Wants to Become the Delaware of DAOs with New Crypto Law for Decentralized Autonomous Organizations" (*Fortune*, March 8, 2024) <https://fortune.com/crypto/2024/03/08/wyoming-dao-a16z-crypto-crypto-blockchain-ooki/> accessed October 19, 2024 (discussing Wyoming's efforts to establish itself as the leading jurisdiction for DAOs, akin to Delaware's status for corporate entities. Wyoming's new crypto law enables DAOs to register as limited liability companies (LLCs), providing them with legal recognition and liability protection, in a move that is intended to attract blockchain and crypto projects by offering a clear and supportive regulatory environment, given the involvement of significant VCs such as Andreessen Horowitz).

2. Comparative Analysis of DAOs, Traditional VC, and Crowdfunding Platforms

DAOs are versatile and have the potential to revolutionize various sectors, including the investment landscape. For instance, MetaCartel Venture DAO is a notable example of a DAO functioning as a collective investment vehicle.[53] Established in 2019, it pooled funds from various investors to support early-stage dApps and blockchain projects. Members contributed capital in exchange for governance tokens, which allowed them to vote on investment decisions.[54] MetaCartel has successfully funded several projects, demonstrating the DAO model's viability in venture funding. However, it operates within a legal framework by registering as an LLC in the state of Delaware,[55] addressing some regulatory concerns.

Beyond using DAOs as investment vehicles, DAOs' applications in other areas, such as real estate and philanthropy, have already been showcased. In the real estate sector, DAOs offer a transformative approach by tokenizing property ownership.[56] Platforms like RealT enable investors to purchase fractional shares of properties, thereby arguably democratizing access to real estate investments. This model enhances liquidity, as tokenized shares can be bought and sold on secondary markets, providing investors with greater flexibility compared to traditional real estate investments, which are often illiquid and require significant capital commitments.[57] The process of tokenization involves converting real estate assets into digital tokens on a blockchain, each representing a fraction of ownership. Investors can then acquire these tokens, which entitle them to a proportionate share of rental income and capital appreciation. By leveraging

[53] "What Is MetaCartel and How Does MetaCartel Work?" (*Blockchain Council*, May 19, 2022) <https://www.blockchain-council.org/dao/metacartel/> accessed October 19, 2024.

[54] "MetaCartel Ventures: Recent Investments" (*Crunchbase*) <https://www.crunchbase.com/organization/metacartel-ventures/recent_investments> accessed October 19, 2024 (according to Crunchbase, MetaCartel Ventures has made 32 investments. Their most recent investment was on February 8, 2024); "DAO-as-a-Service Infrastructure Dora Factory Closed Seed Funding" (*Cointelegraph*, February 7, 2021) <https://cointelegraph.com/press-releases/dao-as-a-service-infrastructure-dora-factory-closed-seed-funding> accessed October 19, 2024 (referencing "newly emerged DAO VCs," such as DuckDAO and MetaCartel Ventures).

[55] "About MetaCartel Ventures, What is Venture DAO?" (*MetaCartel Ventures*) <https://metacartel.xyz/about> accessed October 19, 2024 (stating that "[o]ur DAO is made up of a code and law pairing; with our business LLC entity being tightly coupled with its smart contracts and token technology deployed on the Ethereum main-net"); "MetaCartel Ventures Grimoir" (*MetaCartel Ventures*) <https://assets.website-files.com/5713afec1b6331b577731396/628253fc4e3c6a60cc17f9f8_MCV-Grimoire-Final-All-Exhihbits> accessed October 19, 2024.

[56] Franco Faraudo, "The DAO of Real Estate Investment Management" (*Propmodo*, April 21, 2024) <https://propmodo.com/the-dao-of-real-estate-investment-management/> accessed October 19, 2024 (exploring the evolution and potential of DAOs in real estate investment management. Originating from cryptocurrencies like Bitcoin, and gaining traction with Ethereum's Vitalik Buterin in 2016, DAOs have expanded to physical assets. In 2021, around 6,000 individuals used a DAO to purchase 40 acres in Wyoming, leveraging collective decision-making without traditional administrative costs. Recent developments include GoKey's DAO-controlled cryptocurrency tied to real estate price indexes, which stabilizes token pricing and provides a more stable investment environment).

[57] "The Birth of a DAO to Decentralize the Ecosystem" (*Medium*, April 7, 2024) <https://medium.com/realtplatform/the-birth-of-a-dao-to-decentralize-the-ecosystem-965f58211c13> accessed October 19, 2024 (discussing the creation of a DAO by RealT to decentralize the real estate ecosystem. It highlights the steps taken to establish the DAO, the technology used, and the expected benefits of decentralization in real estate investments, such as increased transparency, reduced costs, and greater investor participation).

a DAO structure, RealT automates the distribution of rental income through smart contracts, ensuring timely and transparent payments to token-holders.[58] One of the key advantages of this model is the reduction of entry barriers. Traditional real estate investments often require significant capital and entail complex legal and administrative processes. In contrast, the tokenization of real estate assets allows smaller investors to participate in the market, promoting financial inclusion. Additionally, the use of blockchain technology ensures that all transactions are recorded on an immutable ledger, enhancing transparency and reducing the potential for fraud.

However, the adoption of DAOs in real estate is not without challenges.[59] Legal and regulatory uncertainties surrounding the tokenization of real estate,[60] and the use of DAOs for investment purposes remain significant hurdles. For instance, questions regarding the classification of tokens as securities and compliance with existing real estate and financial regulations need to be addressed to foster wider adoption.

Similarly to the realm of real estate, in the philanthropy sector DAOs have also been utilized, where the same pooling-of-capital and token-governance mechanics that power collective investment DAOs are repurposed to manage and distribute donations in a transparent and efficient manner.[61] For example, Andreessen Horowitz recently created a donor-advised vehicle that channels part of its carry into grants for underrepresented founders, demonstrating how a mainstream VC can fuse traditional investing with an explicitly philanthropic mandate.[62] Indeed, in the context of funding and sustaining open source software projects, many projects secure funding through donations, which play a crucial role in their development and maintenance, ensuring their long-term sustainability. These donations can come from various sources, including individuals, organizations, or business entities. Blockchain technology offers new possibilities for funding and incentivizing users' contributions in

[58] ibid.

[59] Shermin Voshmgir and Michael Zargham, "Real Estate Tokenization and the Law: The Regulatory Challenges of Security Tokens" (2020) 15 New York University Journal of Law and Business 101, 110 (exploring how security tokens can revolutionize real estate investment by enhancing liquidity and democratizing access but also highlighting significant regulatory hurdles, including securities law compliance and the need for legal frameworks to adapt to these new technologies).

[60] For more on this, "Exploring the Trends in the Tokenization of Real Estate" (*Proptech Jobs*) <https://proptechjobs.com/exploring-the-trends-in-the-tokenization-of-real-estate/> accessed October 19, 2024 (discussing the growing trend of real estate tokenization, which involves creating digital tokens representing ownership in real estate properties. This method increases accessibility, enhances liquidity through secondary markets, and enables fractional ownership. Tokenization also facilitates global investment opportunities and improves transparency and security using blockchain technology. The article highlights regulatory considerations and the potential for increased market efficiency through automation and digitization of real estate processes); also Juliet M Moringiello and Christopher K Odinet, "The Property Law of Tokens" (2022) 74 Florida Law Review 607 (examining the legal challenges and implications of applying traditional property law principles to digital tokens. The authors analyze how tokens, as a form of digital asset, interact with existing property law frameworks and explore potential legal reforms needed to address issues of ownership, transfer, and security in the context of tokenized assets).

[61] Primavera de Filippi and Xavier Lavayssière, "Blockchain Technology: Toward a Decentralized Governance of Digital Platforms?" in Anna Grear and David Bollier (eds), *The Great Awakening: New Modes of Life amidst Capitalist Ruins* (Punctum Books 2020) 202 <https://hal.science/hal-03098502/document> accessed October 19, 2024.

[62] Natasha Mascarenhas, "A16z launches donor-advised fund for underserved founders with $2.2 million in initial contributions" (*TechCrunch*, June 3, 2020) <https://techcrunch.com/2020/06/03/andreessen-horowitz-launches-2-2m-fund-to-invest-in-underserved-founders> accessed April 29, 2025.

commons-based projects. Crowdfunding portals such as Kickstarter, GoFundMe, and Indiegogo likewise demonstrate dual use: the same infrastructure that finances gadgets or indie films is routinely mobilized to raise millions for disaster relief, medical expenses, and other public interest causes. Commons-based projects are collaborative initiatives where a shared resource or asset is collectively owned and managed by a community or group of individuals. These projects involve open collaboration, decentralized decision-making, and the sharing of resources, knowledge, or goods among participants. Examples of commons-based projects include open source software development, Wikipedia, community gardens, and DAOs.[63] For instance, platforms like Giveth—a nonprofit organization and open source platform for decentralized projects—leverage DAO structures to ensure that funds are allocated according to the collective decisions of the community, thereby enhancing trust and engagement among stakeholders.[64] Some venture firms go further and launch or bankroll purpose-built grant DAOs that operate much like decentralized foundations. Big Green DAO, founded by early Tesla backer Kimbal Musk, directs food justice grants through token-based community voting, while Gitcoin Grants, originally seeded by Web3 investors, uses quadratic funding rounds in which several VC funds supply or match the donor pool. In both cases, blockchain governance lets the wider community, rather than a traditional grants committee, decide how the money is allocated.[65]

Giveth operates by allowing donors to contribute funds to specific causes or projects. These funds are then managed through smart contracts that automate the distribution process based on predefined criteria and community votes. This decentralized approach aims to ensure that the transactions are transparent and that funds would be used as intended, arguably reducing the risk of mismanagement and fraud.[66] Therefore, the transparency afforded by blockchain technology is particularly valuable in the philanthropic sector, where concerns about the misuse of funds can deter potential donors.[67] In effect, philanthropic DAOs substitute social impact returns for financial ones while otherwise mirroring the architecture of investment DAOs. Such philanthropic DAOs may also experiment with channeling a portion of their treasuries into mission-driven start-ups—climate tech, health, and financial inclusion ventures. By providing real-time visibility into the allocation and use of donated funds, DAOs can build trust and encourage more people to contribute to charitable causes.

[63] ibid.

[64] Danielle Gennety, "The Giveth DAO: Community GIVernance" (*Giveth Blog*, December 6, 2021) <https://blog.giveth.io/the-giveth-dao-community-givernance-84f55fa1ce36> accessed October 19, 2024.

[65] Thurman, A, "Kimbal Musk's Big Green DAO is a big step for Web 3: Can a DAO founded by Elon Musk's brother solve philanthropy's many pain points?" (*CoinDesk*, November 30, 2021). https://www.coindesk.com/tech/2021/11/30/kimbal-musks-big-green-dao-is-a-big-step-for-web-3> accessed April 29, 2025.

[66] Diana Aguilar, "Sustainability: What Do DAOs Need to Succeed in the Long Run?" (*Cointelegraph*, November 26, 2022) <https://cointelegraph.com/news/sustainability-what-do-daos-need-to-succeed-in-the-long-run> accessed October 19, 2024 (highlighting the role of tokenization and external funding, such as grants and venture capital, in supporting DAOs financially. Additionally, it addresses challenges such as fund transparency and the centralization of power within DAOs, using examples from various projects to illustrate these points).

[67] ibid.

Moreover, the use of DAOs in philanthropy can foster greater community engagement. Donors are not only passive contributors but active participants in decision-making processes, voting on which projects to fund and how resources should be allocated. This participatory model can lead to more effective and responsive philanthropic initiatives, as it aligns funding decisions with the preferences and insights of a diverse group of stakeholders.[68]

Despite these benefits, the implementation of DAOs in philanthropy also faces challenges. Regulatory issues, particularly concerning the classification of DAO tokens or other digital assets, and compliance with charitable organization laws, need to be addressed.[69] Additionally, the technology's complexity can be a barrier to entry for smaller organizations or those without technical expertise, as further described below; notably, these hurdles echo the legal and operational frictions that conventional VC firms can encounter when they launch impact-oriented funds, underscoring that both models must reconcile innovative financing mechanisms with established for-profit and nonprofit rules.

3. Future Developments and Challenges

The future of DAOs is closely tied to technological advancements in blockchain and related technologies. Developments in interoperability, such as cross-chain bridges, will enable DAOs to operate across multiple blockchain networks, enhancing their functionality and reach. Currently, there are numerous blockchain platforms, each with its own protocols, smart contract languages, and consensus mechanisms. For DAOs to function across this fragmented landscape, there must be interoperability between different blockchains.[70] This would allow assets and information to flow

[68] Gennety (n 64) (also stating that Giveth stresses how "[w]e are progressively decentralizing the Giveth decision-making process by building a community and a token-based economy around our platform that recognizes contributions, values participation and rewards altruism").

[69] Joan MacLeod Heminway, "Non-Investment Finance in an NFT World" in Nizan Geslevich Packin (ed), *The Cambridge Handbook of Law and Policy for NFTs* (CUP 2024) (exploring the use of digital assets for raising non-investment funding, particularly in nonprofit and political contexts. While such assets and tokens can facilitate new funding mechanisms by offering digital assets as premiums or rewards, their use raises significant legal issues, and the absence of comprehensive federal regulation and the challenge of valuing such assets and tokens consistently—particularly NFTs—pose barriers to their successful integration in non-investment finance); Nizan Geslevich Packin and Uri Volovelsky, "Digital Assets, Anti-Money Laundering and Counter Financing of Terrorism: An Analysis of Evolving Regulations and Enforcement in the Era of NFTs" in Nizan Geslevich Packin (ed), *The Cambridge Handbook of Law and Policy for NFTs* (CUP 2024) (focusing on anti-money laundering issues associated with tokens and digital assets).

[70] Discussing interoperability in a different context, in the early days of Application Programming Interfaces (APIs), the advantage of platforms that use them, and the network effects that could be generated by this, Peter Menell wrote: "The ability to control interfaces through intellectual property protection, technological protections (such as digital rights management), and contracts became a major part of these industries. Having innovative, competitively-priced products continued to be important, but establishing and building a successful software-based platform became the key to success. Companies could use API strategies to lock in consumers and lock out competitors. … Other computer companies used API strategies to control access to their video game platforms, cell phone networks, replacement parts (such as ink cartridges for printers), and graphical user interfaces. The contours of intellectual property rules governing interoperability strategies … became a major battleground."

seamlessly across networks, enabling more complex financial operations and broader participation. Solutions such as cross-chain bridges and blockchain agnostic protocols are under development, but widespread implementation and adoption remain challenges.

A related issue is the lack of standardization across the blockchain industry. Different platforms have varying standards for smart contracts, token issuance, and transaction formats. For DAOs to integrate with both traditional financial systems and each other, common standards and protocols need to be established. Standardization would facilitate smoother interactions between disparate systems and reduce the complexity of developing DAOs that can operate within the broader financial ecosystem.

Another correlated and relevant issue for DAOs to attract investment from a broad range of participants relates to user experience and accessibility. Indeed, the process of interacting with DAOs is not as straightforward as dealing with traditional and regulated financial services. This includes understanding blockchain transactions, which are more complex and tech-based, and participating in DAO governance. Improving and simplifying user experience and making blockchain technology more accessible to non-technical users is therefore an essential step toward integrating DAOs with the existing financial ecosystem.

There is also the issue of regulatory innovation. The decentralized and global nature of DAOs does not fit neatly into the jurisdictional boundaries of traditional financial regulation. Regulatory bodies around the world are grappling with how to oversee blockchain-based entities, including DAOs, without stifling innovation. Creating a regulatory environment that supports interoperability between DAOs and traditional financial systems while ensuring consumer protection and financial stability requires innovative approaches to financial regulation.[71] Until lawmakers craft clear, harmonized rules that recognize DAOs' unique structure while integrating them into existing capital markets frameworks, widescale adoption of DAOs as full VC substitutes will remain an unresolved—and pressing—challenge for the future.

Additionally, advancements in zero-knowledge proofs and privacy-preserving technologies can address some of the transparency and privacy trade-offs, making DAOs more appealing to a broader range of participants. For example, the pseudonymous nature of blockchain can make it difficult to hold individuals accountable for actions taken within a DAO. Establishing trust and ensuring transparency while respecting privacy is a delicate balance to strike. Furthermore, more needs to be done in connection with auditability and reporting. Indeed, investors in traditional funds expect regular, comprehensive reporting on performance and risk. Developing clear and widely followed standards and practices for DAOs to report their activities and financial health transparently seems crucial for gaining investor confidence.

Peter S Menell, "Rise of the API Copyright Dead: An Updated Epitaph for Copyright Protection of Network and Functional Features of Computer Software" (2018) 31 Harvard Journal of Law and Technology 305, 318–19 (fnn omitted).

[71] Nizan Geslevich Packin, "Show Me the (Data About the) Money!" (2021) Utah Law Review 1277 (writing about interoperability in the context of open banking).

Therefore, to conclude, improvements in user interfaces and experience will lower the barrier to entry, allowing non-technical users to participate in DAOs more easily. Regulatory advancements will also play a crucial role in the growth of DAOs. As lawmakers develop clearer frameworks for DAOs, it will provide the necessary legal certainty to attract more participants and institutional investors. However, even with regulatory clarity, and despite their potential, DAOs face several significant challenges in becoming a mainstream mechanism for collective investment.

3.1. Technological Risks

Smart contract vulnerabilities are a significant technological risk. The operation of DAOs is heavily reliant on smart contracts, which are self-executing contracts with the terms directly written into code. While smart contracts enable trustless transactions and governance, they are also prone to bugs and vulnerabilities,[72] as evidenced by "The DAO" hack in 2016. Ensuring the security of smart contracts is a major challenge.[73] Traditional VC and crowdfunding portals rely on centralized compliance stacks— KYC checks, audited escrow accounts, bank custodians, and manual rollback procedures—protections that disappear when a collective investment DAO's on-chain treasury is governed solely by code. Additionally, commentators have placed much focus on the potential for errors that may arise during upgrades to smart contracts.[74] Catching these types of errors can be extremely challenging given the inherently cryptic nature of the process. Smart contracts can also be impacted by technological errors and human prejudice, introduced through what is known as the "Oracle Problem."[75]

> The term "oracle" in this context pertains to a service or agent that acquires and confirms real-world data for a smart contract on a blockchain. The "Oracle Problem" is the challenge of getting reliable and precise data to use in a smart contract. If the data given by an oracle is inaccurate, the smart contract will be carried out wrongly, and due to the immutable character of the blockchain, the contract cannot be altered or reversed. The potentially resulting losses range from financial and reputational at the individual level, to the perpetuation of social injustices on a societal level.[76]

[72] eg James Grimmelmann, "All Smart Contracts Are Ambiguous" (2019) 2 Journal of Law and Innovation 1, 16 (generally describing smart contracts, and discussing and demonstrating bugs, flaws, and ambiguity in them).

[73] Maksymilian Ewendt, "Leveraging Blockchain Technology in Property Records: Establishing Trust in A Risk-Filled Market" (2017) 19 North Carolina Journal of Law and Technology, 99, 109 (referencing security challenges for smart contracts).

[74] Grimmelmann (n 72) 15.

[75] "Blockchain Oracles Explained: Decentralized Oracles in DeFI" (*Cryptopedia*, February 4, 2022) <https://www.gemini.com/cryptopedia/crypto-oracle-blockchain-overview> accessed October 19, 2024; Nizan Geslevich Packin and Yafit Lev-Aretz, "Decentralized Credit Scoring: Black Box 3.0" (2024) 61(2) American Business Law Journal 91, 93 (describing oracles in detail and the problems associated with them).

[76] Packin and Lev-Aretz (n 75) 94 (fnn omitted).

Because a token-based treasury holds investor capital directly, any oracle failure can trigger automatic, irreversible fund transfers, exposing backers to a level of custodial risk far higher than in a conventional VC fund.

Additionally, as DAOs grow in size and complexity, scalability becomes a concern.[77] A congested chain or fee spike can freeze capital calls and delay portfolio investments, thereby undermining the time-sensitive deal execution that professional VCs routinely manage off-chain. The blockchain platforms hosting these organizations must be able to handle increasing volumes of transactions and urgent needs and interactions without compromising speed or inflating transaction fees.[78]

3.2. Governance Issues

DAOs rely on token-holders to vote on decisions, from investment strategies to operational changes. However, in the context of decision-making efficiency, achieving consensus can be time-consuming, especially in larger DAOs with numerous stakeholders. For a collective investment DAO, every extra day spent tallying on-chain votes can mean missing a term sheet or losing allocation in a competitive funding round.[79] The challenge lies in designing governance models that balance inclusivity and efficiency.

Some investment DAOs can experiment with delegate voting to speed decisions, but those fixes creep back toward a general partnership-style hierarchy and dilute the promise of fully decentralized control. In addition, plutocracy risks are also relevant. Indeed, in many DAOs, voting power is proportional to the number of tokens held. This can lead to a concentration of power among a small number of wealthy participants, undermining the democratic ethos of DAOs and potentially skewing decisions in favor of the few.[80] When the DAO's treasury represents pooled investor capital, this imbalance lets a single "whale" steer community funds toward pet deals, recreating the agency problems that limited partners manage contractually with conventional fund managers—but without the same fiduciary safeguards.

77 eg Colony, "Challenges in DAO Governance" (*Colony Blog*, March 6, 2019) <https://blog.colony.io/challenges-in-dao-governance/> accessed November 4, 2024.

78 Carlo de Meijer, "Blockchain and the Scalability Challenge: Solving the Blockchain Trilemma" (*TreasuryXL*, October 17, 2023) <https://treasuryxl.com/blog/blockchain-and-the-scalability-challenge-solving-the-blockchain-trilemma/> accessed November 4, 2024.

79 High Alpha, "VCs move fast when they want to" (*High Alpha Blog*, June 15, 2021) <https://www.highalpha.com/blog/vcs-move-fast-when-they-want-to> accessed April 29, 2025.

80 eg Cheyenne Ligon, "Mango Markets Exploiter Avi Eisenberg Found Guilty of Fraud and Manipulation" (*CoinDesk*, April 18, 2024) <https://www.coindesk.com/policy/2024/04/18/mango-<markets-exploiter-avi-eisenberg-found-guilty-of-fraud-and-manipulation/> accessed October 19, 2024 (Eisenberg's actions were deemed fraudulent and manipulative, leading to his arrest and a guilty verdict in 2024).

4. Conclusion

DAOs stand at the forefront of a transformative shift in the investment landscape, harnessing blockchain technology to facilitate democratic, transparent, and efficient collective endeavors. Their emergence challenges traditional venture capital and crowdfunding models by democratizing access to investment opportunities, enhancing transparency, and minimizing the need for intermediaries. DAOs have already begun to influence sectors such as corporate governance, real estate, and philanthropy, signaling a potential redefinition of how we organize and allocate resources in the digital age.

The path to widespread DAO adoption faces significant challenges. While DAOs offer inclusive investment opportunities, they also expose participants to risks such as fraud, financial loss, and technological vulnerabilities like smart contract bugs. Additionally, the lack of clear legal protections and regulatory guidance creates uncertainty, deterring investors. To ensure DAOs don't increase risks for less experienced investors, it is crucial to educate participants and implement safeguards against fraud, balancing democratized access with adequate investor protection.

The urgency with which these challenges must be addressed cannot be overstated. As DAOs continue to evolve, there is a critical need for robust investor protection mechanisms, including dispute resolution processes, accountability measures, and safeguards against fraudulent activities. Technological advancements, such as the integration of DeFi, NFTs, and improvements in blockchain scalability, offer promising avenues to enhance the functionality and security of DAOs.

If we are interested in advancing the use of DAOs as collective investment vehicles, policymakers, industry leaders, and technologists must collaborate to develop clear legal frameworks that balance innovation with investor protection, and provide guidance that accommodates the unique characteristics of DAOs without stifling their potential. This includes recognizing DAOs within existing legal structures or creating new classifications that address their decentralized nature. Similarly, future research should focus on developing standardized best practices for DAO governance, security, and investor protection. In addition, if we are interested in advancing the use of DAOs as collective investment vehicles compared to traditional models, more empirical study examining the performance of DAOs must be done to provide valuable insights. Finally, exploring the socio-economic impacts of DAOs on financial inclusion and wealth distribution can inform policies that promote equitable growth.

In conclusion, DAOs possess the potential to be both disruptive and complementary forces in the investment world. By embracing technological advancements and proactively addressing regulatory and governance challenges, DAOs can redefine how we govern, organize, and invest. The success of this emerging paradigm hinges on our ability to foster an environment where innovation thrives alongside robust protections, ultimately contributing to a more diversified, inclusive, and resilient investment ecosystem.

12

Regulating Decentralized Finance

How Financial Regulation Sheds Light on Governing DAOs

Iris H-Y Chiu

1. Introduction

Although the term decentralized autonomous organization (DAO) is of recent vintage, unincorporated associations of people who share a common interest in technological development, are not a new phenomenon. A DAO can be defined as a community of voluntary participants revolving around a project, which, in project management theory, is task-focused toward the delivery of value, and need not be formally organized.[1] An early version of a DAO is the Linux community of software developers, an ongoing association around open source software innovation and development across borders. The coordination of such a community arises in a bottom-up and organic manner, based on participants' commitment to shared values or outcomes, and the organization of participants' work and roles. Where divergences in values or outcomes occur, participants may fork off projects[2] and carry on coordination with other willing participants. At a basic level, a voluntary association that revolves around a project can arise and cease in a self-regulatory manner, and be governed by bottom-up shared principles and the simple option of voluntary exit.

The proliferation of DAOs of late is facilitated by the availability of various permissionless blockchains offering protocols and smart contract templates for different projects to be created and deployed amongst voluntary participants on a distributed basis. As argued by Martino and Borgogno,[3] the transparency and immutable qualities of the distributed ledger and the cryptographic technology underpinning tokenization are novel technological breakthroughs supporting this new form of socio-techno organization. Decentralized applications (Dapps) on permissionless blockchains can bring together voluntary participants anywhere in the world, to join these "open, self-organized collectives coordinated by economic incentives and

[1] John A Bing, "Principles of Project Management" (1994) 8 PM Network 38, 41; Project Management Institute, "The Standard for Project Management" in *A Guide to the Project Management Body of Knowledge (PMBOK® Guide, Seventh Edition) and The Standard for Project Management* (Project Management Institute 2021) para 2.1.

[2] Scott K Peterson, "Governance without Rules: How the potential for forking helps projects" (2019) <https://opensource.com/article/19/1/forking-good> accessed November 15, 2024.

[3] Edoardo D Martino and Oscar Borgogno, "Decentralised Autonomous Organizations: Targeting the Potential Beyond the Hype" (*EBI Working Paper*, 2024) <https://papers.ssrn.com/sol3/papers.cfm?abstract_id=4692754> accessed November 15, 2024.

self-executing code, cooperating around shared goals."[4] Rather than adhering to a specific organizational form, this fluid notion of loose collectivity,[5] often termed as a "DAO," defines itself by what it is not—that is, established legal organizations like companies.

A project developer usually creates tokens associated with smart contracts and issues them to voluntary purchasers who are envisaged to join the Dapp project and contribute their co-development capacities. Tokens are usually freely tradable in secondary marketplaces, so access, ongoing code development, and exit on a self-regulatory basis may arguably be sufficient for Dapp communities. However, Dapp projects and their DAOs do not simply fit into an informal conception of a "project." Many of them, unlike projects with a typical lifecycle, are expected to continue development in an open-ended manner. DAOs may initially revolve around the narrow and deterministic executions of automated code for precise purposes, such as the Bitcoin network which exists to transfer Bitcoin as value among participants.[6] But Dapp projects are often envisaged to be capable of continuing development by participants coordinating in an open-ended shared enterprise.[7] In this manner, the DAO is an organizational incubator, paving the way for an increasingly complex build-out of a techno-social organization.[8]

Dapp projects often provide disintermediated marketplaces where users can directly transact with each other. They may be superior to centralized platforms that have become powerful and rent-extracting oligopolies.[9] For example, Joystream is a DAO providing a media platform for video creators and musicians to monetize their creative work by marketing non-fungible tokens (NFTs).[10] Collector DAOs, such as PleasrDAO, are communities that enable individuals to own fractionalized units of digital creative work whose ownership right is represented in the form of an NFT held collectively by the DAO. Some of the most popular DAOs are decentralized finance (DeFi) DAOs[11] that sustain projects for crypto-asset holders to carry out financialized activities amongst themselves without necessarily being subject to centralized financial intermediaries.

DAOs thus have an organizational character. They are more than informal projects and their disavowal of established legal organizational forms does not mean that they

[4] Tom Bell, "Blockchain and Authoritarianism: The Evolution of Decentralized Autonomous Organizations" in Oreste Pollicino and Giovanni De Gregario (eds), *Blockchain and Public Law* (Edward Elgar 2021) ch 6.

[5] Peder Østbye, "Exploring DAO Members' Individual Liability" (*SSRN*, 2023) <https://ssrn.com/abstract=4045799> accessed November 15, 2024.

[6] Ying-Ying Hsieh and others, "Bitcoin and the Rise of Decentralized Autonomous Organizations" (2018) 7 Journal of Organization Design 14.

[7] Bell (n 4).

[8] Philipp Hacker, "Corporate Governance for Complex Cryptocurrencies? A Framework for Stability and Decision Making in Blockchain-Based Organizations" in Philipp Hacker and others (eds), *Regulating Blockchain: Techno-Social and Legal Challenges* (OUP 2019) ch 7.

[9] Kumar Saurabh, Parijat Upadhyay, and Neelam Rani, "A Study on Blockchain-Based Marketplace Governance Platform Adoption: A Multi-Industry Perspective" (2023) 25 Digital Policy, Regulation and Governance 653.

[10] "A video platform protocol, joystream Lightpaper v1.3" (*Joystream*, 2023) <https://www.joystream.org/lightpaper.pdf> accessed November 15, 2024.

[11] Such as Uniswap, one of the top three DAOs in terms of treasury and number of token holders, "DeepDAO" <https://deepdao.io/organizations> accessed November 15, 2024.

exist in a legal vacuum.[12] Depending on what organizational structures they are in substance, the Law Commission of England & Wales[13] takes the view that relations created in DAOs can be subject to (1) transactional law governing relationships, such as trusts or contracts; and (2) laws relating to certain organizational forms which can give rise to both privileges and obligations. Nevertheless, prior literature in the US and UK has opined that DAOs do not fit neatly with established organizational laws,[14] not least due to the spectrum of collectivity that different DAOs embrace,[15] making it difficult to distill key common organizational characteristics for the purposes of categorizing DAOs. In this manner, applying only transactional characterizations to DAO activities would also be incomplete.

The chapter acknowledges the important context of organizational legal uncertainty as a key legal/regulatory issue for DAOs. However, as the issue remains debated in many jurisdictions, pockets of sectoral regulation that may affect DAOs' activities could become pivotal to regulating DAOs' organizational and governance aspects. DeFi DAOs increasingly attract the attention of global financial regulators.[16] Further, the EU Markets in Crypto-Assets Regulation (MiCAR) would be applicable to DeFi,[17] unless they are "fully decentralized" crypto-asset activities,[18] many of which do not perfectly meet that criterion.[19] In this way, sectoral regulation provides regulatory entry points for certain DAOs and may shape the broader overall regulatory paradigms for DAOs.

The chapter focuses on the application of financial regulation to DeFi, many of which are organized as DAOs. Section 2 provides an introduction to DeFi Dapps and the self-governing nature of these DAOs. Section 3 discusses how emerging regulatory policy developments in the European Union (EU) and internationally may introduce aspects of regulation for DeFi, shaping DAO governance. The section extrapolates possible regulatory thinking for DeFi and more broadly, DAOs. Section 4 concludes.

[12] Also Martino and Borgogno (n 3).

[13] Law Commission, "Decentralised Autonomous Organisations—A Scoping Paper" (Law Commission, July 2024) <https://lawcom.gov.uk/document/decentralised-autonomous-organisations-scoping-paper/> accessed November 15, 2024.

[14] Timothy Nielsen, "Cryptocorporations: A Proposal for Legitimizing Decentralized Autonomous Organizations" (2019) Utah L Rev 1105 discussing the US context. For the UK, Iris H-Y Chiu, *Regulating the Crypto-economy* (Hart Publishing 2023) ch 4.

[15] Østbye (n 5).

[16] Bank for International Settlements, "The Financial Stability Risks of Decentralised Finance—Executive Summary" (*BIS*, August 2023) <https://www.bis.org/fsi/fsisummaries/defi.pdf> accessed November 15, 2024; Financial Stability Board, "The Financial Stability Risks of Decentralised Finance" (*FSB*, February 2023) <https://www.fsb.org/2023/02/the-financial-stability-risks-of-decentralised-finance/> accessed November 15, 2024.

[17] Philipp Maume, "The Regulation on Markets in Crypto-Assets (MiCAR): Landmark Codification, or First Step of Many, or Both?" (2023) ECFR 243; Iris H-Y Chiu, "The Application of the Markets in Crypto-asset Regulation to Decentralised Finance" (2023) 38 Journal of International Banking Law and Regulation 432. Arts 140 and 142 also envisage that the European Banking Authority and European Securities and Markets Authority need to make reports by June 30, 2025 on the appropriate regulatory treatment of decentralised finance, raising questions whether MiCAR already applies to them.

[18] Preamble 22.

[19] Linn-Anker Sørensen and Dirk A Zetzsche, "From Centralized to Decentralized Finance: The Issue of 'Fake-DeFi'" (*SSRN*, 2021) <https://papers.ssrn.com/sol3/papers.cfm?abstract_id=3978815> accessed November 15, 2024.

2. DeFi's Internal Governance and the Need for Regulatory Governance

2.1. A Brief Primer on DeFi

DeFi applications encompass many types of automated or algorithmically matched/executed transactions, usually between crypto-assets, with a view to generating "yield" for crypto-asset holders. What this means is that crypto-asset holders are able to "financialize" and earn a profit on their assets by deploying them in a manner similar to conventional financial functions, such as market-making, lending, fund management, insurance, and so on.[20]

A fundamental tenet of DeFi's business model is to attract pooled participation by individual crypto-asset holders contributing their crypto-assets according to a protocol. Pooled participation brings about network effects, allowing DeFi protocols to enable transactions quickly and easily amongst crypto-asset holders, such as swapping, trading, lending, borrowing, hedging, and so on. In this manner, there is no centralized intermediary bringing assets onto its own balance sheet or investing proprietarily-managed pools of funds. Intermediaries who perform such functions often act as market makers or risk clearing-houses and they extract a rent from other participants for carrying out their roles. DeFi protocols "defy" the need for centralized intermediaries by facilitating pooled arrangements and offering automated protocols to enable peers to transact. Hence, DeFi is usually non-custodial, as participants retain control over their assets, but the rights to their assets are subject to dealing according to the protocols of DeFi systems. Users' crypto-assets are often "locked" by smart contract in order to be subject to the DeFi application's rules for managing risks and settling transactions. Participants also fully retain their own financial risks. In this manner, financial risks are diffused amongst the many willing participants and are not, as in conventional finance, concentrated upon a centralized financial intermediary (which may become too important or systemic to fail).

Empirical research has shown that DeFi business models can generate new efficiencies and welfare for users,[21] hence their innovative value should not be dismissed. These shared enterprises are often organized as DAOs where users are part of a community for code development and governance. Not all DeFi DAOs are completely democratized for user governance, as founder/developers of DeFi projects often envisage being heavily involved until they perceive the DeFi community as being sufficiently mature for a hand-over.[22]

[20] Vincent Gramlich and others, "Decentralised Finance" (*SSRN*, 2023) <https://ssrn.com/abstract=4535868> accessed November 15, 2024.

[21] Katya Malinova and Andreas Park, "Learning from DeFi: Would Automated Market Makers Improve Equity Trading?" (*SSRN*, 2023) <https://ssrn.com/abstract=4531670> accessed November 15, 2024; Yannis Bakos and Hannah Halaburda, "Will Blockchains Disintermediate Platforms? Limits to Decentralization in DAOs" (*SSRN*, 2023) <https://ssrn.com/abstract=4221512> accessed November 15, 2024.

[22] eg Compound.

An example of a highly democratized DeFi project is Uniswap, an automated market maker on the Ethereum blockchain, boasting 30 million users by mid-2023.[23] The Uniswap protocol allows users to collectively create and contribute their assets to liquidity pools. Liquidity pools of asset-pairs are created so that users can easily meet their trading needs against the pools. Crypto-asset holders who contribute their assets to a liquidity pool get UNI tokens in return (Uniswap's native token). These tokens reflect contributors' share of the pool's liquidity and allow contributors to earn a fee for contributing to the pool's liquidity, which incentivizes users' participation. The fees for participating in a liquidity pool are set in three tiers that will be algorithmically adjusted to reflect the conditions of pool liquidity. The ongoing governance needs of Uniswap are met by the fully decentralized system for participation and governance by Uniswap's users, so that users themselves can refine and maintain the decision-making and substantive rules of the project.

All UNI token-holders are members of the DAO and can participate in Uniswap's governance. Users include the Uniswap Foundation, corporate users, and individuals. Users with certain significant thresholds of token-holding can field governance proposals as executable code to the community.[24] Governance protocols include specific periods of time for token-holders to consider and vote on governance proposals. Successful proposals are then executed as algorithmic rules for the platform after a two-day time lock delay.[25] Participants with coding expertise in particular may enjoy an advantage in governance participation.

2.2. The Limits of Internal Governance Developed by DeFi DAOs

This section argues that DeFi DAOs would not cope with users' real governance needs due to their embrace of an ethos that supports distributed, organic governance which is to be gradually developed. Embryonic governance that awaits to be built out would just not be sufficient to deal with anti-sociality, collective harms, and crises. The chapter is also skeptical that DeFi DAOs' governance would be able to address macro-level issues of public interest that affect DeFi projects themselves.

The idealistic vision of fully distributed governance is perceived as a panacea for the self-regulatory DeFi DAO. However, although many DeFi DAOs have significant communities and network effects, as well as distribution of tokens, oligarchic power structures are the norm.[26] One example is MakerDAO. The project is purposed toward creating a stablecoin DAI, initially pegged to the US dollar but envisaged to become a stable store of value for crypto-asset holders based on self-regulation of its supply

[23] Jane Smith, "Uniswap Smashes Records with Over 30 Million Active Users and 15K ETH Burned in a Week" (*Crypto News Flash*, 7 May 2023) <https://www.crypto-news-flash.com/uniswap-smashes-records-with-over-30-million-active-users-and-15k-eth-burned-in-a-week/> accessed November 15, 2024.

[24] <https://docs.uniswap.org/contracts/v3/reference/governance/overview> accessed November 15, 2024.

[25] "Introducing UNI" (*Uniswap Labs Blog*, 2020) <https://blog.uniswap.org/uni> accessed November 15, 2024.

[26] Henrik Axelsen, Johannes Rude Jensen, and Omri Ross, "When Is a DAO Decentralised?" (2022) 31 Complex Systems Informatics and Modeling Quarterly 51. Although the authors acknowledge that full distribution would yield welfare benefits for all users.

and demand levels once a sufficient mass uptake has been achieved.[27] MakerDAO is the governance body for making substantive rules for the DAI project, including the collateralization policies for DAI, the interest earn rate for DAI holders, admissible collateral, and liquidation policies, etc.

Although the Uniswap and Maker DAOs are large and distributed communities, they experience uneven levels of engagement on users' part, turning into timocratic systems instead of distributed and democratic ones.[28] This is not unexpected for distributed systems of governance, as not all users are equally motivated and engaged. Token-holders also enjoy the ease of secondary market exit and may choose exit over engagement.[29] Many DeFi DAOs feature concentration of power amongst certain groups of large, engaged token-holders who are also active in submitting proposals and voting.[30] The governance risk is that these factions of power may be unaccountable and self-serving, while being able to dominate a DAO's governance. It is unlikely that full distribution of power will result from self-regulatory DAO governance, and perhaps more productive for regulation to intervene and address these power structures and their market failures.

Next, many DAOs' starting point of embryonic governance structures means that there are no ex ante frameworks that ensure that exercises of governance power meet social needs such as fairness or considerations of the common good. By default, exercises of power can be completely self-interested. As token-holders can also hold governance tokens in competing DeFi applications and need not disclose these, there are potential conflicts of interests and diverging incentives amongst them. Any token-holder's governance proposal may not be transparent nor in the interests of the DeFi DAO as a whole.

Further, DeFi DAOs by default favor participants with coding expertise and leave plenty of opportunities for less expert participants to be exploited or abused. Consumer-level users[31] who may not be familiar with code or programming may not understand governance proposals written as executable code. This narrow mode of information availability and voice engagement for users is not sufficiently diverse or inclusive, given the ambitions of DeFi governance framed as being ongoing, widely distributed, and accessible to all.

[27] "DAI Whitepaper: Creative and Robust Financial Tools for the Digital Age" (*Coinmarketcap*, 2023) <https://coinmarketcap.com/community/articles/658727241c205e51dc2f7180/> accessed November 15, 2024.

[28] Tom Barbereau and others, "Decentralised Finance's Timocratic Governance: The Distribution and Exercise of Tokenised Voting Rights" (2023) 73 Technology in Society 102251. On MakerDAO, Eleunthia Wong Ellinger and others, "Decentralized Autonomous Organization (DAO): The Case of MakerDAO" (2023) Journal of Information Technology Teaching Cases 1; Xiaotong Sun and others, "Decentralization Illusion in Decentralized Finance: Evidence from Tokenized Voting in MakerDAO Polls" (*SSRN*, 2022) <https://ssrn.com/abstract=3971791> accessed November 15, 2024.

[29] Igor Makarov and Antoinette Schoar, "Cryptocurrencies and Decentralised Finance" (2022) Brookings Papers on Economic Activity 141.

[30] Saqib Sheikh and Imitiaz Sifat, "Built to Last, Not to Scale: The Long Run of Decentralized Autonomous Organizations" (*SSRN*, 2023) <https://ssrn.com/abstract=4335053> accessed November 15, 2024.

[31] Neeraj Khandelwal, "A Billion consumers in Web3 and Defi" (Branded Article in Forbes India Crypto Made Easy) <https://www.forbesindia.com/article/crypto-made-easy/a-billion-consumers-in-web3-and-defi/79297/1> accessed November 15, 2024.

Although most DeFi DAOs have managed governance problems with ex post development of governance solutions, it is questionable this modus sufficiently meets users' needs. Could prevention, in the form of more robust ex ante governance, be preferred? In DeFi applications where concentrations of power have arisen, abusive governance token-holders could submit proposals that hide malicious bugs in executable code so that they may be deployed upon successful voting. Maliciously executed code can drain a DAO's pools of assets and smart contracts can be tampered with to relinquish users of their rights over crypto-assets.[32] DeFi projects tend to attract such malicious and anti-social users particularly because they pool assets and these become attractive targets for rogues. One incident involving a user called "Humpy" on the DeFi platform Balancer[33] involved the deployment of code that allowed Humpy to extract a significant share of rent from the DAO. The rest of the members had to come to a truce with Humpy to cap its rent extraction, as there was no way to expel a rogue member or to affect its token-holding and governance involvement.

Organic development of governance can happen too late to redress issues of exploitation, lack of sociality and fairness, and even threats to the DeFi's viability. In anticipation of potential problems, large DeFi DAOs like Uniswap and MakerDAO use pre-proposal stages to encourage users to screen and comment on governance proposals, so that accountability can be better achieved.[34] Compound, the popular DeFi lending protocol, implements a minimum number of token holdings for proposals to be submitted, as higher stakeholders could be more naturally aligned with the long-term collective good of the application.[35] Maker and Compound also operate delegated voting protocols so that users can delegate their votes to other trusted users who are active in governance, achieving more meaningful voting participation that way. However, these still rely on users' presumed good intentions and the strength of numbers in participation to countervail the possibility of malice.

There is an intractable dilemma with DAOs' model of developmental governance. Arguably, a sound collective governance structure is needed before users can build on effective continuing development. It may be challenging for users to develop optimal continuing governance without certain fundamental structures already in place. Hence commentators opine that[36] what is optimal for DAO governance cannot be completely divorced from already-established doctrines for good private sector governance, such as in corporate governance. Fundamental tenets[37] could include: addressing the agency problem, that is, ensuring that powers that can be exercised over others' assets are checked and monitored; ensuring sufficient representation in

[32] Maya Dotan and others, "The Vulnerable Nature of Decentralised Governance in DeFi" (*arXiv*, 2023) <https://arxiv.org/abs/2308.04267> accessed November 15, 2024.

[33] ibid.

[34] The offchain MakerDAO Forum <https://forum.makerdao.com/> accessed November 15, 2024; Uniswap's proposal discussion platform (*Uniswap Protocol Governance*) <https://gov.uniswap.org/c/proposal-discussion/5> accessed November 15, 2024.

[35] Robert Leshner, "Compound Governance" (*Medium*, 2020) <https://medium.com/compound-finance/compound-governance-5531f524cf68> accessed November 15, 2024.

[36] Hacker (n 8); Jonathan Rohr and Aaron Wright, "Blockchains, Private Ordering, and the Future of Governance" in Philipp Hacker and others (eds), *Regulating Blockchain: Techno-Social and Legal Challenges* (OUP 2019) ch 2.

[37] Such as company law norms that pertain to board and general meetings.

decision-making, such as having minimum thresholds of stakes to propose decisions, processes for instituting effective collective "meetings" or interactions to ensure that participants are on a level playing field, incentives and processes to enable voting and prevent disenfranchisement, having quorums for decision-making and a majority or super-majority rule to pass decisions; and ensuring processes for disseminating information and answering questions so that governance actors are sufficiently informed.[38]

Without pre-instituted governance structures, DeFi DAOs may not generate optimal and fair governance in a *laissez-faire* environment. Instead, such communities are more akin to a game theoretic environment[39] where participants are self-serving and unpredictable in terms of their cooperation or defection. The very developmental nature of internal governance exposes users in DAOs to the risk of being "in a pool of sharks" where they know little about other users' identities, intentions, and conflicts of interests. These could be Hobbesian[40] environments, inherently disposed to creating market failures that cannot be self-correcting unless pre-supplied governance is in place to steer behavior toward collective achievement of the application's shared enterprise.

Further, the developmental nature of DAO governance is arguably ill-equipped to counter a collective crisis or threat to the DeFi application itself, such as the unexpected but adverse outworking of the application's risk management protocol, as occurred with DAI token-holders on the so-called Black Thursday,[41] or cyberhacking, which is a frequent occurrence for DeFi protocols.[42]

On March 12, 2020, a sustained selling of the Ethereum cryptocurrency caused its price to decline significantly, affecting DAI users who collateralized their DAI holdings with Ethereum locked by smart contracts in the DAI protocol. The sustained selling also caused slow settlement traffic on the Ethereum blockchain, so price feeds for Ethereum were delayed to support the DAI collateralization and liquidation protocols. When the price declines ultimately fed through to the DAI protocols, it triggered massive liquidations of users' Ethereum collateral as being insufficient to support their DAI holdings. As liquidations were executed by automated protocols or bots auctioning off Ethereum collateral at the best possible price, including at zero DAI, many users had their collateral completely wiped out. In this manner, while the automated protocols worked as programmed to maintain DAI's stability, they did so without regard for the harm caused to users.[43] Black Thursday showed that governance by code fails to account for unfair or oppressive effects of enforcement. DAO

[38] Colin Gilson and Sarah Bouraga, "Enhancing the Democratic Nature of Voting Processes Within Decentralized Autonomous Organizations" (2024) 26 Digital Policy, Regulation and Governance 169.

[39] Game dynamics is discussed as a model for DAO relations, Jun Aoyagi and Yuki Ito, "Competing DAOs" (*SSRN*, 2023) <https://ssrn.com/abstract=4293846> accessed November 15, 2024.

[40] Uta Kohl, "Blockchain Utopia and its Governance Shortfalls" in Oreste Pollicino and Giovanni De Gregario (eds), *Blockchain and Public Law* (Edward Elgar 2021) ch 2.

[41] Shalini Nagarajan, "Maker firm settles for $1.16M with users liquidated in Covid crash" (*Blockworks*, 2023) <https://blockworks.co/news/maker-settle-black-thursday> accessed November 15, 2024.

[42] Bessie Liu, "The 5 biggest DeFi hacks of 2023" (*Blockworks*, 2023) <https://blockworks.co/news/biggest-defi-hacks-2023> accessed November 15, 2024.

[43] Ryosuke Ushida and James Angel, "Regulatory Considerations on Centralized Aspects of DeFi Managed by DAOs" in Matthew Bernhard and others (eds), *Financial Cryptography and Data Security—FC 2021 International Workshops Lecture Notes in Computer Science*, vol 12676 (Springer 2021) 21–38; also Hacker (n 8); Rohr and Wright (n 36); Bell (n 4); Gilson and Bouraga (n 38).

governance, which is both embryonic and exclusively code-based, cannot pre-provide for eventualities of incomplete contracting.[44]

Users had few options for conventional remedies.[45] In response, MakerDAO collectively adjusted governance protocols by building in longer auction times at collateral liquidation and having minimum auction prices to reduce unfairness to collateralized users. Governance remains code-based, while the need for organizational structures that are more social and open-ended in nature, such as principles of responsibility and accountability for crisis management, remain lacking.[46]

DeFi applications' developmental code may contain bugs which can be exploited by cyberhackers. Martino and Borgogno argue that DeFi DAOs underinvest in long-term operational aspects, such as cybersecurity and ex post crisis management governance as code is developed by a shifting and unpredictable community. For example, the DeFi lending protocol bZx has been hacked several times losing over US$55 million of assets.[47] Cyberhacks targeting DeFi protocols have made away with billions of dollars at the time of writing.[48] Many of these losses are without recourse as users participate in DeFi protocols on a *caveat emptor* basis and transactions are irreversible. DeFi DAOs engage in bug fixes and patching after the fact, but this may not prevent future crises. Not every cyberhack entails the type of extraordinary intervention of hard forking[49] which took place for the Ethereum blockchain in 2016. After the hack of the first financialized DAO (created by SlockIt), a controversial decision was taken to reverse the protocol blockchain to the state before the hack. This type of resolution is increasingly unlikely and would create disruptive uncertainties on major permissionless blockchains such as Ethereum. It is looking increasingly important for both individual DeFi applications and for the DeFi ecosystem to be appropriately governed in view of the links and interdependencies amongst DeFi applications. From regulators' perspective, not only do DeFi projects exhibit deficits in terms of internal governance developments, but they are inherently unable to address:

- broader collective issues such as financial crime or money laundering through DeFi applications;

44 Sheikh and Sifat (n 30).

45 Users' action against MakerDAO Foundation was dismissed as the Foundation was only one of many governance actors. Ultimately, users sued the founder developers Cayman company Maker Ecosystem Growth Foundation Inc. Its connection to MakerDAO is unclear but it settled out of goodwill.

46 Chiu, *Regulating the Crypto-economy* (n 14), exploring how the Öström principles can be further developed into organizational principles for DAOs.

47 James Rubin, "DeFi Lender bZx Suffers Hack for Reported $55M" (*Coindesk*, 2021) <https://www.coindesk.com/business/2021/11/05/defi-lender-bzx-suffers-hack-for-reported-55m/> accessed November 15, 2024.

48 Liu (n 42).

49 David Z Morris, "CoinDesk Turns 10: 2016—How The DAO Hack Changed Ethereum and Crypto" (*Coindesk*, 15 May 2023) <https://www.coindesk.com/consensus-magazine/2023/05/09/coindesk-turns-10-how-the-dao-hack-changed-ethereum-and-crypto> accessed May 30, 2025. SlockIt built a completely decentralized organization (DAO) to pool investors' funds in order to collectively vote for projects the DAO would fund in the crypto-economy. However, an attacker exploited a flaw in the open source code and managed to drain the pool of funds of about US$50 million worth of Ether (ETH). SlockIt and key miners on the Ethereum blockchain decided to remedy the damage by implementing a hard fork so that an application (smart contract) was written to return ETH that had been contributed to the DAO address, and the Ethereum blockchain maintained a ledger clean of the theft.

- issues of interdependence with other DeFi projects and their vulnerabilities, potentially of importance to financial stability; and
- other matters of public interest that individual DAOs would not necessarily take ownership of.

It is well-known that DeFi applications have been used for laundering proceeds of cyberhacking and other organized international crimes.[50] Many applications allow access by users once a wallet has been linked, and there may be no gatekeeping features for checking and preventing DeFi applications from being used for money laundering. Many DeFi applications, wary of creeping regulatory risk, have developed measures of ex post blacklisting of wallet addresses[51] known to be associated with organized crime or sanctions, but this is far from being a comprehensive endeavor.

Further, it is queried if DeFi governance would be able to provide solutions for wider systemic concerns. One example of a DeFi project that may give rise to DeFi interdependencies, and broader issues of systemic stability, is the Lido application.[52] Lido allows Ethereum holders to pool their crypto-assets together, in order to qualify to stake for validation purposes on the blockchain with its move to a Proof-of-Stake validation protocol. This application works to avoid the situation of blockchain validation being dominated by large stakeholders. Lido offers contributors an earn rate on the Ethereum locked in its smart contracts, and participants gain tokens called stETH (staked Ethereum) in return. As stETH tokens are also stakeable in other DeFi applications, such as being used as collateral against borrowing, say stablecoins, Lido users can use their stETH tokens to construct many linkages and interdependencies with other DeFi protocols, such as by borrowing against them. If interdependent tokens experience a sudden decline in value, this can result in stETH liquidations. Would this affect Lido's business model of valid staking, and to what extent would this affect the operational efficiencies of the Ethereum blockchain itself?[53] It is questionable if Lido's own governance protocols are able to address the more "macro" aspects of DeFi interdependencies.

This section has so far argued that DeFi DAOs' embryonic and increasingly code-based models of governance are likely unable to sufficiently address internal governance problems and collective systemic issues. However, financial regulators may not regard it warranted to dedicate resources to provide financial regulation for DeFi systems. The Financial Stability Board[54] (FSB) has taken the view that DeFi is largely

[50] Vladlena Benson, Umut Turksen, and Bogdan Adamyk, "Dark Side of Decentralised Finance: A Call for Enhanced AML Regulation Based on Use Cases Of Illicit Activities" (2024) 32 Journal of Financial Regulation and Compliance 80; Tom Barbereau and Balàsz Bodò, "Beyond Financial Regulation of Crypto-Asset Wallet Software: In Search of Secondary Liability" (2023) 49 Computer Law and Security Review 105829.

[51] Nicholas Say, "Major DeFi Protocols Block Accounts Linked to Tornado Cash" (*Blockonomi*, 2022) <https://blockonomi.com/major-defi-protocols-block-accounts-linked-to-tornado-cash> accessed November 15, 2024.

[52] Sam Kessler, "Lido DAO Democratized ETH Staking, Then Dominated It" (*Coindesk*, 2023) <https://www.coindesk.com/consensus-magazine/2023/12/04/lido-dao-democratized-eth-staking-then-dominated-it/> accessed November 15, 2024.

[53] Adam Morgan McCarthy, "Ethereum restaking could lead to a 'cascade of liquidations,' says JPMorgan" (*DLNews*, 2023) <https://www.dlnews.com/articles/markets/jpmorgan-warns-of-risk-from-ethereum-restaking/> accessed November 15, 2024.

[54] FSB (n 16).

self-referential, involving only crypto-assets and stablecoins, and does not significantly affect traditional financial activities and financial stability risks.[55] However, increasing linkages between traditional finance (TradFi) and DeFi are being observed. Société Générale (SG), for example, is expanding into crypto-funding. Its subsidiary company has now issued bond tokens acceptable as collateral by the MakerDAO governance body to borrow DAI stablecoins.[56] If the subsidiary's solvency or conditions for maintaining the value of collateral becomes questionable and the bond tokens are liquidated by MakerDAO, this could also result in a run on other SG bond instruments in conventional financial markets. Regulators should be alert to such risks and the ongoing problems of consumer and user protection.

Section 3 turns to the paradigm of financial regulatory extension to DeFi, which is being developed especially under the EU's Markets in Crypto-Assets Regulation (MiCAR). The section discusses how key regulatory tenets could shape DeFi and more broadly, DAO regulation.

3. Regulatory Intervention to Address Internal Governance Failures

We have examined the range of risks and problems inadequately addressed by the organic development of DeFi's internal governance. DeFi's internal governance failures may also compromise the future of the shared enterprise, but more adversely, such failures can result in, or fail to cater for, individual and collective harm, and failures in public interest.

It is yet unclear whether existing financial regulations are applicable to DeFi or what specific reforms are needed to address its peer-to-peer transactions, pooling mechanisms, and automated smart contract systems.[57] However, leaving DeFi unregulated may not be justified as DeFi users are not interacting peer-to-peer but rather, peer-to-pool,[58] with pools being governed by transactional and governance protocols. In this manner, the operation of pools can attract regulatory standards and intervention,[59] even if regulation may not attach in the same manner for traditional financial services, that is, to identified financial intermediaries as legal persons.

It is also unclear if MiCAR applies to DeFi. MiCAR requires the European Banking Authority (EBA) and European Securities and Markets Authority (ESMA) to prepare an interim report by June 2025 on the appropriate regulatory treatment of DeFi. This can be interpreted in two ways: either DeFi is already within MiCAR's scope,

[55] Pablo D Azar and others, "The Financial Stability Implications of Crypto-assets" (*SSRN*, 2022) <https://papers.ssrn.com/sol3/papers.cfm?abstract_id=4438746> accessed November 15, 2024.

[56] "Societe Generale—Forge borrows DAI Stablecoin from decentralised finance protocol Maker DAO to extend loan" (*Forge Societe General Group*, 2023) <https://www.sgforge.com/refinancing-dai-stablecoin-defi-makerdao/> accessed November 15, 2024.

[57] Matteo Aquilina, Jon Frost, and Andreas Schrimpf, "Decentralised Finance: A Functional Approach" (2024) 10 Journal of Financial Regulation 1–27.

[58] Andre Wang, "Rethinking the Rule and Role of Law in Decentralized Finance" (2022) IEEE 24th Conference on Business Informatics (CEI).

[59] Guilherme Maia and João Vieira dos Santos, "MiCAR and DeFi" (*SSRN*, 2021) <https://ssrn.com/abstract=3875355> accessed November 15, 2024, who propose regulating the DeFi project itself.

necessitating a review of its application, or it falls outside, prompting consideration of an extension to include DeFi. ESMA, in developing technical standards for Commission legislation[60] implementing MiCAR, suggests that automated market makers (AMMs) such as Uniswap may be captured within the scope of crypto-asset service providers in relation to operating a trading platform.

In another work,[61] I have argued that it is not impossible for MiCAR to be regarded as extending to DeFi. At the basic level, DeFi protocols mostly issue a token in exchange for other crypto-assets to be locked up for financialization purposes, so this means that DeFi protocols could, strictly speaking, fall within the crypto-asset service provider category of "exchanging crypto-assets for other crypto-assets."[62] It can however be argued that no "proprietary capital" is involved in the exchange as the DeFi protocol issues the platform's native token to swap for a participant's crypto-asset, and there is no "taking on" of assets onto a proprietary balance sheet. However, as many DeFi business models involve the redemption of native tokens, and users' financial interest in a centralized asset pool, a national regulator applying the provision can take the wider view that the definition is met.

Although MiCAR's application is unresolved, this chapter suggests it is useful to distill key financial regulatory tenets in terms of how they might shape regulation of DeFi, hence the governance of DeFi DAOs. These reflect the rationales and principles for financial regulation where self-regulation produces shortfalls. This chapter does not delve into the exact textual application of MiCAR to DeFi activities, focusing more on its underlying principles and possible regulatory outcomes.

MiCAR provides the regulatory standards that apply across the board to all crypto-asset service providers, as well as specific standards for certain modes of crypto-asset intermediation such as operating an exchange, provision of advice, and brokerage. The following focuses on across-the-board regulatory standards.

3.1. MiCAR's Key Regulatory Tenets for Crypto-Asset Service Providers

3.1.1. Authorization to operate

First, MiCAR requires that crypto-asset service providers seek authorization if their functions fall with the scope of MiCAR's list.[63] These are functionally described, such as facilitating trading, brokering, providing advice, etc. There is scope for considering wider functional descriptions in order to encapsulate functions of financial intermediation and to protect those users who entrust and rely on these functions. Pre-authorization ahead of carrying out financial functions establishes scope and legitimacy for regulatory oversight.

[60] European Securities and Markets Authority (ESMA), "Second Consultation Paper on the Technical Standards Specifying Certain Requirements of Markets in Crypto Assets Regulation (MiCA)" (*ESMA CP*, 2023) <https://www.esma.europa.eu/document/second-consultation-paper-technical-standards-specifying-certain-requirements-markets> accessed November 15, 2024.

[61] Chiu, "The Application of the Markets in Crypto-asset Regulation to Decentralised Finance" (n 17).

[62] Markets in Crypto-Assets Regulation 2023/1114, Art 3(16), (20).

[63] ibid Art 2(16)–(26).

The need for authorization, however, raises questions for DeFi applicants' legal personhood, as regulators need clarity on whom they are supervising. While MiCAR does not explicitly exclude crypto-asset service providers that are not organized as legal entities, national regulators must be assured that these entities can comply with MiCAR's requirements. I have previously argued that such a condition could render DeFi practically unauthorizable. However, the authorization requirement may incentivize DeFi projects seeking market share and legitimacy in the EU to adopt established legal structures, with the corporate form being the most common choice.[64] Another possibility for DeFi developers who are opposed to adopting the corporate form is to adopt the innovative technological arrangement licensed in Malta.[65] This is an alternative organizational form catering for blockchain-based organizations and could suit DeFi DAOs.

The legal personhood requirement can compel DeFi DAOs to move away from embryonic insufficiency in internal governance. Legal organizational forms provide certain baseline expectations. These also make it easier for regulators to identify to whom regulatory responsibilities should attach. A more innovation-friendly regulatory design could consider authorizing the DeFi project itself,[66] rather than the DAO. However, this could mean that financial regulators, instead of relying on baseline organizational law to cater for the organization's governance needs, would need to work more extensively with each project to achieve an internal governance baseline appropriate for an authorized status.

Regulators should also bear in mind that DeFi projects are crucially reliant on their protocol blockchains for fundamental matters like transaction settlement and validation. It is likely impracticable that protocol blockchains would fall within financial regulators' jurisdictions for authorization purposes. Hence, regulators may find that crucial aspects for user protection fall outside of the DeFi application's boundaries and regulators' ambit. However, regulators could ask DeFi developers to justify their choice of protocol blockchain in seeking authorization for the project. Some blockchains have been susceptible to criminal use, such as Tron[67] and regulators could scrutinize developers' choices carefully.

3.1.2. Identification and qualities of responsible persons and capital providers

MiCAR requires that "members of the management body" and shareholders of crypto-asset providers be of sufficiently good repute and their criminal records should be disclosed for authorization purposes. These regulatory conditions help regulators to identify and address locations of power and responsibility where the authorized entity is a legal person. This may not appropriately apply to DeFi DAOs' governance

[64] DeFi seeks to become compliant in light of MiCA, Shyft Network, "Navigating Regulatory Challenges: MiCA and the DeFi Landscape" (*Medium*, 2023) <https://medium.com/shyft-network/navigating-regulatory-challenges-mica-and-the-defi-landscape-5fd0fe86045d> accessed November 15, 2024.

[65] Maltese Innovative Technology Arrangements and Services Act of 2018 <https://legislation.mt/eli/cap/592/eng/pdf> accessed November 15, 2024.

[66] Maia and dos Santos (n 59).

[67] Scott Chipolina, "$100mn in crypto payments traced to Myanmar-based 'scammers' (*Financial Times*, 25 February 2024) https://www.ft.com/content/fbe27292-4df9-4610-99e0-a93121e06dd3> accessed November 15, 2024, on scammers using the Tron blockchain to transfer cryptocurrency.

token-holders or users as such. This chapter suggests instead that regulators identify the governance needs for DeFi to consider how they can be regulated effectively, without assuming that certain locations of power in a corporate context map onto DeFi. The following subsections explain.

3.1.3. Ex ante regulation of constitutional structure, operational program, and business policies

In traditional financial services regulation, financial services firms must provide upfront clarity on their structures, organizational governance, business purposes, and operational program prior to authorization. These forms of ex ante governance assure regulators and the public that the firm is ready for risk management, to maintain financial soundness, and user protection. This is arguably contrary to DeFi DAOs' vision of ex post developmental and organic governance. Ex ante policies such as business continuity are important to users, for example, in the event of cyberhacking. Business continuity policies demand that developers consider worst-case disruptions to their community and how crises can be managed. These, and the policies discussed in Section 3.1.4., can be optimal for correcting the deficits of developmental DeFi DAO governance.

3.1.4. Ex ante regulation of internal control, technological, and other risk management policies

Regulators demand financial services providers to have in place ex ante risk management plans and policies in order to mitigate harm to users and firms' own financial risks. Many Dapp projects focus on the potential of their ideas and innovation and may underinvest time and effort into risk management. As code flaws emerge, developers and users then patch them. However, as projects evolve from hobbyist enjoyments, and appeal to a wider range of participants, implicating their financial and proprietary rights, this need for better ex ante development of risk control, particularly technological or cyber-risk controls, is warranted.

Ex ante governance compelled by regulation means that DeFi developers need to pre-code certain risk management capabilities to deal with commonly anticipated risks and problems such as cyber-risk. It is queried whether the Digital Operational Resilience Act (DORA)[68] that applies to all traditionally regulated financial services firms can provide some cross-fertilizing insights. The Act provides for procedural regulation and arguably precise standards in best practices that firms must implement to manage the ever-growing threats of technological and cyber-risk. Some requirements may not be completely relevant to DeFi Dapps, such as having back-up data repositories, but useful procedures such as simulation of cyber attacks and stress testing can be relevant. Regulators should consider whether DORA offers lessons for ex ante technological and cyber risk management applicable to DeFi, before a DeFi application can be authorized and operational.

Next, the overriding public interest of combating financial crime also necessitates financial intermediaries to institute control and management policies ex ante to flag

[68] "The Digital Operational Resilience Act (DORA)—Regulation (EU) 2022/2554" <https://www.digital-operational-resilience-act.com/> accessed November 15, 2024.

and report these risks. Crypto-intermediaries and DeFi applications are not immune. The EU Transfer of Funds Regulations 2023[69] now apply to all crypto-asset transfers where one of the payor or payee's crypto-asset service providers is located in the EU. The Regulations[70] require information accompanying crypto-asset transfers to identify the originator's information and its address as well as the beneficiary's information. Missing information should result in service providers rejecting the transfer or following up for more information. Centralized crypto-asset service providers would need to implement internal control procedures in order to ensure that the requisite information is obtained, and to engage in proactively rejecting non-conforming transfers. However, it is questioned how such gatekeeping roles can be imposed in a DeFi context. It is arguable that user to pool transactions can be governed in a similar way, as ex ante programming can be carried out for pool protocols to reject user transactions that are non-conforming. Commentators[71] have increasingly called for DeFi developers to embed anti-money laundering measures to monitor problematic wallet addresses and to be linked with oracles regarding money laundering risk such as provided by Chainalysis,[72] in order to automatically reject suspicious transactions. Barbereau and others[73] argue that it is also possible for coding requirements to be imposed on wallet developers so that wallet information would automatically carry the required information for users interacting with pools. It is an increasingly pressing issue for DeFi applications to develop ex ante programming to comply with anti-financial crime regulation.

The need to develop a variety of ex ante risk management policies in DeFi would compel developers to organize more ex ante governance capacity for risk management. For example, in terms of identifying capable and responsible leaders within the community to undertake specific responsibility for certain contingencies. In this manner, one of the implications for the need to provide ex ante governance demanded by financial regulation is that developers and other responsible persons may be subject to special regulatory responsibilities. For example, commentators call for fiduciary duties of loyalty and care to be imposed on developers due to their influential positions.[74] This is not unwarranted as most developers maintain significant control until governance is handed over to the DAO. Further, duties of loyalty and care could also be imposed on other leaders who have responsibility for contingency or crisis management. These can be in the form of sub-committees of governance formed of individuals who volunteer, are elected, or invited.

Hacker also proposes that miners or validators should be subject to a prohibition from colluding and using their joint power to advance their preferences. However, as miners and validators are beyond the organizational umbrella of any particular DeFi

[69] Regulation (EU) 2015/847.

[70] ibid Art 14 ff.

[71] Aquilina, Frost, and Schrimpf (n 57); Benson, Turksen, and Adamyk (n 50).

[72] "Chainalysis oracle for sanctions screening" <https://go.chainalysis.com/chainalysis-oracle-docs.html> accessed November 15, 2024; <https://www.chainalysis.com/cryptocurrency-address-screening/> accessed November 15, 2024.

[73] Barbereau and Bodò (n 50).

[74] Hacker (n 8); Timothy Nielsen, "Cryptocorporations: A Proposal for Legitimizing Decentralized Autonomous Organizations" (2019) 2019 Utah L Rev 1105.

DAO and work for the protocol blockchain, it may be difficult for financial regulators to extend duties to them.

It may be argued that there is a limit to how much ex ante internal control can be established in a DeFi Dapp as there is no centralized balance sheet or investment fund under a financial intermediary's control. The stability of the DeFi system depends on users' individual risks. Users may take on leverage across DeFi applications and become potential default risks across DeFi applications. In this manner, risk management regulation for DeFi needs adaptation from traditional regulatory designs.

Perhaps what is needed is that the DAO more effectively requires disclosure and management of users' risks, for example by requiring users' leverage disclosures, conflicts of interests (explored below), and perhaps imposing ceilings for their exposures.[75] Another source of collective risk to the DeFi community is insider rogue risk, as reflected in the Balancer episode discussed in Section 2. Regulators should consider requiring DeFi DAOs to have a policy for dealing with them, in terms of expulsion and expropriation/inactivation of their tokens, and facilitating claims against them for anti-social or abusive behavior.

In this manner, financial regulators may be at the forefront of developing basic governance expectations for DeFi DAOs that can be useful for DAOs more broadly, where similar governance problems are experienced. This can be in the form of a blockchain-based governance code,[76] crucially making minimum provisions for developers' duties and users' rights.

A blockchain governance code can also aim to level the playing field between users who are code-savvy and those that are not, as DeFi applications enjoy consumer participation. Additionally, regulators should require initial and periodic code auditing, like that provided in Malta's Innovative Technological Arrangements and Services Act.[77] This is important for all users to ensure that the DeFi project's protocols perform as represented.[78]

Further, regulators may wish to ensure that DeFi's governance frameworks accommodate codifiable as well as non-codifiable governance. Non-codifiable proposals could be in the form of principles or norms for guiding the resolution of future situations that are not completely addressed by code. Non-codifiable governance frameworks also offer greater inclusivity for users who are not technically trained. In this way, the limitations of code-based governance can be mitigated.[79] Code-based governance proposals should be explained in non-technical terms by proposers. Further, code auditing should be extended to proposals to protect non-tech savvy users. This can be done at proposers' expense but distributing cost that way may not incentivize the

[75] Ilya Kokkorin, "The Anatomy of Crypto Failures and Investor Protection under MiCAR" (2023) 18 Capital Markets Law Journal 500.

[76] Hacker (n 8).

[77] "Maltese Innovative Technology Arrangements and Services Act of 2018" <https://legislation.mt/eli/cap/592/eng/pdf> accessed November 15, 2024.

[78] An empirical study found that code deviations from the White Paper, left unscrutinized, begets governance problems in DAOs, Wei Ma and others, "A Comprehensive Study of Governance Issues in Decentralized Finance Applications" (*arXiv*, 2024) <https://arxiv.org/abs/2311.01433> accessed November 15, 2024.

[79] There are inherent limitations to code-based governance being able to address ex ante every possible governance situation for automatic resolution, Rohr and Wright (n 36).

most socially beneficial proposals, as proposers would be incentivized by generating proposals that make them the most gain. In order not to stifle innovation, it could be a constitutional requirement for all DAOs to set up a code auditing fund to which users contribute. All proposals can then be processed through third-party code auditing. Malta has set up a register of accredited code auditors, called "systems auditors," and this is a regulatory design that can inspire greater confidence for wide participation.[80]

Further, regulators can also consider if DeFi DAOs should institute a form of mandatory internal dispute resolution governance. Commentators[81] opine that internal dispute resolution for users is important in order to resolve the gaps of incomplete contracting. Even if regulations provide minimum governance standards, governance in any DeFi DAO inevitably requires building out. One of MiCAR's requirements for crypto-asset service providers is to establish a mandatory complaint-handling procedure. Complaints handling is a fundamental regulatory tenet for traditional financial services firms so that customers may be able to exhaust their private dispute resolution options before going to a public forum. However, as relational issues in DeFi are not necessarily framed as firm–customer but as internal governance problems, complaint handling may not be an appropriate regulatory requirement. In its stead, it is useful for DAO communities to constitutionally provide for ex post mechanisms to deal with governance issues that cannot be provided for or coded completely in an ex ante manner.[82] Internal dispute resolution can be community-based or outsourced, embedding a third party's protocol,[83] such as Aragon[84] which has instituted on-chain courts for adjudication.[85] However, third-party dispute resolution services are self-regulatory, and outsourcing could be a box-ticking form of compliance rather than a meaningful mechanism for dispute resolution. The regulator can require the DAO members to be satisfied, perhaps by a high threshold of consensus, that the third-party dispute resolution mechanisms meet their needs. In the alternative, there may be economies of scale for financial regulators to consider if they should take on the roles of accrediting and registering third-party dispute resolution services for the DeFi ecosystem at large. However, this may not be a matter just for financial regulators but rather, it is cross-sectoral in nature and ultimately part of general business policymaking.

Overall, there is good reason to compel developers to provide more fully-formed governance frameworks at the founding of a DeFi project in order to place the project

[80] "Systems Auditor Guidelines" <https://www.mdia.gov.mt/systems-auditor-guidelines/> accessed November 15, 2024.

[81] Kyung Taeck Minn, "Towards Enhanced Oversight of "Self-Governing" Decentralized Autonomous Organizations: Case Study of the DAO and Its Shortcomings" (2019) 9 NYU J Intell Prop & Ent L 139; Sheikh and Sifat (n 30).

[82] Rohr and Wright (n 36); Sheikh and Sifat (n 30).

[83] Florence Guillaume and Sven Riva, "Blockchain Dispute Resolution for Decentralized Autonomous Organizations: The Rise of Decentralized Autonomous Justice" in Andrea Bonomi and Matthias Lehmann (eds), *Blockchain and Private International Law* (Nijhoff 2022).

[84] "What is Aragon Court" <https://legacy-docs.aragon.org/products/aragon-court/aragon-court> accessed November 15, 2024. External dispute resolution systems may also need accreditation and regulation to ensure that they align with socially accepted norms for procedural justice, due process, and judgment.

[85] José Enrique González-Ávila, "Ethereum On-Chain Arbitration Protocols, Consent & Functionality" (*Linkedin*, 2022) <https://www.linkedin.com/pulse/ethereum-on-chain-arbitration-protocols-consent-gonz%C3%A1lez-%C3%A1vila/> accessed November 15, 2024.

and its DAO on a sound footing. Such governance frameworks could empower and hold accountable leaders who undertake governance roles, but more crucially, regulatory governance forces developers to be more forward-looking and provide for essential frameworks that manage users' risks. It may also be appropriate for governance leadership to be incentivized or rewarded while being responsible and accountable. Hence, an enabling law perspective for DeFi governance should exist alongside the governance tenets, so that innovations can take place for ongoing governance, catering to the specific needs of the project. In this manner, an optimal way forward could be the institution of a basic governance code for each project or DAO that meets financial regulators' concerns, while leaving scope for organic development of more specific needs.

3.1.5. Ex ante regulation of conflicts of interest management policy and disclosure

An important regulatory tenet for financial services firms is that they should identify, manage, prevent, and disclose conflicts of interest. MiCAR identifies these for crypto-asset service providers as existing between them and a range of constituents such as shareholders, users, employees, and management body members, as well as amongst users inter se. This provision is more applicable to centralized crypto-intermediaries where corporate organs and clients are clearly differentiated, and the aim is to prevent clients from being exploited. In a DeFi project, users take on multiple roles in governance and potentially as employees too and are all capital providers as token-holders. However, the spirit of the provision, which is transparency regarding conflicts of interests, and prioritizing the prevention and management of them, is relevant to DeFi. Conflicts of interest may exist vertically between powerful structures and users, but also horizontally amongst users,[86] and possibly requires more extensive unpacking in regulatory provision.

One possible regulatory design is to require DAOs to have screening/admission criteria for governance token purchasers as part of managing insider rogue risk. This could, however, be contrary to the permissionless ethos for access to DeFi Dapps, and would not necessarily be foolproof. The risks of insider rogues or self-interested motivations that could be collectively harmful may be better managed by requiring a full disclosure of conflicts of interest.

First, developers should disclose conflicts of interest, such as their involvement and funding for other projects. Further, as DeFi users are also involved in other DeFi applications and even competing ones, generating interdependencies between DeFi applications, conflicts of interest management can be regarded as serving both user protection and risk management needs for the DeFi application's stability. Regulators can consider providing a menu of options for DeFi communities for conflicts of interest management. For example, continuing disclosure can be required of all users, especially where they make governance proposals or vote. A register could be maintained for such transparency for all users. Governance proposers who notify conflicts of interest may have to explain in non-technical terms whether their proposals benefit other applications or communities and why they are not self-serving. DeFi

[86] Andrej Zwitter and Jilles Hazenburg, "Decentralised Network Governance: Blockchain Technology and the Future of Regulation" (2020) 3 Frontiers in Blockchain 12.

communities may also wish to decide the extent of permissible conflicts of interest that all users can incur, and whether beyond a particular threshold, a token-holders' vote may be frozen or suspended until the conflict is resolved.

A conflicts of interest governance framework is important for protecting users from potential exploitation. Since users and developers may lack the incentive to establish such a framework early on, a regulatory mandate could provide an effective solution.

3.1.6. Duty to act fairly, honestly, and professionally

MiCAR imposes a principles-based regulatory standard for crypto-asset providers to act fairly, honestly, and professionally in relation to users. This is derived[87] from the traditional financial regulation regime which deals with principal–agent problems[88] between centralized financial intermediaries and customers. This regulatory standard allows for ex post enforcement against conduct that cannot be precisely stipulated in an ex ante manner. Adopting this standard is useful for DeFi as a fundamental governance baseline that is non-code-based, therefore also addressing the deficits of exclusively code-based governance in DeFi. This standard should be adapted to the DeFi paradigm, as one that exists amongst users in a peer-to-peer environment, instead of between firm and customer. In reality, DeFi communities can be susceptible to principal–agent problems when there are unequal power structures. Further, DeFi environments are susceptible to being game theoretic in nature.

It has been suggested that developers, as well as identified governance actors responsible for governance actions, should be subject to duties of loyalty and care. These go beyond the standard of fairness and honesty stipulated above. Therefore, the standard of fair and honest dealing can be a minimum standard of conduct applicable amongst all users. It may be argued that this creates uncertainty and can generate frivolous dispute resolution amongst users. However, having a horizontal minimum standard for conduct amongst users can promote civic and even pro-social behavior that is optimal for the collective good of the DeFi application. The open-ended nature of the standard also allows users to adjust and form reasonable and more precise expectations of one another's conduct over time, ideally supported by effective dispute resolution mechanisms.

This section suggests that the minimum standard of honesty amongst users can be met by those users complying with the conflicts of interest management regime suggested above. This is an appropriate balance that avoids stifling users' freedom in terms of their financial management but prevents them from exploiting others in the community and causing harm. An open-ended duty of fairness imposed on each user is not unwarranted, as a basic and civic standard for dealing inter se. This standard can be used against anti-social or abusive users for the purposes of both private and public accountability and can be useful for DAOs generally.

[87] Critically, Maume (n 17).

[88] Alessio M Pacces, "Financial Intermediation in the Securities Markets Law and Economics of the Conduct of Business Regulation" (2000) 20 International Rev of Law and Econs 479.

3.1.7. Prudential regulation

Prudential regulation is a key tenet in financial regulation, mitigating firms' solvency risks and the fallout consequences for their stakeholders. MiCAR requires all crypto-asset service providers to be subject to prudential regulation as well, that is, having a minimum amount of own funds to be authorized and on an ongoing basis. The initial own funds requirement is set at 12 months' worth of fixed overheads for the crypto-asset service provider.

Ongoing prudential regulation, although likely an expensive requirement ultimately borne by all users, can benefit DeFi users in terms of managing exigencies and loss absorption. In particular, such funds can be used to absorb losses occasioned by cyberhacking and also to sustain the continuity of the DeFi application.

First, asking developers to contribute to an own funds' requirement, to a proportion, can improve skin-in-the-game incentives for developers. Further, own funds can be achieved by treating a proportion of users' contribution via token purchases as "ring-fenced" for prudential purposes. There is a need to consider what level of own funds would be sensible to mitigate a DeFi application's viability risk, for example, based on a scenario of cyberhacking and loss of value locked. Own funds can be set at a level of restoring lost value in such a way as to maintain users' confidence and sustain the DeFi community. DeFi governance would also need to provide for "recapitalizations" post loss and how this can be achieved. Hence, the prescriptive standard of 12 months' fixed overheads that is more appropriate for centralized financial intermediaries that are separate legal persons, should not apply to DeFi.

3.1.8. Users' custodial rights over assets

Protecting users' custodial rights over assets is a fundamental tenet of financial regulation, imposed on many non-bank financial intermediaries such as brokers and investment managers, to combat possible abuse as intermediaries manage customers' financial assets. Users' proprietary rights over assets protect them from being subject to financial intermediaries' solvency risks and provides priority in asset realizations even if their proprietary rights cannot be fully traced.

Crypto-asset service providers have to make adequate arrangements to safeguard asset-holders' ownership rights. The safekeeping and segregation of users' assets is particularly pertinent to centralized crypto-exchanges given the scandal at FTX,[89] but as DeFi is non-custodial in nature, it is queried if this requirement is necessary. Users' crypto-assets are locked in smart contracts for collateralization and liquidation purposes, and Black Thursday has shown how users' assets can be dissipated by automated protocols in a volatile trading environment. DeFi applications almost universally carry out overcollateralization of users' assets to mitigate the financial risks of crypto-asset financialization. Regulators need to consider how the needs for overcollateralization protocols to manage risks adequately should be balanced against users' reasonable risk assumption. Perhaps this cannot be overprescribed, but regulators can scrutinize these as part of the authorization process that applies to the

[89] Securities and Exchange Commission, "SEC Charges Samuel Bankman-Fried with Defrauding Investors in Crypto Asset Trading Platform FTX" (*SEC Press Release*, December 2022) <https://www.sec.gov/news/press-release/2022-219> accessed November 15, 2024.

development of ex ante governance. It can be argued that there should be an avenue for users to challenge radically unexpected ex post effects,[90] while bearing in mind the needs for contractual certainty.

3.1.9. Governance regulation as the basis for achieving broad financial regulatory objectives such as consumer protection?

The foregoing discussion shows that key tenets of financial regulation such as prudence and customer protection are relevant to the balanced protection of users' rights and risks, even if these issues are not best implemented by way of traditional regulatory standards of prudence and conduct. Finally, this section argues that consumer protection, which is a significant subject of financial conduct of business regulation, can also be framed and implemented as governance regulation in the DeFi context.

Traditional financial services regulation provides special protections for consumers to compensate for their lack of bargaining power vis a vis powerful financial intermediaries who impose standard terms. For example, in payment services regulation,[91] we see the introduction of reversal of unauthorized or even fraudulent push payment transactions that are adverse to consumers. In distance-selling, online crowdfunding, and crypto-asset offers, cooling-off withdrawal rights are common for consumer protection. However, these modes of consumer protection may be regarded as contrary to the irreversible nature of permissionless blockchain transactions in DeFi. Further, the imposition of conduct standards assumes a business–customer relationship which is inappropriate in a DeFi context where both vertical and horizontal conduct interact in multiple ways. The fundamental issue is whether the weakest participants, that is, consumers, should have their disadvantage balanced/leveled out. This is likely to be a governance issue in terms of how consumers are identified and how DeFi protocols should make precise adjustments for their disadvantages, such as specific risk warnings and frictions toward the process of engaging in DeFi activities. Whether these can be standardized for DeFi governance would also depend on what best practices emerge.

4. Concluding Remarks and Regulatory Insights for DAOs Generally

Financial regulation such as MiCAR, and other regulations like DORA and anti-money laundering regulations, could significantly shape DeFi's organizational and internal governance arrangements. Financial regulation tenets require much more ex ante programming and governance provision to meet regulatory objectives in user protection, public interest, and collective good. Further, the development of governance in DeFi may be the only way to deal with issues of user protection and risk management, how far users wish to secure the viability of DeFi applications, and how

[90] Jonathan Chiu, Charles M Kahn, and Thirsten V Koeppel, "Grasping Decentralized Finance Through the Lens of Economic Theory" (2022) 55 Canadian Journal of Economics 1702 suggests building in open-ended renegotiation protocols to prevent automatic liquidations in disorderly and unfair manners.

[91] Payment Services Directive 2015/2366, Arts 71–74.

consumers are protected within DeFi applications and the DeFi ecosystem. These insights can be generally useful for considering broader and general regulation for DAOs in other sectors.

It is arguable that some of the governance issues experienced generally in DAOs, not just DeFi DAOs, are of a similar nature in terms of conflicts of interests amongst users, governance attacks, unequal power structures, and disadvantages for non-technically savvy users, as well as the need for dispute resolution in view of incomplete contracting. In this manner, the lessons regarding the need for more ex ante development of governance, code auditing, and perhaps a code of conduct for basic governance standards could have traction for all DAOs generally.

In this manner, it is possible to develop generalized and not just sectoral expectations and demands for Dapp developers, DAO founders, and persons who wield significant governance or management influence in Dapps and even protocol blockchains. It is beyond the scope of this chapter to flesh out governance proposals across the blockchain stacks and in different sectors, but such a mapping may be useful, in light of what this chapter argues to be desirable ex ante governance standards for DeFi.

PART IV

THE FUTURE OF DAOs

13
The Law of Digital Organizations
A Prospective

Jason Grant Allen and Peter Hunn

1. Introduction

This chapter explores the (possible) future of social and economic coordination through legal structures, with a focus on the impact of a novel information and communications technology (ICT)—namely distributed ledger technology (DLT)—on the organizational structures currently provided by the legal system to its subjects ("users"). In other words, it examines the influence of DLT, particularly the emergence of decentralized autonomous organizations (DAOs), on legal organizational structures, and the way that DLT interoperates with traditional legal concepts of organization—up to and including the incorporation of a legal entity separate from the humans that make up its membership and act as its organs. Where other contributions in this volume explore the practicalities of DAO governance or statutory recognition, we aim to surface a deeper architectural question: how legal and technical affordances co-constitute the possibility space for organizational design. Our thesis is that, to the extent that features of DLT provide advantages for facilitating economic and social coordination, those features should influence "legal" modes of organization, too. Among other concepts, our thesis builds on the idea of *affordance* and the idea that technological *architecture* has a "regulative" function—following Lawrence Lessig's seminal analysis, embodying the (often tacit) regulatory assumptions of its designers. The intuition behind this thesis is that, despite numerous peaks of expectation, the promise of DLT as a coordination mechanism has failed to materialize because of the lack of intentional engagement at the *interface of law and technical infrastructure*. In our view, "technological regulation" will increasingly impact and influence the legal regulation of organizations, including corporations, but law will continue to be the primary mode of enablement and constraint in the organization of joint undertakings that endure over time. We propose a new approach to organizational law—one that treats legal and technical affordances not as rivals, but as interoperable primitives in the construction of digital companies. Intentional engagement is highly desirable in order to design a more coherent *techno-legal infrastructure*, in which the affordances of both the legal system and DLT are harnessed and designed for effective interoperation. Ideally, this would yield a new set of "digital organizations" (DOs) domesticated within local legal systems, or (to the extent it is any different) a new set of digital tools for "organ-izing" conventional, legally-sanctioned forms of coordinated social and economic action.

The structure of this chapter is as follows. Section 2 sets out the theories of *organization* (including the concept of *incorporation*) and *affordance*. Affordance, in particular, sheds light on both the role of law and technology in coordinating social behavior over time. The legal system provides a set of affordances, embodied in the various legal doctrines associated with the "law of groups." DLT has a set of affordances, too, but these are often seen as a mechanism to circumvent the law rather than as a set of tools that the law might use, or that might interoperate with the affordances of the law. We argue that *techno-legal affordances* determine the features and functions of DOs (and therefore the different types of DO). Section 3 sets out a spectrum or continuum of DOs, from "digitized corporations" to various species of DAO, according to the technical and legal affordances implicated. On this basis, Section 4 sets out a prospective view of the corporation, asking how extensively these techno-legal affordances could be deployed. Section 5 concludes. In short, we argue that the rise of digitally-mediated organizational forms demands not merely the adaptation of existing legal categories, but their re-composition into a coherent set of techno-legal affordances. This shift marks the emergence of a new modality of organizational law—one that treats legal and technical affordances as *interoperable building blocks* in the design of DOs.

2. Organization

Organizations function as governance structures designed to coordinate and align individual efforts toward achieving collective goals.[1] A core idea in organizational theory is that these systems are mechanisms to address coordination challenges that result from task interdependence in pursuit of those purposes:[2] transaction costs,[3] standardization of tasks,[4] incentive alignment,[5] and environmental demands or market factors.[6] Each may contribute to an organization's structure, processes, and governance in varying degrees and combinations.[7]

The law has always played an important role in social and economic coordination—this is what "the law," as a social system, does. Any given legal system provides the agents within its community certain tools to structure relationships with other agents

[1] eg W Richard Scott and Gerald F Davis, *Organizations and Organizing: Rational, Natural, and Open Systems Perspectives* (Pearson 2007); Henry Hansmann and Reinier Kraakman, "The Essential Role of Organizational Law" (2000) 110(3) Yale Law Journal 387.

[2] eg Henry Mintzberg, *Structure in Fives: Designing Effective Organizations* (Prentice Hall 1983); Thomas Malone and Kevin Crowston, "The Interdisciplinary Study of Coordination" (1994) 26(1) ACM Computing Surveys 87.

[3] Ronald Coase, "The Nature of the Firm" (1937) 4(16) Economica 386; Oliver Williamson, "The Economics of Organization: The Transaction Cost Approach" (1981) 87(3) American Journal of Sociology 548.

[4] Henry Mintzberg, *Structure in Fives: Designing Effective Organizations* (Prentice Hall 1983) (identifying mechanisms for standardizing work processes, outputs, skills, and norms).

[5] Michael Jensen and William Meckling, "Theory of the Firm: Managerial Behavior, Agency Costs and Ownership Structure" (1976) 3(4) Journal of Financial Economics 305.

[6] Paul Lawrence and Jay Lorsch, "Differentiation and Integration in Complex Organizations" (1967) 12 Administrative Science Quarterly 1.

[7] eg Paul Adler and Bryan Borys, "Two Types of Bureaucracy: Enabling and Coercive" (1996) 41(1) Administrative Science Quarterly 61.

over time, avoiding some issues through ex ante structures and dealing with other issues ex post. Nowhere is this more clearly illustrated than in the concept of *incorporation*. Incorporation is a legal institution that combines several features from various areas of law, including the law of contract, property, agency, and persons. This mix of legal institutions has its origins in the Romano-canon law of the Middle Ages, but it blossomed as a commercial and financial device in English law toward the end of the early modern period.[8]

Business organization in the pre-industrial age was restricted to relations between persons with a common interest through social structures that the legal system treated as unincorporated ("bodyless") companies and partnerships.[9] These persist to the present day, but play a smaller role in economic life. They bring together individuals with a shared interest in their several, personal capacities; they are something more than the sum of their parts, but they lack any concept of "joint stock" or "share capital" that members own and do not generally provide participants with benefits such as limited liability. Coordination issues, principally through hold-up costs caused by reliance upon specific individuals, often constrain their ability to function effectively for larger enterprises.[10] But, at core, organizations both with and without corporate status involve so many individuals becoming a group by appointing a sub-set of individuals to act for the whole group, structured by a complex web of contracts, financial records, and legal relationships. As this potted discussion suggests, the modern company evolved to include five core legal characteristics:[11] legal personhood,[12] limited liability,[13] investor ownership, transferable interests,[14] and delegated management.[15] Individuals form a group pursuant to a set of agreements inter se; their participation in the group is structured by their contribution of capital and their (apparent) ownership of an interest in the group and its undertaking; the group is made capable of

[8] Jason Grant Allen, "Bodies Without Organs: Law, Economics, and Decentralised Governance" (2019) 4(1) Stanford Journal of Blockchain Law & Policy 53. Not every aspect of its evolution to the dominant (almost default) mode of business organization was linear: Paddy Ireland, "Capitalism Without the Capitalist: The Joint Stock Company Share and the Emergence of the Modern Doctrine of Separate Corporate Personality" (2007) 17(1) Journal of Legal History 41.
Ron Harris, *Industrializing English Law: Entrepreneurship and Business Organization* (CUP 2000).

[9] eg ibid.

[10] Naomi Lamoreaux, "Partnerships, Corporations, and the Theory of the Firm" (1998) 88(2) American Economic Review 66, 67–68 cf 69–70 (corporations may mitigate reliance on individuals by improving exit opportunities); Benjamin Klein, Robert Crawford, and Armen Alchian, "Vertical Integration, Appropriable Rents, and the Competitive Contracting Process" (1978) 21(2) Journal of Law and Economics 297, 304–06; Henry Hansmann and Reinier Kraakman, "The Essential Role of Organizational Law" (2000) 110(3) Yale Law Journal 387, 390–92, 403–05.

[11] Reinier Kraakman and others, *The Anatomy of Corporate Law: A Comparative and Functional Approach* (OUP 2004)1–19.

[12] The Joint Stock Companies Act 1844 enabled formation by registration as opposed to Royal charter, letters patent, or Acts of Parliament. Judicially recognized in the seminal case of *Salomon v A. Salomon & Co. Ltd* [1897] AC 22 (HL) 51 (Lord Macnaghten).

[13] Introduced by the Limited Liability Act 1855. Walter Horrwitz, "Historical Development of Company Law" (1946) 62 Law Quarterly Review 375.

[14] Transferable shares were effectively enabled by a combination of s 8 (Deed of Settlement), s 25 (Register of Shareholders), and s 66 (Legal Consequences of Registration) of the Joint Stock Companies Act 1844. This was formalized in Companies Act 1862, s 22.

[15] Companies Act 1862, Table A Art 66 recognized in *Automatic Self-Cleansing Filter Syndicate Co. Ltd v Cuninghame* [1906] 2 Ch 34, 42 (Cozens-Hardy LJ). Now reflected in Companies (Model Articles) Regulations 2008, SI 2008/3229 Art 3.

collective action through the appointment of "organs"; and the group per se is treated as a legal person in its own right. Together, "these features ... make it possible to structure large-scale enterprise in a way that avoids the frictions that would otherwise arise in managing the relationships among multiple owners."[16]

2.1. Platform and Network Organizations

Technology —in particular, record-keeping technologies such as double-entry book-keeping—enables more complex and sophisticated forms of business organization.[17] Barry Smith observes:

> A document is something that is able to endure self-identically through time ... Pluralities of documents can be chained together ... and combined in other ways to form new document-complexes, whose structures mirror underlying human relations for example of debtor to creditor, of manager to shareholder ... and so on. *Documents thereby make possible new kinds of enduring social relations and new kinds of enduring social entities together allowing the evolution of entire new dimensions of socio-economic reality* (emphasis added).[18]

The evolution of the company from a group of co-adventurers to vast, anonymous networks bound by ownership of shares, complex default and mandatory rules, and the agency of professional managers was the co-evolution of social, economic, and technological trends. This has been structured responsively (at times reactively[19]) by the legal system, with the "long arc" aiming for some kind of public good (generally defined in welfare economic terms).[20] The record-keeping technologies of the eighteenth and nineteenth centuries—particularly, double-entry book-keeping and the printing press—are central to this story.

The technologies of the information age have facilitated new organizational structures. In classical economic and organizational theory (particularly following Coase and Williamson), *markets* coordinate transactions through the price mechanism, while *firms* "internalize" coordination under hierarchical authority to reduce

[16] Henry Hansmann and Reinier Kraakman, "The Essential Role of Organizational Law" (2000) 110(3) Yale Law Journal 387, 390.

[17] In particular, Alfred Crosby, *The Measure of Reality: Quantification in Western* Europe, *1250–1600* (Cambridge UP 1997) ch 10.

[18] Barry Smith, "How to Do Things with Documents" (2012) 50 *Revisti di Estetica* 179, 181; also David Koepsell, "Beyond Human: Smart Contracts, Smart Machines, and Documentality" in Jason Grant Allen and Peter Hunn (eds), *Smart Legal Contracts: Computable Law in Theory and Practice* (OUP 2022) ch 14. Emphasis added.

[19] eg Paddy Ireland, "The Myth of Shareholder Ownership" (1999) 63 Modern Law Review 32 for an insightful revision of the most common assumptions underlying modern corporations law debates—including, to some extent, our own.

[20] eg Frank Easterbrook and Daniel Fischel, "Limited Liabiltiy and the Corporation" (1985) 52 University of Chicago Law Review 89. For many, these justifications ring hollow: Paddy Ireland, "Limited Liability, Shareholder Rights and the Problem of Corporate Irresponsibility" (2010) 34(5) Cambridge Journal of Economics 837.

transaction costs.[21] The emerging *platform paradigm* does neither; instead, platforms outsource production to external actors while maintaining centralized control over the *infrastructure and rules* that govern interactions on the platform.[22] At the core of this model is a digital infrastructure governed by a set of rules—both social and technological—that manage participation and generate (hopefully positive) network effects. A particular form of this paradigm is captured in Benkler's conception of the "digitally networked environment" in which coordination occurs through decentralized, voluntary collaboration enabled by digital infrastructure rather than through market mechanisms or managerial hierarchies:

> [T]he "networked information economy" … is displacing the industrial information economy that typified information production from about the second half of the nineteenth century and throughout the twentieth century. What characterizes the networked information economy is that decentralized individual action—specifically, new and important cooperative and coordinate action carried out through radically distributed, nonmarket mechanisms that do not depend on proprietary strategies—plays a much greater role than it did, or could have, in the industrial information economy.[23]

These structures enable the aggregation of external resources—such as developers, users, or producers—while minimizing ownership and internal control.

Platforms require new forms of governance that blend contractual regulation with behavioral incentives.[24] The theoretical result is a reduction both in the need for hierarchical control (such as traditional employment practices) and for the high transaction costs typically associated with spot market exchanges. By controlling access, orchestrating data flows, and mediating trust through algorithms and reputation systems, platforms and networks may enable scalable coordination without direct ownership of productive assets or commons-based production—for example, in open source developer communities. As such, they represent an emergent mode of governance that blends *market-like openness* with *firm-like control*, challenging the distinction between internal and external coordination that has long structured theories of the firm.[25]

[21] Ronald Coase, "The Nature of the Firm" (1937) 4(16) Economica 386, 390 (economic theory with organizational implications) and Oliver Williamson, "The Economics of Organization: The Transaction Cost Approach" (1981) 87(3) American Journal of Sociology 548, 553 (applying economics to organizational theory). This idea is also related to the notion of the firm as a "nexus of contracts" whose more or less standardized form reduces transaction costs: Frank Easterbrook and Daniel Fischel, "The Corporate Contract" (1989) 89 Columbia Law Review 1416.

[22] Annabelle Gawer, Michael Cusumano, and David Yoffie, "The Platform Organization" in Charles Snow and Øystein Fjeldstad (eds), *Designing Adaptive Organizations* (CUP 2023); Martin Kenney and John Zysman, "The Rise of the Platform Economy"(2016) 32(3) Issues in Science and Technology 61; Nick Srnicek, *Platform Capitalism* (Polity Press 2016).

[23] Yochai Benkler, "Coase's Penguin, or, Linux and the Nature of the Firm" (2002) 112(3) Yale Law Journal 369; Yochai Benkler, *The Wealth of Networks: How Social Production Transforms Markets and Freedom* (Yale UP 2006) 59–63.

[24] Generally Tarleton Gillespie, "The Politics of 'Platforms'" (2010) 12(3) New Media & Society 347.

[25] eg A Gawer, "Digital Platforms' Boundaries: The Interplay of Firm Scope, Platform Sides, and Digital Interfaces" (2021) 54(5) Long Range Planning 102045; WW Powell, "Neither Market nor Hierarchy: Network Forms of Organization" (1990) 12 Research in Organizational Behavior 295.

Platform-based business models have revolutionized the economy across almost every sector. Like many trends driven by commercial imperatives and enabled by technological advances, the platform economy has a paradoxical relationship with the law.[26] Platform actors obviously utilize legal structures and institutions (particularly property and contract) and assume state law wherever they operate; further, with notable exceptions, they generally respect the regulatory regimes of the states in which they are active. Ultimately, every major platform provider today is itself incorporated under some national law. At the same time, platforms are a site of *private regulation*, and bring functions typically performed by state law and its institutions, such as dispute resolution, in-house. Further, many platforms are (in)famous for their oftentimes cavalier attitude toward state law.[27]

The interaction of the technical features of a platform with applicable state law(s) is generally dealt with post hoc and pragmatically rather than intentionally at the design phase—consider, for example, the question of platform "gig economy" worker status under employment law.[28] Much "innovation" derives from the fact that networked computers provide an infrastructure to minimize users' contact with, and even recourse to, state law. The architecture of this infrastructure is generally designed with economic goals in mind, rather than optimizing platform-to-legal system interoperation, which is considered in a pragmatic (often mercenary) fashion when problems arise. (Sometimes, as we have seen, the infrastructure is designed *not* to interact with law at all, although this is a naïve and irresponsible design approach.)

2.2. Affordances (Technical and Legal)

This pattern is amplified in the context of DLT. One of the central propositions of DLT is the ability to coordinate groups of agents without a central, trusted recordkeeper, and with public "tamper proof" records. The concept of *affordance* provides a set of tools for understanding the dynamics between technology and law.[29] Affordance describes the actionable possibilities offered by an environment to an agent. For example, a flat horizontal surface provides the "affordance" of support.[30] As Laurence Diver explains, perceptual psychologist James Gibson first defined affordance as what an artefact provides an animal. Donald Norman later introduced it into the design sphere, defining it as a relationship between the properties of an object and the

[26] There is a significant literature on the point, eg Hannah Bloch-Wehba, "Platform Governance: Private Power in the Shadow of the State" (2019) 72(1) SMU Law Review 27; Clement Salung Petersen, Vibe Garf Ulfbeck, and Ole Hansen, "Platforms as Private Governance Systems: The Example of Airbnb" (2018) 1 Nordic Journal of Commercial Law 1; Elettra Biette, "A Genealogy of Digital Platform Regulation" (2023) 7 Georgetown Law Technology Review 1.

[27] Harry Davies and others, "Uber broke laws, duped police, and secretly lobbied governments, leak reveals" (*The Guardian*, July 12, 2022) <https://www.theguardian.com/news/2022/jul/10/uber-files-leak-reveals-global-lobbying-campaign> accessed May 25, 2025.

[28] eg Cristina Inversi, Tony Dundon, and Lucy-Ann Buckley, "Work in the Gig Economy: The Role of the State and Non-State Actors Ceding and Seizing Regulatory Space" (2022) 37(5) Work, Employment and Society 1279.

[29] We will use "artefact" to include systems as a whole as well as their components, but will disambiguate as necessary.

[30] James Gibson, *The Ecological Approach to Visual Perception* (Erlbaum 1979) 127.

capabilities of the agent that determine how the object could be used. An affordance can be positive or negative, all things considered.[31] The affordances of an environment also depend on the capabilities of the agent—a spider can walk on a window-pane, a human cannot. Affordances are, therefore, *environmentally-derived relationships* that enable and constrain behavior.[32]

The idea that technical systems "regulate" behavior through their design—by enabling or constraining user actions—has gained traction in legal and regulatory theory. Lessig famously framed architecture (both physical and digital) as one of the four "modalities" of regulation, alongside law, non-legal social norms, and markets. Digital affordances, in this sense, operate as regulatory conditions: they shape what users can do, how, and with what friction.[33] Recent scholarship has extended this logic to law itself. Some have argued that legal institutions offer their own sets of affordances: actionable possibilities for users navigating social and economic life.[34] While the concept remains underdeveloped in legal theory,[35] it usefully captures how law structures agency by providing artefacts—such as contracts, corporations, or marriage—that are not merely classificatory, but performative. These institutions shape behavior by establishing default relationships between facts and legal consequences, and by enabling actors to intentionally effect legal change. Our focus is on the how law itself might "use" technological affordances to perform its social function—how the legal system might harness technological affordances to augment or enhance the affordances it provides to its community of users. While we do not attempt a comprehensive theory

[31] Laurence Diver, "Law as a User: Design, Affordance, and the Technological Mediation of Norms" (2018) 15(1) SCRIPTed 4, 8. Citations omitted.

[32] Donald Norman, *The Design of Everyday Things* (MIT Press 2013) 11. Jenny Davis and James Chouinard, "Theorizing Affordances: From Request to Refuse" (2016) 36(4) Bulletin of Science, Technology & Society 241 (recognizing that affordances are a spectrum that guide forms of behavior rather than providing a binary capability). As Diver explains, by reference to the science and technology studies (STS) and post-phenomenology literature, the relational aspect of affordances is fundamental, because a creature's perception of its world and of its own capabilities within that world are shaped by the affordances it perceives in the environment and the artefacts contained in it. While important, we confine the present exploration to a more superficial level. Laurence Diver, "Law as a User: Design, Affordance, and the Technological Mediation of Norms" (2018) 15(1) SCRIPTed 4, 19.

[33] Generally: Eric Posner, *Law and Social Norms* (Harvard UP 2002); Richard McAdams, "The Origin, Development, and Regulation of Norms" (1997) 96 Michigan Law Review 338. Also Melvin Eisenberg, "Corporate Law and Social Norms" (1999) 99 Columbia Law Review 1253; Robert Cooter, "Decentralized Law for a Complex Economy: The Structural Approach to Adjudicating the New Law Merchant" (1996) 144(5) University of Pennsylvania Law Review 1643; Lawrence Lessig, *Code and Other Laws of Cyberspace* (Basic Books 1999) 85–99 (Lessig identifies these four as regulators of behavior). For an alternative view: Roger Brownsword, *Rights, Regulation, and the Technological Revolution* (OUP 2008).

[34] Ryan Calo, "Can Americans Resist Surveillance?" (2016) 83 The University of Chicago Law Review 23, 27; cf Laurence Diver, "Law as a User: Design, Affordance, and the Technological Mediation of Norms" (2018) 15(1) Scripted 4, 23; also Lawrence Lessig, "The New Chicago School" (1998) 27 The Journal of Legal Studies 661; Lawrence Lessig, *Code and Other Laws of Cyberspace* (Basic Books 1999) and *Code: Version 2.0* (Basic Books 2006).

[35] Laurence Diver, "Law as a User: Design, Affordance, and the Technological Mediation of Norms" (2018) 15(1) SCRIPTed 4, 22 ff; also Mireille Hildebrandt, *Smart Technologies and the End(s) of Law* (Edward Elgar 2016) ch 8; Mireille Hildebrandt, "Law as an Affordance: The Devil is in the Vanishing Point(s)" (2017) 4(1) Critical Analysis of the Law 116; Ronald Leenes, "Framing Techno-Regulation: An Exploration of State and Non-State Regulation by Technology" (2011) 5 Legisprudence 143; Ryan Calo, "Privacy, Vulnerability, and Affordance" (2017) 66 DePaul Law Review 591.

here, we outline an account in which legal institutions operate as artefacts that structure action within a normative system.

In our view, legal institutions can be understood as artefacts that afford particular forms of action within the world recognized (and constituted) by the legal system.[36] Consider incorporation: by performing certain formal acts (eg registration), a group gains access to limited liability, separate legal personality, and capital structures. These consequences are not simply symbolic; they instantiate a new social fact that is recognized and enforced across legal and economic systems. In Ruiter's terms, institutions present a "valid picture" of how things ought to be, and in doing so, help bring about corresponding social practices.[37]

This logic generalizes. Legal artefacts such as marriage, trust, or agency provide users with structures for coordination, rights, and protections—often bundled with duties and constraints. For instance, marriage may afford evidentiary privileges in criminal law, just as incorporation affords liability shielding in commercial law. In each case, the legal system constructs a normative world in which agents can plan, act, and be held accountable. The corporation is a particularly clear example. It is a "person" not in any biological or physical sense, but as an artefact of law—an institutional construct whose capacities (eg owning property, contracting, bearing liability) are defined by legal doctrine and mediated by human agents. Corporate forms such as the Ltd or limited liability company (LLC) are, in this light, modular instantiations of a broader legal institution that afford users specific capacities in exchange for procedural compliance. They do not merely reflect economic activity—they constitute it. The law is constitutive of these characteristics and the relationships that flow as a consequence of the corporation *qua* legal institution: they are legal creations.[38]

2.2.1. Toward a concept of "techno-legal" affordances

We need a concept of affordance that explains both (1) the affordances provided *by the law*, as a social system and a set of "artefacts", to its users and (2) the affordances provided by technological artefacts and infrastructures *to the legal system*, positioned as a "user." We have already touched on (1) above; in this section, we will focus on (2), drawing particularly on Diver's work and that of Mireille Hildebrandt. Ultimately, we have to explain how the legal system and technological artefacts interact with each other—in particular, how the legal system responds to technological artefacts that provide affordances *directly* to users in a manner that bypasses, displaces, or competes with the affordances of the legal system.

This points to a concept of *techno-legal affordances*. The crux of the issue is that technological artefacts and systems *mediate* the law, by providing affordances to the legal system, which it, in turn, uses to provide its affordances. This idea has been

[36] This idea is developed further in Peter Hunn, "Only Binary? Atoms and Bits as Objects of Property", manuscript on file with the authors for publication in a handbook on digital assets and the law; also Yochai Benkler, "Networks of Power, Degrees of Freedom" (2011) 5 International Journal of Communications 721, 724–38.

[37] Dick Ruiter, "A Basic Classification of Legal Institutions" (1997) 10(4) Ratio Juris 357, 362.

[38] See *The Case of Sutton's Hospital* (1612) 10 Co Rep 23a, 77 ER 960, in which Coke CJ observed that the corporation is "invisible, immortal and rests only in intendment and consideration of the law."

developed over a period of time by Hildebrandt, in particular, who has stressed the co-evolution of "law as we know it" with technologies of the printing press.[39]

The introduction of new technological artefacts could change the law in desirable or undesirable ways. One of Hildebrandt's concerns is how data-driven ICT affects the rule of law. For example, automation of an official decision-making process might provide the subject with a faster decision—but one which is less transparent and therefore less "interoperable" with the traditional mechanisms of review. Whether the mediation of the law through any technological artefact causes a net positive or a negative change to the legal system is a question of both fact and value that must be made in context, and remains neglected in the legal theory literature.[40]

Technological artefacts can be deployed to *displace* the law by providing affordances that do not seem to interact with the legal system in any meaningful way. DAOs offer an example: The corporation is the paradigm artefact provided to the users of a legal system to coordinate joint action over time. The DAO uses DLT to provide many of the same affordances without relying on the legal artefact of a corporation, or necessarily engaging with the legal system intentionally at all. (It is always open to subjects of a legal system to seek recourse from the law, even when they have actively tried to interact with others in an "extra-legal space.")

In a simple world, the legal system might simply have taken stock of the emerging practice of extra-legal DAOs and tried—successfully or unsuccessfully—to shut it down. It might have done so by issuing commands never to be involved in a DAO, and/or by denying the affordances of its *other* institutions for matters involving a DAO. (This approach was taken, albeit unsuccessfully in the long term, with unauthorised joint stock corporations until the repeal of the Bubble Act (1720)—"An Act to restrain the Extravagant and Unwarrantable Practice of raising Money by Voluntary Subscriptions for carrying on Projects dangerous to the Trade and Subjects of the United Kingdom"—in 1825.) That is, for better or worse, not the way things have gone—DLT-based structures, including DAOs, appear to have been tolerated rather than prohibited and at least some of the ambient affordances of the law have been made available to users of DLT—for example, providing recourse to the courts (in a procedural sense) or property rights protection (in a substantive sense), even where they have been trying to interact in an extra-legal space.

This mode of development is unfortunate, for it has obscured the ultimate concern of this chapter: The affordances of DLT could be useful per se as an underlying technological infrastructure for the legal system itself as a "user" of technological artefacts in order to provide, in turn, better "services" to users of the legal system. This would be a virtuous cycle of interaction between the law and DLT, rather than a haphazard and opportunistic recourse to law when things go wrong. We have already seen that even

[39] As Diver explains, the novelty of Hildebrandt's contribution is to show "how the affordances of a particular technological embodiment of the law, namely printed text, have affected how law has developed in certain ways which have led to the mature and stable set of institutions and concepts we today take for granted; Laurence Diver, "Law as a User: Design, Affordance, and the Technological Mediation of Norms" (2018) 15(1) SCRIPTed 4, 28; *inter alia*, Mireille Hildebrandt, "Legal Protection by Design: Objections and Refutations" (2011) 5 Legisprudence 223.

[40] For further discussion, Aernoud Schmidt, "Radbruch in Cyberspace: About Law-System Quality and ICT Innovation" (2009) 3(2) Masaryk University Journal of Law and Technology 195.

conventional legal artefacts (such as corporations) are to some extent *techno-legal*, relying as they do on technologies for recording numbers and words, in particular, in a stable form over time. In both cases, novel technologies (such as DLT) can be catalysts for important change in the legal system.[41] Pre-empting our ultimate argument, technology-driven innovation often appears intended to harness the affordances of novel technologies to *displace* legal institutions such as contract, property, or the corporation; in our view, however, the more interesting route is *technological mediation* of the law. We return to this issue below, where we explore the affordances of DLT as a law-mediating technology that could power digital organizations "naturalized" within the legal system directly, rather than through current practices such as a legal "wrapper."

The operation of law is mediated through the "materialities of architecture."[42] Diver's notion of the legal system as a "user" of the affordances of technology is key, as it provides a useful gloss on Lessig's "modalities" of regulation (which include "architecture"), tempering arguments for the rise of a "*lex cryptographia*" which is the product of coders rather than lawyers,[43] and inviting us to think about which affordances of DLT any legal system ought to adopt. The aim must be, we say, to provide the users of a legal system with a better suite of *techno-legal affordances* that are integrated within the institutional fabric of the legal system in a coherent way.

This idea requires a little more unpacking, for which Lessig's well-known account is instructive. Lessig's famous argument is that the law is just one kind of lever for regulating the behavior of social actors, along with the market, informal social norms, and architecture.[44] Sometimes the *content* of norms is determined by the designers and builders of the architecture, even when they are not intentionally or consciously coding norms at all. As Lessig observes, we can design cyberspace to protect values that we believe are fundamental, or we can design it in such a way that allows those values to disappear.[45] His concern is, first and foremost, to enliven us to the design and construction of digital architecture as a site for norm construction—often tacit, and therefore both unconsidered by its authors and uncontested by others. In the case of DLT, the problem is less one of unintentionally inaccurate encoding of norms; given the ideology of the crypto movement, architectures are often designed to exclude law intentionally. This situation is both empirically untenable (as users' recourse

[41] Carla Reyes, "Conceptualising Cryptolaw" (2017) 96 Nebraska Law Review 384; cf Rosa Lastra and Jason Grant Allen, "Lex Cryptographia Financiera" in William Blair, Christos Gortsos, and Chiara Zilioli (eds), *International Money and Banking Law post COVID-19* (OUP 2023) ch 7.

[42] Laurence Diver, "Law as a User: Design, Affordance, and the Technological Mediation of Norms" (2018) 15(1) SCRIPTed 4, 7.

[43] Carla Reyes, "Conceptualising Cryptolaw" (2017) 96(2) Nebraska Law Review 384; cf Rosa Maria Lastra and Jason Grant Allen, "Lex Cryptographia Financiera" in Sir William Blair, Chiara Zilioli, and Christos Gortsos (eds), *International Monetary and Banking Law in the post COVID-19 World* (OUP 2023).

[44] Similar ideas are current in more critical accounts, including Bruno Latour's speedbump as a "sleeping policeman" or Peter-Paul Verbeek's account of shortening rake handles to stop city employees from resting on them: Bruno Latour, *Pandora's Hope: Essays on the Reality of Science Studies* (Harvard UP 1999); Peter-Paul Verbeek, *What Things Do: Philosophical Reflections on Technology, Agency, and Design* (Penn State Press 2005); also Langdon Winner, "Do Artifacts Have Politics?" (1980) Daedalus 121.

[45] For the discussion on "code is law" and "architectures of control": Lawrence Lessig, *Code and Other Laws of Cyberspace* (Basic Books 1999) chs 1, 4.

to the law courts demonstrates) and, from the perspective of state law, normatively unacceptable.

2.2.2. Isomorphism at the legal-technical interface

One of us has warned against the unconscious "bleeding" of norms implicit within the design of DLT structures into the legal system through the process of case-by-case remedial accommodation of the type we have seen over the past decade when crypto projects have gone wrong:

> The central thrust of Lessig's "code as law" approach is to prevent the backwards percolation of code-based regulation going unnoticed. In an early contribution, Lessig observed that the newly emerging "space" looked like it was free of legal constraints and that "contract rather than law" governed behaviour there. On this view, cyberspace is an endless new world in which restless subjects can remove themselves to beyond the claim of bothersome "real world" sovereigns. Lessig's compelling argument was that this space, too, is constituted (and therefore conditioned) by rules built into its very "architecture". These rules need to be exposed to the same kind of normative assessment as any others ... In "real space", obligations are conditioned by norms of competition law, consumer protection, principles of equity, and remedies such as rectification: "The cyberspace analogue has no equivalent toolbox. Its obligations are not conditioned by the public values that contract law embraces. Its obligations instead flow automatically from the structures imposed in the code. These structures serve the private ends of the code writer; they are a private version of contract law. But as the Legal Realists spent a generation teaching, and as we seem so keen to forget: contract law is public law. 'Private public law' is oxymoronic." A similar sentiment was expressed by Holt CJ in the early eighteenth century: private subjects cannot dictate changes in the law to the courts by "setting up [a] new sort of specialty" besides the common law which "attempt[s] to give laws to Westminster hall".[46]

Control through novel technological affordances and conventional legal affordances often looks very different. For instance, code often embeds enforcement as a form of inherent, as opposed to ex post, enforcement. Nonetheless, the relationship between law and technology should—all else being equal—be *isomorphic* with legal norms.[47] The law sometimes regulates the design and use of technology directly, seeking to ensure that technology neither brings *prima facie* regulated activities beyond the perimeter of the law nor leaves *prima facie* valid actions unsupported by the existing law. For example, just because a project uses a crypto token rather than a conventional security does not mean that capital markets regulation should not apply; likewise,

[46] Rosa María Lastra and Jason Grant Allen, "Lex Financiera Cryptographia" in William Blair, Chiara Zilioli, and Christos Gortsos (eds), *International Monetary and Banking Law Post COVID-19* (OUP 2023) 169. Citations omitted include Lawrence Lessig, "The Law of the Horse: What Cyberlaw Might Teach" (1999) 113 Harvard Law Review 501, 530; and *Clerk v Martin* (1702) 2 Ld Raym 757, 758 (a case concerning bills of exchange).

[47] Trevor Bench-Capon and Frans Coenen, "Isomorphism and Legal Knowledge Based Systems" (1992) 1 Artificial Intelligence and Law 65; Mireille Hildebrandt, *Smart Technologies and the End(s) of Law* (Edward Elgar Publishing 2015).

private law should (arguably) support property rights in digital tokens and enforce "smart" contracts.[48]

The problem-space could be framed as follows: (1) technological affordances create legal challenges, as they change the way in which subjects within a legal system can act (and interact), because technological systems are not extra-legal; (2) legal norms, including the consequences that flow automatically (and often mandatorily) from the instantiation of a valid legal institution (or the failure of a valid instantiation), create challenges for subjects using the affordances of novel technology. This creates tension between the potentialities afforded by the legal system and the evolving technological state of the art, especially for those who wish to use the latter to "innovate" in a manner that amounts to little more than the avoidance of regulatory perimeters.

The nature of these affordances may look different with respect to organizations constituted through digital infrastructure in whole or in part. In conventional legal theory, organizational forms such as the corporation, partnership, and trust function as *pre-configured* legal artefacts. They offer "modules" such as legal personality, liability shielding, and asset partitioning that can be selected and combined through private legal acts of formation and governance. The law provides a set of mandatory norms within a broader context of default norms that are susceptible to optimization through party autonomy. These forms are deeply embedded in bureaucratic state infrastructure, and their evolution has historically tracked changes in legal doctrine, administrative capability, and economic practice. By contrast, digital infrastructure introduces a new layer of affordances that are at once technical and have legal valence. These *techno-legal affordances* arise not merely from the law per se but from its operationalization in programmable systems: platforms that mediate participation, automate execution, and instantiate rule-like constraints in code. These affordances do not sit atop the law as extralegal "hacks" but increasingly act as substrates through which legal relationships are performed, contested, and recorded. The key shift is that the architecture of the organization is no longer merely *legally* structured—it is also *technically* executed and, to that extent, technically structured as well. Examples include multi-signature arrangements and programmable voting mechanisms that structure collective decision-making; embedded oracles and role-based permissions that operationalize delegation; and token-based structures for capital and access rights that blur the line between membership, governance, and equity. These are not simply technical affordances: They become part of the *legal* architecture when they are used to instantiate, constrain, or express the relationships constitutive of a legally recognized organization.

The affordances of digital infrastructure are thus increasingly constitutive of legal states of affairs. This is reflected, for example, in the debate about whether a DLT ledger can/should be considered a "root of title" or merely evidential.[49] They shape the epistemic, procedural, and allocative dimensions of organization in ways that depart from traditional forms. At the same time, they remain situated within legal

[48] eg *South West Terminal Ltd v Achter Land* [2023] 10 WWR 717.

[49] eg the report of UNIDROIT Study LXXXII – W.G.1 – Doc. 3, "Exploratory Workshop on Digital Assets and Private Law" (Rome and Zoom, September 17–18, 2020) 4 <https://www.unidroit.org/english/documents/2021/study82/wg01/s-82-wg01-03-e.pdf> accessed May 25, 2025.

frameworks—sometimes implicitly, sometimes contestably. As the Law Commission of England & Wales notes in its scoping paper on DAOs, many of the rights and responsibilities arising in such systems will not be determined by the source code alone, but by the interpretation of that code and its interaction with surrounding legal and institutional context.[50]

Understanding digital organizations, then, requires more than cataloguing novel tools. It requires legal theory to grapple with how those tools *instantiate structure*, *distribute power*, and *mediate accountability*. The crucial question is not simply how code can perform legal functions, but how legal functions are being reimagined within coded systems—sometimes in ways that enhance legitimacy and participation, and sometimes in ways that obscure or displace them. This calls for an applied legal theory of techno-legal affordances.

2.2.3. DLT affordances as techno-legal substrates for organizational coordination

Our argument has been that the affordances of DLT embed new techno-legal substrates for organizational coordination. These systems collapse the traditional distinction between legal affordances and technical infrastructure by encoding rules of interaction, governance, and control into executable architecture. The legal significance of these systems lies not only in their capacity to displace intermediaries, but in how they reconstitute legal roles, relationships, and affordances in programmable form. This section outlines three interrelated affordances: *record-keeping*, *operational regulation*, and *tokenization*.

First, the underlying data management characteristics inherent in DLT architectures regulate record-keeping—not just functionally, but institutionally. Peer-to-peer networks and distributed consensus protocols enforce decentralized data replication, while cryptographic proofs—such as hash chains and Merkle trees—support legally relevant qualities including evidentiary integrity, auditability, and immutability.[51] These features collectively enable tamper-evident ledgers that perform functions traditionally associated with institutional records: chain-of-custody, provenance, and transactional finality, without recourse to trusted intermediaries.[52] Mechanisms such as triple-entry accounting, selective replication rights, and programmable validation embed regulatory logic into the architecture itself. In doing so, DLT platforms instantiate a kind of procedural finality: what is recognized across the network constitutes the system's authoritative "local facts." This affordance of enforced visibility—determining not only what is legible but what is actionable—effectively collapses the traditional distinction between legal affordances and technical infrastructure. In this respect, consensus mechanisms such as proof-of-work or proof-of-stake determine

[50] Law Commission, "Decentralised Autonomous Organisations (DAOs): A Scoping Paper" (July 2024) <https://webarchive.nationalarchives.gov.uk/ukgwa/20250109094345mp_/https://cloud-platform-e218f50a4812967ba1215eaecede923f.s3.amazonaws.com/uploads/sites/30/2024/07/DAOs-scoping-paper-110724.pdf> accessed May 25, 2025.

[51] eg Kevin Werbach, *The Blockchain and the New Architecture of Trust* (MIT Press 2018); Ian Grigg, "Triple Entry Accounting" (2024) 17(2) Journal of Risk and Financial Management 76; Jun Dai and Miklos Vasarhelyi, "Toward Blockchain-based Accounting and Assurance" (2017) 31(3) Journal of Information Systems 5.

[52] eg Primavera De Filippi and Aaron Wright, *Blockchain and the Law: The Rule of Code* (Harvard UP 2018) 187, 196–97.

what "counts" as the authoritative state of affairs within the system. The result is a new techno-legal substrate that embeds institutional ordering into a synchronized, decentralized record.

Second, DLT enables what we describe as *operational regulation*:[53] the encoding and embedding of procedural logic such that transactions, obligations, and governance functions are executed automatically upon the satisfaction of pre-specified conditions. Through smart contracts, actions that would traditionally require institutional mediation—such as fund transfers, role updates, or rule changes—are performed with *automaticity* and *atomicity*, reducing discretionary variation and mitigating inchoate performance risks.[54] This automation introduces a form of techno-legal determinism.[55] It facilitates relationships—for example, contractual obligations and governance arrangements—that are not merely *recorded*, but *operationalized* through code. The result is a narrowing of the temporal and discretionary space in which performance can be contested or reinterpreted. What would previously have been modulated through human judgment or legal process is now hardened into the execution logic of the system itself. Such transformations do not automate law per se, but do automate the performance of acts that have traditionally been carried out by fiduciaries, directors, or trustees. This introduces both potential and peril: a redistribution of agency from human actors to software agents, and a reconfiguration of legal responsibility around the design and deployment of such agents rather than their discretionary acts. Legal systems are only beginning to grapple with the implications of a procedural architecture that is both technical and normative, including for liability, redress, and procedural fairness.

Third, *tokenization*—the unitized digital representation of value including rights to things, rights against others, and purely notional value—acts as a substrate for organizational access, control, and coordination.[56] Through smart contracts, tokens digitize and embed value flows into programmable units whose behavior is constrained by the logic of on-chain code. These units regulate by design: encoding the rules of participation, governance, and incentive alignment into their issuance, transfer, and functional use. Tokenization thus "embeds" regulation where governance mechanisms—previously external to the asset or organizational structure—are incorporated into the digital artefacts themselves. One prospective effect is that smart contracts replicate and, in some respects, reconfigure the coordination mechanisms typical of traditional hierarchical organizations. Tokens no longer just represent value; they carry with them roles, responsibilities, and technical permissions.

Crucially, tokenization recasts the legal separation between *ownership* and *control*. Because token management and governance logic are embedded in smart

[53] Peter Hunn, "Smart Contracts as Techno-Legal Regulation" (2019) 7(3) Journal of ICT 269.

[54] eg Konstantinos Christidis and Michael Devetsikiotis, "Blockchains and Smart Contracts for the Internet of Things" (2016) 4 IEEE Access 2292–2303; Nick Szabo, "Formalising and Securing Relationships on Public Networks" (1997) 2(9) First Monday <https://firstmonday.org/ojs/index.php/fm/article/download/548/469> accessed May 25, 2025.

[55] On concerns regarding practical feasibility, Kelvin Low and Eliza Mik, "Pause the Blockchain Legal Revolution" (2019) 69(1) International & Comparative Law Quarterly 135.

[56] Christian Catalini and Joshua Gans, "Some Simple Economics of the Blockchain" (2016) MIT Sloan Research Paper 5191–16.

contracts, the classic division between capital interest and managerial authority can be blurred (or collapsed). Governance functions such as proposal, voting, and resource allocation can be conditioned on rule-based thresholds and automatically executed, eliminating the discretionary space that human agents once occupied. These affordances are already visible in mechanisms such as: (1) staking, where economic actors lock tokens as collateral to secure networks or signal commitment, serving as both governance constraint and enforcement tool; (2) delegated or token-weighted voting, often implemented through proxy mechanisms, enabling scalable decision-making without the friction of traditional quorum or notice requirements; (3) quadratic funding and voting, which embed redistributive or anti-plutocratic principles by weighting votes non-linearly; and (v) continuous organizations, in which treasury inflows and governance cycles are governed by algorithmic rules, dissolving the temporal boundaries of fundraising, budgeting, and payout. Each of these illustrates how tokenization supports modular, persistent, and reconfigurable organizational forms, whose regulatory features are performed by the infrastructure rather than enforced ex post by (state) law.

This shift challenges existing taxonomies: Are these tokens equity, rights, licenses, or something else? The legal system has not yet developed a stable classification scheme for such hybrid artefacts. Yet in practice, they already perform coordination functions that were once mediated by company constitutions, shareholder agreements, and corporate registries. In sum, tokenization marks a high point in the formalization of governance by code to date. It enables digitally-native organizations to operationalize rules for access, action, and value distribution internally—within the system itself—while leaving law to play a residual role in dispute resolution, external recognition, and the drawing of ultimate limits.

Taken together, these affordances—replicated record-keeping, automated execution, and token-based governance—provide the building blocks of a techno-legal infrastructure for digital coordination. They open the possibility of reconstituting the organization itself as a digitally-instantiated artefact. Yet these affordances operate unevenly, and are not always well-composed. If early DAO projects demonstrated the potential for natively digital organization, they also revealed the conceptual and structural gaps that emerge when technical affordances supplement (or supplant) legal ones without adequate integration—where interoperability with the legal system is not part of the design philosophy. To assess what a more stable and functional model might look like, we now turn to the evolving architecture of digital organizational structures with particular attention to hybrids, wrappers, and emergent forms of organization.

3. Techno-Legal Affordances of Digital Organization

Here, we explore how the DLT affordances have been harnessed by DAO projects to date. These experiments illuminate the possibilities and limitations of structuring organizations through digital infrastructure. Our focus is on how these affordances map onto existing and emergent organizational types, from state-recognized legal entities to experimental decentralized collectives. In the next section, we extend this analysis to ask how these affordances might be more deliberately composed to support the development of *natively digital legal organizations*—entities that are both legally recognized and technologically instantiated.

"Digital organization" covers a broad and evolving spectrum of forms, defined by the extent to which their structure, operations, and governance are mediated—or constituted—by digital infrastructure.[57] Traditional organizations increasingly use digital tools to support analogue, bureaucratic processes, but their architecture remains conventional. By contrast, DOs rely essentially on embedded digital affordances for the very expression of roles, procedures, and entitlements. Forms vary in the balance they strike between legal and technological affordances, and are best conceptualized as a continuum—from conventional entities whose operation is digitized to some extent, to organizations whose existence depends on programmable infrastructure.[58]

At one end of the spectrum are conventional legal entities, such as companies incorporated under legislation like the Companies Act 2006 (UK). These entities possess juridical personality, limited liability, and governance structures defined by statute and could, in theory, operate entirely "on paper." Of course, such entities increasingly rely on digital systems—electronic share registers, online filings, and algorithmic trading platforms—but these tools support processes whose legal basis remains exogenous to the technology itself.[59] A share register may be digitized, but the shares it records are not "natively" digital;[60] in fact, the shares themselves *cannot* be at present in many legal systems (including English law); short of statutory reform, functional equivalence with shares would require creative structuring methods such as bespoke contractual architectures.[61] The prevailing legal approach has favored technology neutrality: ensuring that digital representations do not disturb the underlying legal categories. Yet this posture also delays the full realization of digitally-constituted organizational forms.

At the opposite end of the spectrum lies the maximalist vision of the DAO: An organization constituted entirely through technological affordances, especially those provided by DLT, that does not interact with law at all. These entities operate without a formal legal wrapper; that is, with governance, membership, and operations defined

[57] eg Charles Snow, Øystein Fjeldstad, and Arthur Langer, "Designing the Digital Organisation" (2017) 6(7) Journal of Organization Design <https://link.springer.com/content/pdf/10.1186/s41469-017-0017-y.pdf> accessed May 25, 2025.

[58] Law Commission, "Decentralised Autonomous Organisations (DAOs): A Scoping Paper" (July 2024) [2.112] <https://webarchive.nationalarchives.gov.uk/ukgwa/20250109094345mp_/https://cloud-platform-e218f50a4812967ba1215eaecede923f.s3.amazonaws.com/uploads/sites/30/2024/07/DAOs-scoping-paper-110724.pdf> accessed May 25, 2025. discussing the concept of a spectrum in respect of "DAOs." Peter Hunn, one of the authors of this chapter, was a lawyer on the Law Commission for this project.

[59] Under English law, this regime includes but is not limited to: Companies Act 2006; Companies Act 1985; Companies (Audit, Investigations and Community Enterprise) Act 2004; Company Directors Disqualification Act 1986; Financial Services and Markets Act 2000; the Companies (Model Articles) Regulations 2008 (SI 2008/3229); the Companies (Registration) Regulations 2008 (SI 2008/3014) and various other statutory instruments, retained EU law and the UK Corporate Governance Code (non-statutory).

[60] ss 1134 and 1135(1) Companies Act 2006.

[61] UK Jurisdiction Taskforce, "Legal Statement on the Issuance and Transfer of Digital Securities under English Law" [84]–[85] <https://lawtechuk.io/ukjt/legal-statement-on-digital-securities/> and generally for a comprehensive review of the legality of digital issuance and structuring mechanisms such as "stapling" shares to DLT-based tokens.

and executed entirely on-chain. A "pure DAO" is described by the Law Commission as an arrangement "implemented through smart contracts with very limited off-chain activity, no incorporated legal structure and, often, a rejection (deliberately or otherwise) of dependence on law and legal institutions for their existence."[62] These entities do not merely digitize existing structures: they attempt to replace them.

A prominent variation is the decentralized (sometimes "distributed") autonomous corporation (DAC), which seeks to replicate core corporate functions through programmable logic rather than statute or corporate charter. The absence of incorporation means that the legal affordances of the corporate form are intentionally forgone; instead, DACs seek to replicate key features of traditional corporate forms, particularly in relation to capital formation, stakeholder governance, and capital distribution.[63] De Filippi and Hassan characterize this as a shift from "law as code" to "code as law," in which conventional legal frameworks are *intended* to be replaced by technological systems that operate independently of state authority.[64] In our view, no technological system can operate in the mainstream economy *and* exist alegally or extra-legally; some characterization needs be imposed. Depending on its functional attributes, a DAC (or similar arrangement) might be deemed a general partnership,[65] an unincorporated association,[66] trust arrangement,[67] or a network of contractual relationships among participants.[68] In this sense, even the most "autonomous" technical organization is made legible to the law, and liable to claims of jurisdiction, though not necessarily in ways its creators intended.

Between the poles of state-incorporated entities and fully on-chain DAOs lies a growing range of hybrid forms. These entities combine legal and technical affordances

[62] Law Commission, "Decentralised Autonomous Organisations (DAOs): A Scoping Paper" (July 2024) [2.115] <https://webarchive.nationalarchives.gov.uk/ukgwa/20250109094345mp_/https://cloud-platform-e218f50a4812967ba1215eaecede923f.s3.amazonaws.com/uploads/sites/30/2024/07/DAOs-scoping-paper-110724.pdf> accessed May 25, 2025.

[63] Vitalik Buterin, "DAOs, DACs, DAs and More: An Incomplete Terminology Guide" (*Ethereum Foundation Blog*, 2014) <https://blog.ethereum.org/2014/05/06/daos-dacs-das-and-more-an-incomplete-terminology-guide> accessed May 25, 2025; Samer Hassan and Primavera De Filippi, "Decentralized Autonomous Organization" (2021) 10(2) Internet Policy Review <https://policyreview.info/pdf/policyreview-2021-2-1556.pdf> accessed May 25, 2025.

[64] Primavera De Filippi and Samer Hassan, "Blockchain Technology as a Regulatory Technology: From Code is Law to Law is Code" (2016) 21(12) First Monday <https://firstmonday.org/ojs/index.php/fm/article/view/7113> accessed May 25, 2025.

[65] s 1(1) Partnership Act 1890; US decisions: *Sarcuni v bZx DAO*, No 22-618 (SD Cal March 27, 2023) and *Samuels v Lido DAO* No. 3:23-cv-03013 (ND Cal November 18, 2024) (DAOs can be characterized as general partnerships); *Commodity Futures Trading Commission v Ooki DAO* No 3:22-cv-05416 (ND Cal 2023) (DAOs can be characterized as unincorporated associations under federal law); also Maury Shenk, Sven van Kerckhoven, and Jonas Weinberger, "The Crown, the Market and the DAO" (2023) 6(2) Stanford Journal of Blockchain Law & Policy 245.

[66] Following *Conservative and Unionist Central Office v Burrell* [1982] 1 WLR 522, eg, DAOs that involve collective decision-making and pooled resources for a shared non-commercial purpose may be treated as unincorporated associations.

[67] For a discussion of DAOs and trusts under English law: Law Commission, "Decentralised Autonomous Organisations (DAOs): A Scoping Paper" (July 2024) 3.107–3.114 and 5.55–5.61 <https://webarchive.nationalarchives.gov.uk/ukgwa/20250109094345mp_/https://cloud-platform-e218f50a4812967ba1215eaecede923f.s3.amazonaws.com/uploads/sites/30/2024/07/DAOs-scoping-paper-110724.pdf> accessed May 25, 2025.

[68] Carla Reyes and Christine Hurt, "The Contractarian Joint Venture" (2025) 76 Alabama Law Review 221.

in varying configurations, using traditional legal "wrappers" to stabilize DAO-like operations, or embedding automated governance features into legal structures.[69] Unlike "pure" DAOs or DACs, which implicitly displace traditional institutional forms, these hybrids more explicitly engage the boundary between firm and market—often seeking to "engineer" organizational logic through the composition of hybrid affordances themselves. Their structure is not simply legal or technical, but a composite in which governance, control, and participation are shaped by the interplay of contractual design, technical infrastructure, and statutory form.

The appeal of hybrid structures lies less in *compromise* than *strategic composition*: they seek to combine legal affordances (eg legal personality, limited liability, and access to enforcement) with the programmable affordances of digital infrastructure (eg automated execution, decentralized record-keeping, and token-based governance). The premise, central to this chapter, is that legal affordances can be deliberately introduced to mitigate or discipline the legal uncertainties and governance risks posed by purely technical systems. These hybrids do not simply occupy a compromise position; they seek actively to curate the relationship between law and code, offering a design space in which key organizational functions can be either *selectively externalized to law* or *internalized in code*, depending on the combination sought. The idea driving hybrid approaches is to adopt the affordances of *legal* institutions in order to balance the legal challenges raised by the use of *technological* affordances of DLT-based systems.

Critically, these hybrid forms are not invented from scratch: there is no immaculate conception. They often rely on mimicry of established legal forms and the opportunistic use of the affordances provided by the legal system to structure digital systems intended to operate differently to conventional legal forms. Wrapping a DAO in an LLC or foundation, for example, implicitly imports a logic of corporate governance—even where decision-making is technically decentralized. Conversely, importing smart contract logic into a legal entity reshapes the operational meaning of that form. What emerges are hybrid artefacts that embody both legal and technical affordances, and that are shaped by the institutional expectations of both domains. The result is a techno-legal spectrum along which each form enables a different configuration of affordances. Traditional corporations afford clarity of legal responsibility and access to formal remedies, but lack granular programmability and automated compliance. Pure DAOs offer transparency, immutability, and machine-executed governance, but often at the cost of legal uncertainty, enforcement difficulty, and design brittleness. Hybrid forms attempt to select and recombine affordances, using legal structure to anchor the organization in existing institutional frameworks, while experimenting with programmable infrastructure to reimagine how governance, participation, and value distribution are carried out.

An increasingly prominent class of hybrid are DAO-adjacent entities such as so-called base organizations run by governance (BORGs). BORGs are typically structured with legal wrappers—usually LLCs or similar—that explicitly accept their role as operational agents of decentralized protocols. But rather than seeking to enclose

[69] eg Miles Jennings and David Kerr, "How to pick a DAO legal entity" (*a16zcrypto.com*, April 6, 2022) <https://a16zcrypto.com/posts/article/dao-legal-entity-how-to-pick/> accessed May 25, 2025.

the DAO within a legal shell, BORGs position themselves as "modular" governance units: organizations that execute the DAO's will, manage service provision, and interface with regulators, banks, or courts. The governance of the BORG itself is often delegated to the DAO through binding or semi-binding rules encoded into smart contracts or multi-signature arrangements. BORGs thus offer a distinctive hybrid affordance: they are legally recognizable entities that operate under the constraint of on-chain governance. Thus, they instantiate a novel techno-legal relay: translating the DAO's protocol-based instructions into off-chain contractual, administrative, and regulatory action. This allows DAOs to interact with external systems—hire employees, rent office space, sign non-disclosure agreements (NDAs)—without sacrificing their decentralized identity or exposing participants to general partnership liability. At the same time, BORGs clarify the scope of legal responsibility, creating an interface between the procedural constraints of smart contracts and the open-textured demands of legal reasoning.

Over time, states have increasingly stepped in to formalize hybrid structures, responding to demand for legal certainty. Jurisdictions such as Wyoming, Vermont, and the Marshall Islands have introduced DAO-specific legal forms, such as the "DAO LLC," designed to accommodate decentralized governance while offering benefits like limited liability and contractual capacity.[70] These efforts represent a regulatory strategy of *accommodation*: extending the perimeter of organizational law without abandoning its core features. In effect, they offer legal affordances without requiring full legal conformity, allowing experimental governance systems to anchor themselves in recognized institutional forms. However, these frameworks often come with constraints—such as default fiduciary duties, agent designations, or registration requirements—that may be at odds with DAO design philosophy.

These statutory responses reflect not only policy pragmatism but a deeper pattern of institutional isomorphism. By "recoding" the DAO in the language and conceptual framework of the LLC or the foundation, the state seeks to render the unfamiliar legible—and thus governable. Yet, this translation also imposes familiar legal assumptions onto novel technical architectures, raising questions about whether recognition expands or constrains the design-space for future digital entities. It can also bring state law into conflict with the intentions, expectations, and assumptions of innovators.

Finally, it is worth mentioning that the spectrum of DOs (see Table 13.1) also includes platform firms such as Uber, Airbnb, and Amazon Mechanical Turk. (Though it risks stretching a long bow, we have attempted to join the dots between these business models, conventional corporations, and DLT-driven developments above.) These are not decentralized in structure, but they strategically appropriate decentralization logics in order to reconfigure the boundary between firm and market. Rather than building DAOs, these companies use code to control market-based actors through quasi-organizational structures: algorithmic reputation systems, pricing rules, participation constraints, and dispute resolution mechanisms. They govern like firms but deny firm-like responsibilities, a form of tactical brinksmanship that blurs the

[70] One prominent example is the Wyoming legislation of 2021, WY SF0038, being "[a]n Act relating to corporations; providing for the formation and management of decentralized autonomous organizations [and] providing definitions." <https://www.wyoleg.gov/Legislation/2021/SF0038> accessed May 25, 2025.

Table 13.1 Affordances across the spectrum

Form	Legal Affordances	Technical Affordances	Key Features / Trade-offs
Traditional Company	Legal personality, limited liability, statutory governance	Digitized (but not constitutive) infrastructure (eg share registries)	High legal certainty and institutional stability; low flexibility and automation
Platform Firm (eg Uber)	Full legal incorporation with limited liability	Algorithmic control, data-driven governance	Firm-market boundary blurred; high centralization, low participant ownership
Wrapped DAO	Legal wrapper (eg LLC, foundation); capacity for contracting	On-chain governance, smart contract execution	Legal protection + on-chain operation; potential mismatch between legal logic and protocol
DAO-specific Legal Form	Statutory recognition (eg DAO LLC) with tailored obligations	Partial automation, token governance, multisigs	Balanced affordance set; unclear long-term institutional trajectory; "race to the bottom"?
DAO + BORG architecture	Modular separation of legal and technical roles	Delegated on-chain governance over legal execution layer	Service-layer flexibility; improved external legibility; legal exposure varies
Pure DAO/DAC	No formal legal structure; legal effects inferred ex post	Fully autonomous smart contracts; token-based governance	High technical purity; high legal uncertainty; hard to resolve disputes
Digital Legal Entity	Law recognizes code-based affordances as constitutive	Designed from inception to operate on-chain and under legal authority	Promise of integration and normative coherence; still speculative and institutionally emerging

separating coordinated enterprise from open market. These firms illustrate that the affordances of digital infrastructure can be used not only to replace traditional legal organization, but also to evade or reframe the responsibilities traditionally attached to it. As such, they sit uneasily within the spectrum, not because they lack affordances, but because they *weaponize* them against existing institutional categories. They remind us that techno-legal design is not neutral: it can be used both to democratize coordination and to obfuscate power structures.

The emergence of wrapped DAOs, DAO-adjacent entities like BORGs, and platform firms exploiting technical affordances without decentralization reveals a rich ecosystem of techno-legal hybrids. But in our view, these remain transitional forms—adaptations rather than reinventions. At the far end of the spectrum lies a more ambitious prospect: a *natively digital legal entity*. Unlike hybrids that stitch technical features into existing legal forms, the digital legal entity would be constituted intentionally from the outset through a combination of legal and digital affordances, designed to operate natively in both code and law. It would not merely use digital infrastructure to execute functions—it would embody it in its structure, governance, and logic of operation.

Jurisdictions are beginning to explore legal recognition frameworks that anticipate natively digital operation—whether through token-based equity systems, automated compliance architectures, or fully on-chain governance mechanisms. In our view, this conceptual progression reflects more than the blurring of legal and technological categories. It raises fundamental questions about how legal theory must evolve to accommodate governance regimes defined as much by code as by statute. The rise of natively digital entities and techno-legal hybrids suggests that organizational regulation is no longer the exclusive province of the state (if it ever was), but can instead be reimagined and negotiated—the law responding to private initiatives and innovation.

Section 4 takes up this question directly. It sketches the prospective contours of the digital company—not as a fixed model, but as a class of organizational forms that integrate legal and technical affordances by design. Building on the affordance schema, we explore what such a form might entail, how it might be designed for legal legibility and normative legitimacy, and what institutional implications it holds for the future of organizational governance.

4. The Digital Company: A Prospective

The preceding analysis traced how digital infrastructure is reshaping organizational form through decentralized governance mechanisms and automated, programmable execution. These developments pose questions for legal theory and institutional design: What might the institution of the corporation look like if built from the ground up to operate in and through techno-legal affordances? In this section, we sketch two prospective models of "natively digital" company: the *internalization model* and the *externalization model*. These are not fixed proposals but stylized directions for development, each reflecting different strategies for integrating digital affordances into legally recognized organizational forms. In both cases, the central design question is how legal affordances—such as property, agency, contract, fiduciary duty, and liability—might be adapted or reinterpreted in light of digital instantiation. These affordances do not disappear in digital settings; even "pure" DAOs invoke legal concepts when disputes arise or when token-holders assert control over their assets. The challenge is to explore what these affordances could become in a world where code is not merely supportive of (rather than antagonistic to) law, but constitutive of a recognised legal form.

The internalization model envisions a digital company in which the core coordination functions of the corporate form—such as capital formation, control rights, decision-making procedures, and asset distribution—are embedded directly into the technical architecture of the organization. In this model, digital infrastructure does not merely augment legal structure; it *becomes* legal structure. Legal formality is preserved, but translated into digital-native modalities: smart contract logic becomes the site of compliance, token registries replace share ledgers, and cryptographic execution mechanisms substitute for board resolutions or manual filings.

Crucially, this model depends on the reform or reinterpretation of statutory requirements to accommodate DLT-based systems as compliant forms of legal performance. For example, legislation might explicitly recognize the issuance of governance tokens as satisfying the formalities of share issuance; provided adequate identification of the persons involved, the execution of a multi-signature protocol might be treated as equivalent to board consent; or a vote conducted on-chain might be treated as binding under company law. Jurisdictions pursuing this route could adopt a stance of positive formalization, treating certain digital processes as *intrinsically sufficient* for legal effect, rather than simply tolerating them through technology-neutral language.

In this model, the company's techno-legal architecture is internalized into the fabric of the legal entity. It is not just a company that uses DLT—it is a company that is partly *constituted* by DLT. Organizational documents may exist as smart contracts, governance rules may be codified in protocols, and compliance may be ensured through the logic of system design rather than through oversight or ex post enforcement. This allows for new forms of automated accountability, such as conditional compensation flows tied to token-based key performance indicators (KPIs), or programmable vesting schedules that obviate the need for manual monitoring.

From a design perspective, the internalization model offers the greatest potential for legal-technical coherence, since the affordances of digital infrastructure are built into the legal logic of the firm from the outset. But this also raises normative concerns: how will legal systems ensure that such code-based processes remain contestable, fair, and adaptable? What procedural values must be translated into code—and which cannot be? And to what extent should these digitally native structures remain tethered to traditional legal concepts, or move beyond them altogether?

The externalization model approaches the integration of digital affordances more incrementally. Rather than restructuring the legal form of the company itself, this model attaches digital mechanisms to conventional legal entities through modular systems—smart contract suites, governance tokens, or DLT-based compliance tools. These "bolt-ons" function as adjunct layers: they mediate or automate aspects of governance, coordination, or control without being constitutive of the legal entity's status or its core organizational logic.

In contrast to the internalization model, legal formality in the externalization model remains grounded in traditional mechanisms—incorporation, written resolutions, paper registers, and human-authored constitutional documents. But around this legal core, a new layer of programmable functionality emerges: a DAO-like module might manage a community treasury; an automated compliance protocol might trigger disclosures or sanctions in response to financial flows; a token-based governance mechanism might advise or bind a board on certain categories of decision. What is externalized is not governance per se, but the *logic of governance automation*, which operates alongside but not within the firm's legal substrate.

This model lies much closer to existing hybrids like wrapped DAOs. It is more readily compatible with existing law and more likely to be embraced by mainstream commercial actors. It enables firms to experiment with decentralization tactically, without surrendering the protections or recognitions conferred by traditional incorporation. As such, the externalization model is likely to dominate the near-term landscape, particularly among organizations that wish to tap into participatory or community-driven models of governance while retaining centralized accountability and recognizable legal identity. But it is not without complexity. The interface between the digital layer and the legal core can be unstable or ambiguous: is a DAO-controlled treasury *advisory* to the company's board or *binding*? Are token-based votes legally *enforceable* or merely *expressive*? Who is liable if an externally-connected smart contract fails or misbehaves? In effect, the externalization model replicates the hybrid dynamics described in Section 3, but in reverse: rather than importing legal affordances into a digital shell, it exports digital logic into a legal shell, raising parallel questions of alignment, accountability, and co-constitution. While more conservative in legal terms, this model still carries radical potential. By placing programmable infrastructure in functional tension with legal form, it opens up spaces where novel governance modes emerge not through doctrinal change but through interface design. Over time, the proliferation of such externalized components may exert pressure on the core legal form itself, gradually nudging it toward redefinition.

All forms of organization—whether traditional, hybrid, or natively digital—ultimately rest on legal affordances of some kind. Even the most "pure" DAO, in its day-to-day operation, implicates legal concepts: ownership claims over tokens, entitlement to revenue flows, accountability for governance failures, and so on. The critical question, then, is not whether legal affordances are present, but which affordances are structurally necessary, and how they should evolve in response to digital affordances. If the aim is not merely to accommodate digital affordances within traditional organizational forms, but to develop digital companies as robust, recognizable institutions, then it is necessary to specify which legal affordances are mission-critical—and how they might be rendered interoperable with the affordance structures of decentralized digital infrastructure.

We suggest that the set legal affordances most essential to the digital company are those that enable organizational continuity, coordination, and accountability. These affordances must be expressive, stable, and able to interact coherently with the affordance grammar of DLT systems. In our view, there are five broad requirements that must be satisfied for the coherent and stable evolution of digital organizations:

- Constitutive Recognition: At the foundation lies the ability to instantiate a *legal* company through *digital* formalities, such that the resulting entity enjoys legal personality. This does not require replicating paper-based incorporation, but rather creating legally recognized *conditions of existence*—rules that allow smart contracts or other digital architectures to create a legal person when they meet defined thresholds of control, governance, or purpose. This could involve recognizing token-based capitalization or role allocation as substitutes for share registers and directorships. It could also involve defining formalities (such as key-signing thresholds, on-chain votes, or pre-defined contract triggers) as satisfying statutory requirements for formation, amendment, or consent.
- Attribution and Accountability: Second, there must be a way to attribute actions to the digital company—and to determine which persons (if any) are responsible when the architecture fails. This requires rethinking agency in distributed environments. Rather than assuming a centralized board or executive, the digital company must operate with programmable interfaces for agency attribution: roles

defined by smart contract logic (eg proposal submission, execution authority, veto power) that are *legible* to the legal system and capable of giving rise to legal responsibility. This is not merely about liability. It is about enabling the system to produce accountable outputs: the capacity to say who did what, under what authority, and on whose behalf in a distributed or pseudonymous environment.

- Ownership and Control over Capital Structures: The company must be able to hold, manage, and allocate resources. But "ownership" in this context must be redefined to account for programmable control—access through cryptographic credentials, governance rules, or algorithmically gated functions. The legal system must recognize that property claims over digital assets can be constituted through control within a technical system, but that such claims require stabilization through legal categories to create *boundary conditions* for the operation of on-chain logic. The affordances of the institution of "property" here are less about identifying the holder of title than about enabling the system to enforce exclusion, manage access, and support transfer within a legally coherent framework.
- Governance as Infrastructure: Digital companies must be governable. The key here is not merely "voting" or "rule-making," but modularity: the ability to build, adapt, and constrain governance functions through a composable stack. Smart contracts allow for iterative rule-making and self-enforcing constraints, but they require interpretive scaffolding. (What counts as a quorum? What happens if the chain forks?) Law must provide a *meta-affordance*: a legal framework for interpreting and resolving disputes about governance logic, especially when automated outcomes clash with evolving group intent or external norms.
- Limited Liability and Legal Perimeter: A digital company must be able to interact with the external world without exposing every participant to unlimited legal risk. This implies a clear perimeter: a way of saying what "the company" is, where it ends, and which actors are insulated by its legal form. In programmable settings, this may involve defining legal personality based on contract artefacts, or tethering liability shields to the behavior of governance systems. Without it, digital companies remain informal associations: innovative, but legally precarious.

The doctrinal areas of law most directly implicated in this techno-legal affordance stack are, in our view, broadly similar to the ones at the heart of corporations and corporate governance law: property, agency, fiduciary law, and obligations (both contractual and non-contractual). Property remains the cornerstone of economic coordination, but must be reinterpreted to account for socio-technical artefacts like crypto-assets or token-governed vaults. The interplay between property and conventional corporations law is probably not as well-understood as it could (or should) be; neither in historical terms, nor in the sense that shares are universally regarded as a type of "property" but the company is a person, not a thing.[71] The law of agency

[71] There is a strong conceptual argument to be made that it is categorically not possible to own part of a person; *persons* own (ie have certain types of *rights* in) *things*; if something is owned, it is not a person—we refer to "chattel slavery" because systems that allow this practice treat some humans as things (like non-human animals) rather than as persons. Thus, the legal nature of the share is less well-understood than commonly assumed.

must do a lot of heavy lifting for digital processes and entities to be legally intelligible. Without reliable attribution mechanisms, no programmable action can have *legal* effect. This becomes particularly acute in internalization models, where "decisions" may be executed by contract logic without named actors. In a closely related vein, fiduciary law is perhaps the most under-theorized but indispensable element. In conventional corporations, the concept of office explains how individuals can be harnessed as the "organs" of the corporation. Closer engagement is needed with how office operates conceptually and logically in the context of automated decision-making and action. Done well, this could bridge legal institutionalization and programmable roles—grounding responsibility even in structurally distributed systems. The law of contract is the connective tissue: It binds together technical procedures and human relationships, and becomes the fallback where digital affordances run out. Importantly, it is also the interface between law and code: even when "the code is the contract," legal systems need to interpret or override it. Again, in a closely related vein, extra-contractual liability doctrines are necessary to formalize the perimeter: it both enables innovation (through insulation) and tethers experimental systems to norms of accountability. This is essential for maintaining legal legitimacy.

To bring these affordances into dialogue with the affordances of DLT systems is not to discard the normative structure of law. Rather, it is to construct a *techno-legal layer* in which legal norms are not only represented in code, but also remain interpretable by courts, regulators, and human participants. Just as DLT affords transparency, immutability, and automated execution, law affords recognition, interpretation, and legitimation.

This also reframes the firm/market boundary—long a preoccupation of organizational theory—not as a static divide but as a *design surface*. Digital infrastructure enables fine-grained control, dynamic pricing, and conditional coordination that blur the classic distinctions between internal hierarchy and external exchange. The risk is that firms disappear into markets, or worse, that governance responsibilities are effaced in the name of efficiency. But the promise is that new forms of collective organization can emerge—forms that are lean and legally constituted without falling into either centralized dominance or radical decentralization. This invites a new jurisprudential challenge: to reframe legal affordances as composable elements within this programmable terrain—flexible enough to operate in a distributed setting, but stable enough to support organizational coherence, public accountability, and institutional memory. In that sense, the digital company is not simply a technical innovation or a regulatory problem. It is a design question for law itself: how to recompose the foundations of collective economic life in a digital era, using the grammar of law to anchor the possibilities of code.

5. Conclusion

Law and technology are both systems of organization that can be explicated with the concept of affordance. Their interaction does not merely affect the legal treatment of emerging technologies; it informs the evolution of law itself. As organizations become increasingly digital—whether by design or gradual digitization—the legal affordances that constitute them must interoperate with digital affordances, rather than simply absorb them. This interoperation is not unidirectional. While much of the existing literature asks how code can comply with law, we have argued that law, too, must become more programmable in form while remaining normative in function.

DLT, and the technical affordances it enables—programmable execution, shared state, composable control mechanisms, could make possible a new kind of organizational architecture: one that is not merely automated, but structurally reconfigured. In this sense, DLT-based systems reconfigure the boundaries of the firm, blending market-based interaction with infrastructural governance in novel ways. The result is a hybrid zone, where legal and technical affordances must be carefully recomposed to support coordination, control, responsibility, and trust.

This re-composition could signal the emergence of a new branch of organizational law—what we might call the *law of digital organization*. This is not a wholesale replacement of conventional organizational law, but a new modality layered on top of it. It requires lawyers and system designers to work jointly in specifying what organizational affordances must be preserved, which can be delegated or redesigned, and how both types of affordances—legal and technical—can be composed in a way that preserves intelligibility, legitimacy, and normative coherence. At its heart, the challenge is not simply how to regulate DAOs or accommodate tokens in existing law. It is how to redesign the core tools of organizational life—personality, responsibility, property, governance, and liability—for a world in which code increasingly shares responsibility for institutional ordering. In this sense, the digital company is a jurisprudential provocation to revise the conceptual infrastructure of organizational law for the age of software.

14
What Do DAOs Really Contribute?

Edmund Schuster and Kelvin FK Low

1. The Way of the DAO

A decentralized autonomous organization (or DAO) is, despite earlier references predating the introduction of Bitcoin, today generally regarded as "a blockchain-based system that enables people to coordinate and govern themselves mediated by a set of self-executing rules deployed on a public blockchain, and whose governance is decentralised (i.e., independent from central control)."[1] Although some have suggested that Bitcoin is effectively the first DAO,[2] this is not a prevalent view as "the term is today understood as referring not to a blockchain network in and of itself, but rather to organisations deployed as smart contracts on top of an existing blockchain network."[3] DAOs as they are today understood were thus born not out of the Bitcoin blockchain but of newer blockchains that promise more powerful built-in programming interfaces, with the Ethereum blockchain, a so-called "Turing-complete" blockchain network, foremost among these. So dominant is Ethereum that other aspirants—such as Solana, Cardano, Tezos, Polkadot, etc—are touted as Ethereum killers. Unlike Bitcoin, whose consensus protocol is primarily used to authenticate transactions, these more complex blockchain networks deploy their consensus protocols (which run the gamut from the more well-known proof-of-work of Bitcoin to Ethereum's new proof-of-stake protocol circa 2022 to others) to authenticate and run executable code.[4] Although often marketed as an advance on Bitcoin's simpler, more basic system—Ethereum, being the forerunner of such blockchains was conceived of as "cryptocurrency 2.0"[5]—the ability to run so-called decentralized applications (or Dapps)[6] through so-called smart

[1] Samer Hassan and Primavera de Filippi, "Decentralized Autonomous Organization" (2021) 10 Internet Policy Review 1, 2.

[2] See eg Vitalik Buterin, "DAOs, DACs, DAs and More: An Incomplete Terminology Guide" (*Ethereum Foundation Blog*, May 6, 2014) <https://blog.ethereum.org/2014/05/06/dacs-dacs-das-and-more-an-incomplete-terminology-guide> accessed June 6, 2025; Ying-Ying Hsieh and others, "Bitcoin and the Rise of Decentralized Autonomous Organizations" (2018) 7 Journal of Organization Design 14.

[3] Hassan and de Filippi (n 1) 3.

[4] Quinn DuPont, "Experiments in Algorithmic Governance: A History and Ethnography of 'The DAO,' a Failed Decentralized Autonomous Organisation" in Malcolm Campbell-Verduyn (ed), *Bitcoin and Beyond: Cryptocurrencies, Blockchains, and Global Governance* (Routledge 2017) 157.

[5] Laura Shin, *The Cryptopians: Idealism, Greed, Lies, and the Making of the First Big Cryptocurrency Craze* (Public Affairs 2022) 5.

[6] cf Angela Walch, "Deconstructing 'Decentralization': Exploring the Core Claim of Crypto Systems" in Chris Brummer (ed), *Cryptoassets: Legal, Regulatory, and Monetary Perspectives* (OUP 2019) 39.

contracts[7] carries with it its own drawbacks. As one of us has observed:[8]

> The process of coding is highly exacting as it entails formulating precise instructions that describe how to complete a particular task while anticipating all possible variations that might affect its operation. In coding, there is no officious bystander to add lines of code that go without saying or reinterpret code that must have gone awry. Coding has been likened to "writing *War and Peace*—but with no typos". Unfortunately, "[i]ndustry average experience is about 1–25 errors per 1000 lines of code for delivered software". The industry average for "smart contracts" on the ethereum network, the most popular blockchain hosting "smart contracts", is dramatically worse at more than 100 bugs per 1000 lines of code.

It is of course true that bugs may also afflict simpler blockchains—which are essentially just ledgers programmed to run off code—such as Bitcoin's, perhaps most famously with the Bitcoin overflow bug.[9] Software wallets used to hold crypto-assets may also be affected as trials and tribulations of the Ethereum Parity Wallet in the span of a single year demonstrated.[10] But a more complex system like Ethereum's (and those of its competitors) means more code and more code means more bugs, which is perhaps not desirable in a supposedly immutable ledger.

2. "Secure," "Decentralized" Ledgers?

Before we delve further into DAOs in particular, it is necessary to unpack the commonplace description of permissionless blockchains as secure, decentralized ledgers. The adjectives "secure" and "decentralized", it turns out, don't necessarily mean what many assume they mean. As Walch explained in respect of the latter:[11]

> [T]he terms "decentralized" and "decentralization" are misleading in suggesting that permissionless blockchains lack sites of concentrated power and human agency. To the contrary, there have been many actions taken by small, coordinated groups of people that have made pivotal changes to the Bitcoin and Ethereum systems.

The same, we shall see, is true of the supposed decentralization in DAOs. As to blockchains' vaunted security, it turns out that said security "is concerned exclusively

[7] cf Eliza Mik, "Smart Contracts: A Requiem" (2019) 36 Journal of Contract Law 70; Eliza Mik, "Smart Contracts: Terminology, Technical Limitations and Real World Complexity" (2017) 9 Law, Innovation and Technology 269.

[8] Kelvin FK Low and Eliza Mik, "Pause the Blockchain Legal Revolution" (2019) 69 International & Comparative Law Quarterly 135, 173.

[9] Kai Sedgwick, "Bitcoin History Part 10: The 184 Billion BTC Bug" (*Bitcoin.com News*, March 1, 2019) <https://news.bitcoin.com/bitcoin-history-part-10-the-184-billion-btc-bug/> accessed June 6, 2025.

[10] For an account, see Kelvin FK Low, "Confronting Cryptomania: Can Equity Tame the Blockchain?" (2020) 14 Journal of Equity 240, 252–53.

[11] Walch (n 6) 67.

with ex-post ledger edits",[12] that is, immutability. Given that the most prevalent frauds today target end-users rather than the ledger directly, it is not obvious that the so-called security provided by blockchains is a pressing concern. There is a famous expression in cybersecurity by one of the world's foremost experts: "Only amateurs target machines; professionals target people."[13] As one of us has previously observed, "[t]his means that blockchain security is akin to the infamous Maginot Line built by France to deter invasion by Germany before World War II, except that it would be pointed in the wrong direction at Dover."[14] Perhaps even worse:[15]

> Immutability is often promoted as censorship resistance when it is better regarded as change resistance. Change is neither inherently bad (censorship) nor good (rectification). Context is key, and unthinking adoption of the blockchain will impede rectification, the typical remedy for inaccurate ledgers and other judicial remedies.

Not only does the blockchain *not* secure its users from this most pressing of modern security concerns, by inhibiting our current legal responses, it actively *detracts* from this aspect of security.

3. DAOist Misadventures: This Way Lies Madness?

Although there are multiple definitions of DAOs, the following non-definition by Wright suffices to encapsulate their essence: "DAOs are not run by boards or managers, but rather aim to be governed by democratic or highly participatory processes or algorithms."[16] DAOs therefore enjoy two key attributes—automation (through smart contracts) and direct participatory governance (by removing both management and intermediation). Supposedly, "[b]lockchain technology could enable organizations to operate more efficiently by relying on smart contracts to govern and coordinate certain actions and behavior,"[17] with DAOs supposedly being the epitome of the state of the art of blockchain automation.[18] "Governance in a decentralized organization is achieved in a less hierarchical manner and in a way that is generally more reliant on group consensus."[19] Yet these utopian visions fail to address such mundane problems as to how blockchains solve the collective action problem of retail investors

[12] Kelvin Low, "Bitcoin Users Should Not Overlook Cryptocurrency's Fundamental Flaw" (*Nikkei Asia*, June 14, 2022) <https://asia.nikkei.com/Opinion/Bitcoin-users-should-not-overlook-cryptocurrency-s-fundamental-flaw> accessed June 6, 2025.

[13] Bruce Schneier, "Semantic Attacks: The Third Wave of Network Attacks" (*Crypto-Gram*, October 15, 2000) <https://www.schneier.com/crypto-gram/archives/2000/1015.html#1> accessed June 6, 2025.

[14] Low, "Bitcoin Users Should Not Overlook Cryptocurrency's Fundamental Flaw" (n 12).

[15] Kelvin FK Low, "The Emperor's New Art: Cryptomania, Art & Property" (2022) The Conveyancer and Property Lawyer 378, 383.

[16] Aaron Wright, "The Rise of Decentralized Autonomous Organizations: Opportunities and Challenges" (2021) 4 Stanford Journal of Blockchain Law & Policy 152.

[17] Primavera de Filippi and Aaron Wright, *Blockchain and the Law: The Rule of Code* (Harvard UP 2018) 133.

[18] ibid 146.

[19] ibid 137.

who lack the incentives to incur the time and effort costs of voting.[20] Nor do they explain how this "democratized" vision of direct participation will address concerns of minority oppression.[21]

It has been suggested that "[t]he evolution from bureaucratic to algorithmic entities represents a logical continuation of a core human activity."[22] Supposedly, this is because "our world has become increasingly digital,"[23] but this latter observation can be overblown. We may increasingly purchase goods and services digitally but many of these are still delivered and consumed in the real world, as the various supply chain snarl-ups arising out of the Covid pandemic and since repeatedly remind us. Until such time as we live in The Matrix, it is probably advisable not to take digitalization too seriously. The validity of these theoretical posturings often do not match up to the constraints posed by harsh reality, as can be seen by the case of The DAO and other DAOs that followed in its wake.

As mentioned above, the first notable DAO to launch on the Ethereum blockchain was the venture capital fund called, perhaps confusingly, The DAO. Launched to great fanfare and much braggadocio on April 21, 2016, The DAO initially appeared to be a runaway success,[24] though it is questionable how much of its success was the result of its structure as a DAO and how much was the result of crypto-marketers' adeptness at exploiting crypto-investors'—who are shown by some research to have a tendency toward gambling[25]—fear of missing out (FOMO). As DuPont recounts:[26]

> During the initial funding period, the price of DAO tokens rose programmatically (from an initial value of 1:100)—encouraging early buy-in (a masterful sales tactic, encouraging people to "act soon, limited supplies!"); formally, the price increase was to reward the riskier (information-deficient) behavior of early investors.

Tragedy struck on June 17, 2016, when a bug in The DAO's code was "exploited" by an individual whose identity remains unknown to date, using "unintended behavior of the code's logic to rapidly drain the fund of millions of dollars' worth of ETH tokens."[27] This "attack" led to The DAO being drained of about 30 percent of its total funds[28] and the eventual hard fork of Ethereum to recover the "stolen" funds. The DAO's disastrous failure stemmed from the vision by so many in the crypto industry of modeling complex social properties using game theory premised upon rational actors, a vision that has been described as "a sophisticated, if at times blinkered, view of incentive and distributed action."[29]

[20] Kelvin FK Low, Edmund Schuster, and Wan Wai Yee, "The Company and Blockchain Technology" in Martin Petrin and Christian Witting (eds), *Research Handbook on Corporate Liability* (Edward Elgar 2023) 447, 455–56.

[21] Low, "Confronting Cryptomania" (n 10) 268.

[22] Wright (n 16) 153.

[23] ibid 154.

[24] DuPont (n 4) 158 and 174, endnote 1.

[25] Hee Jin Kim and others, "Comparison of Psychological Status and Investment Style Between Bitcoin Investors and Share Investors" (2020) 11 Frontiers in Psychology Article 502295.

[26] DuPont (n 4) 160.

[27] ibid 158, 162–64.

[28] ibid 164.

[29] ibid 171.

While The DAO may be the most infamous of DAOist misadventures, it hardly stands alone. Rather than directly exploiting the smart contract that comprised a DAO, as was the case with The DAO, an attacker could manipulate the price of thinly traded crypto-tokens used by a DAO. This was what Avraham Eisenberg, initially convicted for the Mango DAO "hack,"[30] did in 2022. According to prosecutors, "Eisenberg manipulated Mango Markets futures contracts on Oct. 11, 2022—when he boosted the price of swaps by 1,300% in 20 minutes—and then 'borrowed' against those inflated contracts using anonymous accounts before fleeing Puerto Rico for Israel."[31] Nor is Eisenberg's attack on a DAO by manipulating its oracle unique. These attacks are not hacks in the traditional sense of the word. In an oracle manipulation attack, Chainalysis explained:[32]

> [M]alicious actors [are] able to drain DeFi protocols of funds without actually taking advantage of an error in the protocol's code. These attackers [are] able to do this by manipulating the price oracles DeFi protocols use to ensure the assets available on their platforms are priced in accordance with the wider cryptocurrency market.

Eisenberg was subsequently acquitted by District Arun Subramaniam on one count (wire fraud) whereas his convictions under two other counts were vacated (commodities fraud and commodities manipulation).[33] The order for vacation appears to have been largely driven by venue considerations but the court's decision to order an acquittal for one fraud charge (wire fraud) but not the other (commodities fraud) turned on the fact that the latter did not require proof of material falsehood but could also be sustained by proof of a manipulative device. Perhaps the key takeaway, however, is that the acquittal for wire fraud turned on the absence of terms and conditions in the manipulated Mango Markets apart from the smart contracts that comprised it. The court accepted Eisenberg's argument that "the lack of any terms and conditions on the platform and the fact that Mango Markets was permissionless and automatic, so anything Eisenberg represented to the platform couldn't influence its decision to lend him cryptocurrency."[34] Such a position insulates bad actors such as Eisenberg from some[35] liability for activity that in almost any other context would undoubtedly be regarded as fraudulent. A purely code-based DAO[36] would thus seem to be an invitation to fraudsters to treat themselves to swindling honest participants in the same.

[30] Jonathan Stempel, "Trader convicted of Mango Markets fraud in first US crypto manipulation case" (*Reuters*, April 19, 2024) <https://www.reuters.com/legal/trader-convicted-mango-markets-fraud-first-us-crypto-manipulation-case-2024-04-18/> accessed June 6, 2025.

[31] David Voreacos, "Crypto Trader Searched Web for 'Fraud' Before $110 Million Haul" (*Bloomberg*, April 13, 2024) <https://www.bloomberg.com/news/articles/2024-04-12/crypto-trader-searched-web-for-fraud-before-110-million-haul> accessed June 6, 2025.

[32] Chainalysis Team, "Oracle Manipulation Attacks are Rising, Creating a Unique Concern for DeFi" (*Chainalysis*, March 7, 2023) <https://www.chainalysis.com/blog/oracle-manipulation-attacks-rising/> accessed June 6, 2025.

[33] *United States of America v Avraham Eisenberg*, No 23-CR-10 (AS), 2025 WL 1489248 (SDNY, May 23, 2025).

[34] ibid 29.

[35] Though not all: Eisenberg was not acquitted of commodities fraud and the conviction was vacated for other reasons: ibid 26–27.

[36] The decision appears to suggest that the introduction of rules by Mango Markets post-"hack" would lead to a different conclusion on this issue: see ibid 25.

For proponents of DAOs as paragons of transparency owing to the blockchains they operate on, *Mantra DAO Inc v John Patrick Mullin*[37] should serve as a warning not to place too much confidence in the blockchain. The plaintiffs were two companies that had established a DAO finance project in conjunction with the defendants. However, a dispute subsequently arose between the parties regarding control and ownership of the project. As an interim measure, the plaintiffs sought and obtained an interim order from the Hong Kong courts compelling the defendants to preserve and disclose the project's financial records in their possession dating back to January 2021. Regardless of how the case is eventually resolved, it demonstrates two matters: first, and perhaps most obviously, blockchains do not prevent or reflect off-chain arrangements, and secondly, blockchain transparency is overrated. As David Lok J explained in the course of applying the balance of convenience test in a case of interim relief:[38]

> I agree with Mr Lam that it is difficult if not impossible to quantify the plaintiffs' loss in monetary terms if they have no visibility of the Project's financial operation. They would not be in a position to know the basis of the decisions made by the defendants in the case of any complaint or challenge against the defendants' decisions. The problems are further complicated by the difficulties in tracing transactions in the cryptocurrency field, which are often anonymised.

The failure of DAOs to solve the problem of investor apathy is demonstrated in 2023's "hack" of Synthetify DAO, in which an attacker took advantage of the DAO's inactivity "to vote on—and pass—their own proposal to steal some $230,000 worth of crypto."[39] As *Blockworks* explained:[40]

> Taking advantage of the DAO's inactivity, the exploiter created ten identical-looking proposals and used their own tokens to reach the voting quorum. Nine of the proposals were empty, but the tenth contained code that sent around $230,000 in USDC, mSOL and stSOL to the attacker's address, according to an X thread from the security auditing firm Neodyme.

This attack represents an almost comic evolution of other governance attacks on DAOs. For example, in 2022, an attacker took over the Build Finance DAO "by using an inflated number of votes to pass a self-serving proposal, allowing the minting of millions of BUILD and other coins and a subsequent getaway, effectively killing the DAO."[41] In the case of Tapioca DAO, the governance protocol appears to have been

37 [2024] HKCFI 2099; [2024] 4 HKLRD 215.
38 ibid [13].
39 Jack Kubinec, "DAO on Solana loses $230K after 'attack proposal' goes unnoticed" (*Blockworks*, October 24, 2023) <https://blockworks.co/news/solana-exploit-dao-hacker> accessed June 6, 2025.
40 ibid.
41 Robert Drage, "Build DAO Loses $470,000 Through 'Hostile Governance Takeover'" (*Crypto News Australia*, February 17, 2022) <https://cryptonews.com.au/news/build-dao-loses-470000-through-hostile-governance-takeover-93735/> accessed June 6, 2025.

compromised by simply phishing one of the project's co-founders.[42] The attackers in this case managed to withdraw some 28 million TAP tokens, which they converted first to $1.6 million worth of Ether before converting these to Tether. The selling pressure from the conversions caused the TAP token to lose 95 percent of its value. But as the Synthetify attack demonstrates, one need not even necessarily attack anything or anyone meaningfully to successfully attack a DAO.

Sometimes, actions taken to protect a DAO from such governance attacks may end up attracting them instead. As a result of disagreements within the project, Nouns DAO decided to allow a group of disgruntled investors to fork from Nouns DAO. The community believed that "the option would improve overall governance—as a political innovation, a form of protection for any dissenting movements and a step toward greater decentralization."[43] Instead of serving as an example for other DAOs, the fork has turned into a cautionary tale. As *CoinDesk* reported:[44]

> Instead of protecting Nouns DAO from 51% attackers—a core fear of every decentralized crypto project—it attracted them. Savvy arbitrageurs came around and have since played Nouns DAO's governance game for profit.

Sometimes, DAOs can even fall apart without any discernible attack at all. When Mantra DAO's token, OM, collapsed by 90 percent in mere hours, initial suspicions were that the project had suffered from a rugpull.[45] However, this was vigorously denied and it appears that there may be a more banal explanation for the price collapse. It turns out that the OM token was one with low circulation but high fully diluted value (FDV), the latter being the current price multiplied by the total number of tokens expected to ever circulate. As a *Bloomberg* report explained, the problem with the math of FDV is that it "makes assumptions that a) those future tokens will be priced where the market is right now and b) that all those tokens will ever be in circulation to begin with."[46] Although the FDV of OM was $1 billion post-crash, only $3.2 million of OM had been sent to the Mantra blockchain. The result appears to be that the forced liquidation of some borrowers who had used the token as collateral was sufficient to crash the token's price.

[42] Tim Craig, "Tapioca DAO founder hack drops token value 96% as investors eat losses" (*DLNews*, October 18, 2024) <https://www.dlnews.com/articles/defi/tapioca-dao-tap-token-plummets-after-founder-suffers-hack/> accessed June 6, 2025.

[43] Danny Nelson, "A $27M Crypto Loss Reveals a Toxic Mix of Money-Hungry Traders and DAO Idealists" (*CoinDesk*, September 23, 2023) <https://www.coindesk.com/business/2023/09/21/nouns-daos-27m-revolt-reveals-toxic-mix-of-money-hungry-traders-and-blockchain-idealists> accessed June 6, 2025.

[44] ibid.

[45] Protos Staff, "MANTRA CEO says 'reckless' exchanges caused OM token collapse" (*Protos*, April 14, 2025) <https://protos.com/mantra-ceo-says-reckless-exchanges-caused-om-token-collapse/> accessed June 6, 2025.

[46] Muyao Shen, "A Token's 90% Crash Shows Some Things Never Change in Crypto" (*Bloomberg*, April 18, 2025) <https://www.bloomberg.com/news/newsletters/2025-04-17/a-token-s-90-crash-shows-some-things-never-change-in-crypto> accessed June 6, 2025.

4. Integrating Law and Blockchains: Theory v Reality

Leaving aside flights of fancy in cloud crypto land,[47] even the most avid proponents of the blockchain, provided they are rational, must recognize a residual role for the law. As Werbach explained:[48]

> The blockchain could be the most consequential development in information technology since the Internet. Created to support the Bitcoin digital currency, the blockchain is actually something deeper: a novel solution to the age-old human problem of trust. Its potential is extraordinary. Yet, this approach may not promote trust at all without effective governance. Wholly divorced from legal enforcement, blockchain-based systems may be counterproductive or even dangerous.

Contemplating a world in which "[b]lockchain developers and legal institutions can work together," Werbach considers how blockchains "may supplement, complement, or substitute for legal enforcement."[49] But, perhaps curiously, he does not consider how the law can effectively temper the blockchain when something goes awry when an interface between the blockchain and the law is not predetermined at the outset, such as in the case of The DAO, which is perhaps what led to the extralegal resolution of the DAO hack. Werbach is of course correct that "they are less insulated from the law's reach than it seems."[50] The question though is whether the law's mechanisms for remedying something that has gone wrong with any aspect of a DAO is satisfactory. As one of us has previously observed:[51]

> The law is not powerless in the face of permissionless blockchains but its traditional armoury is lacking. Whilst a permissionless blockchain can be tempered by equity's ancient in personam jurisdiction, it cannot be entirely tamed.

Thus, "even if a blockchain were technically immutable in an absolute sense, it would still be possible to substantially undo the effects of a transaction by way of a further transaction of equal value in reverse."[52] Werbach unfortunately does not appear to address the question of whether the law's remedial armoury is adequate in the face of both blockchain pseudonymity and immutability.

Permissionless blockchain systems pose numerous obstacles in the way of such legal coercion. Take the simple case of post-scam recovery of crypto-assets, perhaps the most common type of crypto disputes to be litigated before the English courts. A commentary on *Jones v Persons Unknown*,[53] the first final judgment on

[47] cf Edmund Schuster, "Cloud Crypto Land" (2021) 84 Modern Law Review 974.

[48] Kevin Werbach, "Trust, But Verify: Why the Blockchain Needs the Law" (2018) 33 Berkeley Technology Law Journal 487.

[49] ibid.

[50] ibid.

[51] Low, "Confronting Cryptomania" (n 10) 269.

[52] Low and Mik (n 8) 145.

[53] [2022] EWHC 2543 (Comm).

a claim to recover crypto-assets in the Commonwealth, provides a flavor of the challenges:[54]

> As is now commonplace in cases of post-scam crypto recovery, victims must first engage an expert in blockchain analytics—in this case, a company called CiRO—to trace what has happened to their cryptoassets. Unless some of these cryptoassets have found their way to a public wallet associated with a known entity, usually an exchange—in this case, the fourth defendant Huobi—recovery is practically impossible because the blockchain is immutable and thus incompatible with traditional judicial remedies such as rectification; instead, the courts are limited to equitable relief *in personam*: Low (2020) 14 J. Eq. 240. This means that the celebratory swagger that has accompanied the decision should be taken with a pinch of salt. It is notable that Jones lost a lot of cryptoassets: by the time of the judgment they were valued at some £1.536 million, more than three times his initial investment. Many other victims who have been defrauded of more modest sums cannot justify such expenses. It was also amazingly fortuitous that all of Jones's Bitcoins were successfully traced to a wallet associated with a known entity (see [15]). This is not often the case, which is also why many victims simply accept their losses.

Following pushback from the crypto intermediaries who have been named as defendants in many of these actions,[55] it is becoming less clear if legal coercion is an effective means of tempering blockchain immutability or simply an exercise of throwing good money after bad. In jurisdictions with less extensive interlocutory relief and/or which are less accommodating of actions brought against "Persons Unknown" than the common law, such as Japan,[56] odds of recovery through the law are even more remote. Nor do blockchain advocates who promote the utility of smart contracts as a means of automated enforcement give adequate consideration of the consequences of smart contracts that go awry, whether because of a bug in their code or because an on-chain condition (eg *x* ether being transferred into/out of *y* wallet) was triggered as a result of an unauthorized transaction. Such wrongly triggered smart contracts can themselves trigger other smart contracts by causing their conditions to be fulfilled when they wouldn't otherwise have been, leading to a cascade of wrongly triggered smart contracts akin to how automated algorithmic trading may have contributed to the Flash Crash of 2010.[57] Absent any ability to temporarily freeze a permissionless blockchain and truly reverse (as opposed to adding an equivalent and opposite transfer) a set of

[54] Timothy Chan and Kelvin FK Low, "Post-Scam Crypto Recovery: Final Clarity or Deceptive Simplicity?" (2023) 139 Law Quarterly Review 379, 380.

[55] eg *Piroozzadeh v Persons Unknown* [2023] EWHC 1024 (Ch), noted by Farhana Hamid Butt, "Tether Tangle and Binance Breaks Free" (2023) 82 Cambridge Law Journal 398; *D'Aloia v Persons Unknown* [2024] EWHC 2342 (Ch), [2025] 1 WLR 821, noted Timothy Chan and Kelvin FK Low, "Crypto Tracing Stumbles at Trial" [2025] Lloyd's Maritime & Commerical Law Quarterly 208.

[56] Kelvin FK Low and Megumi Hara, "The Folk-Law Behind Blockchain Narrative Economics" in John Flood and Lachlan Robb (eds), *Research Handbook on Blockchain and Society* (De Gruyter.forthcoming).

[57] Report of the Staffs of the Commodity Futures Trading Commission (CFTC) and Securities and Exchange Commission (SEC) to the Joint Advisory Committee on Emerging Regulatory Issues, "Findings Regarding the Market Events of May 6, 2010" (September 30, 2010) https://www.sec.gov/news/studies/2010/marketevents-report.pdf.

transactions, automation run amuck may pose greater risks and dangers to participants than simple contractual non-performance necessitating legal action. After all, legal action will still be required, albeit to reverse wrongly triggered smart contracts rather than the enforcement of actual legal contracts, which by and large are already mostly performed without the need for either automation or legal enforcement.

Since DAOs are made up of smart contracts, they pose similar challenges to smart contracts simpliciter. As de Filippi and Wright observed:[58]

> Once deployed, illicit or defective code will operate as planned, even if it contravenes the law or the fundamental purpose of the organization. The code will be automatically enforced by the underlying blockchain infrastructure, with little room for a court or other third party to force an amendment. Because no one has control over the smart contracts underpinning a DAO, no single party can intervene to amend the code or bring it to a halt—even if the code does not work as expected.

These concerns are vividly demonstrated by the various DAOist misadventures enumerated above. However, de Filippi and Wright draw comfort from the Ethereum hard fork that operated to retrieve the "stolen" funds: "Therefore, all is not without hope. Even if DAOs incorporate sophisticated AI systems, they still cannot operate entirely free of humans."[59] But they do not address any of the messy consequences of the Ethereum hard fork or the remarkable series of coincidental alignment of interests that, to a large extent, made coordination across the network easier but which may not exist in future DAOlusional misadventures. The Ethereum hard fork led to the first major permanent fork of a major blockchain, which saw participants opposed to the hard fork maintaining the original blockchain—dubbed Ethereum Classic—in which the attacker of the DAO kept the stolen funds.

But how replicable is the Ethereum hard fork? And is it a just solution? The fork of the Ethereum network into Ethereum and Ethereum Classic did not pose significant problems because at the relevant time, the Ethereum blockchain(s) only recorded endogenous (or crypto-native) tokens. Indeed, the fork may even have been regarded by some as a positive event: "When Ethereum forked in 2016 into Ethereum and Ethereum Classic, the value of the forked assets did not add up to the value of the undivided original, with holders of $100 of Ethereum mysteriously gifted with an additional $16 value. Code evidently cannot count."[60] Yet if DAOs are supposed to overtake the humble corporation in the future, surely by that point, they would be holding real-world assets such as real estate, machinery, raw materials, inventory, and the like. But, to use real estate as an example, "a fork in the blockchain land registry does not create a duplicate Blackacre Classic."[61]

But let us ignore the problem of exogenous tokens recording ownership interests in real-world assets. Let us assume we now live in The Matrix: nothing is real and everything is digital. One of the reasons why the Ethereum hard fork was able to secure

58 De Filippi and Wright (n 17) 155.
59 ibid 155.
60 Low, "The Emperor's New Art" (n 15) 401.
61 Low and Mik (n 8) 164.

such majoritarian support lay in a curious feature of The DAO. The attacker exploited The DAO's "split" function to repeatedly withdraw funds before the DAO's balance could be updated but The DAO had been coded to build-in a seven-day delay window for such "split" withdrawals, during which time the withdrawn funds were trapped in a new child DAO.[62] This meant that any hard fork would not impact any bona fide purchasers of any of the "stolen" funds since, whilst the funds remained trapped in the child DAO, there were no such persons. Even so, this does not necessarily mean that no innocent parties were impacted by the decision to implement the hard fork. After all:[63]

> The hard fork makes investors whole by adding a new set of rules to the Ethereum code. The rules only apply to the accounts associated with The DAO. The software moves all the funds that were initially invested in The DAO to a new address. From there, Ether will be doled out to people based on how much they initially invested.

If, during the short lifespan of The DAO, you'd made a profit, that profit is now wiped out and you are left with only your initial investment. Is this sort of rough and ready justice acceptable?

There is also no assurance that there would be similar support for future hacks. As one of us has previously observed:[64]

> Should a hack be serious, as was the case with the DAO hack, then many users would be affected and more end users would wish to roll back the blockchain despite inflicting losses on a minority. For less serious hacks, supporters of a rolling back of the blockchain will not be able to attain the majority such a legal rule would require.

As a commentator on the Reddit forum put it pithily:[65] "I made a bad contract in the first days ETH was online and lost 2K ETH with it, can I also get it back? Thanks!" Even if a fork were agreed, what assurance is there that the result would be similar to that of the Ethereum fork rather than that for the Nouns DAO? A fork, as the Nouns DAO fork demonstrated, can itself draw attackers to a DAO so that even if it were an acceptable solution, it may be one that is itself a Trojan horse for a further attack.

There is, of course, a way to integrate the law with blockchains but these would be permissioned blockchains, sometimes pejoratively called blockchains in name only (or BLINOs).[66] Essentially blockchains without the key feature of blockchains—immutability—BLINOs *would* be amenable to the implementation of judicial orders and can thus be more easily integrated with the law. However, they "raise completely different questions, specifically, 'Why bother?' and 'What's new?'"[67] It is true that one

[62] DuPont (n 4) 164.

[63] Morgan E Peck, "'Hard Fork'" Coming to Restore Ethereum Funds to Investors of Hacked DAO" (*IEEE Spectrum*, July 19, 2016) <https://spectrum.ieee.org/hacked-blockchain-fund-the-dao-chooses-a-hard-fork-to-redistribute-funds> accessed June 6, 2025.

[64] Low, "Confronting Cryptomania" (n 10) 268–69.

[65] David Siegel, "Understanding The DAO Attack" (*CoinDesk*, June 25, 2016) <https://www.coindesk.com/learn/understanding-the-dao-attack/> accessed June 6, 2025.

[66] Schuster (n 47) 993–96.

[67] Low and Mik (n 8) 270.

can run smart contracts on such blockchains as well. But the idea of smart contracts actually predates the blockchain.[68] Excitement over smart contracts only took off because permissionless blockchains rendered their automation immutable yet using permissioned blockchains removes precisely that attribute. Nor is there any reason why a centralized digital ledger cannot be automated. After all, the first automated clearing service in the world was created by the Dutch *Postcheque- en Girodienst* in April 1965,[69] almost half a century before Satoshi Nakamoto dreamed up the idea of a blockchain and predating non-blockchain-based smart contracts by more than three decades. This is not to say that a *permissioned* blockchain could not work; just that it is difficult to see how it improves upon the judicious use of automation on a similarly mutable centralized ledger. Just as a bicycle with square wheels *can* get you from point A to point B; if an enterprise wanted to keep its accounts using a BLINO, it should certainly be free to do so, just as it could use Quickbooks, which appears to be surprisingly popular in the crypto space.[70]

5. Real DAOs: Going Beyond BLINOs

There are different arrangements that can and have been used to implement DAOs in the real world. They range from "pure" DAOs,[71] akin to the original 2016 DAO conception, entirely decentralized and operating without traditional legal structures, to "hybrid DAOs" that combine a DAO-like governance structure with a "legal wrapper,"[72] typically in the form of a traditional corporation or other incorporated entity.[73] The degree of autonomy that a DAO possesses also lies on a spectrum.[74]

On one end of this spectrum are "mild" implementations, where what are ultimately traditional corporations integrate DLT/blockchain technology for specific corporate functions. For instance, a company may use blockchain-based ledgers for its financial accounting,[75] perhaps in an attempt to provide greater transparency to investors.[76] Similarly, an otherwise traditional corporation may provide for blockchain-enabled voting mechanisms or on-chain shareholder engagement.[77] At the other end

[68] Nick Szabo, "Smart Contracts: Formalizing and Securing Relationships on Public Networks" (1997) 2(9) First Monday.

[69] Dirk de Wit, *The Shaping of Automation: A Historical Analysis of the Interaction Between Technology and Organisation, 1950–1985* (Verloren 1994) 208.

[70] cf Francine McKenna, "The QuickBooks and the dead" (*FT Alphaville*, February 8, 2023) <https://www.ft.com/content/e3ca0898-4f08-48a3-9588-1819ff61a62c> accessed June 6, 2025.

[71] cf Law Commission, "Decentralised Autonomous Organisations (DAOs): A Scoping Paper" (Law Commission, 11 July 2024) 44 <https://lawcom.gov.uk/project/decentralised-autonomous-organisations-daos/#3-Documents> accessed November 7, 2025.

[72] Although the effectiveness of these legal wrappers may be debatable; eg ibid 89.

[73] eg Chris Brummer and Rodrigo Seira, "Legal Wrappers and DAOs" (2022) <https://papers.ssrn.com/sol3/papers.cfm?abstract_id=4123737> accessed June 6, 2025; Low, Schuster, and Yee (n 20) 447; Law Commission (n 71) 83.

[74] Also Law Commission (n 71) at 37.

[75] eg David Yermack, "Corporate Governance and Blockchains" (2017) 21 Review of Finance 24.

[76] eg Institute of Chartered Accountants in England and Wales, "Blockchain and the future of accountancy" (2018) <https://www.icaew.com/-/media/corporate/files/technical/technology/thought-leadership/blockchain-and-the-future-of-accountancy.ashx> accessed June 6, 2025.

[77] The discussion in Low, Schuster, and Yee (n 20).

of the spectrum we have fully autonomous organizations—"Real DAOs"—in which there exists no human-controlled off-chain override and no terms and conditions beyond its smart contract. Here, the DAO's behavior and interaction with outside stakeholders is fully determined by the underlying smart contracts that govern the DAO, and all interactions between the relevant stakeholders—internal and external—are governed exclusively on the basis of the encoded DAO "operating systems." To use a car analogy, "mild" forms of DAOs that supplement traditional corporations with function specific blockchain technology-based mechanisms could be compared to "assisted drive corporations," whereas Real DAOs can be seen as an attempt to create "full self-driving" corporations.

As we have argued elsewhere, "mild" implementations of DAOs—where DLT/blockchain technology is integrated into specific aspects of corporate governance or shareholder interaction—almost inevitably fall into the category of BLINOs discussed above.[78] These implementations do not fundamentally alter the structure of a corporation, but rather use blockchain-based solutions to try improving the management of business data or to streamline interactions of corporate actors. Ultimately, these are not genuine DAOs but traditional corporations leveraging distributed ledger technology for perceived incremental enhancements. These implementations largely represent a "data, but on the blockchain" approach and inevitably remain subject to human overrides in an entity that, in essence, operates as a conventional corporation. The technological solutions proposed to enhance transparency, automate shareholder voting, or streamline real-time financial reporting have, however, long been available in centralized systems. There is no evidence to suggest that blockchain technology unlocks any relevant features unavailable in traditional electronic databases.[79] The fact that functionally equivalent solutions have existed for decades, but have not been widely adopted in the way often proposed now, strongly suggests commercial, rather than technological, constraints explain the status quo.[80] As such, "assisted driving"-like approaches seem to address problems that are largely imaginary with a solution that is principally illusory.[81] DAO-like systems following this approach are thus unlikely to meaningfully disrupt corporate structures, given that they simply replicate—typically less efficiently—functionalities that are already available through centralized digital systems.[82]

By contrast, what we refer to as "Real DAOs"—the "full self-driving corporation"—go an important step further and do in fact differ fundamentally from traditional corporations. Real DAOs have two core features: First, all significant, binding interactions between a Real DAO and its stakeholders happen within the confines of the governing DAO smart contracts, and secondly, no human has the power to discretionarily override the outcomes and outputs of the relevant smart contracts "off-chain"—that is, there is no "superuser." This means that, in a real DAO, governance

[78] ibid; also text to n 66 above.

[79] For instance, it would be trivial, from a technical standpoint, to create tamper-evident electronic ledgers for shareholder voting or for a company's financial records based on traditional, non-blockchain ledgers.

[80] Low, Schuster, and Yee (n 20).

[81] ibid.

[82] Schuster (n 47).

(but not outcomes) must be entirely determined by code, and to the extent that decisions are reversed, rules changed, or outcomes modified, this also happens within as part of the governance model encoded in the DAO "operating system." We use this definition of Real DAOs to distinguish these organizations from DAOs with ultimate discretionary human control, which as we have argued are simply BLINOs, and thus lack the potential for offering anything fundamentally new beyond, at best, what any updated database software does. The question, then, is whether such Real DAOs offer meaningful advantages over traditional firms, at least in principle. We argue that they do not, as legal obstacles make it impractical to design effective autonomous organizations that interact successfully with the off-chain real economy.

6. The Self-Driving Corporation: Legal Obstacles

Even Real DAOs exist within a world governed by law, and all traditional business organizations must engage and interact with the legal system governing its operational environment. This includes the relationship between members or investors and the DAO itself, as well as external relationships with counterparties, creditors, and other legal actors. As is the case with all proposed applications of blockchain technology involving off-chain assets,[83] Real DAOs face the fundamental challenge of maintaining the perceived advantages of decentralization while at the same time interacting meaningfully with the "real world" and the law that ultimately governs its economic interactions.

7. The Conflict Between DAOs and the Rule of Law

As we have argued previously,[84] the immutability, decentralization, and permissionless nature of most public blockchain systems are inherently anti-hierarchical. However, the anti-hierarchical nature of public blockchains, on top of which DAOs are built, creates unavoidable tensions with legal principles: the rule of law is and the legal system as such are built on the assumption that courts and legal systems have the final authority in determining the legitimacy of transactions and the interactions between different economic actors.[85] This authority includes the ability to declare transactions void or voidable, impose liability, or otherwise rectify illegal or unenforceable agreements.[86]

One fundamental limitation of any permissionless blockchain systems lacking a "superuser," and by extension of any Real DAO is, therefore, that no DAO "operating system"[87] can ever fully encode the entirety of the legal system.[88] While smart

[83] Low and Mik (n 8); also ibid.
[84] Low and Mik (n 8); Schuster (n 47).
[85] Schuster (n 47).
[86] eg Low, "Confronting Cryptomania" (n 10) 269.
[87] ie the collection of smart contracts governing a DAO.
[88] More generally, the discussion in Schuster (n 47).

contracts can automate and enforce pre-defined rules, they cannot capture the full complexity of legal rules, which are open to interpretation, context-dependent, and subject to change.[89] Not only is code not law, but law cannot be fully encoded. Every legal system contains mandatory rules that sometimes override private agreements: for instance, most legal systems will not accept that an exercise of voting rights can have legal effect, despite happening under duress; a transfer of shares or economic interest in a DAO will be considered void or voidable where it is the result of fraud. These legal constraints cannot be effectively encoded within smart contracts because (1) legal systems are too complex to be precisely formulated in code-like language, and (2) at least typically, the circumstances rendering an agreement unenforceable or a transfer void will be entirely off-chain, meaning there is no direct way to give full effect to legal rules, as smart contracts cannot be fully responsive to wholly external, off-chain circumstances. This means that Real DAOs built on permissionless blockchains will always face legal challenges, even if the relevant rules *could* be fully encoded in the smart contracts governing a DAO (which clearly they cannot). It follows that Real DAOs cannot autonomously ensure that every transaction executed within their framework, every exercise of governance rights, and every interaction governed by their smart contracts, reliably aligns with, and is acceptable to, the applicable legal rules. A transaction that appears valid within a DAO's smart contract system may be rendered void due to external legal factors such as duress, fraud, or regulatory non-compliance. If the rights or assets concerned exist in the real world, and are thus subject to and dependent on legal rights, legal remedies are, at least in principle, available to the actors.

This leads to what we have described elsewhere[90] as a synchronization problem: If a DAO operates strictly within the constraints of its internal smart contract rules, ignoring external legal considerations, its real-world control over assets and obligations will always be at risk of diverging from the legally recognized position. Over time, this is all but guaranteed to happen. For example, a DAO may automatically transfer digital assets according to its encoded governance rules, but if those transfers violate mandatory legal rules, the transfer will be invalid in the eyes of the legal system. We submit that this possible divergence threatens the DAO's ability to function effectively, unless the DAO is designed to be responsive to the applicable legal rules and can ultimately give effect to court rulings and other determinations made by the legal system.

8. The Need for a Realignment Mechanism

For a DAO to be viably embedded within the legal framework, it thus must incorporate mechanisms to correct and realign the internal state of its smart contracts with the external legal reality that ultimately governs its assets—at least those assets that

[89] ibid.
[90] ibid.

have an existence off-chain.[91] Where a Real DAO fails to realign, the mismatch between the state of the world according to its internal algorithmic governance system and the external legal reality will render it ineffective.

Herein, however, lies the fundamental problem: any realignment mechanism that fully incorporates legal compliance would have to be built atop a BLINO, but this effectively transforms a Real DAO into a DAO in name only ("DINO"). A DAO can try to simply follow a legal system's determinations, that is, give effect to judgments and other forms of external legal enforcement; this can be done, technically in various ways, including on-chain voting, an on-chain dispute resolution mechanisms, or by giving overriding powers to a third party (or the DAO's "board"). If it does so, however, the DAO effectively ceases to be fully autonomous and decentralized, as, at least functionally, matters are now decided outside of its smart contract governance system. But this raises the question what advantage a design based around decentralization and immutability can offer, given that the governing smart contracts are always subject to a *de facto* override by the legal system.

Consequently, DAO design necessarily faces unattractive trade-offs. A DAO can be designed with ex ante human overrides—what we refer to as DINOs. It can retain formal decentralization for some aspects of its operation, but with ultimate discretionary human control. As argued above, this design choice is viable, but does not plausibly offer any real advantage over the status quo.

A DAO can also be implemented as what we refer to as a Real DAO, but it must then ultimately address the synchronization problem. To achieve this, it must either ensure strict adherence to legal and regulatory constraints, thereby reducing its permissionless, decentralized, and immutable nature to a mere mirage. Its structure thus becomes pointless, and the added complexity and limited flexibility imposed by reliance on smart contracts for its governance cannot plausibly offer a meaningful advantage over traditional corporate structures. Finally, a DAO can also fully embrace autonomy and choose not to address the synchronization problem within its governance system. We argue that this design choice will likely render the DAO unattractive, and often useless, as long as it has meaningful assets and/or interactions with the off-chain world, which is governed by law. If a DAO cannot synchronize its internal state with external legal realities, it will simply be unable to effectively control its off-chain assets and relationships—comparable to a thermostat disconnected from its heating system, its internal systems will be ineffective in controlling the world outside its smart contracts.

We submit that this design challenge severely limits the potential of DAOs to substitute traditional corporations. The more DAOs attempt to interact and integrate with the off-chain economy, the more they will have to compromise their decentralized and autonomous nature—leading them back to traditional corporate structures in all but name, or rendering them useless.

[91] The argument is, admittedly, much weaker where a DAO exclusively interacts with native ("naked") crypto-assets: even permanent misalignment between the law and the state of the blockchain ledger (and the DAO smart contracts) may be of limited concern here, absent an effective legal enforcement mechanism.

It is important to note, however, that these limitations only fully apply to DAOs that attempt to own, transact in, or interact with traditional off-chain assets, rights, and obligations. Where a DAO's assets are *entirely* held on-chain, the (practical) importance of a realignment mechanism will effectively vanish. This is because, in relation to native blockchain assets, the governing smart contracts can indeed ensure that transactions are given effect to exactly as provided for in the smart contract code. Code may not be *law*, in these cases, but code equals on-chain *reality*: transactions in native on-chain assets do not depend on anything else happening in the physical world, and do not require legal enforcement to have effect; it is only the ledger entry itself that matters, rather than any correlated legal right. It is therefore perhaps unsurprising that the largest DAOs—and to our best knowledge every DAO that fits the description of a Real DAO—are limited to holding and transacting in on-chain assets.[92] Where "real-world assets" are held by a Real DAO, this must be achieved via a separate asset tokenization process.[93] In these cases, the required tokenization process necessarily introduces the very problem discussed in this section, albeit at the tokenization, rather than the DAO level.

9. Other Legal Challenges

In addition, DAOs face several lower-level technical legal challenges. One major issue arises from conflict of laws rules, which determine the law governing companies across different jurisdictions. Pure DAOs[94] face the risk of being regarded as unincorporated partnerships[95] or associations under various national partnership laws.[96] Even where hybrid DAOs use legal wrappers, the effectiveness of this choice can be unclear: even where a hybrid DAO's home jurisdiction (ie the country of incorporation) allows the creation of a legal wrapper for a DAO, some jurisdictions will determine an organization's applicable law on the basis of "factual" connecting factors, such as the location of business operations or the place of its management and control.[97]

[92] eg Uniswap; Darcy WE Allen and others, "DAOs Are Adaptive Governance Engines" in Kevin Werbach, Eva Micheler, and Bianca Kremer (eds), *Foundations of Decentralized Organizations: Blockchain and the Future of Corporate Law* (OUP 2026) for a detailed discussion.

[93] As is the case for MakerDAO (now called "Sky Ecosystem"). For the description in the Sky Ecosystem/MakerDAO White Paper; MakerDAO, "The Sky Protocol: Sky's Multi-Collateral Dai (MCD) System" <https://makerdao.com/en/whitepaper#the-sky-protocol> accessed June 6, 2025; *contra* Kelvin Low, "The (f)utility of blockchain asset tokenisation" (*The Business Times*, December 1, 2022) <https://www.businesstimes.com.sg/opinion-features/futility-blockchain-asset-tokenisation> accessed June 6, 2025.

[94] Law Commission (n 71).

[95] eg *CFTC v Ooki DAO*; also Ryan Levin, "Bankrupting the Matrix: DAOs and the Code" (2024) 40 Emory Bankruptcy Developments Journal 455, 471; Carla L Reyes, "Autonomous Corporate Personhood" (2021) 96 Washington Law Review 1453; Stephen D Palley, "How to Sue a Decentralized Autonomous Organization" (*Coindesk*, March 20, 2016) <https://www.coindesk.com/markets/2016/03/20/how-to-sue-a-decentralized-autonomous-organization> accessed June 6, 2025; Michael Schillig, "Decentralized Autonomous Organizations (DAOs) under English Law" (2022) 16 Law and Financial Markets Review 68.

[96] Law Commission (n 71), appendix 4, 245 et seq.

[97] eg Carsten Gerner-Beuerle and others, *The Private International Law of Companies in Europe* (Beck 2019) for an overview.

10. DAOs and the Boundary of the Firm

One may argue that the legal obstacles identified above are ultimately solvable and that legislators could—and perhaps should—address some of our concerns. While we ultimately believe this to be an unlikely outcome, particularly in relation to the synchronization problem discussed above,[98] it would in principle be possible for the legislator to provide a reliable legal basis on which Real DAOs could be built.

We submit, however, that *useful* Real DAOs interacting with the off-chain economy do not only face significant legal challenges; it also appears questionable whether DAOs make sense *as an alternative to traditional corporations* from an economic perspective.

First, DAOs do not convincingly solve, and most do not even address, the central problems associated with doing business in the corporate form—that is, the various agency problems corporations give rise to,[99] but instead simply attempt to remove agents without offering a mechanism that allows the organization to replace the benefits stemming from centralized management.[100]

Second, and related to this, DAOs are naturally most suited in situations in which future interactions and likely future states of the world are situated on a well-defined spectrum of possibilities. This is because all relevant interactions must be capable of being encoded within the governing smart contracts, which almost necessarily requires comparatively low levels of complexity. Only where future states of the world can be reasonably well predicted will governance via a rigorous algorithmic governance mechanism be effective. Put differently, Real DAOs must be designed with operating systems that approach fully contingent contracts, allowing their designers to anticipate and address sources of future conflicts.

Additionally, DAOs must likely operate in areas where the value of private information is comparatively low. Where the success of the organization depends on the use of valuable private information, autonomous decision-makers with discretion—akin to the board of a traditional corporation—have a natural advantage. However, implementing meaningful decision-making by "agents" with discretion calls into question the autonomy of a DAO, as key decisions must then naturally occur off-chain, outside the constraints of its governing smart contracts and based on information not available to the DAO's investors. As discussed above, a DAO so organized is better described as a traditional corporation with a blockchain "add on," rather than a genuinely decentralized entity.

This, however, raises the question whether the efficient boundaries of a DAO on the one hand, and the efficient boundaries of a firm, however organized, on the other, are compatible.[101] If one looks at firm boundaries from a Coasian perspective,[102] where

[98] Schuster (n 47) for the discussion as to the breadth of the necessary adjustments.

[99] Low, Schuster, and Yee (n 20), *contra* eg Wulf A Kaal, "Blockchain-based Corporate Governance" (2021) 4 Stanford Journal of Blockchain Law and Policy 5, 6.

[100] Low, Schuster, and Yee (n 20).

[101] On this, also Wright (n 16). Sinclair Davidson, "The Nature of the Dao" <https://ssrn.com/abstract=4808295> accessed June 6, 2025.

[102] Eva Micheler and Daniela Gandorfer, "DAOs: The Theory of the Firm and Ostromian Perspectives" in Kevin Werbach, Eva Micheler, and Bianca Kremer (eds), *Foundations of Decentralized Organizations: Blockchain and the Future of Corporate Law* (OUP 2026).

transaction costs and the costs of contracting determine whether interactions occur through markets or within firms,[103] projects that meet the optimal conditions for DAOs are unlikely to require separate corporate structures in the first place. If an activity can be fully or near-fully encoded with precision and executed at a reasonable cost via an algorithmic governance system, it is likely more efficient for it to function as a tool or service within existing firms rather than as an independent entity.

As a historical analogy, consider the evolution of computing. Before electronic computers, organizations employed human computers for calculations in military, scientific, and commercial applications. At the time, structuring these human computation efforts as standalone businesses made sense due to their complexity. However, once electronic computers emerged, these organizations became obsolete. Rather than survive as micro-organizations, maintaining their existing boundaries but now operating their business as standalone computation entities, the function they provided was naturally integrated into other organizations.

Similarly, where circumstances are ideal for DAOs—that is, predictability, low transaction complexity, and low value of private information—it seems unlikely that such function aligns with the optimal size and scope of an organization.[104] Put differently, any project that can be entirely coded in Solidity will likely lack the complexity required to justify a corporate structure. Instead, such a project is likely to remain what it is today: a tool, function, or protocol, a—perhaps trivial—part of more complex, broader organizations, rather than an independent business organization.

It is then perhaps unsurprising that DAOs are primarily used in decentralized finance (DeFi),[105] where business is confined to on-chain interactions, and where decentralization and immutability, serve a genuine—if perhaps controversial—purpose.

11. Conclusion

In this chapter, we have argued that "assisted driving"-type DAOs are unlikely to revolutionize the way business is conducted via organizations. These "assisted driving"-type DAOs incorporate blockchain-based tools into what are otherwise conventional business organizations, but since blockchain technology offers very little for these applications beyond what can be achieved with centralized ledgers, we argue that there is little they contribute to business organizations.

We have also argued that Real DAOs "full self-driving" type corporations designed to operate truly autonomously and decentralized face several challenges which we believe are ultimately insurmountable. These challenges are primarily legal in nature and stem from a deep-seated conflict between a non-hierarchically designed technology and the inherently hierarchical nature of every legal system. Thus, what we term Real DAOs will, in our view, always struggle to link the on-chain and the off-chain worlds.

[103] Ronald Harry Coase, "The Nature of the Firm" (1937) 4 Economica 386. See also Oliver Hart, "An Economist's Perspective on the Theory of the Firm" (1989) 89 Columbia Law Review 1757.

[104] Micheler and Gandorfer (n 102) regarding the range of possible uses of DAOs on the market–firm spectrum.

[105] eg Schillig (n 95).

In our view, to make Real DAOs suitable for operating businesses connected to the off-chain world, they must necessarily be designed in ways that compromise their autonomy and decentralization. Consequently, Real DAOs face the same design dilemma as crypto-assets more generally: they can either be truly decentralized, or they can be suitable for interacting with the off-chain world, but they cannot be both.

Does this mean that DAOs will completely disappear? No. First, we acknowledge that for some applications, the challenges we identify are of little importance. There are, and may always be, applications such as unregulated prediction markets, gambling platforms, and certain DeFi applications, where the ability to effect *de facto* transfers of value is more important than the ability to "synchronize" the ledger with how the law views the transactions involved. These use cases, however, will likely remain confined to purely on-chain transactions, with little or no interactions with the off-chain world. Secondly, the blockchain community have built up a narrative around its supposed revolutionary potential that seems impervious to critique or even contrary experience. Despite failing to deliver on this potential in more than a decade and a half, a core community clings on to this revolutionary potential despite no evidence that it is any closer to fruition, in part because it shows no interest in engaging with criticisms. The result is that blockchain "innovations" go through boom and bust cycles in which the same thing is tried over and over again expecting different results. DAOs are thus unlikely to play a significant role in the continuing evolution of the legal structures used to organize the majority of businesses.

15
Out of Control: DAOs, AI, and the Question of Autonomy

Kevin Werbach

1. The AI Tidal Wave

Artificial intelligence (AI) is arguably the most important development in technology today.[1] Experts predict that AI will add trillions of dollars of value to the global economy in the coming decade.[2] Over 70 percent of firms surveyed by McKinsey in mid-2024 were already deploying AI.[3] Investment in AI companies has soared since 2023,[4] propelling AI chip leader NVIDIA to the highest market capitalization of any company in the world.[5] AI is not only disrupting massive numbers of jobs across the global economy, but changing the very nature of work.[6] In any forward-looking evaluation of new organizational forms, such as decentralized autonomous organizations (DAOs), it is therefore important to consider what AI might mean.

AI and blockchain seem to be very distinct phenomena, however. The generative AI boom began in late 2022 simultaneously with the scandalous collapse of major cryptocurrency platforms such as FTX. In the popular conversation, AI is "the next big thing" after crypto, often positioned as a technology whose adoption matched the hype in a way blockchain never achieved.[7] Yet there are important connections

[1] Mustafa Suleyman, *The Coming Wave* (Crown 2023); Steven Levy, "It's Time to Believe the AI Hype" (*Wired*, May 17, 2024) <https://www.wired.com/story/its-time-to-believe-the-ai-hype/> accessed April 21, 2025.

[2] Yiwen Lu, "Generative A.I. Can Add $4.4 Trillion in Value to Global Economy, Study Says" (*New York Times*, June 14, 2023) <https://www.nytimes.com/2023/06/14/technology/generative-ai-global-economy.html> accessed April 21, 2025.

[3] McKinsey Quantum Black, "The State of AI in Early 2024" (May 30, 2024) <https://www.mckinsey.com/capabilities/quantumblack/our-insights/the-state-of-ai> accessed April 21, 2025.

[4] Anna Cooban, "AI Investment Is Booming. How Much Is Hype?" (*CNN*, July 23, 2023) <https://www.cnn.com/2023/07/23/business/ai-vc-investment-dot-com-bubble/index.html> accessed April 21, 2025.

[5] Krystal Hur, "Nvidia Surpasses Microsoft to Become the Largest Public Company in the World" (*CNN*, June 19, 2024) <https://www.cnn.com/2024/06/18/markets/nvidia-largest-public-company/index.html> accessed April 21, 2025.

[6] Mark Rayner, "AI: 3 Ways Artificial Intelligence Is Changing the Future of Work" (*World Economic Forum*, August 14, 2023) <https://www.weforum.org/agenda/2023/08/ai-artificial-intelligence-changing-the-future-of-work-jobs/> accessed April 21, 2025; Martin Fleming, "AI Is Changing Work—and Leaders Need to Adapt" (*Harvard Business Review*, March 24, 2020) <https://hbr.org/2020/03/ai-is-changing-work-and-leaders-need-to-adapt> accessed April 21, 2025.

[7] Christopher Mims, "AI Becomes Silicon Valley's Next Buzzy Bandwagon as Crypto Boom Fizzles" (*Wall Street Journal*, 18 February 2023) <https://www.wsj.com/articles/ai-silicon-valley-crypto-boom-blockchain-artificial-intelligence-59622e9c> accessed April 21, 2025.

between blockchain and AI going forward, especially related to DAOs. DAOs may be an important component of the future of AI; AI may be an important component of the future of DAOs; and DAOs may themselves become the most powerful manifestation of the current AI vision.

AI is now reaching a major inflection point of adoption and transformative impact. For a number of decades since the birth of the field in the 1950s, AI research went through boom and bust cycles, as technical breakthroughs held out the potential for commercialization of AI tools able to match or improve on human performance, only to have what seemed soon achievable prove vastly harder in practice.[8] Finally, advances in deep learning, an offshoot of neural networks, taking advantage of the newfound ability to collect and process extremely large datasets, led to radical improvements in AI performance on a range of important problems. By the mid-2010s, at the same time as the Web3 vision of blockchain-based decentralized applications was coming into focus, AI was heralded as a transformational technology.[9]

And then came ChatGPT.

Released initially as a research prototype by the startup OpenAI in November 2022, ChatGPT was, for many, a revelation. A conversational interface that seemed eerily human, and capable of virtually any task one could assign, it was for many people the first realization of AI concepts that were previously the domain of science fiction. Made available freely to the public, ChatGPT reached 100 million users in just two months, faster than any prior application.[10]

ChatGPT is an implementation of generative AI, designed to create novel responses rather than merely classifying or making predictions from existing data, and using an approach called a large language model (LLM). Related tools allowed generation and interpretation of images, music, and videos. Major global technology firms such as Google, Meta, and Baidu, as well as startups such as Anthropic and Mistral, subsequently released competing LLM foundation models and related systems. Major technology providers began incorporating generative AI throughout their products, and enterprises began investing heavily in generative AI implementations across virtually every business function.

As the generative AI arms race progresses, the speed and ceiling of performance improvements is uncertain. To date, generative AI systems have followed scaling laws, where more data and compute produces better performance.[11] The most powerful foundation models require massive computing clusters using high-end graphical processing units (GPUs), with training costs exceeding $100 million.[12] Further increasing

[8] Eliza Strickland, "The Turbulent Past and Uncertain Future of AI" (2021) (October) IEEE Spectrum 26–31.

[9] Shana Lynch, "Andrew Ng: Why AI Is the New Electricity" (*Insights by Stanford Business*, March 11, 2017) <https://www.gsb.stanford.edu/insights/andrew-ng-why-ai-new-electricity> accessed April 21, 2025.

[10] Krystal Hu, "ChatGPT Sets Record for Fastest-Growing User Base" (*Reuters*, February 2, 2023) <https://www.reuters.com/technology/chatgpt-sets-record-fastest-growing-user-base-analyst-note-2023-02-01> accessed April 21, 2025.

[11] Jared Kaplan and others, "Scaling Laws for Neural Language Models" (*OpenAI*, January 23, 2020) <https://openai.com/index/scaling-laws-for-neural-language-models/> accessed April 21, 2025.

[12] Neil C Thompson and others, "The Computational Limits of Deep Learning" (*arXiv*, June 27, 2022) <https://arxiv.org/abs/2007.05558> accessed April 21, 2025.

these costs, high-quality content providers are increasingly demanding licensing fees rather than allow AI providers to scrape their data for free. As a result of these factors, there is great concern about concentration of power in only a handful of massive AI providers.[13]

One important consequence of the rise of generative AI is that it shifts the definition of artificial intelligence. Although the term has been used for decades to describe computerized systems that can replicate human modes of intelligence—thinking, learning, reasoning, expressing emotions, and so forth—a rigorous definition proves surprisingly difficult to achieve. Prior to generative AI, the essence of the field was machine learning. However, a chatbot or image generator is distinguished not by its ability to learn patterns in existing data (though it does so), but by its ability to create new things.

The Organisation for Economic Cooperation and Development's (OECD) definition, which has been largely adopted in the European AI Act and other recent governmental initiative, defines AI as "a machine-based system that, for explicit or implicit objectives, infers, from the input it receives, how to generate outputs ... that can influence physical or virtual environments."[14] The essence of AI under this framing is neither the learning nor the results, but the inference. In other words, AI involves a leap from objectives to outputs. That leap is based on ordinary mathematics and statistics, but not feasibly reducible to simple deterministic calculations.

2. DAOs and AI

AI intersects with DAOs in at least three ways. First, DAOs may be an important element of the future of AI. DAOs potentially represent a native digital, and decentralized, governance mechanism for AI training data and models. Second, AI may be an important element of the future of DAOs. DAO governance functions could be automated through AI, or DAO participation itself could be conducted by autonomous AI agents. Third, DAOs and AI might converge.

2.1. DAOs as AI Governance Mechanisms

One of the critical challenges in AI development and deployment is the integrity and provenance of the data used to train these models. Data provenance is becoming

[13] Federal Trade Commission, "Generative AI Raises Competition Concerns" (June 29, 2023) <https://www.ftc.gov/policy/advocacy-research/tech-at-ftc/2023/06/generative-ai-raises-competition-concerns> accessed April 21, 2025; UK Competition and Markets Authority, "CMA Launches Initial Review of Artificial Intelligence Models" (May 4, 2023) <https://www.gov.uk/government/news/cma-launches-initial-review-of-artificial-intelligence-models> accessed April 21, 2025.

[14] Stuart Russell, Karine Perset, and Marko Grobelnik, "Updates to the OECD's Definition of an AI System Explained" (*OECD*, November 29, 2023) <https://oecd.ai/en/wonk/ai-system-definition-update> accessed April 21, 2025. The OECD definition is the basis for the definition of AI in the European Union's AI Act; Luca Bertuzzi, "EU Lawmakers Set to Settle on OECD Definition for Artificial Intelligence" (*Euractiv*, March 7, 2023) <https://www.euractiv.com/section/artificial-intelligence/news/eu-lawmakers-set-to-settle-on-oecd-definition-for-artificial-intelligence/> accessed April 21, 2025.

increasingly important with the passage of new laws governing AI systems, such as the European Union's AI Act (EU AI Act).[15] The EU AI Act requires the provider of an AI foundation model to "document and make publicly available a sufficiently detailed summary of the use of training data protected under copyright law."[16] Other regulations related to privacy are also relevant, as LLMs incorporate personally identifiable information into their training data. The Italian data protection agency found in early 2024 that OpenAI violated the EU's General Data Protection Regulation (GDPR) by incorporating such information without permission.[17] In the US, the Federal Trade Commission (FTC) has taken steps to investigate generative AI foundation models.[18] Proposed federal and state laws would require disclosures similar to those in the EU AI Act.

Blockchain offers a powerful mechanism for AI data provenance.[19] Blockchains are tamper-resistant ledgers that provide a trusted repository of information.[20] While the training of AI models is extremely computationally and data-intensive, making it unsuitable for processing on a blockchain, the metadata about the sources, ownership, and attributes of data, as well as the various steps in model training, refinement, and evolution, could effectively be handled on-chain. Already, FICO, a major provider of analytics and fraud detection technology, is using blockchains to track AI model development.[21] FICO plans to make the capability available in the near future to its customers. Blockchains for AI data provenance could make information publicly accessible to facilitate auditing, addressing growing demands for transparency.

In addition to tracking data, blockchains can be used to tokenize data assets, facilitating aggregation without giving up ownership and control. One of the reasons for the consolidation of AI platforms is that only a few providers such as Google, Meta, Amazon, and Apple have direct access to sufficiently large datasets from their customer activity, or the resources to license them. And those firms tend not to make their data accessible to others. Blockchain-based solutions such as Ocean Protocol make it possible for companies that own data to contribute it to common pools, receive

[15] Artificial Intelligence Act, European Parliament legislative resolution of 13 March 2024 on the proposal for a regulation of the European Parliament and of the Council on laying down harmonized rules on Artificial Intelligence (Artificial Intelligence Act) and amending certain Union Legislative Acts (COM(2021)0206 – C9-0.

[16] Artificial Intelligence Act, Art 28b(4)(c).

[17] Reuters, "OpenAI's ChatGPT Breaches Privacy Rules, Says Italian Watchdog" (*Reuters*, January 30, 2024) <https://www.reuters.com/technology/cybersecurity/italy-regulator-notifies-openai-privacy-breaches-chatgpt-2024-01-29/> accessed April 21, 2025.

[18] David Hamilton, "FTC Investigating ChatGPT Creator OpenAI Over Consumer Protection Issues" (*Associated Press*, July 13, 2023) <https://apnews.com/article/openai-chatgpt-investigation-federal-ftc-76c6218c506996942282d7f5d608088e> accessed April 21, 2025.

[19] Isabelle Bousquette, "AI Has a Trust Problem. Can Blockchain Help?" (*Wall Street Journal*, January 11, 2024) <https://www.wsj.com/articles/ai-has-a-trust-problem-can-blockchain-help-ba3b26f7#> accessed April 21, 2025; Arjun Kharpal, "Blockchain, the Tech Behind Bitcoin, May Have Found Its "Killer Use Case" by Keeping AI in Check" (*CNBC*, January 21, 2024) <https://www.cnbc.com/2024/01/22/blockchain-tech-behind-bitcoin-can-be-used-to-track-ai-training-data.html> accessed April 21, 2025.

[20] Kevin Werbach, *The Blockchain and the New Architecture of Trust* (MIT Press 2018).

[21] Scott Zoldi, "How to Use Blockchain to Build Responsible AI: An Award-Winning Approach" (*FICO Blog*, October 17, 2023) <https://www.fico.com/blogs/how-use-blockchain-build-responsible-ai-award-winning-approach-0> accessed April 21, 2025.

compensation for its use through smart contracts and tokens, and not give up their ownership rights.[22]

The next step beyond such blockchain-based data management for AI is for DAOs to serve as the governance layer.[23] DAO governance can be used to coordinate decentralized data ownership, executed through smart contracts. This would allow for communities to oversee development of sophisticated AI which otherwise would only be accessible to large companies. Just as DAOs empower collections of individuals to coordinate efficiently to engage in collective action, such as investment pools, they could support targeted AI development in a fair, democratic manner.[24]

An early example of this model is ClimateGPT, a specialized LLM for research on climate change.[25] By integrating key scientific findings, it is designed to provide a resource for understanding climate change and possible mitigation strategies. The Endowment of Climate Intelligence (ECI), which developed ClimateGPT, created a DAO in March 2024 to function as its governance structure.[26] The DAO coordinates policies and funding for development of the model, effectively decentralizing ownership to the community.

This approach might be particularly valuable for open source AI foundation models, which can be customized by those who adopt them. There is currently a strong division of opinion regarding the desirability of releasing highly capable open source models, which could be exploited by bad actors or make it difficult to provide redress for harms.[27] A DAO could provide oversight to verify that a model is

[22] Trent McConaghy, "The Web3 Data Economy" (*Ocean Protocol Blog*, November 22, 2018) <https://blog.oceanprotocol.com/the-web3-data-economy-b6fd8ecac4c4> accessed April 21, 2025; Trent McConaghy, "Ocean Protocol: Tools for the Web3 Data Economy" in Duc A Tran, My T Thai, and Bhaskar Krishnamachari (eds) *Handbook on Blockchain* (Springer 2022) 505–39; Rameez Asif, Syed Raheel Hassan, and Gerard Parr, "Integrating a Blockchain-Based Governance Framework for Responsible AI" (2023) 15 Future Internet 97; "Tokenization of AI Assets: Unlocking Value in the Digital Economy" (*DcentAI Blog*, April 29, 2024) <https://medium.com/sample-dcentai-blog/tokenization-of-ai-assets-unlocking-value-in-the-digital-economy-5ef48d9eff2a> accessed April 21, 2025. For a more detailed analysis of how tokenization can facilitate decentralization, Michael Sockin and Wei Xiong, "Decentralization Through Tokenization" (2023) 78 Journal of Finance 247.

[23] Felix Ng, "AI Will Reinvent DAOs and Tokenized Models Will Be Valuable: Vance Spencer" (*CoinTelegraph*, September 6, 2023) <https://cointelegraph.com/news/ai-reinvent-dao-tokenized-models-valuable-future-framework-ventures> accessed April 21, 2025.

[24] Joshua Tan and others, "Open Problems in DAOs" (*arXiv*, June 12, 2024) <https://arxiv.org/pdf/2310.19201> accessed April 21, 2025, 63 ("We believe DAOs and other coordination technologies can sustain a new, bottom-up form of AI governance that is more responsive and representative of the stakeholders impacted by AI").

[25] David Thulke and others, "ClimateGPT: Towards AI Synthesizing Interdisciplinary Research on Climate Change" (*arXiv*, January 17, 2024) <https://arxiv.org/abs/2401.09646> accessed April 21, 2025; "ClimateGPT is an AI Expert in Global Warming" (*Inquirer.net*, January 27, 2024) <https://technology.inquirer.net/131575/climategpt-is-an-ai-expert-in-global-warming> accessed April 21, 2025.

[26] Tan and others (n 24) 63–65.

[27] Rishi Bommasani and others, "Considerations for Governing Open Foundation Models" (*HAI Policy & Society Issue Brief*, December 2023) <https://hai.stanford.edu/sites/default/files/2023-12/Governing-Open-Foundation-Models.pdf> accessed April 21, 2025; Elizabeth Seger and others, "Open-Sourcing Highly Capable Foundation Models" (*Institute for Law & AI, LawAI Working Paper Series, No 2-2023*, October 2023) <https://law-ai.org/wp-content/uploads/2023/10/open-sourcing-cover-1-combined.pdf> accessed April 21, 2025. The National Telecommunications and Information Administration of the US Department of Commerce issued a report in 2024 concluding that there was insufficient basis for restricting open-weight models at this time, but the government should develop the capacity to assess the risks and

trained or fine-tuned in a certain way, and an asset-bearing contact point when harms occur. DAOs could, in effect, provide the framework for addressing the "alignment problem:" ensuring that sophisticated AI systems act in accordance with human values and interests.[28] They could build on "collective constitutional AI" approaches pioneered by leading generative AI foundation model developer Anthropic, which fine-tune model alignment based on community engagement.[29]

A further step would be for AI inferencing itself, not just the ownership rights or governance activity, to take place on the blockchain. For generative AI systems, users provide queries which are answered through an application programming interface (API) to the AI model. While still computationally demanding, this stage requires far less compute than the initial training of the model, which requires large numbers of high-performance GPUs. As compute requirements for inferencing decrease further, thanks to more advanced algorithms, and computing performance of blockchains increases, processing AI queries on chain becomes feasible.

The DFinity Foundation, creator of the Internet Computer Protocol (ICP), is building a blockchain ecosystem based on highly scalable technology.[30] Dfinity aims to support applications at the scale of existing web-based platforms on a decentralized blockchain foundation. DFinity in late 2023 announced a partnership with SingularityNet to allow developers to run AI models directly on ICP through smart contracts.[31]

take action if significant dangers manifested themselves; National Telecommunications and Information Administration, (*Dual-Use Foundation Models with Widely Available Model Weights*, July 2024) <https://www.ntia.gov/sites/default/files/publications/ntia-ai-open-model-report.pdf> accessed April 20, 2025.

[28] Samantha Marin, "The Future of DAOs is Powered by AI" (*Aragon Blog*, January 19, 2023) <https://blog.aragon.org/ai-daos-the-future-of-daos-powered-by-artificial-intelligence/> accessed April 21, 2025; Richard Ngo, Lawrence Chan, and Soren Mindermann, "The Alignment Problem from a Deep Learning Perspective" (*arXiv*, 2024) <https://arxiv.org/pdf/2209.00626> accessed April 21, 2025; Brian Christian, *The Alignment Problem: Machine Learning and Human Values* (WW Norton 2020); Iason Gabriel, "Artificial Intelligence, Values, and Alignment" (2020) 30(3) Minds and Machines 411; Eliezer Yudkowsky, "AI Alignment: Why It's Hard, and Where to Start" (*Machine Intelligence Research Institute*, December 28, 2016) <https://intelligence.org/2016/12/28/ai-alignment-why-its-hard-and-where-to-start/> accessed April 21, 2025.

[29] Anthropic, "Collective Constitutional AI: Aligning a Language Model with Public Input" (*Anthropic*, October 17, 2023) <https://www.anthropic.com/news/collective-constitutional-ai-aligning-a-language-model-with-public-input> accessed April 21, 2025.

[30] Dean Takahashi, "Internet Computer Blockchain Has Raised $80M" (*VentureBeat*, March 27, 2024) <https://venturebeat.com/games/internet-computer-blockchain-has-raised-77m-dfinity-foundation/> accessed April 21, 2025.

[31] Jason Nelson, "SingularityNET Joins with Dfinity Foundation for AI Models that Run on Smart Contracts" (*Decrypt*, November 20, 2023) <https://decrypt.co/206640/singularitynet-joins-with-dfinity-foundation-for-ai-models-that-runs-on-smart-contracts> accessed April 21, 2025. SingularityNET is in the process of merging with Fetch.ai and Ocean Protocol, two other platforms connecting AI and blockchain. Jose Antonio Lanz, "FetchAI, SingularityNet and Ocean Protocol Propose Merger to Build Largest Decentralized AI Ecosystem" (*Decrypt*, March 27, 2024) <https://decrypt.co/223679/fetch-ai-singularitynet-ocean-protocol-merger-superintelligence-collective> accessed April 21, 2025.

2.2. AI Controlling DAOs

AI could also transform the way DAOs operate.[32] Governance in DAOs involves token-holders voting on proposals that dictate the organization's actions and policies.[33] DAO governance faces several difficult challenges.[34] Participation rates in governance tend to be low, either because governance token-holders are relatively unconcerned about the outcome of most votes, they lack the time and information to make informed decisions, or because they hold the token for its trading market value rather than any desire to exercise voting rights. Token ownership and voting patterns tend to exhibit significant concentration of power, accentuated by low turnout, which results in arrangements inconsistent with the ideal of DAOs as decentralized.[35] DAOs use a number of techniques to address these problems,[36] but they remain significant.

AI can enhance the efficiency, fairness, and transparency of DAO governance by automating and optimizing voting mechanisms for governance tokens.[37] AI systems can analyze vast amounts of data to inform voting decisions. By processing historical voting patterns, proposal outcomes, and market data, AI can provide insights and recommendations to token-holders. This can lead to more informed and strategic voting, improving the quality of governance decisions. AI could also automate the voting process for governance tokens, to achieve high-level goals set by token-holders. Finally, it could also be used by DAO operators to identify and mitigate problems in the voting process. By analyzing voting data, AI could detect patterns that suggest manipulation or disproportionate influence by certain token-holders.

NEAR is a major layer-1 blockchain and decentralized application platform, competing with Ethereum.[38] NEAR's founder, Illia Polushkin, was one of the Google researchers who co-authored the famous 2017 "Attention is All You Need" paper that introduced the transformer architecture used by ChatGPT and other large language

[32] Marin (n 23).

[33] David Gogel and others, "Decentralized Autonomous Organization Toolkit" (*World Economic Forum*, January 2023) <https://www3.weforum.org/docs/WEF_Decentralized_Autonomous_Organization_Toolkit_2023.pdf> accessed April 21, 2025; Aaron Wright, "The Rise of Decentralized Autonomous Organizations: Opportunities and Challenges" (2021) 4 Stanford Journal of Blockchain Law & Policy 152; Wulf A Kaal, "Blockchain-Based Corporate Governance" (2020) 4 Stanford Journal of Blockchain Law & Policy 3.

[34] Gogel and others (n 33).

[35] R Fritsch, Marino Müller, and Roger Wattenhofer, "Analyzing Voting Power in Decentralized Governance: Who controls DAOs?" (2024) Blockchain: Research and Applications 100208, doi: <https://doi.org/10.1016/j.bcra.2024.100208> accessed June 10, 2025; Jungsuk Han, Jongsub Lee, and Tao Li, "DAO Governance" (*SSRN*, February 3, 2023) <http://dx.doi.org/10.2139/ssrn.4346581> accessed June 10, 2025; Rainer Feichtinger and others, "The Hidden Shortcomings of (D)AOs—An Empirical Study of On-Chain Governance" (*arXiv*, February 28, 2023) <https://arxiv.org/pdf/2302.12125> accessed April 21, 2025.

[36] Gogel and others (n 33).

[37] Marin (n 28); Wulf Kaal, Wulf Kaal, "AI Governance via Web3 Reputation System" (2025) 8 Stanford Journal of Blockchain Law & Policy 4 ("In a decentralized autonomous organization (DAO) governed by Web3 principles, AI systems can actively participate in the governance process, contributing to decisionmaking and protocol changes that impact the network. This approach ensures a fair distribution of power, preventing any single entity from exerting undue influence and fostering an environment where decisions benefit all participants").

[38] The NEAR token was the 20th most valuable digital asset according to CoinMarketCap at the time of this writing; <https://coinmarketcap.com/> accessed April 21, 2025.

models.[39] NEAR is experimenting with AI tools to perform a variety of DAO-related functions.[40] For example, an experimental tool uses ChatGPT to evaluate whether proposals for DAO funding grants meet the objectives of the grant program.[41] The decisions would then be executed through smart contracts. Polushkin also announced the creation of the NEAR.ai R&D lab, whose first project will be to build a development tool to create Web3 applications directly through AI.[42]

MakerDAO is the most prominent asset-backed stablecoin.[43] In operation since 2017, it has over $6 billion in value locked in the platform as of mid-2024.[44] Unlike centralized stablecoins such as USDC and USDT, which maintain price stability with traditional assets held by central operators who redeem them in exchange for the stablecoin token, MakerDAO operates as a set of smart contracts on the Ethereum blockchain. Price stability is achieved by overcollateralizing tokens with other assets, including cryptocurrencies, which are locked up and automatically liquidated when prices fall sufficiently.[45]

A key aspect of MakerDAO is, as the name suggests, its DAO structure. Crucial management decisions, such as the ratio of overcollateralization required and the interest rates for those collateralizing assets, are set through governance votes of token-holders.[46] Governance of MakerDAO therefore is responsible not only for the operational management of the organization, but crucial economic decisions. MakerDAO has developed a complex decentralized governance structure, in which essential functions are divided among semi-autonomous "core units."[47]

In May 2023, MakerDAO founder Rune Christiansen published a post titled "The 5 Phases of Endgame," in which he proposed the next evolution of the DAO's governance.[48] In addition to new tokens and a new blockchain, the framework envisions that, "MakerDAO will gradually transform itself into the first genuinely autonomous DAO using artificial intelligence."[49] The key to this vision is Atlas, "a giant governance

[39] Ashish Vaswani and others, "Attention Is All You Need" (*31st Conference on Neural Image Processing Systems*, 2017) <https://arxiv.org/pdf/1706.03762> accessed April 21, 2025.

[40] Andrew Fenton, "Real AI Use Cases in Crypto, No. 2: AIs Can Run DAOs" (*CoinTelegraph*, November 28, 2023) <https://cointelegraph.com/magazine/real-ai-use-cases-crypto-no-2-ai-can-run-dao/> accessed April 21, 2025.

[41] Dmitry Meshkov and others, "Quex—An AI-powered Near grant program treasury" (*NEARCON IRL Hackathon Submission—Devpost*, 2023) <https://devpost.com/software/quex> accessed April 21, 2025.

[42] Illia Polushkin, "User-Owned AI is NEAR" (*NEAR Blog*, May 22, 2024) <https://pages.near.org/blog/user-owned-ai-is-near/> accessed April 21, 2025.

[43] <https://makerdao.com/> accessed April 21, 2025.

[44] <https://defillama.com/protocol/makerdao#information> accessed April 21, 2025.

[45] The MakerDAO structure differs greatly from purely algorithmic stablecoins, such as the infamous Terra Luna, which attempt to maintain stability entirely through supply and demand configuration. Where Terra Luna and other algorithmic stablecoins ultimately collapsed, MakerDAO has weathered dramatic cryptocurrency price movements successfully.

[46] MakerDAO has a two-token structure. The stablecoin DAI is designed to be pegged to the value of the US Dollar, while the governance token MKR floats in price based on trading.

[47] Rune Christiansen, "MakerDAO Has Come Full Circle" (*MakerDAO Blog*, July 20, 2021) <https://blog.makerdao.com/makerdao-has-come-full-circle/> accessed April 21, 2025.

[48] Rune Christiansen, "The 5 Phases of Endgame" (*MakerDAO Forum*, May 2023) <https://forum.makerdao.com/t/the-5-phases-of-endgame/20830> accessed April 21, 2025.

[49] Andrew Fenton, "MakerDAO's Plan to Bring Back "'DeFi Summer'" (*CoinTelegraph*, January 10, 2024) <https://cointelegraph.com/magazine/makerdao-defi-summer-2024-rune-christensen-interview/> accessed April 21, 2025.

rulebook built as a unified data structure containing all principles, rules, processes and knowledge of the entire MakerDAO ecosystem."[50] A set of specialized conversational AI tools will be used to interact with this canonical rulebook, along the lines of retrieval-augmented generation (RAG) approaches used today by enterprises deploying generative AI.[51] According to Christiansen, "The use of AI tools help level the playing field between deeply embedded insiders and more peripheral community members, by making it possible for anyone to participate at a very high level with all relevant facts and nuances available, and audit and verify decisions and actions by insiders in real time."[52]

Any use of AI for DAO decision-making raises some important challenges. AI systems are subject to limitations of accuracy, explainability, cybersecurity, and bias, among areas subject to significant voluntary corporate efforts and proposed regulation around the world.[53] The fact that a DAO decision might be executed immutably through smart contracts creates further pressure for the AI determination to avoid such problems. As Ethereum creator Vitalik Buterin points out, the prospects of adversarial machine learning deliberately sabotaging AI-based DAO inputs is a particular concern.[54]

2.3. DAOs and AI Agents Converge

Finally, DAOs could be the vehicle for the widespread implementation of AI agents, effectively combining the two technologies rather than using one to control the other. There is a deep isomorphism between AI and DAOs. As described earlier, the central attribute of AI is machine-based inference, converting objectives into outputs through a complex hidden process. A DAO is, in a sense, a kind of artificial intelligence. It is a set of software programs, represented through smart contracts, that takes in the desired objectives of its token-holders and produces functionality in the world.

All corporations are treated as artificial persons under the law.[55] However, this legal personhood does not address what kind of entity or entities lies behind the legal fiction.[56] DAOs, like more established forms of AI such as chatbots or predictive models, render decisions through computer software.

[50] ibid.

[51] Patrick Lewis and others, "Retrieval-Augmented Generation for Knowledge-Intensive NLP Tasks" (*NeurIPS*, 2020) <https://proceedings.neurips.cc/paper/2020/file/6b493230205f780e1bc26945df7481e5-Paper.pdf> accessed April 21, 2025.

[52] Christiansen (n 48).

[53] Reid Blackman, *Ethical Machines* (Harvard Business Review Press 2022); Virginia Dignum, *Responsible Artificial Intelligence* (Springer 2019); Olivia Gambelin, *Responsible AI: Implement an Ethical Approach in Your Organization* (O'Reilly Media 2024).

[54] Vitalik Buterin, "The Promise and Challenges of Crypto + AI Applications" (*Vitalik Buterin's Website*, January 30, 2024) <https://vitalik.eth.limo/general/2024/01/30/cryptoai.html> accessed April 21, 2025.

[55] Susan Watson, "Corporations as Artificial Persons in the AI Age" (*SSRN*, September 29, 2023) <https://papers.ssrn.com/sol3/papers.cfm?abstract_id=4588965> accessed April 21, 2025 ("Viewed reductively, the modern company is a legal fiction that operates as an artificial legal person to capture, extract, and transact for forms of value").

[56] Eva Micheler, *Company Law: A Real Entity Theory* (OUP 2021) 1.

For today's DAOs, the software-based functionality is largely executory, with humans retaining the lion's share of decision-making authority both outside and inside the DAO governance processes. If a human proposes that a DAO allocate a certain fraction of its treasury to a specified address, and human token-holders discuss the proposal on forums and then authorize it by majority vote, it makes little sense to talk of the DAO as an artificial actor making that decision. Yet as the degree of human involvement wanes and the level of autonomous AI activity grows, the answer becomes less clear.

The same is true for corporations. John Armour and Horst Eidenmuller have suggested that as AI is used increasingly to substitute for human decision-making, we should speak of "self-driving corporations" and apply legal principles developed for AI modalities such as autonomous vehicles.[57] With ordinary corporations, however, there is typically some residual of human management. A DAO has no such limitation. Shawn Bayern argues that existing corporate legal structures can be applied even to fully machine-based systems, allowing them to operate as functionally "autonomous organizations."[58]

Thus, the ultimate trajectory of AI and DAOs could overlap even more directly.[59] As early as 2014, Ethereum creator Vitalik Buterin, who was one of the first to introduce the concept of DAOs, described AI as the "holy grail" of DAO functionality.[60] And in 2016, Ocean Protocol creator Trent McConaghy, an AI researcher turned blockchain developer, envisioned the development of AI DAOs.[61] In McConaghy's vision, AI DAOs are distinguished from conventional AI systems by the major characteristics of DAOs: They can own and control resources, and they can operate immutably without the possibility of human intervention. So far, while DAOs have become real entities controlling billions of dollars of assets, these visions have remained hypothetical. Yet, the decade since they were conceptualized has witnessed incredible advances in both the capabilities and real-world adoption of AI. AI systems are now moving steadily closer to the kinds of functionality that would connect them to DAOs.

A defining characteristic of DAOs is that, like corporations, they can represent collective human interests or intent, coordinate actions, control resources, and act in the world. Blockchains themselves and smart contract-based decentralized applications alone lack such capabilities. They can record information immutably and respond dynamically to inputs based on their coding, but it is still humans outside the blockchain who control the assets and execute the operations. Similarly, AI models themselves

[57] John Armour and Horst Eidenmuller, "Self-Driving Corporations?" (2020) 10 Harvard Business Law Review 87.

[58] Shawn Bayern, *Autonomous Organizations* (CUP 2021).

[59] Marin (n 28).

[60] Vitalik Buterin, "DAOs, DACs, DAs and More: An Incomplete Terminology Guide" (*Ethereum Blog*, May 6, 2014) <https://blog.ethereum.org/2014/05/06/daos-dacs-das-and-more-an-incomplete-terminology-guide> accessed April 21, 2025. Buterin first used the term "DAO" in 2013; a short time earlier, Daniel Larimer, a blockchain entrepreneur, described a similar concept as a distributed autonomous corporation (DAC). Vitalik Buterin, "Why Cryptoeconomics and X-Risk Researchers Should Listen to Each Other More," Response to Jeffrey Evans' comment (*Medium*, July 5, 2016) <https://medium.com/@VitalikButerin/i-invented-the-term-in-2013-and-daniel-larimer-came-up-with-dacs-s-organization-corporation-a-ef86db1524d5> accessed April 21, 2025.

[61] Trent McConaghy, "AI DAOs, and Three Paths to Get There" (*Medium*, June 18, 2016) <https://medium.com/@trentmc0/ai-daos-and-three-paths-to-get-there-cfa0a4cc37b8> accessed April 21, 2025.

have no agency. They make decisions and predictions, or generate a response to a prompt, but humans determine what happens next. AI agents, however, add a further layer of automation.

Agents are one of the hottest areas of AI development, seen by many as the next step beyond conversational chatbots.[62] Though the term does not have a precise definition, agents are AI systems able to take actions in the world, through a combination of planning and interacting with other systems. So, for example, instead of giving you a recommendation for a hotel on your vacation in Morocco, the agent could plan the entire trip, including making bookings on your behalf.[63]

According to Accenture, "Over the next decade, we will see the rise of entire agent ecosystems—large networks of interconnected AI that will push enterprises to think about their intelligence and automation strategy in a fundamentally different way."[64] Agent-based systems use generative AI to coordinate various tools to achieve results, such as developing a software program or analyzing a potential acquisition target. An Accenture survey found that 96 percent of executives believed AI agent ecosystems would be a significant opportunity for their organizations in the next three years.[65]

DAOs themselves can function as agents because they are machine-based systems, which interact with the world through smart contracts on a blockchain. Those smart contracts identify users on the basis of cryptographic security measures. An authorized user is one whose digital signature matches the relevant account or indicates control of the relevant assets. There is no direct mechanism to verify that user is a human, as opposed to another machine-based system with access to the keys.[66] A DAO participant may be an AI system programmed to achieve a higher-level goal, acquiring and voting its tokens dynamically to achieve that purpose.

[62] Will Knight, "Forget Chatbots. AI Agents Are the Future" (*Wired*, March 14, 2024) <https://www.wired.com/story/fast-forward-forget-chatbots-ai-agents-are-the-future/> accessed April 21, 2025; Kelsey Piper, "AI 'Agents' Could Do Real Work in the Real World. That Might Not Be a Good Thing" (*Vox*, March 29, 2024) <https://www.vox.com/future-perfect/24114582/artificial-intelligence-agents-openai-chatgpt-microsoft-google-ai-safety-risk-anthropic-claude> accessed April 21, 2025.

[63] McKinsey & Company, "What Is an AI Agent?" (*McKinsey & Company*, March 25, 2025) <https://www.mckinsey.com/featured-insights/mckinsey-explainers/what-is-an-ai-agent accessed April 21, 2025; Lareina Yee, Michael Chui, and Roger Roberts, "Why Agents Are the Next Frontier of Generative AI" (*McKinsey & Company*, July 24, 2024) <https://www.mckinsey.com/capabilities/mckinsey-digital/our-insights/why-agents-are-the-next-frontier-of-generative-ai> accessed April 21, 2025.

[64] Accenture, "Technology Vision 2024" (January 9, 2024) <https://www.accenture.com/us-en/insights/technology/technology-trends-2024> accessed April 21, 2025.

[65] ibid.

[66] For regulatory or oversight reasons, human failsafes may be built into the system, such as through mandatory Know Your Customer (KYC) verification, technical "proof of humanity" mechanisms, or hard-coded backdoors assigned to humans. Distinguishing humans from artificial agents is an important task in an AI era, which a number of blockchain-based projects are seeking to address. Paula Berman and Divvya Siddarth, "An Internet for Humans: Proof-of-Personhood Explained" (*Coindesk*, October 27, 2020) <https://www.coindesk.com/tech/2020/10/27/an-internet-for-humans-proof-of-personhood-explained/> accessed April 21, 2025; RT Watson, "How Blockchain Can Help Solve Proof of Personhood" (*The Block*, December 26, 2023) <https://www.theblock.co/post/268446/how-blockchain-can-help-solve-proof-of-personhood> accessed April 21, 2025; Andrew R Chow, "How Blockchain Could Solve the Problem of Digital Identity" (*Time*, January 28, 2022) <https://time.com/6142810/proof-of-humanity/> accessed April 21, 2025; Andrew R Chow, "What to Know About Worldcoin and the Controversy Around It" (*Time*, August 3, 2023) <https://time.com/6300522/worldcoin-sam-altman/> accessed April 21, 2025.

Vitalik Buterin's original vision of DAOs described the "dream of science fiction"[67] of fully autonomous agents, what we would today call artificial general intelligence (AGI), as the building blocks for the "holy grail" of AI DAOs. Primavera de Filippi and Aaron Wright, in their early work on blockchain and law, similarly envisioned autonomous DAO agents controlled purely through software, not human oversight.[68] We may now be at the point where it is feasible to realize that vision at scale. But should we? Along with the potential of AI DAOs comes, as with other AI activity, very serious risks. Whereas corporate law is primarily about protecting those associated with the firm, such as its investors, managers, and other stakeholders, AI regulation is increasingly oriented toward risks to third parties.[69]

3. The Question of Autonomy

The connection point between AI regulation and DAO governance is the concept of autonomy. Autonomy refers to an entity's capacity for self-determination. In the context of technological forms of persuasion that threaten autonomy, it has been described as "the capacity to make one's own choices, with respect to both existential and everyday decisions."[70] Autonomy is a foundation of both fundamental rights and attribution of responsibility for actions. The dynamics of autonomy for AI, DAOs, and corporations highlight the emerging legal questions as DAOs and AI converge.

3.1. Autonomy for AI and Corporations

AI models are capable of making complex decisions independent of direct human oversight, taking actions in the world, and controlling other systems. Autonomous AI agents, however, raise two broad classes of issues. First, they may act in ways not aligned with the desires of their human creators.[71] Second, they may be held morally or legally responsible for their actions.[72] These issues have been at the forefront of debates over AI safety for advanced AI models, and the bounds of AI regulation around the world. As DAOs incorporate more AI functionality, the degree of autonomy will prove a central question for legal considerations.

In the corporate context, the question of autonomy is complicated by controversy over the nature of the corporate entity. A thing might be autonomous; a group or an idea will never be. Corporations can be viewed as collective entities, established either

[67] Buterin (n 60).

[68] Primavera de Filippi and Aaron Wright, *Blockchain and the Law: The Rule of Code* (Harvard UP 2018) 148.

[69] Margot E Kaminski, "Regulating the Risks of AI" (2023) 103 Boston University Law Review 1347.

[70] Daniel Susser, Beate Roessler, and Helen Nissenbaum, "Online Manipulation: Hidden Influences in a Digital World" (2019) 4 Georgetown Law Technology Review 1, 35.

[71] See n 28.

[72] Ian Ayers and Jack Balkin, "The Law of AI is the Law of Risky Agents without Intentions" (2024) Oxford Business Law Blog, July 10 <https://blogs.law.ox.ac.uk/oblb/blog-post/2024/07/law-ai-law-risky-agents-without-intentions> accessed November 3, 2025; Iria Giuffrida, "Liability for AI Decision-Making: Some Legal and Ethical Considerations" (2019) 88 Fordham Law Review 439.

through private contractual arrangements or a grant of rights from the state to an artificial vehicle. Or they may be considered real entities in their own right.

Under the real entity theory, "the company is a legal entity allowing an organization to act autonomously in law and company law establishes procedures facilitating autonomous organizational decision-making."[73] Whatever answer one gives to the ontological question of what a corporation "is," there is no dispute that corporations are granted legal personhood by the state. This legal status means, among other things, that they can own property, enter into contracts, sue, and be sued. Legal personhood provides corporations with autonomy to operate as independent entities. They can make strategic decisions, invest resources, and pursue business opportunities without direct approval from their shareholders or other individuals. This autonomy is essential for the functioning of a modern corporate entity.

Corporate autonomy, however, comes with a complex web of responsibilities, both at the firm and individual levels. A key function of corporate governance is to manage and sometimes restrain this autonomy to ensure that corporations act ethically, legally, and in the best interests of their stakeholders. Fiduciary duties, for example, do not restrain the autonomy of directors to make their own decisions, but they impose legal obligations on how those directors do so, lest they and their firms be held liable for undesirable consequences.

Regarding AI, traditionally legal responsibility for actions has been attributed to human actors. In the context of AI, determining responsibility becomes more complex. If an AI system operates with high autonomy, questions arise about whether the system itself, its developers, or its operators should be held accountable for its actions.

One of the contentious issues in AI law is whether AI systems can be granted a form of legal personhood, similar to corporations.[74] Legal personhood would allow AI systems to be held accountable for their actions in a manner analogous to humans or corporate entities. However, this concept is controversial and raises numerous philosophical and legal challenges, including the nature of agency, intentionality, and moral responsibility.

In the development of the EU AI Act, the first comprehensive AI regulatory framework, autonomy was originally an essential element in the definition of AI systems subject to the Act. In the final text, however, this requirement was removed. AI systems were defined, following the OECD, as inference engines, with responsibility tied to risk rather than degree of autonomy.[75] Similarly, US frameworks such as the Biden administration's AI Executive Order frequently refer to "automated" decision-making, which is a step below autonomous.[76]

[73] Micheler (n 56).

[74] Lawrence B Solum, "Legal Personhood for Artificial Intelligences" (1992) 70 North Carolina Law Review 1231; Eliza Mik, "AI as a Legal Person?" in Reto Hilty and Kung-Chung Liu (eds), *Artificial Intelligence & Intellectual Property* (OUP 2020); Carla Reyes, "Autonomous Corporate Personhood" (2021) 96 Washington Law Review 1453.

[75] The OECD definition specifies that, "Different AI systems vary in their levels of autonomy and adaptiveness." "Explanatory Memorandum on the Updated OECD Definition of an AI System" (2024) OECD Artificial Intelligence Papers No 8 <https://doi.org/10.1787/623da898-en> accessed April 21, 2025.

[76] The White House, "Executive Order on the Safe, Secure, and Trustworthy Development and Use of Artificial Intelligence" (30 October 2023). Although the Executive Order provides a definition of artificial intelligence, many of the substantive provisions cover "automated or algorithmic systems," including AI as a subset.

3.2. Autonomy and DAOs

"Autonomous" is the middle term in the acronym "DAO." Yet virtually no DAOs in operation today are autonomous in any real sense.[77] Even when DAOs are operationally decentralized, in that no individual actor can control their functionality, their freedom of action is highly constrained. The smart contracts controlled through DAO governance votes may be able to change particular parameters of a decentralized application or direct funds to certain accounts, but only in limited ways and only at the explicit direction of the DAO's token-holders. Prominent DAO advocates, such as Aaron Wright, highlight the potential benefits of DAOs for improving human coordination and management of organizations, not for replacing the humans entirely.[78]

DAOs are also not immune from the autonomy constraints of the legal system, as described throughout this volume, whether through explicit embodiment in an established corporate legal wrapper or through *de facto* determinations by courts or regulators.

Some point out that DAOs can have a range of autonomy.[79] Wright, for example, describes "algorithmic" DAOs, which "defer entirely to software to structure and coordinate social interactions,[80] as contrasted with "participatory" DAOs controlled by humans. However, his algorithmic category mainly encompasses base-layer blockchains such as Bitcoin and Ethereum, which are DAOs in a conceptual sense but quite different from the purpose-built entities usually considered. These algorithmic DAOs generally achieve their autonomy from human overseers by limiting the autonomy of their code. The Bitcoin software, for example, is designed to be absolutely reliable and predictable in its actions. In contrast to the traditional financial system of commercial and central banks, Bitcoin is entirely autonomous from human managers. Yet in other ways it is radically non-autonomous. If something goes wrong, the system has no capacity to alter its behavior.

A similar lack of flexibility was the root of the infamous controversy in 2016 over The DAO, the Ethereum-based crowdfunding platform that was successfully exploited by a hacker who took advantage of a smart contract bug to drain funds.[81] Because The DAO had no means of autonomously responding to the exploit, the only

[77] Ann-Sofie Cloots, "Decentralised Finance, Decentralised Organisations and the Future of the Firm" in Christopher M Bruner and Marc Moore (eds), *A Research Agenda for Corporate Law* (Edward Elgar 2023); Kevin Tai, "DAOs Are Meant to Be Completely Autonomous and Decentralized, but Are They?" (*CoinTelegraph*, February 5, 2022) <https://cointelegraph.com/news/daos-are-meant-to-be-completely-autonomous-and-decentralized-but-are-they> accessed April 21, 2025.

[78] Wright (n 33).

[79] Nathan Tse, "Decentralized Autonomous Organizations and the Corporate Form" (2020) 51 Victoria University of Wellington Law Review 313, 320. For an effort to map the autonomy levels of different DAOs, Steven A Wright, "Measuring DAO Autonomy: Lessons From Other Autonomous Systems" (2021) 2(1) IEEE Transactions on Technology and Society 43.

[80] Wright (n 33) 6.

[81] Kint Finley, "A $50 Million Hack Just Showed that the DAO Was All Too Human" (*Wired*, June 18, 2016) <https://www.wired.com/2016/06/50-million-hack-just-showed-dao-human/> accessed April 21, 2025; Robbie Morrison, Natasha CHL Mazey, and Stephen C Wingreen, "The DAO Controversy: The Case for a New Species of Corporate Governance?" (2020) 3 Frontiers in Blockchain 25; Quinn DuPont, "Experiments in Algorithmic Governance" in Malcolm Campbell-Verduyn (ed), *Bitcoin and Beyond* (Routledge 2017) 157.

options were to allow the thief to succeed (taking a substantial percentage of all the Ether in circulation at the time) or to fork the entire Ethereum blockchain with an upgrade that reversed the transaction.

The convergence of AI and DAOs would make possible DAOs that are more substantially autonomous, both from their human operators and from the legal system. If AI agents are holding the tokens involved in DAO governance votes, their actions will be implemented by the smart contracts of the DAO without human involvement. And if the DAO is given significant flexibility in its scope of action, it starts to resemble Vitalik Buterin's original "dream of science fiction."[82]

4. Governing Autonomous DAOs

4.1. DAO Legal Responsibility

DAOs today are subject to legal responsibility under normal principles of corporate law. If the DAO has a legal wrapper such as a Delaware limited liability company (LLC) or a Caymans Foundation, that structure forms the entity entitled to personhood and therefore the subject of legal obligations.[83] If the DAO is wrapperless, courts may still impose a legal form, such as a general partnership, and treat the DAO as a legally responsible entity that way.[84] These scenarios today, however, involve human-controlled DAOs. When DAO participants make the relevant decisions, either directly or mediated through explicit token votes, saying that the DAO engaged in some harmful act is no different than making the same statement about a conventional corporation. In both cases, it is possible to imagine imposing liability on either the entity itself, the human decision-makers personally, or both. The question becomes murkier as more of the autonomous decision-making behind the challenged action is the work of AI.

In AI regulation, there is generally an effort to identify responsible human parties, even when the AI systems they build or deploy act with autonomy.[85] Thus, if a corporation implements an AI system for hiring which violates antidiscrimination laws, the fact that the AI acted independently of its human overseers is immaterial: The firm is legally responsible. In fact, AI legal frameworks, such as the EU AI Act, are to a large extent designed to concretize the obligations of such AI developers and deployers. They have specified obligations, such as being subject to a conformity review for high-risk systems, conducting audits, and providing disclosures. Even if liability under

[82] Buterin (n 60).

[83] Christopher J Brummer and Rodrigo Seira, "Legal Wrappers and DAOs" (*SSRN*, May 30, 2022) <http://dx.doi.org/10.2139/ssrn.4123737> accessed April 21, 2025; Wright (n 33); Gogel and others (n 33).

[84] Brummer and Seira (n 83); Sam Reynolds, "The Liability of DAOs and Their Founders Has Been Put to the Test in Court" (*Coindesk*, March 29, 2023) <https://www.coindesk.com/business/2023/03/29/the-liability-of-daos-and-their-founders-has-been-put-to-the-test-in-court/> accessed April 21, 2025; Carla Reyes, "If Rockefeller Were a Coder" (2019) 87 George Washington Law Review 373.

[85] Even when not mandated by law, attribution of responsibility to humans is common as what Elish calls a "moral crumple zone." Madeleine Clare Elish, "Moral Crumple Zones: Cautionary Tales in Human-Robot Interaction" (2019) 5 Engaging Science, Technology, and Society 40.

private law is uncertain, such regulations ensure there are legal obligations flowing back to the humans.

The liability question becomes more difficult in the case of generative AI foundation models. These models, such as OpenAI's GPT-4o and Google's Gemini, are pretrained on structures such as human language, but not limited to a specific function. Instead, they are provided either directly to users or indirectly through application programming interfaces to respond to queries. The Foundation model developers do not know or control all the ways their customers (or *their* customers) will use the system. Therefore, they argue strenuously that they should not be legally liable when things go wrong. This dispute nearly undermined the passage of the EU AI Act at the last minute, until a compromise was struck to impose mainly limited transparency duties on all but the most powerful foundation models.[86]

Today's DAOs are not like generative AI foundation models, in that they are generally designed for a particular purpose. A decentralized finance (DeFi) DAO might be subject to financial regulation, while a DAO for allocating work to freelancers might be subject to employment law, because those involved in setting up the DAO would have appropriate notice of the relevant legal regime. A more autonomous, AI-driven DAO would likely still be established with similar limitations. On the other hand, if generative AI models control DAO tokens and engage in voting, their decision-making would not necessarily be so constrained.

As a practical matter, attributing moral or legal responsibility solely to the DAO raises significant challenges. Unlike corporations, which have human directors and executives who can be held accountable, DAOs operate through decentralized, often anonymous, networks of participants. Identifying responsible parties within a DAO can be difficult, as decision-making is distributed among token-holders and executed through smart contracts. This decentralization complicates the assignment of individual liability and raises questions about the effectiveness of holding the DAO itself accountable.

In corporate criminal law, doctrines such as "failure to prevent" have been created to assign liability to organizations even when there is no specific culpable actor.[87] These are controversial, however, and the UK Law Commission recommended against expansion of failure to prevent broadly to economic crimes.[88] Moreover, for DAOs there is not only no identifiably responsible actor, there may be no identifiable actors who might have taken steps to prevent the harm. If an action is brought against the DAO itself, consequences would require the human actors with collective control over the DAO's multi-signature wallets (potentially all DAO governance token-holders through their voting power) to take affirmative steps to satisfy the judgment.

[86] Tate Ryan-Mosley, "Why the EU AI Act was so Hard to Agree On" (*Technology Review*, December 11, 2023) <https://www.technologyreview.com/2023/12/11/1084849/why-the-eu-ai-act-was-so-hard-to-agree-on/> accessed April 21, 2025; Emilia David, "EU May Fail to Pass Its AI Act in 2023" (*The Verge*, October 23, 2023) <https://www.theverge.com/2023/10/23/23929273/eu-ai-act-generative-regulation-models> accessed April 21, 2025.

[87] Failure to prevent was first established in the UK in the Bribery Act 2010. Liz Campbell, "Corporate Liability and the Criminalisation of Failure" (2018) 12(2) Law and Financial Markets Review 57.

[88] Law Commission, "Corporate Criminal Liability: An Options Paper" (Law Com No 195, 2022).

Morally, the concept of DAO responsibility hinges on the idea that entities capable of autonomous decision-making should be accountable for their actions. If a DAO operates with a high degree of autonomy, making decisions and executing transactions without direct human intervention, it could be argued that the DAO bears some moral responsibility for its actions. However, this perspective challenges traditional notions of moral agency, which typically require intentionality and the capacity for moral reasoning—attributes that DAOs, as algorithmic entities, lack.

4.2. Regulation for Autonomous Harms

A related question is whether the potential for harm from autonomous DAOs calls for prophylactic regulation. In addition to corporate governance obligations, corporations are subject to various forms of regulation based on their activities. In the US, a toy company must adhere to product safety regulations of the Consumer Product Safety Commission; a bank is subject to supervision to ensure safety and soundness by the Comptroller of the Currency, Federal Reserve, and other banking agencies; a mobile phone carrier is subject to telecommunications regulation by the Federal Communications Commission. These regulatory structures, however, generally assume that prescriptive rules and post hoc enforcement are sufficient to mitigate risks. Autonomous systems pose greater challenges.

Consider, for example, autonomous weapons systems.[89] Nations are developing technologies that put AI systems in control of drones and other weapons.[90] The potential military benefits are considerable.[91] In the "fog of war," relying on human commanders to make decisions about whether to take out an enemy, or even which enemies to target, may limit effectiveness significantly. A drone with a facial recognition camera that detects a known terrorist may have only a short time window in which to act.

On the other hand, autonomous weapons raise very serious concerns. Should we defer life-and-death judgments to AI systems? Will those systems truly align with the choices human commanders would make? Will autonomous weapons lower ethical standards in the conduct of war and other hostilities, by divorcing humans from the decision to kill? And what if the system malfunctions, either due to a flaw or an external attack—can there be an effective "kill switch" to prevent friendly fire? These questions have led to a variety of debates and attempts, so far unsuccessful, to address autonomous weapons systems through international law.[92]

[89] Nehal Bhuta, Susanne Beck, and Hin-Yan Liu (eds), *Autonomous Weapons Systems: Law, Ethics, Policy* (CUP 2016); Armin Krishnan, *Killer Robots: Legality and Ethicality of Autonomous Weapons* (Routledge 2016); Kai Fu Lee, "The Third Revolution in Warfare" (*The Atlantic*, September 11, 2021) <https://www.theatlantic.com/technology/archive/2021/09/i-weapons-are-third-revolution-warfare/620013/> accessed April 21, 2025.

[90] David Adam, "Lethal AI Weapons Are Here: How Can We Control Them?" (*Nature*, April 23, 2024) <https://www.nature.com/articles/d41586-024-01029-0> accessed April 21, 2025.

[91] For a more detailed overview of potential benefit and drawbacks of autonomous weapons, Amitai Etzioni and Oren Etzioni, "Pros and Cons of Autonomous Weapons Systems" (2017) (May–June) Military Review 27.

[92] Ingvild Bode and others, "Prospects for the Global Governance of Autonomous Weapons: Comparing Chinese, Russian, and US Practices" (2023) 25 Ethics & Information Technology 5.

Autonomous DAOs raise similar questions. Because DAOs can directly control financial resources in the form of the tokens in their treasuries, and can even to some extent control humans by incentivizing them to take certain actions, they could effectively provide a real-world offramp for AI agents.[93] More concerning, the AI systems involved need not be superintelligent to create significant risks.[94] A DAO provides a kind of force multiplier to the value and dangers of AI agents, even with today's technology. An AI system could engage in a phishing attack to obtain bank account credentials and use them to steal funds, but the damage could be mitigated by the existence of centralized human controls. With a DAO, the assets are all fully digital and on-chain, with no human capable of stopping or reversing transactions on the blockchain. Thus, it may be necessary to consider some of the more serious regulatory impositions being proposed for frontier AI models, such as mandatory kill switches, extensive disclosure, private legal liability, or pre-deployment licensing, for autonomous DAOs. Such mandates are controversial in the AI context, because of their potential to restrain innovation, especially for open source models.[95]

So far, AI regulatory efforts have become hung up on the proper definition of autonomy. The question is at what point a system is sufficiently automated. For example, the EU's GDPR has requirements for "fully-automated processing" to make important decisions based on personal data.[96] Although this provision seems quite significant, in practice it has had limited impact. One reason is that companies tend to argue their determinations, though informed by algorithms, are not fully automated. Similarly, analysis of New York City Local Law 144, which mandates that firms publish bias audits for algorithmic hiring, shows that few companies actually do so, because they take the position the hiring is not entirely done by the algorithm.[97]

[93] Vitalik Buterin acknowledged that a significant inspiration for his invention of the DAO concept was the 2006 novel *Daemon* by Daniel Suarez, which envisioned an autonomous program created by a dying software genius, which ultimately restructured society by incentivizing various activities among the humans it recruited to act on its behalf. Buterin (n 60).

[94] Thus, autonomous AI DAO risks are not the same as the "superalignment" problem that frontier AI developers such as OpenAI and Anthropic are focused on, which is that AI systems smarter than humans may seek to achieve their own goals, rather than acting in the interests of humanity. Nick Bostrom, *Superintelligence* (OUP 2014); Eliza Strickland, "OpenAI's Moonshot: Solving the AI Alignment Problem" (*IEEE Spectrum*, August 31, 2023) <https://spectrum.ieee.org/the-alignment-problem-openai> accessed April 21, 2025; Cade Metz, "OpenAI Co-Founder, Who Helped Oust Sam Altman, Starts His Own Company" (*New York Times*, June 19, 2024) <https://www.nytimes.com/2024/06/19/technology/ilya-sutskever-openai-safe-superintelligence.html> accessed April 21, 2025.

[95] Kelsey Piper, "The AI Bill that Has Big Tech Panicked" (*Vox*, June 14, 2024) <https://www.vox.com/future-perfect/355212/ai-artificial-intelligence-1047-bill-safety-liability> accessed April 21, 2025; Gabriel Weil, "The Pros and Cons of California's Proposed SB-1047 AI Safety Law" (*Lawfare*, May 8, 2024) <https://www.lawfaremedia.org/article/california-s-proposed-sb-1047-would-be-a-major-step-forward-for-ai-safety-but-there-s-still-room-for-improvement> accessed April 21, 2025.

[96] Regulation (EU) 2016/679, of the European Parliament and the Council of 27 April 2016 on the protection of natural persons with regard to the processing of personal data and on the free movement of such data, and repealing Directive 95/46/EC (General Data Protection Regulation) [2016] OJ L119, Art 22.

[97] Lucas Wright and others, "Null Compliance: NYC Local Law 144 and the Challenges of Algorithm Accountability" (*FAccT '24*, 2024) <https://dl.acm.org/doi/10.1145/3630106.3658998> accessed April 21, 2025; Lauren Weber, "New York City Passed an AI Hiring Law. So Far, Few Companies Are Following It." (*Wall Street Journal*, January 22, 2024) <https://www.wsj.com/business/new-york-city-passed-an-ai-hiring-law-so-far-few-companies-are-following-it-7e31a5b7> accessed April 21, 2025.

4.3. Humans in the Loop

One common response to concerns about AI-driven systems is to mandate human oversight at critical points—a technique referred to as "humans in the loop."[98] Dozens of government policies already require human involvement or oversight of algorithmic decisions.[99] As Rebecca Crootof, Margot Kaminski, and Nicholson Price point out, however, these efforts often fail to address the problems with machine-based decisions, or even make them worse. Humans and machines each do certain things better than the other, and human superiority is highly contextual for the application. An autonomous vehicle transferring control to a human driver shortly before an accident may give the human insufficient time to act to prevent an accident, for example. And when humans are placed in the loop, they may serve many different functions, ranging from preventing or correcting errors, to increasing legitimacy, to establishing a point of accountability, to introducing deliberate friction to improve decision-making. Requirements for human involvement must therefore specify with some precision what goals are to be served, and must consider carefully where the humans really add value.

Humans in the loop is an important element of the corporate law and governance regime. Internally, fiduciary duties and similar concepts mean that boards and officers are potentially legally responsible individuals for the actions of the firm. Externally, public companies are subject to regulated financial audits, which in practice brings in additional humans to review and certify financial statements. And legal requirements such as the Sarbanes-Oxley mandate that CEOs and CFOs personally attest to financial statements place humans even more directly on the hook.

There are, moreover, downsides to putting humans in the loop. The more decisions need to wait on explicit human involvement, the less the system can benefit from the speed and efficiency of automated algorithmic decision-making. Moreover, research shows that human oversight of machine decisions can actually worsen problems such as bias, because human determinations about when to overrule the machine, or to rely on it to begin with, are themselves biased.[100]

In the DAO context, there may also be regulatory implications. The arguments that DAOs should not be subject to obligations of financial regulation usually assert that DAOs are decentralized environments, not human-controlled transactional platforms analogous to regulated exchanges and other service providers. In its post-mortem determination that The DAO was an unregulated securities exchange, the Securities and Exchange Commission (SEC) highlighted the significant roles of human curators and

[98] Rebecca Crootof, Margot E Kaminski, and W Nicholson Price, "Humans in the Loop" (2023) 76 Vanderbilt Law Review 429.

[99] Ben Green, "The Flaws of Policies Requiring Human Oversight of Government Algorithms" (2022) 45 Computer Law & Security Review 9–14.

[100] Ben Green and Yiling Chen, "Disparate Interactions: An Algorithm-in-the-Loop Analysis of Fairness in Risk Assessments" (Proceedings of FaCCT 2018) 90–99; Sandra Mayson, "Bias in, Bias Out" (2018) 128 Yale Law Journal 2218; Green (n 99); Saar Alon-Barkat and Madalina Busuioc, "Human–AI Interactions in Public Sector Decision Making: "Automation Bias" and "Selective Adherence" to Algorithmic Advice" (2023) 33 Journal of Public Administration Research & Theory 153; Diag Davenport, "Discriminatory Discretion: Theory and Evidence From Use of Pretrial Algorithms" (*SSRN*, September 22, 2023) <http://dx.doi.org/10.2139/ssrn.4580390> accessed April 21, 2025.

developers in the operation of the system.[101] Even if human oversight of AI DAOs is normatively desirable, therefore, it might not be a viable approach for DAO communities without changes to the legal environment.

Nonetheless, DAOs may provide an effective vehicle for more effective humans-in-the-loop obligations. DAOs are, by their nature, mechanisms for human collective action. Even when designed to operate autonomously, there is still an opportunity to structure the DAO with strategic interventions by humans in the loop. Figuring out what such mechanisms should look like, and how they might be incorporated into either corporate structures or regulatory oversight of DAOs, will be an important challenge as AI and DAOs develop.

5. Conclusion

The growing connections between AI and DAOs will call for new regulatory approaches that draw on corporate law and governance, on the one hand, and the emerging world of AI regulation, on the other. DAOs could also, though, prove extremely valuable as a means of addressing important concerns about AI, by establishing robust mechanisms for data provenance and alternatives to relentless consolidation.

Both DAOs and AI push on our traditional concept of a corporation by potentially replacing humans with machines. The pace and extent to which AI enhances DAOs, DAOs enhance AI, and autonomous AI DAOs take off remain to be seen. Even if DAOs never grow beyond the DeFi applications and collective investment vehicles which are substantial today, or fizzle out entirely as a concept, they will provide an environment for experimentation with both the governance mechanisms and legal considerations that will have growing stakes as AI development continues. Understanding the appropriate scope of autonomy will be essential to address the challenges that will arise.

101 Securities and Exchange Commission, Securities Exchange Act of 1934, Report of Investigation Pursuant to Section 21(a) of the Securities Exchange Act of 1934: The DAO, Release No 81207 (25 July 2017).

Index

For the benefit of digital users, indexed terms that span two pages (e.g., 52–53) may, on occasion, appear on only one of those pages.

A

Aberdeen Railway Co v Blaikie Bros, 54
Accountability
  algorithmic hiring audits, 322
  challenges in DAOs, 69, 71, 201
  code of conduct enforcement, 202
  fiduciary duties and, 91–92
  role of legal wrappers, 276–77
  via humans in the loop, 323–24
  via reputation systems, 208
Accreditation authority, 15–16, 25
Adams, Hayden, 132
Administrative decentralization, 116
Affordances, 264–66
  DLT as techno-legal substrate, 271–73
  legal vs. technical, 278*t*
  tokenization as, 272–73
Agency costs, 69–70, 125–26, 137, 187, 234
  reduction via DAOs, 61, 69–70, 125–26
  in traditional corporations, 66–67
Agency law, 282–83
Agents (AI)
  convergence with DAOs, 313–14
  definition and capabilities, 314–15
  legal responsibility, 319–20
Agreements on jurisdiction. *See* Choice of court agreements
Airdrops, 68, 136
  governance distribution, 133
  Optimism (OP token), 136
  regulatory implications, 229–30
  Shapeshift (FOX token), 131
  Uniswap (UNI token), 133
Algorithmic entities, 288, 321
Algorithmic governance, 163–64
  challenges of, 243
  experiments in, 138
  limitations of, 298
Alignment problem (AI), 309–10
Alternative dispute resolution (ADR), 25–26, 208
  on-chain arbitration, 251
  DAO-specific mechanisms, 204–8
  Kleros, 205
Alternative venture capital (AVC), 217
Amazon Mechanical Turk, 277–78
Anarcho-capitalists, 106, 107–8
  decentralization and, 114
  influence on DAOs, 145
Andreessen Horowitz (a16z), 93, 132–33, 228–29
Anonymity. *See* Pseudonymity
Anthropic, 309–10
Anti-money laundering (AML), 221
  DeFi compliance, 248–49
  regulatory risks, 25
Antitrust issues, 238
Appraisal rights, 73
Aragon DAO
  on-chain courts, 251
  dispute with Aragon Association, 195–96
Arbitration
  arbitrability of corporate disputes, 205
  on-chain protocols, 204–7
  corporate statutes (Switzerland), 179–80
  enforceability of awards, 202
  Immunefi rules, 206–7
  Kleros, 202, 205
  London Chamber of Arbitration and Mediation (LCAM), 206–7
  writing requirement, 206
Artificial intelligence (AI)
  agents, 314–16
  alignment problem, 310
  controlling DAOs, 311–13
  convergence with DAOs, 313–14
  foundation models, 306, 319–20
  generative, 306
  governance of, 308–10
  human oversight (human-in-the-loop), 323–24
  legal personhood, 317
  legal responsibility, 319–21
  regulation of, 309–10, 321–22
Asset partitioning, 150–51, 282
Assets
  in bankruptcy estates, 150–51
  custodial rights, 254–55
  digital, nature of, 2
  off-chain, 186–87, 190, 199–200, 299, 300
  real-world assets (RWA), 300
  tokenization of, 227–28

Audits
algorithmic bias, 322
code, 221, 250
financial, 323
smart contract, 24, 250
Authority
centralized, 69
conflicts in DAOs, 196–97
legal vs. algorithmic, 298
Automation, 148–50, 287
governance and, 67–68
limits of, 293–94
transaction costs and, 117
Autonomous weapons systems, 321
Autonomy, 109–13, 316–19
algorithmic DAOs, 318
corporate, 316–17
definition in AI context, 322
ideological, 109–10
legal vs. technical, 297–98
smart contracts, 110–13
Avoidance actions (bankruptcy), 157–58
fraudulent transfers, 158
immutability conflict, 157–58
preferences, 158

B
Balancer, 241, 250
Bankless DAO, 146
Bankruptcy, 143
automatic stay, 153
avoidance powers, 157–58
creditors, 151–53
disclosure requirements, 156–57
eligibility of DAOs, 154
governance during, 155–56
involuntary, 160–61
liquidation (Chapter 7), 150, 155
petition filing authority, 155
policy implications, 159
reorganization (Chapter 11), 150, 155
trustees, 155–56
Barlow, John Perry, 107
Base organizations run by governance (BORGs), 276–77
Bean, Tom, 90
Beliefs, community, 103–4, 106
Benkler, Yochai, 262–63
Big Green DAO, 228–29
Bitcoin
as algorithmic DAO, 4, 285–86, 318
core developers, 84–85
developers as fiduciaries, 84–88
genesis of, 1
overflow bug, 286
white paper, 84
BitDAO, 148–49
BitLicense (New York), 128
Black Thursday (MakerDAO), 193–94, 242–43, 254
Blockchain-based limited liability companies (BBLLCs), 18–19
Blockchain in name only (BLINO), 295–96
Blockchains
affordances of, 271–73
consensus protocols, 286
governance codes, 250
immutability, 157–58, 286
layer 2 networks, 134
permissionless vs. permissioned, 288
record-keeping, 66
security limitations, 286–87
scalability, 233
Board of directors
absence in DAOs, 68, 191
fiduciary duties, 54
Brussels I Regulation, 172, 173, 176
exclusive jurisdiction, 205
Bubble Act of 1720, 48
Bugs. *See* Smart contracts, bugs
Build Finance DAO, 290
Business judgment rule, 66
Buterin, Vitalik, 2, 109, 125, 131, 132, 187, 312–13, 314, 315
bZx DAO
bankruptcy implications, 152
CFTC enforcement action, 90–92
governance disputes, 201
hacking incident, 243
legal classification, 168

C
California Corporate Code, 91
Capital lock-in, 46
smart contracts and, 51–52
Cayman Islands foundation companies, 21–22
Centralization
risks of, 240
trends in governance, 71
Centralized Autonomous Organization (CAO), 125
CFTC v Ooki DAO, 13–14, 79, 90, 152, 202, 207
Chainalysis, 248–49, 289
ChatGPT, 306, 310, 311–12
Choice of court agreements
DAO-related disputes, 178–82
disputes with third parties, 176–78
effects on courts, 173–74
exclusive vs. non-exclusive, 172–73
formal validity, 172, 175
internal disputes, 174–76
validity requirements, 171–73
Choice of law rules, 177, 301
Christensen, Rune, 71, 312–13

Civil law partnerships, 24, 167, 174–75
ClimateGPT, 309
COALA DAO Model Law. *See* DAO Model Law (COALA)
Coase, Ronald, 101, 123–24, 260, 302–3
Code as law, 45–46, 193, 269, 275, 298
  challenges to, 193
Code audits, 221, 250
Code of conduct, 250
Coding errors. *See* Smart contracts, bugs
Collective investment
  challenges, 220
  crowdfunding comparison, 217–18
  democratization of, 218–19
  investor protection, 221
  technological risks, 232–33
Colony, 111, 208
Commodity Exchange Act of 1936, 13–14, 90–91
Commodity Futures Trading Commission (CFTC)
  enforcement actions, 208
  Ooki DAO case, 13–14, 90, 200
Common pool resources, 102–3
  corporation as, 103
  Ostrom's principles, 102
Community building, 111
Companies Act of 1862 (UK), 50, 261–62
Companies Act of 2006 (UK), 79, 274
Compliance, automated, 276, 280
Compound, 149, 241
Conflict of laws, 169–70
  connecting factors, 169–70
Conflicts of interest, 71, 79–80
  DeFi applications, 240
  disclosure, 251–52
Consensus mechanisms, 271–72
  holographic consensus, 146
Constitution DAO, 62, 135, 186–87
Consumer protection, 255–56
Contract law, role in DAOs, 45, 282
  incomplete contracts, 250
Contracts
  legal capacity of DAOs, 176
  smart (*see* Smart contracts)
Coordination
  costs, 238
  social and economic, 260–62
Corporate form
  bankruptcy eligibility and, 147
  evolution of, 261–62
  spectrum of digital organizations, 274–79
Corporate governance, 65–69, 82, 127, 276, 282–83, 317
Corporate personhood, 62–63, 317
  digital entities, 281
Corporate Transparency Act (US), 39–40
Corporations
  as artificial persons, 313
  history of, 47–52
  self-driving, 297–98
Creditors, in DAO bankruptcy, 151–53
  government creditors, 152
  lenders, 151
  token-holders as, 151
  tort claimants, 152
  trade creditors, 151–52
Cross-chain bridges, 230–31
Crowdfunding, 114, 217–18, 229–30
  regulation of, 218
Crypto-anarchy, 106, 145
Crypto-arbitration, 205
Crypto-asset Service Providers (CASPs)
  authorization in the European Union, 246–47
  prudential regulation, 253
Crypto-secession, 114
Curve DAO, 68, 146, 207
Custodial rights, 254–55
Cyberhacks. *See* Hacks and exploits
Cypherpunks, 106–7, 145

D
DAO Model Law (COALA), 15–16, 96–98
  privacy provisions, 203–4
Decentraland, 114–15
Decentralization, 114–17
  administrative, 116
  as aspiration, 115
  degrees of, 148–50
  dimensions of, 116
  financial, 116
  illusion of, 288
  misleading nature of term, 286
  political, 116
  progressive, 184–85
Decentralized applications (dApps), 1–2, 235–36
Decentralized autonomous corporations (DACs), 2, 275
Decentralized Autonomous Organizations (DAOs)
  as adaptive governance engines, 137–40
  as AI agents, 315
  algorithmic vs. participatory, 67–68, 318
  autonomous, 318–19
  constitutions, 113, 250
  definitions, 14, 61, 125–26, 285–86, 318
  evolution of, 127–37
  as general partnerships, 17, 77–78, 94, 147
  hybrid forms, 275–77
  legal forms, 13–26
  origins, 2
  pure, 94–95, 168, 274
  purpose, 3, 105
  as social organizations, 165–68

Decentralized exchanges (DEXs), 128, 238
Decentralized finance (DeFi), 8, 236
  authorization, 246–47
  governance limits, 239–45
  hacks, 243
  interdependencies, 244
  regulation of, 245–56
  risks, 238
Decision-making. *See* Governance
Declaration of Independence of Cyberspace, 107
Deed of settlement companies, 47, 48
Delaware General Corporation Law, 80
Delegated voting, 192, 241, 272–73
Democratization of finance, 51–52, 218–19
Design principles (Ostrom), 102, 120
Developers
  as fiduciaries, 84–89
  legal responsibility, 319–20
  role in DAOs, 115–16
DFinity Foundation, 310
Digital assets
  in bankruptcy, 150–51
  definition, 2
  property rights, 281
Digital legal entities, 278*t*
Digital nomads, 114–15
Digital Operational Resilience Act (DORA) (EU), 248
Digital organizations (DOs)
  affordances, 278*t*
  concept, 259–84
  spectrum of, 274–79
Digital signatures, 28–29
Directors
  duties, 79–80
  liability, 54
Disclosure
  bankruptcy requirements, 156–57
  conflicts of interest, 251–53
  mandatory, 64–65
  smart contract parameters, 15–16
Dispute resolution
  arbitration, 205–7
  challenges, 200–2
  external disputes, 199–200
  hurdles, 200–2
  internal disputes, 191–98
  mechanisms, 163–64, 204–8, 250–51
  on-chain vs. off-chain, 204–8
  spectrum of, 204–8
Distributed ledger technology (DLT). *See* Blockchain
Dolphin CL, LLC, 198
Domicile, legal, 25–26, 169
dOrg, 68
Double-spending problem, 30, 186
DUNA (Decentralized Unincorporated Nonprofit Association), 20
dYdX trust, 22–23

E
Eisenberg, Avraham, 289
Emergency DAOs, 207–8
Employees, DAO contributors as, 68
Enforcement
  of judgments, 182–83
  smart contract automation, 111
ENS (Ethereum Name Service), 146, 199–200
  eth.link dispute, 199
  legal wrapper (ENS Labs), 200
Entity status. *See* Legal personality
Ethereum, 2, 285–86
  hard fork, 294–95
  The DAO hack, 45–46, 193, 288–89
Ethereum Classic, 2
Ethereum Name Service (ENS), 199–200
European Banking Authority (EBA), 245–46
European Securities and Markets Authority (ESMA), 245–46
European Union
  AI Act, 309–10, 318
  GDPR, 308–9, 322
  MiCA Regulation (*see* Markets in Crypto-Assets Regulation)
Exchange Act of 1934 (US), 64–65
Exit rights, 112
  rage quit, 194–95, 204
Extropians, 107

F
Fei Protocol, 193–94
FICO, 308
Fiduciary duties, 71–74, 77–78
  academic debate, 81–84
  breach of, 80–81
  developers, 84–89
  duty of care, 80
  duty of loyalty, 79
  exclusion of, 96–98
  implied covenant of good faith, 74
  opt-in approach, 97
  UK vs US standards, 79–81
Financial distress. *See* Bankruptcy
Financial regulation
  anti-money laundering, 248–49
  authorization, 246–47
  conflicts of interest, 251–53
  consumer protection, 255–56
  prudential regulation, 253
Financial Stability Board (FSB), 244–45

Forks, 15–16, 82, 85, 89, 112, 235, 282, 294–95
as dispute resolution, 204
Nouns DAO, 195, 290–91
Steem fork into Hive, 192–93
Forum selection. *See* Choice of court agreements
Foundation companies (Cayman), 21–22
Foundations (legal wrapper), 135
Fraud, 289
Mango Markets, 289
Freedom of contract, 33–34, 37–38
Fritch, Robin, 115, 191–92
FTX, 9, 144, 154, 254, 305–6

G
General Data Protection Regulation (GDPR), 307–8, 322
General partnerships, 47, 93–94
DAOs as, 24, 83, 93, 147
implied fiduciary duties, 81
liability in, 17, 77–78
Generative AI, 306
Gitcoin, 112, 134–35, 228–29
Giveth, 228–30
GoDaddy, 199
Gogel, David, 115
Governance
adaptive, 137–40
algorithmic, 163–64
bankruptcy and, 155–56
centralized elements, 115–17
conflicts of interest, 251–53
corporate comparison, 66–67
customization, 74–75
decentralized, 239–45
disputes, 191–93
iterative, 136–37
off-chain, 113, 134
on-chain, 113, 133
participation rates, 68–69
polycentric, 98–99
tokens, 2, 42–43, 62, 133, 191
Grantee Accountability Protocol (GAP) DAO, 208
Griffith, Virgil, 199, 200
Guernsey Special Purpose Trust (SPT), 22–23

H
Hacks and exploits, 193–95, 243, 288–91
liability for, 91
restitution via fork, 294–95
Hague Convention on Choice of Court Agreements, 171–74
Hard fork. *See* Forking
Hats Protocol, 196
Hector DAO
bankruptcy of, 144, 150–51, 154
litigation against, 144
High-frequency trading, 293–94
History of corporate law, 46–58
Hive, 146, 193
Human in the loop, 323–24
Hybrid DAOs, 275–77, 296
BORGs, 276–77

I
Immunefi, 206–7
Immutability, 1, 157–58, 286–87, 293–94, 295–96
Incorporation, history of, 49–50
Indiegogo, 218
Information asymmetries, 56–67
Insolvency. *See* Bankruptcy
Institutional economics, 123–27
Internal controls, 248–49, 250
International Chamber of Commerce (ICC), 206
Internet Computer Protocol (ICP), 310
Investment DAOs
challenges, 220–26
comparison with venture capital, 220–25
Isomorphism, legal-technical, 269–71

J
Joint Stock Companies Act of 1844 (UK), 50
Joint stock companies, 47
Jones v Persons Unknown, 292–93
Joystream, 236
Jurisdiction, 164–65
challenges in locating, 168–70
choice of court, 171–74
personal, 77–78

K
Kaal, Wulf A., 115
Kickstarter, 218
Kistner, Kyle, 90
Kleros, 112, 202, 205
Klima DAO, 3
Know Your Customer (KYC), 90–91, 129–30, 201, 221

L
Larimer, Dan, 2, 124–25
Law Commission (UK) DAO Scoping Paper, 88–89, 274–75
Layer 2 networks, 134
Legal capacity, 169, 176–78
Legal personality, 44–45, 62, 178, 263
absence in pure DAOs, 166
digital entities, 281
Legal wrappers, 33, 49, 117, 167, 204, 275–77, 301

Lessig, Lawrence, 265–66, 268–69
LexPunk, 206–7
Liability
failure to prevent, 320
general partners, 77–78
joint and several, 13–14, 17
limited, history of, 50–51
software developers, 84–89
Lido DAO, 92–94, 197–98
class action, 197–98
general partnership classification, 93–94
systemic risks, 244
Limited liability, 44–45
history of, 50–51
Limited Liability Companies (LLCs)
blockchain-based (Vermont), 18–19, 30–31
DAO LLCs (Wyoming/Tennessee), 19, 20, 36
flexibility of, 33–36
operating agreements, 34–36
series LLCs, 38
Liquidation (bankruptcy), 153–54
Liquidation (collateral), 243
Liquidity pools, 132, 239
Lugano Convention, 170–73

M
MakerDAO, 71, 239–40, 312–13
AI governance proposal (Endgame), 312–13
Black Thursday, 194, 242–43
trademark registration, 152
Malicious code, 241
Mango Markets exploit, 289
Manifold Finance, 199
Mantra DAO, 291
Mantra DAO Inc v John Patrick Mullin, 290
Markets in Crypto-Assets Regulation, 53, 246–55
and DAOs, 14
and DeFi, 246
implications for DAOs, 53
Marshall Islands DAO Act, 25–26, 277
May, Timothy C., 107, 145–46
McConaghy, Trent, 314
Membership
rights, 19
token-based, 62
Mergers and acquisitions (M&A), 189
MetaCartel Ventures, 227
Metropolitan Bank v Heiron, 55
MiCA. *See* Markets in Crypto-Assets Regulation
MiCAR. *See* Markets in Crypto-Assets Regulation
Miners, 85, 116, 249–50
Minority protection, 195
Nouns DAO fork, 195–96
Model Law (COALA). *See* DAO Model Law
MolochDAO, 112, 151, 194–95, 205
Mt. Gox, 128–29
Multi-signature (Multisig)
authorization and hierarchy, 116, 187
as investor protection, 221
wallets, 98, 116, 221

N
Natively digital companies, 273–74
externalization model, 280–81
internalization model, 279–80
NEAR Protocol, 311–12
Network effects, 238, 262–63
Network states, 107–8
New institutional economics, 123
New York Convention, 205, 206
Non-fungible tokens (NFTs), 150, 230, 236
Nouns DAO, 195, 291

O
Ocean Protocol, 308–9, 314
Off-chain assets, 300–1
disputes regarding, 199
Ooki DAO, 17, 90–92
CFTC enforcement action, 200, 202, 207
governance disputes, 201
OpenAI, 306
Open source software, 83, 88–89, 106 , –310
Operational regulation, 272
Optimism (DAO), 128*t*, 134–37, 311
bicameral governance, 135
governance minimization, 136
iterative governance, 136–37
mediation mission, 204
Oracles, 163–64, 233
manipulation of, 289
Ostrom, Elinor, 102–5
application of theories to DAOs, 119–20
design principles, 102
Ownership
data, 308–9
digital organizations, 281
separation from control, 66–67, 272–73

P
Parity Wallet, 286
Participatory DAOs, 67–68, 318
Partnership Act of 1890 (UK), 48–49, 81
Partnerships. *See* General partnerships
Permissionless blockchains, 4, 41–42, 286
Philanthropy, DAOs in, 228–30
Plasma Group, 134–35
Platform firms, 278*t*
PleasrDAO, 3, 236–37

Political decentralization, 116
Polushkin, Illia, 311–12
Polycentric governance, 98
Principal-agent problem, 8–9, 54, 253
Privacy, 39, 231
Private international law, 7, 168–70
Proof-of-stake, 244
Proof-of-work, 271–72
Property rights, digital, 281
Prudential regulation, 253
Pseudonymity, 7, 39, 157, 201
  bankruptcy disclosure and, 156–57
Public benefit corporations, 62, 135
Public goods funding, 110, 134–35
Pure DAOs, 278*t*

Q
Q Protocol, 206
Quadratic voting, 70, 146, 192, 228–29, 272–73

R
Rage kick, 205
Rage quit, 112, 161, 194–95, 204, 205
Rari Capital, 193–94
Real DAOS, 297–98
Record-keeping, distributed, 1, 271–72
Regal (Hastings) Ltd v Gulliver, 56
Regulation
  AI, 309–10, 321–22
  by enforcement, 225–26
  financial, 245–56
  prudential, 254
  securities, 64–65, 225–26
Regulatory equivalence, 15, 78, 98–99
Reputation systems, 208
Revised Uniform Limited Liability Company Act (RULLCA), 33
Risk management, 248–50
Rule of law, conflicts with DAOs, 298

S
Samuels v Lido DAO, 92–94, 197–98
Sarcuni v bZx DAO, 93, 94–95
Securities Act of 1933 (US), 77–78
  Section 12 liability, 93–94
Securities and Exchange Commission (SEC)
  DAO Report (2017), 129, 234, 323–24
  public offerings, 64
  Shapeshift settlement, 131
Securities, tokens as, 63–65, 77–78, 225–26
Security councils, 207–8
Self-driving corporations. *See* Corporations, self-driving
Service of process, 157, 201
Shapeshift, 109, 128*t*, 128–32
  membership model, 129–30
  transition to DAO, 131
SingularityNet, 310
Slock.it, 45–46, 124, –49
Smart contracts, 2, 110–13, 285–86
  bugs and exploits, 193–95
  definition, 2, 14
  limitations, 111
  as techno-legal regulation, 272
Snapshot, 113, 134, 163–64, 181, 192
Social organizations, DAOs as, 165–68
Software developers. *See* Developers
South Sea Bubble, 47
Srinavasan, Balaji, 107
Stablecoins, 150, 239–40, 312. *See* also MakerDAO
Staking, 92, 197–98, 244, 272–73
Standardization
  Financial, 67, 231
  governance, 74–75
Steemit, 192–93
Sun, Justin, 192–93
Superusers, 297–99
Sushi DAO, 149
Swiss association, 5, 23–24, 178
  as legal wrapper, 25–26, 167, 178
  suitability for DAOs, 25
Swiss DAO regulation, 23–25
Synchronization problem, 299–300
Synthetify DAO, 290

T
Tapioca DAO, 290–91
Technological neutrality, 28–29, 37
Technology-mediated social structures, 41
Tennes*See* DAO LLC law, 20, 36
Terrorism financing, 77
Tezos, 94
The DAO (2016), 2, 45–46, 63, 68, 91, 124–25, 149, 199, 221, 288–89, 294–95
  hack, 112, 288–89, 318–19
Theory of the firm, 101–2
  application to DAOs, 117–18
Tokenization, 227–28, 235–36, 272–73, 301
Tokens, 2, 273
  and DAO classification, 48–49
  in DAO governance, 2, 5–6, 22, 42–43, 62, 67–71, 72–73, 191, 241, 311, 319
  as financial resources, 322
  and legal responsibility, 320
  not imposing fiduciary duties, 72
  as securities, 63–64
Tornado Cash, 93

Transaction costs, 45, 74–75, 101, 117, 123–26, 136–37, 262–63, 302–3
Transparency, 98–99, 113, 157, 202–4, 229–30, 290
  bankruptcy and, 156–57
  DAO Model Law, 96–97
  paradox, 200, 202–4
  zero-knowledge proofs, 231
Treasury management, 194–96
Tribe DAO, 193–94
Trusts, 47
  Guernsey SPT, 22–23
Tulip Trading Ltd v van der Laan, 6, 56–57, 77–78, 84–88, 89
Turing completeness, 32, 285–86
Tyrrell v Bank of London, 55

U
Uber, 118, 277–78
Ukraine DAO, 109, 114
Unichain, 193, 197, 203
Uniform Commercial Code (UCC), 150
Unincorporated associations, 13–14, 17, 39, 77–78, 91, 202, 235, 261–62
Uniswap, 64–65, 128*t*, 132–34, 147, 149, 239, 245–46, 313
  UNI token, 133, 191–92
United States v Eisenberg, 289
Utah DAO Act, 20–21
Utility tokens, 63–64, 151

V
Validators, 92, 116, 249–50
Venture capital (VC), 216–17
  comparison with DAOs, 220–26
Vermont blockchain-based LLC, 18–19, 30–31
VitaDAO, 107, 109–10
Voorhees, Erik, 128
Voting
  delegated, 192, 241, 244
  mechanisms, 191–93
  off-chain, 113
  problems with, 70–71
  quadratic, 70, 146, 192, 228–29, 272–73

W
Web3, 163, 215
Whales, 115
White papers, 41–42, 43, 69, 181
Wrapped DAOs, 278–79, 280–81
Wrappers, legal. *See* Legal wrappers
Wright, Aaron, 298, 316, 318
Wright, Craig, 84
Wyoming DAO LLC, 18–19, 51–52, 178, 186, 226

Z
Zero-knowledge proofs, 107, 201, 231
Zuzalu, 107–8